HAZARDOUS WASTE PROCESSING TECHNOLOGY

HAZARDOUS WASTE PROCESSING TECHNOLOGY

By

YEN-HSIUNG KIANG
AMIR A. METRY

ANN ARBOR SCIENCE
PUBLISHERS INC / THE BUTTERWORTH GROUP

230 Collingwood, P.O. Box 1425, Ann Arbor, Michigan 48106

Library of Congress Catalog Card Number 81-69070
ISBN 0-250-40411-7

Manufactured in the United States of America

Butterworths, Ltd., Borough Green, Sevenoaks
Kent TN15 8PH, England

PREFACE

The U.S. Environmental Protection Agency (EPA) estimates that in 1980 at least 57 million metric tons of the nation's total waste load could be classified as hazardous. Only 10% of the hazardous wastes are properly managed and disposed. Many dangerous materials that society has thrown away over recent decades have endured in the environment—making household words of "Love Canal" and "Valley of the Drums."

In 1976 Congress passed the Resource Conservation and Recovery Act (RCRA), a law that established a national program to protect human health and the environment from improper handling of solid waste and to encourage conservation of natural resources. Directed by RCRA to take the lead in developing strict controls, EPA issued a national "cradle-to-grave" control system to track all significant quantities of hazardous waste from wherever they are generated to their final disposal.

The "cradle-to-grave" control system classifies hazardous waste activities into five categories: generation, transportation, storage, treatment and disposal. The purpose of this book is to present the state-of-the-art of treatment (or processing) technologies for hazardous wastes. There are two basic processing technologies: thermal and chemical/physical/biological, and one ultimate disposal method—land disposal.

Thermal processing technology is used to destroy organic waste without posing a threat to the environment. Thermal incineration technology is the most advanced and proven technology. A properly designed thermal incineration system will include not only hazardous waste disposal capability, but the possibility of recovering valuable but wasted heat and by-products. Other thermal processing methods are catalytic incineration, wet air oxidation and pyrolysis.

Three kinds of treatment processes can be used to render hazardous waste less hazardous or nonhazardous:

1. physical processes, such as carbon or resin adsorption, centrifuging, flocculation, sedimentation, reverse osmosis, and ultrafiltration;

2. chemical processes, such as fixation, neutralization, ion exchange, oxidation reduction and precipitation; and
3. biological processes, such as activated sludge, composting and land application.

These various options can reduce the degree of hazard and the amounts of waste that must be disposed directly on land, a crucial concern since the land available for disposal is decreasing, while waste tonnages are increasing. Land disposal includes secure chemical landfilling, secure burial and deep well injection. All the above techniques are covered in this book.

This book is divided into two parts. Part 1 discusses the thermal processing technologies, and Part 2 presents treatment and disposal technologies.

Chapter 1 is a general introduction and overview of hazardous waste management and regulations. Chapter 2 is a review of regulations, waste management and technologies governing thermal processes. Also included in Chapter 2 are waste classifications, applicability of processes and process development for system design.

Chapter 3 discusses the evaluation of incineration systems and waste handling technologies. The design of incinerator equipment is discussed in Chapter 4. Chapter 5 deals with special topics involving theory, design, research and development, and instrumentation, control and measurement of incineration systems. The recovery of waste heat and byproducts is discussed in Chapter 6. Also presented in Chapter 6 are air and water pollution aspects and treatment. Other thermal processing technologies, such as catalytic incineration, wet air oxidation and pyrolysis are discussed in Chapter 7. The developing technologies—molten salt incinerator and plasma reactor—will also be included. Chapter 8 is an overview of treatment processes and disposal site selection requirements. Chapter 9 is devoted to a discussion of physical treatment processes. Chemical treatment processes are discussed in Chapter 10, and Chapter 11 presents biological treatment processes.

It is the objective of this book to consolidate present state-of-the-art hazardous waste processing technologies into one comprehensive volume. It is hoped that this book will be used as a reference book for professionals involved with hazardous waste activities.

The authors wish to acknowledge the support and encouragement of the Trane Company, IU Conversion Systems Inc. and Roy F. Weston Inc. for their cooperative assistance in typing, duplicating and myriad other tasks associated with the preparation of this work. We thank Ms. Connie Raymond and Ms. Joan McElmoyle for their typing of the manuscript. We also thank Ms. Louise Miller for her review and technical editing of the manuscript.

The authors wish to express their thanks to the Trane Company, E. I. DuPont DeNemours & Co., Boeing Engineering and Construction Co., Deltak Corporation, Astra Metallurgical Co., Zimpro, TRW Corporation, and Penn Power and Light for their supplying materials to us for preparation of the manuscript.

Yen-Hsiung Kiang
Amir A. Metry

Kiang

Metry

Yen-Hsiung Kiang joined the Trane Company, Process Division, in 1974 as Process Engineer, and is currently Manager of Process Technology, responsible for concept development, process engineering, product and process development, technical consultations, and R&D laboratory operation.

Dr. Kiang received his BSChE from Cheng Kung University, Taiwan, China, and his MS and PhD from the University of Florida, Gainesville. He is also a registered Professional Engineer.

Dr. Kiang is the author of several books and more than 20 articles and other publications covering waste disposal, energy recovery and air pollution control, and has been a lecturer for the APCA Annual Meeting since 1978.

Dr. Kiang has more than seven years of comprehensive experience in the fields of combustion, heat transfer, waste incineration, energy recovery and air pollution control. He is the holder of U.S. Patent No. 4,192,659, "Method for Hot Gas Cooling and Gaseous Contaminant Removal."

Amir A. Metry is currently Vice President, Residuals Management, Roy F. Weston, Inc., West Chester, Pennsylvania. Prior affiliations include Vice President of Research and Systems Engineering, IU Conversion Systems, Inc., Horsham, Pennsylvania; Research Associate, Drexel University; and Project Manager with the firm of Naim Mahfonz, Cairo, Egypt.

Dr. Metry has 18 years of experience in the fields of industrial and hazardous waste and environmental resources management, including process development and design, conceptual engineering, waste disposal facilities siting and design, hazardous waste management, and utility waste management and disposal.

Dr. Metry received his MS and PhD in environmental engineering from Drexel University, and his BS in mechanical engineering and MS in engineering management from Cairo University. He is a member of the American Society of Civil Engineers, National Society of Professional Engineers, the Water Pollution Control Federation and the Institute of Environmental Sciences, and is a diplomate of the American Academy of Environmental Engineers.

Dr. Metry is the author of several books and more than 50 articles in the fields of environmental resources and waste management.

To my wife Patty and son Gary
Yen-Hsiung Kiang

To my wife Nawal and sons Adam and Robert
Amir A. Metry

CONTENTS

Part 1
Thermal Processing Technologies

Part 2
Treatment Technologies

CHAPTER 1

INTRODUCTION AND BACKGROUND

EVERYBODY'S PROBLEM: HAZARDOUS WASTE

Every year, billions of tons of solid wastes are discarded in the United States. These wastes range in nature from common household trash to complex materials in industrial wastes, sewage sludge, agricultural residues, mining refuse and pathological wastes from institutions such as hospitals and laboratories.

The U.S. Environmental Protection Agency (EPA) estimated in 1980 that at least 57 million metric tons of the nation's total wasteload can be classified as hazardous. Unfortunately, many dangerous materials that society has "thrown away" over recent decades have endured in the environment—making household words of 'Love Canal' and 'Valley of the Drums.' These two incidents are not unique. The EPA has on file hundreds of documented cases of damage to life and the environment resulting from the indiscriminate or improper management of hazardous wastes. The vast majority of cases involve pollution of ground water—the source of drinking water for about half of the U.S. population—from improperly sited or operated landfills and surface impoundments (pits, ponds and lagoons). In addition to polluting ground water, the improper handling or disposal of hazardous waste can cause several other kinds of environmental damage, as illustrated by these case histories (often involving more than one form of damage) from EPA records.

Hazardous Waste Can Pollute Ground Water

- The water supplies of Toone and Teague, Tennessee, were contaminated in 1978 with organic compounds when water leached from a nearby landfill. When the landfill closed, about six years earlier, the site held some 350,000 drums, many of them leaking pesticide wastes. Because the towns no longer have access to uncontaminated ground water, they must pump water in from other locations.

- Ground water in a 30-square-mile area near Denver was contaminated from disposal of pesticide waste in unlined disposal ponds. The waste, from manufacturing activities of the U.S. Army and a chemical company, dates back to the 1943–1957 period. Decontamination, if possible, could take several years and cost as much as $80 million.

Hazardous Waste Can Contaminate Rivers, Lakes, and Other Surface Water

- At least 1500 drums containing waste, primarily from metal-finishing operations, were buried near Byron, Illinois, for an unknown number of years until about 1972. Surface waters (and soil and ground water as well) were contaminated with cyanides, heavy metals, phenols and miscellaneous other materials. Wildlife, stream life and local vegetation were destroyed. The disposal site suffered long-range damage from the toxic pollutants that drained into the soil.
- About 17,000 drums littered a 7-acre site in Kentucky which became known as 'Valley of the Drums.' Some 6000 drums were full, many of them oozing their toxic contents onto the ground. In addition, an undetermined quantity of hazardous waste was buried in drums and subsurface pits. In 1979, EPA analyses of soil and surface water in the drainage area about 25 miles south of Louisville identified about 200 organic chemicals and 30 metals.

Hazardous Waste Can Pollute the Air

- In 1972, waste containing hexachlorobenzene (HCB), one of the family of toxic organic compounds that contains chlorine, was disposed of in a landfill near Darrow and Geismar, Louisiana. The HCB vaporized and subsequently accumulated in cattle over a 100-square-mile area. Some cattle had to be destroyed. This incident represented direct and indirect economic losses of over $380,000. Elevated, although subtoxic, levels of HCB in blood plasma were found in some area residents.
- A truck driver was killed in 1978 as he discharged waste from his truck into one of four open pits at a disposal site in Iberville Parish, Louisiana. He was asphyxiated by hydrogen sulfide produced when liquid wastes mixed in the open pit. The area was surrounded by water and had a history of flooding.

Hazardous Waste Can Burn or Explode

- A fire broke out in 1978 at a disposal site in Chester, Pennsylvania, where 30,000 to 50,000 drums of industrial waste had been received over a 3-year period. The smoke forced closing of the Commodore Barry Bridge and 45 firemen required medical treatment, mostly as a result of lung and skin irritation from chemical fumes. A number of homes are located within three blocks of the site; drummed waste was kept only 20 feet from a natural gas storage tank, and liquefied natural gas tanks were about 100 yards away. Waste was emptied directly on the soil of the 3-acre site; some probably drained to the tidal section of the adjacent Delaware River. Waste may even have been dumped into the river.
- A bulldozer operator was killed in a 1975 explosion at a landfill in Edison Township, New Jersey, as he was burying and compacting drums of unidentified chemical waste. Of the 200 truckloads of waste the landfill received daily, about 50 were industrial waste.

Hazardous Waste Can Poison Via the Food Chain

- In 1970, three children in an Alamogordo, New Mexico, family became seriously ill after eating a home-slaughtered pig that had been fed corn treated with a mercury compound. Local health officials found several bags of similarly treated corn in the community dump.
- Over a 4-month period in 1976, an Indiana family consumed milk contaminated with twice the maximum concentration of polychlorinated biphenyls (PCB) considered safe by the Food and Drug Administration. The milk came from the family's cow, which had been grazing in a pasture fertilized with the city of Bloomington's sewage sludge. The sludge contained high levels of PCB from a local manufacturing plant. A Federal law passed in 1976 banned production of PCB after January 1, 1979.

Hazardous Waste Can Poison by Direct Contact

- The health of some residents of Love Canal, near Niagara Falls, New York, was seriously damaged by chemical waste buried a quarter of a century ago. As drums holding the waste corroded, their contents percolated through the soil into yards and basements, forcing evacuation of over 200 families in 1978 and 1979. About 80 chemicals, a number of them suspected carcinogens, were identified.
- In 1979, cattle on a Kansas feedlot were contaminated with PCB after waste oil was used in animal backrubbers. The waste oil (from electrical transformers) had been purchased from a salvage yard in 1972, before the effects of PCB were widely known. Inedible byproducts

> from 54 head of cattle had been shipped to a number of states and had to be traced and disposed of properly; another 112 head had to be destroyed.

These examples provide dramatic evidence of damage to life and the environment from mismanagement of hazardous waste. It was in large part to prevent such tragedies that, in 1976, Congress enacted Subtitle C of the Resource Conservation and Recovery Act (RCRA), Public Law 94–580. This law imposes strict controls over the management of hazardous waste throughout its entire life cycle. The costs for proper environmental controls will be higher than amounts spent in the past to manage these wastes. But the astronomical costs of cleaning up damage caused by poor disposal practices should be eliminated. An ounce of prevention, in this instance, is a sound investment.

A 1979 EPA study indicated that cleaning up abandoned hazardous waste sites and those operating under environmentally unsound conditions could cost as much as $44 billion, only part of which is likely to be paid for by the owners of the sites. The remainder would have to come from other sources. But in many cases it is impossible to assign dollar values to the long-term harm to health and the environment that has resulted from improper management of hazardous waste.

The National Program to Control Hazardous Wastes

In a report to Congress in 1973, the EPA recommended passage of a federal law to regulate the handling of hazardous waste. The EPA reported that although existing federal legislation was adequate to protect the air, surface waters and oceans from improper disposal of hazardous waste, there were no national controls over its disposal on land. Morever, the air and water pollution laws requiring industry to adopt environmentally acceptable treatment and disposal practices had increased the amounts of hazardous waste being dumped on the land, a relatively unregulated outlet for disposal. Thus, a law was needed to close the circle of federal environmental protection by providing, for the first time, control over disposal of hazardous waste on land.

Congress responded by including hazardous waste provisions in RCRA—the law that established a national program to protect human health and the environment from improper handling of solid waste and to encourage conservation of national resources. Directed by RCRA to take the lead in developing strict controls, the EPA began a three-pronged effort to attack the nation's hazardous waste problem.

The first phase, the regulatory program under RCRA, is intended to help states prevent any Love Canals in the future. Central to this program is a national "cradle-to-grave" control system to track all significant quantities of hazardous waste from wherever it is generated to its final disposal. The regulatory program includes:

- identification of hazardous waste,
- standards for generators and transporters of hazardous waste,
- performance, design and operating requirements for facilities that treat, store or dispose of hazardous waste,
- a system for issuing permits to such facilities and
- guidelines describing conditions under which state governments can be authorized to carry out their own hazardous waste management programs.

Along with its authority under RCRA, the EPA is using regulatory authorities under several other acts it administers. These include the Clean Water Act, the Safe Drinking Water Act, the Toxic Substances Control Act and the Refuse Act. Under certain provisions of these acts, the EPA has been able to:

- fund the development of programs for management and enforcement of hazardous waste activities by state and local governments,
- fund cleanup of disposal sites,
- approve landfills and incinerators for PCB disposal and treatment and
- provide technical assistance to state and local officials to help them analyze and remedy existing or potential problems caused by improper hazardous waste management.

The second phase of the national hazardous waste management effort consists of EPA investigations to identify dangerous abandoned or uncontrolled dump sites, which the agency estimated in 1979 to number as many as 2000. Under RCRA, the EPA can force the owner to clean up a hazardous waste disposal site if it causes an "imminent and substantial" danger to human health and the environment. The EPA has stepped up its efforts under this provision to discover, investigate and clean up abandoned disposal areas.

Unfortunately, the owners of dangerous sites often cannot be found. Even when they are found, they may not have the finances necessary for cleanup, or they may deny any legal liability for damages attributed to the site. Thus innocent victims must resort to long and costly legal proceedings under the state laws, and government agencies are faced with cleanup expenses.

The third phase of the attack on hazardous waste is a 1979 legislative proposal, termed the "superfund," developed by the EPA and others to rectify the limitations of the imminent hazard provision. The main purpose is to provide funds that will permit federal and state governments to move quickly and effectively to deal with the consequences of uncontrolled and abandoned disposal sites, as well as spills of oil and hazardous substances.

The Public Role

Of special importance in RCRA is a provision stating that "public participation in the development, revision, implementation, and enforcement of any regulation, guideline, information, or program under this Act shall be provided for, encouraged, and assisted" by the EPA and the states. This booklet is an example of the kind of information the EPA makes available to the public. It is intended to help build an understanding of the hazardous waste problem and thus promote effective public participation in the development of federal and state programs for bringing the problem under control.

HAZARDOUS WASTE DEFINED

RCRA defines a hazardous waste as a solid waste that may cause or significantly contribute to serious illness or death, or that poses a substantial threat to human health or the environment when improperly managed. Hazardous wastes are among the leavings of a highly technological society and come from many segments of that society—industry, hospitals, research laboratories, and all levels of government. Industry is by far the largest source, generating these wastes to manufacture cars, fuel, paper, plastics, clothing, rubber, paint, pesticides, medicines and a host of other products that Americans need or expect in their day-to-day lives.

Working from the RCRA definition, the EPA has compiled and proposed a list of hazardous wastes. Listing is the most common method of defining hazardous waste in European countries and in some state laws. The EPA has also proposed that a hazardous waste be identified by testing it to determine if it possesses any one of four characteristics. If it does, it will be subject to regulation under RCRA. Three of the characteristics selected by EPA produce acute effects likely to cause almost immediate damage; the fourth creates chronic effects most likely to appear over a longer time period. The four characteristics are:

1. ignitibility, which identifies wastes that pose a fire hazard during routine management. Fires not only present immediate dangers of heat and smoke, but also can spread harmful particles over wide areas.
2. corrosivity, which identifies wastes requiring special containers because of their ability to corrode standard materials, or requiring segregation from other wastes because of their ability to dissolve toxic contaminants.
3. reactivity (or explosiveness), which identifies wastes that, during routine management, tend to react spontaneously, to react vigorously with air or water, to be unstable to shock or heat, to generate toxic gases or to explode.
4. toxicity, which identifies wastes that, when improperly managed, may release toxicants in sufficient quantities to pose a substantial hazard to human health or the environment.

Several of the methods used to test for these characteristics are identical to those used by the U.S. Department of Transportation in its program to control transport of hazardous materials.

The EPA may add to or delete from the list of hazardous wastes or characteristics identifying a hazardous waste. Any changes will be published in the Federal Register, and the public will be given an opportunity to comment on proposed changes.

HAZARDOUS WASTE MANAGEMENT

Good Management: There Are Better Ways

The Love Canal tragedy, contamination of ground water in Toone, the dumping of PCBs along North Carolina's roads, the thousands of drums piled high in Kentucky's "Valley of the Drums" and similar incidents served to focus attention on what can happen when hazardous waste is improperly managed. Although technologies exist for environmentally sound management, they have not been widely used because of their higher costs and because there was no legal requirement for their use.

Proper management means more than just careful disposal. It means consideration of a range of options that depend on such factors as characteristics, volume and location of the waste. In order of priority, the desired options for managing hazardous waste are:

- minimize the amounts generated by modifying the industrial process involved;
- transfer the waste to another industry that can use it;
- reprocess the waste to recover energy or materials;

- separate hazardous from nonhazardous waste at the source and concentrate it, which reduces handling, transportation and disposal costs;
- incinerate the waste, or subject it to treatment that makes it nonhazardous; and
- dispose of the waste in a secure landfill (one that is located, designed, operated and monitored—even after it is closed—in a manner that protects life and the environment).

Transferring a hazardous waste to another industry is an option that is receiving increased attention. Operating on the principle that one company's waste may be another's raw material, this option can take two forms: the materials exchange, which is equipped to handle, treat and physically exchange wastes and the information exchange, which acts only as a clearinghouse, leaving generator and potential purchasers to negotiate directly.

The first information exchange started in The Netherlands in 1972. Since then, the idea has spread quickly in Europe and is beginning to spread in the United States. At least 20 information exchanges and 3 materials exchanges are now in operation in the United States. The first information exchange in the United States was established in 1975 by the St. Louis Regional Commerce and Growth Association. Typically, information exchanges are run by chambers of commerce or other nonprofit groups. In contrast, materials exchanges are usually operated by profit-oriented private concerns.

Probably only a small percentage of hazardous waste is suitable for exchange. Purer, less-contaminated wastes stand the best chances of being exchanged. Also, waste is more likely to be exchanged where the purchaser is in the same or a nearby locality, which minimizes transportation costs. The waste exchange, though not a panacea, makes a valuable contribution by reducing the amounts of material to be managed by less desirable options.

Related to the exchange option is the recovery of energy or materials. With shortages of raw materials and tighter restrictions on disposal of wastes, recovery will become a more viable alternative. Many wastes contain valuable basic ingredients. And the extraction of materials from concentrated wastes requires less energy—and generates less water and air pollution—than the mining and processing of virgin materials. Consequently, when energy or materials are recovered from hazardous waste, natural resources are conserved and the environment is protected.

Incineration is a proven method of destroying organic waste without posing a threat to the environment. The EPA has conducted a number of research and field-scale projects on incineration methods for chemical wastes. Two successful projects carried out in 1979 involved several types of commercial incinerators and 20 different chemical wastes, including 9 pesticides. These wastes were almost totally detoxified or destroyed. The successful use of cement kilns to destroy chlorine- or bromine-containing organic waste—which is very toxic because it resists degradation and accumulates in living tissues—is one of the more important results of the EPA's demonstration project. The chlorine or bromine in the waste reduces the alkalinity of the residue left after combustion, simplifying disposal. The heat value of the waste also replaces some of the fuel needed to manufacture cement.

Another promising approach to disposing of chlorine- or bromine-containing organic waste is to burn it at sea aboard special incinerator ships. This technique, pioneered in Europe, has been used on several occasions by the United States, including the disposal of the Air Force's surplus stock of Herbicide Orange, the defoliant used in Vietnam. The incineration was aboard a Dutch vessel, the Vulcanus. The possibility of building American incinerator vessels is being considered.

Three kinds of processes can be used to render a hazardous waste less hazardous or nonhazardous:

1. physical processes, such as carbon or resin adsorption, distillation, centrifuging, flocculation, sedimentation, reverse osmosis and ultrafiltration;
2. chemical processes, such as fixation into solids that are more readily disposed of, neutralization, ion exchange to remove heavy metals, oxidation and precipitation; and
3. biological processes, such as activated sludge treatment to destroy organic compounds, composting of organic-rich wastes, trickling filters to promote decomposition, and controlled application on land ("landfarming") to degrade organic compounds.

Use of these processes can reduce the amounts of hazardous waste that must be disposed of directly on land—a crucial concern because the land available for disposal is decreasing, while waste tonnages are increasing. The hazardous waste management industry, major waste-generating industries and the EPA are devoting increased attention to development of new, improved and less expensive treatment technologies. But even with new technology, some hazardous waste always will be destined for land disposal.

Bad Management = Environmental Disasters

Sound technologies may be available to manage hazardous wastes, but EPA studies of 17 industries between 1975 and 1978 indicate they are not being used for 90% of the waste generated. The predominant practice is disposal in unlined impoundments (pits, ponds and lagoons) and landfills. Up to 80% of hazardous waste is disposed of on the generator's property.

The least expensive environmentally sound method of disposal is a secure landfill; however, only a limited number of secure landfills are in operation in the United States. Many commercial incinerators pollute the air when they burn hazardous waste. Dumping at sea, an inexpensive alternative for companies holding the required EPA permits, will be sharply reduced in 1981 when all provisions of the 1972 Marine Protection, Research, and Sanctuaries Act are in effect. The cheapest alternative of all is the "midnight dumper." With only a truck and a total disregard for public safety, midnight dumpers take hazardous waste off generators' hands for relatively modest fees and then dispose of it in any one of a number of ways; flushing it into sewers and ditches, dumping it in lakes and rivers, dropping it off ships at sea, burying it in farmland, concealing it in municipal waste for disposal in sanitary landfills and storing or dumping it on open lots or fields.

The common practice of open storage has led to some of the most damaging incidents caused by mismanagement of hazardous waste—the "Valley of the Drums" and a site in Lowell, Massachusetts, being flagrant examples. The Lowell site dates back to 1970, when a private corporation was set up to salvage and reprocess waste from area industries. In 1977, the company declared bankruptcy, leaving some 20,000 barrels, many rusted and leaking, containing 1 million gallons of toxic waste. Some of the barrels were only a few hundred feet from a stream that flows into the Concord River, a tributary to the Merrimack. Several communities get their drinking water from the Merrimack. Another 250,000 to 300,000 gallons were left in leaking storage tanks. This 5.2-acre site was located only a few hundred yards from some residences in the town of Lowell. With the company bankrupt, the State of Massachusetts had to appropriate $1.5 million to clean up the site.

RCRA: Moving Toward a Safer Environment

Harm to human health and the environment caused by past mismanagement of hazardous waste led to incorporation in RCRA of a "cradle-to-grave" control system. This system calls for regulation of hazardous waste from the time it is first generated through transport to final treatment or disposal. The concept uses a pathways approach, so-called because the movement of hazardous waste destined for storage, treatment or disposal is constantly monitored and controlled. This approach is basically different from that used to regulate air and water pollution, where specific standards are tailored for each industrial category. The pathways approach was chosen because hazardous waste is mobile and can be disposed of at locations far from where it was generated. In contrast, sources of industrial air and water pollution are fixed and relatively easy to identify.

The Congress intended that the individual states develop their own hazardous waste control systems, subject to EPA approval. To receive approval, the state program must be equivalent to the national regulatory program developed by EPA. EPA handles the program only in states that choose not to implement their own programs or that fail to get approval.

The EPA has developed and proposed a set of six regulations to control all stages of the hazardous waste management cycle, whether the waste is managed at an "off-site" waste management facility. Promulgation of all of the hazardous waste regulations in final form was scheduled for 1980, to take effect six months later. Proposed regulations are always subject to change; therefore, the following discussion focuses on basic requirements under the Act.

Generators

Those who generate potentially hazardous waste in their operations are required to determine if the waste is hazardous under the RCRA definition. Thus, the definition of hazardous waste is the cornerstone of the national regulatory program. Once a waste is identified as hazardous, RCRA requires that all significant quantities be tracked throughout their life cycle by means of a transport manifest and by stringent recordkeeping and reporting requirements. In order to identify a waste as hazardous, the generator refers to a list of wastes or tests the waste against the characteristics in the final regulations. Or, the generator may simply declare the waste to be hazardous. Generators disposing of their waste on-site must be issued a permit but do not need a manifest because no transportation is involved.

Generators are the key linked in the transport control system. Under the proposed RCRA regulation, they must:

- originate a transport manifest, describing the amount, composition, origin, routing and destination of each shipment;
- use approved containers and label them properly;
- select a responsible company to transport the waste;
- specify the facility to which the waste is to be delivered and ensure that it has a valid permit;
- confirm that a waste reaches the intended facility;

- keep records of information in the manifest and report them to an authorized State or to the EPA; and
- notify authorities of international shipments.

Transporters

Transporters must deliver hazardous waste shipments to the facility designated by the generator, keep appropriate records, and report any spills en route. Hazardous waste transporters do not need permits in the federal system, but some states require transporters to register.

Many of the major problems in the past have been caused by irresponsible actions of some transporters. After being paid to take hazardous waste to disposal facilities, they have instead merely dumped the waste indiscriminately, without regard for the effects of their actions. For example, the sewage treatment plant in Louisville, Kentucky, had to be shut down for several months in 1977 after a local transporter dumped several tons of pesticide waste into the sewer system. During the clean-up, which cost federal, state and local agencies $3 million, raw sewage had to be discharged directly into the Ohio River. The manifest system is designed to prevent such practices because generators can quickly notify authorities if the designated facility does not receive a shipment.

Some portions of the RCRA regulation on transporters overlap with provisions of the Hazardous Materials Transportation Act (HMTA) administered by the U.S. Department of Transportation (DOT). Regulations issued under HMTA have been amended to make them more compatible with the RCRA regulation, thus avoiding duplication of administrative and enforcement activities. Overlapping provisions of the two acts, covering labeling, packaging and placarding of hazardous waste by generators, are being administered similarly. The EPA and DOT jointly enforce regulations when they share authority. EPA regulations take effect if DOT lacks authority.

Standards and Permits for Facilities

Owners and operators of facilities that treat, store or dispose of hazardous waste must comply with minimum standards for ensuring that the facilities operate safely. These standards cover containing, testing and destroying wastes so that they cannot contaminate ground water, surface water or the atmosphere. There are also standards for safety and emergency measures to be used if hazardous waste is accidentally discharged, for training personnel for emergency situations and for keeping records and filing reports. Owners and operators of facilities also are required to demonstrate financial responsibility for their operations.

The owner of a hazardous waste facility must apply for a permit within a specified time. Under the RCRA regulation, the applicant must provide information on the site and the amounts and types of hazardous waste to be handled. To receive a permit, an applicant must meet the standards set for the specific type of facility. The permit describes the terms, conditions and schedules of compliance, as well as monitoring, recordkeeping and reporting requirements.

Many procedures of the permit program under RCRA are similar to permit requirements under other EPA-administered laws. The agency has consolidated these programs into one set of regulations. The EPA's objective is to move in the direction of processing an applicant's hazardous waste permit simultaneously with other required permits. The EPA's consolidated permit program includes:

- the hazardous waste management program under RCRA;
- the underground injection control program under the Safe Drinking Water Act;
- the national pollutant discharge elimination system under the Clean Water Act;
- the dredge or fill program under the Clean Water Act; and
- the program for prevention of significant deterioration of air quality under the Clean Air Act.

States must be authorized by the EPA to conduct their own hazardous waste management programs. In order to receive authorization, the state program must be equivalent to the national program. Among other things, the state must have legislation and regulations that are no less stringent than the federal standards, and the state must show that it has the resources to administer and enforce the program. If a state's program does not fully comply with EPA requirements, the EPA may grant the state interim authorization for two years, during which time the program should be further developed to meet all authorization requirements.

CONCEPTUAL FRAMEWORK FOR EFFECTIVE HAZARDOUS WASTE MANAGEMENT*

The potential for damage of public health and to the environment from mismanagement of hazardous wastes justifies the need for implementation of an effective hazardous waste management program.

Current EPA air and water legislation concerning pollution discharges focuses on industrial stationary-source emissions by requiring new

*This section is digested from: "State Decision-Makers Guide for Hazardous Waste Management"—U.S. Environmental Protection Publication (SW-612), 1977.

source performance standards and effluent limitation guidelines. Such requirements on industrial categories are Congressionally mandated. Emission controls appeared necessary because:

- man-made ambient "controls" (other than water dilution) are impossible;
- sources are geographically fixed, that is, each plant is faced with an immediate problem of treatment; and
- surveillance and enforcement of emission limits are much more practical than is waste-load allocation or ambient-air modeling.

In other words, with regard to air and water discharges, plants are stationary and emit to a moving receiver (air or water). Thus, regulation at the receiving end (ambient levels) is very difficult. Sampling the emissions into the receiving medium and exercising control at the discharge site is not only logical but is, perhaps, the only practical approach. Also, with a moving receiving medium (air or water), it is difficult to establish a direct link between a specific plant's emission in terms of its effect on the environment and public health. In the case of air, this is due to such variables as wind velocity and direction as well as the ambient levels to which the plant is contributing. Similar vagaries exist with water discharges. Streams have different flow rates, bottom sediments have differing sorption characteristics, etc.

Land disposal, on the other hand, is a more readily controllable medium. The sink (the land) is fixed, and the wastes entering it are the variables subject to control in terms of the capabilities of a particular site to accept specific amounts of certain wastes.

Waste Management

Industrial hazardous wastes (whether solids, powders, cakes, sludges, slurries, liquids or contained gases) are a unique problem because they are transportable, and they may be immediate polluters of the land as well as future hazards in the air and water media on both a short- and long-term basis. Thus, the integrity of the pathways which wastes seek (land deposition, incineration, chemical treatment, etc.) is the critical environmental factor to be controlled.

Several important trends are evident from industry-oriented hazardous waste studies. First, many wastes have similar characteristics in terms of the disposal options selected. Waste disposal practices are usually determined by the physical properties of the waste (liquid, sludges, etc.) rather than by its chemical properties. Analysis of the studies shows more variation within an industry segment in terms of treatment/disposal methods than between the industry segments surveyed. Also characteristics of several diverse wastes often can be exploited beneficially at waste treatment/disposal centers.

Second, since wastes often are transported for treatment/disposal, and off-site treatment and disposal are a significant private-sector business, waste streams are not "stationary" in the sense that air and water emissions are.

Because economic waste treatment/disposal usually requires an accumulation of sufficient quantities for processing, the prospect of waste movement and the environmental integrity of such transport is a major source of regulatory concern.

Finally, land deposition is the most popular waste-disposal option. Current technological variety is minimal at present; for many wastes, land disposal is the process that needs regulation, not industrial process streams. However, there is a finite amount of land available for disposal of hazardous wastes.

A hazardous waste management program should result in creation of a system with certain characteristics: adequate treatment and disposal capacity, lowest cost to society consistent with public health and environmental protection, equitable and efficient allocation of cost to those responsible for waste generation, and conservation of resources achieved by recovering materials and energy from wastes.

The system should combine on-site (point of generation) treatment of some wastes, off-site (central facility) treatment for hazard elimination, and secure land disposal of residues that remain hazardous after treatment.

Waste Disposition Hierarchy

Due to their high potential for public health and environmental damage, some hazardous wastes require special control procedures. Management of these wastes means awareness and control over them from the time of generation through their transportation, temporary storage, treatment and disposal (so-called "cradle-to-grave" control). This comprehensive management of hazardous wastes should be conducted or coordinated at the state level so that wastes may reach environmentally sound treatment and disposal facilities. Several states have adopted waste transportation control systems involving manifests or "trip tickets" to monitor these waste flows. Such systems appear to be the most effective method to ensure proper handling and tracking of wastes from generation to ultimate disposal. Effective identification and labeling of wastes by the generators is essential to the effective operation of any manifest-based system. A discussion of these topics is contained in this guide.

In addition, management of hazardous waste means more than careful disposal. It implies consideration of alternate methods and schemes, both institutional and technical, to reduce the degree of hazardousness of wastes.

A hierarchical structure of waste management options is offered below, based primarily on environmental concerns, which recognize that economics will play a major role in the waste generator's decision process.

Reuse, energy recovery and material recovery as well as treatment are desirable prior to ultimate disposal, especially land disposal. Thus, the desired waste management options are (in order of priority):

- waste reduction,
- waste separation and concentration,
- waste exchange,
- energy/material recovery
- waste incineration treatment, and
- secure ultimate disposal.

1. Waste Reduction. Reducing the amount of hazardous waste at the source, through process changes, is desirable. Reduction of hazardous chemicals used in operations, substitution of less hazardous materials, and better quality control to reduce production spoilage are all examples of possible actions that would reduce the amount of hazardous waste requiring disposal. The less hazardous the waste to be disposed of, the less risk of environmental damage.

2. Waste Separation and Concentration. Even with the minimum amount of waste, it is possible to isolate the more hazardous or toxic waste streams from the mixtures in which they occur. Waste separation early in process-stream flows, as well as simple isolation of similar wastes into separate disposal containers, can reduce waste handling and disposal costs. Moreover, isolation of such hazardous wastes in separate storage areas would permit operating personnel to focus their attention on careful management of those wastes.

Concentration of wastes by dewatering (with appropriate air-pollution controls) will reduce the amount of wastes requiring treatment or disposal. This process not only reduces the cost of ultimate disposal but, more significantly, minimizes transportation costs, which are frequently the major variable in total waste-management costs.

3. Waste Exchange. Next in priority is the concept of waste clearing-

houses where pretreated or untreated hazardous wastes are transferred. These clearinghouses operate on the principle that "one man's waste can be another man's feedstock." At least six waste exchanges in Europe and ten formally organized waste exchanges in the United States testify to the feasibility of this concept under a variety of institutional arrangements. Such clearinghouses are desirable but may only be feasible at a state or multi-state level. An EPA report on this subject is available from the National Technical Information Service, Springfield, Virginia. Since this concept is relatively new, additional information is provided in the next section.

4. Energy/Material Recovery. Recovery of potentially useful substances, energy or materials from hazardous wastes is desirable. Many wastes contain valuable basic materials, some of which are in short supply, making material recovery logical from both resource conservation and environmental viewpoints. Extraction of materials from concentrated waste usually requires less energy, and generates far less air and water pollution than the mining and processing operations required to produce the material from virgin resources. As material shortages become more widespread, material recovery from hazardous waste will become more attractive.

Likewise, the combustion of such wastes to recover energy or heat value for other purposes is endorsed. Such operations usually require special high-temperature equipment with emission control systems and effluent monitors. Other limitations are imposed by the "quality control" aspects of waste utilization for energy. The user facility must have an adequate supply of fuel with consistent heat value on a regular or full-time basis. Also, some provisions must be made for standby or emergency operations. These limitations must be carefully considered and integrated into the planning for any system using industrial wastes for fuel.

5. Incineration/Treatment. Incineration even without energy recovery is desirable—in its proper order of priority—mainly to destroy organic wastes. Other nonburnable wastes should be detoxified and neutralized to the greatest extent possible through physical, chemical and biological treatment. Careful attention to environmental emissions, using control equipment and monitoring devices, is still required regardless of the process employed. Alternative treatment techniques are being investigated by the Office of Solid Waste and several reports will be forthcoming.

6. Secure Land Disposal. For those hazardous wastes not amenable to recovery, treatment or destruction, volume reduction to minimize land-use requirements should be performed prior to secure land disposal. Secure land disposal either through encapsulation of small quantities of waste or through the use, on a larger scale, of a chemical waste landfill is

recommended. In general terms, a chemical waste landfill provides complete long-term protection for the quality of surface and subsurface waters from hazardous waste deposited therein, and prevents hazards to public health and the environment. Such sites should be located or engineered to avoid direct hydraulic continuity with surface and subsurface water flow into and out of the disposal area. Monitoring wells should be established, and a sampling analysis program conducted. Air emissions should be controlled and monitored as well.

Waste Transfer Concepts (Waste Exchange)

Waste transfer is both similar to and different from the purchase and reuse of industrial by-products. In both cases an industrial process generates, in addition to its principal product, some material that is not usable by the generating company, but which can be sold economically for reuse by another company. When the material has a well-recognized value that justifies the costs of recovery, handling and transportation, it is known as a by-product. When the material has a value which has not been recognized, it is a potentially transferable waste.

As long as disposal is easy and inexpensive, disposal will be the waste generator's economically preferred course. Transfer to another plant or industry is economically attractive only when disposal presents major problems, as will increasingly be the case with tighter restrictions and higher costs. Transfers can occur only after many conditions have been established for both generator and user. Each, depending on his own business and perspective of what is important, must consider the following:

- Technical feasibility: the matching of the chemical and physical properties of available waste streams with the specifications of raw materials they might replace;
- Economic feasibility: balancing of disposal costs foregone and raw material costs saved against the administrative and transport costs of implementing a waste transfer;
- Institutional and marketing feasibility: guarantees of supply and anonymity; and mutual confidence among generator, user and transfer agent and
- Legal and regulatory feasibility: protection of confidentiality, legality, and unlikelihood of liability suits.

ACKNOWLEDGMENT

The material in this chapter is derived in part from information in the U.S. EPA publications: "Everybody's Problem: Hazardous Waste," SW-826 (1980) and "State Decision-Makers Guide for Hazardous Waste Management," SW-612 (1977).

PART 1

THERMAL PROCESSING TECHNOLOGIES

CHAPTER 2

THERMAL PROCESSING REQUIREMENTS

Hazardous chemical wastes in the environment represent one of the most serious problems facing society today. According to the United States Environmental Protection Agency [1], in 1980 at least 57 million metric tons of the nation's total wasteload could be classified as hazardous. Of this 57 million tons of hazardous waste, almost 60% [2] is organic in nature and can be destroyed by available thermal processing methods, such as incineration, catalytic incineration, pyrolysis, calcination and wet air oxidation. The aforementioned methods also can be applied to treat carbon monoxide and those inorganic chemicals which are oxidizable, such as hydrogen sulfide. Certain thermal processing methods are used primarily for volume reduction purposes, such as evaporation and steam stripping. In general, "thermal processing" is defined as [3] "the treatment of hazardous waste in a device which uses elevated temperatures as the primary means to change the chemical, physical or biological character or composition of the hazardous waste".

Some thermal processing methods, such as thermal incineration, are well-developed and well-understood technology; others such as plasma technology are in developing stages. In most cases, a properly designed and operated thermal processing system has the following advantages [4]:

- volume reduction, especially for bulky solids with a high combustible content and waste water;
- detoxification, especially for combustible carcinogens, pathologically contaminated material, toxic organic compounds, or biologically active materials which would affect sewage treatment plants;
- environmental impact mitigation, especially for organic materials which would leach from landfills, generate landfill gas or create odor nuisances;

- energy recovery, especially where large quantities of waste are available and reliable markets for by-product fuel or steam are nearby; and
- by-product chemical recovery.

These advantages have justified the development and application of a variety of thermal processing systems of widely different complexity and function to meet the needs of any specific application.

Operating contrary to these advantages are the following disadvantages for thermal processing [4]:

- Cost: in most instances, thermal processing is a costly waste treatment step, both in initial investment and in operation.
- Operation: variability in waste composition and the severity of the processing environment result in many practical waste handling problems, high maintenance requirements and equipment unreliability.
- Staffing: the low status often accorded to waste disposal makes it difficult to obtain and retain qualified supervisory and operating staff.
- Secondary Environmental Impacts: many thermal processing systems generate sulfur dioxide, hydrogen chloride, nitrogen oxides, fly ash and submicron particles. The waste waters from air pollution control systems are often highly acid and contain dissolved and suspended solids.
- Public Sector Reaction: Thermal processing systems, especially incinerators, commonly arouse concern, close scrutiny and hostility from the public.
- Technical Risk: Since changes in waste characteristics are common and process analysis is difficult, a definite risk exists that a new system may not work well, or in extreme cases may not work at all.

However, the technology disadvantages have been reduced through technology development and proper management of system design and operation. There are many cases where properly designed and managed thermal processing systems are effective. Thus, thermal processing has persisted as an important concept in waste management.

THERMAL PROCESSING TECHNOLOGIES

A wide variety of thermal processing technologies is available for hazardous waste treatment, but no single technology is a cure-all. Each technology has advantages and disadvantages that must be evaluated before selection. Technology must be matched with specific waste application.

Incineration is an engineered process that uses thermal oxidation to convert an organic waste to a less bulky inorganic material. Generally, only organic and organic-inorganic wastes are candidates for incineration. Incineration offers the benefits of reducing waste volume, completely eliminating harmful bacterial and viral contaminants, destroying toxic organic compounds and affording the opportunity for waste heat and by-product chemical recovery.

Catalytic incineration systems are used primarily for destruction of gaseous wastes. They are generally sensitive to temperature, having a maximum operating temperature of about 1500°F, and therefore cannot be used on extremely rich fume. Generally, catalytic incinerators are considered for operation with waste containing hydrocarbon levels that are less than 75% of the lower explosive limit.

Oxygen incineration is a recently developed technology, which makes use of oxygen, instead of air, as oxidant for incineration.

Pyrolysis processes partially oxidize waste organic compounds and form combustible gas, which is discharged from the furnace. The low-Btu gas may be used as fuel in an external combustion chamber with heat recovery.

Calcination makes use of cement kilns to treat toxic chemical industrial wastes. Generally, cement kilns have a temperature in excess of 2500°F and have residence time of 15 seconds or more, and thus are viable hazardous waste treatment systems.

Power plant *boiler* also can be used to coincinerate hazardous organic wastes.

Wet air oxidation is a unique process that has been applied successfully to aqueous solutions containing oxidizable compounds in relatively low concentrations. The process operates under the principle that the rate of oxidation of organic compounds is increased significantly at high pressures. Thus, by pressuring an aqueous organic waste, heating it to an appropriate temperature and then introducing atmospheric oxygen, a complete liquid phase oxidation reaction is produced, which destroys most of the organic compounds.

Distillation systems are used to segregate, separate, purify or recover organics.

Steam distillation is a process for removing water-immiscible, volatile organic chemical compounds from waste streams. It is used also to recover heat-sensitive, high boiling, water soluble components from waste streams.

Evaporation systems usually are used to concentrate solid waste and wastewater containing organic or inorganic compounds by drying out the water. The heat source can be steam or hot gases. The equipment may be direct contact or indirect heat exchangers.

Steam stripping systems usually are applied to wastewater containing high volatiles. Steam is used to convert the high volatile materials into vapor phase for further processing or recovery.

Molten salt reactors recently have been developed to pilot-plant and demonstration scale for oxidizing organic wastes. Wastes such as liquids, free-flowing powders and shredded materials may be fed directly to molten salt reactors.

Plasma arc pyrolysis is a newcomer in the waste treatment field. It makes use of a plasma torch to gasify and pyrolyze wastes.

Microwave discharge systems have been explored for destruction of toxic compounds in gaseous, liquid and solid forms. Currently, the system has been found successful, with some inherent limitations, for treating certain toxic organic compounds.

WASTE CLASSIFICATION

Hazardous wastes are numerous in kind and defy easy definition. It is difficult to classify waste materials into a neat package that follows all the rules. However, there are three basic classification methods, which are combined to form a waste classification system. This classification system is directly related to thermal processing requirements and focuses on the information needed to select, design and operate a thermal processing system.

1. Physical classification identifies the physical state of the waste. This classification is needed for the selection and design of waste handling systems and the choice of processing equipment.
2. Chemical classification is the key to selection of proper process design parameters, selection of materials of construction, choice of concentration equipment, design of incinerator hardware, the possibility of by-product recovery, and the requirement of flue gas and discharge water treatment systems.
3. Thermal classification is used to determine energy requirements for processing and to select system configuration.

Based on physical characteristics, typical waste materials are classified as: gaseous, liquid, slurry, sludge, solid and containerized waste.

Based on chemical characteristics, the waste materials can be classified as:

- Clean waste: this group covers hydrocarbons which contain only carbon, hydrogen and oxygen. The oxidation products are considered clean and can be discharged into the atmosphere.

- Wastes generating gaseous contaminants: the oxidation products of this type of waste containing gaseous contaminants, such as hydrogen chloride, etc. Flue gas and discharge water treatment systems generally are required.
- Waste containing heavy metals: the oxidation products of the metals are usually in the solid state at typical processing temperatures. This characteristic affects the selection and design of processing equipment and flue gas treatment systems.
- Waste containing alkali metals: depending on the processing temperature, this type of waste generates solid, liquid or gaseous particulates. The selection and design of processing equipment and the choice of proper process design parameters are critical for trouble-free operating systems.

The elementary constituents of the waste materials for different types of chemical classifications are listed in Table 2-1. It must be noted that chemical classification is applicable only to the oxidation subset of thermal processing technologies.

Based on thermal properties, typical waste materials are classified as:

- Combustible wastes: this group covers wastes which will sustain oxidation reaction without additional energy requirements.
- Noncombustible wastes: this group represents low-Btu value wastes which will not sustain oxidation reaction without aditional energy requirement. The noncombustible wastes can be classified further into two categories: (1) noncombustible waste with no low volatiles (the organics in the waste contain no low volatiles which, when heated, will evaporate) and (2) noncombustible waste with low volatiles (the organics in the waste are heat sensitive and readily vaporized when heated).

Table 2-1. Chemical Classification of Waste Materials

Waste	Element Constituents
Clean Wastes	C,H,O
Wastes Generating Gaseous Contaminants	C,H,O,N,S,F,Cl,Br
Wastes Containing Heavy Metals	C,H,O,N,S,F,Cl,Br Heavy metals, Si
Wastes Containing Alkali Metals	C,H,O,N,S,F,Cl,Br Heavy metals, Si, alkali metals, P,B

These two classifications give important information for the designing of evaporation and steam stripping systems. They are also important factors in the selection of preconcentration equipment of wastes.

The successful application of thermal processing systems requires accurate and reliable information about the composition and characteristics of any waste to be processed. Such data are essential to an understanding of the process and selection of process equipment. The basic waste data required are presented in Table 2-2.

Table 2-2. Basic Waste Data

Parameter	
Ultimate Analysis	C,H,O,N,H_2O,S and Ash
Metals	Na,K,Cu,Ca,V,Ni,Fe,Pb,Hg, etc.
Halogens	F,Cl,Br,I
Others	P,B, etc.
Heating Value	Btu/lb
Solids	Size, form and quantity
Liquids	Viscosity, specific gravity
Gases	Density
Organic Composition	Compound, percent
Special Data	Corrosiveness, reactivity, flammability decomposition, polymerization
Disposal Rate	Peak, average, normal, minimum
Water Content	% Water

APPLICATION OF TECHNOLOGIES

A matrix matching the physical classifications against the thermal processing technologies is presented in Table 2-3. This matrix offers a broad picture of the types of wastes that can be handled by the various thermal processing systems.

The typical operation parameters of the thermal processes are illustrated in Table 2-4.

GENERALIZED SYSTEMS

The generalized thermal processing system is illustrated in Figure 2-1. In the generalized system, wastes together with air, fuel and other utilities, if required, are introduced into the thermal processing unit. The

Table 2-3. Technology Application Matrix

Technology	Waste					
	Containerized	Solid	Sludge	Slurry	Liquid	Fume
Incineration	x	x	x	x	x	x
Catalytic Incineration						x
Pyrolysis	x	x	x	x	x	x
Calcination	x	x	x	x	x	x
Wet Air Oxidation				x	x	
Distillation					x	
Steam Distillation					x	
Evaporation		x	x	x	x	
Steam Stripping					x	
Molten Salt Reactor	x	x	x	x	x	
Plasma Technology	x	x	x	x	x	
Microwave Discharge	x	x	x	x	x	x

Table 2-4. Operating Parameters for Thermal Processing Technologies

	Temperature Range (°F)	Residence Time Range
Incineration	1400–3000	0.1 sec–1.5 hr
Catalytical Incineration	600–1000	1 sec
Pyrolysis	900–1500	12–15 min
Wet Air Oxidation	300– 500 (1500 psig)	10–30 min
Molten Salt Reactor	1500–1800	0.75 sec

product gases from the processing unit are then passed into waste heat recovery systems. The heat recovery system can be gas-to-gas heat exchangers, boilers and others. The exhaust gas from the heat recovery units is then introduced into the chemical recovery system and passed through the air pollution control system, before discharge into the atmosphere. The water discharged from air pollution control systems may or may not require water treatment before final discharge.

It must be noted that Figure 2-1 illustrates the possible components and one possible combination of a thermal processing system. The actual system is dependent on each individual system requirement. For example, the heat recovery system can be used to preconcentrate the waste, as illustrated in Figure 2-2. Also, the chemical recovery can be integrated

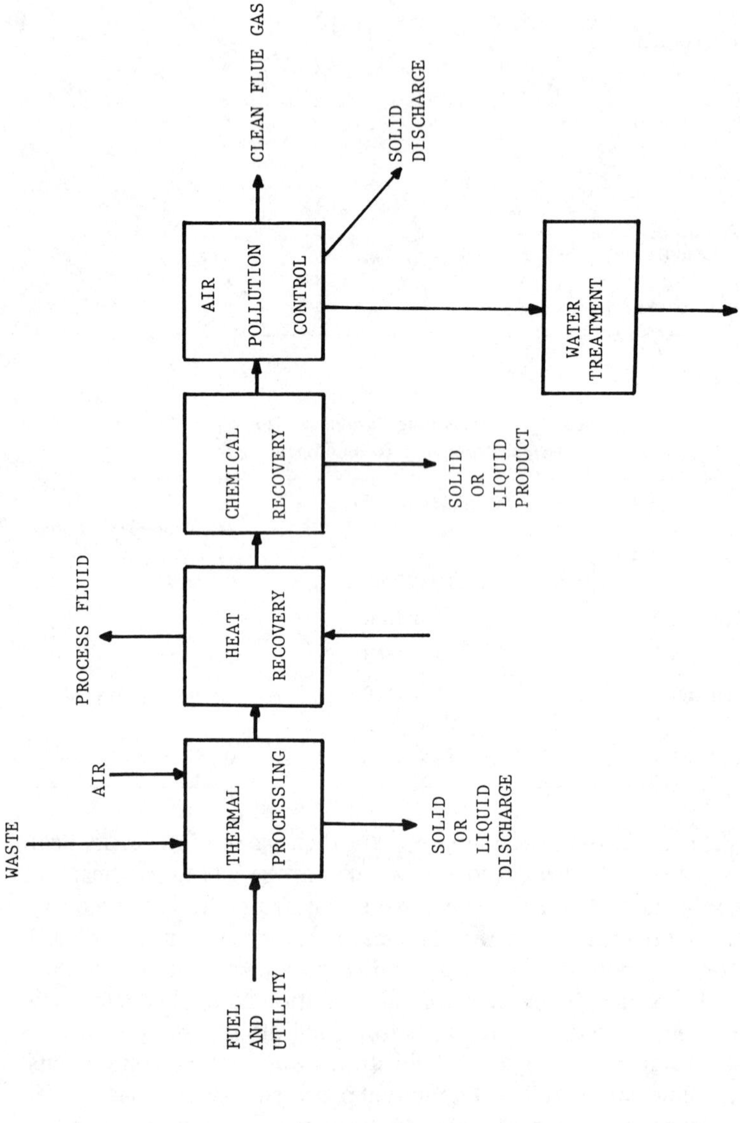

Figure 2-1. Generalized thermal processing system.

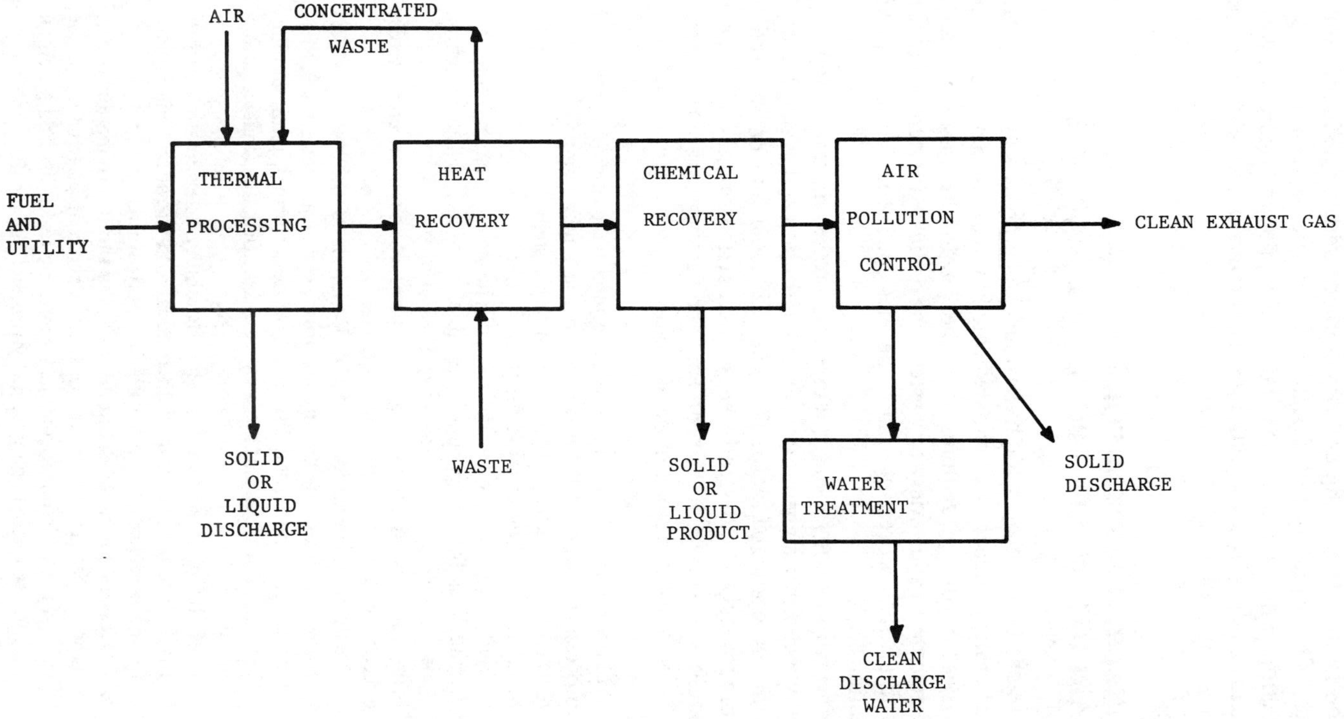

Figure 2-2. Alternate of generalized thermal processing system.

into the thermal processing unit or combined with air pollution control systems. The actual system design is the result of front-end process engineering, which requires the balance of capital and operating cost as well as the study of the integration of the thermal processing system into the production process.

ENGINEERED SYSTEM FOR HAZARDOUS WASTE PROCESSING

There are two concepts for hazardous waste processing; the general purpose system concept and the dedicated system concept. The generalized system concept requires that the hazardous waste processing system handle a wide variety of wastes. The dedicated system concept requires that the processing plant be designed for certain specific applications.

Engineered systems for hazardous waste processing can be defined as systems which are designed, after careful definition and evaluation of the problem, for optimal hazardous waste treatment and energy and by-product recovery. The design of engineered systems requires a coherent methodology to approach the problem. The key steps are summarized in Table 2-5 and are described in detail below.

1. Problem definition is used to broadly establish the goals of the thermal processing systems. This should include, at a minimum:
   a. the type of wastes to be treated in this system,
   b. the degree of destruction for these wastes,
   c. guidelines of air, water and solid discharge requirement, and
   d. guidelines for energy and by-product recovery, such as potential uses of the recovered energy and materials.
2. Front-end process engineering is the heart of the engineered system concept. It consists of the following steps:
   a. Waste characterization, a detailed analysis of the wastes, is performed to determine the physical form, chemical constituents, thermal ratings and treatability of the wastes. Normal, minimum and maximum flow rates of the waste are identified. Seasonal variations are defined for chemical constituents, thermal ratings and flow rates. It must be noted that the treatability determination derives from past experience and theoretical consideration. Pilot plant testing is recommended for new types of wastes.
   b. Process requirement definition involves the determination of the basic process design parameters, the degree of destruction of the wastes, the emission requirements and the feasibility and potential uses for recovered energy and by-product chemicals.

Table 2-5. Engineered System Methodology

1. Problem Definition – what will be accomplished in the thermal processing systems
2. Front-End Process Engineering
   - A. Waste Characterization
   - B. Process Requirement Definition
   - C. Process Concept Development
   - D. Process Design Calculations
   - E. Process Control Philosophy Development
   - F. Process Flow Diagram Preparation
   - G. Preliminary Piping and Instrumentation Diagram Preparation
   - H. Process Equipment Sizing
3. Technical Evaluation
4. Economic Evaluation
5. System Selection

c. Process concept development defines the alternative systems that can be developed to satisfy the waste and process requirement. As with the treatability, the basic process design parameters of the systems are determined by past experience only. New wastes or new processes require pilot plant tests.
At this stage, wastes are grouped, based on their chemical constituents, physical properties and compatibility into several feedstreams. The grouping of the waste is a very critical step. The consideration should include not only physical properties and compatibility, but also chemical constituents in conjunction with process requirement. Process concept development is a prescreening step to determine the feasible systems.

d. Process design calculation involves material and energy balance for system design. The hardware characteristics and limitations are also developed.

e. Process control philosophy development is used to determine the minimal instrumentation and control required for the processes to achieve the waste treatment and process requirement purposes.

f. A process flow diagram then is developed as the result of previous work. A typical process flow diagram is illustrated in Figure 2-3, for an incineration system.

g. A preliminary piping and instrumentation diagram covering the basic process equipment and process control philosophy then will be developed from information obtained thus far. Illustrated in Figure 2-4 is typical preliminary piping and instrumentation diagram for an incineration system.

h. Process equipment, such as incinerators, reactors and scrubbers are then sized.

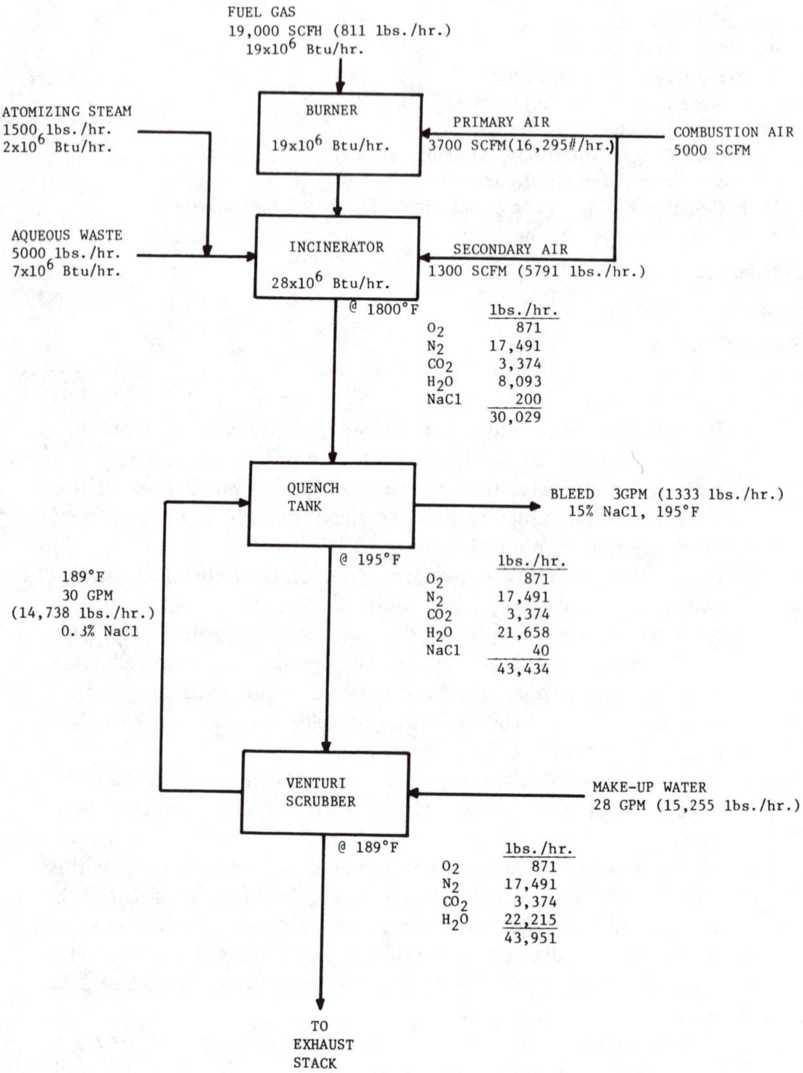
FUEL GAS
19,000 SCFH (811 lbs./hr.)
19x10^6 Btu/hr.
BURNER
19x10^6 Btu/hr.
ATOMIZING STEAM
1500 lbs./hr.
2x10^6 Btu/hr.
PRIMARY AIR
3700 SCFM(16,295#/hr.)
COMBUSTION AIR
5000 SCFM
AQUEOUS WASTE
5000 lbs./hr.
7x10^6 Btu/hr.
INCINERATOR
28x10^6 Btu/hr.
SECONDARY AIR
1300 SCFM (5791 lbs./hr.)
@ 1800°F
lbs./hr.
O2 871
N2 17,491
CO2 3,374
H2O 8,093
NaCl 200
30,029
QUENCH
TANK
BLEED 3GPM (1333 lbs./hr.)
15% NaCl, 195°F
@ 195°F
189°F
30 GPM
(14,738 lbs./hr.)
0.3% NaCl
lbs./hr.
O2 871
N2 17,491
CO2 3,374
H2O 21,658
NaCl 40
43,434
VENTURI
SCRUBBER
MAKE-UP WATER
28 GPM (15,255 lbs./hr.)
@ 189°F
lbs./hr.
O2 871
N2 17,491
CO2 3,374
H2O 22,215
43,951
TO
EXHAUST
STACK

Figure 2-3. Typical process flow diagram.

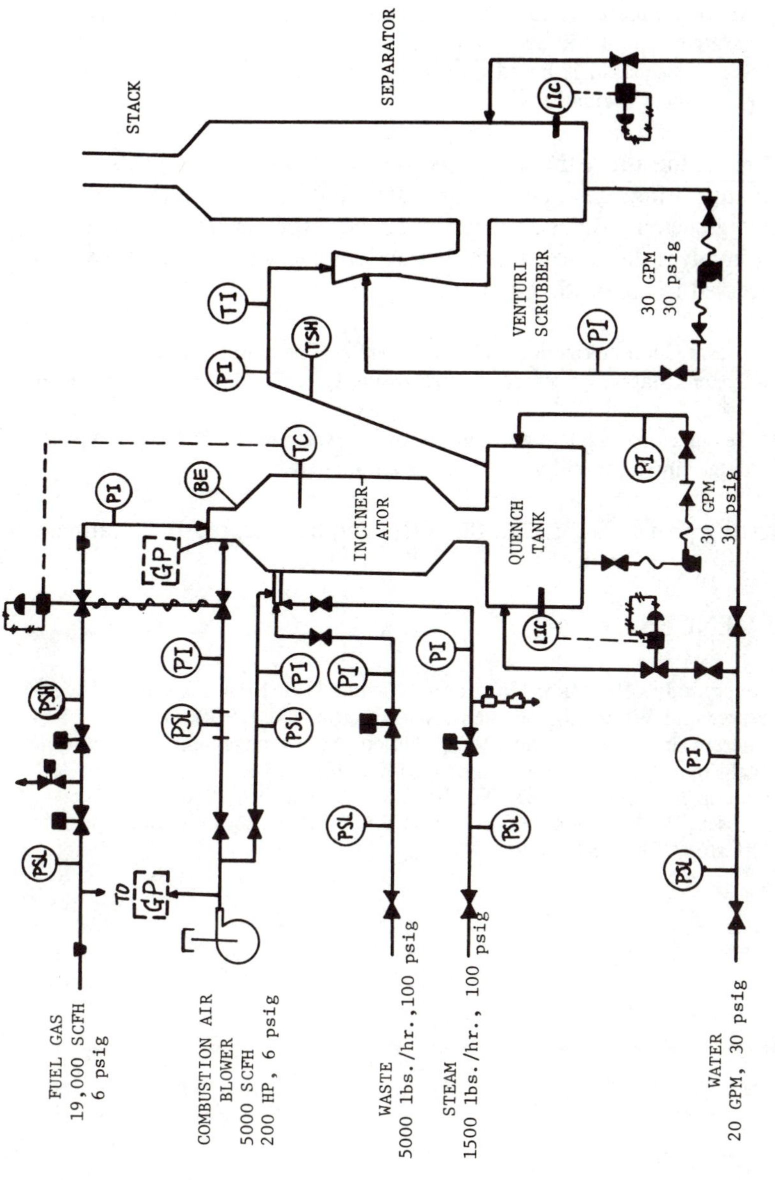

Figure 2-4. Preliminary piping and instrumentation diagram.

3. Technical evaluation is performed next to determine the advantages and disadvantages of the various systems.
4. An economic evaluation then is performed to determine the comparative capital and operating costs of all the systems.
5. System selection is based on the balance between the technical and economical evaluations.

Following the above methodology, the optimal system can be selected. Pilot plant testing, detailed system design and installation then follow.

The engineered system application concept for hazardous waste processing involves the following three steps for every new type of waste to be processed in an existing system.

Step 1. Waste Characterization: determine the pertinent waste characteristics.
Step 2. System Matching: match the processing system and the waste characteristics.
Step 3. Testing: process a small quantity of the waste in the designated system, determine treatability and process parameters.

If testing proves successful, the waste can be accepted for treatment.

REFERENCES

1. "Everybody's Problem: Hazardous Waste," U.S. EPA SW-826, Office of Water and Waste Management, Washington, DC (1980).
2. Cheremisinoff, P. N., and W. F. Holcomb. "Management of Hazardous and Toxic Wastes," Poll. Eng., (April 1976), p. 24.
3. Federal Register, Vol. 45, No. 98, Book 2, May 19, 1980.
4. Niessen, W. R. "Combustion and RCRA," AIChE 86th National Meeting, Houston, TX April 1979.

CHAPTER 3

THERMAL INCINERATION FUNDAMENTALS

Thermal incineration is an engineered process that uses high-temperature thermal oxidation to convert a waste to a less bulky, less toxic or less noxious material. The principal products of incineration are carbon dioxide, water vapor and ash. The hazardous products of incineration are compounds containing sulfur, nitrogen, halogens and heavy metals (mercury, arsenic, selenium, lead and cadmium) [1–3].

If the gaseous combustion products of incineration contain undesirable compounds, air pollution control equipment is required. The solid and liquid effluents may require treatment prior to ultimate disposal or discharge [4,5].

Generally, only organic wastes are candidates for incineration, although some inorganics can be thermally degraded. Incineration offers the benefits of reducing waste volumes and eliminating hazardous organic compounds while affording the opportunity for by-product and waste heat recovery.

EVOLUTION OF INCINERATION TECHNOLOGY

The practice of incineration goes back to the discovery of fire and the generation of combustible wastes. A typical old-fashioned incineration system is illustrated in Figure 3-1. Wastes and air are mixed in a refractory lined furnace where organics are oxidized. Hot combustion product gases are then discharged into the environment. This type of incineration system serves its purpose when the wastes generated are simple. As waste characteristics become more complex and environmental effects are

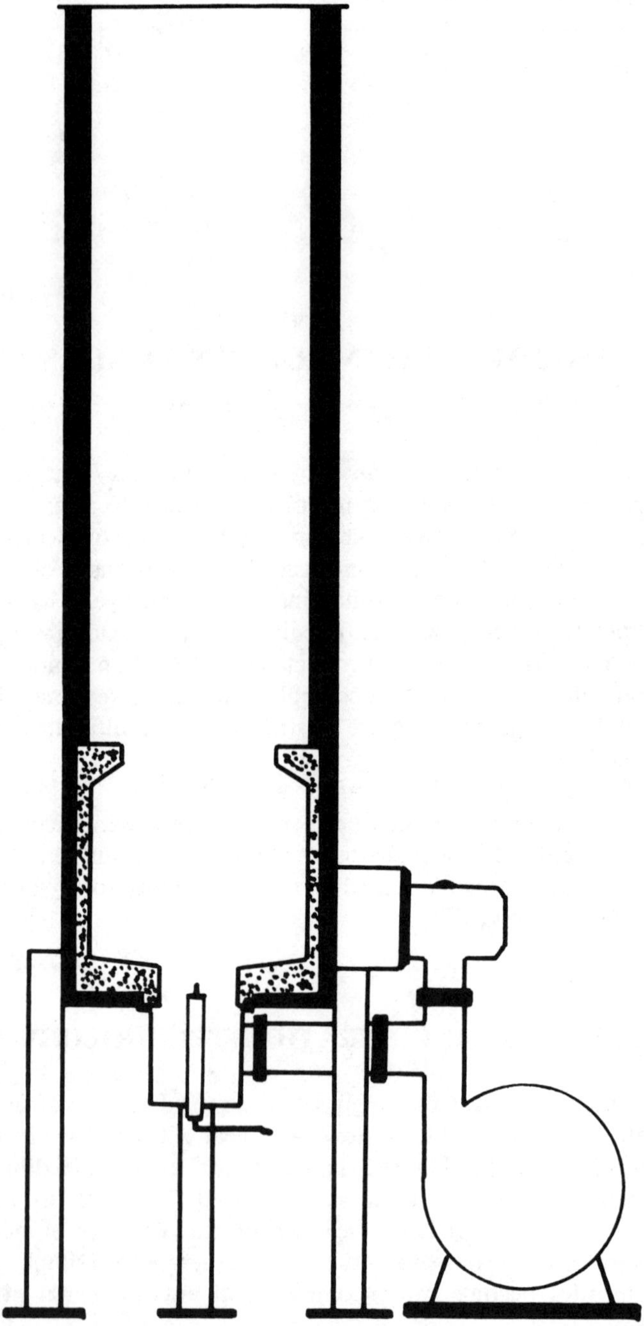

Figure 3-1. Open incinerator (reproduced courtesy of The Trane Company, La Crosse, WI).

taken into account, air pollution control equipment has been introduced into incineration systems to ensure a clean stack. For example, packed tower and venturi scrubbers are used for gaseous and solid particulate removal, as shown in Figures 3-2 and 3-3. With the shortage of energy and raw materials, waste heat and by-product recovery have been gradually integrated into incineration systems as in Figures 3-4 to 3-6 [6,7]. Thus, a modern incineration system (Figure 3-7) has become a complex chemical processing plant, and bears little resemblance to its ancestor, Figure 3-1.

WASTE HANDLING

The first step in incineration is the introduction of wastes into the incerator. Methods vary with the types of wastes.

Solid Wastes

Solid waste introduction is a four-step method as illustrated in Figure 3-8. To begin with, a waste pit provides a staging area for safe and convenient holding of wastes. In a properly designed pit, waste from numerous sources can be mixed to provide a degree of homogeneity of feed for the incinerator. For hazardous waste handling, the waste pit must be maintained at a negative pressure. The exhaust gases can pass through an activated carbon filter to remove hazardous organic materials. The exhaust gases can also be used as combustion air in the incinerator. Fires occasionally develop in the waste pit, so the pit area should be equipped with fire hoses. The entire pit should be watertight and sloped to drains for dewatering. The drain water must be properly treated to avoid the discharge of hazardous materials. Special caution must be taken to avoid the mixing of noncompatible wastes in the pit.

Cranes are usually used to transport the waste to the charging hoppers, and to mix and distribute the solid waste in the pit. This mixing results in a more uniform burning material and better utilization of pit capacity. The crane types most commonly used are the monorail crane and the bridge crane. The monorail is a fixed unit suspended from a single rail that crosses the pit in only one horizontal direction. The bridge crane can maneuver horizontally in two directions. Incinerator cranes usually use a closed scoop bucket or a grapple. The closed scoop is a clamshell with heavy steel lips usually equipped with short teeth. The grapple is similar to a clamshell but has much longer teeth called tines. For hazardous waste applications, the crane should be operated remotely or automatically.

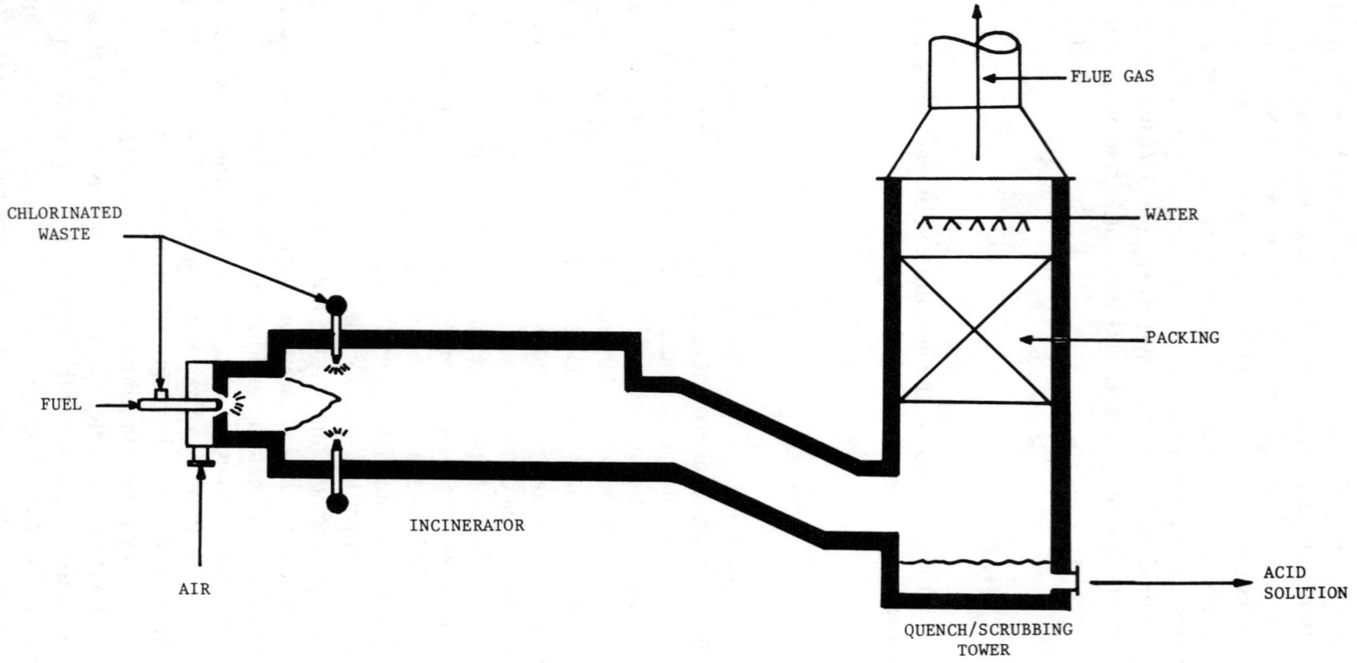

Figure 3-2. Chlorinated hydrocarbon incineration system (reproduced courtesy of The Trane Company, La Crosse, WI).

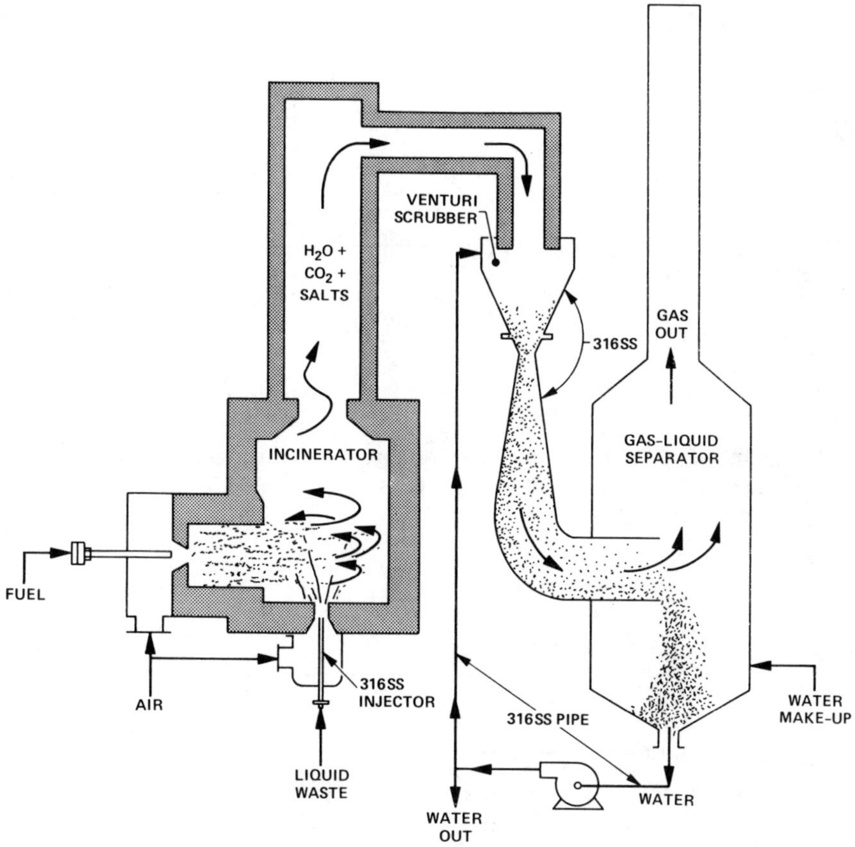

Figure 3-3. Incineration system with metallic compounds (reproduced courtesy of International Nickel Co., New York).

Charging hoppers are used to maintain a supply of solid waste to the incinerator. In batch-feed furnaces, a gate separates the charging hopper from the furnace and supports the solid waste while the furnace is burning the previous charge. In a continuous feed furnace, the waste-filled hopper and chute assist in maintaining an air seal to the incinerator as well as providing a continuous supply of waste. Most charging hoppers have the shape of an inverted, truncated pyramid. The size of the hopper opening should be large enough to prevent arching of oversized material across the hopper bottom.

The charging chutes connect the hopper to the furnace. The discharge of waste into the furnace can be achieved by gravity, reciprocating, vibrating or ram feed mechanisms. The charging chute, because of its

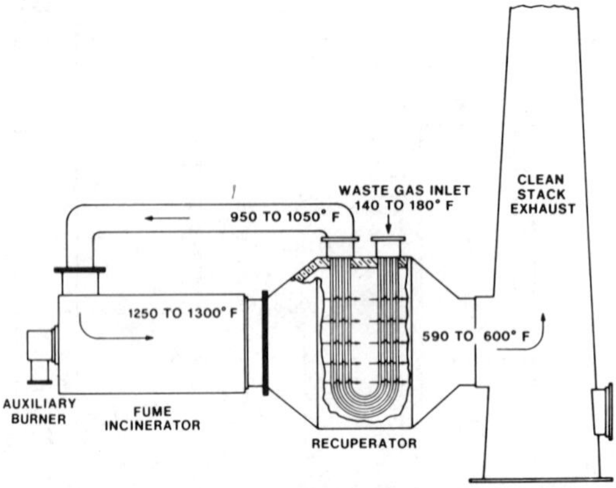

Figure 3-4. Incineration system with gas preheating (reproduced courtesy of The Trane Company, La Crosse, WI).

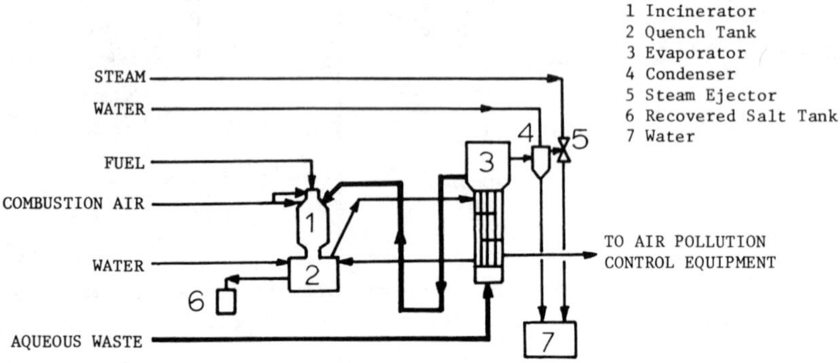

Figure 3-5. Incineration system with waste preconcentration (reproduced from Reference 5, courtesy of Chemical Engineering Progress, New York).

proximity to the furnace, is exposed to extreme heat. For this reason, chute walls are often water jacketed. A hopper cover or other means of closure is provided for ending a burning cycle in a continuous feed furnace.

A typical installation is described in Figure 3-9.

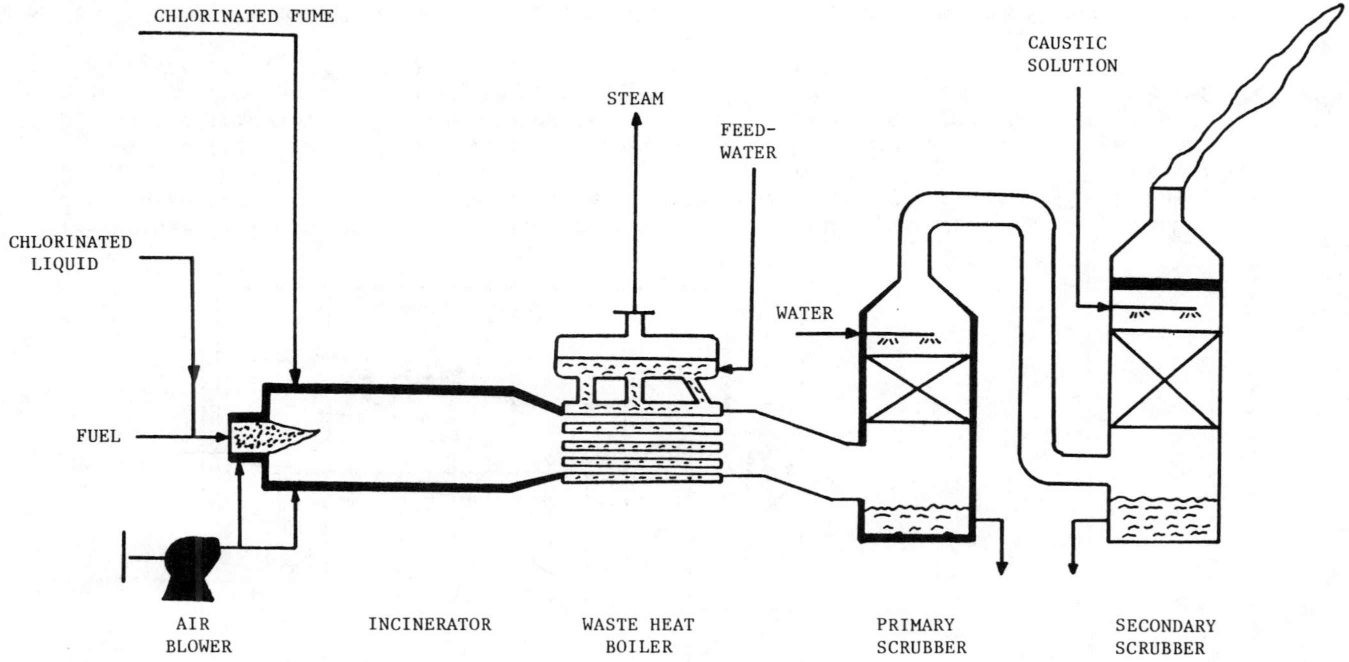

Figure 3-6. Chlorinated hydrocarbon incineration with waste heat and by-product recovery (reproduced from Reference 13, courtesy of Marcel Dekker, Inc., New York).

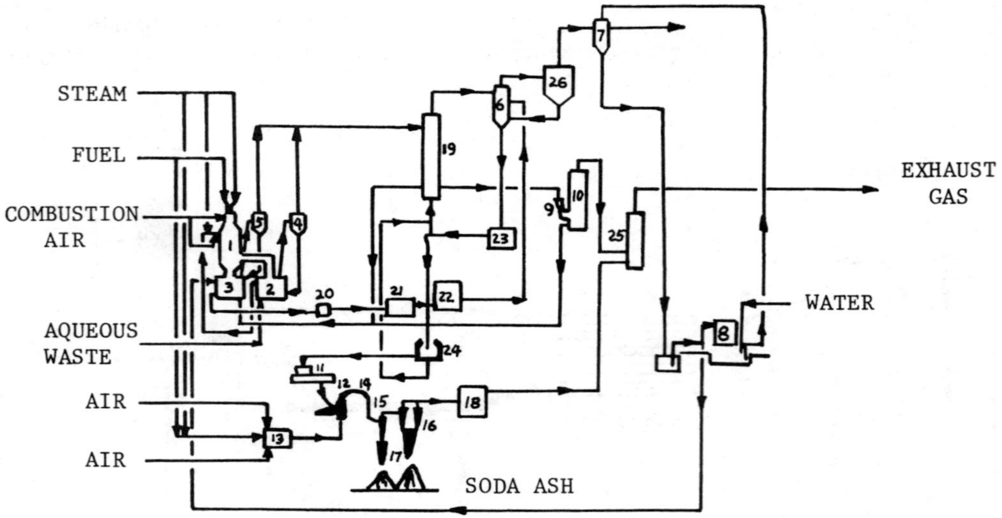

1 - burner-incinerator	8 - cooling tower	15 - primary cyclone	22 - tank
2 - concentrator	9 - venturi scrubber	16 - secondary cyclone	23 - tank
3 - quench tank	10- separator	17 - rotary valve	24 - centrifuge
4 - mist eliminator	11- screw conveyor	18 - baghouse	25 - stack
5 - mist eliminator	12- crusher	19 - heat exchanger	26 - mist eliminator
6 - flash drum	13- air heater	20 - tank	
7 - condenser	14- dryer	21 - filter	

Figure 3-7. Waste disposal and sodium carbonate recovery system (reproduced from Reference 5, courtesy of Chemical Engineering Progress, New York).

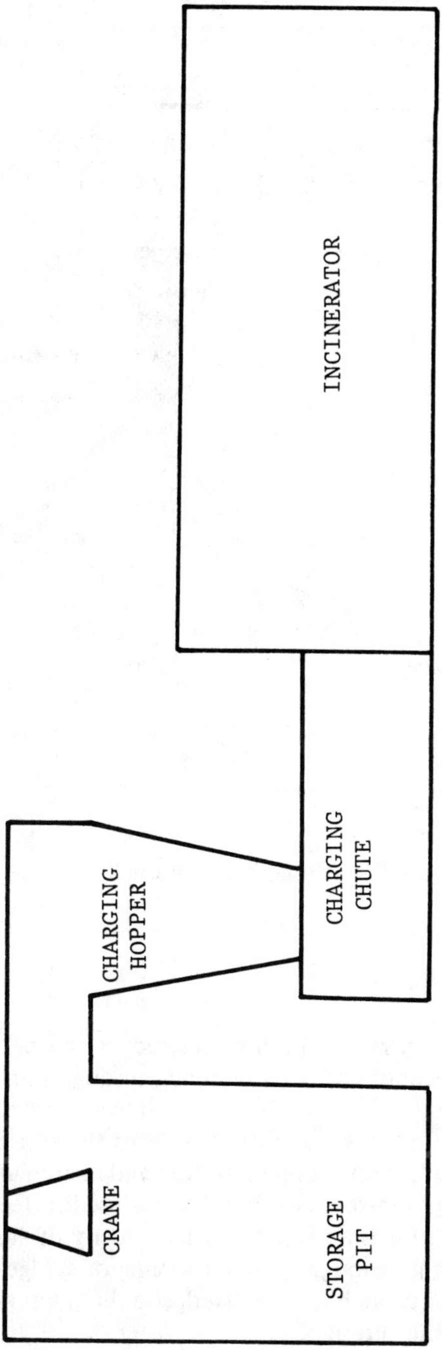

Figure 3-8. Solid waste handling system.

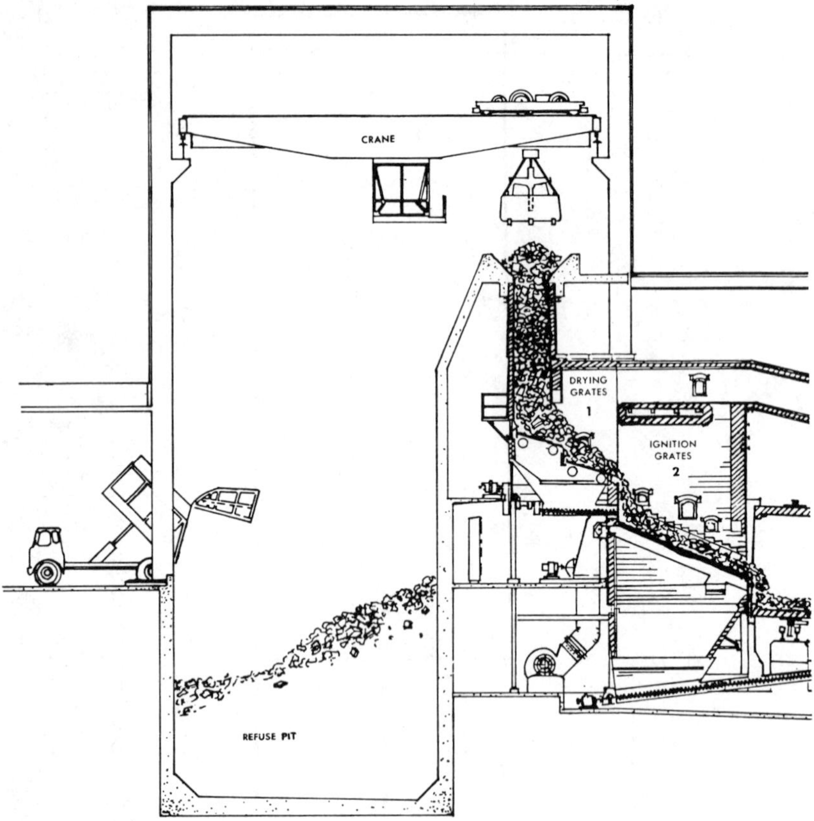

Figure 3-9. Typical installation of solid waste handling system.

Sludge and Slurry Wastes

Unless a sludge or slurry has been dewatered, it can be transported most efficiently and economically by pumping through pipelines [8].

There are two systems which can be used to introduce sludges into an incineration system. Illustrated in Figure 3-10a is the system normally used for pumpable sludges. A pumping station and recirculation line are used to keep the sludges mixed. A split stream is used to feed the waste into the incinerator through an injector. The velocity of sludges in the split stream must be high enough to avoid settling of sludges. Thus, the pipe size must be small enough to avoid sludge settling, but large enough to permit sludge passing through.

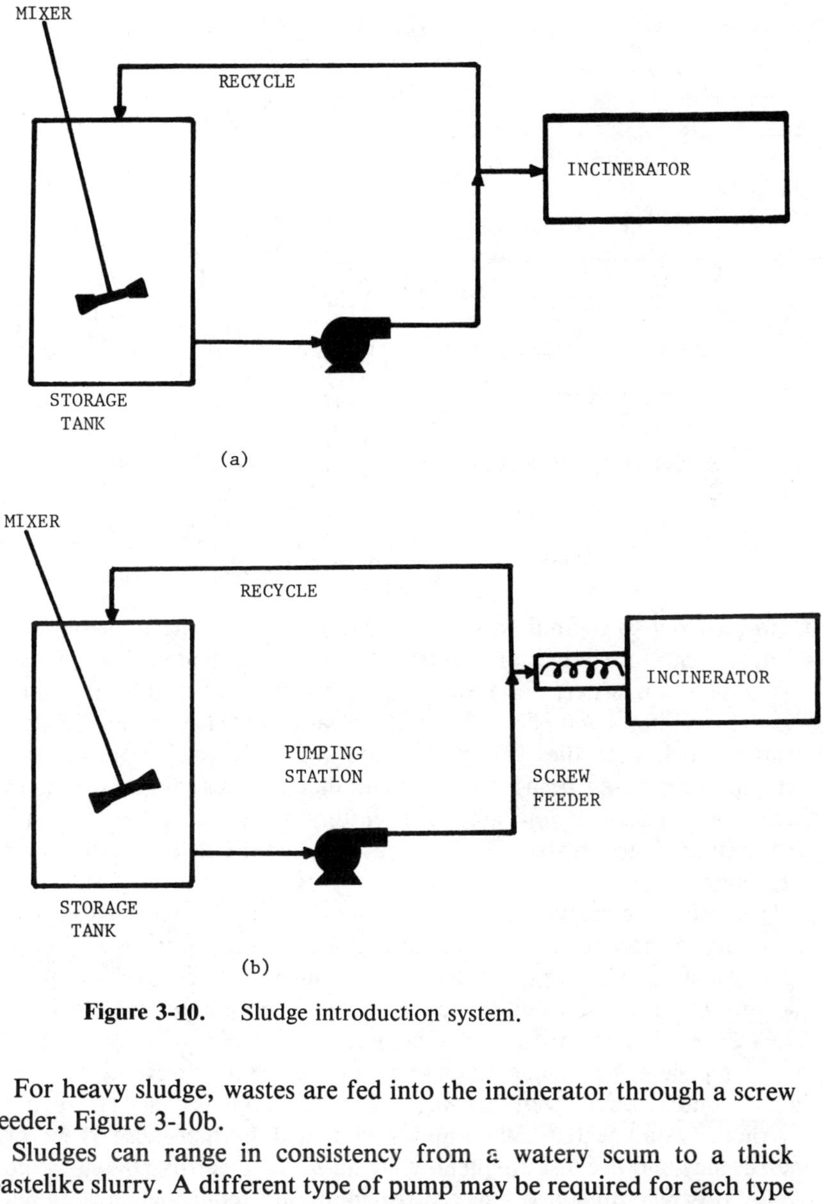

Figure 3-10. Sludge introduction system.

For heavy sludge, wastes are fed into the incinerator through a screw feeder, Figure 3-10b.

Sludges can range in consistency from a watery scum to a thick pastelike slurry. A different type of pump may be required for each type of sludge. Pumps which are currently utilized for sludge transport include centrifugal, torque flow, plunger, piston, piston/hydraulic diaphragm, progressive cavity, rotary, diaphragm, ejector and air lift pumps.

A *centrifugal pump* (Figure 3-11) consists of a set of rotating vanes in a housing or casing. The vanes may be either open or enclosed. The vanes

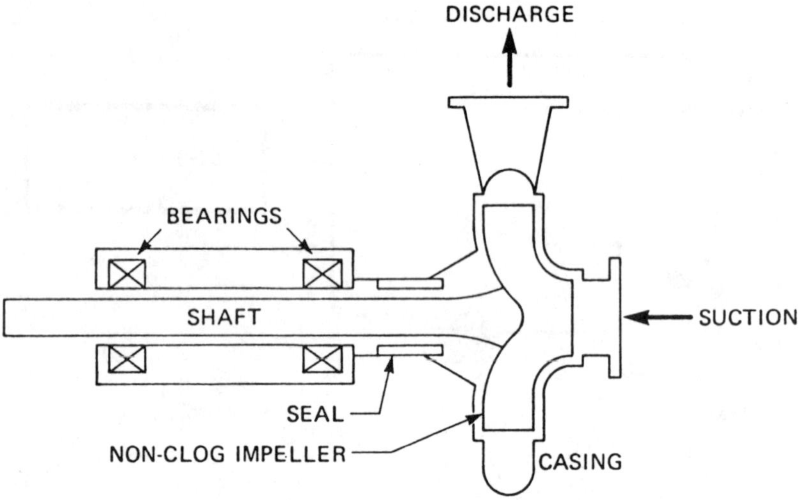

Figure 3-11. Centrifugal pump [8].

impart energy to a fluid through centrifugal force. The nonclog centrifugal pump for sludges, in comparison to a centrifugal pump designed to handle clean water, has fewer, but larger and less obstructed, vane passageways in the impeller; has greater clearances between impeller and casing; and has sturdier bearings, shafts and seals. Such nonclog centrifugal pumps may be used to circulate digester contents and transfer sludges with relatively low solids concentration. The larger passageways and greater clearances result in increased reliability at a cost of lower efficiency.

The basic problem with using any form of centrifugal pump on sludges is choosing the correct size. At any given speed, centrifugal pumps operate well only if the pumping head is within a relatively narrow range; the variable nature of sludge, however, causes pumping heads to vary. The selected pumps must be large enough to pass solids without clogging of the impellers, yet small enough to avoid diluting the sludge by drawing in large quantities of overlying water. Throttling the discharge to reduce the capacity of a centrifugal pump is impractical, both because of energy inefficiency and because frequent clogging of the throttling valve would occur. It is recommended that centrifugal pumps requiring capacity adjustment be equipped with variable-speed drives. Fixed capacity in multiple-pump applications is achieved by equipping each pump with a discharge flow meter and using the flow meter signal in conjunction with the variable-speed drive to control the speed of the pump. Seals last longer if back suction pumps are used. Utilizing the back of the impeller for suction removes areas of high pressure inside the pump casing from the location of the seal and prolongs seal life.

Propeller or mixed-flow centrifugal pumps are sometimes used for low head applications because of higher efficiencies.

A *torque flow pump* (Figure 3-12), also known as a recessed impeller or vortex pump, is a centrifugal pump in which the impeller is open-faced and recessed well back into the pump casing. The size of particles that can be handled by this type of pump is limited only by the diameter of the suction or discharge openings. The rotating impeller imparts a spiraling motion to the fluid passing through the pump. Most of the fluid does not actually pass through the vanes of the impeller, thereby minimizing abrasive contact and reducing the chance of clogging. Because there are no close tolerances between the impeller and casing, abrasive wear within the pump is further reduced. The price paid for increased pump longevity and reliability is that the pumps are relatively inefficient compared with other nonclog centrifugals: 45 vs 65% efficiency is typical. The pumps must be sized accurately so that excessive recirculation does not occur at any condition at the operating head. Capacity is adjusted and controlled as for other centrifugal pumps.

Plunger pumps (Figure 3-13) consist of pistons driven by an exposed drive crank. The eccentricity of the drive crank is adjustable, offering a

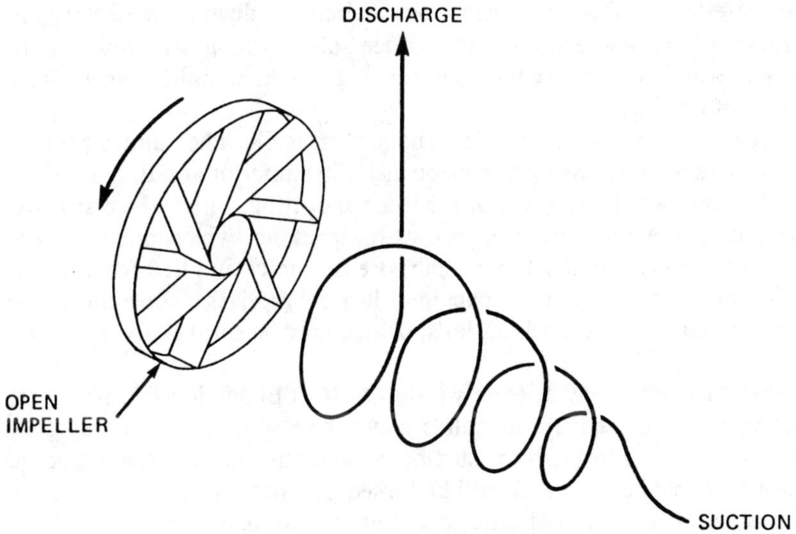

Figure 3-12. Torque flow pump [8].

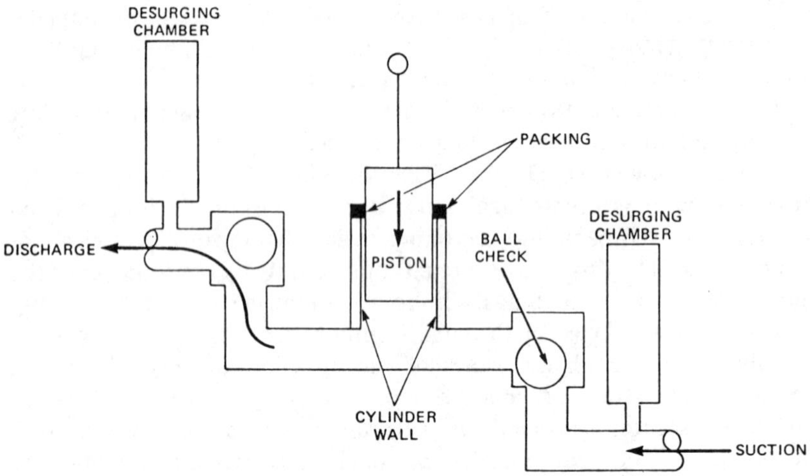

Figure 3-13. Plunger pump [8].

variable stroke length and hence a variable positive displacement pumping action. The check valves, ball or flap type, are usually paired in tandem before and after the pump. Plunger pumps have constant capacity regardless of large variations in pumping head, and can handle sludges up to 15% solids if designed specifically for such service. Plunger pumps are cost-effective where the installation requirements do not exceed 500 gpm, a 200-ft discharge head, or 15% sludge solids. Plunger pumps require daily routine servicing by the operator, but overhaul maintenance effort and cost are low.

The plunger pump's internal mechanism is visible. The pump's connecting rod attaches to the piston inside its hollow interior and this "bowl" is filled with oil for lubrication of the journal bearing. Either the piston exterior or the cylinder interior houses the packing, which must be kept moist at all times. Water for this purpose is usually supplied from an annular pool located above the packing; the pool receives a constant trickle of clean water. If the packing fails, sludge may be sprayed over the surrounding area.

Plunger pumps may operate with up to 10 ft of suction lift; however, suction lifts may reduce the solids concentration that can be pumped. The use of the pump with the suction pressure higher than the discharge is not practical because flow will be forced past the check valves. The use of special intake and discharge air chambers will reduce noise and vibration. These chambers also smooth out pulsations of intermittent flow. Pulsation dampening air chambers, if used, should be glass lined to avoid destruction by hydrogen sulfide corrosion. If the pump is operated when the discharge pipeline is obstructed, serious damage may occur to the pump, motor or pipeline; this problem can be avoided by a simple shear pin arrangement.

Piston pumps are similar in action to plunger pumps, but consist of a guide piston and a fluid power piston (see Figure 3-14). Piston pumps are capable of generating high pressures at low flows. These pumps are more expensive than other types of positive displacement sludge pumps, and are usually used in special applications such as feed pumps for heat treatment systems. As for other types of positive displacement pumps, shear pins or other devices must be used to prevent damage due to obstructed pipelines.

A variation of the piston pump has been developed for use where reliability and close control are needed. The pump utilizes a fluid power

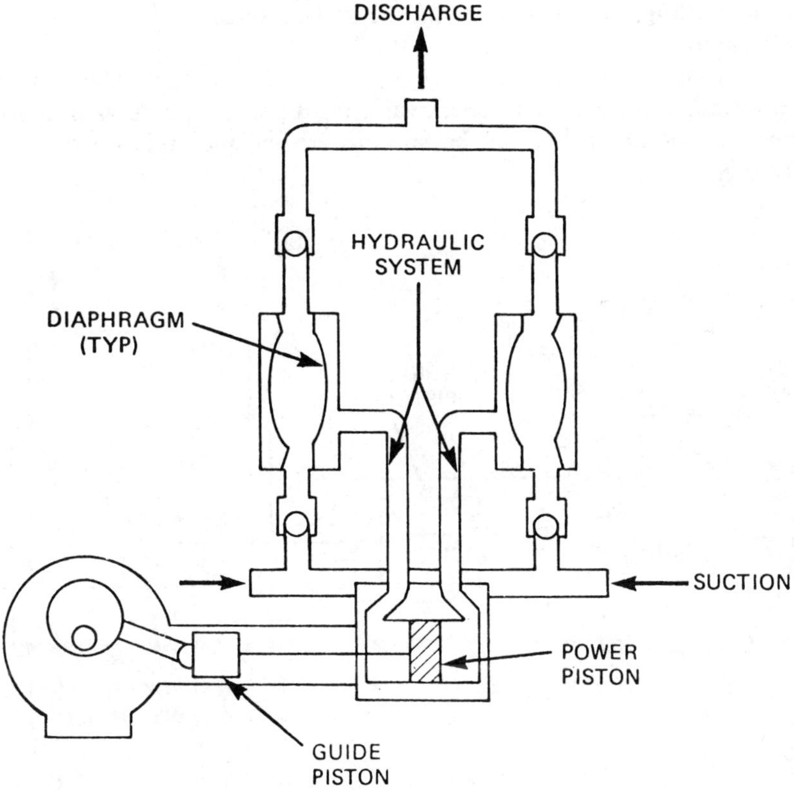

Figure 3-14. Piston pump [8].

piston driving an intermediate hydraulic fluid (clean water), which in turn pumps the sludge in a diaphragm chamber (Figure 3-15). The speed of the hydraulic fluid drive piston can be controlled to provide pump discharge conditions ranging from constant flow rate to constant pressure. This special pump has the greatest initial cost of any piston pump, but the cost is usually offset by low maintenance and high reliability.

The *progressive cavity pump* (Figure 3-16) has been used successfully on almost all types of sludge. This pump comprises a single-threaded rotor that operates with an interference clearance in a double-threaded helix stator made of rubber. A volume or "cavity" moves "progressively" from suction to discharge when the rotor is rotating, hence the name "progressive cavity". The progressive cavity pump may be operated at discharge heads of 450 ft on sludge. Capacities are available to 1200 gpm. Some progressive cavity pumps will pass solids up to 1.125 in. in diameter. Rags or stringy material should be ground up before entering this pump.

The rotor is inherently self-locking in the stator housing when not in operation, and will act as a check valve for the sludge pumping line. An auxiliary motor brake may be specified to enhance this operational feature.

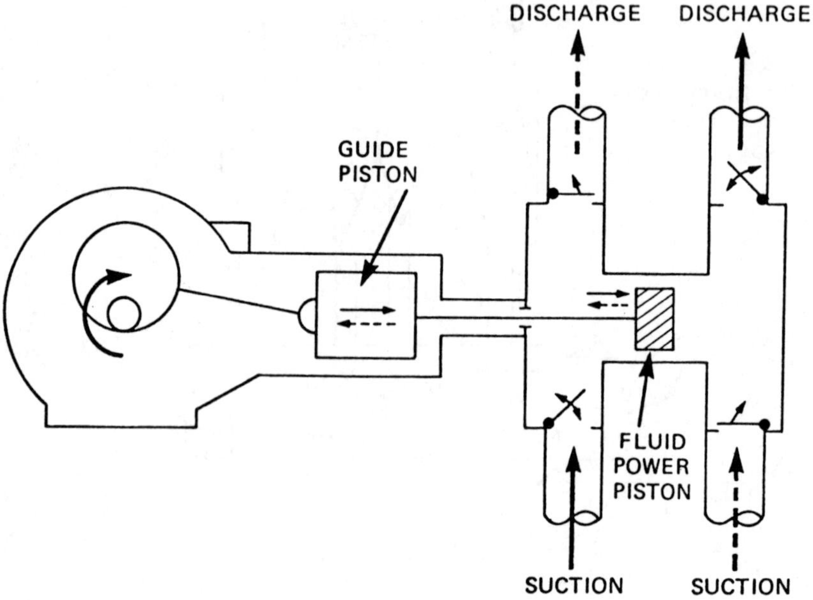

Figure 3-15. Combination piston/hydraulic diaphragm pump [8].

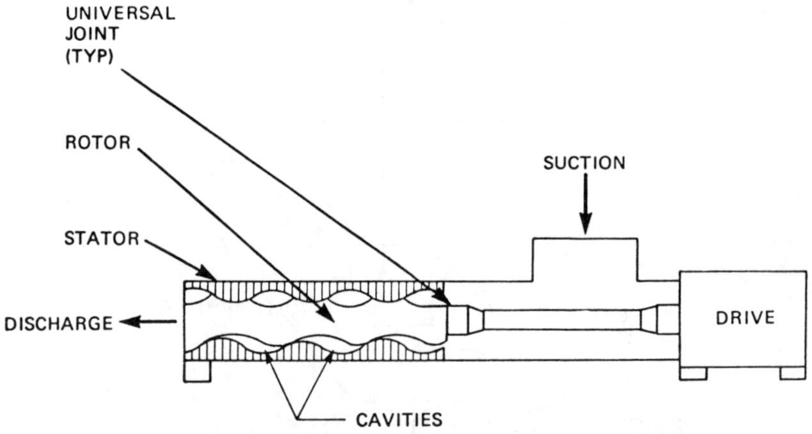

Figure 3-16. Progressive cavity pump [8].

The total head produced by the progressive cavity pump is divided equally between the number of cavities created by the threaded rotor and helix stator. The differential pressure between cavities directly relates to the wear of the rotor and stator because of the slight "blow by" caused by this pressure difference. Because wear on the rotor and stator is high, the maintenance cost for this type of pump is the highest of any sludge pump. Maintenance costs are reduced by specifying the pump for one class higher pressure service (one extra stage) than would be used for clean fluids. This creates many extra cavities, reduces the differential pressure between cavities and consequently reduces rotor and stator wear. Also, speeds should not exceed 325 rpm in sludge service, and grit concentrations should be minimized.

Since the rotor shaft has an eccentric motion, universal joints are required between the motor shaft and the rotor. The design of the universal joint varies greatly among different manufacturers. Continuous duty, trouble-free operation of these universal joints is best achieved by using the best quality (and usually most expensive) universal gear joint design. Discharge pressure safety shutdown devices are required on the pump discharge to prevent rupture of blocked discharge lines. No-flow safety shutdown devices are often used to prevent the rotor and stator from becoming fused due to dry operation. As previously mentioned, these pumps are expensive to maintain. However, flow rates are easily controlled, pulsation is minimal and operation is clean. Therefore, progressive cavity pumps are widely used for pumping sludge.

Diaphragm pumps (Figure 3-17) utilize a flexible membrane that is

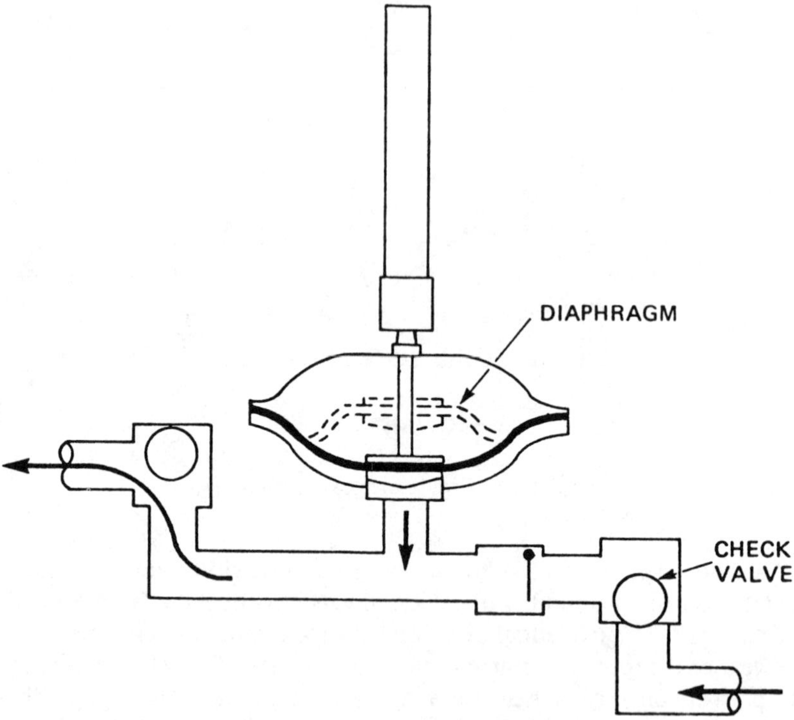

Figure 3-17. Diaphragm pump [8].

pushed or pulled to contract or enlarge an enclosed cavity. Flow is directed through this cavity by check valves, which may be either ball or flap type. The capacity of a diaphragm pump is altered by changing either the length of the diaphragm stroke or the number of strokes per minute. Pump capacity can be increased and flow pulsations smoothed out by providing two pump chambers and utilizing both strokes of the diaphragm for pumping. Diaphragm pumps are relatively low head and low capacity units; the largest available air-operated diaphragm pump delivers 220 gpm against 50 ft of head. The distinct advantage of the diaphragm pumps is their simplicity. Their needs for operator attention and maintenance are minimal. There are no seals, shafts, rotors, stators or packing in contact with the fluid; also, diaphragm pumps can run in a dry condition indefinitely.

Flexure of the diaphragm may be accomplished mechanically (push rod or spring) or hydraulically (air or water). Diaphragm life is a function of the dicharge head and the total number of flexures rather than of the abrasiveness or viscosity of the pumped fluid. Power to drive air-driven diaphragm pumps is typically double that required to operate a mechanically driven pump of similiar capacity. However, hydraulically operated (air or water) diaphragms generally outwear mechanically driven diaphragms by a considerable amount. Hydraulically driven diaphragm pumps are suitable for operation in hazardous explosion-prone areas; also, a pressure release means in the hydraulic system provides protection against obstructed pipelines. In some locations, high-humidity intake air will cause icing problems to develop at the air release valve and muffler on an air-driven diaphragm pump. A compressed air dryer should be used in the air supply system when such a condition exists.

The overall construction of some diaphragm pumps, the common "trash pump" is such that abrasion may cause the lightweight casings to fail before the diaphragms, since the pumps are not designed for continuous service.

Rotary pumps (Figure 3-18) are positive displacement pumps in which two rotating synchronous lobes essentially push the fluid through the pump. Rotary pump lobe configurations can be designed for specific applications. Rotational speed and shearing stresses are low. It is not recommended that the pumps be considered self-priming or suction lift pumps, although they are advertised as such. The pump operates best

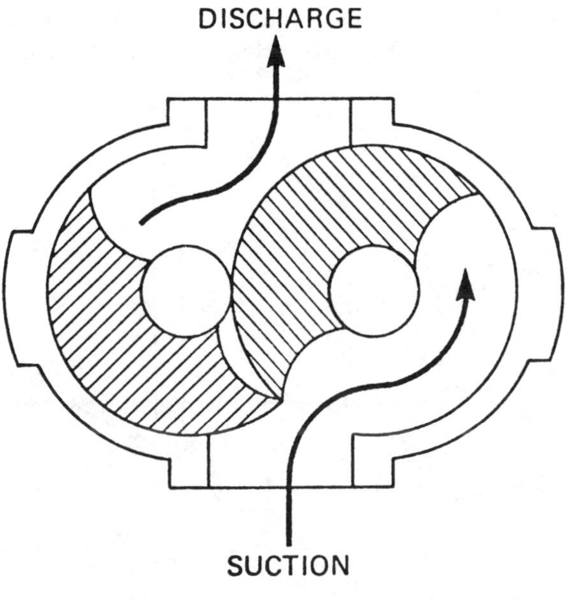

Figure 3-18. Rotary pump [8].

with a bottom suction and top discharge. Only very limited operational data are available for rotary pumps used on sludge. Two manufacturers now advertise hard metal two-lobed pumps for sludge usage. Lobe replacement for these pumps appears to be less costly than rotor and stator replacement on progressive cavity pumps. Rotary pumps, like other positive displacement pumps, must be protected against pipeline obstructions.

Sludge ejectors use a charging pot which is intermittently discharged by a compressed air supply (see Figure 3-19). Ejectors are more applicable for incoming average flow rates less than 150 gpm.

Gas lift pumps use low pressure gas released within a confined riser pipe with an open top and bottom. The released gas bubbles rise, dragging the liquid up and out of the riser pipe. Air is commonly used, in which case the pump is called an air lift pump. Gas lift sludge pumps are usually limited to lifts of less than 10 feet. The capacity of a lift pump can be varied by changing its buoyant gas supply. Reliable gas lift pumping requires the gas supply to be completely independent of outside flow or pressure variables. Gas lift pumps with an external gas supply and circumferential diffuser can pass solids of a size equivalent to the internal diameter of the confining riser pipe without clogging. When the gas is supplied by a separate inserted pipe, the obstruction created negates this nonclog feature. Gas lift pumps, because of their low lifting capability, are very sensitive to suction and discharge head variations, and to variations in the depth of buoyant gas release. Special discharge heads are

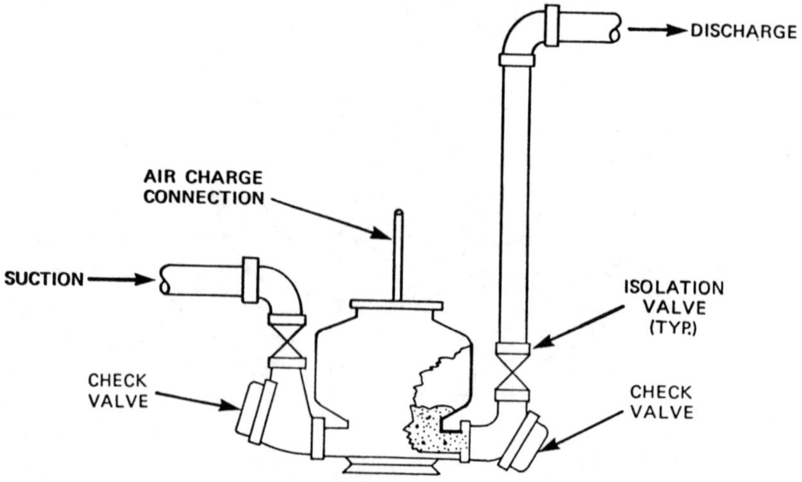

Figure 3-19. Ejector pump [8].

usually required to enhance the complete separation of diffused air once the discharge elevation has been reached.

Water eductors use the suction force (vacuum) created when a high-pressure water stream is passed through a streamlined confining tube (venturi). Like the air lift pump, water eductors have no moving parts.

Sludges can be introduced into the incinerator by a pump of the type described above, through an open pipe. Dilute sludges can also be "sprayed" into the incinerator with the externally atomized injector described in the liquid waste section. A screw feed mechanism (Figure 3-20) is another means for introducing the sludges into the incinerator chamber.

Liquid Wastes

The typical liquid waste handling system is illustrated in Figure 3-21. The storage tank provides pneumatic or mechanical mixing of the wastes to avoid stratification. A pump is used to transport the waste liquid to the point of injection. Recirculation is provided to prevent stratification of liquids in the line.

The injector atomizers used to inject waste into the combustion zone or the oxidation chamber are critical equipment. The main purposes of injecting the liquid as a spray are to:

1. break up the liquid waste into fine droplets, and
2. introduce the liquid waste into the incinerator in a specific location

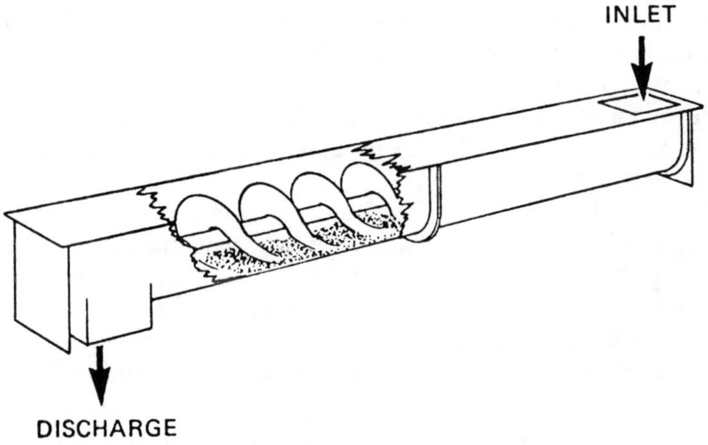

Figure 3-20. Screw feeder [8].

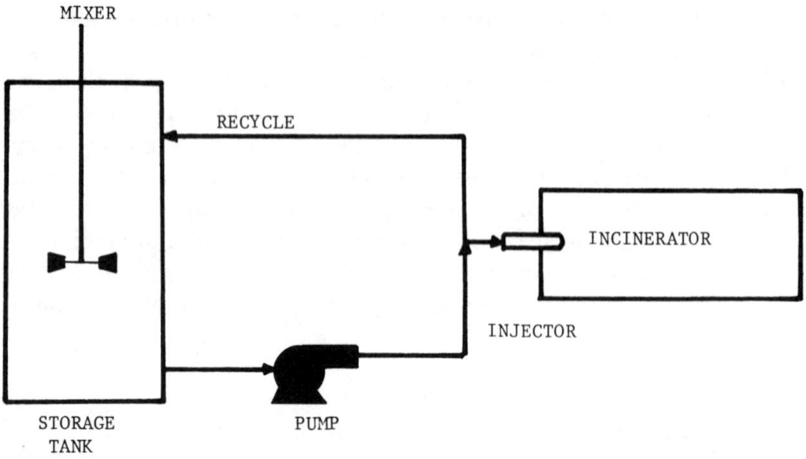

Figure 3-21. Liquid waste handling system.

with a specific pattern, with sufficient penetration and kinetic energy, and at a specific flow rate.

Therefore, it is important that the nozzle design maintain these important features so that evaporation and oxidation will be completed.

The major problems that occur in nozzles are plugging, erosion and corrosion. Proper nozzle design is necessary to prevent plugging and erosion (and proper selection of materials is necessary to minimize or prevent erosion and corrosion). The following information must be provided to the incinerator designer to ensure proper nozzle selection: flow rate, specific gravity, viscosity curve, chemical analysis, solids content and maximum particle size.

There are three basic designs classified by the form of energy supplied to the nozzles: (1) hydraulic, (2) pneumatic, and (3) combination of hydraulic and pneumatic [9,10].

In thermal incineration applications, the primary purpose of the injector is to break up the liquid into droplet sizes as small as possible to provide maximum surface area for heat and mass transfer. Fine droplet size leads to rapid evaporation, superheating, ignition and oxidation. This is sometimes not possible with waste liquids containing solids (sludges). However, nozzles have been developed to produce particle sizes as low as one or two microns.

In atomizers, where atomization is solely by hydraulic pressure, liquid break-up is usually caused by the collapse of unstable sheets or jets. Centrifugal pressure nozzles impart a swirling motion to the liquid by tangential passages, slots or cores. The swirling film of liquid then emerges through a circular orifice as a thin hollow conic sheet. Since it is unstable, it immediately collapses into ligaments which break up into small droplets of various sizes. Such devices produce droplets ranging from one or two microns up to several hundred microns. Although it is desirable to have all the droplets of equal size, this is usually not possible in conventional atomizer design.

In most cases, as nozzle capacity increases, the droplet size increases also. Coarser droplets generally result (as metering passages are enlarged to allow greater liquid throughput). Finer droplets usually result from larger spray angles. Droplet size may vary even with a given spray pattern. In hollow cone sprays, for example, there is usually a preponderance of larger droplets at the outside of the pattern. Other factors being equal, cone spray nozzles usually produce somewhat finer droplets than do flat spray or flooding nozzles.

Droplet size usually is reduced by the increasing of atomizing pressure. As an approximate rule of thumb, droplet size may be assumed to vary as the -0.03 power of pressure. However, the exact effect is strongly dependent on nozzle design and other operating variables. At very high pressures, a further increase in pressure usually has a negligible effect on atomization.

Droplet size is quite sensitive to the viscosity of the liquid wastes. Higher viscous forces must be overcome by the energy supplied to the nozzle. This detracts from the energy available for liquid break-up, resulting in coarser droplets. With very viscous materials, satisfactory atomization becomes difficult and high operating pressures are usually required.

Liquid wastes having high surface tension are more difficult to atomize. Compared with viscosity, surface tension has a relatively minor effect, because it normally varies over a much smaller range. The density of liquid waste and ambient also affect the size of droplets. Agglomeration caused by clustered spray units can be a factor. Poor atomization can occur with a plugged or contaminated or worn out nozzle.

The pneumatic nozzle has been developed to overcome some of these limitations of hydraulic nozzles. For pneumatic atomizer, the shearing force required to break up the liquid sheet is attained by either air or steam pressure. The kinetic energy supplied by the atomizing air or steam causes the liquid steam to be broken apart into droplets.

Illustrated in Figure 3-22 is a typical pneumatic nozzle, the external atomized tip, for highly viscous materials. The design requires only low-pressure liquids, thereby minimizing the problems of pumping very high

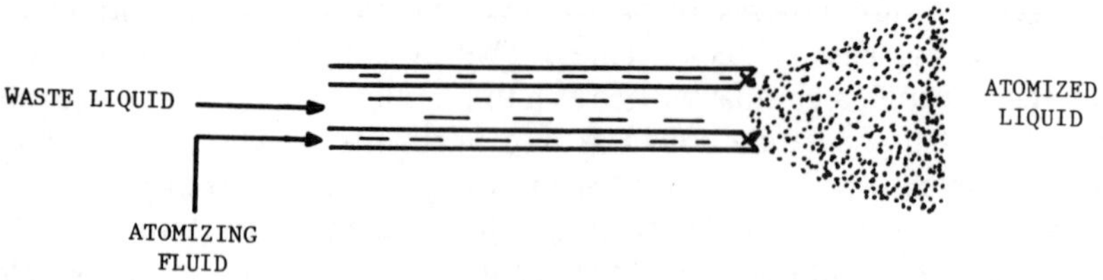

Figure 3-22. TEAT nozzle (reproduced courtesy of The Trane Company, La Crosse, WI).

viscosity materials. Normally, the liquid waste pressure required is <20 psig and in most cases is ~5 psig. The air or steam orifices are directed at the liquid stream on the external surface, creating a vortex action. Sometimes, the atomizing fluid also can be directed at the center of the stream, breaking it up and developing the required spray angle.

These nozzles have been used on materials with viscosities as high as 4500 seconds saybolt universal at 300°F. One advantage of this design is that the atomizing media flow rate is fixed for the flow rate of the liquid waste stream. At reduced flow rates, atomizing fluid rate remains constant and minimizes control problems. The rate of atomizing fluid to the process fluid is in the range of 0.2 to 0.5 lb of steam or air/pound of waste fluid.

Illustrated in Figure 3-23 is a dual liquid nozzle [10]. Using this type of nozzle, incompatible liquids can be introduced into the combustion chamber separately, without requiring multiple injectors. The gaseous wastes usually are introduced through the outer ring of the injector.

This type of injector generates a solid cone. Combustion rates usually are slowed down because of poor combustible air mixing in the center waste mass.

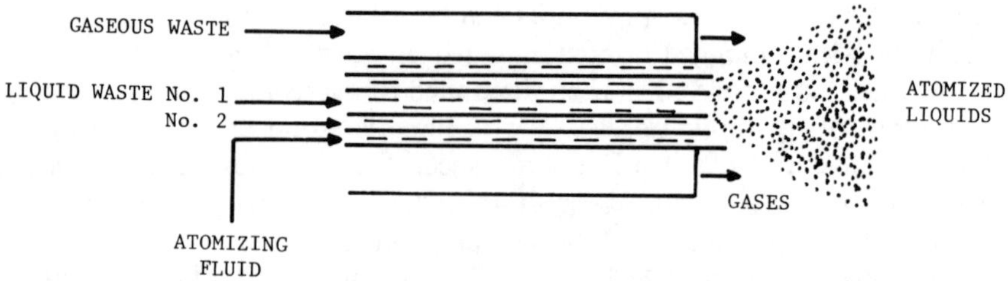

Figure 3-23. Dual fluid TEAT nozzle (reproduced courtesy of The Trane Company, La Crosse, WI).

Illustrated in Figure 3-24 is a different type of externally atomized tip. The spray generated by this type nozzle is hollow cone.

Another form of pneumatic nozzle, the sonic nozzle, depends on sonic atomization to break up viscous liquids. Liquid breakup is achieved in an intense field of sonic energy instead of a small orifice. Any liquid delivered to the sonic energy field can be atomized. Again, these nozzles are activated by a pressurized gas, either steam or compressed air. The gas passes through the nozzle's inner bore at high velocity and into a resonator cavity. The sonic atomizers are relatively unaffected by viscosity variations. The characteristics of a sonic nozzle are the soft, plume-shaped spray with low mass droplets, low forward velocity and low impingement characteristics. Their fine atomization provides uniform distribution of the liquid with minimum overspray and waste. Large liquid ports permit the atomization of contaminated fluids without clogging or malfunction. Low liquid pressures considerably reduce wear and performance degradation with continuous use.

The position of the nozzle with respect to a gas flow pattern within the incineration chamber should be considered carefully. In certain applications, a vortex action created by the gases within the incinerator tends to destroy the major advantages of the sonic nozzles, i.e., changing the soft, low forward velocity plume into a sheet, and, thus, causing the atomized droplets to agglomerate into larger droplets. Therefore, it is important to determine the proper nozzle location. It is also important to study the combined effect of the low forward velocity, soft and plume-shaped spray with the velocities generated within the incineration chamber. Another feature of the sonic nozzles is a narrow angle of

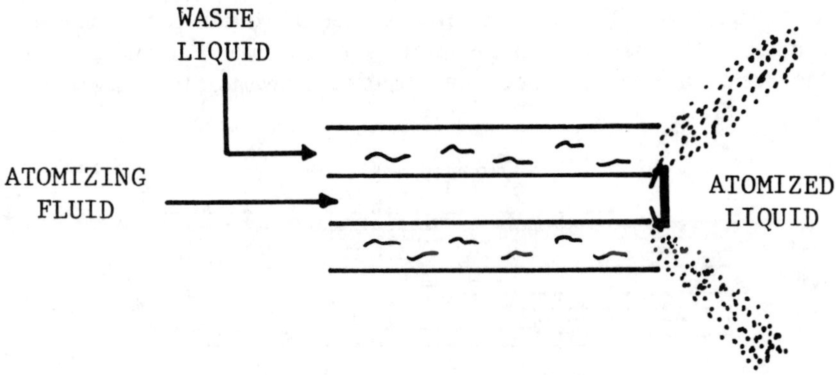

Figure 3-24. HEAT nozzle (reproduced courtesy of The Trane Company, La Crosse, WI).

atomization. This also should be reviewed in determining nozzle location within an incinerator chamber.

The combination hydraulic and pneumatic nozzle with internal atomization is used where materials of low viscosity and minimum solids content are to be incinerated.

Figure 3-25 illustrates a typical design of an internal mix nozzle for wastes at pressures up to 150 psig with steam pressure at 90–100 psig. These nozzles operate basically as a hydraulic nozzle at the maximum flow rate. Minimal atomizing medium flow rates are required at this operating point. As the flow rate is decreased, the atomizing medium flow is increased to maintain a constant differential pressure across the outer tip openings.

The advantage of this type of nozzle is that it will give a turndown ratio of 3:1 to 4:1 at a pressure level of 150 psig. The hydraulic nozzles require pressures of 1000–1500 psig to maintain the same turndown. However, the incinerator nozzle does require sufficient quantities of steam or air at the low flow rate to maintain good atomization. At this point, the pressure of the waste is at a minimum level of 60–80 psig and the break-up of the liquid particles is accomplished by the swirling motion of the steam or air.

In the selection of nozzles, the following parameters are critical to proper material choice: operating temperature, operating pressure and internal flow areas.

The most important parameter is the operating temperature. Hydraulic-type nozzles usually are cooled by the liquid while in operation. However, radiation from the incineration chamber, which may be in the range of 1400–3000°F, will affect the metal temperature of the nozzle. It is important to know the operating temperature during operation, as well as at shutdown. Temperature level is caused by radiation from the chamber into which the nozzle is spraying, convection of air and gases at the face of the nozzle, and cooling effects by the waste, atomizing steam and/or air.

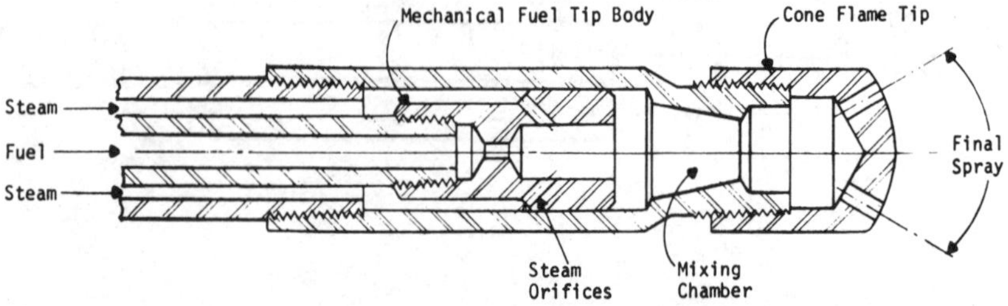

Figure 3-25. Internal mixed nozzle (reproduced from Reference 9, courtesy of Chemical Engineering Progress, New York).

Chemical reactions take place at the face of the nozzle between the hot gases in the chamber and the waste being injected. For example, if water is sprayed into an incineration chamber, the cooling effect of the spray nozzle can cause condensation of the hot incineration gases along the wall of the spray nozzle. These gases, if acidic, will then react with the metal if at or below the dewpoint of the acid. Therefore, it is important to know that the temperature of the metal will be kept at a safe level to prevent acid condensation and corrosion. If this cannot be determined, it will be necessary to use a material resistant to the particular acid.

Another example is the reaction between the waste being sprayed and the gases in the incinerator chamber. Velocities normally used at the exit of a nozzle will cause recirculation of the hot gases from the chamber into the waste spray. If the gases contain a material that can be absorbed in the spray – for example, an aqueous waste spray in a chamber containing chlorine or hydrochloric acid gases – the water will react immediately with the gases (in this example, to form a hydrochloric acid mist in the fine spray droplets). These will be recycled into the turbulent zone at the nozzle exit and come in direct contact with the nozzle body. Under the right metal temperature conditions, the acid attack of metal will begin almost immediately. Material selection of the nozzle is thus very-important.

To prevent nozzle plugging, the velocity, temperature and chemical analysis of the waste are important to nozzle design. Pluggng will occur with wastes which contain polymers. In these cases, the materials of construction are not as important as the internal flow passages and orifices which may create deterioration of the nozzle performance. A very small opening will cause rapid blockage and deterioration of spray angle, atomization and, finally flow. The effect of the orifice size of the nozzle can be seen in Figure 3-26; in the smaller opening a slight deposit of polymer restricted the area by 77%. With the larger nozzle, the same deposit of polymer on the circumference of the nozzle decreased the flow area by 44%.

GENERALIZED SYSTEM

The possible components of an incineration system are illustrated in Figure 3-27. The actual system is dependent on each individual application requirement. It may consist of one or more of the components.

The heart of an incineration system is the incinerator which is used to oxidize hazardous organic substances in the wastes. In the incinerator, auxiliary fuel, combustion air, atomizing and cooling medium are used.

To minimize auxiliary fuel requirement, waste preconcentration such

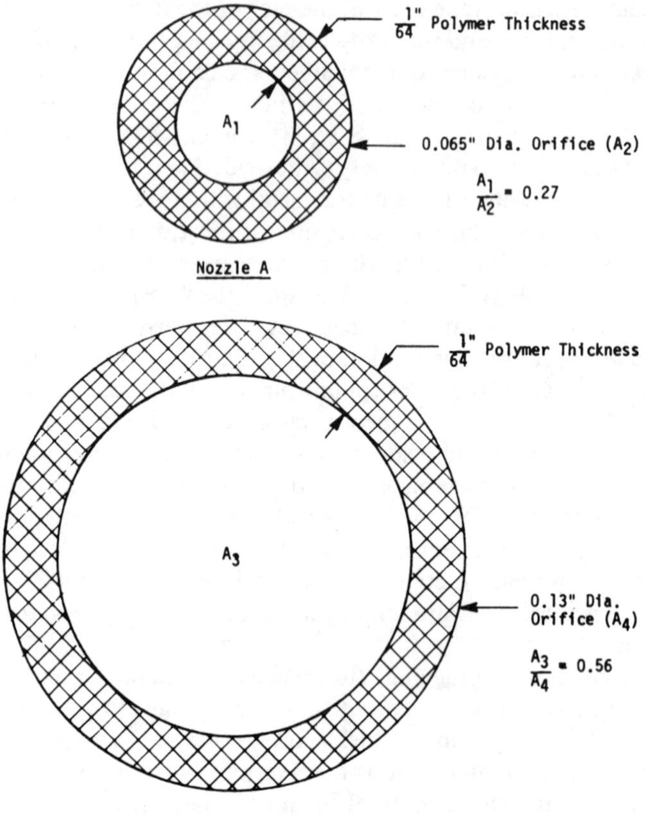

Figure 3-26. Effect of blockage on nozzle orifices (reproduced from Reference 9, courtesy of Chemical Engineering Progress, New York).

as removal of water, and preheating systems can be used. Heat recovery systems can be used to recover waste heat as steam or other usable form. The exhaust gases from incinerator and/or waste heat recovery equipment are then cooled in a gas cooling system. By-product recovery and air pollution control system are then used to treat the exhaust gases for recovery of valuable materials or to ensure clean exhaust gases. The gas cooling, by-product recovery and air pollution control systems can be integrated into a single piece of equipment or be designated into several pieces of equipment.

The solid residue discharged from the incinerator, waste heat recovery system, gas cooling equipment and air pollution control system can be landfilled or treated before landfilled, depending on process requirement. The liquid from the gas cooling system and air pollution control

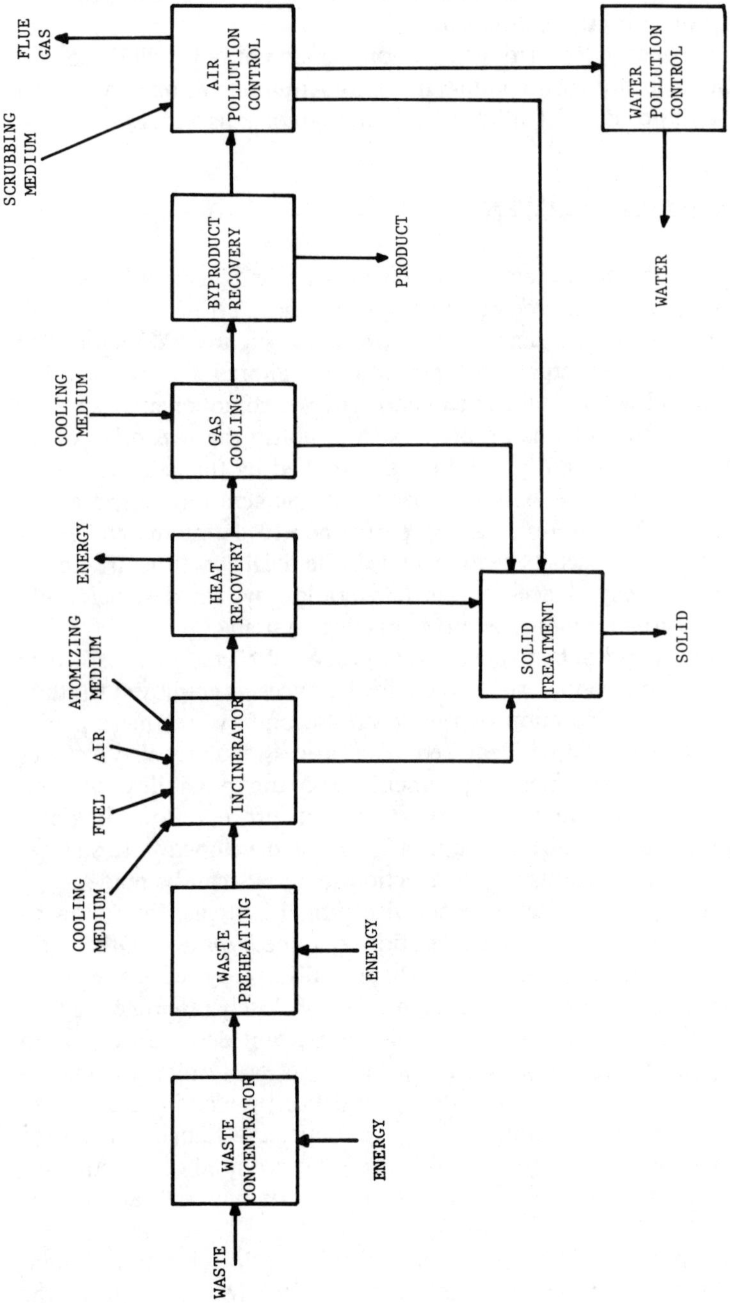

Figure 3-27. Generalized system.

equipment can be either discharged or treated before discharged, also depending on process requirement.

Thus, a properly designed incineration system not only will dispose of wastes, but also will ensure minimal energy requirement, maximum heat recovery and no harmful solid, liquid and gaseous discharges.

SYSTEM DEVELOPMENT

Developing the most practical and energy-efficient incineration system with optimal design parameters is not an easy task. To achieve this goal, a programmatic system development program (Figure 3-28) should be followed [11]. The actual program will be tailored to each specific application and will contain one or more of the comoponents.

The initial phase of this program is to establish the *feasibility* of incineration. Waste stream properties, as supplied by the generators, are used to determine the best approach for incineration purposes. If necessary, bench scale tests can be performed to determine characteristics of the wastes, such as heating values, chemical constituents, etc. At this stage, past experiences of the incineration system designer are a valuable tool to determine the most practical system.

The second step will be to *develop the process*. Process analysis, which utilizes computerized material and energy balances, is employed to study options for the incineration of the waste. Secondary treatment equipment requirements will be identified. The process analysis also includes the minimization of fuel requirements and the possibility of heat recovery and by-product recovery. A set of process flow diagrams (PFD), which present different options, will be developed in this stage, and preliminary selections of construction materials can be made.

If adequate past experience exists with similar systems, the following two steps – pilot plant test and operation – can be bypassed. Otherwise, they will be conducted to ensure a reliable full-scale system.

The *pilot plant* selected for testing must very closely resemble the full-size unit. Pilot plant testing will provide important design information concerning waste handling system, waste injection system, mixing requirements, incineration temperature, residence time and excess air requirement. The three definable design parameters – temperature, time and excess air – can be optimized to provide the required combustion efficiency and destruction efficiency. Construction materials also can be selected and tested in this phase.

A continuous pilot plant operation is conducted in this phase. Potential problems can be identified and corrected before the design of the final system.

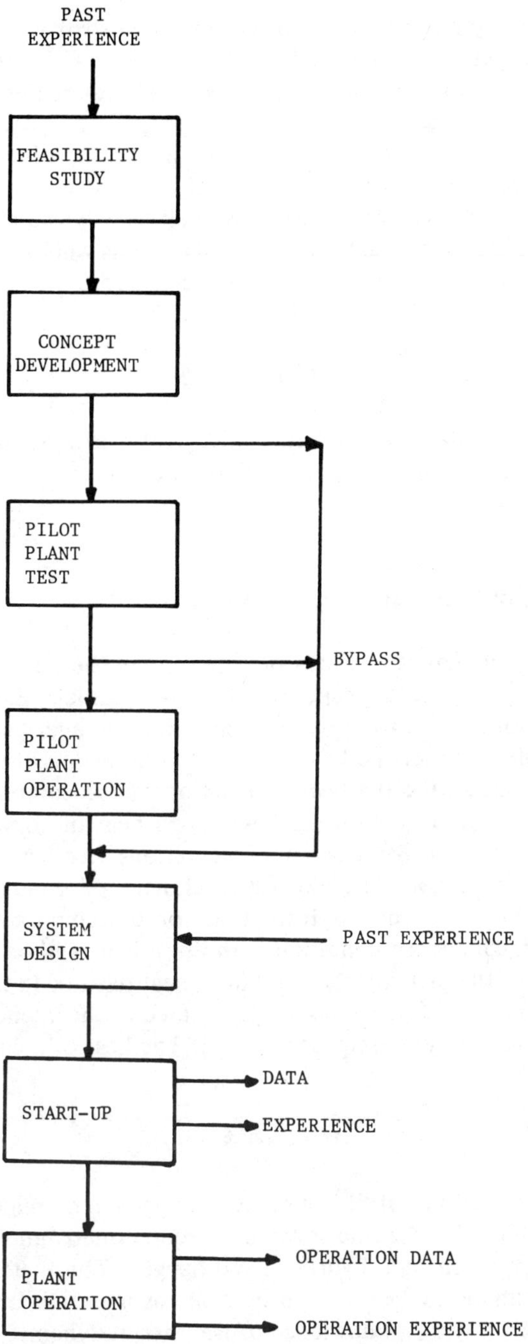

Figure 3-28. System development program.

At this stage, using the information obtained from previous phases and past experiences, the final system will be *engineered and designed*.

During startup, more information will be gathered and built into the supplier's experience data bank.

When the system reaches steady-state operation, it is necessary to collect as much *operation data* as possible: flows, temperatures, pressures, compositions and emissions. Process analysis will also be performed on the operating system. All these data and analysis will then be fed back into the designer's data bank for future reference.

COMBUSTION FUNDAMENTALS

The design of an incinerator must center around the combustion process. Selected topics on combustion fundamentals are discussed in the following sections.

Heat of Combustion

There are different methods of determining the heat of combustion, one of the fundamental properties of waste materials. Experimentally, a bomb calorimeter can be used to determine the high heating values of combustible materials [12]. The heat of combustion also can be determined by calculating the heat of reaction of the combustion reaction, through heat of formation [13]. Although heat of combustion can be determined rigorously, feasibility calculations frequently must be performed without complete experimental heat of combustion data or knowledge of the heats of formation for the compounds being considered. Under these conditions, an empirical method is used which makes use of the fact that the amount of heat released in the oxidation of a wide range of compounds is closely related to the quantity of theoretical combustion oxygen required [14-17]. The heat of combustion can be estimated by

$$H_C = 6000\,R, \text{ Btu/lb}$$

where R = pounds of stoichiometric oxygen requirements/pound of combustibles. This method is valid for compounds and waste streams containing only carbon, hydrogen and oxygen. This method can also be used to estimate the heat of combustion for materials containing other elements. However, a knowledge of the thermodynamic equilibrium of the combustion process and the thermal oxidation operating conditions is necessary; then a reasonably accurate estimate of the stoichiometric oxygen demand can be made and the heat of combustion can be estimated.

Material Balance

A material balance is a quantitative expression of the law of conservation:

$$\text{input} = \text{output} + \text{accumulation}$$

Stoichiometric analysis is usually used as the simplified approach to explain incineration material balances. The stoichiometric analysis is an overall material balance which considers the incineration process as an idealized chemical reaction which chemically combines combustible materials and air to form the product of composition.

A typical incineration material balance can be illustrated by the incineration of propane in air.

$$C_3H_8 + 5O_2 + 19.13N_2 \rightarrow 3CO_2 + 4H_2O + 19.13N_2$$

By developing this equation, the following information on incineration is determined:

1. the stoichiometric oxygen demand: for propane the oxygen demand is 3.63 lb/lb waste;
2. the stoichiometric fuel air ratio: for propane this ratio is 1 to 15.81 by weight;
3. the stoichiometric combustion products: for propane the products are carbon dioxide, water vapor and oxygen and
4. the stoichiometric gas analysis: for propane the analysis is:

Flue Gas Component	Wt/Unit Wt Waste	Weight %	Volume %
N_2	12.17	72.40	73.18
CO_2	3.00	17.85	11.48
H_2O Vapor	1.64	9.75	15.34
Total	16.81		

This basic analysis is the heart of incineration process design.

Energy Balance

Energy balance relevant to incineration involves the heat of combustion and the temperature. Temperature is a state function representing an instantaneous property of the reactants and the products of incineration. The heat of combustion relates to the temperature and wastes. Since temperature is a state function, it is not necessary to determine the actual process of the incineration. Any convenient method is satisfactory to perform incineration energy balance. Figure 3-29 illustrates the simplest model. The wastes and air at temperature T(input) are cooled to a reference temperature T(reference), where the heat of combustion can be determined. The oxidation reaction takes place at temperature T(reference), and the heat released by both the cooling and the oxidation then is used to heat the product gases to the final temperature T(incineration). This is a rather simplified approach. However, it gives results identical to those of the true paths of the incineration process. The energy balance, Figure 3-29, is

$$\Delta H_S + \Delta H_C = \Delta H_T$$

The equation can be used to determine the incineration temperature, given wastes, or to determine auxiliary fuel or cooling medium requirements at a given incineration temperature.

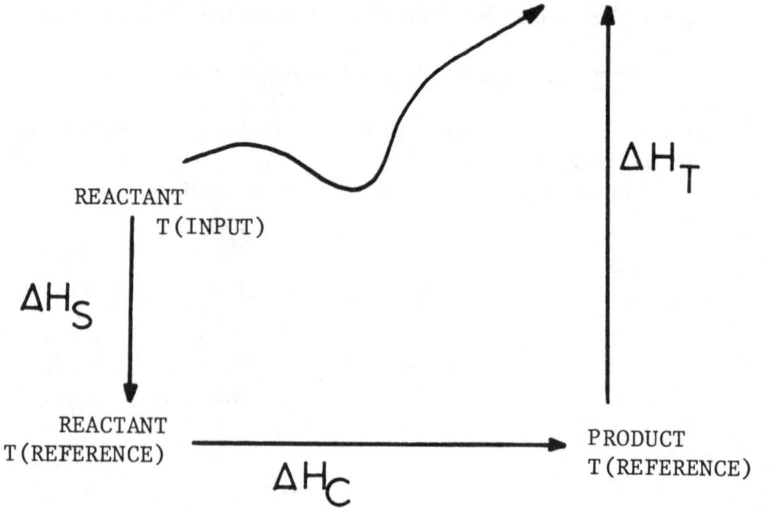

Figure 3-29. Incineration energy balance.

Incineration Process Calculation

The incineration process calculation makes use of the following equations:

- material balance equations
- energy balance equations
- pressure balance equations, and
- reaction equilibrium equations.

The basic criterion for the thermochemical equilibrium is that the Gibbs free energy, G, be a minimum for the system, that is

$$dG = 0$$

The temperature and chemical composition determined by considering all the possible chemical products and maintaining material and energy balance give minimum Gibbs free energy and the optimal solution to the system. There are computer programs available for these calculations [18].

This calculation is based on the assumption that the process reaches thermal equilibrium. However, in practice, incineration reactions proceed at a finite rate depending on temperature and the concentrations of the reacting species. It also should be recognized that in most practical incinerators, reaction rate does not control incineration rate. In typical cases, temperatures are maintained high enough that reactions proceed rapidly in comparison to the mean residence time, and other slower processes are rate-limiting, usually the mixing rate of wastes and oxygen.

PRODUCTS OF INCINERATION REACTION

The end product gases of incineration reaction are a function of the incineration temperature, and the elements found in the wastes. The major products are discussed here [19].

The product of incineration of carbon is carbon dioxide gas.

The product of incineration of hydrogen is water vapor. If the halogens fluorine and chlorine are present, some of the hydrogen may be present as hydrogen fluoride gas or hydrogen chloride gas.

The product of incineration of organic nitrogen is primarily gaseous nitrogen. However, appreciable amounts of nitrogen oxides may exist.

The product of incineration of organic phosphorus is gaseous phosphoric pentoxide.

The product of incineration of organic sulfur is gaseous sulfur dioxide.

The product of incineration of organic fluorine is hydrogen fluoride gas. The formation of hydrogen fluoride depends on the presence of hydrogen in the incineration material. If hydrogen is not present in sufficient quantity to combine with all the fluorine, the balance of the fluoride will appear as carbon tetrafluoride or possibly COF_2, unless other elements (such as metals) are present. Additional hydrogen in the form of auxiliary fuel should be added to eliminate the formation of carbon tetrafluoride and COF_2. Any metals in the incineration product gases will combine with fluoride to form metallic fluorides.

The product of incineration of organic chlorine is hydrogen chloride gas. Because oxygen and chlorine are of comparable electronegativity, the possibility of forming elemental chlorine gas exists.

The product of incineration of organic bromine is hydrogen bromide gas with appreciable amount of bromine gas.

The product of combustion of organic iodine is elemental iodine.

Depending on the elemental species in the incineration products and incineration temperature, metals may form halides, sulfates, phosphates, carbonates, hydroxides, oxides, etc.

REFERENCES

1. Ross, R. D. "The Burning Issue: Incineration of Hazardous Wastes," *Poll. Eng.* (August 1979), p. 25.
2. Hitchcock, D. A. "Solid Waste Disposal: Incineration," *Chem. Eng.* (May 21, 1979), p. 185.
3. Shen, T. T., M. Cher and J. Lauber. "Incineration of Toxic Chemical Wastes," *Poll. Eng.* (October 1978), p. 45.
4. Kiang, Y. H. "Controlling Vinyl Chloride Emissions," *Chem. Eng. Prog.* 72(12):37 (1976).
5. Kiang, Y. H. "Liquid Waste Disposal Systems," *Chem. Eng. Prog.* 72(1):71 (1976).
6. Kiang, Y. H. "Technologies for the Utilization of Waste Energy," IES 23rd Annual Meeting, Los Angeles, April 1977.
7. Santoleri, J. J. "Chlorinated Hydrocarbon Disposal and Recovery Systems," *Chem. Eng. Prog.* 69(1):70 (1973).
8. "Process Design Manual for Sludge Treatment and Disposal," U.S. EPA 625/1-79-011 (September 1979).
9. Santoleri, J. J. "Spray Nozzle Selection," *Chem. Eng. Prog.* 70(9):84 (1974).
10. Kiang, Y. H. "Total Hazardous Waste Disposal Through Combustion," *Ind. Heating* 14(12):9 (1977).
11. Kiang, Y. H. "RCRA Compliance Incineration Test and System Development," paper presented at the AIChE 73rd Annual Meeting, Chicago, IL November 1980.

12. "ASTM Standards for Bomb Calorimetry and Combustion Methods," (Philadephia, PA: American Society for Testing and Materials, 1974).
13. Kiang, Y. H. *Waste Energy Utilization Technology,* (New York: Marcel Dekker, Inc. 1980).
14. Perry, J. H. *Chemical Engineering Handbook,* 4th ed. (New York: McGraw-Hill Book Company, 1963).
15. Ross, R. D. *Industrial Waste Disposal* (New York: (Reinhold Book Corp., 1968).
16. Weast, R. C. *Handbook of Chemistry and Physics,* 50th ed. (Cleveland, OH: CRC Press, Inc., 1975).
17. Cudahy, J. J., and W. E. Wass. "New Technique for Estimating Heat of Combustion Needed for Waste Disposal," *Poll. Eng.* (February 1979), p. 45.
18. Steffensen, R. J. "A FORTRAN IV Program for Thermochemical Calculations Involving the Elements, Al, Be, C, F, H. Li, Mg, N, and O and Their Compounds," Ph.D. Thesis, Purdue University, Purdue, IN (1966).
19. "Thermodynamic Data for Industrial Incinerators," National Bureau of Standards, Washington, DC (1972).

CHAPTER 4

THERMAL INCINERATION EQUIPMENT

There are several types of incinerators available today that may be used for thermal processing of hazardous wastes [1,2]. The basic types of incinerators are:

1. multiple hearth
2. fluidized bed
3. liquid injection
4. fume
5. rotary kiln
6. multiple chamber
7. cyclonic
8. auger combustor
9. ship mounted

Each of these incinerators has advantages and disadvantages that must be evaluated before final process selection. The major design and operating features and applications for each type of incinerator are discussed in this chapter.

Residence times and operating temperature ranges for the various types of incineration equipment are listed in Table 4-1. The parameters are general, as each specific application should be considered individually, taking into account unique design and engineering problems.

A matrix matching waste types against incineration equipment is presented in Table 4-2. This matrix offers a general guideline for the application of various types of incinerators to types of wastes.

Table 4-1. Operating Parameters for Incinerators

Incinerator Type	Temperature Range (°F)	Residence Time
Multiple Hearth	1400–1800	0.25–1.5 hr
Fluidized Bed	1400–1800	Seconds-hours
Liquid Injection	1800–3000	0.1–2 sec
Fume	1400–3000	0.1–2 sec
Rotary Kiln	1500–3000	Liquids and gases: seconds Solids: hours
Multiple Chamber	1000–1800	Liquids and gases: seconds Solids: minutes
Cyclonic	1800–3000	0.1–2 sec
Auger Combustor	1400–1800	Seconds-hours
Ship-Mounted	1800–3000	0.1–2 sec

Table 4-2. Matrix of Incinerator Application

	Waste					
Incinerator	Solid	Sludge	Slurry	Liquid	Fume	Containerized
Multiple Hearth	x	x	x	x		
Fluidized Bed	x	x	x	x	x	
Liquid Injection			x	x	x	
Fume					x	
Rotary Kiln	x	x	x	x	x	x
Multiple Chamber	x	x	x	x	x	x
Cyclonic		x	x	x	x	
Auger Combustor	x	x	x	x	x	
Ship-Mounted		x	x	x		

MULTIPLE HEARTH INCINERATOR

The multiple hearth furnace is usually for the disposal of low Btu value wastes. A typical multiple hearth incineration system is illustrated in Figure 4-1.

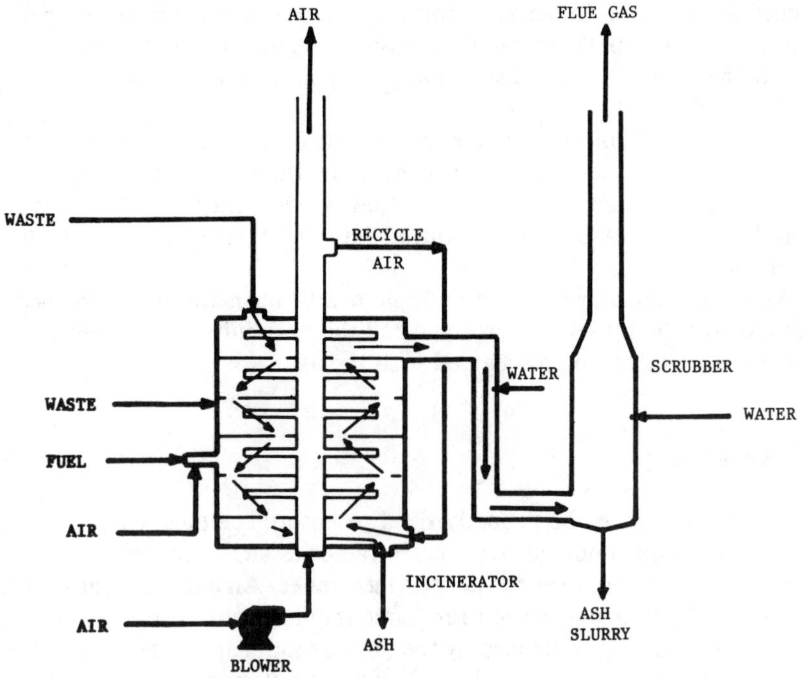

Figure 4-1. Multiple hearth incinerator [3].

Operating Principle

The multiple hearth incinerator is a cylindrical steel shell lined with refractory material. This refractory-lined chamber is divided into smaller zones, or hearths, which are created by self-supporting refractor arches. Waste is introduced through the top of the furnace. The waste is moved by rabble teeth attached to arms and a vertically positioned central shaft which rotates and plows the waste either inward or outward across the hearth floor to the drop opening where it falls to the next hearth. Ultimately, there is one peripheral opening at the bottom which connects to the ash removal system. The direction of rotation is the same for both the rabble arms and teeth. Sometimes back rabbling is accomplished by reversing the angles of the teeth.

The furnaces are refractory lined. The central shaft is made of cast iron or steel with refractory insulation. Alloy materials usually are used for the rabble arms and teeth, with exact materials of construction depending on specific wastes. Rabble arms normally are air cooled, with the cooling air usually used as the combustion air. Rabble arms and teeth are high maintenance items. Large, heavy solid wastes should not be introduced into the furnace.

Auxiliary fuel burners and air are introduced through the walls of the furnace; the exact locations are dependent on the requirement of specific wastes. Air and combustion products flow opposite the flow of the waste. Liquid wastes usually are introduced into the furnace through liquid burners.

Major disadvantages of the multiple hearth incinerators are the high capital cost, high fuel and air usage and the possibility of partially combusted materials being discharged with the ash.

Process Design

The furnace must be properly sized to ensure complete combustion, minimize flame impingement on refractories and provide adequate temperature control over the desired feed range. An adequate supply of solids on the hearth is needed for flame impingement protection [4].

Residence time is controlled by the rabble tooth pattern design and the rotation speed of the central shaft. The incineration temperature usually is adjusted by burner firing rate and air rate. Mixing of waste and air is very limited. The burning rate of a typical multiple hearth incinerator ranges from 8 to 15 $lb/ft^2/hr$ and is dependent on the waste being processed.

The temperature profile for a multiple hearth incinerator is such that the temperature drops through each hearth as the gas rises from hearth to hearth. The temperature in the top hearth, however, may be higher than the temperature in the lower hearths. Typically, the temperature is controlled by using excess air or auxiliary fuel which are both fed at the bottom of the combustion zone.

A typical temperature profile is illustrated in Figure 4-2. The use of either excess air or auxiliary fuel shifts the temperature profile to the left or right, respectively, from the profile derived from the incineration of feed without the use of excess air or auxiliary fuel. The temperature difference across each hearth is dependent on such factors as gas flow, the solid mass in each hearth and the furnace's heat release.

The simplest method for determining the residence time of the gas phase is to assume plug flow through the incinerator. Thus [3],

$$t = \frac{V}{W}$$

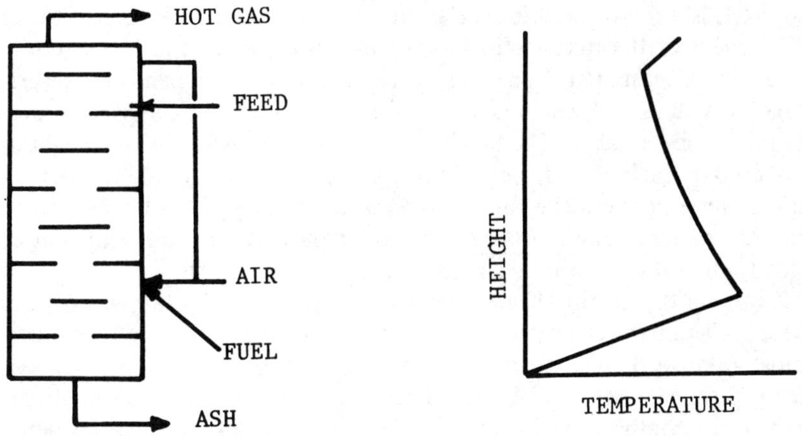

Figure 4-2. Temperature profile in a multiple hearth incinerator [3].

where t = residence time
V = volume of multiple hearth incinerator
W = volumetric flow rate of air.

Residence time so determined is the total residence time and not the effective residence time, which is important for estimating organic compound destruction.

Vapors generated from the solid wastes are assumed to be swept through the incinerator at the same flow rate as the air fed to the incinerator. Therefore, the residence time of vapor generated in a given hearth depends on the vertical location of that hearth.

As mentioned previously, the solid waste moves across each hearth in a spiral. The expression describing the movement of the solid material across the hearth in polar coordinates is:

$$r = \pm a\theta$$

where r = distance from center of the hearth
a = distance of teeth from the center of hearth (assuming they are evenly spaced)
θ = angle
$\pm$ = whether the material is moving toward or away from the center of the hearth (+ for an "out-hearth"; − for an "in-hearth").

If r = radius of hearth and θ_2 = angular velocity, then the time for the solid traverse across the hearth, t, is:

$$t = \frac{r}{Ea\theta_2}$$

where E is a factor describing the slip of solid matter with respect to the movement of the rake teeth. For liquid wastes, E depends on viscosity and can be estimated. For solid wastes, the slippage depends on several factors such as size, shape and moisture content of the materials, and is estimated less readily. The height of the dead-bed, which is the height of material on each hearth, also affects the slippage of material. The further the material is from the rake teeth, the greater slippage of material, so that the material on the floor of the hearth moves across the hearth more slowly than the material closer to the rake teeth.

Scale-up of rotating hearth incinerators is limited by the necessity of keeping angular velocity low, so as not to increase velocity of the outermost rake teeth beyond acceptable values. The relationships between incinerator capacity and hearth diameter, incinerator height and rotational speed are complicated by the dependence of solids and gas residence times not only on incinerator height and diameter but also on the rake teeth configuration (angle, spacing, etc.) and the properties of the solids. The probability of developing useful generalized scaling laws for multiple hearth incinerators is not high.

Process Application

The multiple hearth incinerator is most suitable for materials which are difficult to burn or for waste containing valuable metals, such as silver, which can be recovered. The best approach for multiple hearth incinerator is a large central installation where various wastes with different heat contents can be blended to achieve optimum combustion and minimal auxiliary fuel requirement.

FLUIDIZED BED INCINERATOR

Fluidized bed incinerators are versatile devices which can be used to dispose of solid, liquid and gaseous wastes. This technique was first used commercially in the United States in 1962, and has found limited use in the petroleum and paper industries and for processing nuclear wastes. A typical fluidized bed incinerator is shown schematically in Figure 4-3.

Operating Principle

A fluidized bed incinerator consists of a vertical refractory-lined vessel containing a bed of inert granular material [5]. Combustion air is intro-

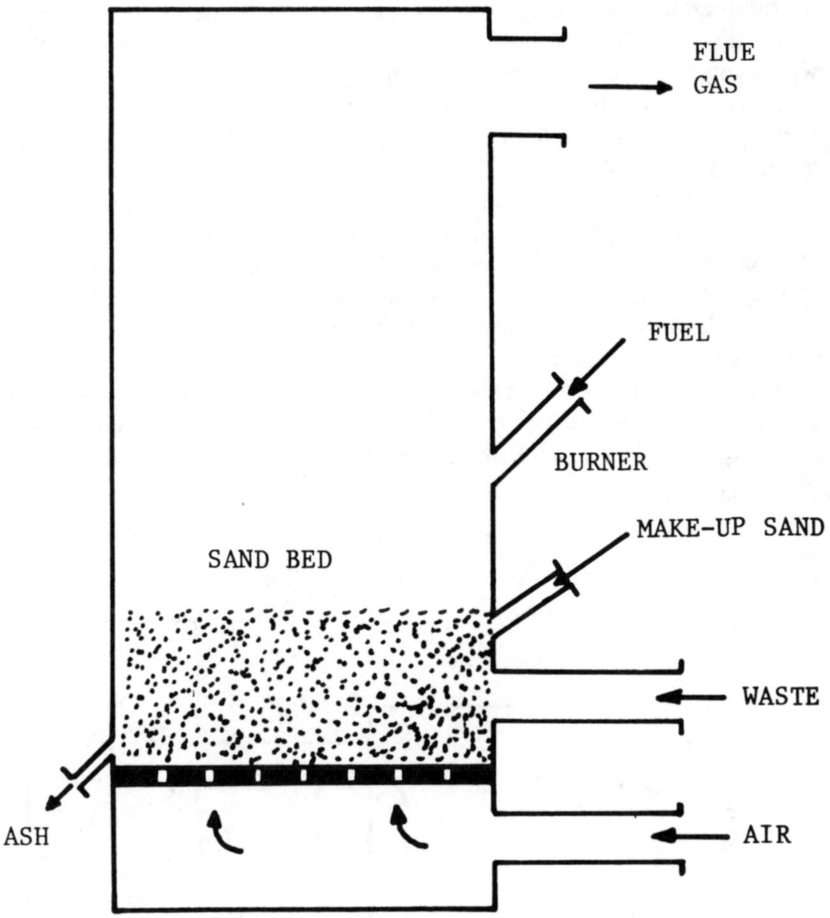

Figure 4-3. Fluidized bed incinerator.

duced through a plenum at the bottom of the incinerator and rises vertically through a distributor plate into the granular bed. Sand is typically used as the bed material. If the waste contains inorganic materials, the bed can be replaced gradually with the inorganic material generated through incineration. Continuous bed material removal is necessary for this situation.

The upward flow of air through the bed results in turbulent mixing and causes fluidization of the bed material. Waste material is injected into the bed and combustion occurs within the bubbling bed. Air passage through the bed produces strong agitation of the bed particles. This promotes rapid and uniform mixing of the waste material and air within the fluidized bed. Normally, the combustion of waste material is restricted inside the bed. The freeboard area above the bed usually is used for separating the inert particles from coming out of the incinerator.

A different design, which utilizes the flowing of bed material, also has been developed. A schematic diagram of this type of incinerator is illustrated in Figure 4-4.

Heat is transferred from the bed into the injected waste materials. The waste rapidly reaches ignition temperature, and the heat released then transfers back into the bed. Continued bed agitation by the fluidizing air allows larger waste particles to remain suspended until combustion is completed. Elutriated fines are carried off the bed and freeboard area by the exhausting flue gases.

Preheating of the bed to start up temperature can be achieved either by a burner located above the bed and impinging down on the bed or by air preheating. Auxiliary fuel usually is injected through nozzles within the bed.

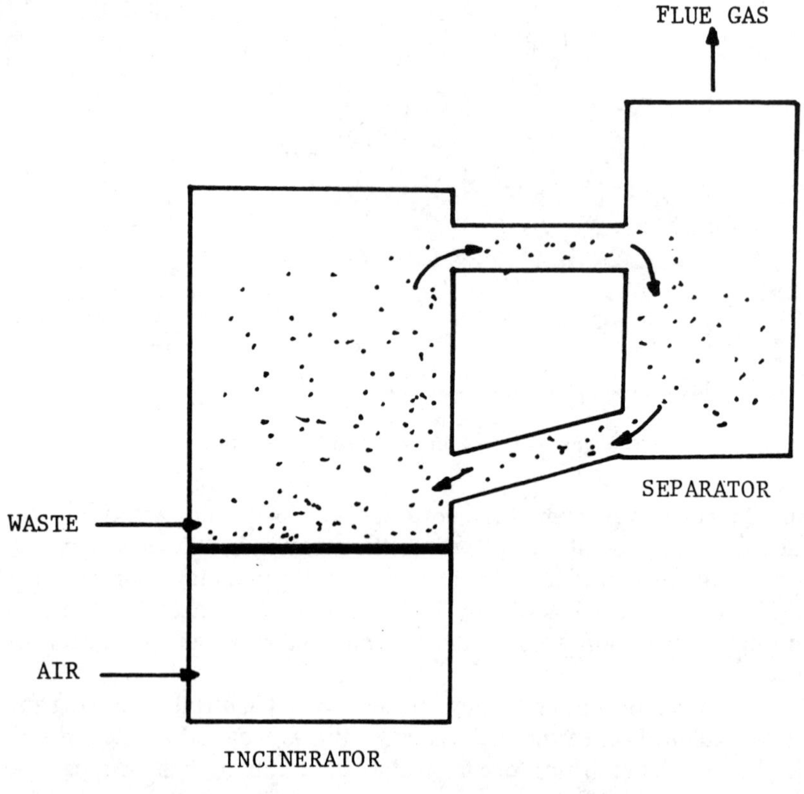

Figure 4-4. Fluidized bed incinerator with transported bed.

Process Design

The basic design parameters for a fluidized bed incinerator are superficial gas velocity, bed depth, bed temperature, freeboard area, air distribution design and bed material selection.

The superficial gas velocity through a solid bed determines whether a bed will remain stationary, acquire a vertical velocity temporarily or acquire and maintain that velocity. This fluidization phenomenon is described in Figure 4-5. There are various conditions, enumerated as follows, which exist in a bed of fairly uniform particles when a gas is passed through that bed:

1. The rate of gas flow is low, and the gas passes between the particles without significantly disturbing the bed structure.
2. The rate of gas flow is sufficiently high so that the particles start to lift.
3. As the particles are lifted, the distances between the particles increase. The velocity of the gas decreases. The particles remain in motion at these gas velocities. The bed acts like a fluid and possesses quite a violent motion.
4. The rate of gas flow reaches the terminal velocity of the particles and the vertical velocity of particles becomes permanent.
5. The rate of gas flow exceeds the terminal velocity of the particles and the particles are swept along by the gas stream. The expression for terminal velocity is:

$$U_t = \frac{4g(\varrho_p - \varrho_g)\, d_p}{3\varrho_g C_D}$$

where U_t = terminal velocity
g = gravitational constant
ϱ_p = density of particle
ϱ_g = density of fluid
d_p = particle diameter
C_D = drag coefficient, dimensionless (a function of Reynolds number and the shape of the particle).

Illustrated in Figure 4-6 is the relationship between the superficial gas velocity and the bed pressure drop.

The fluidization superficial gas velocity is in the range of 1 to 15 ft/sec, depending on the particle sizes. For incineration applications, the superficial gas velocity is maintained between 5 and 8 ft/sec.

Bed depths range from about 16 in. to several feet. Variations in bed depth affect particle residence time and system pressure drop. Therefore, it is necessary to minimize the bed depth to maintain complete combustion

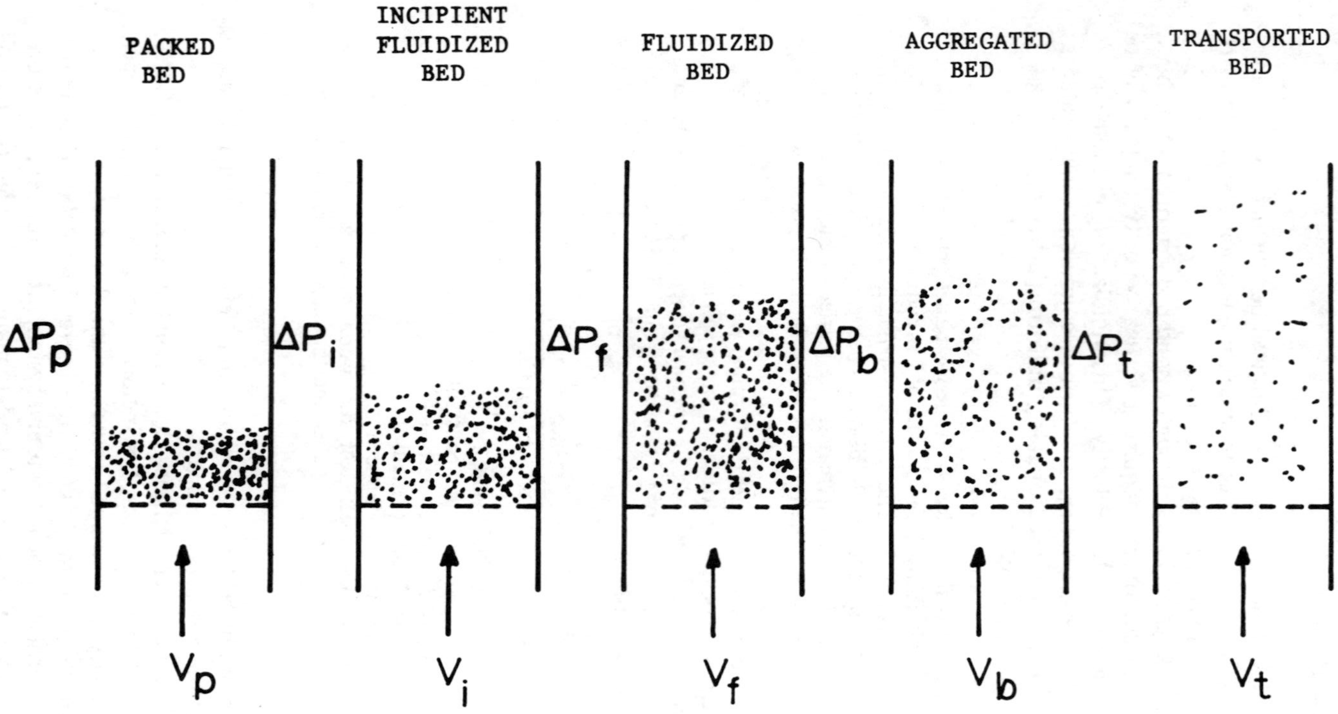

Figure 4-5. Fluidization phenomena.

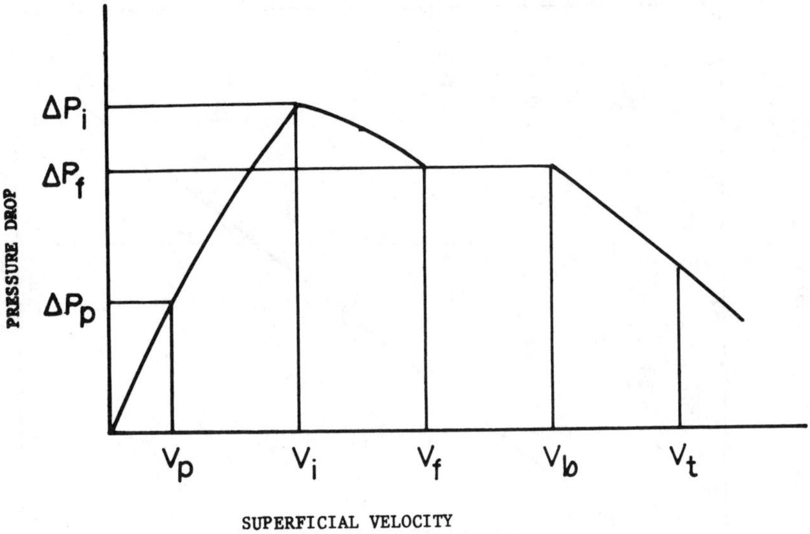

Figure 4-6. Fluidized bed pressure drop [6].

of waste with minimal excess air. The height of the expanded bed is a function of gas superficial velocity and is illustrated in Figure 4-7.

Bed temperature is normally quite uniform throughout the bed. The temperature requirement usually is determined by the waste material to be incinerated. The incineration temperature must be high enough to ensure complete combustion of wastes; however, it must also be low enough to avoid the formation of an eutectic mixture which will cause bed defluidization. This is a major factor limiting the application of fluidized bed incinerators.

The freeboard area above the bed is a space used to control particulate carryover and to allow room for bed expansion. The height requirement of the freeboard area is illustrated in Figure 4-8.

The functions of the air distributor are to ensure even distribution of the combustion air over the entire bed, to support the bed in fluidizing or in slumping, and to provide trouble-free operation: free from weeping (dripping of particles into the plenum), plugging (obstruction of gas passages into the bed), clinkering (fusion of ashes due to local hot spots), overheating (excessive temperature gradients and thermal stresses) and air blasting (poorly aimed air jets touching solid surfaces, which may cause erosion). The design of an air distributor can be found in Reference 7.

For perforated plate, the pressure drop ratio between the distributor and bed for fair air distribution is between 0.1 to 0.3. The minimal distri-

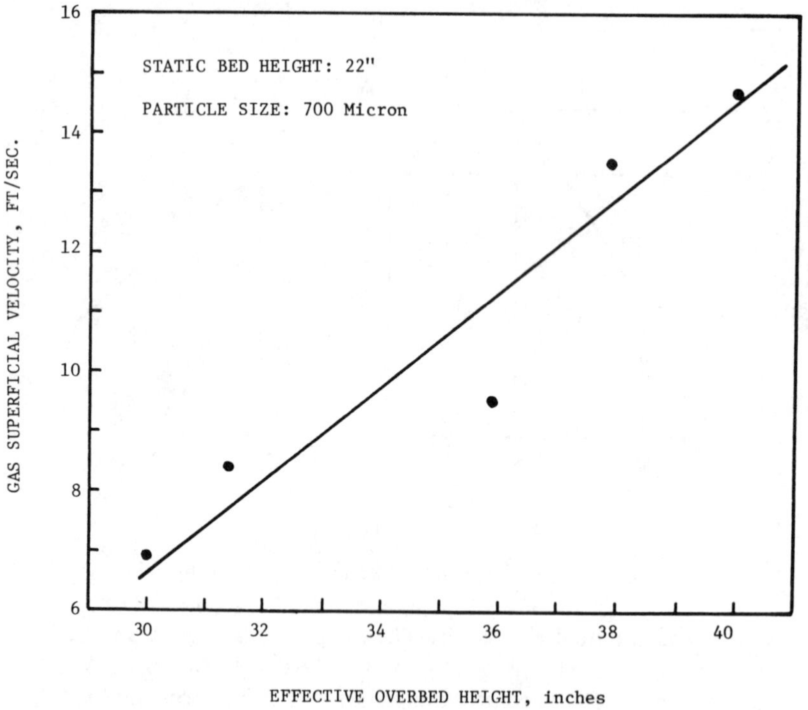

Figure 4-7. Fluidized bed expansion [6].

butor pressure drop is 14 in. water column. Illustrated in Figure 4-9 is the basic design requirement for perforated plate distributor. A different distributor plate is illustrated in Figure 4-10, which makes use of bubble cap design for air introduction. Refractory or bed materials are used to insulate the plates to minimize radiation, mechanical and thermal stress.

As mentioned before, sand is usually used as the bed material; however, for some applications, depending on waste characteristics, special bed materials may be used. Limestone can be used to control sulfur dioxide emission when burning waste containing sulfur. Soda ash has been used for wastes generating soda ash as a product of incineration. A specially formulated bed mixture 95% by weight of SiO_2/Al_2O_3 and 1% by weight of Na_2O/K_2O was used to control chlorine and hydrogen chloride emissions as well as to avoid defluidization [8] in one instance.

Process Application

The fluidized bed incinerator is particularly well suited for the incineration of high-moisture wastes, sludges, and wastes containing large quantities of ashes.

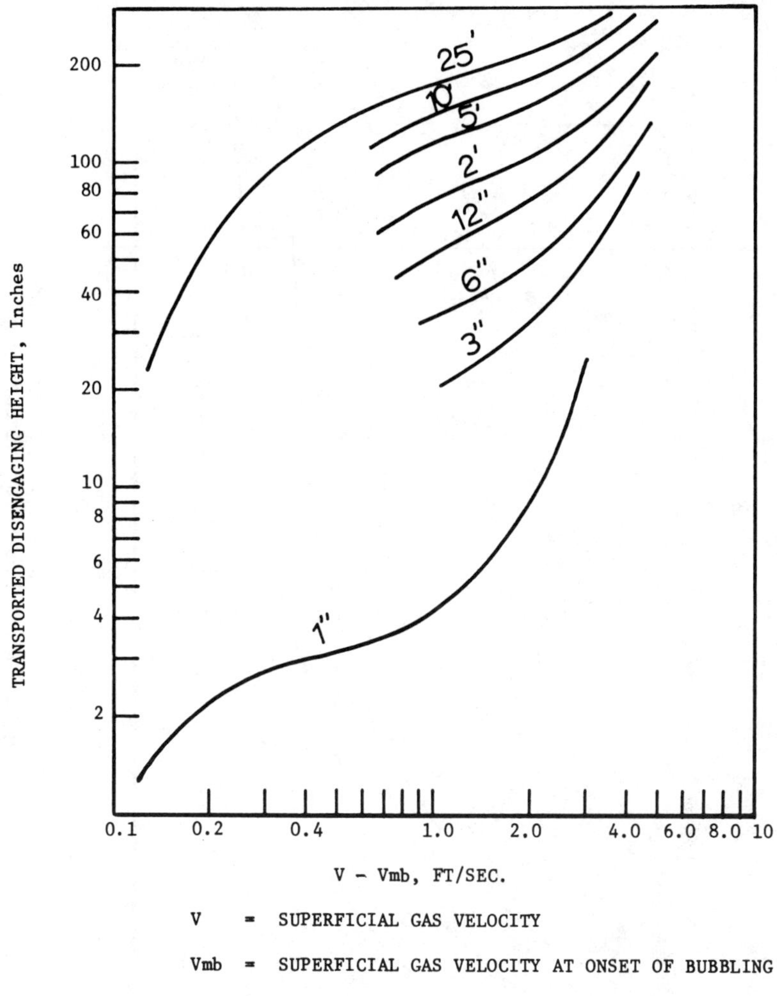

Figure 4-8. Fluidized bed free board height requirement [6].

Because of the low bed temperature of the typical fluidized bed incinerator, the exhaust gases usually contain low nitrogen oxides.

The presence of sodium chloride in the wastes usually causes operating difficulties [9], sodium chloride can form eutectic mixtures with sodium sulfate and sodium carbonates (Figures 4-11 to 4-13) with a melting temperature < 1200°F. Therefore, bed temperatures must be controlled below these temperatures to avoid bed defluidization. However, incomplete combustion usually occurs at this low temperature. In this case, a chemical additive such as Kaolin clay [10], can be used to control the ash fusion temperature.

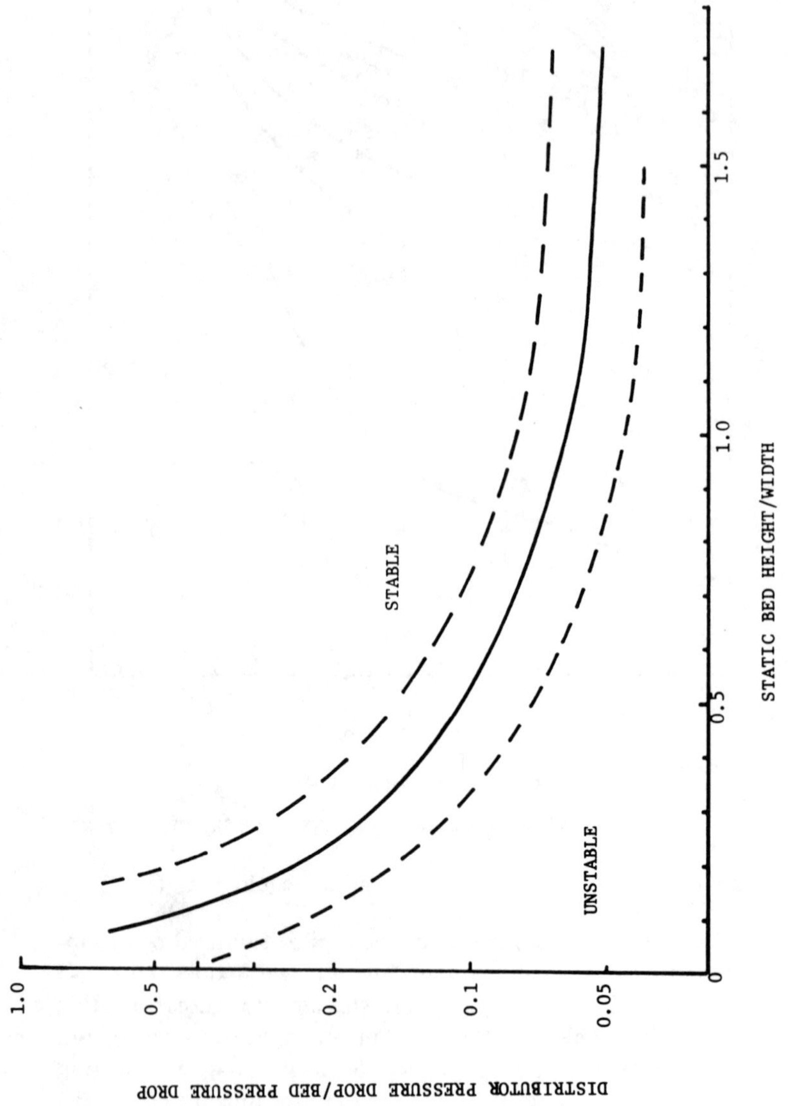

Figure 4-9. Pressure drop of perforated plate.

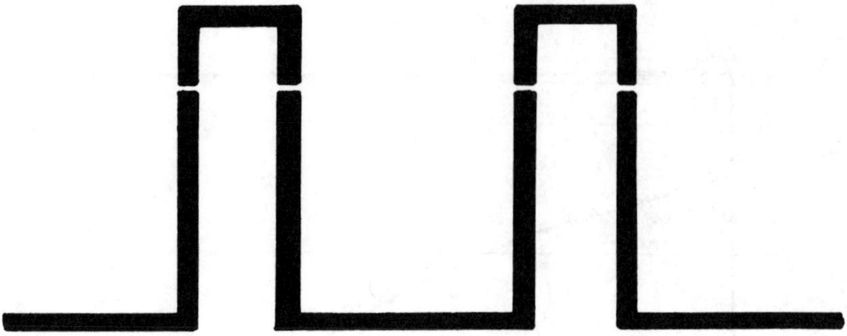

Figure 4-10. Bubble cap type distribute plate.

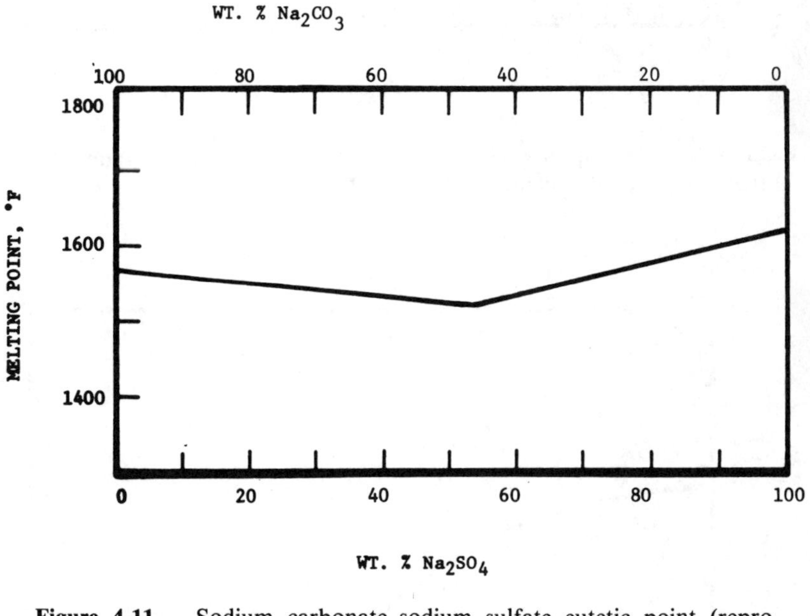

Figure 4-11. Sodium carbonate–sodium sulfate eutetic point (reproduced from Reference 4-9; courtesy of Marcel Dekker, New York).

A thorough understanding of the variations in the physical and chemical characteristics of waste material is necessary for a properly designed system. Liquids and small solids can be fed readily into the incinerator. Larger and denser material will make the bed more sensitive to feed distribution.

A pilot plant test usually is required to determine the process design parameters. Ash fusion study is necessary for the selection of bed material

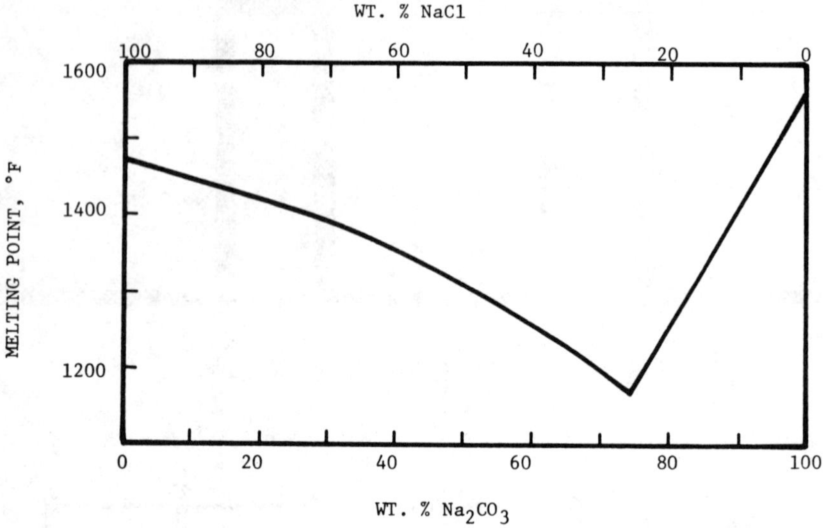

Figure 4-12. Sodium chloride–sodium carbon eutectic point (reproduced from Reference 4-9; courtesy of Marcel Dekker, New York).

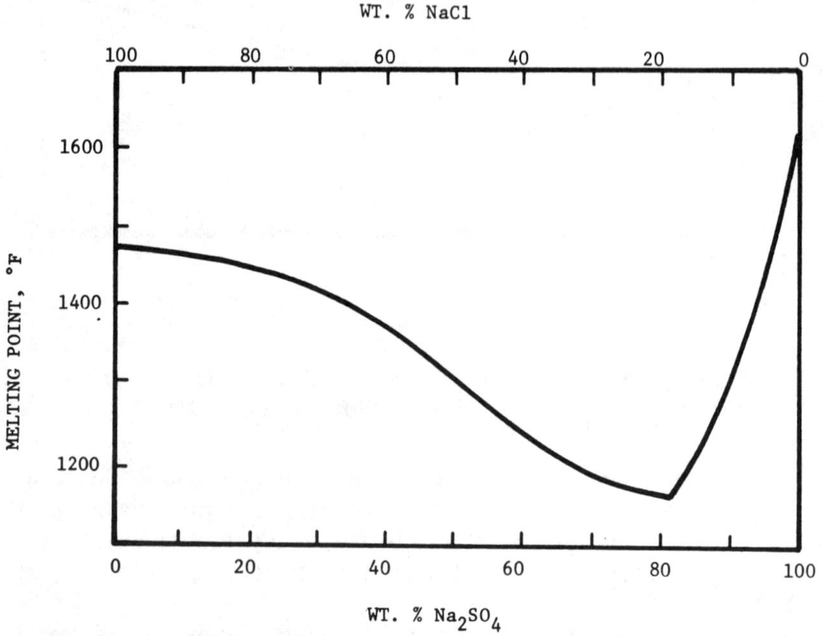

Figure 4-13. Sodium chloride–sodium sulfate eutectic point (reproduced from Reference 4-9; courtesy of Marcel Dekker, New York).

and chemical additives. A word of caution: the scale-up of fluidized bed incinerators is an art. At the present time, a five-time scale-up is the maximum limit.

LIQUID INJECTION INCINERATOR

Liquid injection incinerators are versatile devices which can be used to dispose of virtually any pumpable wastes and fumes. There are a wide variety of liquid injection incinerators in operation in the United States. Liquid injection incinerators find applications ranging from complete combustion of normally noncombustible wastes, such as contaminated water, to combustion of totally organic compounds, such as waste solvents. A typical liquid injection incineration system is illustrated in Figure 4-14.

Operating Principle

The heart of a liquid injection incinerator is the waste atomization device or nozzle. Details of injectors are discussed in Chapter 3.

Normally, liquid injector incinerators consist of two stages. The primary chamber is usually a burner where combustible liquid and gaseous wastes are introduced. Noncombustible liquid and gaseous wastes usually bypass the burner and are introduced downstream of the burner into the secondary chamber. A schematic diagram of a two-stage system is shown in Figure 4-15. Single-stage incinerators are used for systems handling only combustible wastes.

In general, waste liquid cannot be oxidized efficiently in conventional burners. A high heat release, Vortex type burner is usually necessary for complete combustion of liquid wastes. Forced draft units usually have better combustion characteristics than natural draft units. The burners must be located to prevent flame impingement on walls and, in the case of multiburner systems, interference with one another. Where multiple injectors are located within a single air register, performance suffers.

The configuration of a liquid injection incinerator can be horizontal, vertical upfired, vertical downfired or sloped. The selection of configuration usually depends on the characteristics of wastes [11]. Liquid injection incinerators contain no moving parts and require the least maintenance of all types of incinerators.

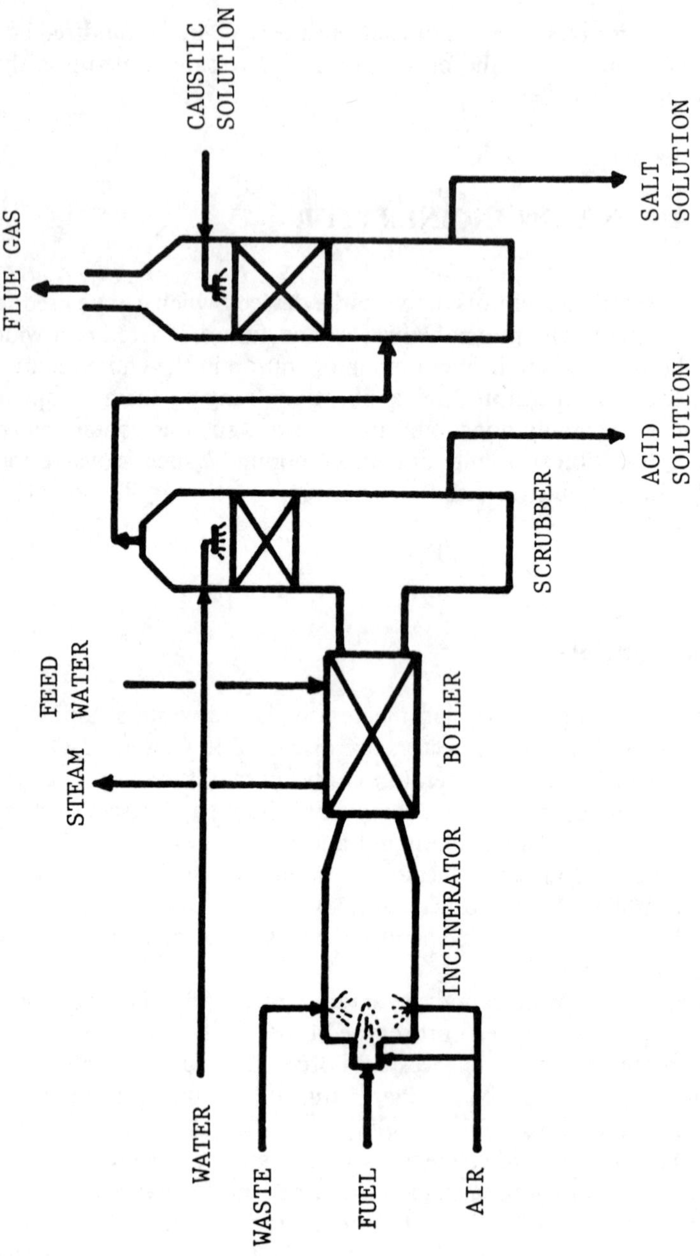

Figure 4-14. Liquid injection incineration system.

Process Design

The operating temperature of liquid injection incinerators ranges from 1800 to >3000°F, and residence time ranges from ½ to 2 sec. The time, temperature and excess air requirement are highly dependent on the design of the mixing system, the selection of the burner and the waste characteristics. It is a general rule that a short flame burner application requires less time and excess air for complete combustion of wastes when operating at the same temperature as a long flame burner [11]. Most conventional units have combustion chamber volumes which provide for a heat release of approximately 25,000 Btu/hr-ft^3. However, the vortex type incinerator has a heat release of about 100,000 Btu/hr-ft^3.

It is necessary to test a waste in a pilot plant to determine the process design parameter requirement [12]. Usually, the scaled-up unit performs better for liquid injection incineration, because it is more difficult to design mixing systems for smaller units.

Process Application

Liquid injection incinerators are generally applicable to the ultimate disposal of organics in pumpable liquid wastes and represent proven technology.

This type of incinerator also can be used to dispose of solid wastes, either by melting or by dissolving into a liquid material. When preheating a waste, it is essential to ensure that undesirable preliminary chemical reactions such as polymerization, nitration, etc. will not occur. Provision also should be made to prevent the release of gases during heating.

Liquid injection incinerators are highly sensitive to waste composition and flow changes. Thus, storage and mixing tanks are necessary to ensure a reasonably steady and homogeneous waste flow.

FUME INCINERATOR

Fume incinerators are similar to liquid injection incinerators in basic principles. The only difference is in waste injection method; fumes do not require atomization.

Operating Principle

A fume incinerator can be a single-stage or two-stage device. Rich fumes (high Btu content fumes) are normally used in the burner as fuel.

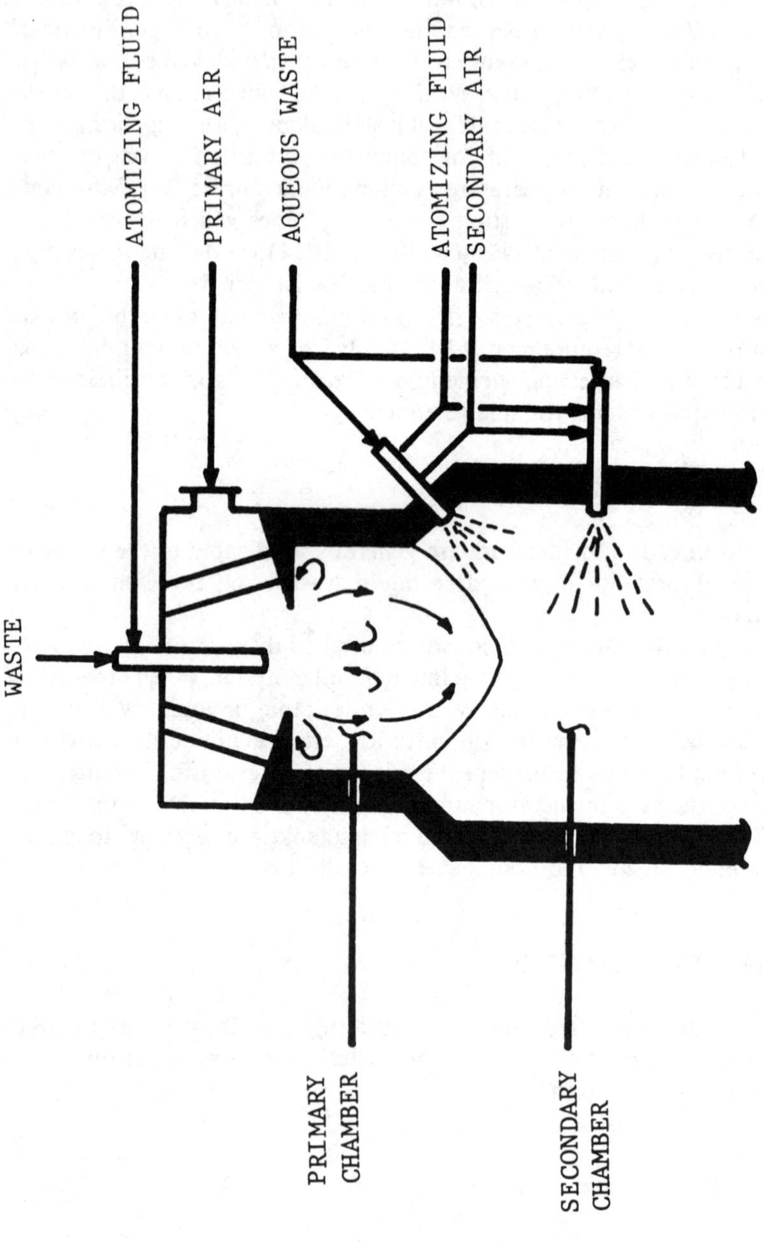
WASTE
ATOMIZING FLUID
PRIMARY AIR
AQUEOUS WASTE
ATOMIZING FLUID
SECONDARY AIR
PRIMARY CHAMBER
SECONDARY CHAMBER

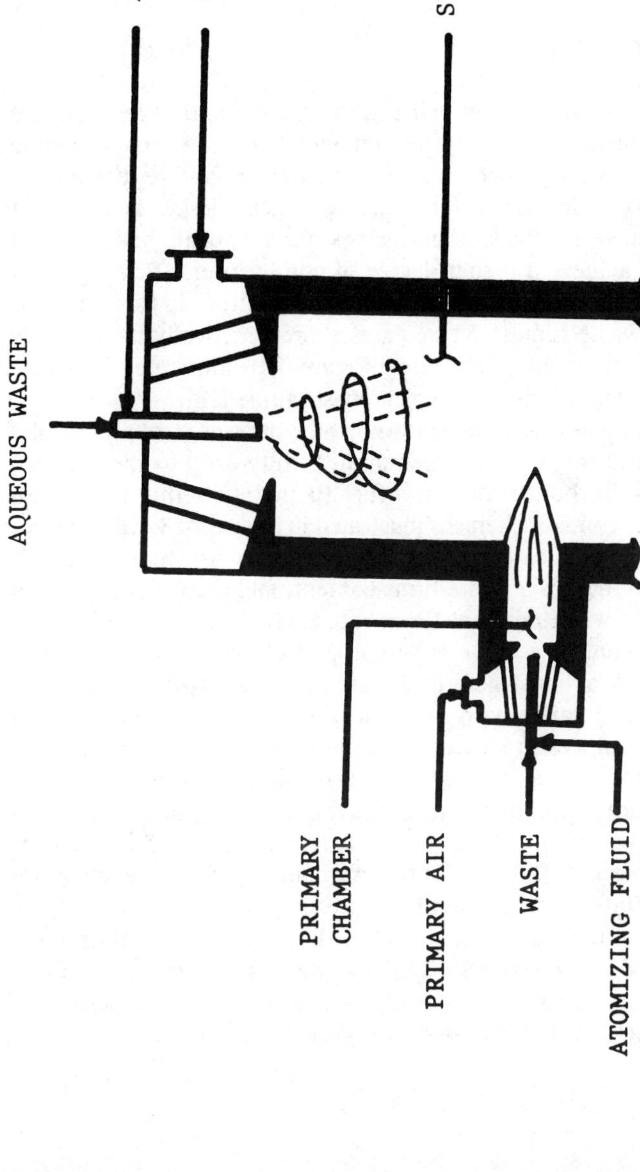

Figure 4-15. Two-stage incinerator.

Dilute fumes (low Btu content fumes) must bypass the burner and be introduced into the secondary chamber.

The greatest variation among different fume incinerator designs is in how well the fumes reach the required temperature and maintain it for the required time.

Fume supply lines are usually equipped with a flame arrester. It is required that waste fumes must be maintained below lower explosion limit (LEL).

Process Design

Incineration temperature, residence time, mixing and excess air rate govern the performance of a fume and incinerator. Normally, fume incineration temperature is between 1400 and 3000°F, and residence time varies between 0.1 and 1 sec. The mixing system design is the most important parameter. When other factors are identical, better mixed incinerators will achieve a higher degree of combustion efficiency.

Fume incinerators are extremely sensitive to variations in flow rate and composition of waste fumes. Waste gases characteristically have a wide range of compositions and flow rates. Figure 4-16 illustrates flow rate and composition variations of a typical waste fume [13].

In order to compensate for the variations, the basic control philosophy of a fume incinerator is to let the system heat duty drop to the minimal firing rate, then introduce auxiliary fuel to maintain this firing rate (Figure 4-17). The control scheme is illustrated in Figure 4-18. The temperature controller is used to cut the combustion air when temperature is decreasing due to the lower waste fume content, and then to increase the auxiliary fuel rate when minimal firing rate is reached.

Although the control scheme is simple and effective, unsatisfactory control may occur, as illustrated by Figures 4-19 and 4-20, as the incineration temperature varies with excess air. There are two temperature solutions to the temperature/excess air relationship, one above and one below the stoichiometric air/fuel ratio. It is possible that the control may shift from the true control point "a" to the false control point "b", due to unsteady-state operation. When the control reaches this false control point, it is difficult to shift it back to the true control point by temperature control alone. Thus, a check point is necessary to ensure satisfactory excess air operation. This can be achieved through the control of stack oxygen. When the oxygen content controller detects the deficiency of air, it will override the temperature controller and do whatever is necessary to correct it. This scheme is illustrated in Figure 4-21.

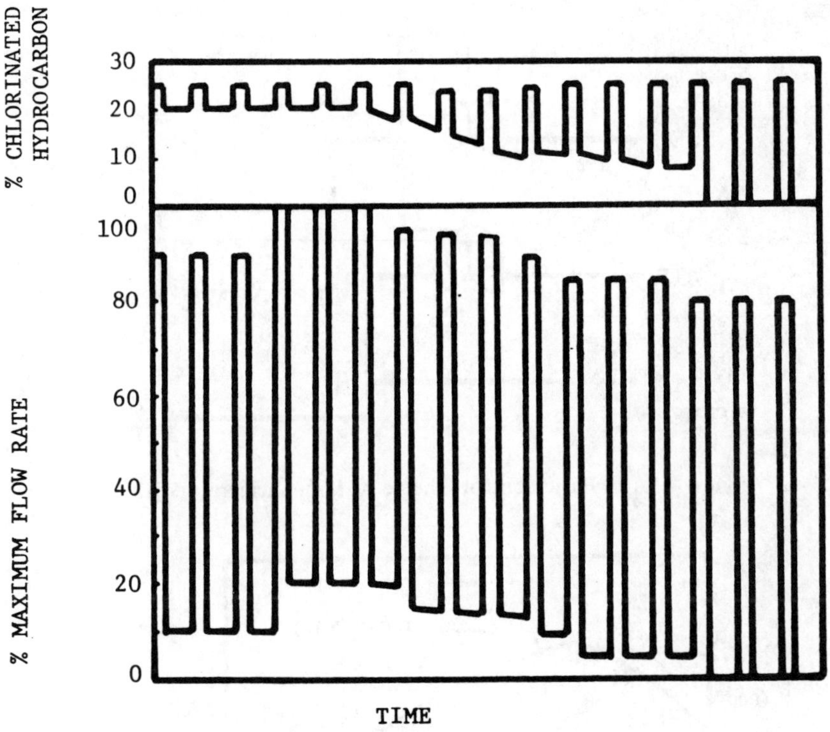

Figure 4-16. Typical PVC plant waste fumes [13].

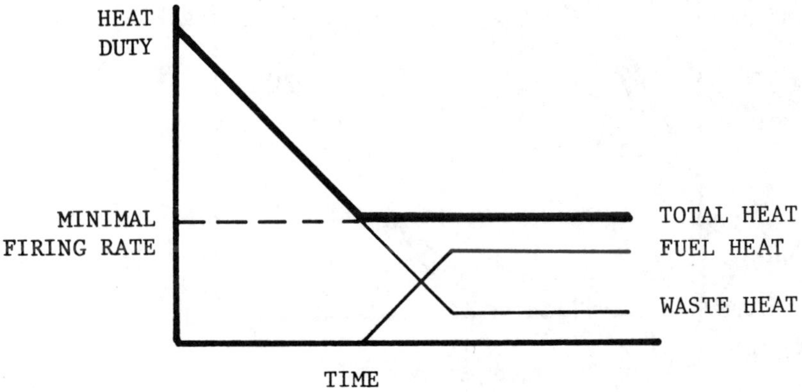

Figure 4-17. Basic control philosophy of fume incinerators [13].

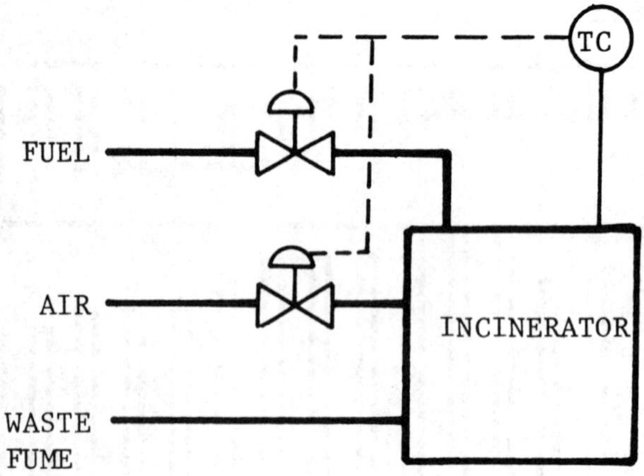

Figure 4-18. Basic control scheme of fume incinerators [13].

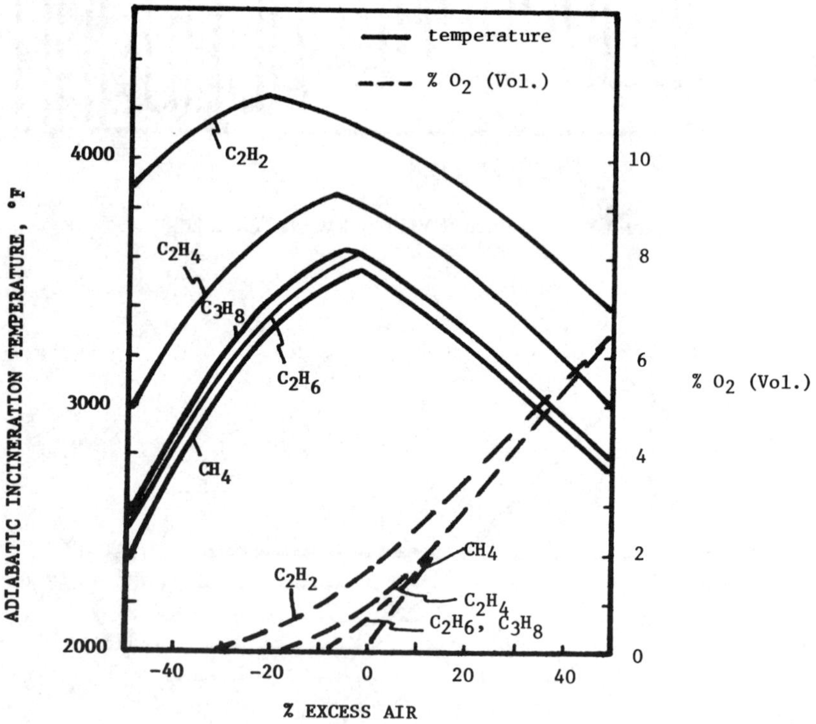

Figure 4-19. Temperature/excess air relationship of typical gases [13].

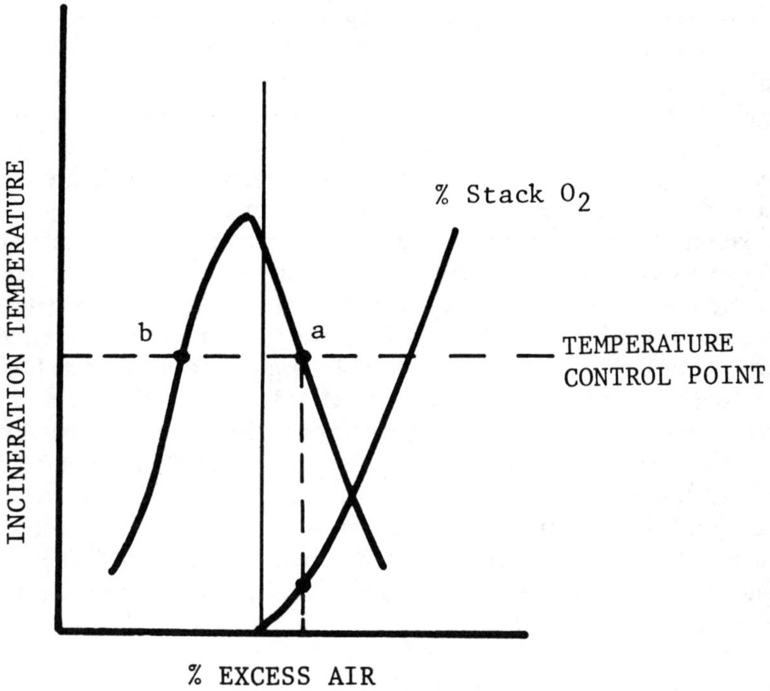

Figure 4-20. Temperature control points for fume incinerator [13].

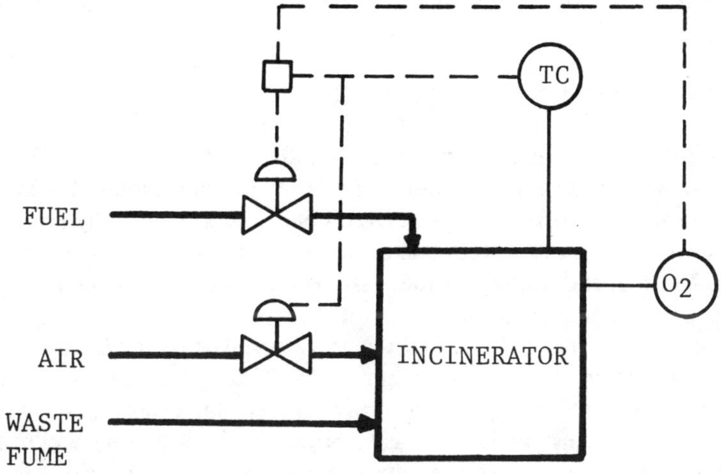

Figure 4-21. Modified control scheme for fume incinerator [13].

The residence time of the system can be determined by the mass flow rate of the input gases. Since it is not practical to control waste gas flow, only an alarm function is built into the residence time indication.

The systems described are capable of controlling incinerators which handle waste fumes with a gradual change in heat content. When waste heat changes are more rapid, as in the system described in Figure 4-15, the control system response is not fast enough to compensate for the variation. Thus, the control scheme must be modified. A simple and effective way to maintain combustion stability is to baseload the incinerator; that is, overpower the system by introducing a minimal fixed amount of auxiliary fuel. The quantity is usually determined by the system minimal firing rate. Thus, irrespective of the variation in the waste fume, high quality combustion is always maintained (Figure 4-22). For a small incinerator, baseload may be a good approach. However, when baseload heat duty requirements are higher, fuel consumption may prohibit its use. Then a different solution approach, the dual burner system, can be used (see Figure 4-23). The secondary burner is used as ignition source when the main burner firing rate drops below the minimal firing rate. Thus, the combustion quality is not sacrificed, and the base usage quantity of fuel is relatively small.

ROTARY KILN INCINERATOR

Rotary kiln incinerators are versatile units which have sufficient design flexibility for incineration of a wide variety of liquid and solid wastes.

Operating Principle

The rotary kiln incinerator is a cylindrical refractory-lined shell mounted with its axis at a slight slope from the horizontal. It can be fueled by natural gas, oil or pulverized coal. The kilns usually are very long, so that the combustion zone occupies a small portion of the incinerator. Most of the heating of the waste is due to heat transfer with the combustion product gases and the walls of the kiln.

There are two types of rotary kiln incinerators. The basic type of rotary kiln incinerator is illustrated in Figure 4-24. This system consists of the rotary kiln and a secondary combustion chamber. Solid wastes, heavy tar, sludges, waste drums and liquid wastes can be fed into the rotary kiln. As the solid waste moves down the kiln, organic matter is destroyed. Liquid and gaseous wastes and purchased fuels are used as auxiliary fuel in both the kiln and the secondary chamber.

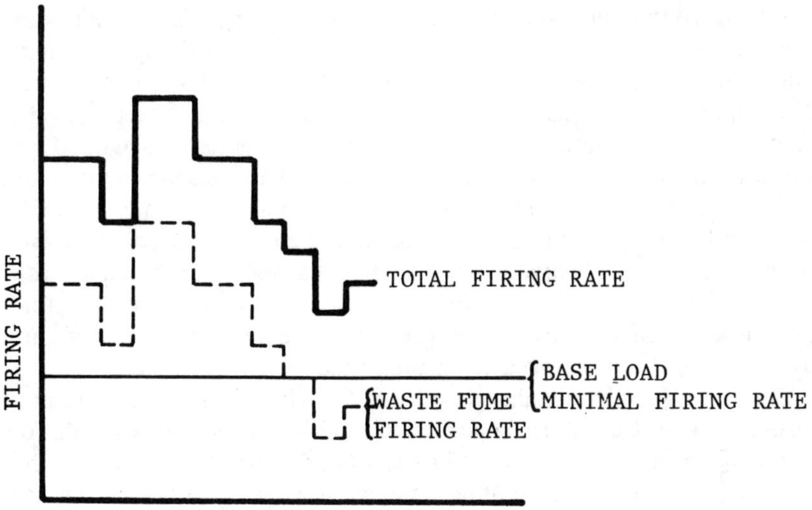

Figure 4-22. Baseload fume incineration system [13].

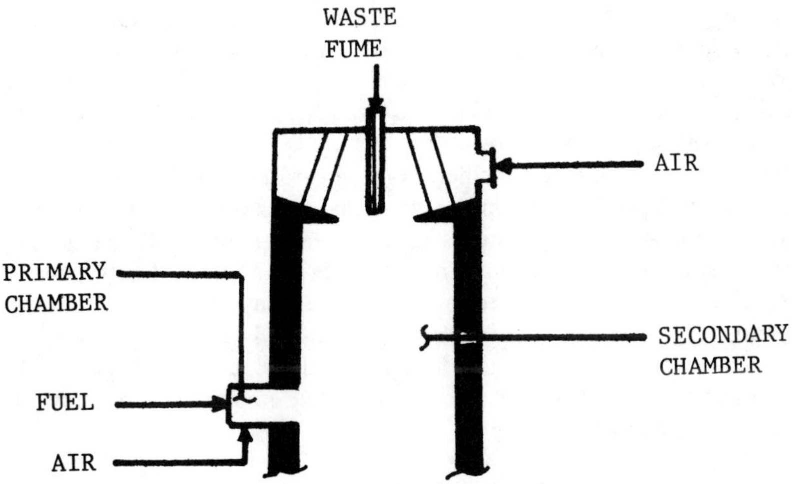

Figure 4-23. Dual burner system for fume incineration [13].

Illustrated in Figure 4-25 is the other type of rotary kiln, which can be used to handle large volumes of solid wastes along with any entrained liquid. In the drying section, water and volatile organics are vaporized. The vaporized materials then bypass the rotary kiln and feed into the secondary combustion chamber. The solid materials are ignited on traveling grates before entering the kiln. Liquid and gaseous wastes can be introduced into the kiln or the secondary combustion chamber.

In both configurations, the secondary chamber ensures complete combustion of volatile organics and organics carried by airborne particles.

The ashes leaving the unit are made up primarily of slag and other nonburnables such as drums and other metallic material. The ashes are usually cooled and removed from the system.

Since the drive mechanism is outside the kiln, maintenance requirements are low. Care must be exercised in sizing the kiln to provide for adequate accommodation of solid wastes and maximize refractory life. As kiln size decreases, the unit becomes increasingly sensitive to excessive heat release, and temperature control becomes more difficult.

Process Design

Rotary Kiln incinerators generally have a length to diameter ratio (L/D) between 2 and 10. Lower L/D ratios result in less particulate carryover. Rotation speed of the kiln is usually in the range of 1 to 5 rpm; variable speed drive can be used to control the rotation. Both the L/D ratio and the rotation speed requirements are strongly dependent on the type of waste being incinerated. In general, high L/D ratios along with slower rotation speeds are used when the waste material requires longer residence times in the kiln. The kilns usually are designed with 1/16 to 1/4 in. per foot incline ratio.

The residence time and incineration temperature required for proper incineration depend totally on the waste material's combustion characteristics. Incineration temperatures usually range from 1600 to 3000°F. Required residence times vary from seconds to hours: a finely divided propellant may require 0.5 sec, but bulk solids may require 5, 15 or even 60 min.

The residence time of solids depends on the slope of the rotary kiln axis and on the rotation speed of the kiln. The empirical correlation for time of passage is [14]:

$$\theta = 0.19(L/D)/(sN)\,(\text{min})$$

where L, D = kiln length and diameter
s = slope of kiln (m/m)
N = rpm.

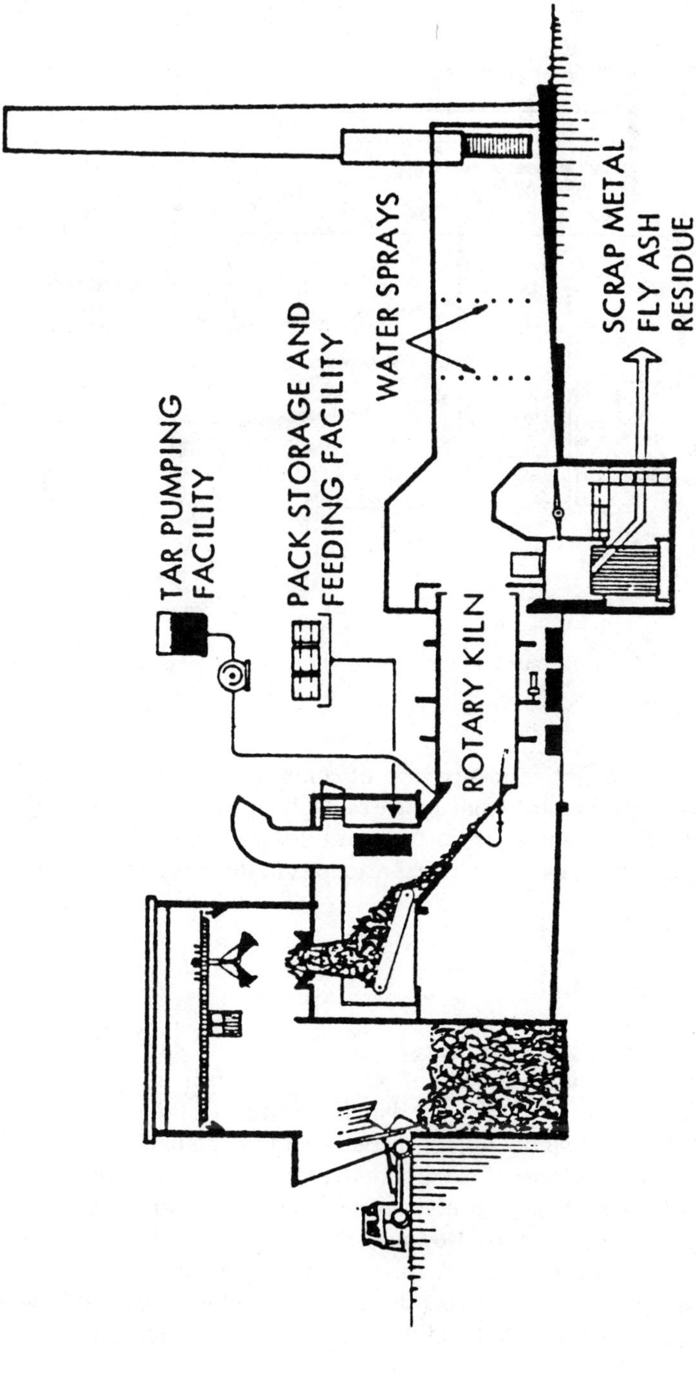

Figure 4-24. Basic rotary kiln incinerator [4].

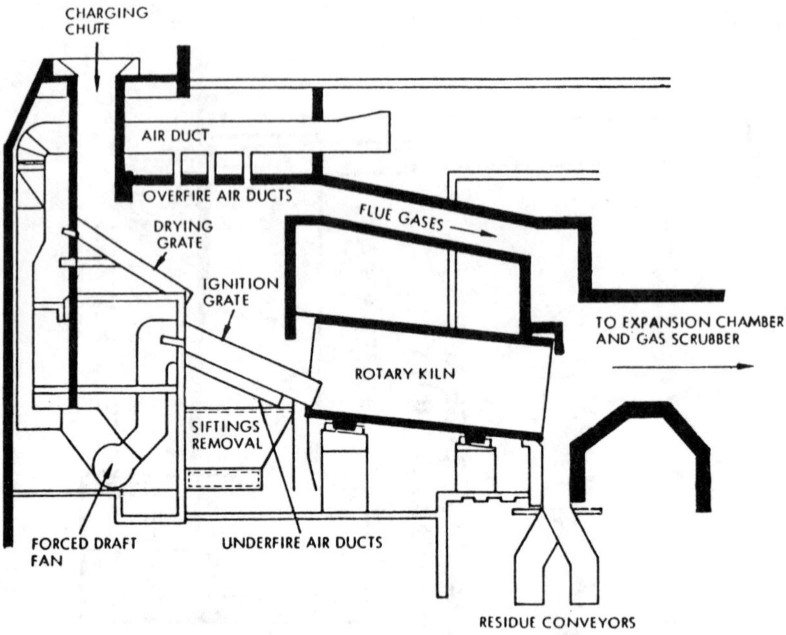

Figure 4-25. Rotary kiln incinerator with waste drying and ignition sections [4].

Evaluation of the residence time of combustion gases of the auxiliary fuel is straightforward, that of gases evolving from the waste is more difficult. Mass transfer from the waste to gas stream will have to be addressed, as well as the chemical reactions in the waste and in the gases.

Process Application

Rotary kiln incinerators are especially effective when the size or nature of the waste precludes the use of other types of incineration equipment. Kilns usually are designed for batch feeding. Continuous feeding is possible if a reasonably homogeneous feed is available.

Turndown, the ratio of maximum to minimum thermal capability of a rotary kiln, represents a problem due to leakage of air throughout the system. Fuel efficiency is also lower due to the air leakage.

Drying and ignition sections are required when burning wastes containing large quantities of volatile and combustible materials; otherwise these wastes, if fed into the kiln directly, may cause explosion.

Drying and ignition grates can become clogged with plastic melt plugging grates and grate mechanisms.

MULTIPLE CHAMBER INCINERATOR

The configuration of modern multiple chamber incinerators falls into two general types as illustrated in Figures 4-26 and 4-27. These are the retort type, named for the return flow of gases through the "U" arrangement of component chambers; and the in-line type, so-called because of the linear arrangement of the component chambers.

Operating Principle

The combustion process in a multiple-chamber incinerator proceeds in two stages: primary or solid fuel combustion in the ignition chamber, followed by secondary or gaseous-phase combustion. The secondary combustion zone is composed of two parts, a downdraft or mixing chamber and an up-pass expansion or combustion chamber.

The two-stage multiple-chamber incineration process begins in the ignition chamber and includes the drying, ignition and combustion of the solid refuse. As burning proceeds, the moisture and volatile components of the fuel are vaporized and partially oxidized in passing from the ignition chamber through the flame port connecting the ignition chamber with the mixing chamber. From the flame port, the volatile components of the waste and the products of combustion flow down through the mixing chamber into which secondary air is introduced. The combination of adequate temperature and additional air, augmented by mixing chamber or secondary burners as necessary, initiates the second stage of the combustion process. Turbulent mixing, resulting from the restricted flow areas and abrupt changes in flow direction, furthers the gaseous-phase reaction. In passing through a curtain wall port from the mixing chamber to the final combustion chamber, the gases undergo additional changes in direction accompanied by expansion and final oxidation of combustible components. Fly ash and other solid particulate matter are collected in the combustion chamber by wall impingement and simple setting.

The essential features of the two types of multiple chamber incinerators are:

1. *Retort Type*
   a. The arrangement of the chambers causes the combustion gases to flow through 90° turns in both lateral and vertical directions.

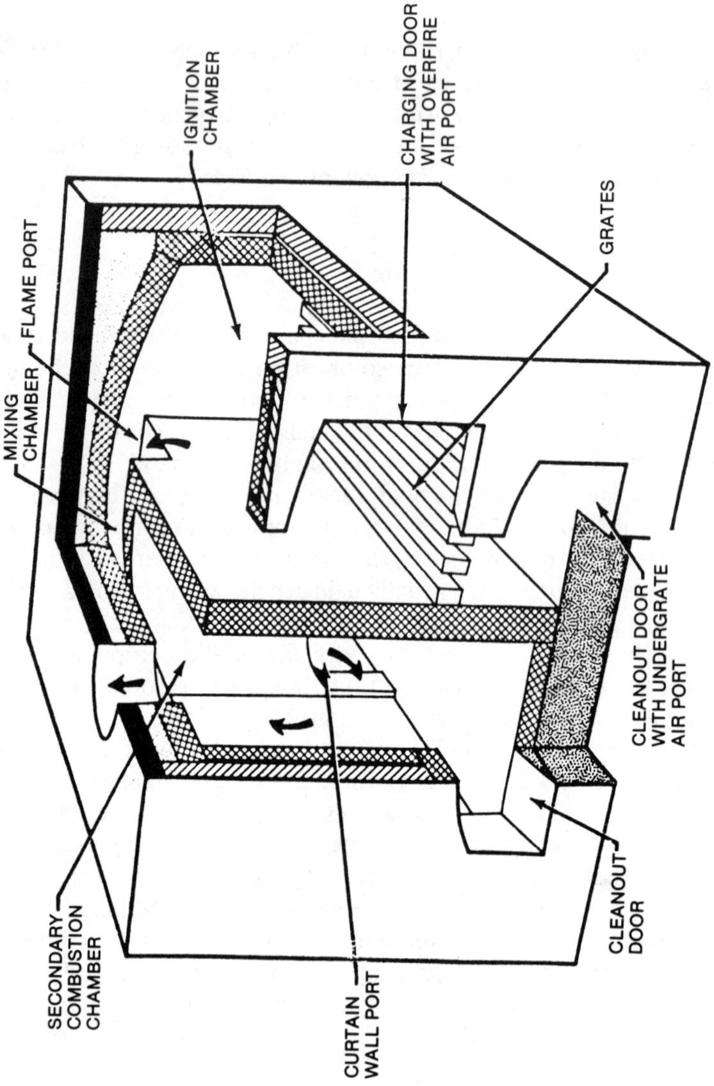
IGNITION CHAMBER
CHARGING DOOR WITH OVERFIRE AIR PORT
GRATES
FLAME PORT
MIXING CHAMBER
CLEANOUT DOOR WITH UNDERGRATE AIR PORT
SECONDARY COMBUSTION CHAMBER
CURTAIN WALL PORT
CLEANOUT DOOR

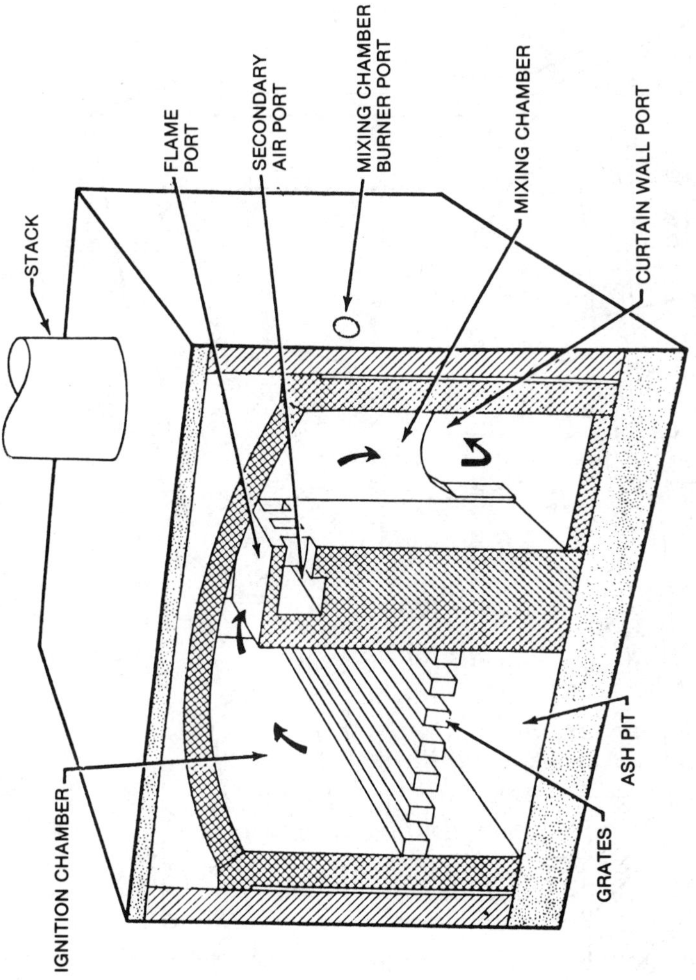

Figure 4-26. Retort type multiple chamber incinerator [15].

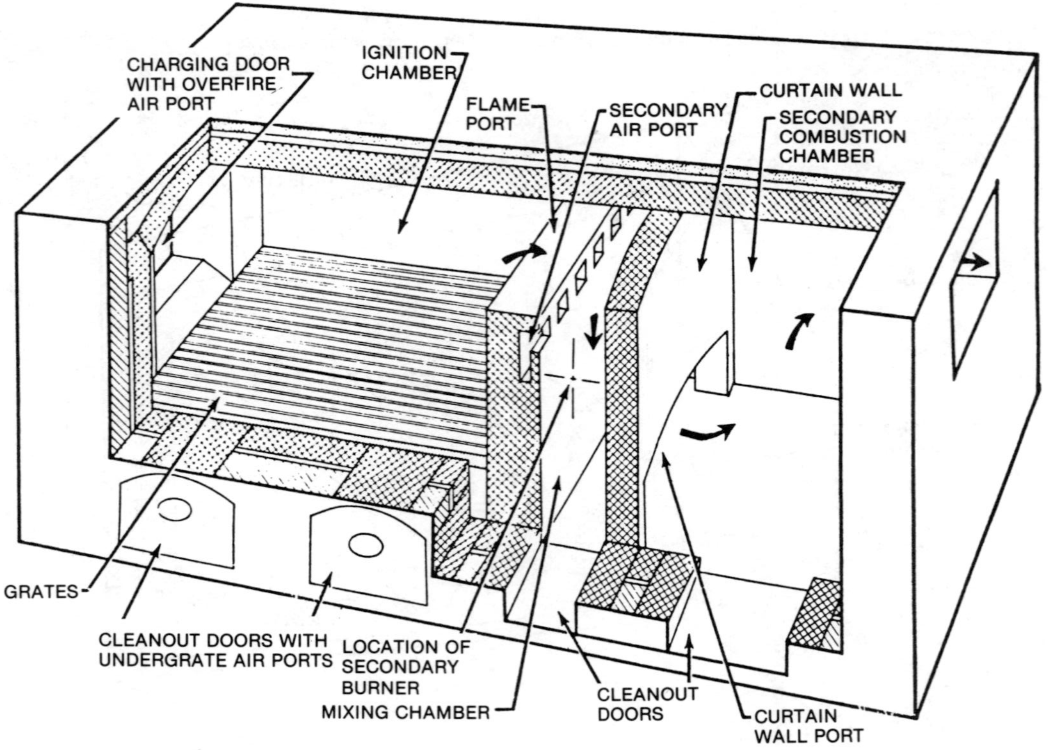

Figure 4-27. In-line type multiple chamber incinerator [15].

b. The return flow of the gases permits the use of a common wall between the primary and secondary combustion stages.
c. Mixing chambers, flame ports and curtain wall ports have length-to-width ratios in the range of 1:1 to 2.4:1.
d. Bridge wall thickness under the flame port is a function of dimensional requirements in the mixing and combustion chambers. This results in construction that is somewhat unwieldy in the size range above 500 lb/hr.

2. *In-line Type*
   a. Flow of the combustion gases is straight through the incinerator with 90° turns only in the vertical direction.
   b. The in-line arrangement is readily adaptable to installations that require separated spacing of the chambers for operating, maintenance or other reasons.
   c. All ports and chambers extend across the full width of the incinerator. Length-to-width ratios of the flame port, mixing chamber and curtain wall port flow cross-sections range from 2:1 to 5:1.

During the evaluation and development phases of the multiple-chamber incinerator, different incinerator configurations with variations in the sizes and shapes of the several chambers and ports were tested. The results of these tests defined the optimum operating limits for the two basic styles. Each style has certain characteristics with regard to performance and construction that limit its application.

The basic factors that cause a variance in the performance of the two types of incinerators are: (1) proportioning of the flame port and mixing chamber to maintain adequate gas velocities within dimensional limitations imposed by the particular type involved, (2) maintenance of proper flame distribution over the flame port and across the mixing chamber and (3) flame travel through the mixing chamber into the combustion chamber.

A retort incinerator in its optimum size range offers the advantages of compactness and structural economy because of its cubic shape and reduced exterior wall length. It performs more efficiently than its in-line counterpart in the capacity range from 50 to 750 lb/hr. In these small sizes, the nearly square cross-sections of the ports and chambers function well because of the abrupt turns in this design. In retort incinerators with a capacity ≥ 1000 lb/hr, the increased size of the flow cross section reduces the effective turbulence in the mixing chamber and results in inadequate flame distribution and penetration and in poor secondary air mixing.

No outstanding factors favor either the retort or the in-line configurations in the capacity range of 750–1000 lb/hr. The choice of retort or in-line configuration in this range is influenced by personal preference, space limitations, the nature of the refuse, and charging conditions.

The in-line incinerator is well suited to high-capacity operation, but is not satisfactory for service in small sizes. The smaller in-line incinerators are somewhat more efficient in secondary-stage combustion than the retort type. In in-line incinerators with a capacity of < 750 lb/hr, the shortness of the grate tends to inhibit flame propagation across the width of the ignition chamber. This, along with thin flame distribution over the bridge wall, may result in the passage of smoke from smoldering grate sections straight through the incinerator and out of stack without adequate mixing and secondary combustion. In-line models in sizes ≥ 750 lb/hr have grates long enough to maintain burning across their width, resulting in satisfactory flame distribution in the flame port and mixing chamber. The shorter grates on the smaller in-line incinerators also create a maintenance problem. The bridge wall is very susceptible to mechanical abuse because usually it is not provided with a structural support or backing and it is thin where the secondary air lanes are located. Careless stoking and grate cleaning in the short-grate in-line incinerators can break down the bridge wall in a short time.

The upper limit for the use of the in-line incinerator has not been established. Incinerators with a capacity < 2000 lb/hr may be standardized for construction purposes to a great degree. Incinerators of larger capacity, however, are not readily standardized since problems of construction, material usage, mechanized operation with stoking grate, induced-draft systems and other factors make each installation essentially one of custom design. Even so, the design factors advocated herein are as applicable to the design of large incinerators as to the design of smaller units [16].

Process Design

Control of the combustion reaction, and reduction in the amount of mechanically entrained fly ash are most important in the efficient designing of a multiple-chamber incinerator. Ignition chamber parameters are regarded as fundamental, since solid contaminant discharges can only be function of the mechanical and chemical processes taking place in the primary stage. Other important factors include the ratios of combustion air distribution, supplementary air and temperature criteria, residence time and the secondary-combustion-stage velocity and proportion factors. Some of these factors are functions of the desired hourly combustion rate and are expressed in empirical formulas; some are assigned values that are independent of incinerator size; and others are functions of the wastes.

Table 4-3 lists the basic parameters, evaluation factors and equations for designing multiple-chamber incinerators and gives the minimum values for each [15, 16]. The allowable deviations should be interpreted with caution to avoid consistently high or low deviation from the optimum values. Application of these factors to design evaluation must be tempered by judgment and by an appreciation of the practical limitations of construction and economy.

The values determined for the several parameters are mean empirical values, accurate in the same degree as the experimental accuracy of the evaluation tests. The significance of exact figures is reduced further by the fluctuation of waste composition and conditions. For purposes of design, permissible variations from the optimum mean are ± 10%, and velocities may deviate as much as 20% without serious consequence.

The formulas governing ignition chamber design were tentatively postulated from data available through tests of units of varying proportions burning at maximum combustion rates. Optimum values of the arch height and grate area may be determined by using the gross heating value of the refuse to be burned and interpolating between the upper and lower curves in Figures 4-28 and 4-29. An allowable deviation of these values of ± 10% is considered reasonable. Rather than establish formulas for both the upper and lower curves of these figures, which represent ≥9000 Btu/lb and ≤7500 Btu/lb respectively, a formula for the average values of the two curves has been given. This curve corresponds to a gross heating value of 8250 Btu/lb.

The ignition mechanism should be one of waste bed surface combustion. This is attained by the predominant use of overfire combustion air and by charging in such a manner as to attain concurrent travel of air and waste with minimum admission of underfire combustion air. Limiting the admission of underfire air and thereby maintaining relatively low fuel-bed temperatures is important. With a relatively high air rate through the waste bed, the stack effluent contains appreciable quantities of metallic salts and oxides in microcrystalline form. A probable explanation is that vapor phase reactions and vaporization of metals take place in high waste bed temperatures with resultant condensation of particles in the effluent gases as they cool upon leaving the stack.

To accomplish waste bed surface combustion through use of overfire air, the charging door should be located at the end of the ignition chamber farthest from the flame port, and the waste moved through the ignition chamber from front to rear. This way, the volatiles from the fresh waste pass through the flames of the stabilized and heated portion of the

Table 4-3. Multiple-Chamber Incinerator Design Parameters [15]

Item and Symbol	Recommended Value	Allowable Deviation
Primary Combustion Zone		
Grate loading, L_G	10 Log R_c; lb/hr-ft^2 where R_c equals the	±10%
Combustion chamber, V_{CC}	waste combustion rate in lb/hr	
Grate Area, A_G	R_c/L_G : ft^2	±10%
Average Arch height, H_A	$4/3\ (A_G)^{4/11}$ ft	–
Length-to-width ratio (approx.):		
Retort	Up to 500 lb/hr, 2:1; >500 lb/hr, 1.75:1	–
In-line	Diminishing from ~1.7:1 for 750 lb/hr to ~1:2 for 2000 lb/hr capacity. Oversquare acceptable in units of >11 ft ignition chamber length.	–
Secondary Combustion Zone		
Gas Velocities:		
Flame port, V_{FP}	55 ft/sec	±20%
Mixing chamber, V_{MC}	25 ft/sec	±20%
Curtain wall port, V_{CWP}	~0.7 of mixing chamber velocity	–
Combustion chamber, V_{CC}	5 to 6 ft/sec; always <10 ft/sec	–
Mixing chamber downpass length, L_{MC}, from top of ignition chamber arch to top of curtain wall port.	Average arch height (ft)	±20%
Length-to-width ratios of flow cross-sections:		
Retort, mixing chamber, and combustion chamber	Range: 1.3:1 to 1.5:1	–
In-Line	Fixed by gas velocities due to constant incinerator width	–
Combustion Air		
Air requirement batch-charging operation.	Basis: as required. 50% air requirement admitted through adjustable ports: 50% air requirement met by open charge door and leakage.	
Combustion air distribution:		
Overfire air ports	70% of total air required	–
Underfire air ports	10% of total air required	–
Mixing chamber air ports	20% of total air required	–
Air inlet ports oversize factors:		
Primary air inlet	1.2	
Underfire air inlet	1.5 for >500 lb/hr to 2.5 for 50 lb/hr	

Table 4-3, continued

Item and Symbol	Recommended Value	Allowable Deviation
Secondary air inlet	2.0 for >500 lb/hr to 5.0 for 50 lb/hr	
Incineration Temperature	As required	

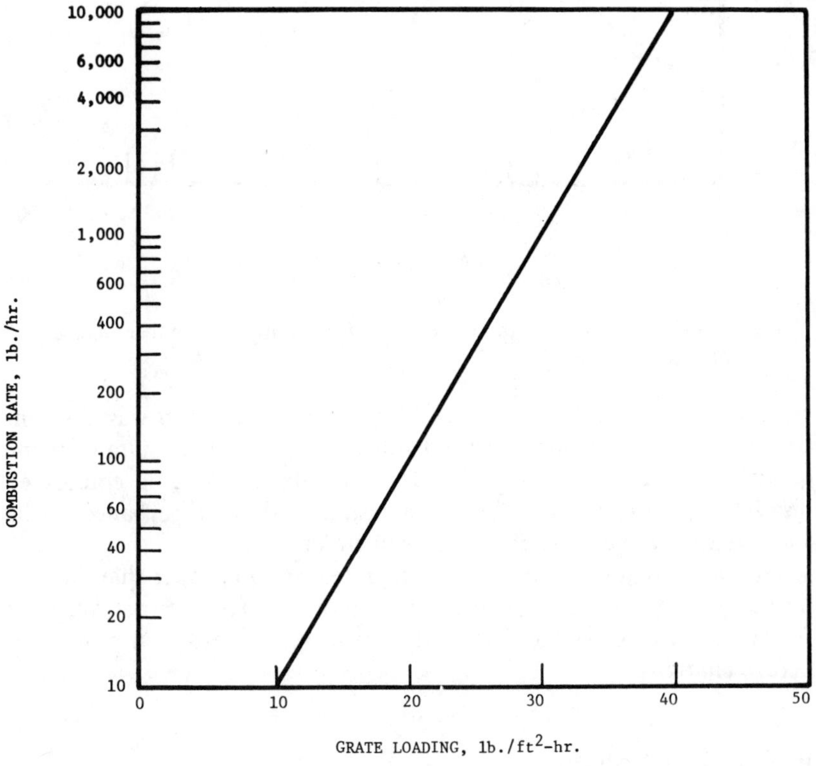

Figure 4-28. Grate loading combustion rate for multiple chamber incinerator [15].

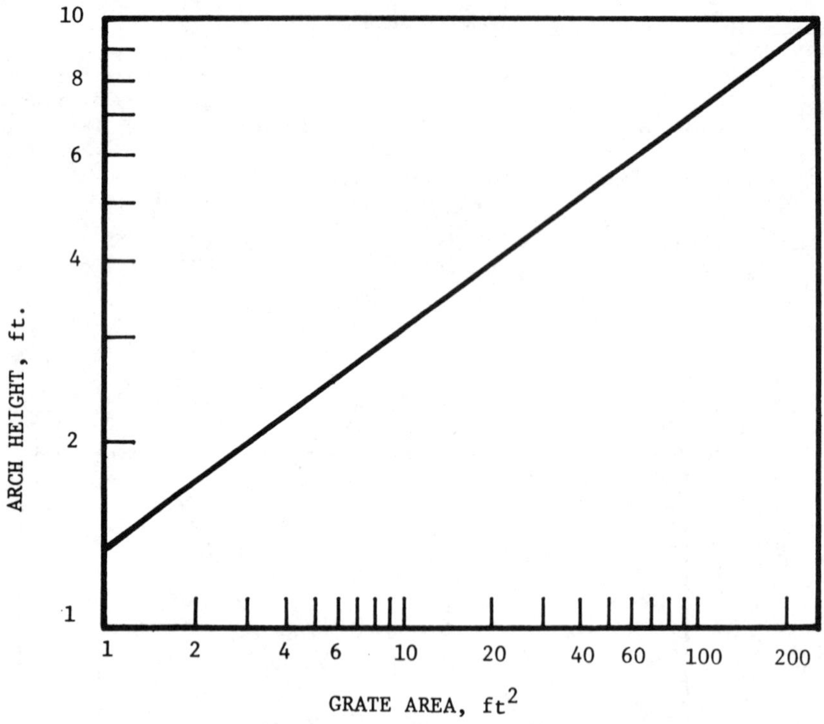

Figure 4-29. Arch height/grate area for multiple chamber incinerator [15].

burning waste bed. Also, the rate of ignition of unburned waste is controlled, which prevents flash volatilization with its resultant flame quenching and smoke creation. Top or side charging is considered disadvantageous because of the suspension of dust, disturbance of the stabilized waste bed and the additional stoking required.

With good regulation of the burning rate through proper charging, air port adjustment and the use of an ignition or "primary" burner, the need for stoking can be reduced to that necessary for waste bed movement before charging.

Process Applications

Generally, multiple chamber incinerators are used for solid wastes. Flowable materials, such as sludges, liquids and gases, can be used in a multiple chamber incinerator only if a proper burner is used.

Multiple chamber incinerators are usually batch-fed equipment. A ram-type feeding system is normally used. For wastes containing high volatiles, frequent feeding of small batches is necessary.

CYCLONIC INCINERATOR

The cyclonic incinerator can be considered as a large burner combustion chamber. Figure 4-30 illustrates the schematics of a cyclonic incinerator.

Operating Principle

A cyclonic incinerator is a cylindrical, refractory lined furnace. Combustion air is injected through a manifold along the sides of the incinerator; the waste is also injected through the sides via single or multiple nozzles. Auxiliary fuel can be injected with wastes or through separate nozzles or a pilot burner as required.

The distinctive feature of a cyclonic incinerator is the means of air injection. The tangentially admitted air produces a cylinder of flame which spirals out of the furnace. Very small diameter cyclonic units may have combustion intensities equal to that of the Vortex type burner (10^6 Btu/hr/ft^3). Larger units are rated at 10^5 Btu/hr/ft^3.

Process Design

The residence time, incineration temperature and excess air requirements are functions of the wastes to be incinerated and should be pilot tested for each new waste application.

Process Application

The cyclonic incinerator can handle gaseous, liquid and sludge wastes. The air injection method makes it a staged combustion chamber, that is, the front end of the incinerator operates fuel-rich and the exhaust end operates fuel-lean. This feature makes it especially adaptable to wastes containing nitrogen for nitrogen oxide control [17].

AUGER COMBUSTOR SYSTEM

The Auger Combustor Energy Recovery System, Figure 4-31, was developed by the Boeing Engineering and Construction Company of

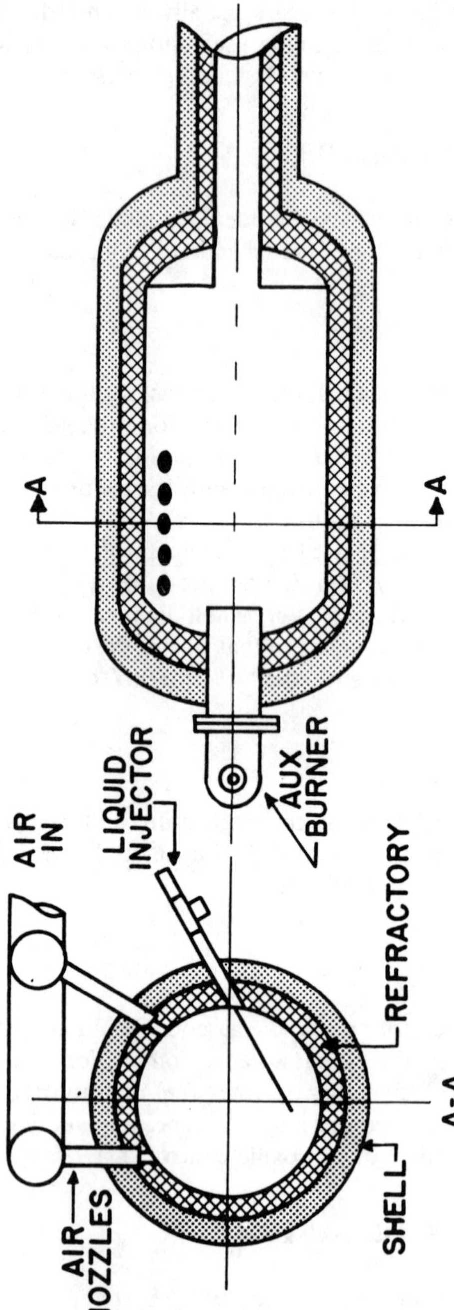

Figure 4-30. Cyclonic incinerator (reproduced courtesy of E. I. DuPont de Nemours and Co., Wilmington, Delaware).

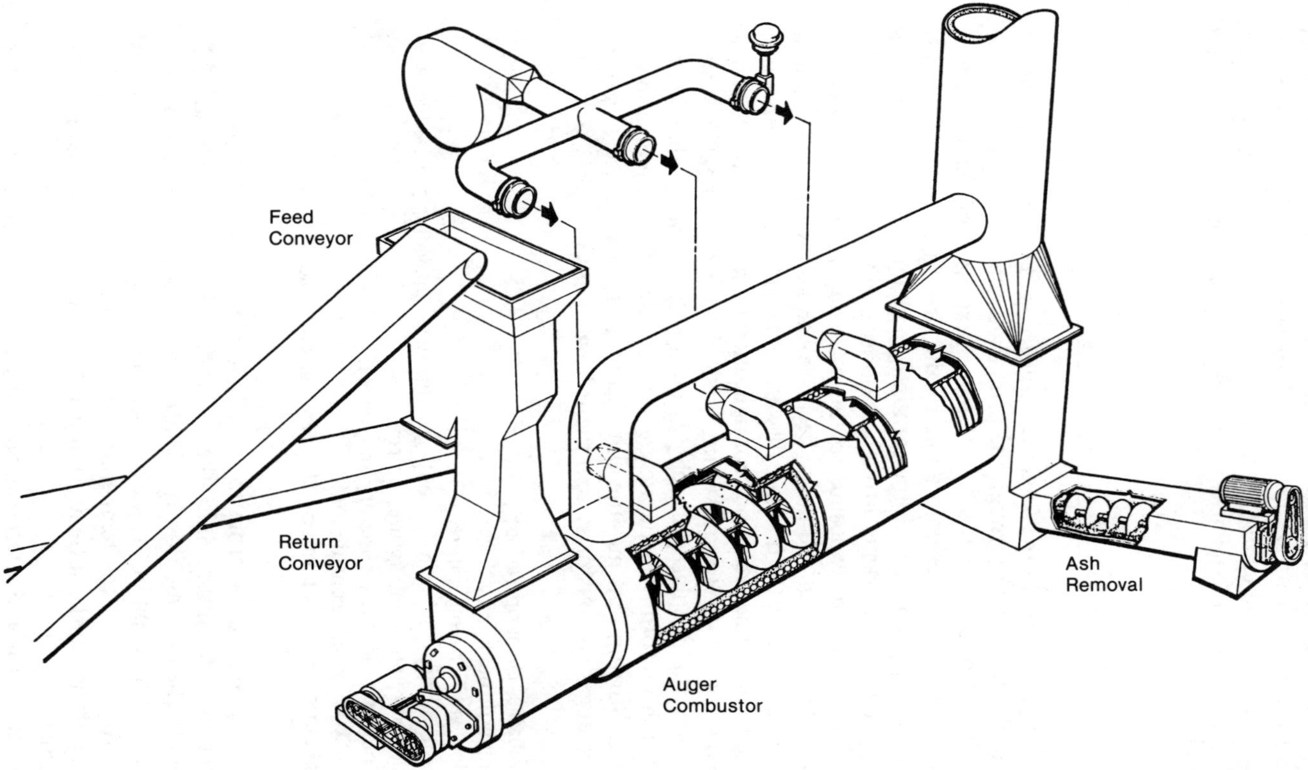

Figure 4-31. Auger combustor incinerator (reproduced courtesy of Boeing Engineering and Construction Company, Seattle, Washington).

Seattle, Washington. It employs a starved-air combustion technique, partially combusting or gasifying solid waste in the primary chamber, then passing the combustible gases to an afterburner where sufficient air is added to complete combustion and to maintain appropriate exit gas temperatures [18].

Operating Principle

The unique feature of the Auger Combustor is the variable-pitch auger which moves the waste through the primary combustion chamber. The waste, shredded to a size of 90% <8 in., enters the combustor at a controlled rate and is shaped into a pile by the first auger flight. It then is pushed and tumbled through the combustion chamber by the auger. As the auger moves the waste through the horizontal cylinder, it stirs the material to maximize exposure to the oxidizing air injected into the chamber. The pitch of the auger decreases along the path of material flow to accommodate the decrease of waste bulk as the material combusts. The ability to manage waste-bed configuration permits control of forced-draft combustion air to gasify nearly all the waste without complete combustion taking place, thereby allowing the primary chamber to operate at a uniformly moderate gas temperature. This combination of waste-bed stirring and air injection with precise temperature control gives the auger combustor system the following advantages:

- reliable, clean operation;
- high throughput;
- low gasifier temperature;
- afterburner combustion of only gaseous fuels, providing precise flame structure and temperature control;
- long material life (refractory and anger);
- fully automatic control; and
- ability to combus a variety of heterogeneous solid wastes.

Exhaust gases exiting from the combustor pass upward through the hot duct and downward into the afterburner, where combustion is completed. The cyclonic flow of the afterburner also serves to remove a significant proportion of the particles carried over from the combustor. The afterburner exit gas temperature is controllable to a level safely below lowest ash initial softening temperature by the air injected into the afterburner.

Both combustor and afterburner are regeneratively cooled; that is, the air injected into each vessel first passes through the structure to cool the structure and heat the air, reducing heat loss and improving performance.

Conventional superheater, waste-heat boiler, and economizer can be used for heat recovery. Commercially proven gas clean-up equipment is incorporated to meet applicable emission standards for particulates or gaseous emissions. Cleaned gases exit through the stack. Ash from the afterburner, boiler sections and precipitator is wet sluiced to the combustor ash pit and blended with combustor ash for removal and disposal.

Process Design

The auger combustor includes the refractory-lined, cylindrical, combustor shell, infeed section, outfeed section, plenums, ash collector and variable pitch auger. Underfire air is supplied through holes in the refractory by tubes embedded in the refractory and installed circumferentially from a steel plenum in the roof of the combustor.

The infeed and outfeed sections attached to the chamber are fabricated of mild steel plate. The infeed section has no refractory or tubes. The outfeed section has refractory but no tubes.

The wet ash collector is attached to the bottom of the outfeed section. This collector includes a conveying device for removal of the combustor ash after quenching in a water sump that also acts as an air seal for the chamber.

A variable-pitch screw auger rotates within the combustor shell to convey the refuse derived fuel. The auger consists of a water-cooled pipe shaft, with a single solid flight followed by several ribbon flights of temperature resistant metal attached to the shaft by standoffs. Cooling water to the shaft is supplied and returned through a Johnson joint. The auger shaft and first two inches of standoffs are refractory coated.

Combustion air is supplied both underfire and overfire. Control of both underfire and overfire air is divided into three zones (primary, secondary and tertiary) to provide for more precise regulation of air/fuel ratio as the fuel is sequentially processed in its travel through the combustor.

The afterburner completes combustion of fuel gas generated by partial oxidation of the solid waste in the substoichiometric primary chamber. The incinerator gas is routed to the afterburner by hot ducting lined with refractory. The afterburner is a vertically installed, double-walled, firebrick-lined cylinder. Forced draft is introduced through multiple ports in the shell. An ash collection hopper, a sluicing box and a hot gas outlet are included.

Steam can be generated by a modular waste-heat watertube boiler, with superheater if required, and economizer suitable for service with the auger combustor. Soot blowers and trim appropriate to this service also are provided. Both superheater and boiler are bare-tube heat exchangers, but the economizer has finned tubes for more efficient heat transfer at the lower temperatures prevailing in that section. Boiler feedwater treatment is provided as necessary, with the deaeration optimized for best cycle performance in the given process plant system.

Cleaning of the exhaust gas stream can be accomplished by an electrostatic precipitator or a baghouse to remove particulates. A low-energy scrubber for removal of gaseous pollutants can be added, if required.

The major portion of the ash comes from the auger combustor. At all of the other ash-generating points, a sluice funnel installed beneath the hopper mixes the ash with water and moves it into the sluice piping. The sluice pipe directs the ash water mixture to the combustor ash sump. Sluice water is recirculated out of the sump and boiler blowdown may be added for make-up. The ash moves out of the sump by screw conveyor and dumps onto a belt conveyor, which conveys it to a bin for pick-up and disposal.

Process Application

The auger combustor system can be used to dispose of sludge and shredded solid wastes. At the present time, the auger combustor system is used primarily for disposal of municipal solid waste and recovery of waste energy. However, its design does offer potential for use in the processing of hazardous wastes.

SHIP-MOUNTED INCINERATOR

A ship-mounted incinerator is an alternative to a land-based incinerator. The basic incinerator design is similar.

The "at-sea" incineration concept is attractive because of public resistance to burning toxic wastes, such as polychlorinated biphenyls (PCB), on land.

At-sea incineration is a relatively new disposal technique and little is known about its long-term effects. It has been practiced in Europe since 1969. The first U.S. experiment was conducted during 1974 and 1975 in the Gulf of Mexico on waste generated during the production of glycerine, vinyl chloride, epichlorohydrin and epoxy resins [19]. In this test, wastes were incinerated at a temperature of 2400°F. The stack gases contained 25–75 ppm carbon monoxide, 9–12.5% oxygen, 5.2–6.2% hydrochloric acid and <200 ppm chlorine [2,18]. Destruction efficiencies of toxic organics were reported to be in excess of 99.9%.

The second test was performed on Agent Orange in the Pacific Ocean during 1977 and 1978. This test proved that the destruction efficiency is >99.99% for most of the toxic substances tested. The toxic substances tested were 2,3,7,8-tetrachlorodibenzo-p-dioxin, isooctyl ester of 2,4,5-trichlorophenoxyacetic acid, normal butyl esters of 2,4-dichlorophenoxyacetic acid and of 2,4,5-trichlorophenyacetic acid. The incineration temperature was maintained at 2280°F [20]. The total residence time in the furnace was ~1.05 sec. The stack gases contained 7.5–13.2% oxygen, 5.9–11.9% carbon dioxide, 4–13 ppm carbon monoxide and 8–110 ppm total hydrocarbon emissions.

A typical ship-mounted incinerator is exemplified by M/T Volcanus. Two vertical upfired incinerators are located at the stern of the ship, each lined with silica firebrick and each with an 18 ft o.d. and a 15.75 ft i.d. The total height of the incinerators is 34.25 ft and the volume of each combustion chamber is 3100 ft^3. Each incinerator is equipped with three burners located roughly symmetrically around the bottom of the furnace. These burners have a rotating cap fuel-injection system that provides vortex turbulence and distribution of feed throughout the entire chamber. No air pollution control equipment is used in the system; the incinerators exhaust directly into the atmosphere. The basic principle of ship-mounted incineration is that any residue, such as hydrochloric acid and trace metals, would be dispersed and diluted in the air and water to undetectable concentrations within a few hours of emission.

Ship-mounted incineration presents an attractive alternative to land-based incineration and is encouraged by the U.S. Environmental Protection Agency as a means of disposal of toxic substances which could not be disposed of on land due to public resistance. However, questions remaining unanswered about at-sea incineration include: the long-term impact on marine life, the safety and health of crew members and the effect of hydrochloric acid discharge into the atmosphere. These questions cannot be answered now, and they will become problems if the number of ship-mounted incinerators should skyrocket.

REFERENCES

1. Manufacturing Chemists Association. "A Guide for Incineration of Chemical Plant Wastes," Washington, DC (1974).

2. Hitchcock, D. A. "Solid-Waste Disposal: Incineration," *Chem. Eng.* (May 21, 1979), p. 182.
3. "Hazardous Material Incinerator Design Criteria," NTIS, Washington, DC (1979).
4. Petura, R. C., "Operating Characteristics and Emmission Performance of Multiple Hearth Furnaces with Sewer Sludge," Proceeding of 1976 National Waste Processing Conference, Boston (May 1976), p. 313.
5. *Disposal of Industrial Wastes by Combustion, Vol. IV,* (New York: American Society of Mechanical Engineers, 1977).
6. "Fluidized Bed Combustion," George Washington University, Course No. 494 (1979).
7. Qureshi, A. E., and D. R. Creasy. "Fluidized Bed Gas Distributors," *Powder Technol.* 22: 113 (1979).
8. Fujiu, M., and T. Hilda. "Method for Incineration of Organic Chlorine Compound and Incinerator Used Therefor," U.S. Patent No. 4,231,303 (November 4, 1980).
9. Kiang, Y. H. "Waste Energy Utilization Technology," (New York: Marcel Dekker, Inc., 1981).
10. Wall, C. J., J. T. Graves, and E. J. Roberts. "How to Burn Salty Sludges," *Chem. Eng.* (April 14, 1975), pp. 77–82.
11. Kiang, Y. H. "Total Hazardous Waste Disposal Through Combustion," *Ind. Heating,* 44 (12):9 (1977).
12. Kiang, Y. H. "RCRA Compliance Incineration Test and System Development Program," paper presented at the AIChE 73rd Annual Meeting, Chicago, November 1980.
13. Kiang, Y. H. "Incineration of Waste Gases," Paper No. 79-5.4, Air Pollution Control Association, 72nd Annual Meeting, Cincinnati, Ohio, June 1979.
14. Perry, J. H. "Chemical Engineering Handbook," 4th ed. (New York: McGraw-Hill Book Company, 1963).
15. "Air Pollution Engineering Manual," U.S. Department of Health, Education and Welfare, Cincinnati, OH (1967).
16. Rose, A. H., and H. R. Crabaugh. "Incinerator Design Standards: Research Findings," Publication 60, Los Angeles County Air Pollution Control District, Los Angeles (1955).
17. Monroe, E. S., and D. E. McKee. "The Incineration of Nitrogen Compound," Proceedings of 1976 National Waste Processing Conference, Boston (May 1976), p. 531.
18. Boeing Engineering and Construction Company. "The BEC Auger Combustor System" (1981).
19. Ricci, L. T. "Offshore Incineration Gets Limited U.S. Backing," *Chem. Eng.* 83:86 (1976).
20. "At Sea Incineration of Herbicide Orange Onboard the M/T Vulcanus," U.S. EPA Research Permit No. 770DH001R (August 1977).

CHAPTER 5

THERMAL INCINERATION SPECIAL TOPICS

As described in previous chapters, a wide variety of incinerators can be used for hazardous waste processing. Although these incinerators differ in design and application, they have in common certain general principles which are discussed here as special topics.

INCINERATOR HARDWARE

There are three distinct features of any incinerator: the incinerator orientation (the direction of hot gas flow), the incinerator chamber configuration and the draft system.

The orientation of an incinerator is dependent on the type of incinerator and the waste characteristics. The basic orientations are illustrated in Figure 5-1. The orientation of a multiple hearth incinerator usually is upfired, as is the fluidized bed incinerator. The rotary kiln incinerator normally is in a sloped, downfired orientation. The multiple chamber incinerator normally is horizontally fired. Liquid injection, fume and cyclonic incerators can be in any form, depending on the wastes to be incinerated. When salts are present in the combustion product, downfired or sloped downfired designs are required to allow salts to clear out of the system.

Incinerators can be cylindrical, square or rectangular boxes. Cylindrical design is required for multiple hearth, fluidized bed, rotary kiln, cyclonic and auger combustor incinerators. Although liquid injection, fume and multiple chamber incinerators can be of either square or rectangular design, a cylindrical chamber is the preferred configuration. The roof refractory design of a square or rectangular design is usually very difficult.

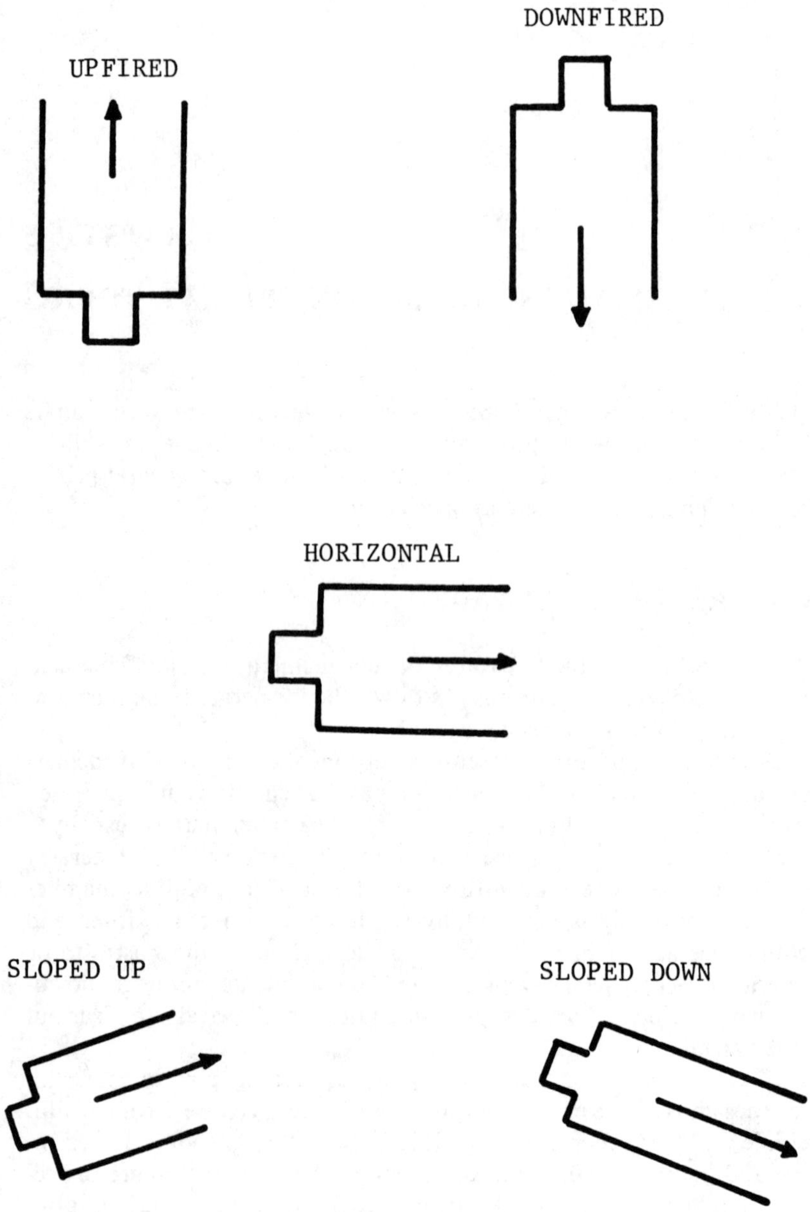

Figure 5-1. Incinerator orientation.

Theoretically, there is little difference between a forced draft system and an induced draft system (Figure 5-2). The advantage of using an induced draft system is safety. The corrosive acidic gases, generated in incineration systems, are always contained in the system because of the vacuum operation. However, there are practical implementation problems such as induced fan selection, since the corrosive exhaust gas is detrimental to the fan. Also, in practice, the induced system usually requires a higher excess air rate, increasing the size of the equipment and the auxiliary fuel usage. In most cases, waste incineration requires high-intensity combustion, which can be achieved only by forced draft. Thus, a forced draft system is usually the preferred design.

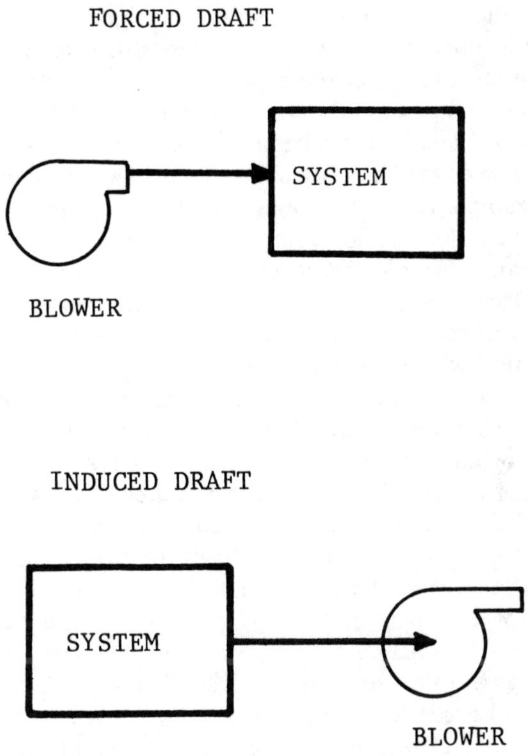

Figure 5-2. Incinerator draft system.

MATERIAL OF CONSTRUCTION

There are two critical areas in the incinerator for material selection: the waste injectors and the combustion chamber refractory.

Injector

In the selection of nozzles, the following are critical to proper material selection: operating pressure, internal flow areas, operating temperature and the chemistry of the fluids.

Most important of these is the operating temperature. Nozzles that operate hydraulically are cooled by the liquid while in operation; however, radiation from the incinerator chamber, which may be in the range of 1400 to 3000°F, will affect the metal temperature of the nozzle. In selecting the material for the nozzle, it is important to know the temperature during operation, as well as at shutdown. Temperature level is caused by radiation from the chamber into which the nozzle is spraying, convection of air and gases at the face of the nozzle, and cooling effects of the liquid, steam and/or air. Chemical reactions take place at the face of the nozzle between the hot gases in the chamber and the liquid being injected.

An example is water cooling sprays in a chamber containing high-temperature products of combustion. The cooling effect of the spray nozzle can cause condensation of the hot gases along the wall of the nozzle. These gases, if acidic, then react with the metal if at or below the dewpoint of the acid. Therefore, it is important to know that the metal temperature will be at a safe level to prevent acidic corrosion. If this cannot be determined, it will be necessary to use a material resistant to the particular acid. Tables 5-1 and 5-2 list typical materials to use in incinerator nozzles for various acids and gases [1–6].

Another reaction is between the liquid being sprayed and the gases in the oxidation chamber. The velocities normally used at the exit of a nozzle cause recirculation of the gases from the chamber into the liquid spray. If the gases contain a material that can be absorbed into the spray—for example, an aqueous waste spray in a chamber containing chlorine or hydrochloric acid gases—the water will react immediately with the gases to form a hydrochloric acid mist in the fine spray droplets. These will be recycled into the turbulent zone at the nozzle exit and result in direct contact with the nozzle body. If metal temperature conditions are right, attack will begin almost immediately. It is important to realize that if these conditions can occur, they most often will. Material selection of the nozzle is very important.

Table 5-1. Materials with Increasing Corrosion Resistance to Liquids

Hydrochloric Acid <1% (Room Temperature)	Hydrochloric Acid <1% (Boiling Point)	Sulfuric Acid 5% (Boiling Point)
Carpenter 20B	Inconel 600	Ni-Resist
Inconel 600	Nickel	316 S.S.
Nickel (air free)	Monel (air free up to 0.5% HCl)	Inconel 600
Monel (air free)		Nickel 200
Hastelloy B	Hastelloy D	Duremit 20
Hastelloy D	Hastelloy C	Carpenter 20B
Hastelloy C	Hastelloy B (chlorine free)	Nionel-825
		Hastelloy C
		Lead
		Hastelloy D
		Monel 400
		Aluminum Bronze
		Hastelloy B

Refractories

Refractories are the most vulnerable materials of any high temperature system, especially in those units where a variety of wastes are oxidized [5]. The major features affecting the life of refractories are: mode of operation, refractory design, and material selection. It is important that each of these be analyzed to achieve a minimum cost for maintenance of an incineration system [7].

Mode of Operation

In a waste disposal system utilizing high temperature incineration, there are a variety of operation problems which tend to minimize the life of the refractory. Typical of these are the following:

1. *Intermittent Operation.* Units which operate intermittently are most likely to see a very short refractory life. The operator is anxious to get the unit up to operating temperature as quickly as possible and, on completion of the burning cycle, will cool the unit down quickly to minimize fuel usage and save time.

2. *Operation with Minimum Safeguards to Prevent Thermal Shock in the Incinerator.* A typical example is a unit operating with aqueous wastes being sprayed into the incinerator chamber. Upon the loss of

Table 5-2. Materials with Increasing Corrosion Resistance to Gases [7]

H_2S	Sulfur	SO_2	HCl	Cl_2
Nickel	Nickel, Copper	Nickel	Copper	Tantalum
Mild Steel	Mild Steel	Iron	Monel	Aluminum
Iron	Iron	Cu-10 Mg	Mild Steel	Copper
Iron Manganese	Fe-14 Cr	Fe-15 Cr	Fe-18 Cr-8 Ni	Mild Steel
Inconel	Cu-Mn	Tantalum	Fe-18 Cr-8 Ni-Mo	Platinum
Copper	80 Ni-13 Cr-6.5 Fe	Copper, Brass	Hastelloy C	Fe-18 Cr-8 Ni
Fe-15 Chromium	Mn	Aluminum Alloys	Hastelloy B	Monel
Fe-25 Chromium	Cr	Mo, V	Inconel 600	Hastelloy C
Chromium	Fe-17 Cr	Fe-30 Cr	Nickel	Hastelloy B
18 Cr-8 Ni	Fe-18 Cr-8 Ni	Fe-18 Cr-8 Ni		Inconel 600
22 Cr-10 Al	Hastelloy	Inconel		Nickel
Copper-10 Mg	Al, Mg	Copper-12 Al		
Fe-12 Al, Ni-15 Al		Zirconium		
Ta, Mo, V				
Al, Mg				

auxiliary fuel, caused by low fuel pressure, low air pressure or flame failure, the incinerator temperature will drop immediately if aqueous waste continues to flow into the unit. The cold spray striking the refractory walls will cause immediate spalling and ultimate failure.

3. *Operation in an Atmosphere with Contaminated Combustion Air Source.* The air can be contaminated with dust such as phosphate, lime, etc., which can attack the refractories in the combustion chamber, if the material selection does not take this into consideration.

4. *Operation without Control of Excess Air Rate.* Operation under reducing conditions has led to failure of refractories not designed for this type of operation.

5. *Operation with Liquid Wastes Containing Abrasive Solids or Chemical Compounds.*

6. *Operation at High Pressures.* High operating pressures can cause diffusion of the combusion products through the refractories.

Refractory Design

One of the major, sometimes critical, problems in a refractory installation is the soundness of the design. When refractory lining failures occur rapidly, this may not always be caused by operation or by material selection. The proper design for adequate expansion, anchoring and support often determines the life of a refractory lining. As mentioned above, if the lining could operate without cycling, the need for maintenance would be minimized; however, this is not always the case. During startup of a new system, the refractory lining goes through many cycles and upsets caused by unscheduled shutdowns due to problems in debugging a process or new system. Frequently, more damage is done during the startup than during any other part of the operation of an incineration system.

The most important characteristics in proper refractory design are as follows:

1. *Refractory Properties*

a. Heat Conductivity. Heat conductivity in the material is the ability of the material to transfer heat through its thickness, thereby causing a temperature variation between the front and back wall of the lining. This affects the heat loss by condution and eventually radiation from the shell. Heat conductivity plays a part in refractory design since it controls the temperature difference between the inner and outer face of the brick or castable refractory. The greater this difference, the more tendency there is for spalling and fracturing to occur because of thermal stresses which can develop in the lining. In many cases, these stresses are greater than the allowable stresses in the refractory material. Heat conductivity plays a part in spalling, since it is directly related to density of the material, and density in turn is related to the spalling characteristics of the material [8].

Engineering calculations generally show it is preferable to use more courses of thin brick rather than fewer courses of thick brick. Heat conductivity plays a part in the amount of heat loss to the surroundings. Most chamber designs attempt to minimize this heat loss. This allows faster warmup and cooldown. By proper selection of refractory, the heat storage in the lining is maintained over the shutdown period; thereby reducing heat-up time and fuel requirements for the next startup.

b. Hot Strength. A major physical requirement of a refractory lining is the ability to stand up under load at elevated temperatures. In most thermal incinerators, these stresses occur within the structure itself. As a guide in the selection of refractories, load tests give some indication of the conditions to be expected. In Figure 5-3, the short-duration load test for various materials indicates the amount of expansion or contraction at various temperature ranges. The sustained load test for 100 hr operation (Table 5-3) aids in determining the overall hot strength of a material over a long period of time. It is important to determine from the short range test, the amount and uniformity of expansion to the point of maximum expansion. Low uniform thermal expansion minimizes difficulties with the mechanical distortion of the structure. At the point where expansion ceases, softening under load begins.

The shrinkage which occurs during the period the material is under load is also of great importance. Contraction of the material can be interpreted directly in terms of an incinerator life. Contractions of 5% are classified as failures, since this is a 7/16-in. slump of the 9-in. long brick, usually enough to lose keying, wedging or arching action in a modular unit.

c. Thermal Shock. The physical properties of the refractory material influence the development and distribution of thermal stresses. Tensile strength, thermal conductivity, modulus of elasticity and thermal expansion are characteristics that determine how well a material will resist thermal shock. Low thermal expansion is desirable, since it prevents non-uniform expansion to a great degree. The thermal expansion of a typical high-temperature material is shown in Figure 5-4. For most materials, the expansion rate is fairly constant over the range of 400 to 2500°F. However, there is an inversion with a large volume change between the different forms of silicate at high temperatures. This is shown in Figure

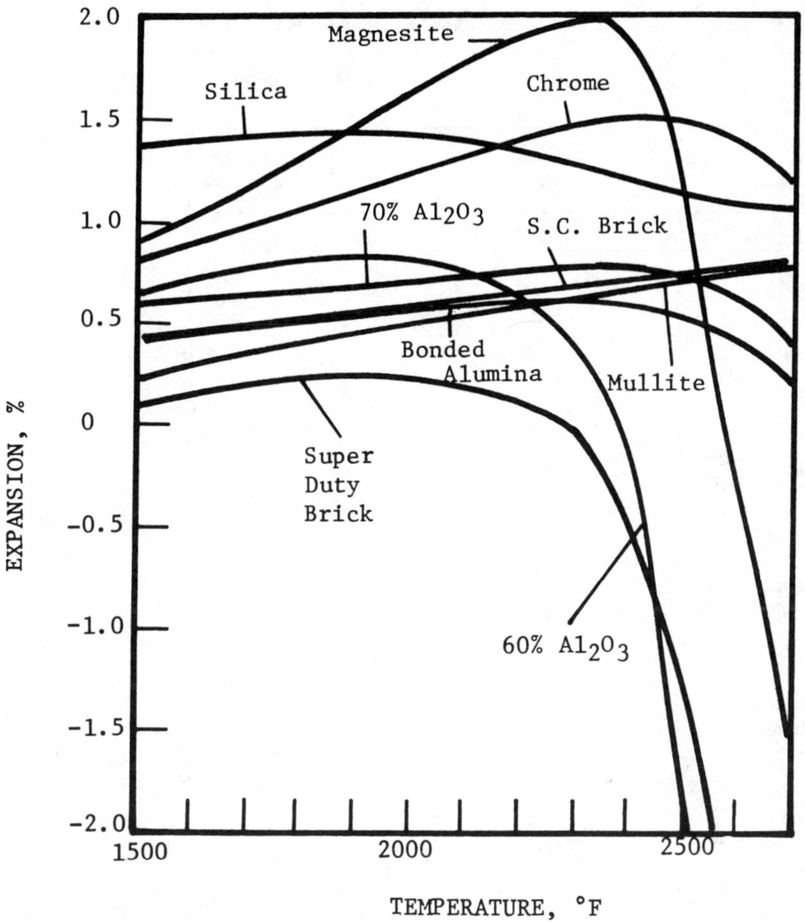

Figure 5-3. Refractory short duration load tests [7].

5-5. Since most refractories contain some silica in the body or the bond, this inversion must be coped with to minimize thermal spalling in most high-temperature materials.

Following are some suggested procedures for handling the problem. After a refractory vessel is lined, a proper curing procedure is required for the lining. This is best done with thermocouples installed in various locations throughout the refractory to monitor refractory temperatures. A measure of the gas temperature in the incinerator is not an indication of the refractory temperature. In the initial cure, refractory should be brought up to a temperature of between 170 and 230°F and maintained

Table 5-3. Refractory Sustained Load Tests [7]

	Load (psi)	Deformation After 100 Hours (%) — Temperature (°F) 2192	2462	2732
Fireclay	6.25	0.30	3.9	
	12.5	0.23	4.3	
	25.0	0.32	11.3	
	50.0	–	>10.3	
Semi-Silica	6.25	–	1.19	
	12.5	–	3.14	
	25.0	–	5.03	
	50.0	1.19	–	
Silica	6.25			–
	12.5			nil
	25.0			0.13
	50.0			0.25
High-alumina Fireclay	6.25	–	2.8	–
	12.5	–	2.4	–
	25.0	0.87	7.7	–
	50.0	1.30	9.9	–
Bonded Alumina	6.25		+0.20	2.51
	12.5		+0.04	3.73
	25		0.25	8.68
	50		1.08	10.58
Mullite	6.25			
	12.5			
	25			
	50		nil	nil
Silicon Carbide	6.25			0.40
	12.5			0.40
	25.0			0.58
	50.0			0.78

at this temperature for a period of at least 10 hr. This ensures that the water in the refractory will be steamed out. In the design of the lining, sufficient openings should be provided for the steam to escape; if it is trapped, it may cause premature refractory failure by steam expansion behind the refractory. If the lining has been held at a temperature in the range of 200 to 230°F, the temperature can be raised from this level to 1000°F at a rate of 100°F/hr. The temperature should be held at 1000°F in the combustion chamber for ~10 hr. After this period, the

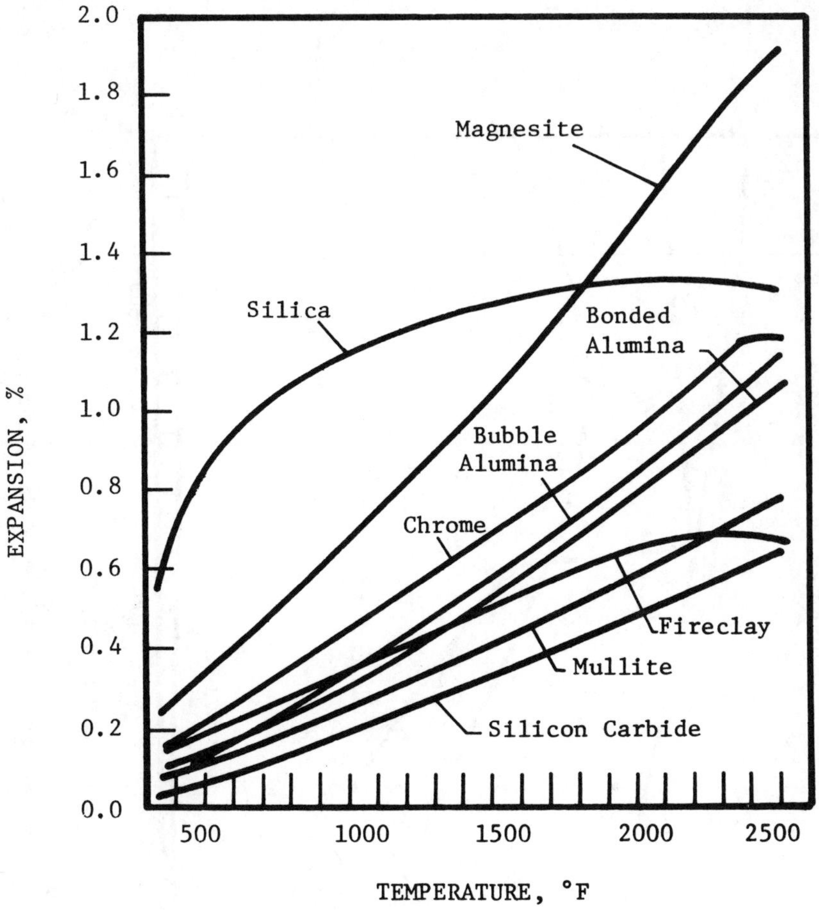

Figure 5-4. Thermal expansion of high temperature materials [7].

temperature is steadily increased to the operating level at a rate not to exceed 200°F/hr.

During the refractory curing, it is imperative that there be no decrease in the combustion chamber temperature. The temperature should be held at a constant level and gradually increased during the curing operation. Temperature oscillations frequently result in improper curing and subsequent failure of refractories. After reaching the curing temperature, cooling can be effected by gradually reducing the temperature ~200°F/hr. This temperature reduction is maintained until the temperature reaches 800°F. After the initial cure, the combustion chamber or oxidation chamber can be safely heated or cooled at a rate of 300°F/hr

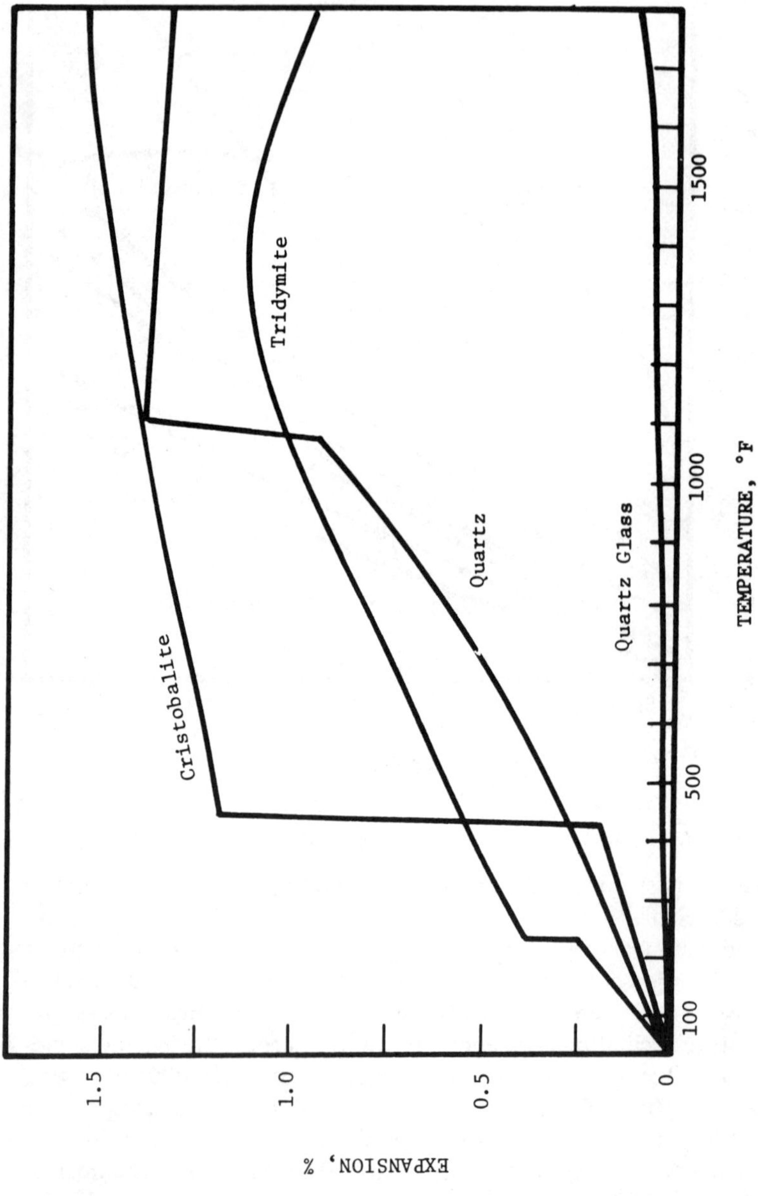

Figure 5-5. Thermal expansion of different forms of silica [7].

between 500 and 1100°F. In heating beyond 1100°F up to the working temperature, or in cooling down, a higher rate of ~400°F/hr may be safely employed. It is important to be very careful in heating and cooling in the low temperature range between 200 and 600°F because cristobalite—the form in which silicate is likely to be present—undergoes a reversible transformation at ~400°F that is accompanied by a large change in volume. Therefore, if the materials are carried through this initial range too rapidly, induced tensile strength may cause cracking or spalling. From room temperature to ~500°F, a heating rate ≤100°F/hr is best. This isn't always possible, but knowing these danger points is helpful [9].

In summary, it is not as important to adjust the heating and cooling rate to an average temperature rise over the entire range from ambient temperature to operating temperature over a certain period of time. It is more important to concentrate on maintaining a closely controlled, gradual rise on the lower end of the temperature range. Once the temperature level of 500°F is reached, a much higher rate can be tolerated. Required temperature can be reached, and at the same time stresses within the incinerator components are kept to a minimum.

d. Chemical Resistance. Chemical reaction is one of the great factors leading to the destruction of high-temperature materials. Most often in incinerator applications, damage is caused by reaction of combustion products with the basic refractory materials. Most often, damage occurs during startup or shutdown, when condensation of the products of combustion can occur.

With the variety of wastes disposed of by thermal incineration, it is most important to know the analysis of the combustion products and the variation that can occur during operation. Products of combustion normally contain CO_2, H_2O, N_2, O_2 and other substances, depending upon the waste material being oxidized. These other products can be sulfur dioxide, sulfur trioxide, vanadium pentoxide, carbon monoxide, hydrogen, hydrogen chloride, chlorine, sodium oxide, sodium carbonate, sodium sulfate, etc. The reactions between these products and the refractory materials have to be studied, and may require a design using special mortar in brickwork or a resilient lining in the interface between the refractory and the steel. It is important to know the expansion rate of the refractory versus the steel. It is also important to know how the steel can best be protected from corrosion from these combustion products. The premeability of the refractory is also important, especially in a unit operating at pressure. Under these conditions, gases can attack the steel lining during operation, and not necessarily during shutdown.

e. Permeability. Permeability of the refractory lining of an incinerator chamber determines the attack on the outer enclosure by the bases in the chamber. The more porous the lining, the greater chance there is of attack to the outer shell. A dense inner lining prevents penetration by liquids. However, this also requires an insulating back-up lining to keep heat loss to a minimum. Design of this inner lining requires maintaining good joints to prevent leakage.

f. Abrasion Resistance. In selecting abrasion resistant materials, a major point is an understanding of the two basic types of abrasion: an impingement by fine solids suspended in air, gas or liquid, and direct abrasion by a mass of wet or dry solids moving across or at the surface. The grade of abrasion depends on variables such as size, hardness, shape, weight and concentration of particles; velocity and direction of impact; operating temperature and corrosive nature of the abrading material; and atmosphere. Extreme toughness and hardness of the lining material is demanded when abrasion and corrosion are combined. If hardness prevents a breakdown by abrasion, chemical attack is retarded; however, if chemical attack destroys the bond, nothing can prevent the granular segments from being washed away.

In designing for high-velocity areas within combustion chambers, it is well to know the maximum velocities that various materials can withstand. Most dense materials (≥ 100 lb/ft^3) should withstand velocities up to 100–150 ft/sec at high temperatures (2000–3000°F) without erosion problems. In some fume incinerator designs where a lightweight refractory may be used (1400–2000°F insulating brick or castable refractory), certain areas may operate with velocities up to 50 ft/sec. In cases where higher velocities are generated, a coating of 40% solution of sodium silicate will permit operation without erosion of the lightweight porous refractory up to ~ 150 ft/sec. Lightweight insulating firebrick has been used up to 300 ft/sec with coating of refractory paint. In some cases, alloy liners may be used with an insulating material as a back-up in the interest of using a low conductivity material of low density [9].

g. Refractoriness. In selecting a 1500–3500°F material for application in incinerators, the resistance to heat should be the last product characteristic to be considered. In too many cases, materials are chosen only on the basis of temperature without consideration for the characteristics and conditions outlined above. The pyrometric cone equivalent (PCE) is usually a guide in the selection of materials. However, safe working temperatures are often well below the PCE value. Some materials (fired clay, insulating brick and high alumina fired clay) begin to soften well below their indicated PCE values because of exceptional purity and structure and emphasis on development of crystal and such structure.

Electric furnace material such as alumina, mullite, silicon carbide and a few of the gas bodies give service at temperatures much closer to their PCE values.

2. *Refractory Anchoring Systems.* Many recent refractory linings for furnaces have been monolithic refractories rather than brick linings, in the interest of labor saving. Originally, monolithic materials were used to quick-patch or temporarily repair small areas of brickwork. The technique for holding the patch involved curing the brickwork surrounding the repair area to key in the monolithic refractory. This practice proved successful in larger repair areas where attempted, but the keying-in method was not sufficient to hold larger masses of material, leading to the development of metallic anchors. Common forged bolts were welded to the furnace shell with the heads projecting into the refractory slab. Holding ability was improved by bending approximately 2 in. of the bolt head in 90°.

All these systems have been replaced with modern sophisticated designs using steel, alloys and prefired high-alumina ceramic shapes. The increased acceptance of refractory monolithic linings in the furnace industry shows the importance anchoring systems play in the success of any refractory installation. As a result, specifications for installation practices and techniques are becoming more exacting. Advanced systems had to be developed to meet present-day operating demands on furnaces subjected to increased firing rates and more severe processes.

Various densities of monolithic linings are used to serve different purposes. A lightweight castable lining is used for thermal insulation, a dense and impermeable material for corrosion protection, and a high-strength material for wear resistance. In incinerator application, the lining system is usually a combination of a dense and impermeable material for temperature and corrosion protection and a lightweight castable back-up material for thermal insulation. It is important that these linings act as a monolithic structure to protect the incinerator shell from temperature and corrosion. The anchoring system function is to hold this structure to the shell or supporting structural work. Modern anchoring systems for refractory slabs function only as a holding device and not as a reinforcing element for the slab.

There are basically three main anchor categories: prefired refractory shapes used with metallic holders, V-type alloy metallic foundry castings, and V-type alloy metallic rods (see Figure 5-6). To select the proper anchor and spacing the design conditions are dependent on the following:

- maximum furnace operating temperatures (hot face and cold face),
- refractory lining thickness and the number of lining components,

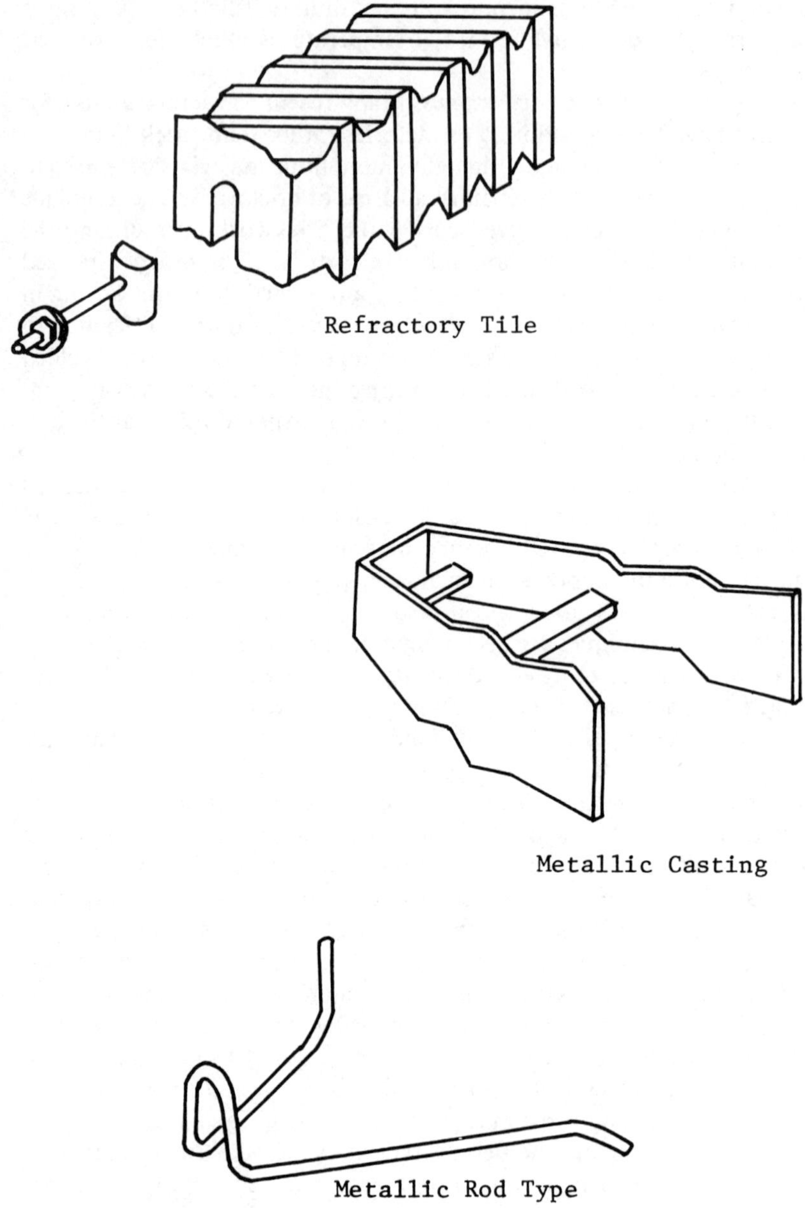

Figure 5-6. ~~Monolothic~~ refractory anchors [7]. Monolithic

- incinerator geometry,
- installation method (for example, rammed plastic, castable or gunning),
- vibration and/or severity of incinerator operation conditions,
- structural stability of the incinerator shell, linings or supporting steel work, and
- installation technique of refractory anchors where arc welding is considered.

All of these factors must be taken in combination and properly evaluated.

Incinerators are designed for specific functions. Many times the geometry is determined without fully considering that the final major step in completing the installation is the application of anchoring systems and refractories without disrupting the combustion features and functions of an incinerator design. A slight shift of minor change in the contour of a nose section or wall detail can greatly improve the ease of applying anchoring systems, and, in turn, gain a more secure refractory lining.

Material Selection

In order to select the proper refractory materials for an application, an understanding of the typical data sheet available for all refractories should be considered. The technical data most often supplied for a refractory is as follows:

- pyrometric cone equivalent (PCE)
- hot load strength
- panel spall loss
- porosity
- bulk density
- modulus of rupture
- crushing strength and chemical analysis.

Of these, the three most important are PCE, panel spall loss and porosity, with the latter two having a direct relationship. The more dense the brick, the greater the spalling characteristics. Considering these data, if a refractory application required maximum temperature resistance combined with maximum strength and abrasion resistance, and the application was one where spalling might well be a factor, a very high alumina would perhaps be the most desirable product. If, on the other hand, economics entered into consideration, all of the above service conditions should be reevaluated with the objective of finding a more economical product that would perform adequately. For example, it might be found that abrasion resistance was the most important factor, that temperature considerations had received too much emphasis, and that the equipment would operate more constantly than originally anticipated, thus reducing the likelihood of spalling. THis review might then result in selection of a lower alumina material because of its higher bulk density and low porosity. Normally, the alumina content of a material is directly related to the cost of brick, especially when looking at super-duty and better type firebrick. With regard to the chemical analysis of brick, it is sometimes important to know the other components, such as ferric oxide, titanium, calcium oxide, magnesium oxide and alkali. In acid incineration systems, the higher the alkali content of the back-up brick the more problems result when condensation takes place in the lining. Normally, insulating brick is used. The difference between the alkali content of various bricks should be investigated to be certain that these bricks will not deteriorate when condensation takes place.

The operating pressure of an incinerator will affect refractory selection. Those with minimum porosity and maximum density will be the best selection for a high pressure application. This prevents crushing of the materials on the interface and maintains stability of physical dimensions. It also prevents bypass leakage of the products through the refractories to areas where corrosion or overheating could take place.

In the selection of refractories, the atmosphere to which the refractories are exposed is certainly critical to the materials selected [10–15].

1. *Oxidizing Atmospheres.* Most oxide-base and fire clay materials are inert to oxidation whether caused by CO, CO_2, H_2O or O_2 (even CO can cause oxidation in certain materials). Carbon and graphite materials are the most susceptible to oxidation. Under some conditions, carbon from the breakdown of carbon monoxide into carbon and carbon dioxide can be deposited within incinerator linings. This carbon builds up around iron impurities in the refractory materials and sets up severe disrupting forces. Thus, it is necessary to select low-iron-content materials or materials where the iron impurities have been tied up in chemical complexes.

2. *Hydrogen Atmosphere.* In molecular form, hydrogen will not cause damage to the refractory materials; however, from 2500 to 3000°F, molecular hydrogen breaks down into nascent or atomic hydrogen. In this form, hydrogen will attack silica or iron, causing reactions that destroy silica-containing materials. Hydrogen in atomic form can attack silicon carbide, silica, zircon, mullite, fire clay and clay-bonded alumina. The high-temperature material which best withstands attack from atomic hydrogen is pure alumina. When hydrogen is present, commercial varieties of bonded alumina are unsuitable for temperatures >2700°F. These materials are available, however, in forms that contain ≥ 98–99%

bonded alumina. Other materials that can withstand atomic hydrogen are magnesia and zirconia.

3. *Chlorine Atmosphere.* These gases attack silica-containing materials above 1200°F. The end product is silicon tetrachloride. In most incinerator applications, the problem is to convert the chlorine to HCl so that the chlorine is essentially eliminated as a gas. The high temperature HCl gas can then be resisted by a high-alumina brick, castable or rammed lining. At lower temperatures, acid brick, where the silica content is 10% greater than in commercial firebrick, can be used. Fire clay, acidproof materials have low permeability and are highly resistant to corrosion. The only disadvantage with acid brick is its low thermal shock resistance. Therefore, in high temperature applications where thermal shock is a definite requirement, the high alumina materials have given the best service.

4. *Reducing Atmospheres.* In many thermal incinerators, a combination of reduction and oxidation takes place. Under reducing conditions, CO and H_2 will attack certain types of refractory material, as well as mortar. To eliminate this attack, a low-iron and low-silica content material should be used. It has been found that a phosphate bonded material for both low and high temperature strength minimizes the attack of CO and H_2 on the bonding agents. Another effect of a reducing atmosphere on a refractory is the lowering of the softening point.

5. *Alkali Atmosphere.* Alkali compounds carried into the combustion chamber are potentially very harmful to the refractory. Potash, soda and lithium are all about equally destructive. Alkalis form a series of low melting compounds with the ingredients of fire clay and high alumina refractories. The reactions between alkali compounds and the ingredients in the refractories result in the formation of new alkaline minerals accompanied by expansion. Distress due to alkali attack may be seen as glazing or dripping of the refractories if the temperature is high enough, or at low temperatures as a shelling or decrepitation of the surface.

PROCESS DESIGN ASPECTS

The goal of hazardous waste incineration is the complete destruction of organic hazardous constituents, which is related to, but not identical with, the complete combustion of the fuel and the combustible waste components. The destruction efficiency of organic hazardous constituent (OHC) is defined as:

$$DE_{OHC} = \frac{W_{in} - W_{out}}{W_{in}} \times 100$$

where DE_{OHC} = destruction efficiency of specific organic hazardous constituent, %
W_{in} = mass feed rate of organic hazardous constituent to the incinerator
W_{out} = mass emission rate of organic hazardous constituent

The Resource Conservation and Recovery Act regulation designates the destruction and removal efficiency (DRE) of principal organic hazardous constituents (POHC) as the requirement for incinerator design [16,17]. The DRE of an incineration system is defined as:

$$DRE = \frac{W_{in} - W_{out}}{W_{in}} \times 100$$

where DRE = destruction and removal efficiency, %
W_{in} = mass feed rate of the principal organic hazardous constituent(s) to the incinerator
W_{out} = mass emission rate of the principal organic hazardous constituent(s) to the atmosphere (as measured in the stack prior to discharge).

Thus, destruction and removal efficiency calculations are based on the combined efficiencies of destruction in the incinerator and removal from the gas stream in the air pollution control system. The potential presence of principal organic hazardous constituents in incinerator bottom ash or solid/liquid discharges from air pollution control devices is not accounted for in the destruction and removal efficiency calculation as currently defined by regulation.

The regulations require a DRE of 99.99% for all principal organic hazardous constituents of a waste unless it can be demonstrated that a higher or lower destruction and removal efficiency is more appropriate based on human health criteria.

Specification of the principal organic hazardous constituents in a waste is subject to best engineering judgment, considering the toxicity, thermal stability and quantity of each organic waste constituent. DRE normally is measured only during trial burns and occasional compliance tests, and is used as a basis for determining proper incineration system operation parameters.

Process Design Parameters

The destruction efficiency of organic hazardous constituents by incineration depends on the exposure of organic components to oxygen at a sufficiently high temperature for a sufficient time. The four important process design parameters are: residence time, incineration temperature, excess air (stack oxygen) and mixing. The first three are definable and finite parameters. However, the mixing aspects are not finite but empirically different for each incinerator and each waste.

To study the effectiveness of an incinerator, that is, the interrelationship between destruction efficiency and process design parameters (time, temperature, excess air and mixing) analytical models of the incinerator have to be developed. There are two approaches for modeling: the two-reactor method and the zone method [18].

In the two-reactor method, the incinerator is divided into two sections (Figure 5-7). The first section is the perfect stirred reactor (PSR), where fuel, waste and air are mixed. In this section, all reactants are assumed to be perfectly mixed and are at a uniform temperature. The gas stream leaves the perfect stirred reactor with the same temperature and composition. The function of perfect stirred reactor section is to ensure ignition, stable flame holding and instantaneous and uniform distribution of reactive species. The second section is the plug flow reactor, where enough residence time must be allowed to complete the combustion. The division between these two sections is purely theoretical. For single-stage incineration, the dividsion is made on the basis of visible flame boundary observation. For two-stage incineration, the division is downstream of the secondary waste injector (Figure 5-7). The overall residence time is defined as:

$$RT = \frac{V}{S}$$

where RT = overall residence time, sec,
V = incinerator volume, ft^3, and
S = combustion gas flow rate, ft^3/sec.

However, the overall residence is a meaningless parameter. The real important parameter is the effective residence time (ERT) as defined by:

$$ERT = \frac{V_{PFR}}{S}$$

where ERT = effective residence time, sec, and
V_{PFR} = volume of plug flow reactor section, ft^3.

Usually, the effective residence time is not attainable because of the difficulty of defining the division plane.

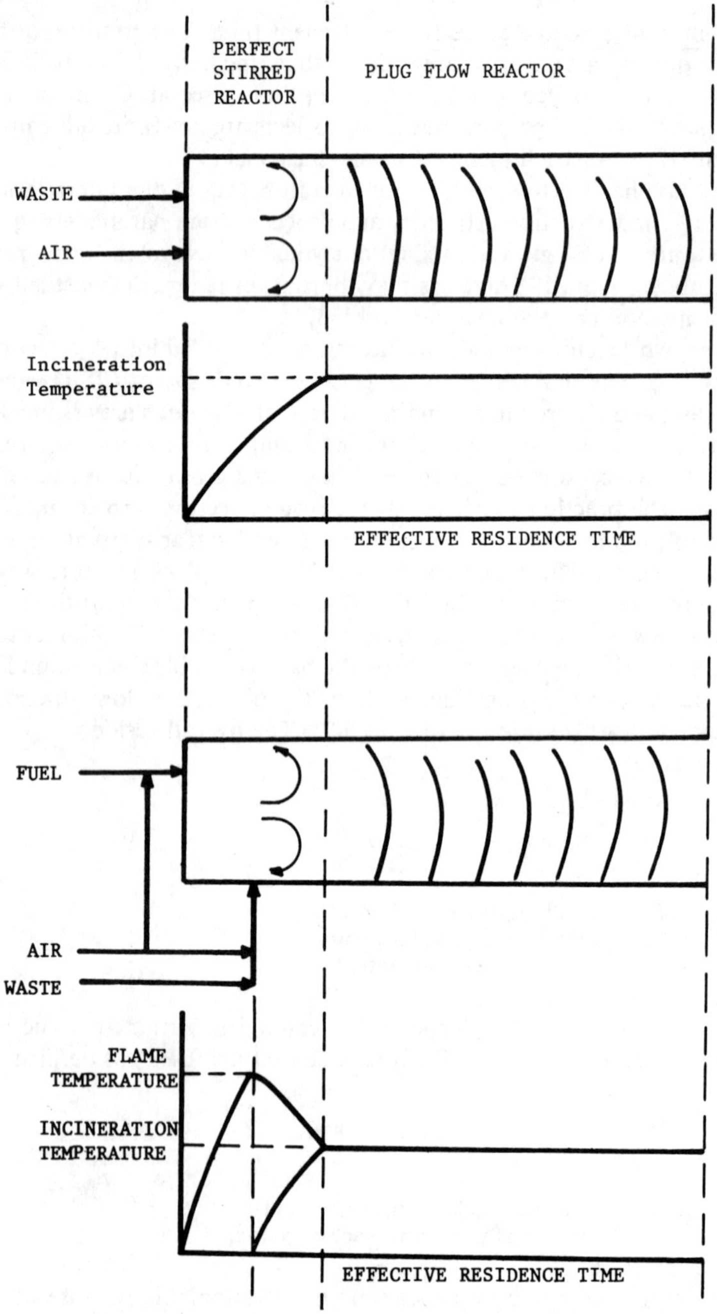

Figure 5-7. Two reactor model of liquid injection incinerators.

The zone method provides a more detailed model of an incinerator. However, the initial point is again an assumed knowledge of the fluid flow patterns, the chemical reactions and the radiation characteristics of the gases and solid particles (if any).

The model is established as follows: the incinerator volume and its walls are divided into a number of gas and surface zones. In each zone, the temperature and properties are assumed to be uniform and the gas flows in and out of each zone. A schematic of the model is shown in Figure 5-8. Material and energy balances are then developed for each zone, taking into account all forms of energy transport, heat of reaction and reaction kinetics. The solution of the many simultaneous equations yields the temperature and composition distribution in the incinerator. Since the flow patterns, including perfect mixing inside each zone, were assumed to be known a priori, all four process design parameters are now known, hence the destruction efficiency can be derived. The difficulties stem from the underlying assumptions more than from computational difficulties encountered in solving the large number of strongly nonlinear simultaneous equations. The initial assumption that recirculation patterns in the incinerator are known is weak, and so is the knowledge of the radiative properties of gases during combustion. Therefore, the development of a good, predictive zone model for any incinerator depends to a large extent on the amount of data available from similar devices and on the skill of the analyst in using that data to fine tune the model.

Mixing Aspects

Since the two-reactor model is simple and straightforward, it is used in this section for discussion. The temperature profile of an ideal liquid injection incinerator along the combustion gas travel direction is illustrated in Figure 5-7, for both a single- and two-stage unit. At the same overall residence time, the smaller the mixing zone, the longer the effective residence time.

One approach to reducing the mixing zone is to reduce the flame length in the burner. This phenomenon is illustrated in Figure 5-9. Assuming identical incinerator volume, short flame burner application has higher turbulence and heat transfer.

Illustrated in Figure 5-10 is the effective residence time comparison for liquid injection incinerators with either short- or long-flame burner applications, assuming identical size of incinerators, same excess air and identical flame temperature. Since the flame length is short, the short-

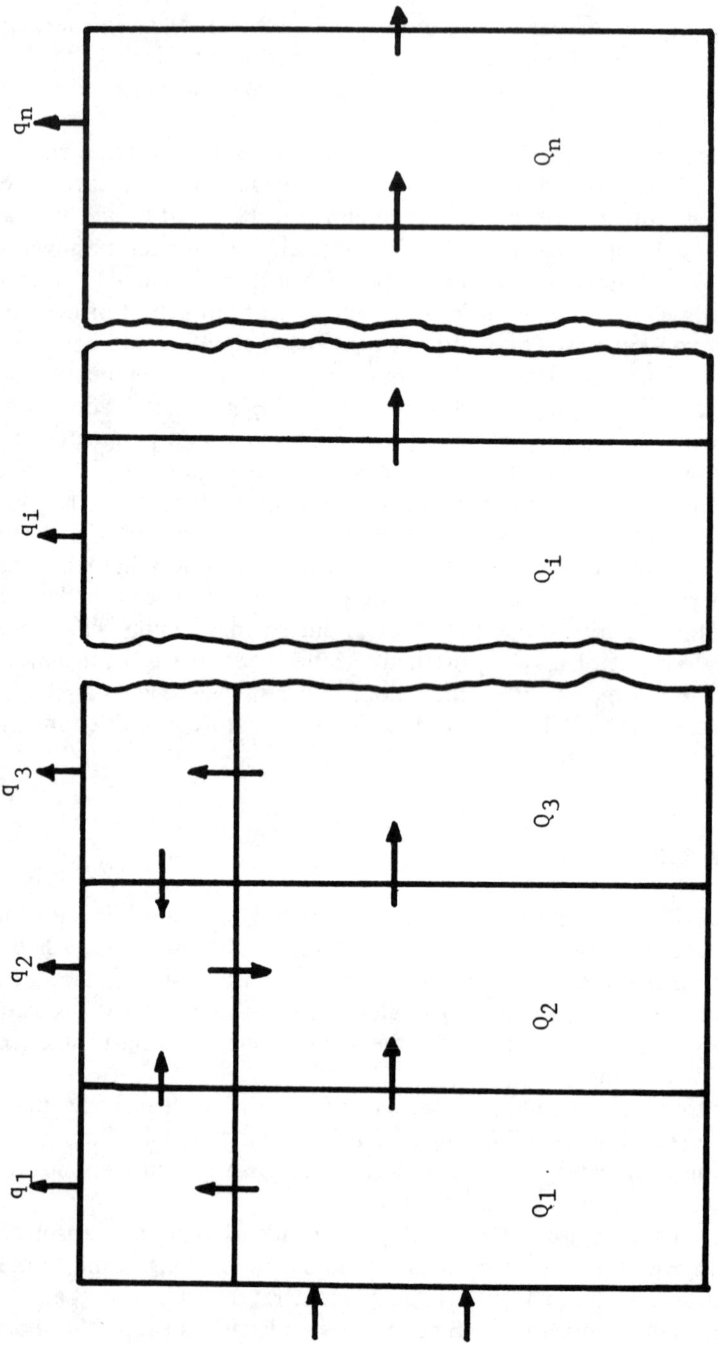

Figure 5-8. Zone model of liquid injection incinerators [18].

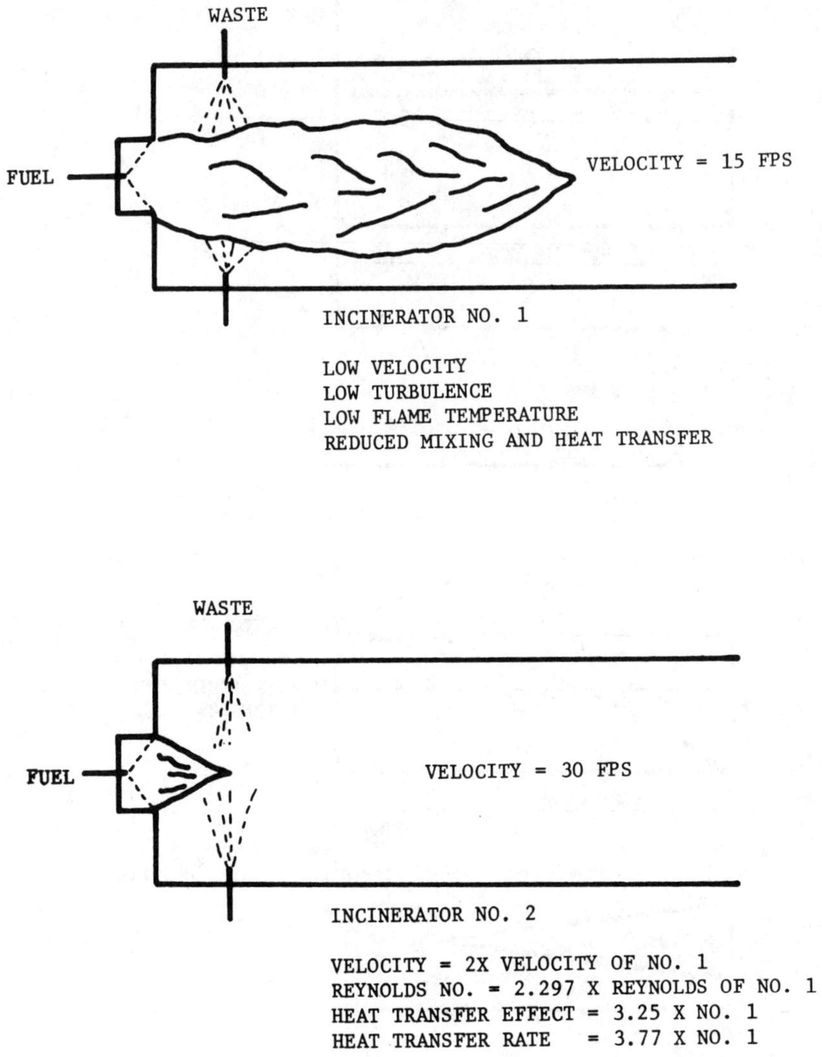

Figure 5-9. Flame length and incineration characteristics.

flame burner reaches flame temperature faster and thus the average incineration temperature is higher. Usually, the incinerator chamber size or overall residence time of short-flame burner application can be designed smaller than that of a long-flame burner.

For two-stage incinerators, assuming identical injection points and

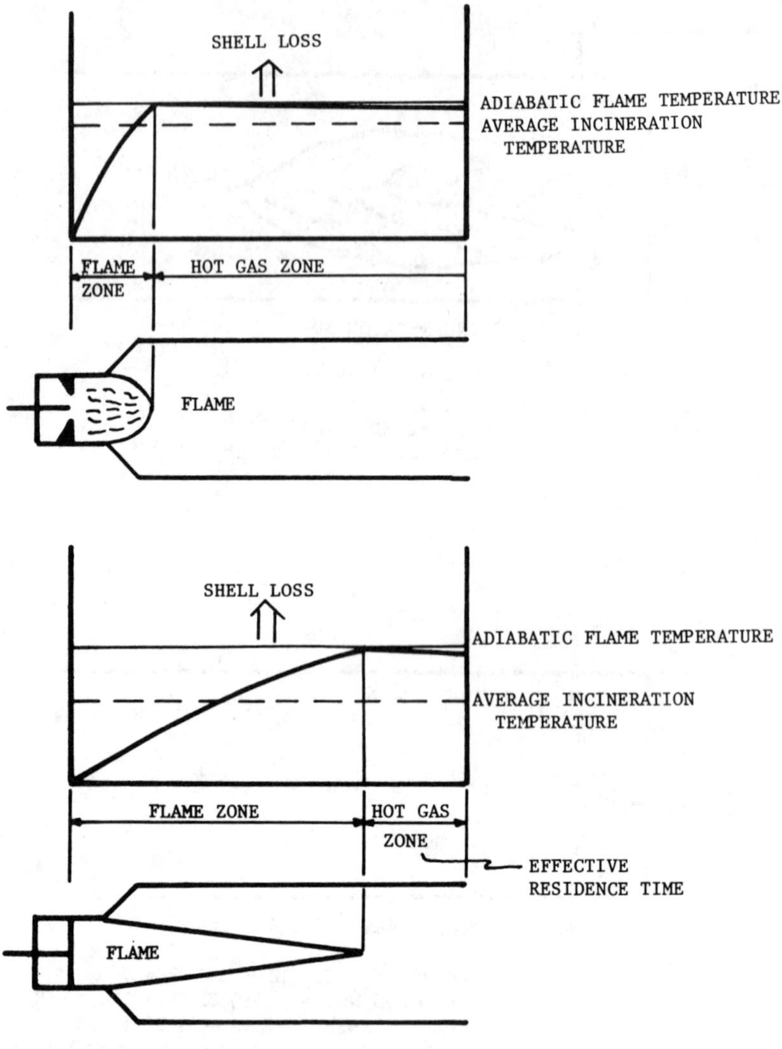

Figure 5-10. Flame length and effective residence time—single-stage incinerator.

mixing time in the secondary chamber, the comparison of the effective residence time for incinerators using short- and long-flame burners is illustrated in Figure 5-11. Note that for the long-flame burner the introduction of secondary wastes into the flame zone may result in incomplete combustion. Thus, when using a long-flame burner as the primary chamber, the injection point of the secondary wastes should be further down-

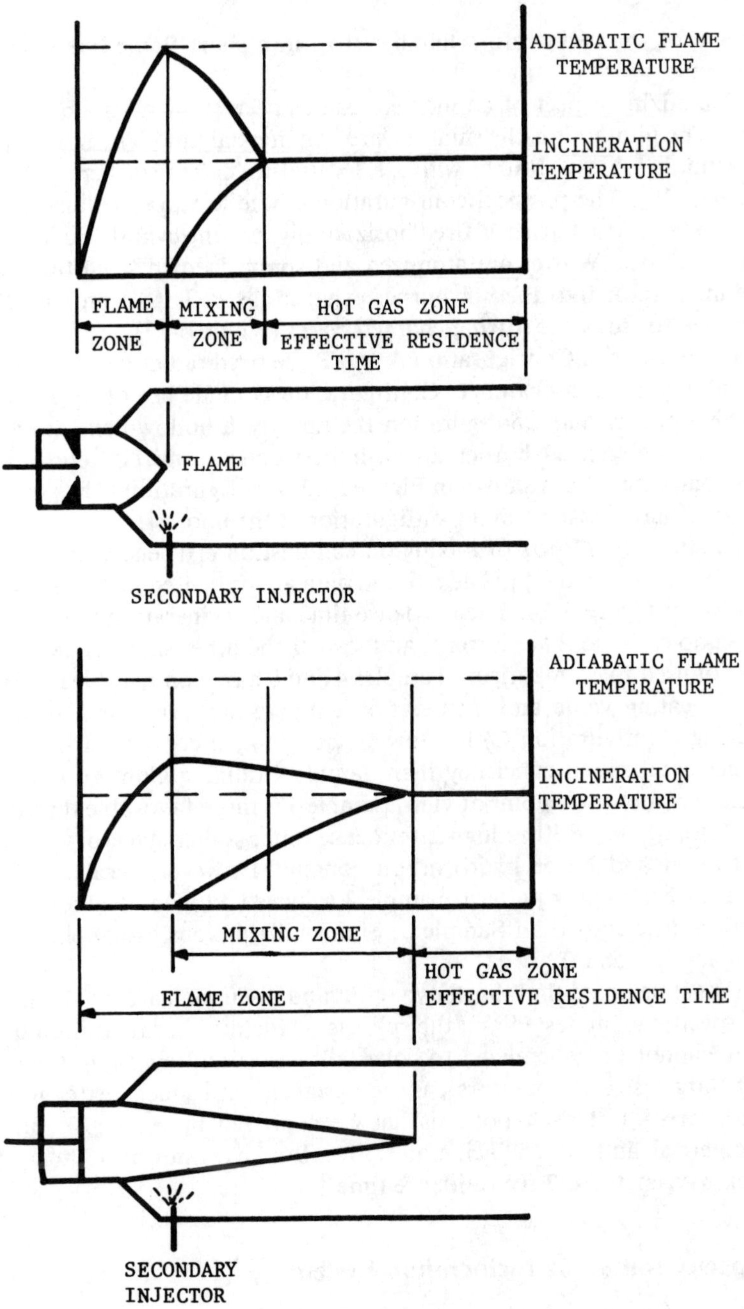

Figure 5-11. Flame length and effective residence time—two-stage incinerator.

stream of the incinerator chamber than in a short-flame burner application.

The mixing aspect of an incinerator has been studied on a pilot plant [19]. The pilot unit is the smallest size commercial unit. The heat duty of this unit is 1.3×10^6 Btu/hr with a 1.3×10^6 Btu/hr Trane Thermal Vortex Burner [10]. The physical configuration of the test unit is illustrated in Figure 5-12. The burner is fired horizontally into the cylindrical incineration chamber. Wastes are atomized and sprayed down from the top of the incinerator into the hot burner exhaust gases. Three configurations are used to study the mixing characteristics (Figure 5-13).

The burners in Configuration A and B are fired radially into the cylindrical incineration chamber. Configuration A made use of a solid-cone waste atomizer and Configuration B employed a hollow-cone atomizer. A tangentially fired burner and a hollow-cone atomizer were used in Configuration C. As shown in Figure 5-13, Configuration C has the best mixing characteristics, and Configuration B the poorest.

To study the effects of mixing on combustion efficiency, the original data were averaged [19]. The reduced data are presented in Table 5-4 and plotted in Figure 5-14. The residence time and incineration temperature of Samples 1 and 2 are lower than those of the other samples and, thus, are not used for comparison. Samples 4 and 8 have comparable residence time, heating value and incineration temperature. Although Sample 8 (mixing Configuration C) has lower stack oxygen content, it has much higher combustion efficiency than Sample 4 (mixing Configuration B). From a combustion point of view, Sample 3 is more favorable than Sample 7, i.e., Sample 3 has higher residence time, higher stack oxygen concentration and lower hydrocarbon content. However, because of the difference in mixing pattern, Sample 7 achieved a higher degree of combustion efficiency than Sample 3. Similar discussions are applicable to Samples 5, 8 and 9.

It must be noted that the above result and discussion are valid only for the specific waste tested and the specific incinerator configuration used. They cannot be generalized to cover all wastes and configurations. In fact, larger size incinerators can be designed with much better mixing characteristics. This hypothesis has been proved in a 30×10^6 Btu/hr commercial unit which incinerates 1340 Btu/lb wastes at 1800°F, 4% stack oxygen and 0.7 sec residence time.

Capacity Rating of Incineration System

During the design phase of an incineration system, composition and flow rate of waste materials must be fixed for design purposes. However,

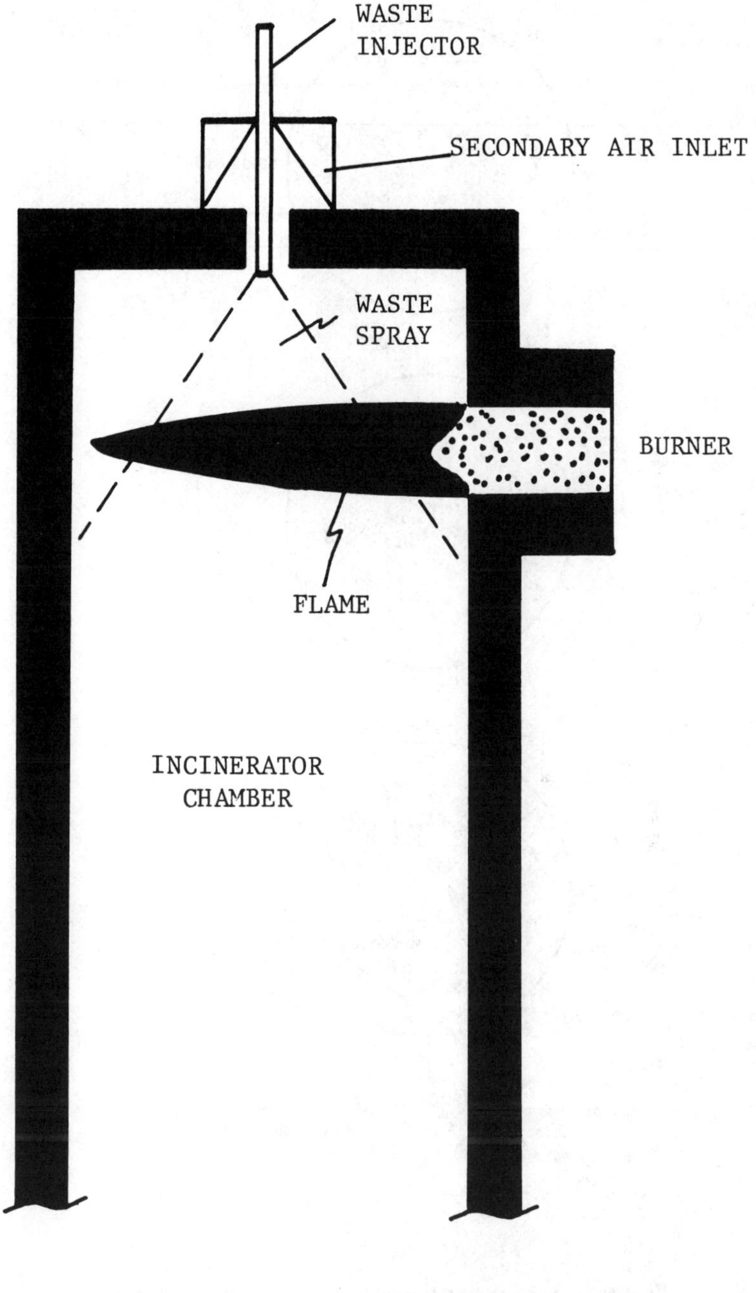

Figure 5-12. Test incinerator hardware [19].

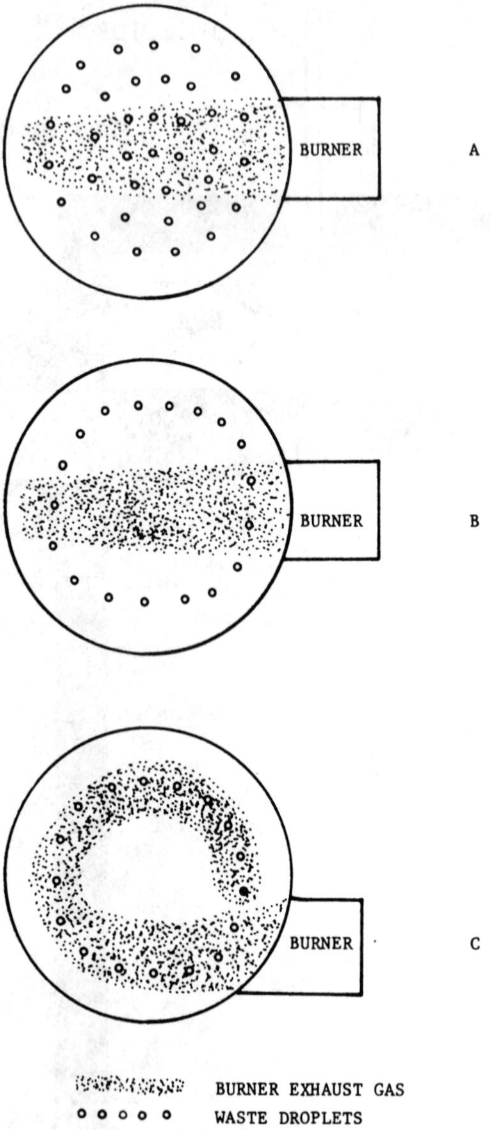

Figure 5-13. Test incinerator mixing configuration [19].

Table 5-4. Reduced Pilot Plant Test Data [19]

Sample Number	Waste High Heating Value (Btu/lb)	Residence Time (sec)	0_2 (%)	Incineration Temperature (°F)	Combustion Efficiency (%)
1	1350	0.64	5.83	1685	94.49
2	1350	1.15	5.83	1685	94.62
3	300	1.38	5.3	1800	99.53
4	3200	1.38	5.2	1754	96.46
5	1000	1.52	5.37	1800	99.61
6	590	1.44	0.8	1800	99.82
7	590	1.32	4.6	1800	99.96
8	3000	1.39	4.0	1800	99.96
9	3000	1.47	4.96	1790	99.91

in the real world, it is impossible to maintain a consistent composition. Thus, it is necessary in the design phase to define not only the design flow rates, but also the capacity rating of the system.

Capacity rating analysis is a very complex procedure; there are so many interrelated parameters to be maintained; for example, maximum and minimum rating of the burner used; minimal excess air rate and residence time; air leakage into the system; constant incineration temperature; line sizes which restricted the flow rates of waste, fuel and air; and blower sizing. Sometimes, additional parameters are necessary for specific applications. All these constraints must be taken into account. The following systematic analysis procedure can be used for rating analysis.

1. Define the design parameters and system sizing.
2. Determine the constraints of the system. The constraints should include both hardware and process requirement.
3. Perform material and energy balance to determine the rating parameters.
4. Plot all the rating parameters and enter into operating manual. The assumptions made for calculations have to be stated also.

To illustrate the procedure, a liquid injection aqueous waste incineration system is used:

1. The design conditions of the system are:
   28 gpm aqueous waste with 5% organics,
   30% design excess air rate and minimal excess rate of 25%,
   incineration temperature fixed at 1800°F and
   minimal residence time is 1 sec.

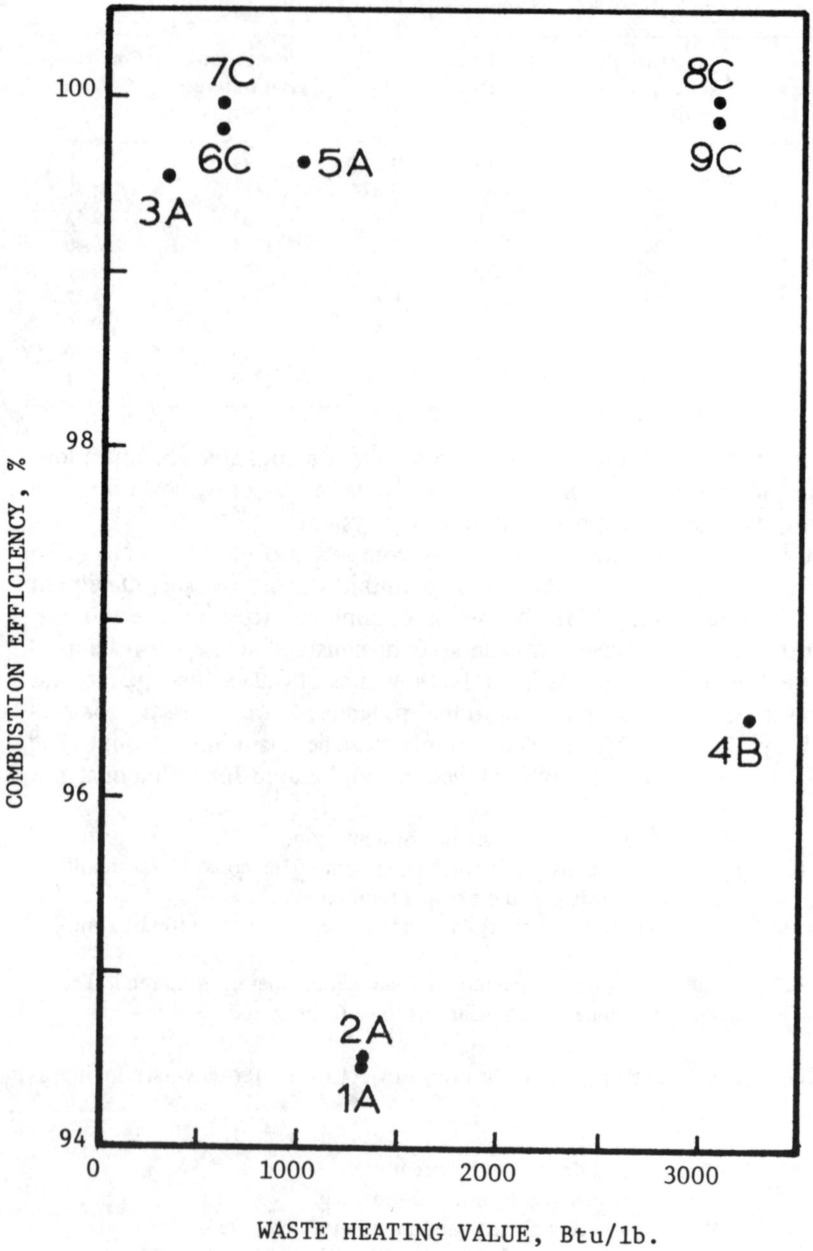

Figure 5-14. Combustion efficiency vs waste heating value [19].

The system sizes are:
burner: 50×10^6 Btu/hr maximum and
total combustion air—11,000 scfm.

2. The constraints of the system are:
maximal burner input is 50×10^6 Btu/hr (burner constraint),
minimal burner input is 16×10^6 Btu/hr,
maximal aqueous waste flow rate is 30 gpm (line size constraint),
minimal secondary air rate is 1000 scfm (waste injector design),
maximal total air rate is 11,000 scfm (blower sizing),
minimal residence time is 1 sec (design requirement),
incineration temperature is 1800°F (design requirement) and
minimal excess air rate is 25% (design requirement).
3. Material and energy balances are then performed, using the concentration of the aqueous waste as variable.
4. The capacity rating curve for this system is illustrated in Figure 5-15. The assumption for developing these curves is that the heating value (or composition) of the organics is a constant.

THERMAL CHEMICAL PRINCIPLES

The incineration process is a high-temperature oxidation reaction. The basic principles governing the oxidation reactions are the chemical reaction equilibrium and kinetics. In order to better understand the design and operation of a thermal incinerator, knowledge of these fundamental thermal chemical principles is required.

Chemical Reaction Equilibrium

The fundamental chemical reaction principle states that there is no complete reaction; that is, some unreacted materials always remain. Furthermore, all other possible chemical reactions involving the primary reactants, the primary products and all the intermediates will take place. Many of the possible reactions are neglected, because either the reaction rate is too slow to produce significant amounts of products, or the quantities of species involved are so small as to be insignificant. The fundamental chemical principles used to study the final composition of a reaction are the chemical reaction equilibrium principles.

The basic reaction equilibrium parameters is the equilibrium constant, at constant pressure, Kp, which is a function of temperature and is defined as

$$Kp = \frac{\pi\, p_{P_i}^{\beta_i}}{\pi\, p_{R_i}^{\alpha_i}}$$

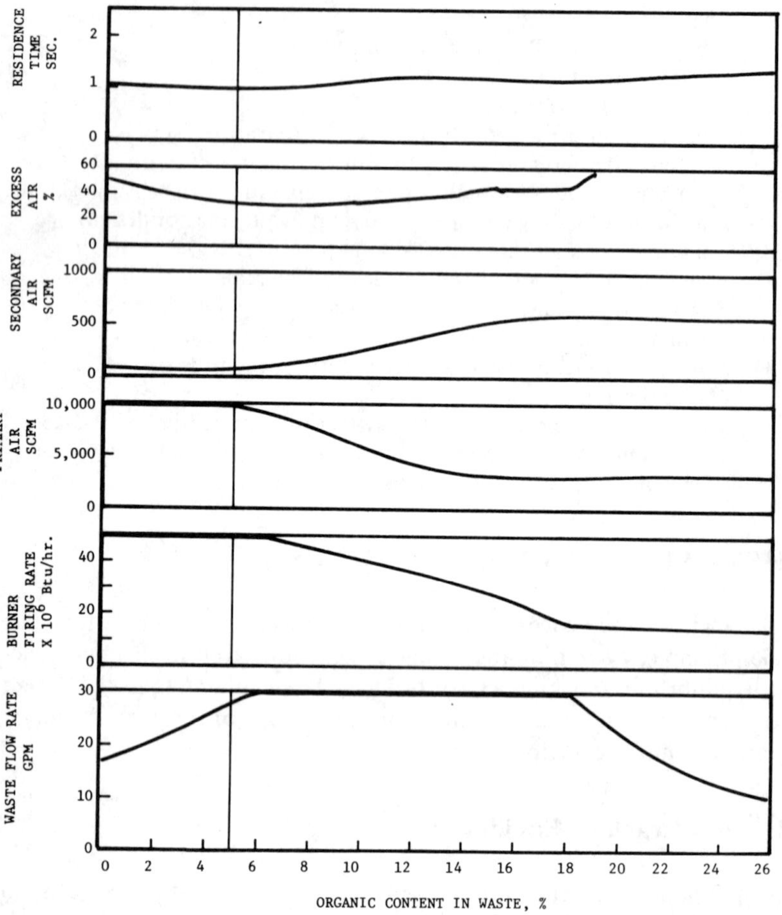

Figure 5-15. Example of incineration system capacity rating curve.

for the reaction

$$\alpha_1 R_1 + \alpha_2 R_2 + \cdots + \alpha_m R_m \rightleftharpoons \beta_1 P_1 + \beta_2 P_2 + \cdots + \beta_n P_n$$

where p is the partial pressure.

The equilibrium constants can be determined from free energy data.

$$K_p = e^{-\Delta E/RT}$$

where $\Delta E = \Sigma^{\beta_i E_i}(\text{products}) - \Sigma^{\alpha_i E_i}(\text{reactants})$ = change in free energy due to reaction

E_i = free energy of component i.

The equilibrium constants can be generated for most any desired reaction by using the thermochemical data contained in the JANAF Tables [20]. The equilibrium constants for reactions common in incineration systems, Table 5-5, are presented in Figure 5-16.

Equilibrium analysis is usually performed to provide information on the formation of trace organic compounds. There are computer programs available to perform equilibrium analysis [22,23]; however, in order to make use of these programs, the basic chemistry of the reactants has to be understood. The computer programs are used to calculate equilibrium compositions for large numbers of components by minimizing total free energy for the system.

Table 5-5. Reaction Equilibria Shown in Figure 5-16

A. Carbon Reactions	
1. $\frac{1}{2}C_2(g) \rightarrow C(s)$	8. $CO + \frac{1}{2}O_2 \rightarrow CO_2$
2. $C(g) \rightarrow C(s)$	9. $CO + H_2O \rightarrow CO_2 + H_2$
3. $C + \frac{1}{2}O_2 \rightarrow CO$	10. $CH_4 \rightarrow C + 2H_2$
4. $C + \frac{1}{2}N_2 \rightarrow \frac{1}{2}C_2N_2$	11. $\frac{1}{2}C_2H_4 \rightarrow C + H_2$
5. $C + 2H_2O \rightarrow CO_2 + 2H_2$	12. $HCHO \rightarrow CO + H_2$
6. $C + H_2O \rightarrow CO + H_2$	13. $\frac{1}{2}C_2H_2 \rightarrow C + \frac{1}{2}H_2$
7. $C + CO_2 \rightarrow 2CO$	14. $\frac{1}{3}C_3O_2 + \frac{1}{3}H_2O \rightarrow CO + \frac{1}{3}H_2$
B. Nitrogen and Oxygen Reactions	
15. $O_3 \rightarrow \frac{3}{2}O_2$	18. $NO + \frac{1}{2}N_2 \rightarrow N_2O$
16. $\frac{1}{2}N_2 + \frac{1}{2}O_2 \rightarrow NO$	19. $H_2 + \frac{1}{2}O_2 \rightarrow H_2O$
17. $NO + \frac{1}{2}O_2 \rightarrow NO_2$	20. $\frac{1}{2}N_2 + \frac{3}{2}H_2 \rightarrow NH_3$
C. Sulfur Reactions	
21. $\frac{1}{2}S_2(g) \rightarrow S(\ell)$	24. $\frac{1}{3}SO_2 + \frac{2}{3}H_2S \rightarrow \frac{1}{2}S_2(g) + \frac{2}{3}H_2O$
22. $SO_2 \rightarrow SO + \frac{1}{2}O_2$	25. $H_2S \rightarrow HS + \frac{1}{2}H_2$
23. $SO_2 + 3H_2 \rightarrow H_2S + 2H_2O$	26. $CO + H_2S \rightarrow COS + H_2$
D. Radical Reactions	
27. $C + \frac{1}{2}N_2 \rightarrow CN$	31. $2O \rightarrow O_2$
28. $CH_4 \rightarrow CH_3 + \frac{1}{2}H_2$	32. $2H \rightarrow H_2$
29. $2N \rightarrow N_2$	33. $\frac{1}{2}H_2 + O_2 \rightarrow HO_2$
30. $N + O \rightarrow NO$	34. $OH + O \rightarrow HO_2$
	35. $OH + \frac{1}{2}H_2 \rightarrow H_2O$

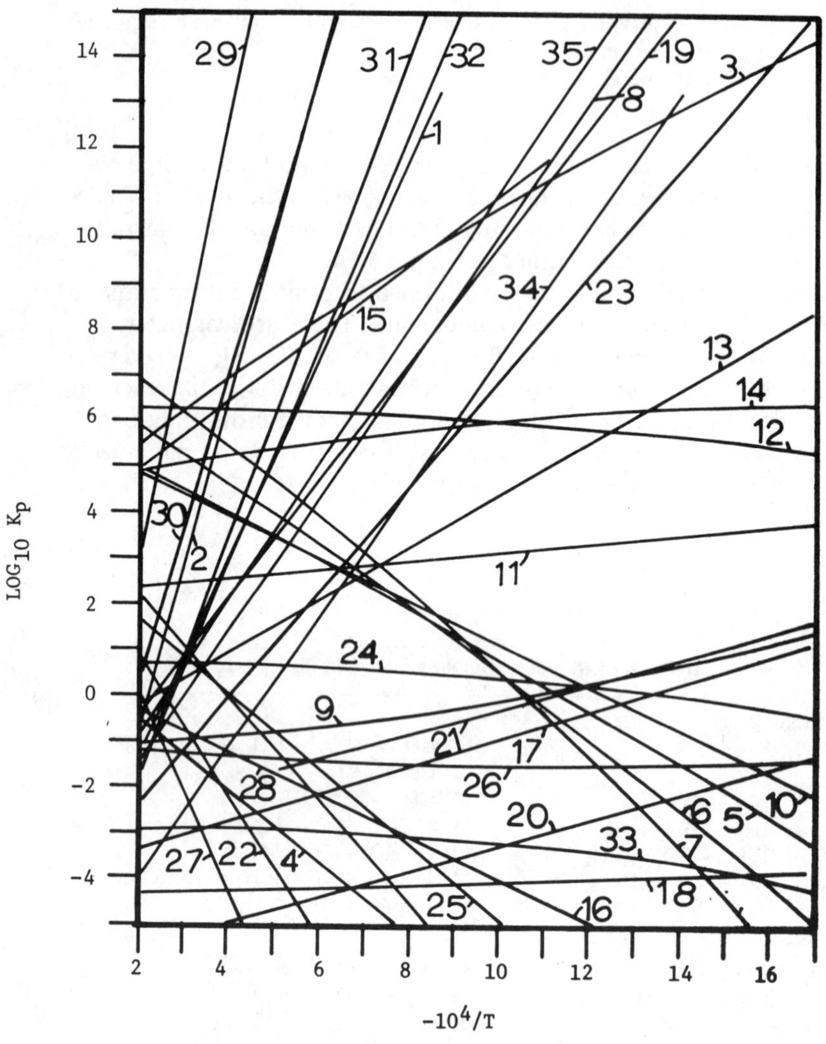

Figure 5-16. Equilibrium constants for reactions common in combustion systems (reproduced from Reference 21, courtesy of Marcel Dekker, New York).

Chemical Reaction Kinetics

The chemical reaction sequence which takes place in the destruction of organics by thermal incineration is a complicated process. It involves a series of decomposition, polymerization and free radical reactions. Intermediate products will appear before reaching final chemical reaction equilibrium. Hence, a time kinetic model should include many kinetic constants to take all of these reactions into consideration.

However, most of the intermediate products exist for only a short time, and for engineering purposes the overall reaction rate can be satisfactorily described by the following analysis.

The gas incineration reaction can be simplified as

$$W + O_2 \xrightarrow{k} \text{products}$$

the rate equation can be described as

$$\frac{dC_w}{dt} = -kC_wC_x$$

where C_w = the concentration of the organic compounds,
C_x = the concentration of the oxygen,
t = time and
k = the kinetic rate constant defined by the Arrhenius equation.

$$k = Ae^{-E/RT}$$

where E = the activation energy,
R = the universal gas constant and
T = the temperature.

This is the simplified kinetics model. The actual combustion reaction is a very complex process and is different for each waste compound studied.

The model described above is an empirical model which requires laboratory determination of all the kinetic constants. A laboratory apparatus has been developed for this purpose [24–26]. A schematic of the apparatus is illustrated in Figure 5-17. There are several types of designs of this unit. The apparatus illustrated in Figure 5-17 describes the basic requirement for kinetic study. The heart of this device is the quartz tube reactor. The quartz tube is twice folded and located within the central portion of a three-zone tube furnace. The three-zone tube furnace is required to ensure a uniform temperature profile [25]. The oxidants, oxygen mixed with inert gases, passed through the sample vaporizer for liquid and solids or mixed directly with gas as samples are introduced into the quartz tube reactor. Samples are taken before and after the reactor and reaction kinetic constants can then be determined. Researchers at the University of Dayton Research Institute [24,26] used this system to study the

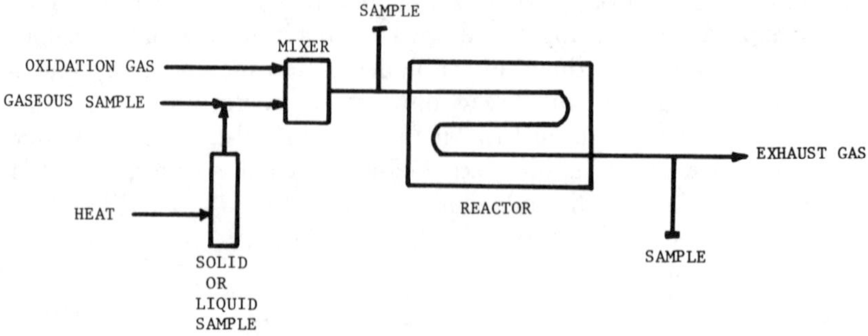

Figure 5-17. Laboratory apparatus for high-temperature organic compound oxidation kinetic studies.

thermal degradation and oxidation of Kepone® and polychlorinated biphenyl. So far, the only kinetics data available are for dilute fume oxidation [25,27], that is, a small quantity of organic vapors in a large quantity of air. In this case, the oxygen concentration can be assumed to be constant.

It must be noted that the empirical kinetic equation model assumes that the reactants are completely mixed. In most cases, the reaction rate does not control the rate of incineration. Typically, temperature, residence time and excess air maintained high enough that reactions proceed rapidly and other factors, such as the mixing characteristics, become rate limiting.

Theoretical Kinetic Models

The reaction kinetic models described in previous section is an empirical model, requiring experiment kinetic data. In this section, actual mechanisms involved in oxidation process are discussed.

1. *Free Radical Flame Reactions* [6]. Within flames, oxidation does not take place by reaction of molecular oxygen with fuel, but rather through free radical mechanisms [6]. This reflects the near-zero activation energy of free radical oxidation reactions. For instance, the activation energy for the oxidation of carbon monoxide by OH radicals

$$CO + OH \rightarrow CO_2 + H$$

is only 1800 Btu/mole, whereas that for the direct oxidation by molecular oxygen

$$CO + O_2 \rightarrow CO_2 + O$$

is 86,400 Btu/mole. In addition, in flames, the OH, O, and H radical concentrations are orders of magnitude higher than would be predicted by the dissociation equilibrium for H_2O, O_2 and H_2. This can be explained by the high rates for the chain branching reactions (two radicals produced for every one involved).

$$H + O_2 \rightarrow OH + O$$

$$O + H_2O \rightarrow OH + OH$$

$$O + H_2 \rightarrow OH + H$$

$$H + H_2O \rightarrow H_2 + OH$$

A partial equilibrium is quickly established between radicals via these reactions and their reverse. However, the much slower three-body recombination reactions,

$$OH + O + M \rightarrow H_2O + M$$

$$H + H + M \rightarrow H_2 + M$$

$$O + O + M \rightarrow O_2 + M$$

where M represents the third (energy absorbing) body, do not return the system to complete equilibrium with molecular species until sometime after all wastes have been consumed. Typically, peak OH concentration in flames (3000°F) are in the range of 1 to 5 mol %. The corresponding equilibrium mole percentages are one or two orders of magnitude lower, 0.1–0.2. At lower temperatures, the equilibrium values are even lower, e.g., 10^{-5} mol % of OH at 1400°F. Combustion reaction can be quenched by a drop in temperature which drastically reduces rates or by the presence of a high concentration of third bodies, e.g., high surface area of inert molecules.

Radicals can be generated by slow initiation reactions between fume and fuel. However, in continuous flow incinerators, these initiation steps are not very important since radicals are carried from burning regions to unburned regions by mixing and diffusion.

Initial attack of the vaporized fuel molecule in an oxidizing flame is probably by an OH radical. For methane, this is

$$CH_4 + OH \rightarrow H_20 + CH_3$$

Then the chain continues

$$CH_3 + O_2 \rightarrow CH_2O + OH$$

or

$$O + CH_3 \rightarrow CH_2O + H$$

forming formaldehyde. This reacts further to give CO by the reactions

$$CH_2O + OH \rightarrow H_2O + CHO$$

and

$$CHO + OH \rightarrow H_2O + CO$$

CO is then oxidized to CO_2 via the following reaction

$$CO + OH \rightarrow CO_2 + H$$

All evidence points to CO oxidation as the slowest step in oxidation of hydrocarbons.

Hydrocarbons composed of more than one carbon will undergo a similar sequence, with organic acids and aldehydes appearing as intermediates. With hydrocarbons of more than 3 or 4 carbons, the radical formed in the equivalent of reaction

$$CH_4 + OH \rightarrow H_2O + CH_3$$

is unstable and is likely to undergo pyrolytic decomposition (endothermic) and/or dehydrogeneration.

$$RCH_2CH_2 \rightarrow R'CH = CH_2 + R''$$

$$RCH_2CH_2 \rightarrow RCH = CH_2 + H$$

As a result, aldehydes containing more than two carbon atoms are not likely to be found in flames. Aldehyde concentration in flames is generally very low since all steps except the oxidation of CO to CO_2 are very fast at flame temperatures. If concentrations of O and OH are low (poor mixing or fuel rich flames), dehydrogenation may be accompanied by polymerization to yield material of a high C/H ratio—smoke and soot. Steam is often injected to reduce soot formation. This helps to increase OH concentration via reactions

$$O + H_2O \rightarrow OH + OH$$

and

$$H + H_2O \rightarrow H_2 + OH.$$

2. *Low Temperature Oxidation* [6]. At very low temperatures, oxidation rates can be taken as zero. However, for temperatures between 500°F and the ignition temperature, relatively slow chain reactions occur which yield "cool flames" for combustible mixtures. As in high-temperature flames, OH radicals are a major oxidizing species, but in this case their concentration is much lower, and peroxide radicals (HO_2) play a major role.

Methane is used as an example to illustrate cool flame mechanisms. Initiation occurs by

$$CH_4 + O_2 \rightarrow CH_3 + HO_2$$

which is very slow. A chain reaction is set up with initial attack on CH_4 via

$$CH_4 + OH \rightarrow H_2O + CH_3$$

and

$$CH_4 + HO_2 \rightarrow H_2O_2 + CH_3$$

then methyl radicals react with oxygen to give formaldehyde.

$$CH_3 + O_2 \rightarrow CH_2O + OH$$

which leads to branching by

$$CH_2O + O_2 \rightarrow CHO + HO_2$$

Formaldehyde can also react with OH and HO_2 radicals

$$CH_2O + OH \rightarrow H_2O + CHO$$

$$CH_2O + HO_2 \rightarrow H_2O + CHO$$

The oxidation continues to CO via

$$CHO + O_2 \rightarrow CO + HO_2$$

CO oxidation is very slow at low temperatures but probably occurs via an ozone intermediate or other excited species.

$$CO + O + M \rightarrow CO_2 + M$$

As can be seen, some of the reaction steps are the same as low and high temperatures. However, the rates are much slower, and concentrations of OH and O are much lower. As a result, the less active peroxide radicals play an important role. Also, aldehydes are much more prevalent and provide for chain brancing through the reaction.

$$CH_2O + O_2 \rightarrow CHO + HO_2.$$

Higher hydrocarbons follow a similar sequence with corresponding aldehydes, acids, alcohols, and peroxides formed as intermediates. As with higher temperature processes, large hydrocarbon molecules tend to decompose following the initial hydrogen abstraction step.

3. *Thermal Oxidation in the Absence of Flame* [6]. The above discussion shows the important role free radicals play in the oxidation of hydrocarbons to CO_2 and H_2O. It has also been pointed out that radical concentrations in flames are one or two orders of magnitude above equilibrium values with correspondingly high reaction rates.

For thermal oxidation in the absence of flame, radical concentrations are expected to be much closer to equilibrium values once excess levels from the supplemental fuel burner have decayed. Chain branching reactions dominate only while fuel is being consumed. Within the combustion chamber, combustible concentration in the fume will determine the amount by which radical concentrations can exceed the overall equilibrium values set by the temperature and concentrations of water and oxygen. Radicals generated by reactions such as

$$CO + OH \rightarrow CO_2 + H$$

or remaining from the fuel burner will tend to recombine by the following reactions

$$OH + O + M \rightarrow H_2O + M$$

$$H + H + M \rightarrow H_2 + M$$

$$O + O + M \rightarrow O_2 + M$$

rather than branching. The lower the concentration of combustibles, the nearer the radical concentrations will be to overall equilibrium values since chain terminating collisions of radicals with third bodies are more likely than reacting collisions with hydrocarbon molecules.

4. *Elementary Reactions—Kinetic Models.* Prediction and extrapolation can also be done by using a model based on the actual mechanisms involved in the combustion. This involves using the elementary reaction steps (free radical reactions) discussed before. Computer programs for integrating large systems of nonlinear differential equations can be adapted to handle reaction rate expressions. Heat generation and simple mixing processes can be accommodated. This type of model cannot be used for a prior prediction of reaction rates but it holds much promise as a semiempirical tool. Difficulties involved with a completely theoretical approach lie mainly in determining the reaction mechanism (to decide which elementary reactions should be included in the model), and in determining the reaction rate constants. Methods are available for estimating these rate constants for simple reactions (e.g., hydrogen abstraction) and many rates have been determined through mass spectrometer studies of flames or in non-flame experiments. Some data are given in References 28 and 29. It is most likely, however, that this type of model will be utilized for interpreting experimental results and making them useful in design. In this way, a minimum amount of experimentation will be required and interpolation and extrapolation can be done with confidence.

Incinerability of Hydrocarbons

During the incineration feasibility study phase, the incinerability of organic hazardous constituents is an important factor for the preliminary selection of incinerator type, residence time, incineration temperature and excess air requirement. To determine the incinerability of organic compounds, the high temperature chemical reaction kinetics of that specific compound have to be known. At the present time, only limited kinetic data are available. Thus, it is necessary to correlate the limited data with known combustion parameters, such as heat of formation, heat of combustion and autoignition temperature. Then, the correlation will give an indication of the incinerability of specific organic compounds.

The kinetic data for fifteen compounds obtained by Lee et al. [27] were used. The incinerability indicators used were the temperature required to achieve 99.99% destruction efficiency at 1 and 2 sec residence time. Attempts were made to correlate the basic combustion parameters with the incinerability indicators. Of the parameters tested, only autoignition temperature offers a reasonable correlation (Figure 5-18). Thus, it appears that autoignition temperature can be used to rank incinerability. However, this ranking of incinerability is an approximation and not a definitive method. The experimental data used are for cases where organic vapors were carried by an abundance of oxygen. More test work is required to determine the effect of oxygen content in ranking by autoignition temperature. Furthermore, the characteristics of liquid and solid wastes also play a very important role in incinerability. Volatile organics are usually easier to incinerate than nonvolatile organics, where solid or liquid droplet combustion mechanism controls.

MATHEMATICAL MODELING

The four basic process design parameters of a hazardous waste incinerator are residence time, incineration temperature, excess air and mixing. Three of these four parameters—time, temperature and excess air—can be readily established through measurements and calculations; however, the evaluation and control of mixing are more difficult to attain. At the present time, mixing design is highly dependent on past experience and overdesign. Two approaches can be used to develop more knowledge of mixing: mathematical modeling of heat and mass transfer mechanisms, and chemical reaction kinetics within the incinerator; and collection of voluminous data and application of regression analysis and other statistical methods. The chance of success with either of the aforementioned is very small. The most promising approach is to apply a mixture of mathematical models and experimental data to fine tune these models. Using this approach, the mixing aspect of waste incineration can be gradually developed. In the following discussion, the present state of knowledge of modeling and scale-up is summarized.

Swirl and Craya-Curtet Numbers

Incineration is a combustion process which involves flame and the heat transfer between the flame and the secondary injected wastes. In the

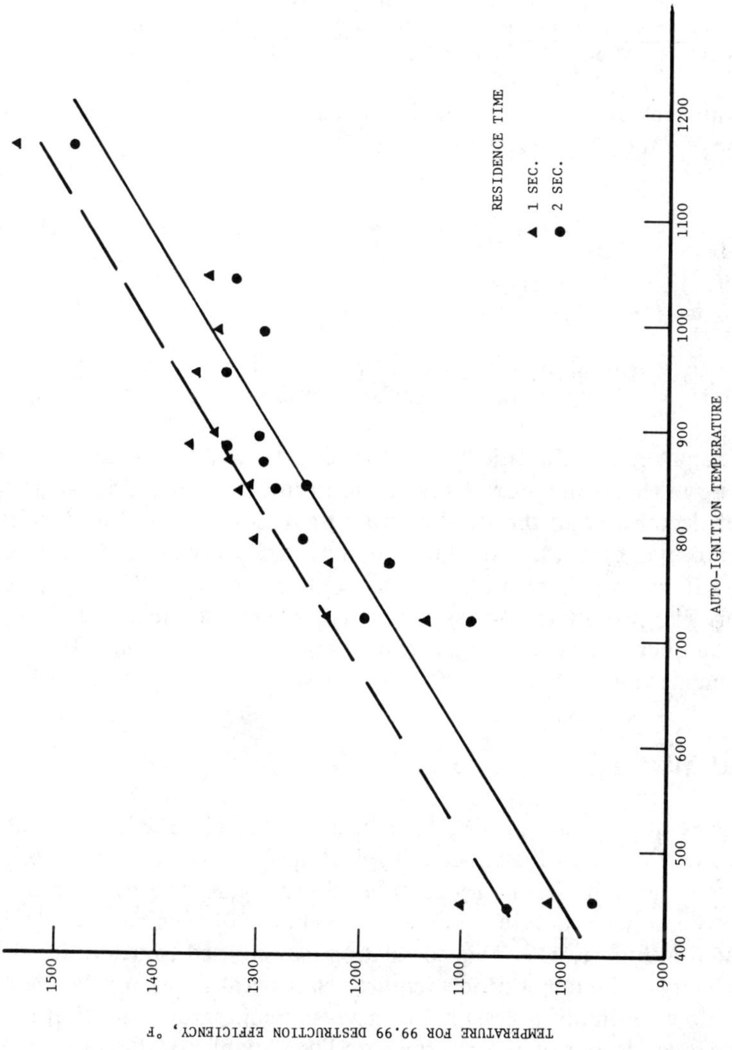

Figure 5-18. Incinerability correlation for selected compounds.

combustion field, the swirl number has been used as the indicator for turbulence mixing. The swirl number is defined as

$$S = \frac{2\,G_{\phi}}{G_x D_e}$$

where G_{ϕ} = axial flux of angular momentum through the opening
G_x = axial flux of linear momentum through the opening
D_e = diameter of the opening.

The interrelationship between the flame and the incinerator can be described by the Craya-Curtet number (C_t):

$$C_t = \frac{1}{\sqrt{m}} \tag{5-31}$$

where $m = \dfrac{U_d^2 - 1/2\,U_k^2}{U_k^2}$
U_d = dynamic mean entry velocity
U_k = velocity of total flow uniformly distributed.

The parameter, m, is a ratio that describes how well the flame will stir things up in the incinerator. As the ratio m increases, the Craya-Curtet number decreases and the swirl number increases. A long flame in an incinerator will have a low swirl number and high Craya-Curtet number. A short flame will have a high swirl number and a low Craya-Curtet number. The two dimensionless constants, the swirl number and Craya-Curtet number, can be used together to characterize the mixing efficiency of an incinerator.

Gas Jet Mixing

In incinerator design, gas jets have been used to mix the hot combustion gas and cold gas introduced. Typical applications are dilute fume incineration and the secondary chamber downstream of a rotary kiln.

A correlation was developed by Carlson et al. [30]. The basic model is illustrated in Figure 5-19. This correlation can be used to determine the size, velocity and number of jets required to penetrate and mix the mainstream flow to obtain a designed transverse temperature variation at a given distance downstream from the jets. The variables of the correlation are presented in Figure 5-20 and Table 5-6. The basic correlations are jet centerline penetration (Figure 5-21), centerline mixing ratio (Figure 5-22) and jet spreading (Figure 5-23).

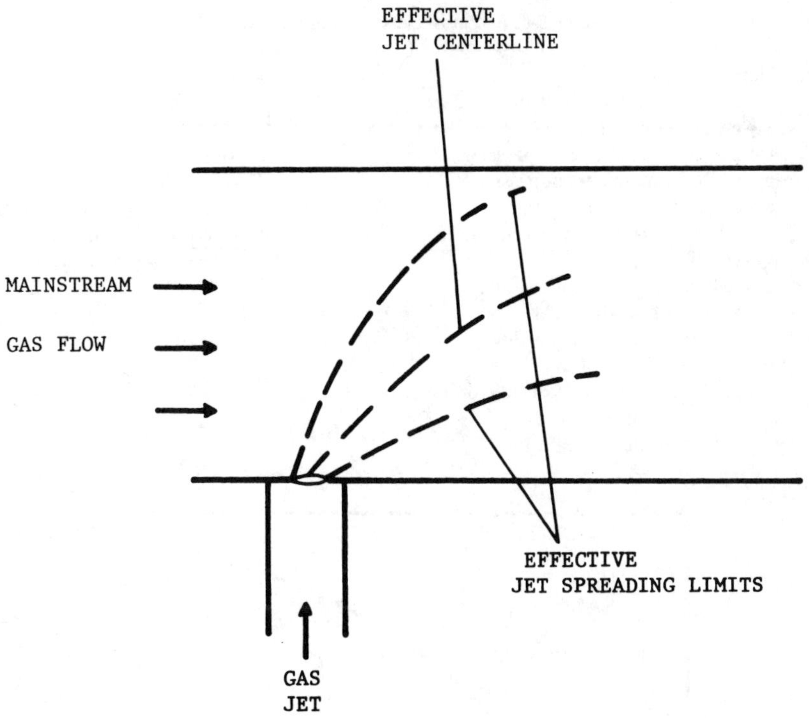

Figure 5-19. Schematics of gas jet mixing system [30].

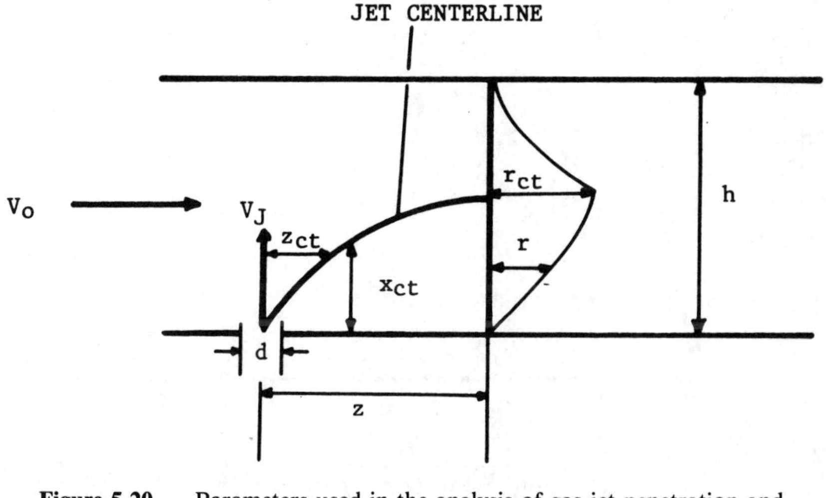

Figure 5-20. Parameters used in the analysis of gas jet penetration and mixing [30].

Table 5-6. Parameters for Figure 5-20

Variables	Dimensionless Variables
z—distance downstream from jet hole	$Z = z/\sqrt{cd}$
x—penetration distance	$X = x/\sqrt{cd}$
h—height of main stream passage	$H = h/\sqrt{cd}$
b—width of main stream passage	$B = b/\sqrt{cd}$
d—diameter of holes	$G = \varrho_j V_j / P_o V_o$ = mass velocity ra
$\sqrt{cd}$—effective diameter of jet holes	$R = W_j/W_o$ = mixture ratio
V_j—velocity of jet	$W_T = \pi G/4BH$ = total flow ratio
V_o—velocity of main stream fluid	$K = 1.54\ W_T = 12.1\ G/BH$
ϱ_j—density of jet fluid	subscript
ϱ_o—density of main stream fluid	ct = centerline
n—number of jet holes	
c—discharge coefficient of hole on tube	
W_j—weight of jet fluid	
W_o—weight of main stream fluid	

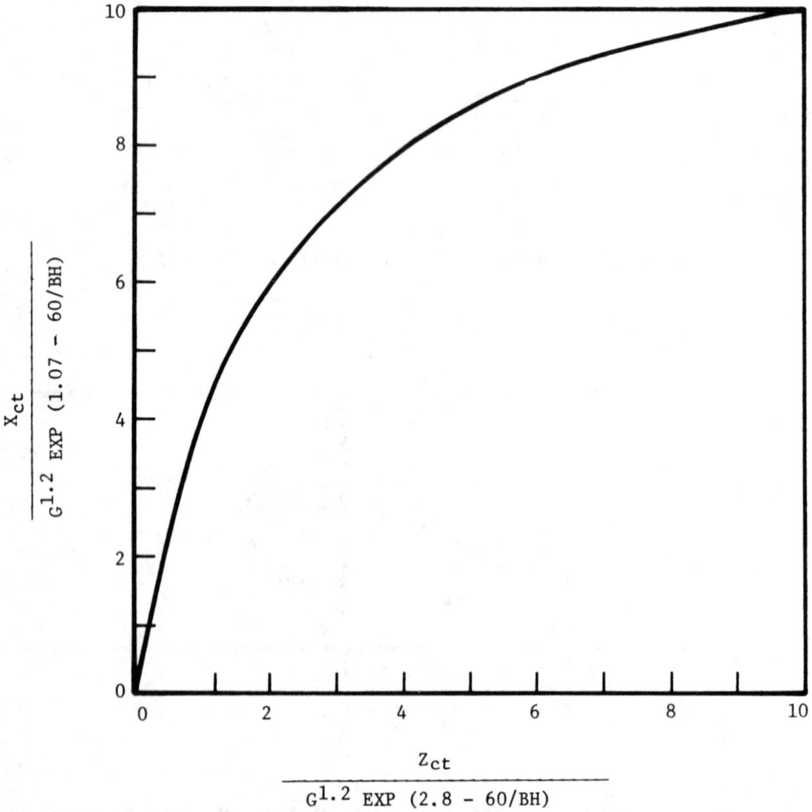

Figure 5-21. Correlation for jet centerline penetration [30].

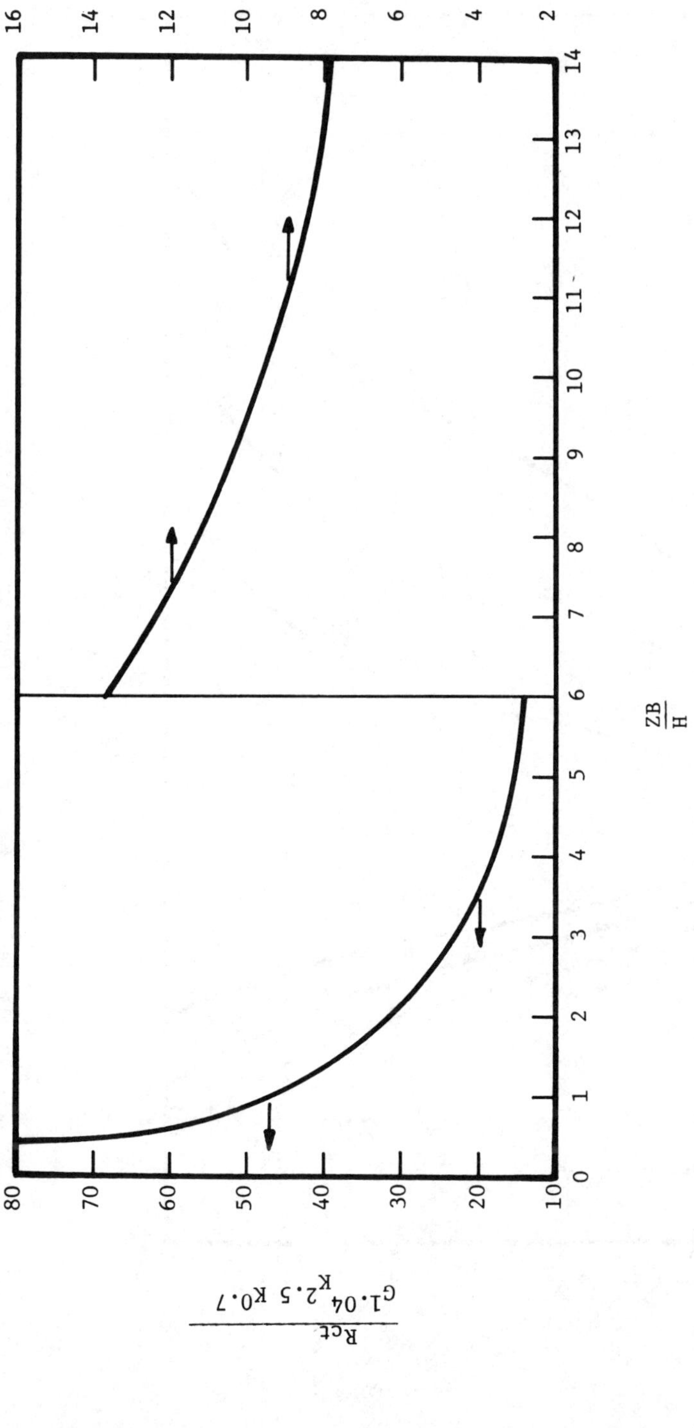

Figure 5-22. Correlation for centerline mixing ratio [30].

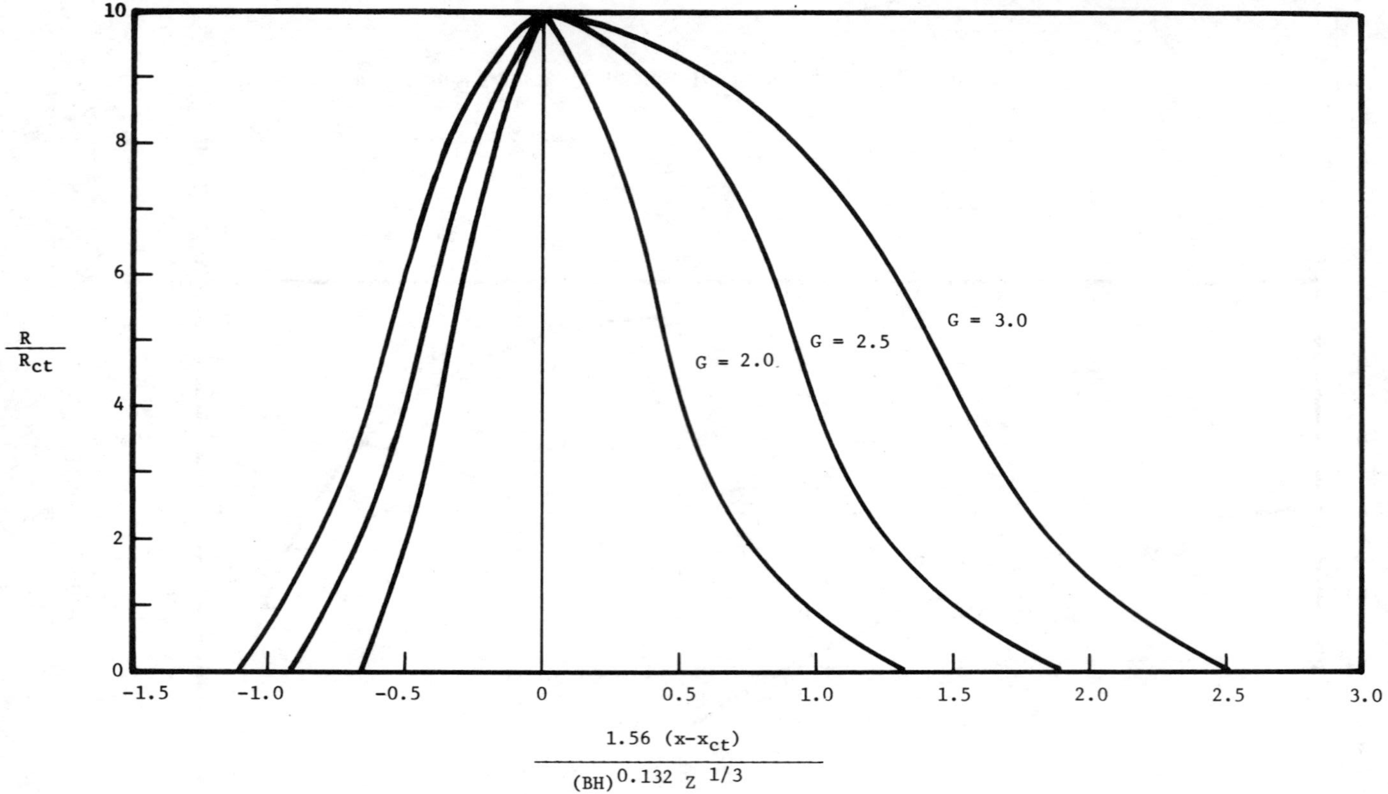

Figure 5-23. Correlation for jet spreading from centerline [30].

Using the three basic correlations (Figures 5-21 to 5-23), given any jet diameter, velocity and density, and any mainstream velocity and density together with the main passage width and height, the variation of mixing ratio and temperature across any given downstream cross section can be calculated.

Liquid Waste Incineration

Liquid waste incineration requires two additional steps, atomization and vaporization, when comparing to gaseous waste incineration. The related topics on liquid waste incineration are atomization, jet penetration and vaporization, and liquid droplet combustion.

1. *Atomization—Liquid Droplet Size.* The mechanism of droplet formation by pneumatic atomization can be considered to be a balance between the forces that resist droplet formation (e.g., surface tension, expansion force, drag force and force due to tensile viscosity) and those which cause drop formation (e.g., forces due to gravity and kinetic energies of liquid and gas). Thus it is seen that the average drop diameter produced by pneumatic atomization can be a complex function of several variables, e.g., densities, viscosities and flow rates of liquid and gas, surface tension, relative velocity, nozzle size and configuration, etc. The effects of these variables on the average droplet diameter as given by empirical studies agree only qualitatively. Nevertheless, it is now well established that the droplet diameter increases with decreasing relative velocity between the gas and the liquid jet and increasing ratio of liquid to gas flow rates. The increase in gas pressure or gas density seems to decrease the droplet diameter due to greater dynamic head causing the liquid break-up. An increase in droplet diameter can be achieved by decreasing liquid density, increasing liquid surface tension and increasing liquid visocity [31].

The simplest method of estimating the droplet size produced by pneumatic atomization is to use the well-known Weber number criterion which says that the droplet will shatter at a critical value of the Weber number (We = $\rho_g v_r^2 d/2\sigma$). Calvert suggested a critical value of Weber number to be about 12. Thus, a crude but simple approximation to the drop diameter is:

$$d = \frac{12\sigma}{\rho_g V_r^2}$$

where V_r = relative velocity,
σ = surface tension,
ρ_g = gas density and
d = droplet diameter.

An empirical correlation by Nukiyama and Tanasawa can be used to estimate the droplet size. This is given [31] by:

$$d = \frac{0.585}{Vr}\sqrt{\frac{G}{P_l}} + 5.32 \times 10^{-3}\left(\frac{\mu_l^2}{\sigma \rho_l}\right)^{0.225}\left(\frac{Q_l}{Q_g}\right)^{1.5}$$

where Vr = relative velocity
σ = surface tension
ρ_l = liquid density
μ_l = liquid velocity
Q_l = mass rate of liquid
Q_g = mass rate of gas.

A more comprehensive correlation was recently developed by Kim and Marshall which is given by[31]:

$$d = \frac{249\sigma^{0.41}\mu_l^{0.32}}{(\rho_g V_r^2)^{0.56} A_a^{0.36} \rho_l^{0.16}} + 1260\left(\frac{\mu_l^2}{\sigma \rho_l}\right)^{0.17}\frac{M^\eta}{V_r^{0.54}}$$

where $\eta = 1$ if $M < 3$
$\eta = 0.5$ if $M > 3$
A_a = cross-section area at the point of liquid injection.

The units to be used in the above equation are: for σ, dyne/cm; for μ_l, CP; for V_r, ft/sec; for ρ, g/cm^3; and for A_a, in^2.

The importance of the existence of the various correlations is that for any given injector, the operating conditions can be manipulated to obtain the same atomization characteristics with different wastes; for instance, by heating a viscous waste, altering the atomizing gas velocities or by using waste mixtures, so as to maintain invariant the Weber and Reynolds Numbers. Thus, invariant liquid spray characteristics can be ensured for wastes with different physical properties.

2. *Jet Penetration and Droplet Vaporization.* Jet penetration into an air stream was developed by Ingebo [32] to depend on the Weber and Reynolds Numbers and on the liquid-to-gas velocity ratio. The maximum penetration distance X_{max} is related to the maximum droplet diameter D_{max}

$$\frac{X_{max}}{D_{max}} = 0.08\,\mathrm{ReWe}^{-0.41}\left(\frac{V_g}{V_l}\right)^{0.29}$$

Another comprehensive model was developed by Rahman [33]. The analytical formulation is described here. When liquid drops are introduced into a duct by an injection in the form of a jet, a jet strength is defined as

$$\lambda = \frac{V_{jo}}{U}$$

where V_{jo} = the velocity of the jet at the inlet port
U = the main gas stream velocity.

The physical configuration and the parameters are illustrated in Figure 5-24. The velocity of the jet will decrease gradually from V_{jo} to a value at which the horizontal component $V_j \cos\beta$ is nearly equal to the main stream velocity U at that location, then the jet will cease to exist.

The ratio of the centerline velocity of any location (V_j) to the injected mean velocity at the inlet port is given by [34]

$$\frac{V_j}{V_{jo}} = \frac{\sin\phi}{\cos(\beta - \phi)}$$

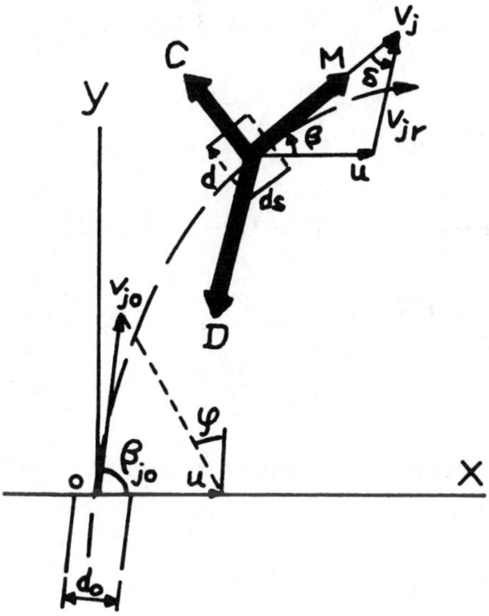

Figure 5-24. Parameters used in the analysis of liquid jet penetration [33].

where ϕ can be determined by the following correlation

$$\phi = \tan^{-1}\frac{[1 - \lambda \cos(\beta_{jo})]}{\cos(\beta_{jo})}$$

For the case of a jet injected at 90° to the main stream, $\beta_{jo} = 90°$, the value of β varies according to [35]

$$\beta = \tan^{-1}\left[0.327\lambda^{0.9113}\left(\frac{x}{d_o}\right)^{-0.6654}\right]$$

And the locus of the jet centerline is given by the relation

$$\frac{y_i}{d_o} = 0.9772\lambda^{0.9113}\left(\frac{x}{d_o}\right)^{0.3346}$$

The above equations are only applicable to those cases where the incinerator diameter is considerably longer than the nozzle diameter.

The rate of mass entrainment due to turbulence, U_f, can be obtained from

$$(1 + U_f)^{1/2} - 1 = \frac{-\cos\phi}{8}\int_{\beta_{jo}}^{\beta_j}\frac{\tan(\beta_j - \phi)}{\sin\beta_j\cos(\beta_j - \phi)}E^* d\beta_j$$

where

$$E^* = 0.2\lambda^{-0.6}\left(\frac{S}{d_o}\right)^{1.37} \quad \text{for} \quad \beta_{jo} = 90°$$

The mass entrained by the vortices U_v is expressed by

$$U_v = -\ln\left[\frac{\tan\left(\beta - \frac{\phi}{2} + \tan\frac{\phi}{2}\right)}{\tan\left(\beta - \frac{\phi}{2} + \cot\frac{\phi}{2}\right)}\right]\left[\frac{\tan\left(90 - \frac{\phi}{2} + \cot\frac{\phi}{2}\right)}{\tan\left(90 - \frac{\phi}{2} + \tan\frac{\phi}{2}\right)}\right]$$

The time rate of change of the droplet radius, r, is [36]:

$$\frac{dr}{dt} = \frac{Sh\,D}{zr_l\beta_l}\,\frac{P_s}{R_f T_s}$$

where D = mass diffusion coefficient
r_l = droplet radius
ρ_l = liquid density

P_s = saturation pressure
R_f = gas constant of the vapor
T_s = saturation temperature
Sh = Sherwood number.

The Sherwood number is composed of two parts [37]: the conduction and the convection numbers. The conduction number is 2 for spherical drops. For droplets with significant internal circulation, the convective Sherwood number is defined as

$$\mathrm{Sh} = 0.895\left(\frac{U_o}{U_s}\right)^{1/2}\mathrm{Pe}$$

$$= 0.895\left(\beta_1\frac{1-\phi^{5/3}}{\nu}\right)^{1/2}\mathrm{Pe}^{1/2}$$

where U_o = velocity of the drop equation
U_s = ensemble velocity (average velocity of the cluster of droplets relative to the main stream velocity)
Pe = Peclet number.

and β_1 is defined as

$$\beta_1 = \frac{\mu_g}{\mu_1 + \nu}$$

where μ_g = coefficient of viscosity outside the droplet
μ_1 = coefficient of viscosity inside the droplets.

The parameter ν is the interfacial viscosity and is due to impurities such as dust particles. If no impurities are presented, $\nu = 0$.

The factor ϕ is the volume fraction occupied by the droplets and Y is defined as

$$Y = 2 + 2\beta_1 + \phi^{5/3}(3 - 2\beta_1)$$

For droplets with negligible internal circulations, the convective Sherwood number is [38]

$$\mathrm{Sh} = 1.037\left(\frac{1-\phi^{5/3}}{1+3/2\,\phi^{5/3}}\right)\mathrm{Pe}^{1/3}$$

To calculate the Peclet number, Pe, the ensemble velocity has to be evaluated at any location. This can be obtained by the vectorial subtraction of $(V_j - U)$.

The convective Sherwood Number also can be determined as [39]

$$Sh = 0.6(Sc)^{1/3}(Re)^{1/2}$$

where Sc = Schmidt Number.

The spray penetration into the incineration chamber also can be calculated [40] by drag coefficients of evaporating droplets, C_D:

$$C_D = 27\ Re^{-0.84} \qquad 0 \le Re \le 80$$

$$C_D = 0.271\ Re^{0.271} \qquad 80 < Re \le 10^4$$

$$C_D = 2.0 \qquad R > 10^4$$

3. *Droplet Combustion.* The combustion of a spray of liquid fuel involves the combustion of fuel vapors and of the discrete droplets that make up the spray.

Liquid fuel combustion involves sequential vaporization and burning in the gas phase so the problem has been extensively studied [41]. The rate at which liquid droplets vaporize and burn is dependent on droplet size and the rate at which heat can be transferred to the surface. Rapid mixing and radiation of heat from the combustion chamber walls or flame give a high rate of heat transfer. The simplest model of droplet combustion is the diffusion-controlled model of an isolated spherical droplet, when gas velocities are relatively low. This model is applicable to dilute sprays only. In dense sprays, complete evaporation of the droplets may precede burning, which then is controlled by the diffusion of the vapor into the air or by gas-gas mixing.

For dilute sprays, i.e., isolated droplets in quiescent air, a droplet evaporates and the fuel vapor and the air burn in a diffusion flame which surrounds the droplet. The mass burn rate M_L is related to the decrease in droplet diameter D such that [41]

$$M_L = \frac{d}{dt}\left(\pi \frac{D^3}{6} \rho_L\right)$$

which can be rewritten as

$$\frac{d}{dt}(D^2) = \frac{4M_L}{\pi \rho_L D}$$

It has been shown experimentally that M_L is proportional to D, so that the above equation can be integrated to yield

$$D^2 = D_o^2 - Kt$$

In the above equation, the constant K must be obtained from experiment or by solving conservation equations for global mass, species mass, energy and momentum.

Solution of the conservation equations is possible provided some major assumptions are made. These assumptions include: infinitely rapid chemical reaction rate and simplified chemical reactions, such as, Fuel + O_2 → products, or Fuel + Oxygen → CO followed by CO + Oxygen → CO_2.

The solutions depend on whether fixed or variable transport properties are used. A widely used model, assuming fixed properties and a Lewis number of one, results in a burning rate coefficient K

$$K = \frac{8k}{C_p \rho_L} \ln(1 + B)$$

where the transfer number B is

$$B = \frac{1}{L} [C_p (T_\infty - T) + Q\phi]$$

and

k = thermal conductivity of the gases
Q = fuel heating value
L = latent heat of evaporation
C_p = specific heat of gases
ϕ = equivalence ratio (air/fuel)/(air/fuel) stoichiometric.

The results markedly depend on the values assigned to the thermal conductivity k and the specific heat C_p of the gases; these depend on gas temperature and composition, neither of which is known a priori. Usually k and C_p are computed on the basis of air or nitrogen properties at the log mean temperature between the liquid and the flame temperature, though somewhat more sophisticated approaches have been proposed.

Incinerator fuels are mostly mixtures of hydrocarbons and other more or less volatile compounds, rather than a single component liquid. An expression for the burning rate coefficient of binary mixtures was derived by Wood et al. [42] and numerical calculations have been carried out for multicomponent heavy fuel oils [43]. The method proposed in the latter work could be used to compute the evaporation and combustion of a given hazardous waste contained in a liquid fuel. The compound could be liquid or a suspended solid, or a solid formed by fuel cracking, such as occur in heavy fuel oils. However, the computation is cumbersome and a large computer is needed.

The droplet burning equation $D^2 = D_o^2 - Kt$ is valid for a droplet burning in quiescent air, whereas in most incinerators, air velocities must be high enough to promote mixing. A correction of the burning rate coefficient to take into account forced convection has been proposed [44].

$$K = K_o[1 + 0.278 Re_L^{1/2} Pr^{1/2} (1 + 1.237/Re_L Pr^{4/3})^{-1/2}]$$

This equation is possibly valid for $10 < Re_L < 800$ but has not been experimentally verified outside of the range $1.3 < Re_L < 2.2$.

A simplified correlation for vaporization and destruction of original hydrocarbon is [45]

$$t = \frac{29800\, Mwd_o^2}{P_{O2} T^{1.75}}$$

where P_{O2} = oxygen partial pressure, atm
d_o = original drop diameter, cm
T = °K
M_w = molecular weight.

None of the proposed predictive methods can take into account transient burning effects or change in combustion mode, such as the transition, above a critical gas velocity, from a diffusion flame all around the droplet to a wake flame (i.e., no burning on the droplet surface and combustion in the wake behind the droplet). Still more important is the fact that the single droplet combustion model does not really represent spray combustion.

4. *Spray Combustion.* It has been shown that droplets exist in a relatively small volume, close to the injector nozzle and that most droplets do not burn individually, but that the fuel vapor from the droplets burns in a jet, essentially as a gas diffusion flame. This was proven in experiments conducted with a light distillate oil [46] and with heavy fuel oil [47]. The "mixed is burned" principle applies well to a diffusion flame, i.e., the turbulent mixing of fuel vapor and air is the combustion rate controlling mechanism. Therefore, one would consider characterizing the droplet shrinking shown in the equation $D^2 = Do^2 - Kt$, by heating and evaporation only and omit the fuel heat release time term $Q \times \phi$ in the transfer number B; i.e.,

$$B = \frac{C_p}{L}(T_\infty - T)$$

when modeling the incineration mechanisms as a spray, i.e., a gas-diffusion flame [48].

Particle Combustion

The combustion of particles is a two-step process: heating/evaporation and combustion. In the heating/evaporation step, solid particles are heated, light hydrocarbons are vaporized. The heated particle is then oxidized in the presence of oxygen.

For small particles, the time required to heat particles to incineration temperature is small when compared to the actual particle burning time. This is shown in the Nusselt Number correlation when the particulate is moving at the same velocity as the gas:

$$h_c = \frac{2k}{d}$$

where h_c = heat transfer coefficient
k = gas thermal conductivity
d = particle diameter.

For spherical carbonaceous particles, the combustion rate is [21,49]

$$q = \frac{P_{O2}}{1/K_s + 1/K_d}$$

where q = the rate of carbonaceous particle reaction ($g/cm^2\ sec^{-1}$)
P_{O2} = the partial pressure of oxygen (atm)
K_s = the kinetic rate constant for the consumption reaction
K_d = the diffusional rate constant.

For small particles of diameter d (centimeters), the diffusional rate constant at temperature T (K) is approximately given by:

$$K_d = \frac{4.35 \times 10^{-6} T^{0.75}}{d}$$

The kinetic rate constant is given by:

$$K_s = 0.13 \exp\left\{-\frac{35{,}700}{R}\left(\frac{1}{T} - \frac{1}{1600}\right)\right\}$$

where R is the gas constant (1.986 cal/g mol K).

There are three kinetic models for solid particle combustion [18]:

1. The continuous reaction/constant size model is applicable to reactions in which a solid is consumed uniformly throughout the particle. The gas diffusion into the particle is much faster than the gas-solid reaction.
2. The unreacted core/constant size model (also known as the shell model) is applicable to cases where both or either the gas-solid reaction and the gas diffusion through the residual solid shell are controlling.
3. The shrinking particle model is applicable to the cases where oxidation leaves no solid residue, i.e., a case very similar to droplet combustion. Here either gas-through-gas diffusion or surface reaction can be controlling.

For the continuous reaction model, the progress of conversion of solid reactant B is independent of particle size as a first approximation (a uniform concentration of oxygen is implicit in the fast gas diffusion assumption). The rate of conversion of the solid reactant B is

$$\frac{dX_B}{dt} = K_v C_A (HX_B)$$

where X_B = fraction of B converted
C_A = concentration of oxygen (constant)
K_v = rate coefficient based on the volume of solid.

The continuous reaction model usually applies to very small particles. Note that the residence time required to completely oxidize the particle is independent of particle size.

The unreacted core/constant size model includes several mechanisms:

1. Oxygen diffuses through the boundary layer surrounding the particle to its surface.
2. Oxygen diffuses through the product layer to the reaction front.
3. Oxygen reacts with the solid in a narrow reaction zone.
4. Gaseous products diffuse to the main gas stream.

The chemical kinetics for heterogeneous oxidation of a spherical particle are represented as first order in oxidant [50]. The governing equation for the unreacted core/constant size model is

$$-\frac{dN_A}{dt} = 4\pi r_c^2 K (C_A)_S \left\{1 + \frac{r_c k}{d_e}\left(1 - \frac{r_c}{r_s}\right)\right\}^{-1}$$

where N_A = moles of oxygen
t = time
r_c = radius of particle at the reaction zone
K = kinetic rate constant (first-order irreversible reaction)
$(C_A)_S$ = concentration of oxygen at r_s
r_s = radius of spherical particle
D_e = effective diffusivity of oxygen through the solid product layer.

For the shrinking particle model, according to the spherical geometry of the particle, the governing equation is:

$$\frac{dr_c}{dt} = \frac{bM_BK(C_A)_S}{\rho_B}\left\{1 + \frac{r_sK}{D_e}\frac{r_c}{r_s}\left(1 - \frac{r_c}{r_s}\right)\right\}^{-1}$$

where r_c = particle radius
r_s = initial particle radius
ρ_B = density of B
M_B = molecular weight of B
b = stoichiometric constant.

The above can be integrated to yield the time necessary for a particle to completely disappear. For cases where both the reaction kinetics and diffusion through the product layer represent rate limiting steps, this equation must be solved using numerical methods. When either the chemical kinetics or diffusion controls the rate of reaction, an analytical solution is possible.

Kinetic controlled: $r_sk \ll D_e$

$$t = \frac{\rho_B r_c}{bM_BP_k(C_A)_s}$$

The time needed to consume a particle, i.e., the residence time needed to completely react a particle is proportional to the particle radius.

Diffusion controlled: $r_sk \gg D_e$

$$t = \frac{\rho_B r_c^2}{2bM_B(C_A)_sD_e}$$

In this case, the residence time for complete particle oxidation is proportional to the particle radius squared.

The shrinking particle model is very similar to the model for liquid fuel drop burning and differs from the unreacted core only in that the controlling diffusion rate is now that of the oxygen diffusing through a gas layer.

Heat Transfer Model of Rotary Kiln Incinerator [18]

The mathematical treatment of high temperature rotary kilns found in the literature is limited to specific applications, such as cement kilns or ore dryers and does not lend itself to generalization. Exceptions are a model presented by Sass [51] which includes a preheat section wherein the solids are heated to the boiling point of the liquid, and an isothermal section where the liquid is evaporated, followed by a final section where the solids are heated to a desired discharge temperature; and a very useful treatment by Imber and Paschkis [52] in which dimensionless parameters were used. A schematic diagram of the heat flow paths in a cross-section of a rotary kiln is shown in Figure 5-25 taken from the work of Imber and Paschkis. Sass includes some heat loss to the ambient air.

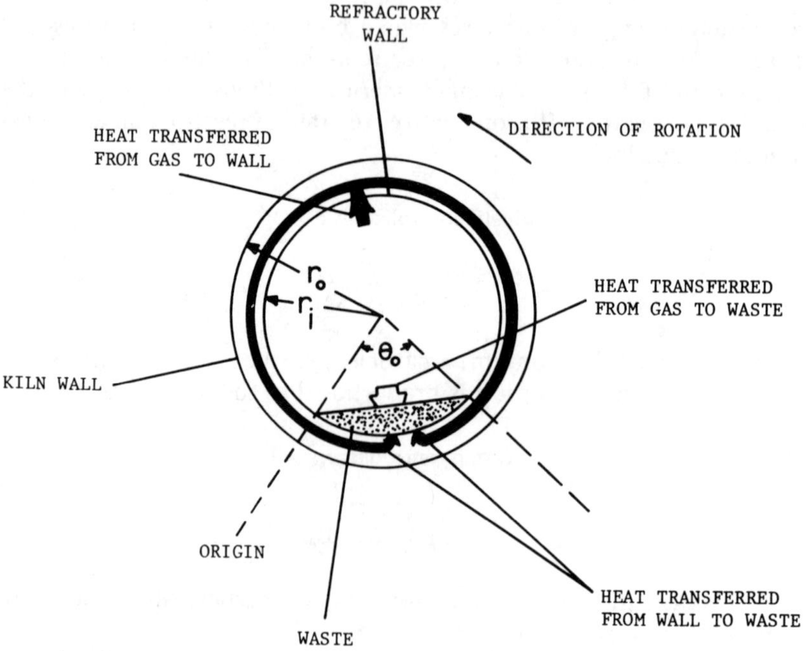

Figure 5-25. Parameters used in the analysis of rotary kiln incinerator [33].

The heat transfer equations from gas to kiln wall to the charge used by Sass are shown in Table 5-7.

The most salient feature of these equations is the use of the empirical correlation

$$h = 0.05\left(\frac{C_g}{S_x}\right)^{0.67} + 0.173E_g\left(\frac{T_g^4 - T_w^4}{T_g - T_w}\right)$$

for gas-to-wall heat transfer and

$$h = 0.25\left(\frac{C_g}{S_x}\right)^{0.67}$$

for the corresponding wall to waste heat transfer. These correlations are at best applicable as a rule of thumb, useful to calculate an approximate kiln length.

Solids and gas emissivity calculations also present some difficulties because of gas-borne particle radiation and uncertainties of the emissivities of solids in the charge. When better documented heat and mass transfer correlations are developed, an analytical treatment of the heat transfer in the rotary kiln incinerator will become possible because the problem then will be reduced to solving a periodic heat conduction problem which is defined by classical nondimensional parameters, a Fourier number and two Biot numbers, as discussed below.

Heat is received from the gases by the kiln wall, and transported to the waste mass. If a section $rd\theta$ of the kiln wall is followed from the position marked "origin" on Figure 5-25 as it emerges from contact with the waste mass and is rotated through the angle $(2\pi - \theta o)$, that wall element will be progressively heated by the combustion gases. Initially, the temperature distribution in that element was $T_o(r)$, after a rotation of $(2\pi - \theta o)$, i.e., after a time period of $2\pi N$ sec (N is the number of revolutions per second), the temperature distribution in the element is $T_1(r)$. Neglecting axial conduction, the equations describing the heat transfer are:

$$\frac{\partial T}{\partial t} = \alpha \nabla^2 T = \alpha\left(\frac{\partial^2 T}{\partial r^2} + \frac{1}{r}\frac{\partial T}{\partial r} + \frac{\partial^2 T}{\partial \theta^2}\right)$$

$$\frac{\partial T}{\partial r} = h_1(T_g - T) \quad , r = r_1$$

$$T = T_o(r,\theta) \quad , t = o$$

Table 5-7. Rotary Kiln Incinerator Heat Transfer Coefficient Correlations[a] [18,53]

Heat Transfer Path	h_i
Gas to inner kiln wall	$h_1 = 0.05\ (G_g/S_x)^{0.67} + 0.173 \times 10^{-8}\ E_g(T_g^4 - T_w^4)/(T_g - T_w)$
Gas to solid	$h_2 = 0.05\ (G_g/S_x)^{0.67} + 0.173 \times 10^{-8}\ E_g(T_g^4 - T_s^4)/(T_g - T_s)$
Inner kiln wall to solid	$h_3 = h_{3cc} + h_{3RAD}$ $h_{3cc} = 0.25\ (G_g/S_x)^{0.67}$ $h_{3RAD} = 0.173 \times 10^{-8}\ fE_s(T_w^4 - T_s^4)/(T_w - T_s)$
Inner kiln wall to outer kiln wall	$h_4 = r_o - r_i$
Outer kiln wall to ambient air	$h_5 \approx 2.5$[b]

[a]E_g + gas emissivity
E_s = solid emissivity
f = correction factor
k = thermal conductivity of insulating brick
S_x = cross-sectional area of kiln
Θ = fill angle as shown in Figure 5-25
T_s = solid temperature
T_g = gas temperature
G_g = mass flow rate of wet gas
G_s = mass flow rate of wet solid
T_w = wall temperature

[b]Approximate value used to obtain initial estimate of outer-wall temperature. With this estimate, a more accurate value of h_5 was computed.

where α is the thermal diffusivity of the brick. If $(\partial^2T/\partial\theta^2)$ is small compared to the radial derivatives, the solutions will be of the form

$$\frac{T - T_g}{T_o - T_g} = f(Fo, Bi)$$

where Fo = the Fourier number = $\alpha t/\bar{r}^2$
Bi = the Biot number = $h_1\bar{r}/k$

Close form solutions are cumbersome and require simplifying assumptions because radiation causes the heat transfer coefficient to depend on temperature.

Numerical solutions are quite readily accessible. At the end of the time period $(2\pi - \theta_o)/2\pi N$ the kiln wall element, $\bar{r}d\theta$, reaches the upper border of the wastes. The temperature distribution in the element is known, and heat is transferred from the element to the (cooler) wastes. The equations for the wall in contact with the waste is:

$$\frac{\partial T}{\partial t} = \alpha \nabla^2 T$$

$$\frac{\partial T}{\partial t} = h_s(T - T_s), \quad r - r_i$$

$$T = T(Fo_1, Bi_s), \quad t = \frac{1}{N}\,\frac{2\pi - \theta_o}{2\pi}$$

where $Fo_1 = (\alpha/\bar{r}_i^2)\{(2\pi - \theta)/2\pi N\}$, $Bi_s = h_s\,\bar{r}/k$.

A steady state will be reached when the temperature distribution after one whole revolution is the same as the assumed initial distribution $T_o(r)$.

The steady-state solution depends on one Fourier number: $\alpha(2\pi-\theta_o)/2\pi N\bar{r}^2$, and on two Biot numbers: $h_1\bar{r}/k$ and $h_s\bar{r}/k$. The heat transfer coefficient h_1 must include gas and particulate (dust) radiation and convection. Gas radiation, mainly due to carbon dioxide and water vapor, can be readily calculated; particular radiation is less accessible since dust loading and dust size distribution inside the kilns are hard to measure. The convective transfer can be described by conventional Nusselt, Reynolds Prandtl number correlations. The heat transfer to the solids is less well defined and generally must account for all three heat transfer mechanisms. Furthermore, direct heat flow from gas to charge must be accounted for.

Mass transfer and/or chemical reactions are not included here, and these mechanisms introduce another set of parameters that influence the destruction of hazardous components.

Similarity and Scale-up

There has been very little work done on the similarity and scale-up of the incinerators. The similarity and scale-up principles are very critical in answering the following questions: "If a given waste can successfully be burned in Incinerator A, can it be safely burned in Incinerator B?" [53].

In order to relate the results of tests on one incinerator to another incinerator, it is necessary to establish rules for similarity. It is well known that similarity of fluid flow in two geometrically similar systems is achieved if the Reynolds numbers are the same in both systems, assuming that the fluid is incompressible and gravitational forces are small. If these assumptions do not apply, the Mach and Froude numbers also must be replicated. It has been shown also that to achieve a similarity in convective heat flux between a flowing fluid and a surface, the Nusselt number must be reproduced. The relationship $Nu = f(Re, Pr)$ can be derived through dimensional analysis or by examination of the Navier Stokes and the energy equations. In the case of incineration of hazardous waste, the similarity should be viewed in light of the objective of the incinerator. A potential definition of similarity is as follows [53]:

> Two geometrically similar incinerators of different capacity are deemed similar if, when burning the same type of waste, they produce the same level of destruction and their stack gases and residues, respectively, have the same composition.

Development of criteria for allowing comparison of data between incinerators is more complicated. It is not difficult to design two units (of differing size) to provide the same mean temperature, mean residence time and mean excess air in each portion. However, the mixing characteristics are the major factors which provide the difference in operation between units. These two units should behave in the same manner if their heat transfer characteristics and turbulence conditions are the same. Dimensional analysis should be a satisfactory method of comparing such systems. Dimensional analysis is a technique of reducing the heat transfer and flow systems to a series of dimensionless numbers which, when they are equal for the two systems, indicate similarity of that property. Examples of such dimensionless numbers are Reynolds and Mach numbers for fluid flow or Prandtl and Nusselt numbers for heat transfer. There are many other such dimensionless numbers. The difficulty in their use for complex flow systems comes in choosing the proper dimension of the system to use: i.e., which length dimension determines the desired Reynolds numbers for two incinerators.

The validity of this approach is reinforced by recent findings by Lee at all. [27]. Using a simple reactor, Lee determined reaction rate and time data for 15 compounds. By analyzing these data, it was shown that above a relatively low critical temperature, a compound's destruction proceeds by a first-order reaction mechanism in the presence of a large excess of oxygen. This suggests that, for purposes of comparing data from one incinerator to the next, the exact kinetics of destruction are unimportant; two units would behave in a similar manner if their mean temperature, residence time and excess air are the same and if certain key dimensions which govern heat transfer rates and mixing are also the same.

An example of similarity is the rotary kiln incinerators and reported by Weitzman [53]. From the equations,

$$h = 0.05\left(\frac{C_g}{S_x}\right)^{0.67} + 0.173E_g\left(\frac{T_g^4 - T_w^4}{T_g - T_w}\right)$$

and

$$h = 0.25\left(\frac{C_g}{S_x}\right)^{0.67}$$

it becomes apparent that the heat transfer coefficients are related to the approximately two-thirds power of the gas velocities. Similarly, they are related by approximately the cube of the temperature difference between the waste and flame when radiant heat transfer predominates as would be the case in most incinerators. When comparing two incinerators, it thus becomes clear that increasing the flame temperature will sharply increase the heat transferred to the waste and reduce the kiln length needed.

In summary, the state of the art of scaling up incineration equipment is at best very crude and, in most cases, nonexistent. The analytical model described in this section should be fully developed before a similarity study is attempted, and experimental data are necessary to verify the similarity principles.

CHARACTERISTICS OF SPECIAL WASTES

As discussed before, the characteristics of wastes affect incinerator design. The purpose of this section is to present the design requirements for incinerators handling certain types of waste.

Chlorinated Hydrocarbon Waste

Chlorinated hydrocarbon wastes are generated by a wide variety of industrial chlorination processes. In the incineration of a chlorinated hydrocarbon waste, hydrochloric acid will be presented in the exhaust gas, as well as some free chlorine. An example of such a reaction is the incineration of vinyl chloride. If it is burned with air, it will follow the following reaction:

$$C_2H_5Cl + 3O_2 + 11.29N_2 \rightarrow 2CO_2 + 2H_2O + HCl + 11.29N_2$$

Another example is to incinerate trichloroethylene:

$$CHCl = CCl_2 + 2O_2 + 7.52N_2 \rightarrow 2CO_2 + HCl + Cl_2 + 7.52N_2$$

The hydrochloric gas formed can be removed by scrubbing with water, but relatively insoluble chlorine will require caustic scrubbing. By the addition of fuel, water or steam, the chlorine might be converted to hydrogen chloride by the following reactions:

$$CHCl = CCl_2 + 3.5O_2 + 13.17N_2 \rightarrow 3CO_2 + 3HCl + H_2O + 13.17N_2$$

and

$$CHCl = CCl_2 + 1.5O_2 + H_2O + 5.64N_2 \rightarrow 2CO_2 + 3HCl + 5.64N_2$$

The latter equation is really not possible because of the low temperature achieved by the combustion reaction. The following reaction is typically required in the incinerator design.

$$CHCl = CCl_2 + 3.5O_2 + H_2O + CH_4 + 13.17N_2 \rightarrow$$

$$3CO_2 + 3HCl + 2H_2O + 13.17N_2$$

Depending on the heating value of the waste, auxiliary fuel may or may not be required. Figure 5-26 shows the relation between the percentage chlorine content and the heating value of the waste.

For practical correlation purposes, the hydrogen chloride to chlorine distribution in the combustion product is assumed to follow the equilibrium equation

$$Cl_2 + H_2O \overset{K_p}{\rightleftharpoons} 2HCl + 1/2O_2$$

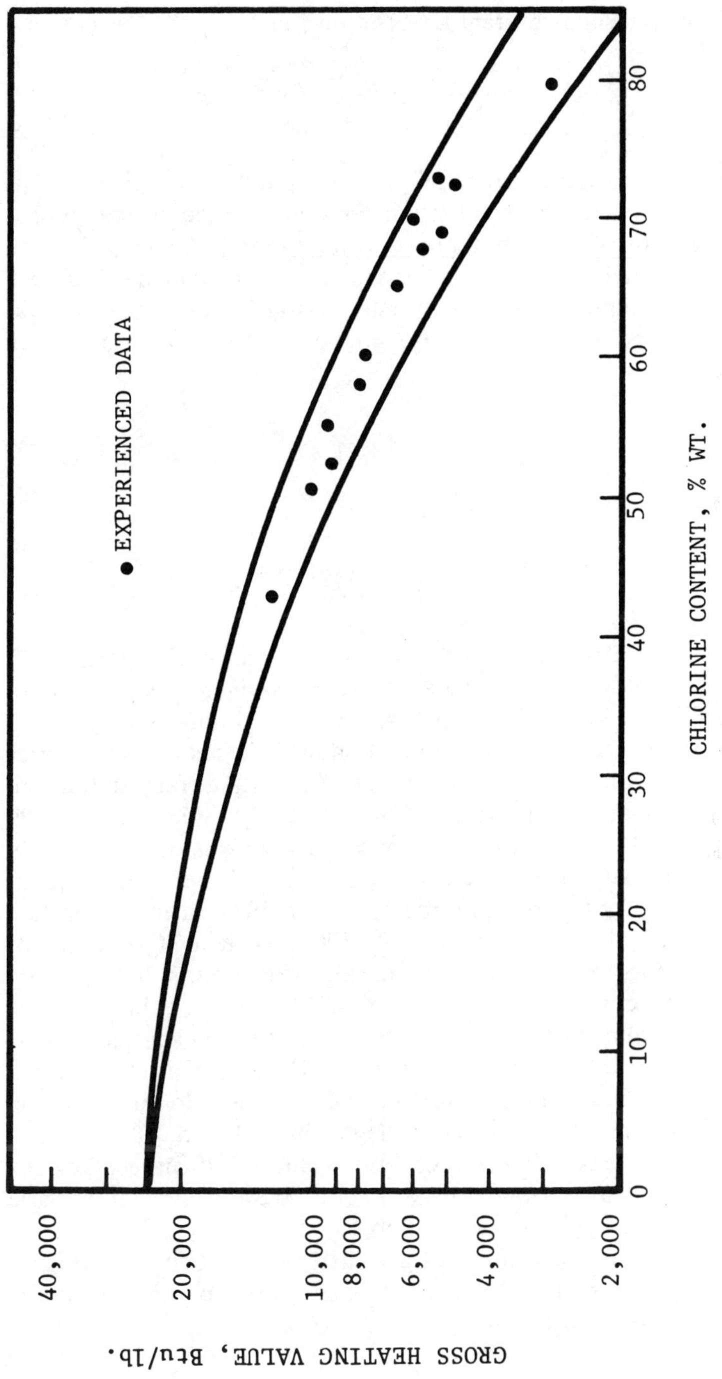

Figure 5-26. Heat of combustion of chlorinated hydrocarbons (reproduced courtesy of The Trane Company, La Crosse, WI).

where the equilibrium constant Kp is defined as

$$Kp = \frac{P_{HCl}{}^2 P_{O_2}{}^{1/2}}{P_{H_2O} P_{Cl_2}}$$

where P is the partial pressure of the corresponding compounds. The relationship between the equilibrium constant K_p and temperature is shown in Figure 5-27. To minimize chlorine formation, the combustion reaction must take place at a high temperature, with minimal free oxygen and with maximal water content. It must be noted that at high temperature, the chlorine will be formed through the decomposition of hydrogen chloride.

$$HCl \rightleftharpoons H + Cl$$

$$Cl + Cl \rightleftharpoons Cl_2$$

$$2H + 1/2O_2 \rightleftharpoons H_2O$$

In the design of a chlorinated hydrocarbon incineration system, it is necessary to analyze the formation of free chlorine. The curves illustrated in Figures 5-28 and 5-29 are examples of this analysis [54].

As an example, Figures 5-28 and 5-29 show the results of the chlorine generated from the combustion of a waste fuel with a composition containing 70% chlorine by weight, 3.5% hydrogen by weight and 26.5% carbon by weight. This waste fuel has a heating value of 4500 Btu/lb, contains principally dichloroethylene, trichloroethane, carbon tetrachloride, chloroform and dichorobutane. With 10% excess combustion air, the theoretical flame temperature is 3100°F, with an H to Cl ratio of 1.77. Under these conditions, the chlorine formation is 300 ppm. By introducing water to the system, the H to Cl ratio will rise; however, the chlorine formation, as well as the flame temperature, will decrease. Auxiliary fuel also can be introduced to boost H to Cl ratio and heating value. Also included in Figures 5-28 and 5-29 are the chlorine formation data based on fuel addition to raise the heating value to 6500 Btu/lb.

By reviewing the curve on H to Cl ratio vs chlorine discharge, the optimum point in either case (operating at 10 or 25% excess air with the basic water material) is approximately 4–5 to 1.

This ratio becomes insignificant when fuel is used to boost up the heating value. It must be noted that in the calculations no dissociation of combustion gases is considered.

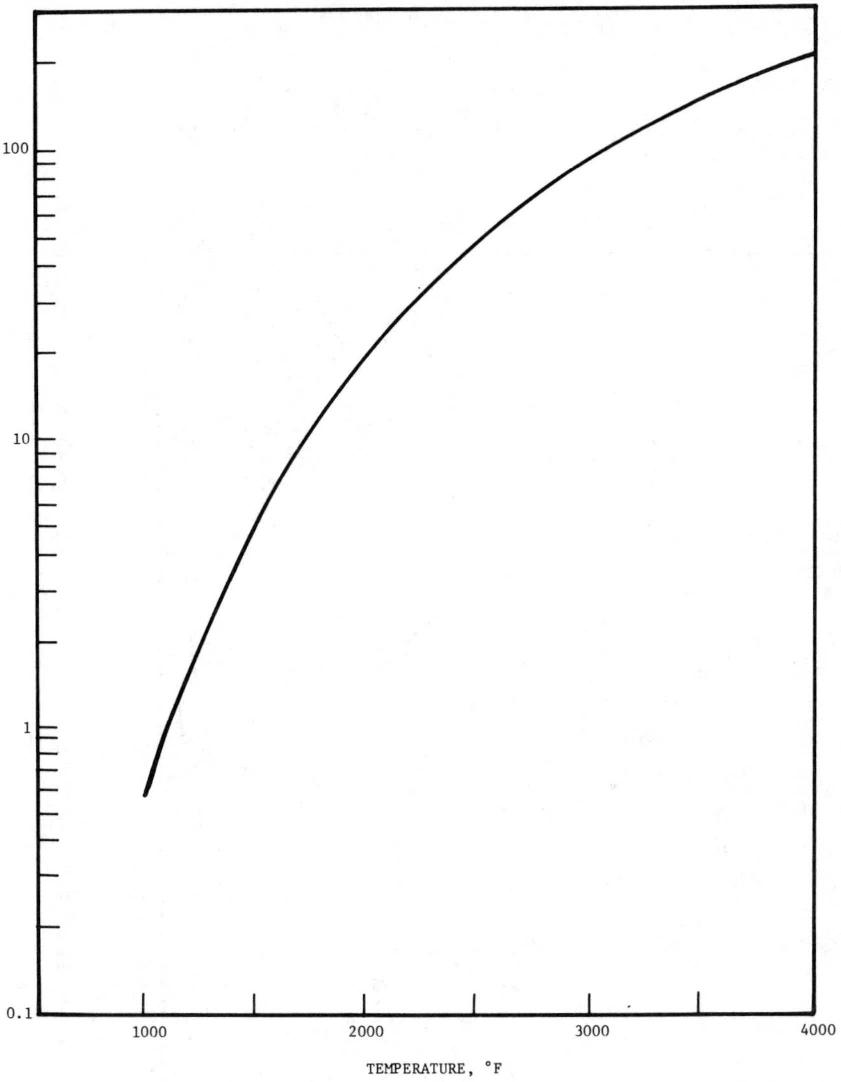

Figure 5-27. Equilibrium constants for hydrogen chloride and chlorine system.

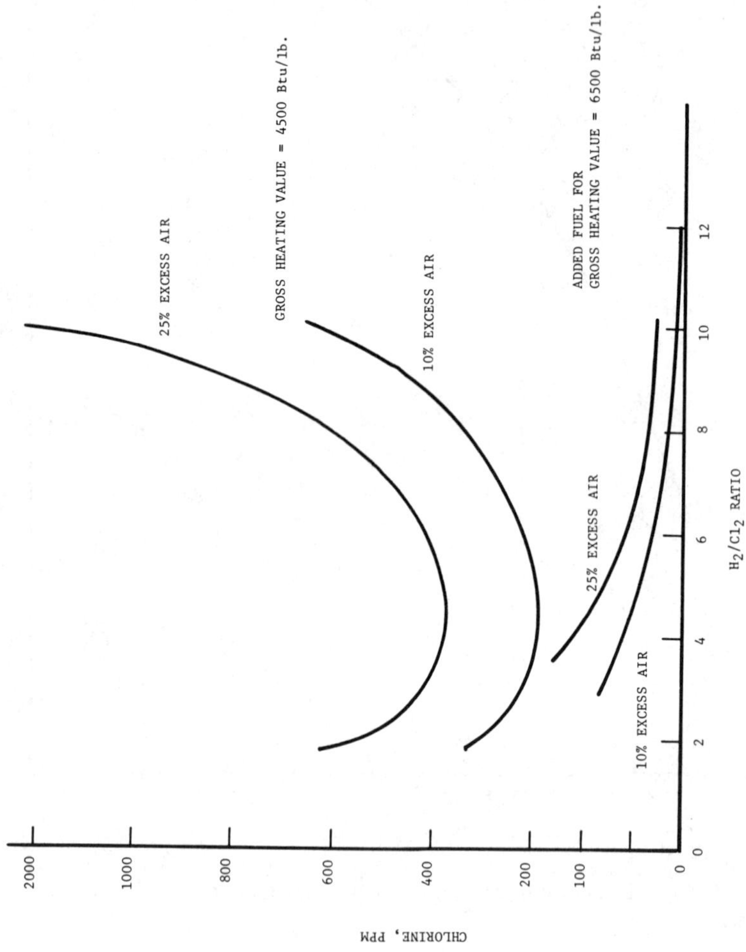

Figure 5-28. Chlorine formation as a function of hydrogen to chlorine ratio (reproduced courtesy of The Trane Company, La Crosse, WI).

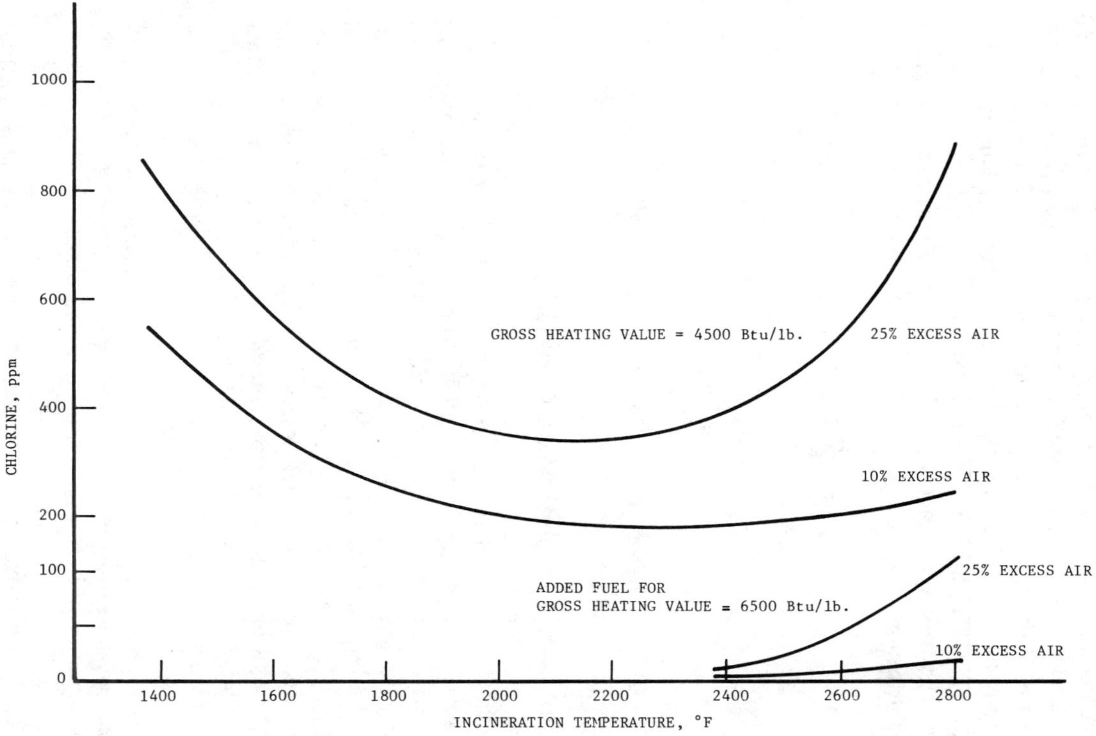

Figure 5-29. Chlorine formation as a function of incineration temperature (reproduced courtesy of The Trane Company, La Crosse, WI).

Other Halogenated Hydrocarbon Wastes

This group of wastes consists of hydrocarbons containing fluorine, bromine and iodine. In general, substituted hydrocarbons are more difficult to incinerate, especially the brominated compound. Bromine is one of the most effective flame retardant compounds. A halogenated hydrocarbon with 50% of combination chlorine and bromine is not self-combustible, although the theoretical flame temperature can be as high as 3000°F. The formation of free halogens is also dependent upon the halogens. The following reaction equilibrium is generally used to model HX/X_2 distribution.

$$X_2 + H_2O \overset{K_p}{\rightleftharpoons} 2HX + 1/2O_2$$

where

$$Kp = \frac{P_{HX}^2 \, P_{O_2}{}^{1/2}}{P_{X_2} \, P_{H_2O}}$$

The equilibrium constants are illustrated in Figure 5-30.

Prevention of Hydrochloric Acid Corrosion

Hydrochloric acid and free chlorine exist in the incinerators which process wastes containing chlorinated hydrocarbon. The formation of hydrochloric acid causes the shell corrosion problems in the incinerator. In a poorly designed incinerator, a carbon steel shell may corrode out in a matter of a few months. Figure 5-31 illustrates the cutaway of a typical incinerator, which consists of three sections: the steel shell, the insulating refractory and the hot face refractory. Because most refractories are porous, the hydrogen chloride can penetrate the refractory and contact the shell. Thus, the causes of steel shell corrosion when burning chlorinated hydrocarbons are:

1. high temperature reaction between the steel shell and hydrochloric acid gas, and
2. condensation of hydrochloric acid on the steel shell.

The acid corrosion, once started, cannot be stopped. Thus, it is essential to use preventive measures. The preventive action is best performed during the initial design stage.

Since the corrosion mechanisms caused by hydrogen chloride are high-temperature reaction and low-temperature condensation, the approaches

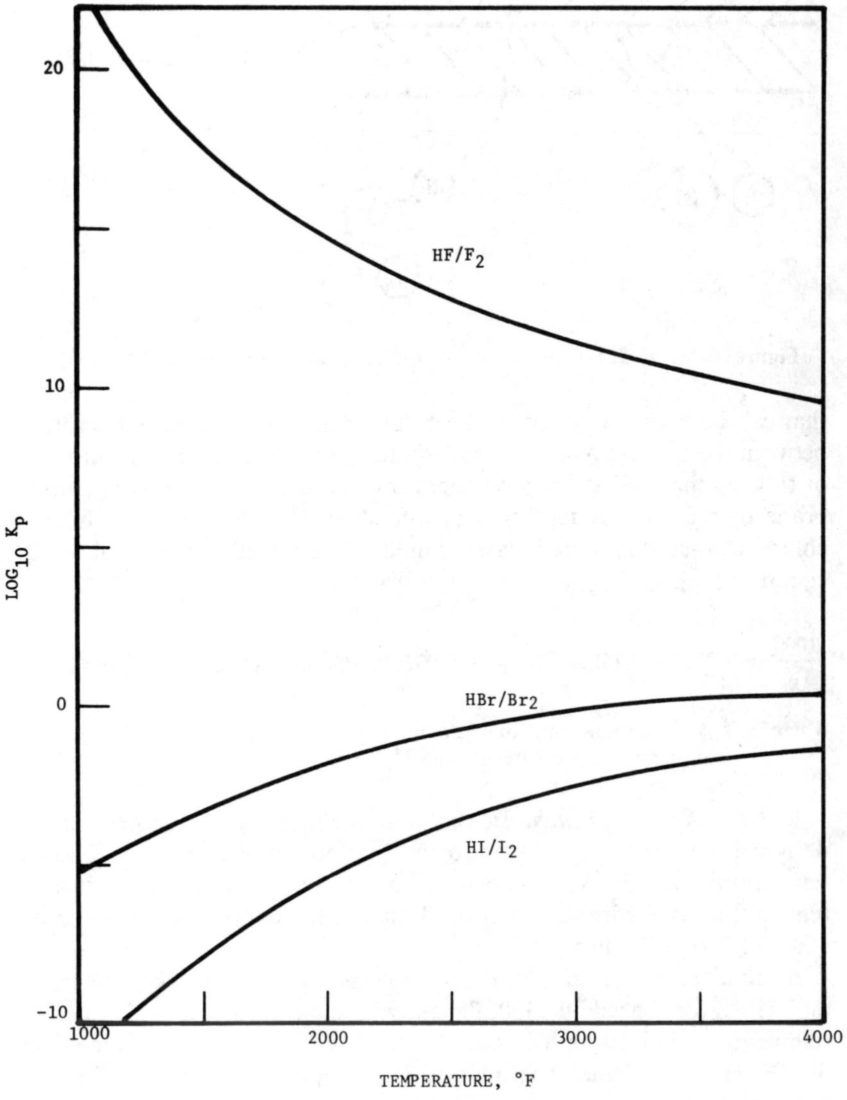

Figure 5-30. Equilibrium constants of hydrogen halide and free halogen systems.

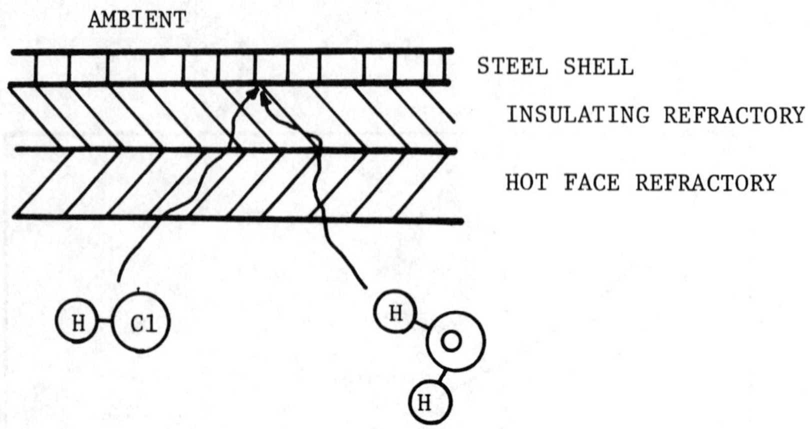

Figure 5-31. Cut-away view of typical incinerator refractory [55].

that can be taken are either to keep this shell at a medium temperature between the reactive and condensation temperature of hydrogen chloride, or to keep the shell at a low temperature and use a nonpermeable membrane to prevent condensation on the shell. The dewpoints of hydrochloric-acid-contaminated gases can be determined by the following equation [56]:

$$\frac{1000}{T_{DP}} = 3.7368 - 0.1591 \ln(P_{H_2O}) - 0.0326 \ln(P_{HCl}) + 0.00269 \ln(P_{H_2O}) \ln(P_{HCL})$$

where T_{DP} = the dewpoint in °F, and
P = partial pressures in mm Hg.

1. *Hot Shell Approach.* In this approach, the shell temperature is designed so that of all the operating conditions, the steel shell temperature will be kept above the dewpoint and below the reactive temperature of hydrogen chloride. Usually, the temperature is between 300 and 700°F (Figure 5-32).

As an illustrative example, Figure 5-33 shows the design parameters of an incinerator. Based on 2500°F incineration temperature, 50°F ambient temperature and 50-mph wind, the shell temperature is calculated at 360°F. However, when the incineration temperature varies or the ambient conditions change, the shell temperature may move into a corrosive zone. Thus, the selection of the design case is critical, as well as the physical design of the incinerator. In the hot shell design, the operating procedures of the unit are also important. It is necessary to burn aux-

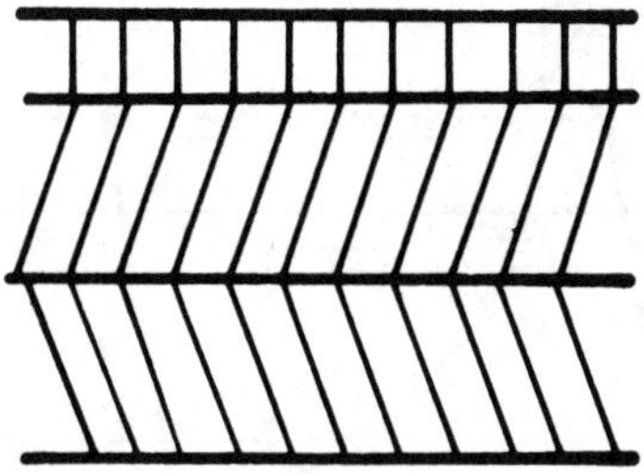

Figure 5-32. Hot shell refractory design [55].

iliary fuel prior to shutdown to remove any hydrogen chloride residue which might be condensed after cooldown.

2. *Lined Shell Approach.* In this approach, the shell is lined with a nonpermeable membrane. A typical membrane may only tolerate moderate temperatures, such as 250°F. Continuous refractory protection is essential for a trouble-free membrane surface temperature. Because of the low temperature, any hydrogen chloride penetrating the refractory will be condensed on the membrane, Figure 5-34.

The incinerator design in Figure 5-35 shows a possible problem with the lined shell approach. Any sustained change in incineration temperature or other ambient conditions which cause high membrane face temperature will damage the lining and leave the metal shell without protection. Thus, the designer must consider several possibilities carefully before the final design. Other problems related to the lined shell approach are different expansion coefficients between the steel shell and the membrane; and curing of the lining. The lined shell approach is more costly than the hot shell approach, and usually does not offer a higher level of confidence.

3. *The Ultimate Solution.* When necessary, the shell can be made of corrosion-resistant alloys such as Hastelloy® (a registered trademark of Cabot Corporation, Kokomo, IN) or Inconel® (a registered trademark of the International Nickel Co., New York). This approach is the surest and is usually the most costly. Most of the time, it is not economical and may not be necessary, because a well-designed and carefully operated incinerator, with a carbon steel shell may last as long as one using exotic materials.

The comparison of these three approaches is shown in Table 5-8. The use of exotic materials is the most expensive. The increased cost in the lined shell approach does not show up in the increasing of confidence level.

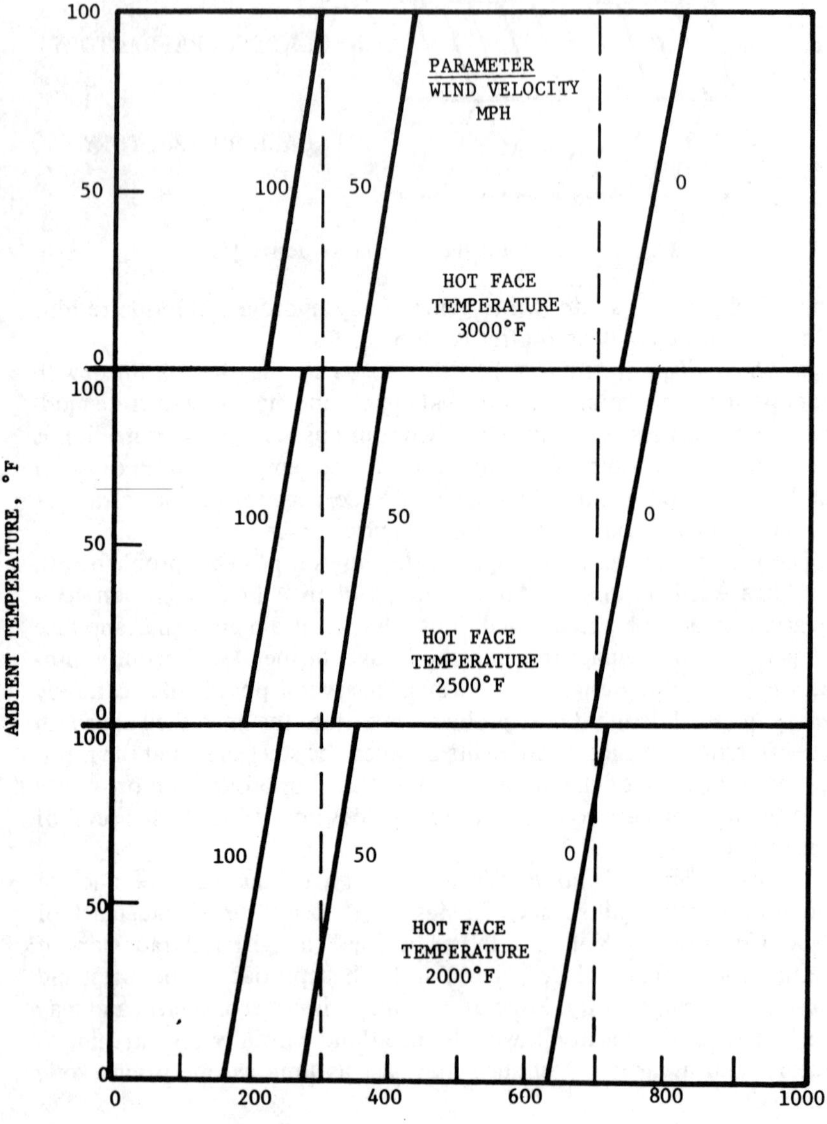

Figure 5-33. Hot shell refractory temperatures [55].

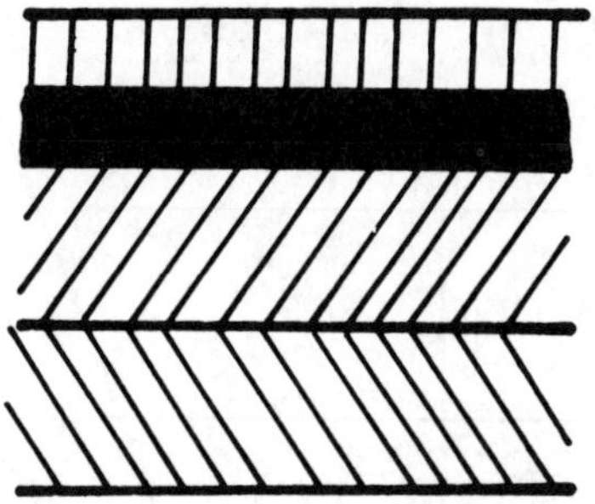

Figure 5-34. Lined shell refractory design [55].

Besides the design requirement, shell corrosion prevention also requires a properly written and followed operating procedure. For the hot shell approach, it is necessary to burn clean fuel prior to system shutdown to purge residual hydrogen chloride.

Waste Containing Metals

Depending on the incineration temperature, the type of metal and other contaminants, the combustion products of metals can be in solid, molten or vapor states. Usually, the heavy metals form solid compounds and do not affect the design of the incinerator. One group of wastes, the alkali metal-containing wastes, are the most critical wastes for incineration applications.

The operating temperature of the incinerator is a basic design criterion. For multiple hearth, fluidized bed, rotary kiln and multiple chamber incinerators, the incineration temperatures are usually low so that the salts are often in solid form. A major problem with this approach is the eutectic compound formed by a mixture of salts [57]. The eutectic compound usually has a lower melting point. Thus the incineration temperature must be low enough to ensure solid material, but this most often results in incomplete combustion.

For liquid injection incineration, the optimum incineration temperature is found to be between 1600 and 1800°F, and the chamber is usually in vertical downfired design. The temperature and downfired design are required to ensure that the salts are in the molten state and flow down the refractory wall into the salt cooling chamber. This temperature selection is critical because too low a temperature will cause the salt to freeze on the walls and possibly block the incinerator discharge, and too high a

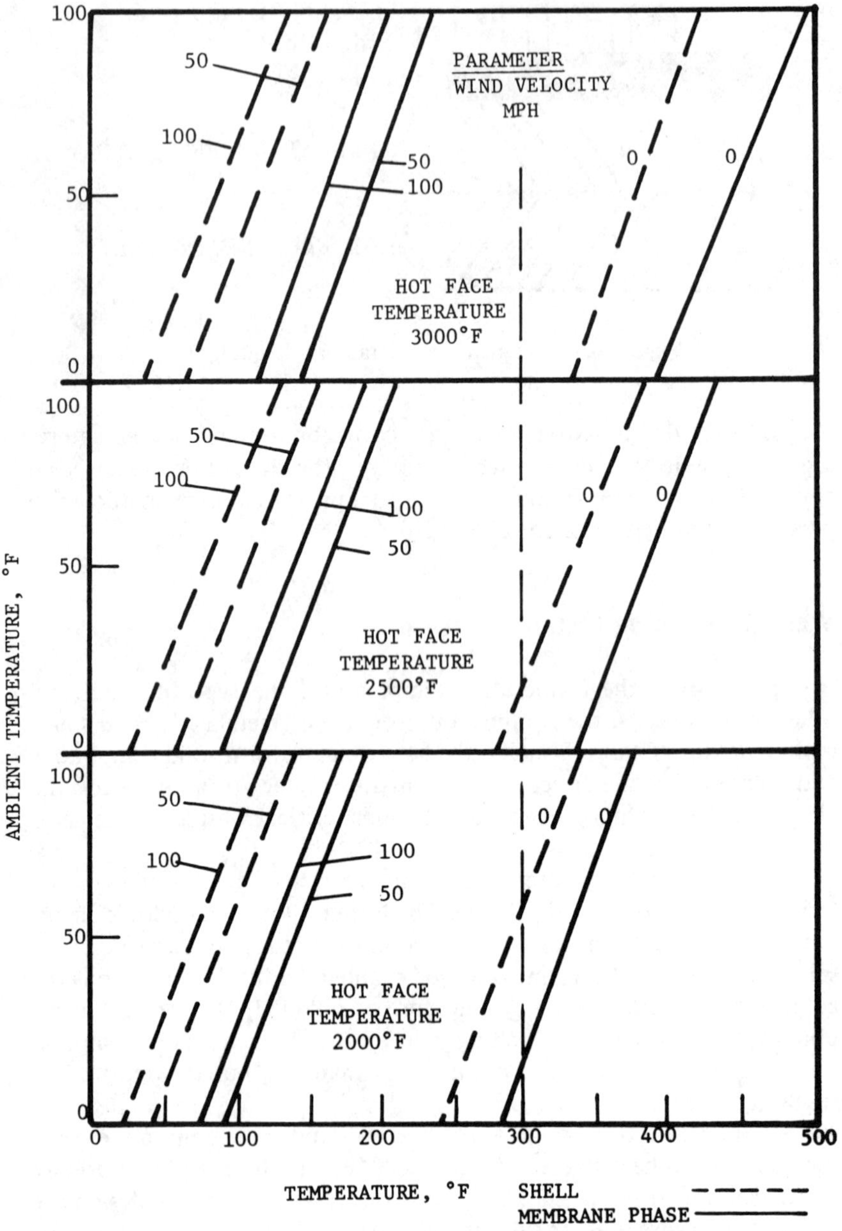

Figure 5-35. Lined shell refractory temperature [55].

Table 5-8. Rating of Shell Corrosion Prevention Methods

	Hot Shell	Lined Shell	Exotic Material
Cost	+	+ +	+ + +
Design Effort	+ +	+ + +	+
Size	+	+ +	+
Confidence	+ +	+ +	+

temperature will produce alkali oxide vapor (Figure 5-36), which will react with refractory material and cause spalling. The typical reactions between alkali salts and common refractory materials are presented in Table 5-9 [58]. Thus the selection of refractory is critical in an incinerator with alkali salts. Usually, low porosity refractory material is required.

Two other elements, although not metals, are worth discussion. The first compound is phosphorus. At typical incineration temperature, phosphorus will form phosphorus pentoxide which is a gaseous phase.

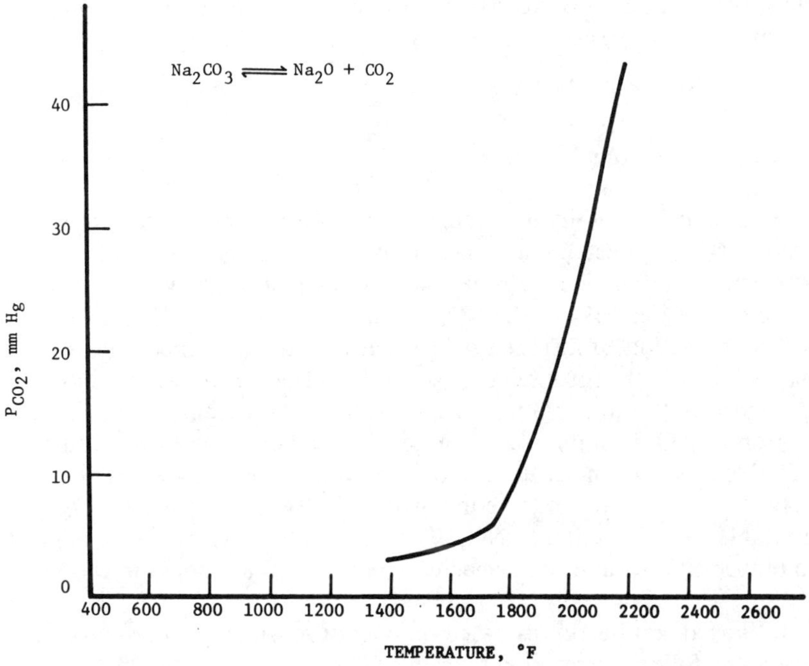

Figure 5-36. Carbon dioxide and sodium carbonate equilibrium.

Table 5-9. The Reaction of Sodium Compounds with Refractory Materials

Sodium Compound	Refractory Constituent	Temperature (°F)	Results
Sodium Oxide	Chromium	1350	liquid formation
Soda Ash	Alumina	1350	volume expansion
Sodium Silicate	Alumina	1375	liquid formation
Sodium	Silicate	1475	liquid formation
Soda Ash	Magnesia	1550	volume expansion
Soda Ash	Alumina	2000	volume expansion

After cooling, the phosphorus will form phosphoric acid mists with particle sizes in the submicron range. Thus, the selection of particulate removal equipment is critical.

The second compound is silica. In the incineration chamber, silica will form crystobalite, a form of silicon dioxide, which has a melting point of ~2700°F. Also, the particle size of molten silican dioxide is <0.1 micron; thus, the incinerator outlet usually has plugging problems. This must be taken into consideration when designing an incinerator.

Waste Containing Nitrogen

When wastes containing organic bonded nitrogen are burned, nitrogen oxides (NO_x) are usually discharged into the environment. For chemical waste incineration, ~5–10% of organic bonded nitrogen will form nitrogen oxides. Over 95% of the NO_x is emitted as NO and <5% as NO_2.

The formation of nitrogen oxides is a very complex mechanism. One major factor in the formation of NO_x is the difference in the way nitrogen is bonded in the waste [59]. For a volatile nitrogen compound, the formation of NO_x is minimized because of the inherent two-stage combustion. However, for nonvolatile nitrogen compounds, the residue nitrogen may be released later in the combustion processes when more oxygen is available for conversion to NO_x. Two control techniques can be applied to reduce NO_x formation: staged combustion and ammonia injection.

1. Staged combustion is based on operation with a rich primary zone where the following reaction takes place.

$$NO + HC \rightarrow N_2 + CO_2 + H_2O$$

In the first zone, the combustion air is usually controlled between 65% stoichiometric to stoichiometric oxygen requirement. The temperature is usually controlled at ~2400 to 2600°F. In the secondary chamber, secondary air is injected to quench the hot gas rapidly to 1800°F and oxidize unburned hydrocarbons and soot (Figure 5-37).

2. The Thermal $DeNo_x$ Process relies on the selective reaction between NH_3 and NO_x to produce nitrogen and water. The reaction requires the presence of oxygen and proceeds within a critical temperature range [60]. The overall NO_x reduction and production reactions are summarized in equations below:

$$NO + NH_3 + 1/4O_2 \rightarrow N_2 + 3/2H_2O$$

$$NH_3 + 5/4O_2 \rightarrow NO + 3/2H_2O$$

The first equation dominates at temperatures around 1740°F. For temperatures >1830°F, the second equation becomes significant. As temperatures are reduced to <1600°F, the rates of both reactions slow down and the ammonia flows through unreacted.

In addition to temperature, the process is also sensitive to initial NO_x and NH_3 concentrations. Other variables affecting performance are excess oxygen and available residence time at the reaction temperature.

The reaction temperature can be reduced by introducing more hydrogen relative to NH_3. At H_2/NH_3 ratio on the order of 2:1, the NO_x reduction reaction can be forced to proceed rapidly at 1290°F. By judiciously selecting the H_2/NH_3 injection ratio, flue gas treatment can be accomplished over the range of 1290–1830°F.

FLUE GAS CONDITION AND COOLING

As described before, the flue gas of an incinerator usually contains contaminants that must be removed before final release into the atmosphere. Air pollution control systems are required to remove these contaminants. There are two types of air pollution control equipment, dry and wet. In both, the temperature of the flue gases must be reduced to <400°F before passing into the air pollution control systems. Thus, flue gas conditioning and cooling systems are required to reduce the temperature. When a waste heat boiler is used in the system, some of the cooling requirement can be achieved by the boiler.

When a dry system, such as a bag filter, electrostatic precipitator, etc., is used for air pollution control, a cooling chamber is required. Air,

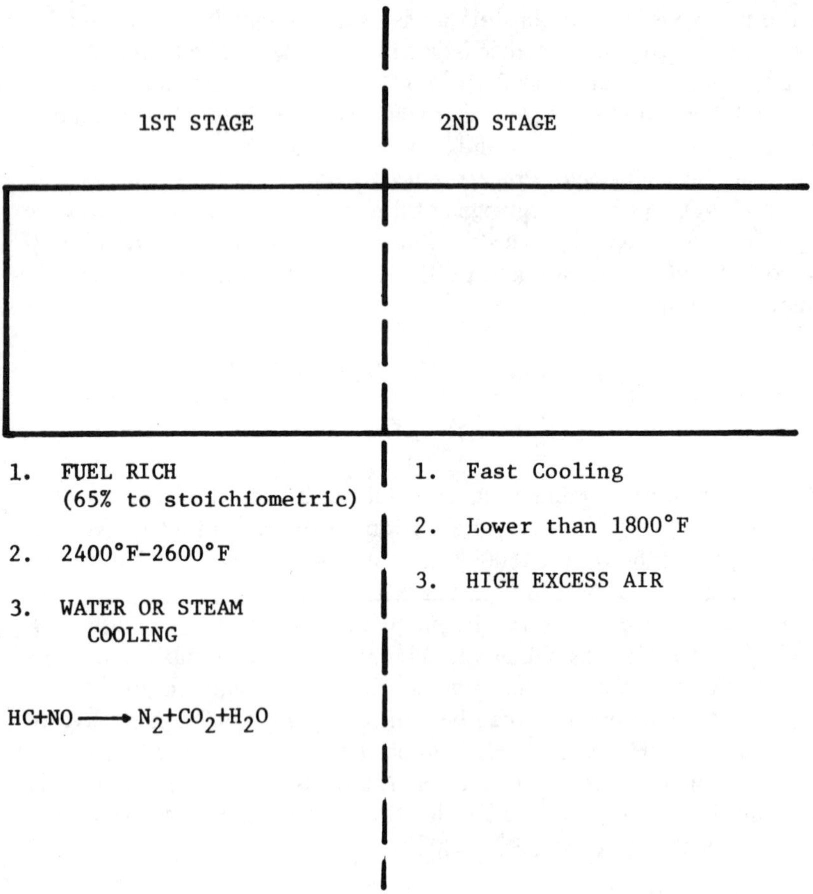

Figure 5-37. Two-stage combustion for nitrogen oxides reduction.

water and steam are introduced into the cooling chamber to reduce the temperature to the desired level (Figure 5-38). The chamber can be cylindrical, and the orientation can be upfired, downfired or horizontal. The amount of air and water required is determined by the temperature of the flue gases leaving the incinerator or boiler. The ratio of air and water has to be adjusted to avoid condensation inside the air pollution control equipment. Sometimes, recycled flue gas can be used to cool the gases (Figure 5-38b).

When wet type air pollution control systems such as scrubbers are used, the cooling requirement becomes complicated. The equipment has

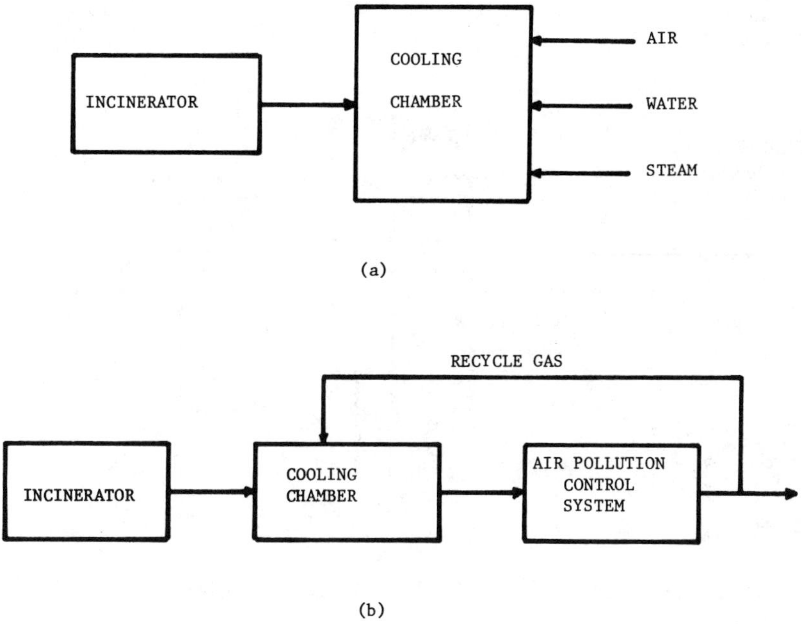

Figure 5-38. Schematics of hot gas cooling systems.

to be able to cool the flue gases from up to 3000°F to <190°F. The system must also be able to handle both hot and cold, as well as dry and wet, environments. The different types of hot/cold interface are presented in the following discussions.

Cooling Tower

This type of hot/cold interface makes use of either a countercurrent or a cocurrent tower (Figures 5-39, 5-40). If countercurrent design is used, the tower can be a packed bed or a spray quench tower. A spray quench tower can be used in the cocurrent design. When packed bed towers are used, they can also serve as an acid scrubbing tower.

The cooling tower is a composite vessel which is usually made of acid-proof brick within a lined steel shell. If a packed bed tower is used, the internals are usually made from inert materials such as graphite and ceramic. A typical cooling tower is illustrated in Figure 5-41.

The critical design part of the cooling tower is at the hot gas inlet throat. Special design features must be built into the inlet so that the liquid,

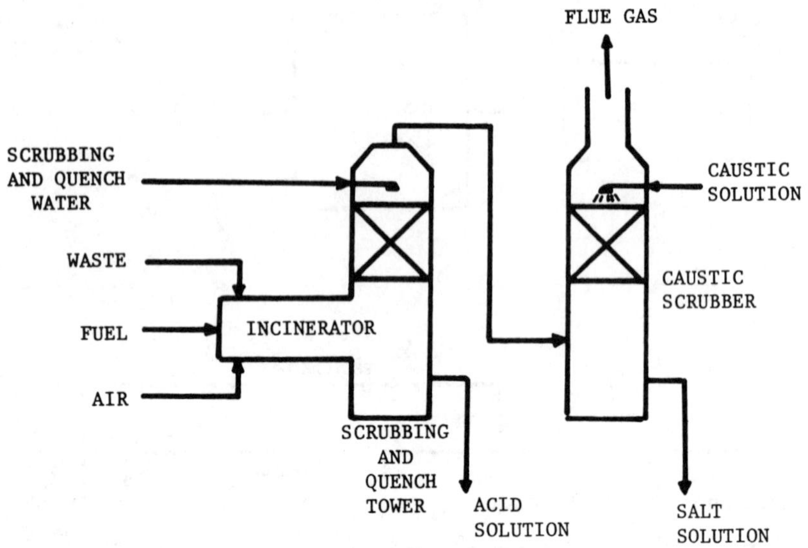

Figure 5-39. Countercurrent hot gas cooling system.

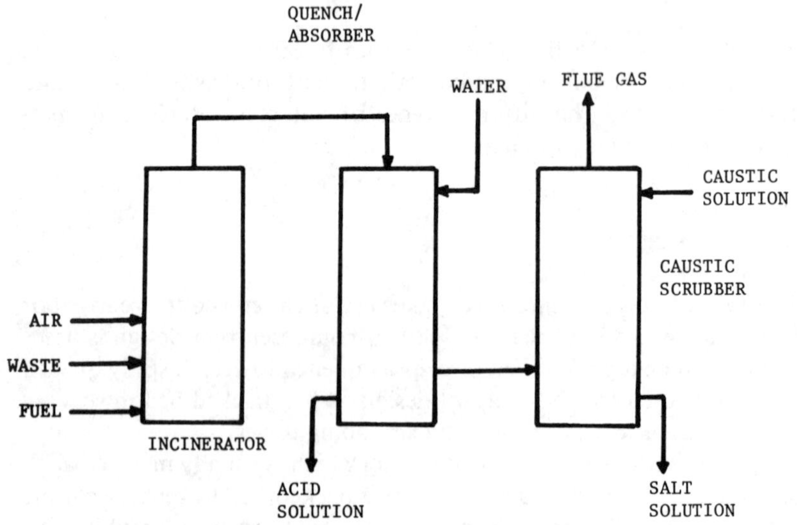

Figure 5-40. Cocurrent hot gas cooling system.

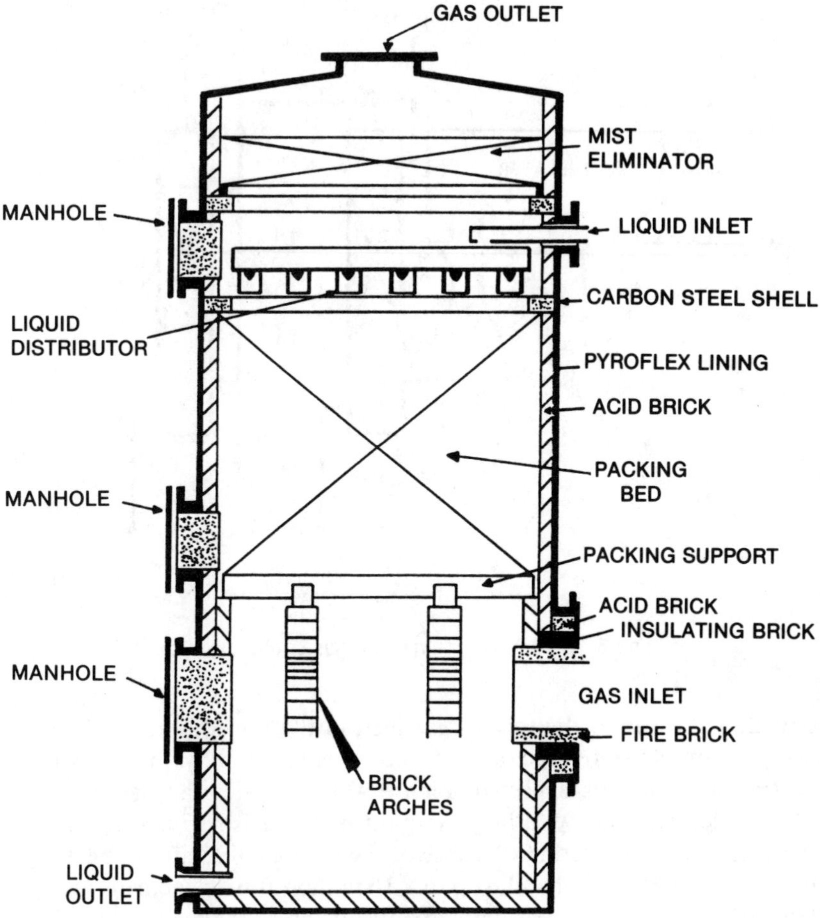

Figure 5-41. Schematics of a composite packed tower (reproduced from Reference 5-59, courtesy of Marcel Dekker, New York).

usually acidic, will not backflow into the incinerator. Also, safety must be incorporated so that emergency water can be used in case of quench water failure.

Venturi

A venturi scrubber can be used as the quench system. A typical system is illustrated in Figure 5-42. The venturi is usually a composite vessel con-

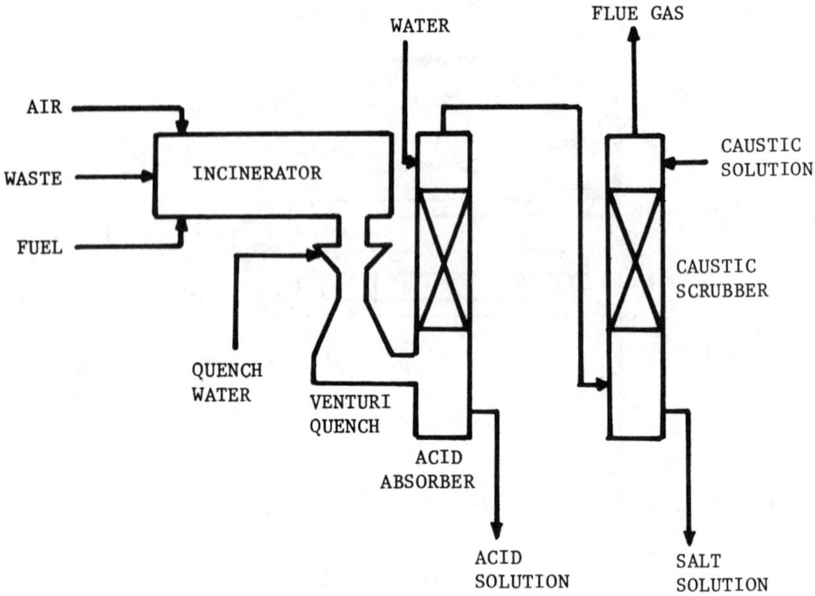

Figure 5-42. Venturi-type hot gas cooling system.

struction, similar to the tower described in the previous section. Some manufacturers use fiberglass reinforced plastics or alloys, if a low concentration of acid is expected. Figure 43a illustrates the basic venturi quench design. Usually, a large amount of water is required to protect the shell from overheating. Because of the physical limitation, the design in Figure 43a can only handle up to a 10 million Btu/hr incineration system. Also, the fixed throat limits the turndown of the quench. The configuration in Figure 43b can be used to increase the capability of the venturi quench. The central piece can be moved to compensate for process variations. Similarly to the wall, the central piece has to be water covered and made of corrosion-resistant material. The design of the movable parts is also critical. If the flue gas contains particulates, this system can be used to cool the hot gases and remove particulates.

Submerged Exhaust Cooling System

In this design, hot gases pass through a downcomer and exhaust below the water bath level inside the tank. Several types of design are available for this system.

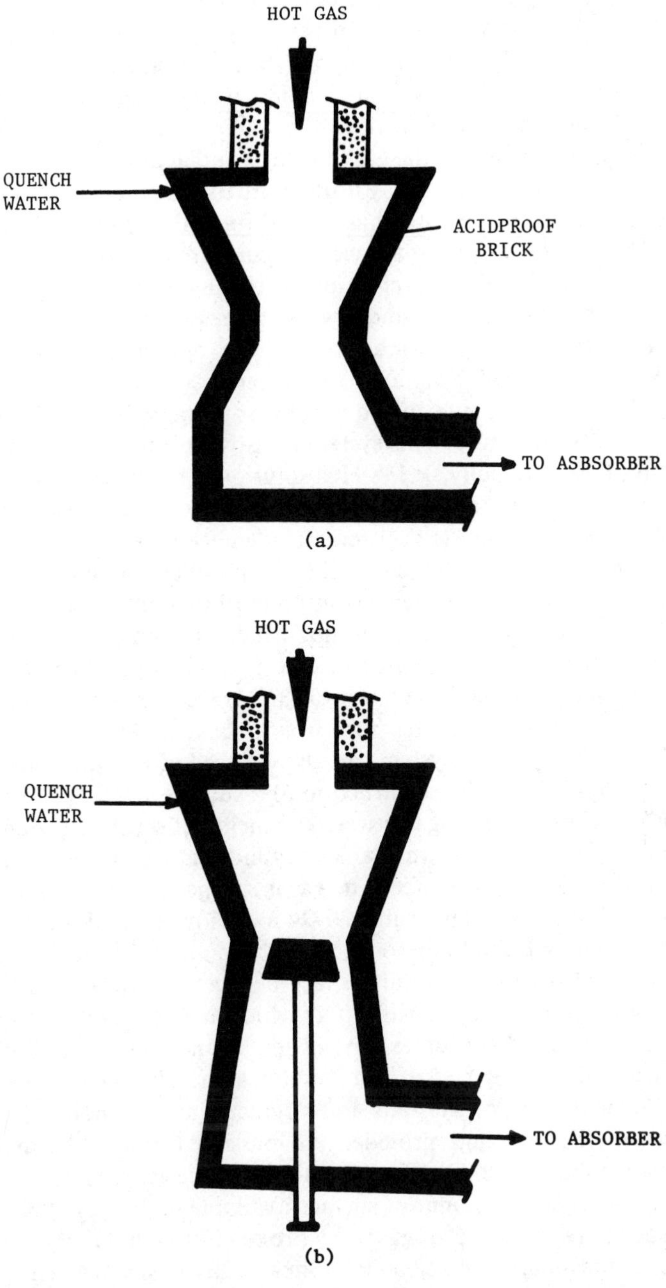

Figure 5-43. Venturi vessel.

Illustrated in Figure 5-44 is a low immersion Sub-X® system, used almost exclusively in PVC plant incineration systems. It is a compact unit and the size is usually between one and five million Btu/hr heat duty range. The hot combustion gases are introduced into a quench tank by an alloy downcomer and sparge through the water bath formed by the weir (Figure 5-45). At this point, the gas reaches its adiabatic end point and is saturated with water vapor. Spray nozzles are used in the chamber above the water bath. The water spray has several functions: to cool the downcomer tube, to cool the gas to a lower temperature and to scrub gaseous contaminants. The hydrogen chloride scrubbing efficiency is >90%. This type of design is compact and low cost. The pressure drop across the quench/absorber is ~5 in. water column. To operate the system, the water supply has to be reliable. If the water is lost, due to the nozzle plugging, lost pressure, etc., the downcomer and tank lining will be subjected to high temperature. This system is also not suitable for high concentration of HCl. Usually, <1% HCl solution is the maximum concentration the alloy downcomer and weir can handle. The quench tank is usually lined with Kynar® (a registered trademark of Pennwalt Corp.).

In the submerged quench system, the hot products of combustion do not come in contact with the quench liquid until they enter the liquid as a gas bubble. The refractory lining in the furnace is maintained at the furnace temperature. The incinerator discharge is not in contact with the liquid at any point, so there is no wet-dry interface on the refractory and none of the problems connected with it as discussed before.

A full emersion Sub-X® system can also be used as the hot/cold interface. Figure 5-46 shows the construction of a sub-X® system. The downcomer tube is the flow passage between the incineration chamber and the liquid in the quench tank. In this tank, a cylindrical weir is installed concentric with the downcomer tube. The gas is sparged into the liquid from the bottom of the downcomer tube; 20–24 in. below the tank water level. This permits many bubbles to form, which rise and mix with the evaporating water vapor in the annular space between the downcomer tube and the weir. This creates an airlift effect which moves the liquid over the outer surface of the downcomer tube. The gas and water vapor will be disengaged at the upper end of the annular area. The separated liquid will flow over the top of the weir and circulate into the bottom of the weir through the openings provided. In passing through the annular space between the weir and the downcomer tube, the gas transfers heat to the liquid via the large amount of surface available in the gas bubbles. It has been estimated that 1 ft^3 of gas when broken into bubbles of 0.001-in. diam represents an area of 72,000 ft^2 of heat transfer surface. The gas is cooled to within 10°F of the liquid discharge temperature. The down-

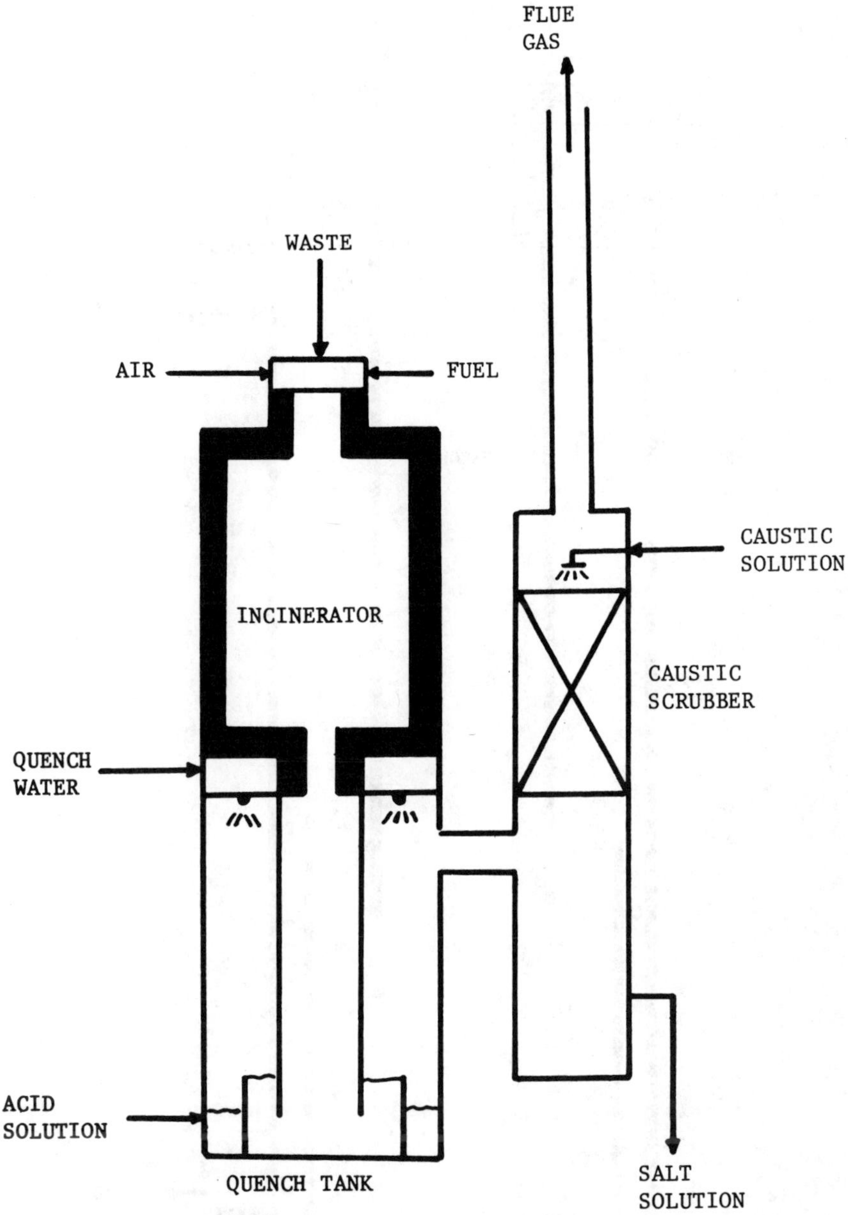

Figure 5-44. Sub-X® incineration system (reproduced courtesy of The Trane Company, La Crosse, WI).

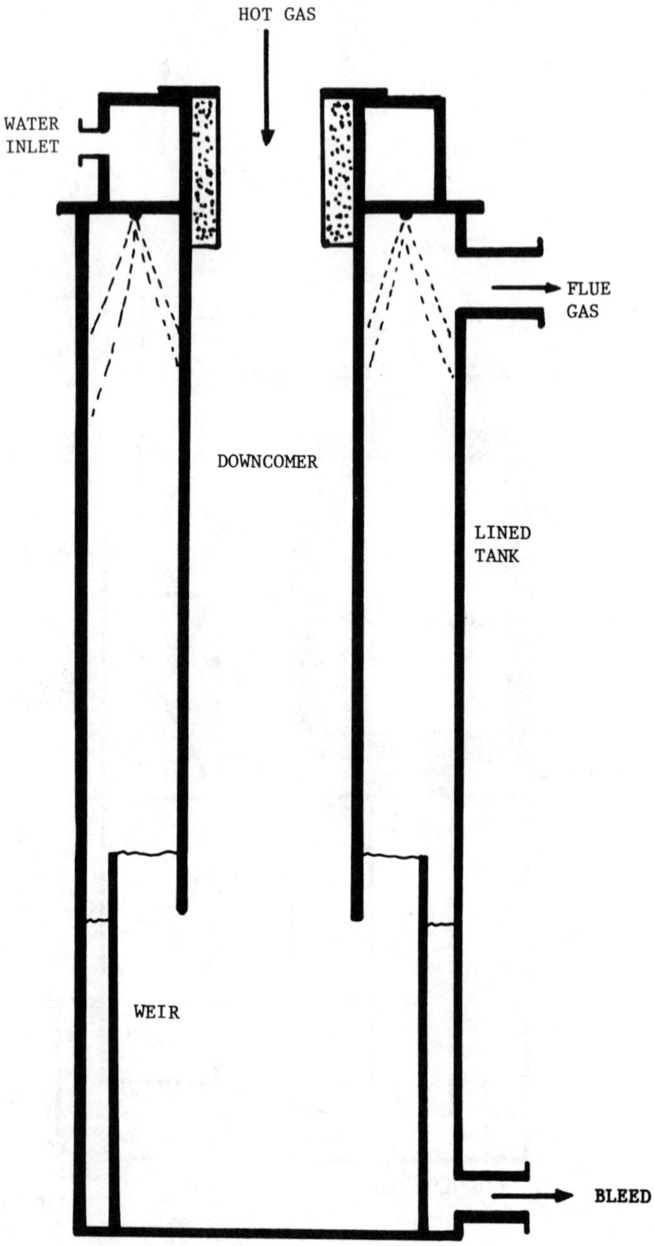

Figure 5-45. Sub-X® cooling tank—minimal emersion (reproduced courtesy of The Trane Company, La Cross, WI).

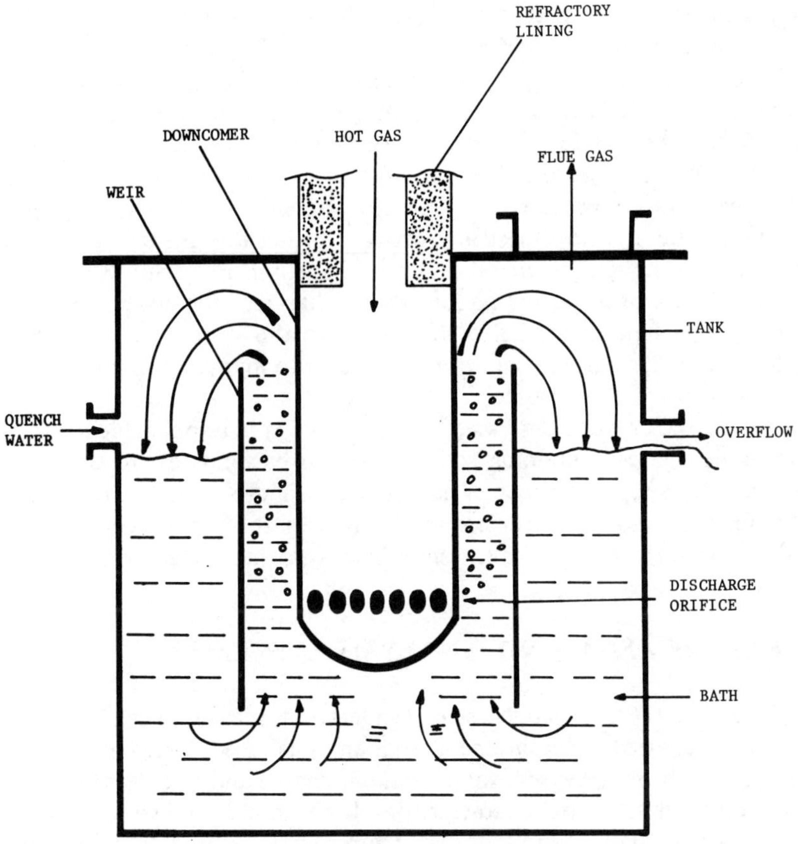

Figure 5-46. Sub-X® cooling tank—full emersion (reproduced courtesy of The Trane Company, La Crosse, WI).

comer tube is maintained at a relatively constant temperature by the external cooling effect of the quench tank. The major portion of the incinerator with the discharge duct is not in contact with the liquid at any point, so that there is no wet-dry interface on the refractory.

The downcomer tube is usually a graphite or alloy tube designed to withstand attack by the incinerator gases and the quench liquid. This downcomer tube operates at a temperature level between the bath temperature and the combustion gas temperature. Selection of materials is dependent upon this operating temperature and bath solution quality. Where high acid concentration results, graphite tubes have been used with a great degree of success.

The tank construction is usually dependent on the solution inside. For high concentrations of acid, a steel tank lined with rubber and acid brick has been successful. Kynar® lined steel can also be used.

This type of design usually is the most costly in both capital and operating categories. However, its advantages usually warrant selection of this design. As described before, there is no refractory hot-cold interface, a major maintenance problem. Because of the construction material, it can give continuous corrosion-free operation. In all the other quench methods, there is no time delay between losing the quench water and overheating the quench chamber. In the full-submersion Sub-X® design, there is 24 in. of water bath above the discharge of the hot gas. Even if other safety equipment failed to shut down the system, there may be more than a 30-min time lag for the operator to manually shut down the system or correct the problem.

The Sub-X® system described in Figure 5-46 is not applicable to incinerator flue gases containing solid or molten particulates. In this case, an open tube type downcomer can be used, Figure 5-47. In this design, the solid or molten particles usually bypass the sparge orifices and exhaust into the water bath through the downcomer tube opening.

MEASUREMENT AND ANALYSIS SYSTEMS

To establish the effectiveness of incineration, measurement and analysis are required. Measurement and analysis needs for incineration usually center on the waste, solid/liquid discharge and stack gas analysis.

To establish the waste characteristics, both simple and exotic chemical and physical analyses are required. Simple analysis usually involves the determination of heating value, total analysis, ash content, viscosity, moisture content, etc. The analytic method is well developed. More exotic chemical analysis often is required to determine the organic constituents in the wastes. Usually, gas-chromatography/mass-spectrometry (GC/MS) methods are required [61,62]. Both the equipment and analytical procedure are very costly. This type of analysis is necessary for establishing the wastes for incineration, but it is not cost effective for regular quality assurance. At the present time, the measurement and analytical needs for quality assurance of waste materials are not available. Fundamental research is required to develop quality assurance programs.

The measurement and analytical needs for solids discharged from an incineration system are similar to those of raw waste materials, if trace organic constituents are to be determined.

When scrubbers are used in incineration systems, the organic contents of the scrubber water will give an indication of the completeness of incin-

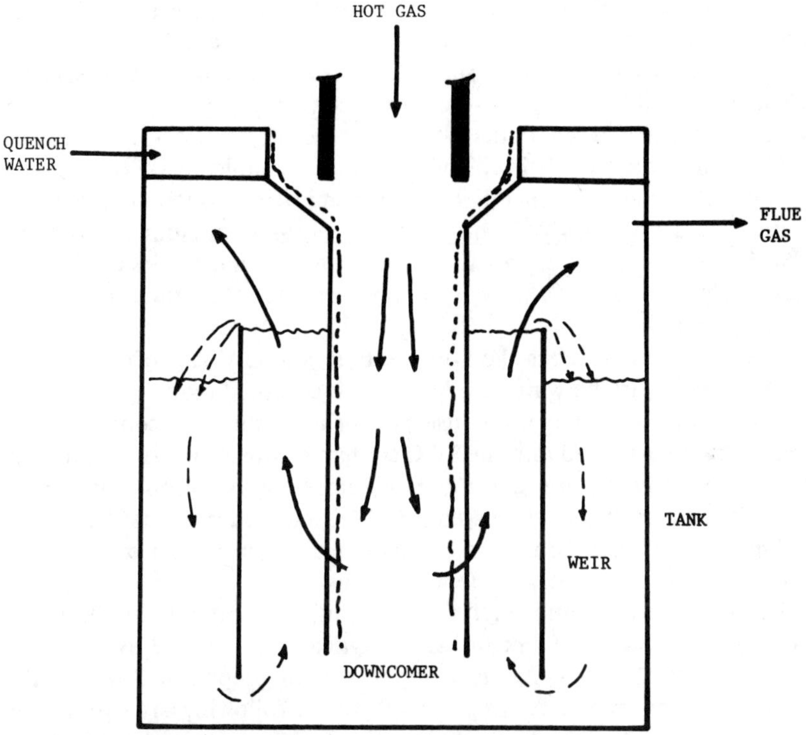

Figure 5-47. Sub-X® cooling tank—salt application (reproduced courtesy of The Trane Company, La Crosse, WI).

eration. There are two types of analysis requirements for scrubber water: specific organic compound concentration and total organic concentration.

To determine the specific organic compounds in the scrubber water, the sample preparation and analysis procedures developed for priority pollutant must be followed [63]. The procedure involves solvent extraction of trace quantities of organic compounds. Then GC/MS can be used to determine the organic content. Sometimes carbon adsorption and solvent regeneration methods also can be used for sample preparation.

There are three methods available to determine total organic content in scrubber water: biochemical oxygen demand (BOD), chemical oxygen demand (COD) and total organic carbon (TOC) [64]. The BOD method relies on the biological activity of bacteria to reduce the dissolved oxygen level of water after a typical five-day incubation period [65]. The reduction in oxygen is defined as BOD. The BOD method, although widely used, is not an efficient technique for total organic content determination. Besides the long time delay (5 days), inorganic materials such as sulfides, sulfites, etc., will register as BOD. Organic compounds, such as pesticides, antibiotics, toxic inhibitors, etc., might destroy or reduce biological activity to render the BOD result meaningless. Also, refractory-type organic compounds may not decompose completely.

The COD method depends on the chemical oxidation of materials present by a powerful oxidizing agent, such as potassium dichromate [66]. Similar to the BOD method, interference by inorganics and chlorides presents a major obstacle for applying the COD method to incineration systems.

The TOC method is based on the catalytic combustion process wherein all the organics in the water are oxidized to carbon dioxide [66]. A non-dispersive infrared analyzer is used to measure the CO_2 content. This value is then correlated into the TOC content of the water. Acid sparging is used to remove the inorganic carbon before the oxidation chamber.

Of the three methods discussed, the TOC method presents the fastest and most practical method for total organic concentration determination in incineration system discharge water.

The measurement and analysis of organic compounds in the stack gases are the most difficult tasks. Analytical methods are available to determine the organic content; however, sample preparation and conditioning systems are not fully developed. In the following discussion, the present state of the art of stack gas sampling and analysis methods is presented.

Stack gas can be analyzed continuously with on-line instruments. The instruments which have been used successfully are the conventional oxygen analyzer, chemiluminescent nitrogen oxides analyzer, nondispersive infrared analyzers for carbon monoxide, carbon dioxide and sulfur dioxide analysis, flame ionization detector for total hydrocarbon analysis and on-line gas chromatograph for specific hydrocarbons. Most of the analyzers can operate effectively provided the sample is delivered to the instrument dry and resembles the stack concentration. The exception is that the flame ionization detector is not applicable for determining the presence of aldehydes.

The present state of the art of stack sample conditioning systems is illustrated in Figure 5-48. A rugged sintered sampling probe with integral filters is used in the stack. The sample is then transported to the dryer through a heated sample line. The sample line maintains the gas above its dewpoint until it reaches the dryer. This portion of the system is kept clean by frequent blowbacks. In addition, a high gas flow is used to minimize particle deposition between blowbacks, with a bypass arrangement

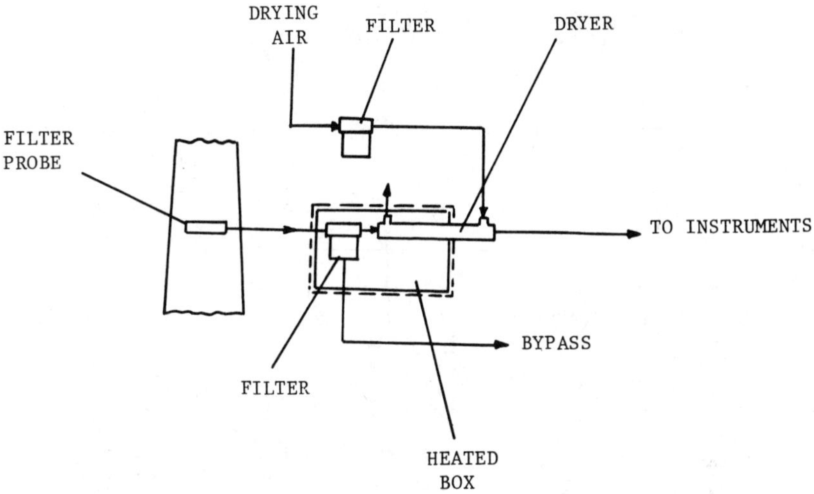

Figure 5-48. Stack sample handling and conditioning system.

used to reduce the flow to the analyzers. The dryers use permeation membranes (tubular) which allow the removal of water vapor so that the sample gas is never in contact with condensate.

For most hydrocarbons and chlorinated solvents, the dryers are an effective means to separate out water. However, alcohols, ketones, esters and certain organic acids will permeate the dryer and thus cause erroneous reading on hydrocarbon analyses.

Stack organic compounds can also be sampled by the source assessment sampling system (SASS) developed by EPA [67]. The SASS train consists of a stainless steel probe connected to three cyclones and a filter in an oven module, a gas treatment section and an impinger section (see Figure 5-49). The gas treatment is comprised of four components: the gas cooler, the sorbent trap, the aqueous condensate collector and a temperature controller. Organic materials are collected in a cartridge (or trap) containing XAD-2 sorbent. The collected organic materials are then regenerated and analyzed by gas chromatography or GC/MS. At the present, this sampling train is not fully developed for organic compound evaluation; extensive studies are required to perfect the procedure.

SAFETY AND PROCESS CONTROL

An incineration system is a combustion system; and regular combustion safety control requirements, such as automatic shut-off of fuel and

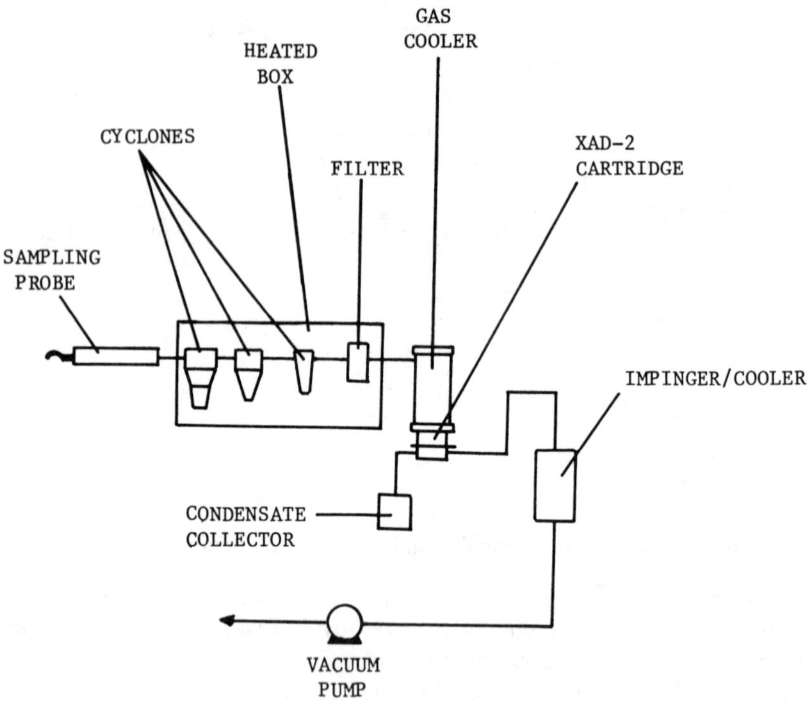

Figure 5-49. EPA source assessment sampling system (SASS).

waste, flame safety devices, etc., are required. Comprehensive combustion safeguard systems are discussed in References 68–70. The combustion safety control requirements are centered on explosion prevention. In incineration applications, it is necessary to ensure that the waste is destroyed. As described before, for a specific incinerator, the destruction efficiency is a function of incineration temperature, excess air rate and residence time. Thus, the present state of the art of incineration system control involves the measurement of air, fuel and waste flow rates, incineration temperature, stack oxygen and carbon monoxide concentrations (Figure 5-50). Note that this system is above and beyond the regular combustion safety control systems required.

The waste rate usually is manually set. Fuel and air rates are adjusted to maintain the desired incineration temperature. Sometimes cooling water and steam also can be used and controlled. Stack oxygen measurement is used to override the temperature controller, to ensure that an adequate amount of air is introduced into the incinerator. Residence time

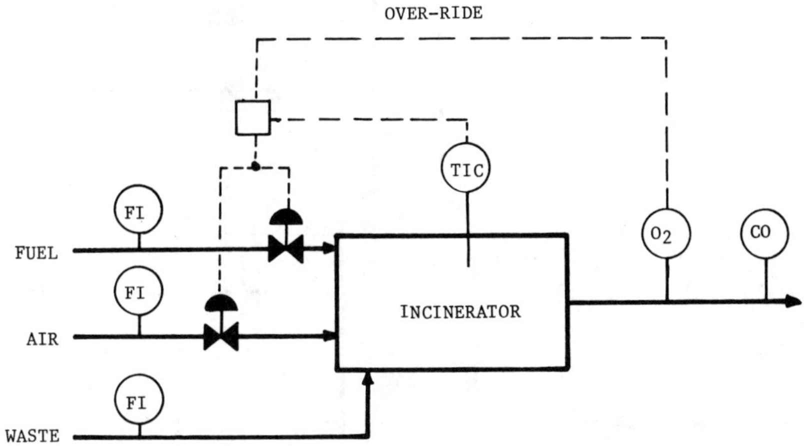

Figure 5-50. Incineration process control.

can be estimated by the knowledge of waste, air and fuel flow rates and incineration temperature. The overall combustion efficiency is determined by measurement of stack carbon monoxide concentration. Experience has shown that carbon monoxide is the most sensitive indication of combustion operation [19]. Usually, carbon monoxide monitor is connected to an alarm system. In case the stack carbon monoxide level is over the preset safety level, operators are alerted to investigate the cause.

When air pollution control systems are used in an incineration system, safety systems must be used to protect the downstream equipment from excessively high temperature. The most critical item is loss of water in the quench system. A typical safety system is illustrated in Figure 5-51. The quench system is protected by three sets of safeguards: temperature, cooling water flow rate and low water level. In the event of an abnormal condition in any one of these parameters, the incinerator is shut down and emergency water is introduced.

To avoid nuisance shutdowns, an alarm is used before the system shutdown. For example, the level control system provides a low level alarm and a low low level switch. If the water level drops, an alarm sounds so that corrective action can be taken by the operator before system shutdown. However, if the level continues to drop, the low low level switch then shuts down the system.

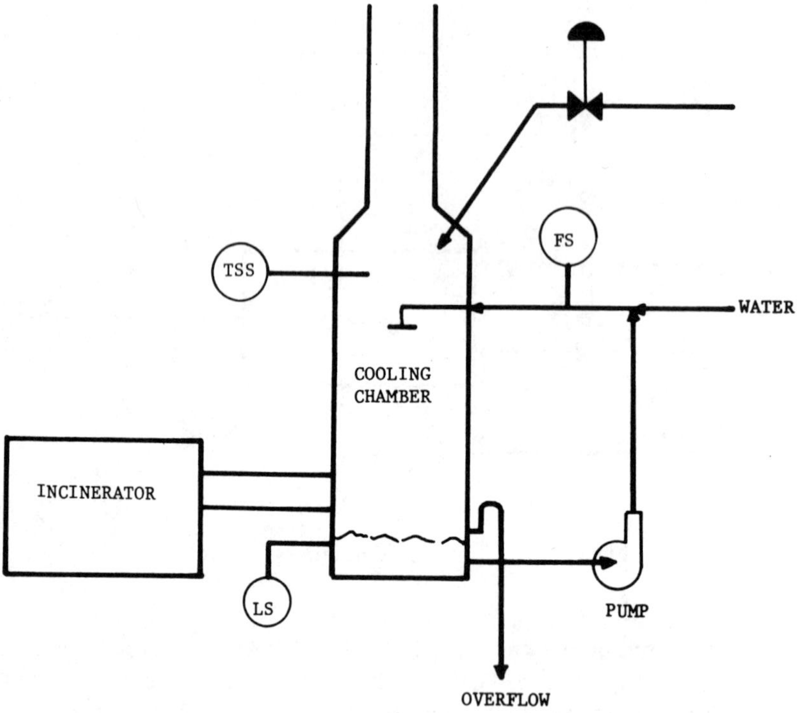

Figure 5-51. Hot gas cooling system safety control.

REFERENCES

1. International Nickel Company. Corrosion Eng. Bulletins CEB-1, CEB-3 (1972).
2. Carpenter Steel Company. No. 20cb Bulletin (1972).
3. Haynes Stellite Company. "Corrosion Resistance of Haynes Alloys," (November 1958).
4. *Corrosion Data Survey,* 1967 ed., National Association of Corrosion Engineers.
5. Kubaschewski, O., and B.E. Hopkins. "Oxidation of Metals and Alloys," (London: Butterworth and Co., 1962).
6. Rolke, R. W., et al. "Afterburner System Study," NTIS, PB-212 562, (August 1972).
7. Santoleri, J. J. "Industrial Waste Disposal Material Selections for Combustion Chambers," paper presented at the AIChE 76th Annual Meeting, Tulsa, OK (March 1974).
8. Brown, R. W. "High Temperature Non-Metallics," *Chem. Eng.* (April 21, 1968).

9. Babcock and Wilcox Company. Private correspondence (1972).
10. Kiang, Y. H. "Liquid Waste Disposal Systems," *Chem. Eng. Prog.* 72(1): 71 (1976).
11. Criss, G. H., and R. R. Schneider. "Effect of Flue Gas Contaminants on Refractory Structures at S/Rated Temperatures," ASME 63-WA-258 (December 1963).
12. Vogrin, C. M. "High Temperature Stability of Insulating and Refractory Castables in Reducing and Oxidizing Atmosphere," ASME 55 PET 31 (1972).
13. Read, G. W. and F. M. Veater. "Acidproof Concrete Lining for Steel Stacks or Power Plants," *Combustion* (March 1972).
14. Pierce, W. "Fundamentals for Ceramic Linings," American Institute of Chemical Engineers 49th Meeting, March 1963.
15. Crowborg, M. S., and J. F. Wygant. "Acid Resistant Concrete," American Institute of Chemical Engineers 54A, November 1967.
16. Bonner, T., et al. "Engineering Handbook for Hazardous Waste Incineration," U.S. EPA, Washington, DC (November 1980).
17. Federal Register, Vol. 46, No. 15, 40 CFR Parts 122, 264, and 265 (January 23, 1981).
18. "Hazardous Material Incinerator Design Criteria," NTIS, Washington, DC (1979).
19. Kiang, Y. "Incineration of Hazardous Organic Wastes," Proceedings of 1980 National Waste Processing Conference, Washington, DC (1980), p. 93.
20. Dow Chemical Company. "JANAF Thermochemical Tables" (1964).
21. Niessen, W. P., "Combustion and Incineration Processes," (New York: Marcel Dekker, Inc. 1978).
22. Steffensen, R. J. "A FORTRAN IV Program for Thermochemical Calculations Involving The Elements Al, B, Be, C, F, H, ...," Ph.D. Dissertation, Purdue University, Lafayette, IN (1966).
23. TRW. "Thermal Degradation of Military Standard Pesticide Formulations," TRW Report No. 24768-60/8RV-00 (December 1974).
24. Carnes, R. A., et al. "A Laboratory Approach to Thermal Degradation of Organic Compounds," Paper No. 77-19.3, Air Pollution Control Association 70th Annual Meeting, Toronto, Canada, June 1977.
25. Lee, K. C., et al. "Thermal Oxidation Kinetics of Selected Organic Compounds," Paper No. 78-58.6, Air Pollution Control Association 71st Annual Meeting, Houston, TX, June 1978.
26. Duvall, D. S., et al. "Applications of the Thermal Decomposition Analytical System (TDAS)," Paper No. 80-8.1, Air Pollution Control Association 73rd Annual Meeting, Montreal, Canada, June 1980.
27. Lee, K. C., et al. "Predictive Model of the Time Temperature Requirements for Thermal Destruction of Dilute Organic Vapors," Paper No. 79-10.1, Air Pollution Control Association 72nd Annual Meeting, Cincinnati, OH, June 1979.
28. Hochstim, A. R., Ed. *Bibliography of Chemical Kinetics and Collison Processes* (New York: IFI/Plenum Publishing Corporation, 1969).
29. Brokaw, R. S., and D. A. Bittker. "Carbon Monoxide Oxidation Rates Computed for Automobile Exhaust Manifold Reactor Conditions," NASA Technical Note TN-D-7024 (1970).

30. Carlson, C. W., et al. "The Penetration and Mixing of Air Jets Directed Perpendicular to a Stream," paper presented at the American Society of Mechanical Engineers WAM, New York, December 1968.
31. Goel, K. C. "Analysis and Optimum Design of Venturi Scrubbers," Ph.D. Thesis, University of Waterloo, Waterloo, Ontario (April 1975).
32. Ingebo, R. D. "Penetration of Drops into High Velocity Air Streams," NACA TM X-1363 (1966).
33. Rahman, A. A. "Liquid Drops Evaporation in a Jet Penetration in a Hot Cross Flow," presented at the American Society of Mechanical Engineers WAM, New York, December 1979.
34. Le Grives, F. "Mixing Process Induced by the Velocity Associated with the Penetration of a Jet into a Crossflow," *Trans ASME J. Eng. Fluid Power,* (July 1978).
35. Fearn, R., and R. P. Western. "Vortiaty Associated with a Jet in a Crossflow," AIAA Journal, 12:12 (1974).
36. Elkotb, M. M. and N. M. Rafat. "Fuel Spray Trajecting in Diesel Engines," *Trans. ASME, J. Eng.* for Power (April 1978).
37. Levich, V. G. "Physichemical Hydrodynamics," (Englewood Cliffs, NJ: Prentice-Hall, Inc., 1962).
38. Yaron, I., and B. Gal-Or. "Convective Mass Transfer from Size Distributed Drops, Bubbles or Solid Particles," *Int. J. Heat Mass Transfer* (1971).
39. Ranz, W. B., and W. R. Marshall. "Evaporation from Drops," *Chem. Eng. Prog.* 48:141 (1952).
40. Dickerson, R. A., and M. D. Schuman. *J. Space Craft* 2:99 (1956).
41. Williams, A. "Combustion of Droplets of Liquid Fuels: A Review," *Combust. Flame* 21:1 (1973).
42. Wood, B. A. et al. *Combust. Flame,* 4:235 (1960).
43. Shyu, R. R., et al. "Behavior of Combustible Fuel Drops at High Temperature," *Fuel* 51:135 (1972).
44. Faeth, G. M., and R. S. Lazar. *AIAA J.*, 9:2165 (1971).
45. "Control Techniques for Particulate Air Pollution," U.S. National Air Pollution Control Administration, Publication AP-51 (1969).
46. Onuma, Y. and M. Ogasawara. "Studies on the Structure of a Spray Combustion Flame," 15th International Symposium on Combustion, Tokyo, Japan (1974), p. 453.
47. Beer, Y. M., Comment to Ref. 5.
48. William, A., "The Mechanism of Combustion of Droplets and Sprays of Liquid Fuels," *Oxid. Combust. Rev.* 3:1 (1968).
49. Field, M. A., et al. "Combustion of Pulverized Coal," British Coal Utilization Research Assn., Leatherhead, Surrey, England (1967).
50. Kunil, D., and D. Levenspiel. "Fluidization Engineering," (New York: John Wiley & Sons, Inc., 1969).
51. Sass, A. "Simulation of the Heat Transfer Phenomena in a Rotary Kiln," *I&EC Proc. Design* Devel., 4:6 (1967).
52. Imber, M., and V. Paschkis. "A New Theory for a Rotary Kiln Heat Exchanger," *Int. J. Heat Mass Transfer* 5:623 (1962).
53. Weitzman, L. "Scale-up Criterion for Incinerators," Paper No. 80-84, Air Pollution Control Association 73rd Annual Meeting, Montreal, June 1980.

54. Santoleri, J. J. Private correspondence.
55. Kiang, Y. H. "Prevent Shell Corrosion for Chlorinated Hydrocarbon Incineration," paper presented at the Seminar on Corrosion Problems in Air Pollution Control Equipment, Sponsored by APCA, IGCI, and NACE, Atlanta, GA, January 1978.
56. Kiang, Y. H., "Prediction Dewpoints of Acid Gases," *Chem. Eng.*, 88(3):127 (1981).
57. Wall, C. J., et al. "How to Burn Salty Sludges," *Chem. Eng.*, (April 14, 1975), p. 77.
58. C.E. Refractory, Private communication
59. Martin, C. B., and J. S. Boneu. "NO_x Control Overview," paper presented at the International Symposium on NO_x Reduction in Industrial Boilers, Heaters and Furnaces, Houston, TX, October 1979.
60. Bartok, W., and G. M. Varga. "Applicability of the Thermal DeNO_x Process to Coal Fired Utility Boilers," paper presented at the International Symposium on NO_x Reduction in Industrial Boilers, Heaters and Furnaces, Houston, TX, October 1979.
61. Shrader, S. R. "Introducing Mass Spectrometry," (Boston, MA: Allyn and Bacon, Inc., 1971).
62. McFadek, W. H. "Techniques of Combined Gas Chromatography/Mass Spectrometry: Applications in Organic Analysis," (New York: John Wiley and Sons, Inc., 1973).
63. Heller, S. R., et al. "Trace Organics by GC/MS," *Environ. Sci. Technol.* 9:210 (March 1975).
64. "Methods for Chemical Analysis of Water and Wastes," U.S. EPA (1974).
65. *1977 Annual Book of ASTM Standards: Pat 31 Water* (Philadelphia, PA: American Society for Testing and Materials, 1977).
66. Small, J. W. "All About TOC Analysis," *Poll. Eng.* (September 1980), p. 63.
67. Rimberg, D. B. "Sampling Particulate Emissions from Exhaust Stacks," *Plant Eng.* (October 1980), p. 69.
68. Factory Insurance Association (Industrial Risk Insurers). "Recommended Good Practice for Combustion Safeguards on Single Burner Boiler-Furnace," Chicago, ILL (1963).
69. Factory Mutual Engineering, *Handbook of Industrial Loss Prevention,* 2nd ed. (New York: McGraw-Hill Book Company, 1967).
70. National Fire Protection Association. "NFPA No. 66," Boston, MA.

CHAPTER 6

THERMAL INCINERATION PERIPHERAL SYSTEMS

As described in Chapter 3, modern incineration systems include not only incinerators for waste disposal, but also energy and by-product recovery systems, as well as air and water pollution control systems. These peripheral systems are now designed as an integrated part of incineration systems.

HEAT RECOVERY

Incineration is an energy-intensive process in which an appreciable amount of waste heat is generated. Wastes to be incinerated fall into two broad categories: (1) rich wastes, those with high enough heating values to be burned like fuel and (2) lean wastes, those that require auxiliary fuel to maintain incineration chamber temperature.

There are two different approaches in heat recovery [1]. For both rich and lean wastes, heat can be recovered for process plant use. For lean wastes, heat also can be conserved by reducing the fuel required for incineration.

Process plants can make use of wasted heat from incineration systems in various ways. Modes of heat recovery and typical in-plant usage are illustrated in Table 6-1.

Heat Recovery Arrangement for Process Plant Usages

Typical block diagrams for rich waste incineration with waste heat recovery are illustrated in Figure 6-1. Typical heat transfer equipment

Table 6-1. Mode of Heat Recovery

Mode of Heat Recovery	In-Plant Uses
Hot Water Heating	Boiler feedwater Building heat supplement Washing water Process water
Process Fluid Heating	Process heat supplement
Steam Generation	Process heat supplement Building heat supplement
Air Heating	Make-up air Process air
Process Gas Heating	Process heat supplement
Heat Transfer Oil Heating	Process heat supplement
Cryogenic Fluid Vaporization	Process heat supplement

types are gas-to-gas heat exchanger, gas-to-liquid heat exchanger, boiler, condensing type heat exchanger and direct-contact heat exchanger. The selection of heat recovery mode depends on the characteristics of the application; the process plant requirement, and economic considerations.

The location of the incineration system related to the process plant is critical if waste heat is to be recovered. Insulation requirements and heat losses have to be considered as factors in site selection.

Another inherent problem is timing. Incineration systems usually are operated continuously. However, heat requirement has peaks and valleys. Thus, a systematic approach is needed for process plant energy management [1].

Energy Management for Lean Waste Incineration

Two types of heat recovery approaches can be used for lean waste incineration: for process plant usage, and for incineration fuel requirement. The latter is discussed in this section.

For gaseous wastes, fuel can be reduced through air preheating, waste gas preheating or a combination of both (Figure 6-2). When waste gas preheating is used, special care must be taken to avoid ignition of waste gases in the recuperator and interconnecting ducts.

To minimize fuel requirement for solid and liquid wastes, the water content of the wastes must be reduced. Illustrated in Table 6-2 is the en-

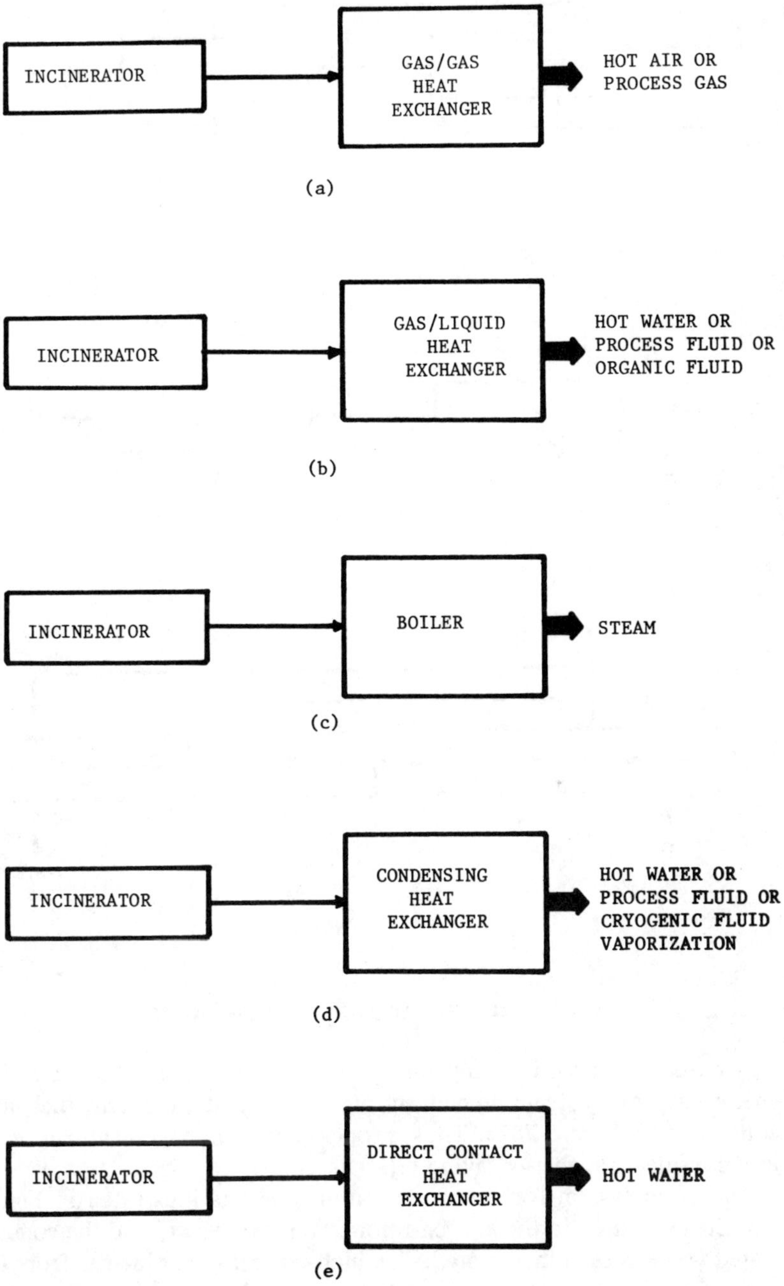

Figure 6-1. Heat recovery arrangement for rich waste incineration.

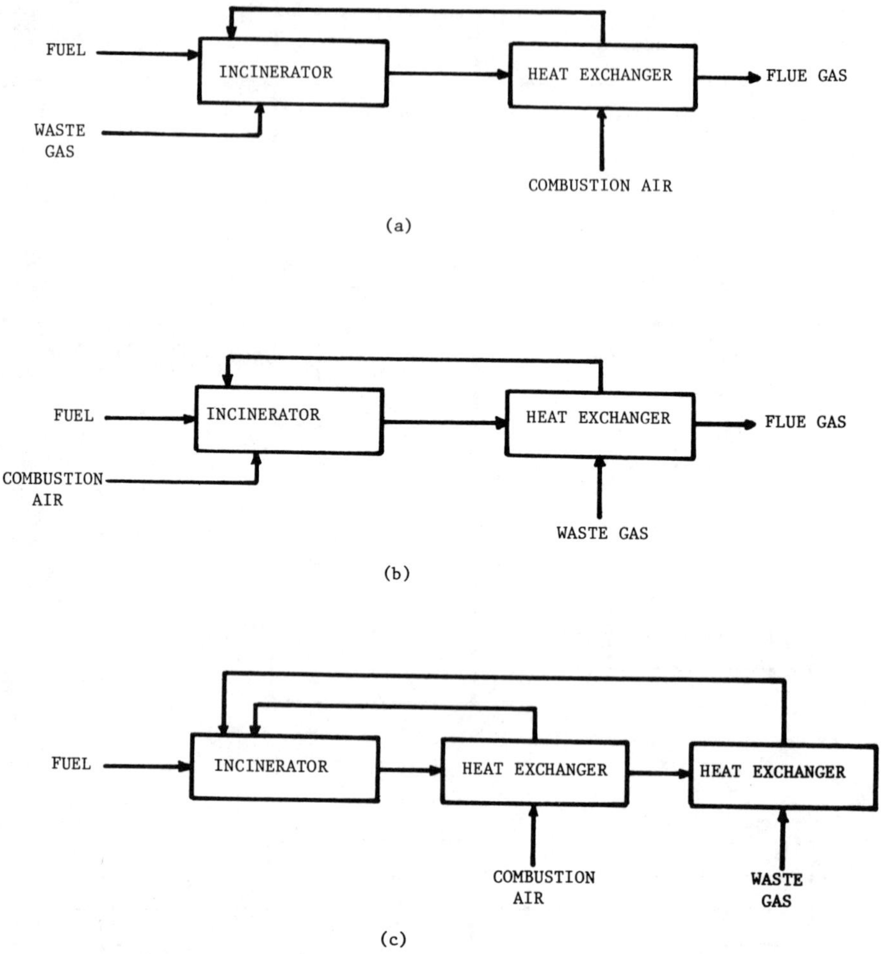

Figure 6-2. Heat recovery for waste gas incineration.

ergy requirement for incineration of a waste containing 95% water. The energy savings by steam preconcentrate on the waste, reducing the water content to 85%, is >70%. Thus, proper energy management can result in a considerable energy saving [2].

The basic system for preconcentrating waste is illustrated in Figure 6-3. Steam is used in the concentrator to remove water, and the concentrated waste is then incinerated. The high-temperature flue gas from the incinerator can then be used in a waste heat boiler or other heat transfer equipment for heat recovery.

Table 6-2. Energy Management Study [2]

	Energy Requirement (Btu/lb waste)		
	Fuel	Steam	Total
Case 1[a]	3150	0	3150
Total			3150
Case 2[b]			
Concentration	0	800	800
Incineration	100	0	100
Total			900

[a]Basis: waste containing 95% water, 5% organics; incineration temperature = 1800°F.
[b]Preconcentration from 95% water to 85% water.

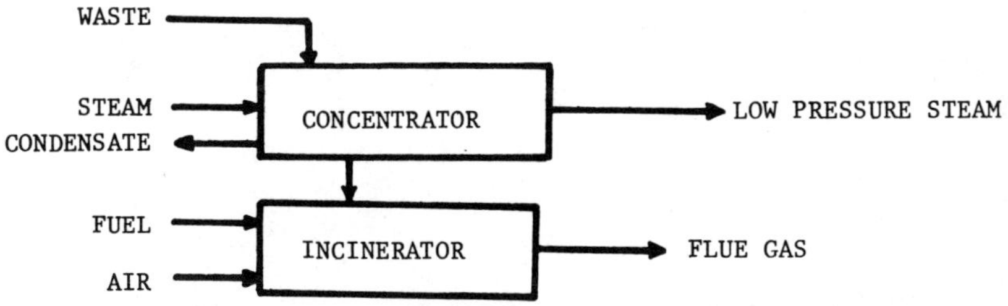

Figure 6-3. Energy management for lean waste incineration.

Depending on the constituents in the waste, the low-pressure steam coming out of the concentrator may or may not require further treatment. If the waste contains no volatile compounds, the low-pressure steam either can be used as plant steam or can be condensed and discharged. If the waste contains volatile organic compounds, further treatment of the contaminated low-pressure waste steam is required. It can be condensed and treated in a biological treatment plant or treated by incineration. Typical waste steam incineration systems are illustrated in Figure 6-4.

An alternative waste preconcentration scheme is illustrated in Figure 6-5. In this system, heat generated by incineration is used to evaporate water from the waste. The low-pressure steam can be either discharged or treated in systems described in Figure 6-4.

Water in the waste also can be removed by air stripping (see Figure 6-6). The saturated air, together with any organic compounds, can be

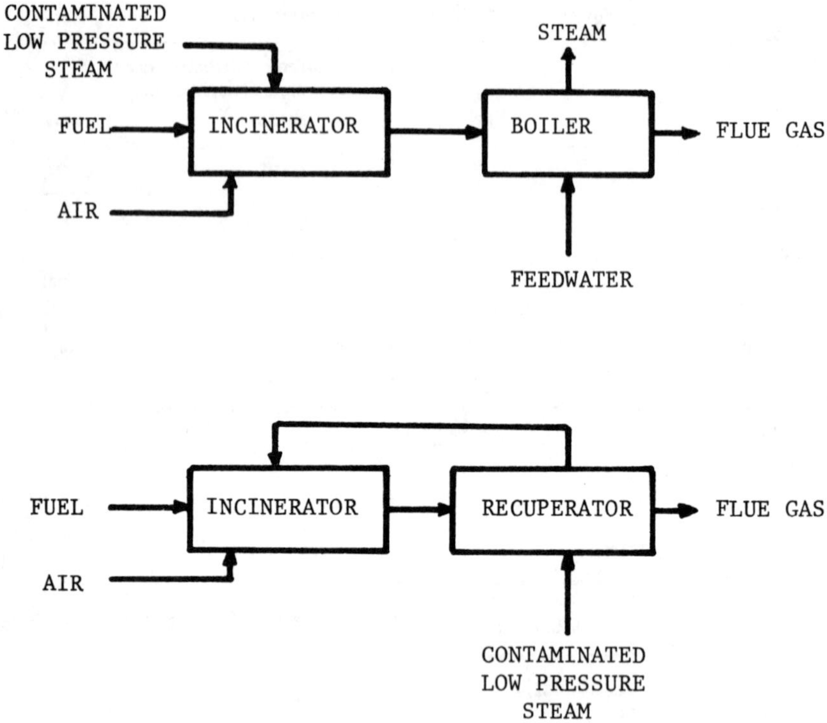

Figure 6-4. Energy management for low volatile control.

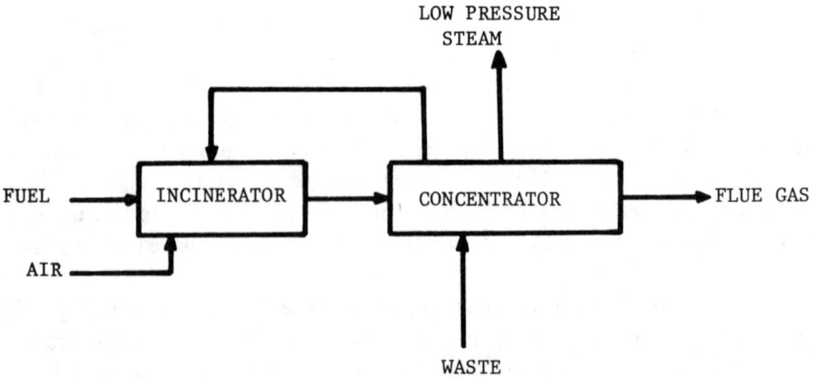

Figure 6-5. Energy management for lean waste with low melting point ash and without low volatiles.

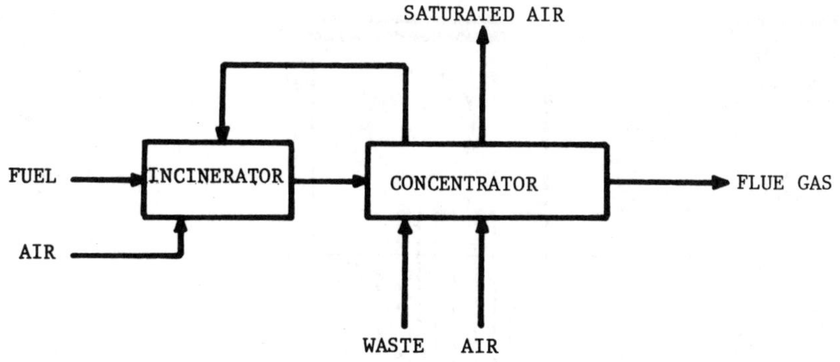

Figure 6-6. Energy management for lean waste with low melting point ash and with low volatiles.

used as combustion air for the incinerator or can be disposed of by fume incineration.

Waste Heat Boiler for Specific Waste Application

At the present time, carbon steel waste heat boiler applications are limited to specific wastes and are highly sensitive to the chemistry of the waste material; corrosion is a major problem.

For chlorinated hydrocarbon incineration, carbon steel fire tube boilers are used successfully; a typical boiler for this application is illustrated in Figure 6-7. This type of waste heat boiler usually has an external steam drum.

Since hydrogen chloride exists in the combustion flue gases, the important design feature of a boiler for chlorinated hydrocarbon applications is to maintain the boiler tube wall temperature to avoid hydrogen chloride high-temperature attack and low-temperature condensation [3]. A carbon steel boiler is satisfactory for a chlorinated hydrocarbon incineration application provided that (1) the tube is kept clean; (2) the metal temperature is maintained in the 400–500°F range; (3) the boiler is purged during shutdown and (4) the combustion system is designed to keep chlorine formation at a minimum. Without deposits on tube surfaces, corrosion of the carbon steel tubes by hydrogen chloride in the flue gas is negligible unless the metal temperature is >600°F. If the flue gases contain ash and there is an ash deposit on the tube surface, free chlorine can be formed from hydrogen chloride under the influence of catalysts in

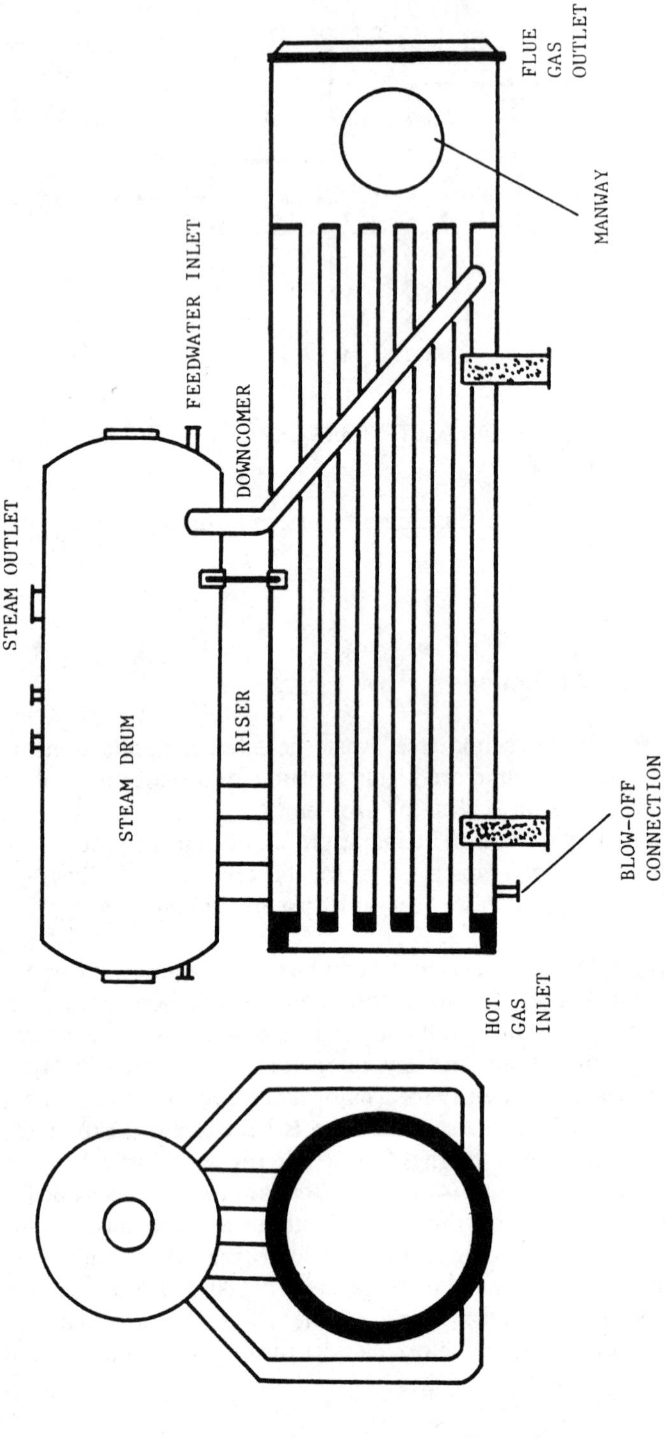

Figure 6-7. Waste heat boiler for chlorinated organic waste incineration (reproduced from Reference 1, courtesy of Marcel Dekker, NY).

the deposit. The free chlorine then will react with the tubes to start corrosion at a moderate metal temperature. If the deposit is not removed before boiler shutdown, it serves as a sponge to collect the condensate, and low-temperature acid corrosion cannot be avoided. Moreover, high concentrations of chlorine in flue gases are also harmful to boiler tubes. Thus, chlorine must be minimized by combustion process adjustment as described in Chapter 5. If the tube metal temperature is maintained in the 400–500°F range, the flue gas temperature at the tube wall will still be far above the dewpoint. In order to achieve desirable metal temperature ranges, the pressure within the boiler should be between 200 and 500 psig.

Purging the flue gas from the boiler tubes during shutdown will help protect the tubes. Corrosive gases are removed from the tubes before the tube metal temperature drops below the dewpoint of the gas. In the present state of the art, the maximum inlet flue gas temperature for the chlorinated hydrocarbon waste heat recovery boiler is 2200°F. This limitation is required to ensure trouble-free tube sheets. This low temperature can be achieved by cooling the flue gas through the injection of water or steam, or through flue gas recycling. The introduction of a cooling medium will decrease the steam generation rate. Flue gas recycling has no effect on steam generation; however, it requires a larger boiler and a compressor for hot, acid-laden gases. Attempts have been made to use exotic alloys as tube material. To do this, one must study the expansion effect to avoid overstressing in the tubes, shell or tube sheets.

There are no known applications for carbon steel boilers with respect to halogens other than chlorine. There have been unsuccessful attempts to use carbon steel boilers with phosphoric-acid-laden flue gases. The dewpoint of the phosphoric acid vapor can be as high as 850°F.

For wastes containing metallic compounds, boiler conditions must be studied in detail. The flue gas temperature has to be kept below the melting point of the metallic compounds to prevent sticky particle deposition on the heat transfer surfaces. For solid particles, soot blowers generally are required. For molten particles, it is necessary to reduce the flue gas temperature to solidify the particles before introducing them into the boiler. Enough residence time is needed to allow complete particle solidification. For example, when sodium salts exit in the flue gas, the "sticky" temperature is between 1200 and 1350°F. Thus, cooling is required to lower the temperature to <1200°F, and a refractory-lined chamber becomes necessary to provide time for sodium salts to solidify (Figure 6-8). Water tube boilers are the most logical choice for this type of application. Soot blowers are required to clean the shell side periodically.

The salt cooling chamber is the critical element in heat recovery for

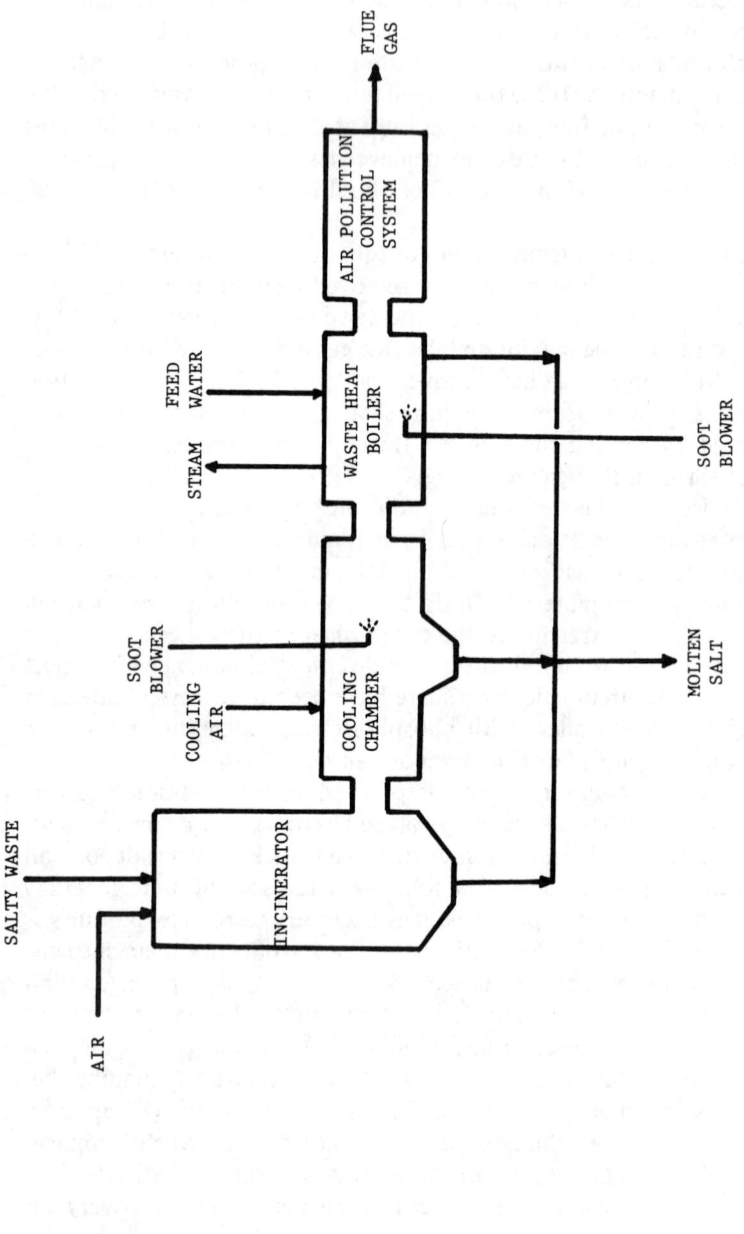

Figure 6-8. Waste heat recovery for alkali waste incineration.

alkali-containing waste incineration. The cooling chamber provides a cooling medium to reduce incinerator flue gas temperature below the solidification temperature. It also provides enough residence time for the molten salt particle to be completely solidified. Both temperature and time are critical design parameters. If insufficient time is allowed, the salt particles will solidify outside and melt inside. When the salt particles hit the boiler tubes, the solid shell will break and the molten salts will stick on the boiler tubes. The cooling medium of the salt cooling chamber can be radiant cooling, recycle flue gas cooling, air and water cooling.

When there are mixed salts in the incinerator flue gases, eutectic compounds are usually formed that have a lower melting point than pure compounds. This effect can be observed through the melting point of $Na_2CO_3-Na_2SO_4$, $NaCl-Na_2CO_3$, and $NaCl-NO_2SO_4$ systems (as presented in Figures 4-11-4-13, later in this section). Thus, care must be taken when evaluating the melting point of the salts generated through incineration [4].

A typical water tube boiler for high solid loading application is illustrated in Figure 6-9, a Deltak DERVISH boiler [5]. In this design, only the heat exchanger is in the potentially corrosive gas stream. The expensive steam drums are outside the system. The heat exchanger is in sections, each of which may be removed individually by lifting upward through the opened roof. The tubes are bare. Square pitch provides straight gas lanes for operation and for soot blowing. The vertical lanes are straight too, so that solids can drop clear to the bottom hoppers. Dust build-up on a drum, as it occurs in conventional designs, is eliminated because the mud drum is outside the gas stream. Suspended tubes vibrate and provide a self-cleaning mechanism. Soot blowers would use air only; steam might condense and should be avoided.

Recovery of waste heat through the use of steam boilers has become a fairly common practice in the industrial community. One effect of using waste heat boilers is to replace some existing plant boiler duty, which in turn results in energy savings. If the process plant does not have an existing steam generation facility, the additional cost of a boiler feedwater treatment system has to be included in the economic evaluation.

Boiler Corrosion Mechanism

The discussion above is centered on waste heat boiler applications for specific wastes only. When a boiler is required for general purpose incineration, the boiler design becomes more complicated. In this section, the corrosion mechanism of boilers is discussed. Understanding of the boiler

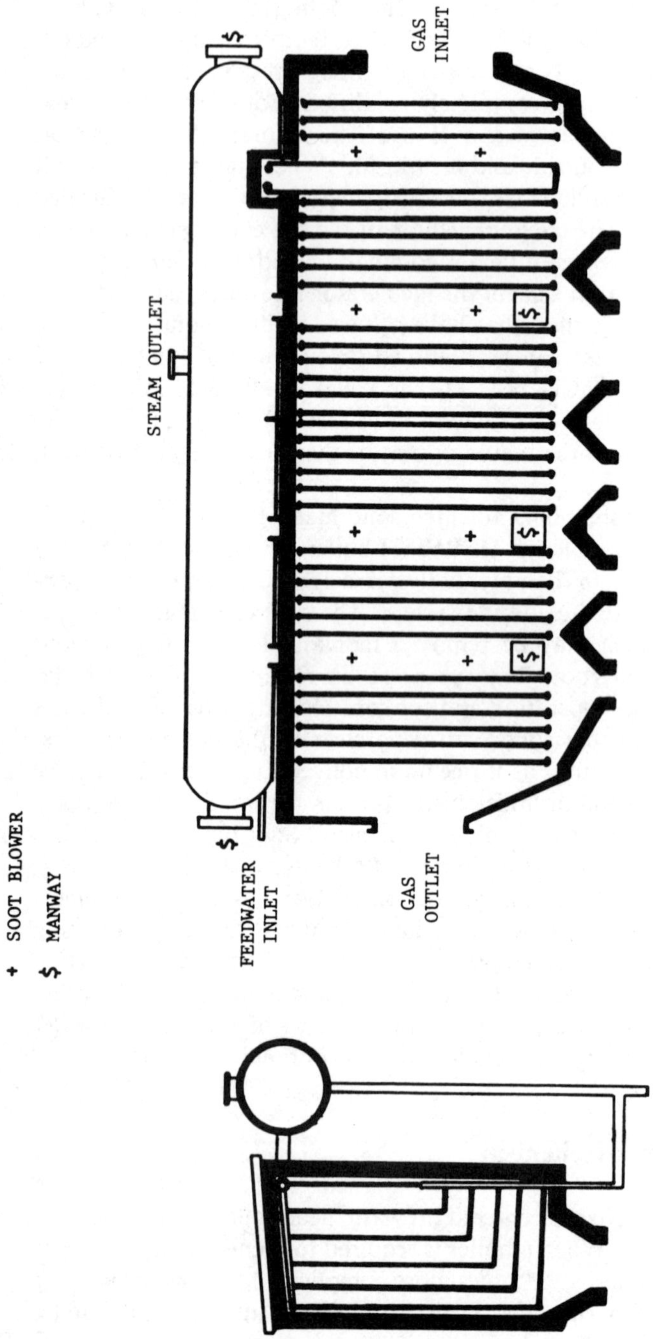

Figure 6-9. Waste heat boiler for high solid loading flue gases (reproduced, courtesy of Deltak Corp., Minneapolis, MN).

corrosion mechanism is an important step in the design of a waste heat boiler for incineration applications.

The causes of boiler corrosion are the presence of chlorine compounds, sulfur compounds and particles in the incinerator flue gases [6]. Hydrogen chloride is produced by the following mechanisms:

1. burning of chlorinated hydrocarbon in the incinerator,
2. hydrolysis of alkali chlorides at temperature starting around 750°F ($2NaCl + H_2O \rightarrow Na_2O + 2HCl$) and
3. reaction between acid sulfates and alkali chlorides at temperature starting around 400°F.

Chlorine is formed by the following catalytic reaction at low temperature:

$$2HCl + 1/2O_2 \underset{4}{\overset{480\text{–}930°F,\ catalyst}{\rightleftarrows}} Cl_2 + H_2O$$

The actual course of corrosion is explained as follows. Ash from the incinerator deposits on the boiler tube. If the ash contains alkali chlorides and sulfates, trace metals in the ash act as catalysts to promote reaction processes described above. Also, hydrogen chloride and water vapor are absorbed by the ash deposits. Chloride in the incinerator flue gases either is formed through catalytic reaction or is absorbed by the ash deposits.

Hydrogen chloride and chlorine are then diffused through the ash deposits to the tube surface, where they can react with the surface oxides and metals of the boiler tubes to form iron chlorides at temperatures between 660 and 750°F. Because of the low tube temperature, the reaction is possibly a hydrolysis process. The iron chloride diffuses toward regions of higher temperature in the tube deposit and is decomposed to iron oxides, gaseous hydrogen chloride and chlorine, which will then start the corrosion process again. The process of hydrogen chloride and chlorine corrosion is illustrated in Figure 6-10 [6].

Although large quantities of hydrogen chloride can be formed in incinerators, the corrosion of boiler tubes cannot be ascribed to this corrosion mechanism alone. Sulfate corrosion is another very important mechanism.

The phenomena of sulfate corrosion are observed primarily in coal-fired boilers and have been described in the literature [6]. Nelson and Cairn [7,8] described a sufate corrosion mechanism and showed that the formation of alkali-iron sulfates is responsible for the corrosion. Although these investigations were carried out on coal-fired boilers, the results explain the corrosion of incinerator-boiler systems, since a complete

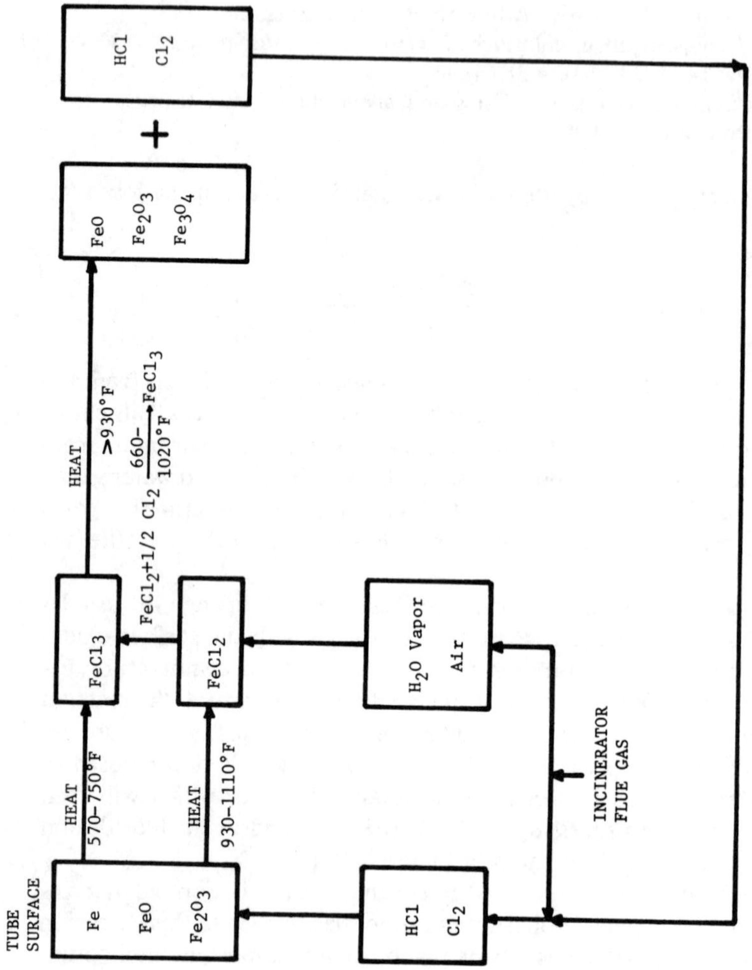

Figure 6-10. Hydrogen chloride and chlorine corrosion mechanism [6].

dissociation of the alkali salts at flame conditions is independent of the materials to be burned.

The basic corrosion reaction is

$$3Fe + 2O_2 \xrightarrow[1020\text{–}1290^\circ F]{\text{alkali-iron sulfate}} Fe_3O_4$$

that is, only a small amount of alkali-iron sulfates is necessary to produce a major corrosive attack.

The detailed mechanisms are:

1. In the incinerator flue gas, alkali oxides react with sulfur trioxide to form alkali sulfates.

$$K_2O + SO_3 \rightarrow K_2SO_4$$

2. At temperature between 600 and 900°F, alkali pyrosulfates form, then react with iron oxide to form complex alkali-iron sulfates.

$$3K_2SO_4 + 3SO_3 \xrightarrow{600\text{–}900^\circ F} 3K_2S_2O_7$$

$$Fe_2O_3 + 3K_2S_2O_7 \longrightarrow 2K_2Fe(SO_4)_3$$

3. The alkali-iron sulfates then react with tube materials and form iron oxides.

$$Fe + K_3Fe(SO_4)_3 \xrightarrow{1020\text{–}1290^\circ F} Fe_2O_3 + K_2SO_4 + FeS$$

   This is an oxidation-reduction reaction in which the iron of the tube materials reduces the sulfate radical to sulfide, and the iron is oxidized to iron oxide.

4. The sulfide formation is only an intermediate step with oxygen and sulfur dioxide in the flue gas; the complex sulfate formation is again possible.

$$3FeS + 5O_2 \rightarrow 3SO_2 + Fe_3O_4$$

$$SO_2 + 1/2O_2 \rightarrow SO_3$$

This closes the corrosion loop. The corrosion mechanism is illustrated in Figure 6-11.

The presence of alkali salts is not a prerequisite for tube wall corrosion. A direct attack on the iron by sulfur or sulfur dioxide at temperatures prevailing in the boiler is possible (Figure 6-12).

Thus, at the tube wall temperature, a pure sulfur oxide corrosion is possible. However, the corrosion attack is amplified with the presence of alkali sulfate or chloride.

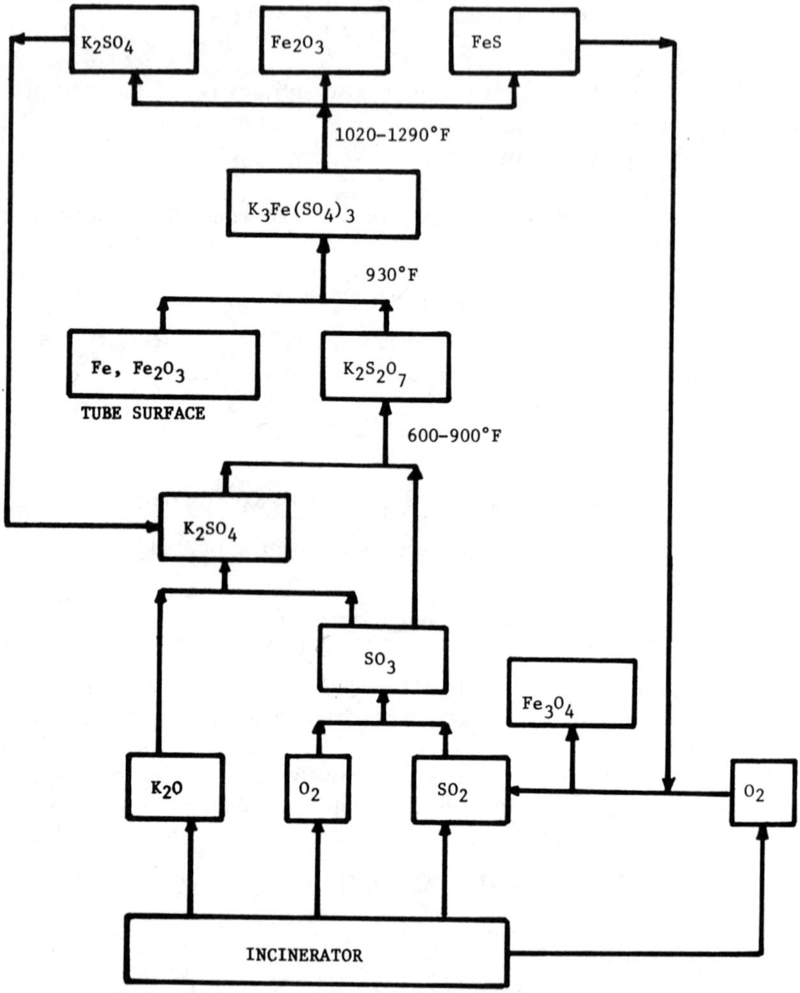

Figure 6-11. Sulfate corrosion mechanism [6].

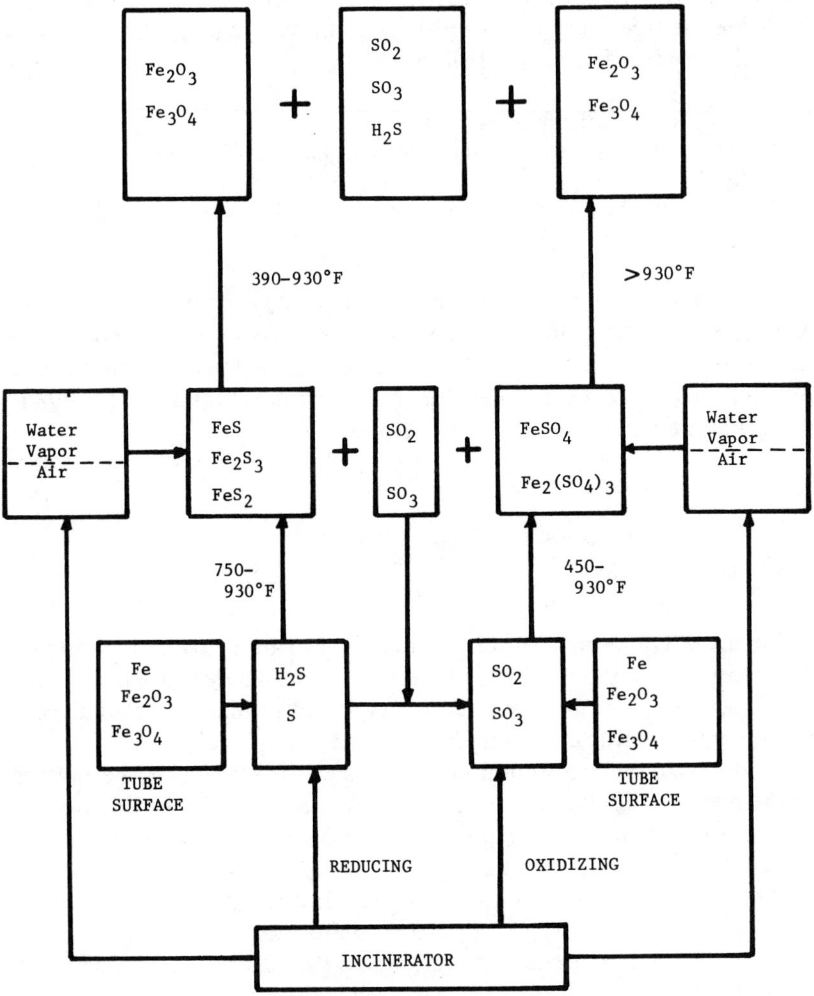

Figure 6-12. Sulfur corrosion mechanism [6].

In summary, the severity of corrosion attack in a waste heat boiler is determined primarily by the tube wall temperature, the temperature gradients between the flue gas and the tube wall, and the chemistry of incinerator flue gases. Below the dewpoint of the flue gases, an electrochemical corrosive attack (acid corrosion) occurs. Above a critical temperature, high temperature corrosion begins. In this region, three types of corrosion mechanisms are possible.

1. corrosion via the pure gas phase,
2. corrosion as a result of iron chloride or alkali-iron sulfate formation, and
3. corrosion as a result of iron chloride or alkali-iron sulfate decomposition.

For practical applications, the corrosion mechanism can be studied by analysis of deposits. However, the components found in the deposits are the result and residue of reactions that have previously taken place in service; thus, prediction of the chemical reaction is required with fundamental and advanced chemical principles.

Alkali Waste Incinerator/Waste Heat Recovery Systems

For alkali-containing waste, waste heat can be recovered through a waste heat boiler as described in Figure 6-8. Alternative waste heat recovery systems also can be used. Those developed primarily for alkali containing aqueous wastes [9] are discussed here.

To minimize fuel consumption, aqueous waste can be preconcentrated before introduction into the incinerator. Waste heat in the incinerator exhaust gas can be used as the preconcentration medium. Three basic preconcentration schemes can be used.

The first makes use of a Sub-X® direct contact concentrator as illustrated in Figure 6-13. The incinerator exhaust gas bypasses the quench tank and feed into the concentrator, where the hot gases are cooled and the heat contained in the gases is used to evaporate water from the waste. This system makes use of a direct contact evaporator, eliminating the possibility of heat transfer surfaces fouling. This system is not applicable to waste containing high vapor pressure organics.

The second type makes use of a condensing type evaporator (see Figure 6-14). In the evaporator, water saturated exhaust gas from the quench tank is cooled and water vapor is condensed. The heat released

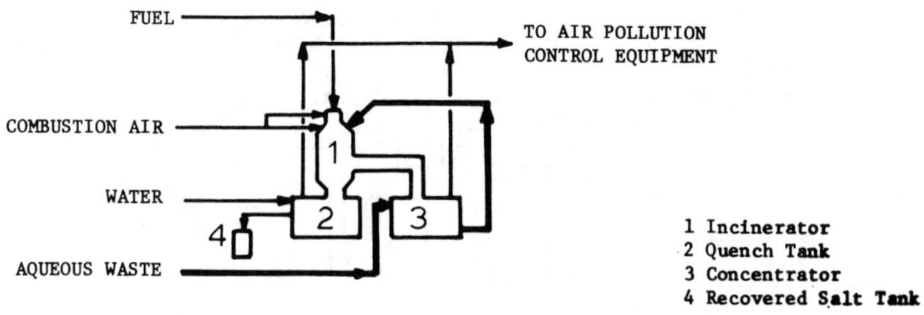

Figure 6-13. Aqueous waste preconcentration through the Sub-X® concentrator (reproduced from Reference 9, courtesy of Chemical Engineering Progress, NY).

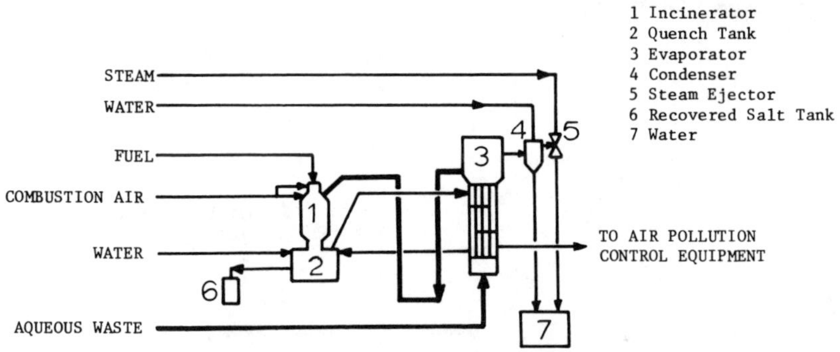

Figure 6-14. Aqueous waste preconcentration through the evaporator (reproduced from Reference 9, courtesy of Chemical Engineering Progress, NY).

by the condensed water vapor is transferred to the incoming aqueous waste. A vacuum is maintained to evaporate water from the waste. A double-effect evaporator can also be used, as illustrated in Figure 6-15.

The third type, Figure 6-16, is used for waste liquids containing large percentages of volatile organics. Liquid waste is preheated in the same manner as in the second type. A stripping tower removes volatile materials which are then oxidized in the incinerator. Combustion air is the stripping medium.

These three preconcentration schemes can be used individually or in combination. The system illustrated in Figure 6-17 is a version of a combination of two evaporators and one Sub-X® concentrator to concentrate highly dilute aqueous waste.

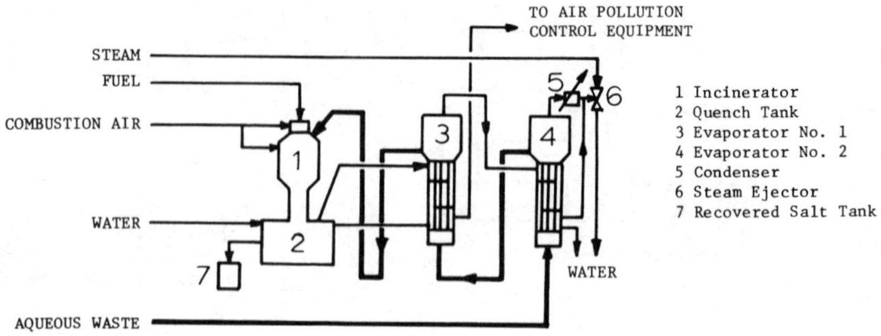

Figure 6-15. Aqueous waste preconcentration through the double-effect evaporator (reproduced from Reference 9, courtesy of Chemical Engineering Progress, NY).

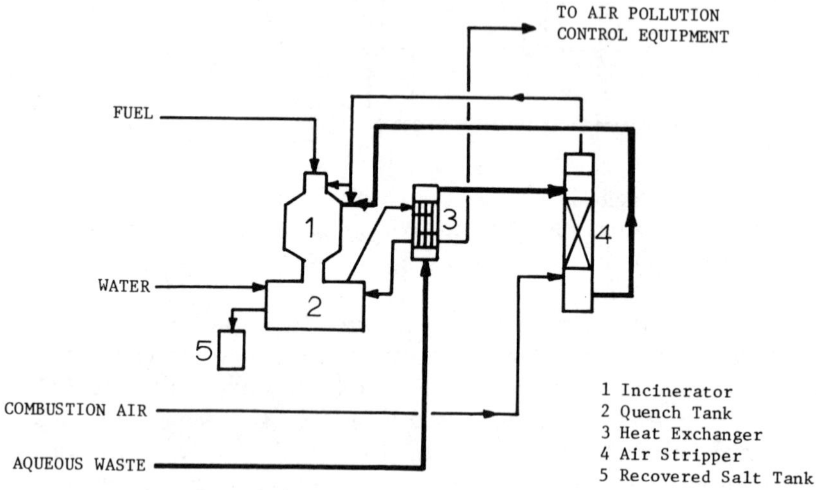

Figure 6-16. Aqueous waste preconcentration through air stripper (reproduced from Reference 9, courtesy of Chemical Engineering Progress, NY).

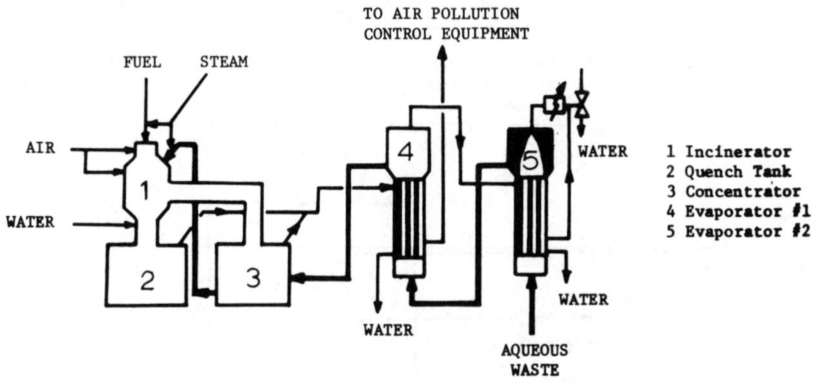

Figure 6-17. A combination waste preconcentration scheme (reproduced from Reference 9, courtesy of Chemical Engineering Progress, NY).

Waste preconcentration is one form of heat recovery. In another form, using the same type of heat exchange devices mentioned above, waste heat can be used to concentrate or crystallize the salt product of the system. Thus, salt solution or crystals of a high concentration and purity can be produced from this system for process plant reuse or sale. The waste heat also can be used to heat process fluid, and to concentrate or crystallize process chemicals (Figure 6-18).

The heat exchange device used in this system is different from conventional exchangers, which use steam or hot gas as the heating medium. The heating media are the saturated gases at a temperature between 180 and 200°F.

To make use of this heat, the exchangers are designed to lower the temperature of the gas and thus condense the water vapor. The heat available from one pound of saturated air by decreasing the temperature from 190 to 180°F is equivalent to the heat released by reducing the temperature of one pound of hot dry air by 850°F. Since the temperature is relatively low, evaporation must be carried out under reduced pressure, and the heat transfer surface requirement is relatively large. The heat exchanger design must take into consideration the condensing in the presence of noncondensibles.

BY-PRODUCT RECOVERY

As incineration technology evolves, a modern incineration system performs not only the waste disposal function, but also resource recovery,

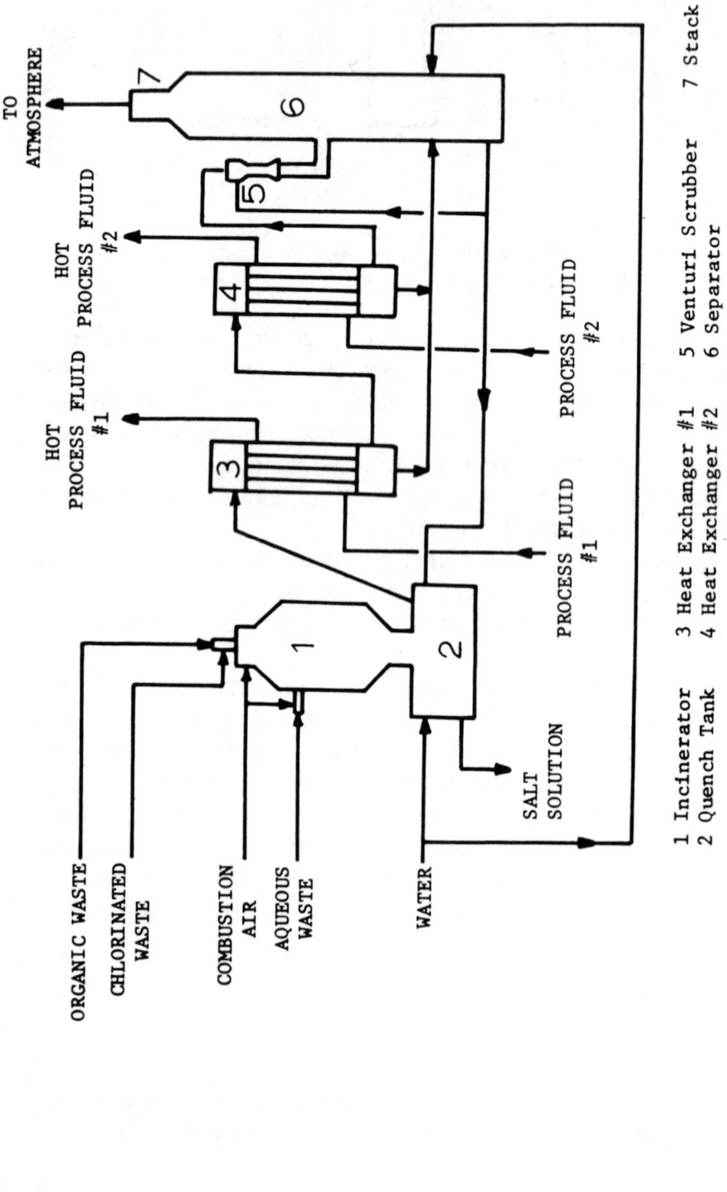

Figure 6-18. An integrated waste disposal/heat recovery plant (reproduced from Reference 9, courtesy of Chemical Engineering Progress, NY).

such as heat and by-product recovery. Heat recovery is the subject of the previous section. In this section, by-product recovery is presented.

HYDROCHLORIC ACID RECOVERY

Chlorinated hydrocarbon waste constitutes a large proportion of industrial wastes [10]. As described in Chapter 5, the product of the incineration of chlorinated hydrocarbons contains hydrochloric acid gas. Thus, recovery of commercially usable hydrochloric acid is possible. In this case, the incineration plant is actually a production plant for hydrochloric acid where chlorinated hydrocarbon wastes are the raw material.

Because of the heat content in the incinerator flue gases, it is difficult to recover hydrochloric acid at a concentration greater than the azeotropic mixture (20% by weight of hydrogen chloride). A typical hydrochloric acid recovery system is illustrated in Figure 6-19. Here, the quench and scrubbing tower (shown in Figure 5-39) is divided into two stages: (1) the cooling section where incinerator flue gases are cooled, using concentrated hydrochloric acid and (2) an absorber where 20%

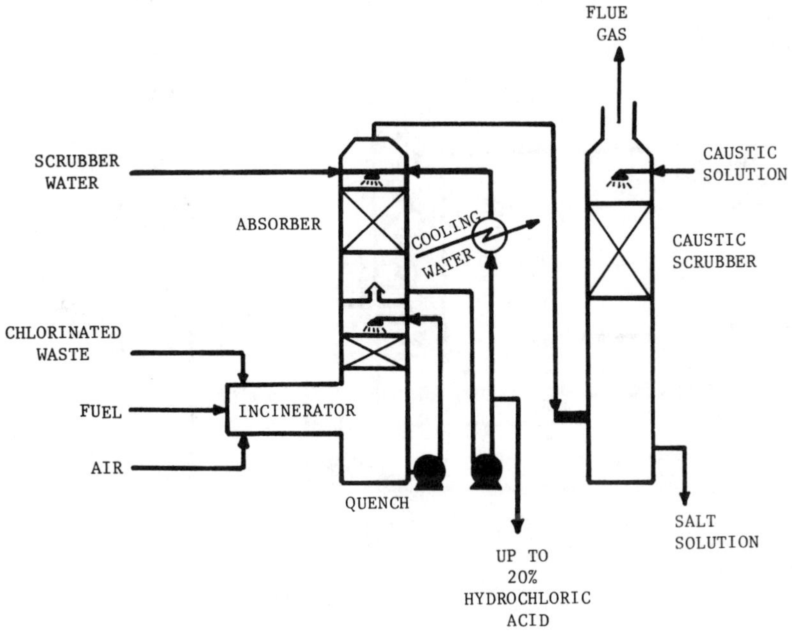

Figure 6-19. Basic hydrochloric acid recovery system (20% by weight) (reproduced courtesy of The Trane Company, La Cross, WI).

hydrochloric acid is produced. The requirement of the cooling heat exchanger is dependent on the acid content of the system and the heat content of the flue gases. An alternative system (Figure 6-20) also can be used. In this arrangement, the dilute acid coming out of the second stage is concentrated in the first stage. Up to 20% hydrochloric acid also can be recovered by using the system described in Figure 6-21, with or without the recycle and heat exchanger.

In order to recover hydrochloric acid at a higher concentration than the azeotropic composition from chlorinated hydrocarbon incineration, several proprietary systems are available.

In a system developed by Nittetu Chemical Engineering of Tokyo, Japan, an extractive distillation process is used in combination with the Sub-X® system [10] for transferring heat from the incinerator exhaust gases by the direct contact of the gases with the solvent, such as calcium chloride or sulfuric acid. The combination of the Sub-X® system and the extractive distillation tower provides a method for reaching hydrochloric acid concentration >60%. The waste heat is used to reconcentrate the solvent before use in the extractive distillation tower, thereby eliminating the need for a separate reheater.

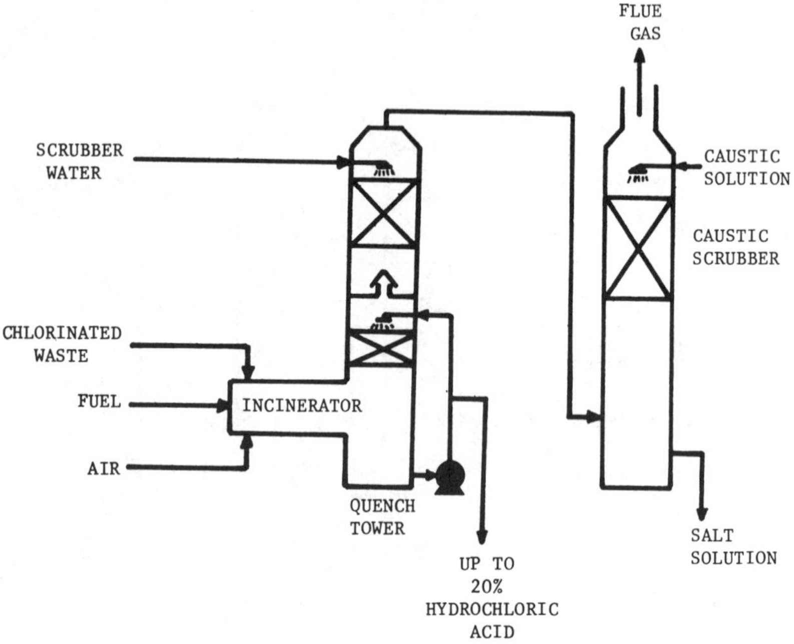

Figure 6-20. Alternative hydrochloric acid recovery system (20% by weight) (reproduced courtesy of The Trane Company, La Crosse, WI).

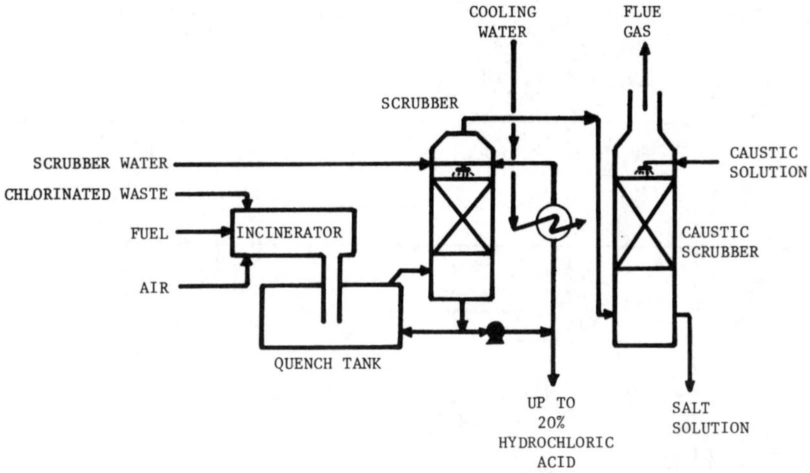

Figure 6-21. Sub-X® hydrochloric acid recovery system (reproduced courtesy of The Trane Company, La Crosse, WI).

Systems that can be used for recovery of concentrated hydrochloric acid are illustrated in Figures 6-22 and 6-23. Figure 6-22 shows the recovery of 35% acid and Figure 6-23 shows the recovery of anhydrous hydrogen chloride. In either case, the system described in Figure 6-21 is the basic system except that the quench liquid in the Sub-X® tank is the water solution of the stripping solvent. For 35% acid, the dilute hydrochloric acid from the absorption tower and the concentrated solvent solution from the quench tank are fed to the extractive distillation tower top. A sufficient amount of heat is then supplied through the reboiler installed in the bottom of the tower to permit hydrochloric acid vapor at ~60% concentration to be distilled from the top of the tower. The acid thus generated is sent to the water-cooled condenser where it is condensed and absorbed by adding water to reach the 35% concentration. When this system is used, a mist separator is installed between the Sub-X® tank and the absorption tower. This prevents any carryover of the concentrated solvent into the absorption tower. The extractive distillation tower can be a packed tower. Its shell is constructed of rubber-lined steel with acidproof brick or impregnated graphite carbon.

In order to produce anhydrous hydrogen chloride, the overhead vapor leaving the extractive distillation column is cooled through water condensers and eventually through brine coolers to ~14°F.

Illustrated in Figure 6-24 is the UCAR hydrogen chloride recovery system [11]. The combustion product gas from the incinerator, contain-

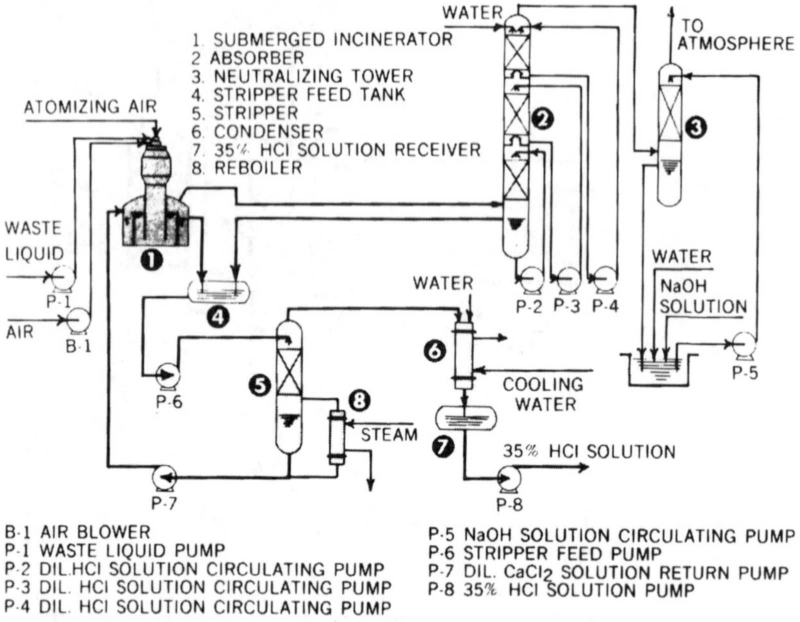

Figure 6-22. Nittetu hydrochloric acid recovery system (35% by weight) (reproduced from Reference 10, courtesy of Chemical Engineering Progress, NY).

ing as little as 3% by volume of hydrogen chloride, is sprayed with filtered product hydrochloric acid, reducing the temperature from 3000 to 700®F. These vapors then are fed to the primary falling film absorber. At the bottom of the primary absorber, 27% hydrochloric acid is discharged to the strong acid intermediate storage tank. The gas discharging from the bottom of the primary absorber still contains unabsorbed hydrogen chloride. This gas is fed to the secondary falling film absorber, and its hydrogen chloride content is further reduced by absorption in the dilute acid which comes from the tertiary absorber. The gas from the secondary absorber is taken to the tertiary falling film absorber for similar scrubbing. The liquid make-up to the tertiary absorber can be fresh water, very dilute acid or 21% acid from a stripper (if anhydrous gas is being generated) or a combination of these. The vent scrubber is a packed column designed to remove the last traces of hydrogen chloride and chlorine from the gas stream.

When anhydrous hydrogen chloride is desired, the 27% acid made in the absorption equipment is fed to a conventional packed column stripper. A reboiler and bottom acid cooler are required to provide heat

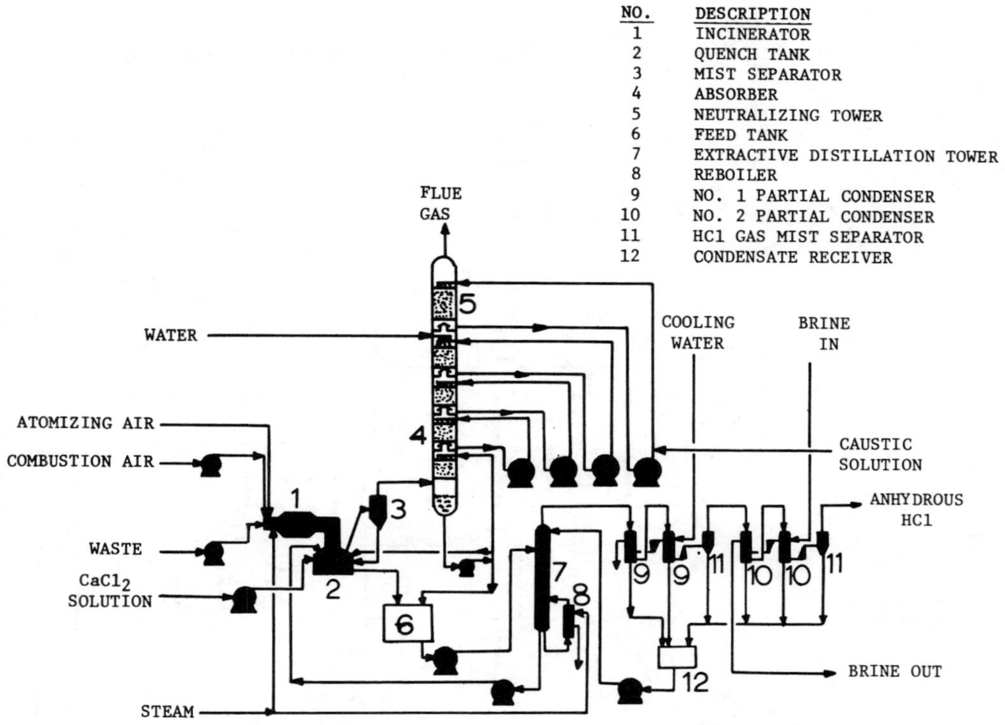

Figure 6-23. Nittetu anhydrous hydrochloric acid recovery system (reproduced from Reference 10, courtesy of Chemical Engineering Progress, NY).

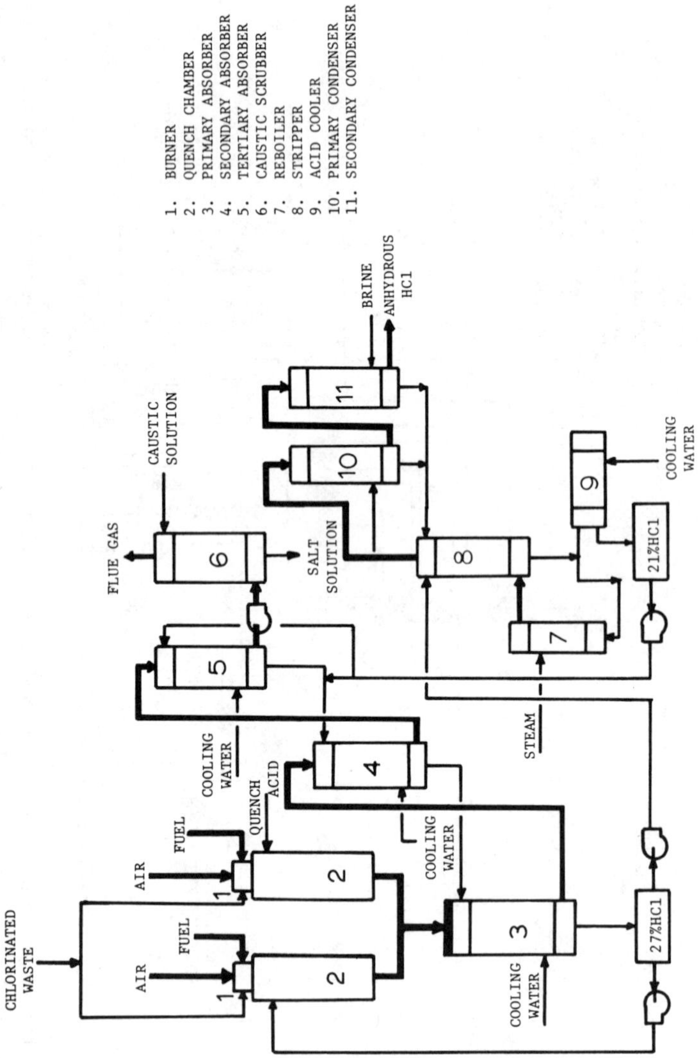

Figure 6-24. UCAR hydrochloric acid recovery system [11] (reproduced, courtesy of Union Carbide Corporation, Cleveland, OH).

for stripping and cooling of the azeotropic acid. The cooled azeotropic acid is recycled to the absorption system to pick up another load of hydrogen chloride which is then processed in the stripping system.

Vapors generated in the stripper are 75–80% hydrogen chloride and are fed to a water-cooled condenser which increases the gas concentration to ~99% HCl. Condensate formed in this condenser is 35–40% hydrochloric acid and is returned to the stripping column. The 99% HCl vapor is processed in a refrigerated condenser where the gas temperature is lowered to ~10®F and the moisture content reduced to <50 ppm.

The material of construction for the falling film absorbers, the stripper reboilers, bottom acid cooler, the two stripper overhead condensers and the transfer pump is "Karbate" impervious graphite. The quench chamber is monolithic graphite and the duct from the quench chamber to the primary absorber is "Karbate". Other than this duct, interconnecting process piping and vapor ducts can be plastic, lined steel or fiberglass reinforced plastics (FRP).

There are other HCl recovery processes, such as the Rhone Poulenc system shown in Figure 6-25 [12].

Acid Recovery

Acids other than hydrochloric acid also can be recovered from an incineration system. For example, the system illustrated in Figure 6-19 has been used to recover hydrobromic acid. Phosphoric acid also can be recovered by system described in Figure 6-26.

As a general rule, if the acid in the flue gas is in a gaseous state, an absorption tower is used for acid recovery. If the acid is in mist or solid form, a venturi scrubber is used for acid recovery.

Salt and Metal Recovery

The basic system described in Figure 6-14 can be used to recover salt and metals, such as 15% soda ash solution. This type of system is especially suitable to be used as a catalyst recovery system. Organic contaminated catalyst can be combusted in the incinerator; the catalysts, in either element or oxide form, can then be recovered for future reuse.

The system described in Figure 6-27 is a complete system for the disposal of aqueous waste containing sodium compound, and the recovery of dry soda ash.

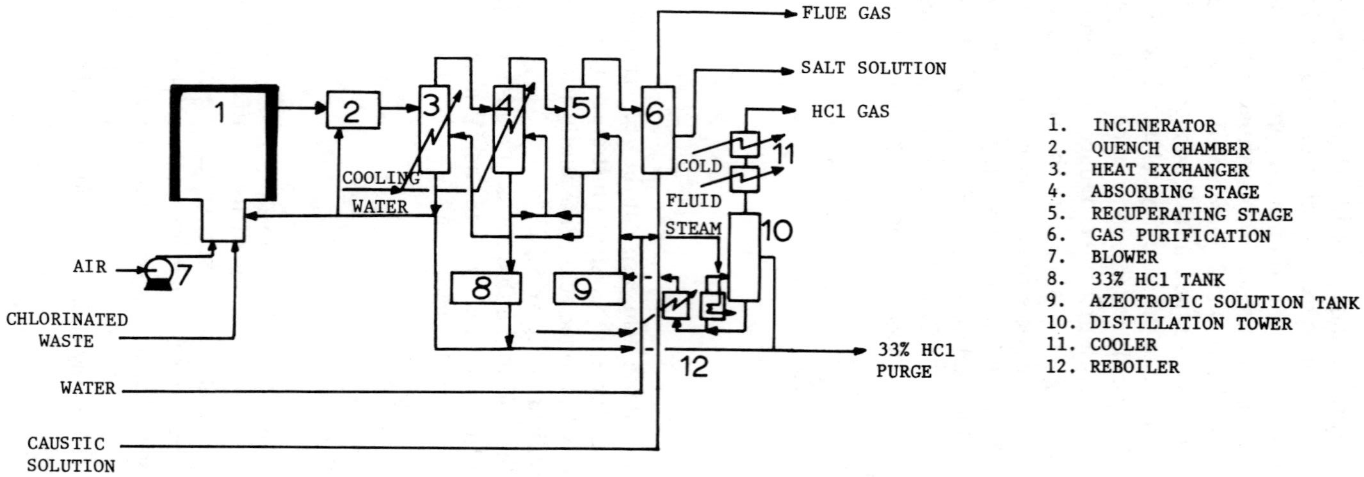

Figure 6-25. Rhone Poulenc hydrochloric acid recovery system (reproduced from Reference 12, courtesy of The Gulf Publishing Co., Houston, TX).

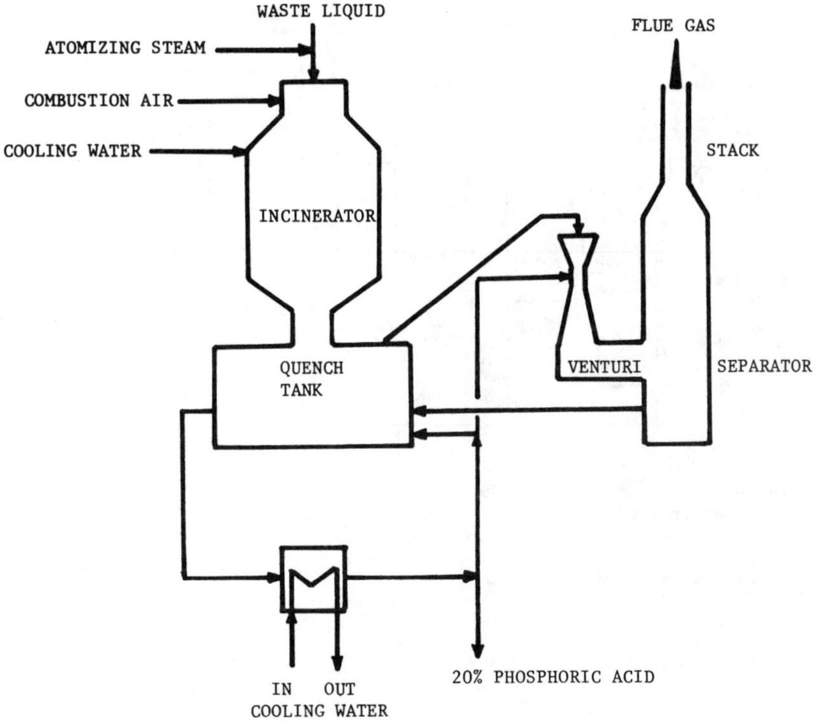

Figure 6-26. Trane thermal phosphoric acid recovery process (reproduced, courtesy of National Industrial Publishing Co., Pittsburgh, PA).

AIR POLLUTION CONTROL

The sources of air pollutants in a hazardous waste incinerator are:

1. incomplete combustion of organic constituents and
2. conversion of certain inorganic constituents present in the waste and other system inputs.

Two other nuisance factors, steam plume and mist carry-over from the incineration system exhaust stack, also require consideration.

The products of incomplete combustion include carbon monoxide, carbon, hydrocarbons, amines and other waste constituents or their partially degraded products. In well-designed and well-operated incinerators, these incomplete combustion products are emitted only in insignificant amounts.

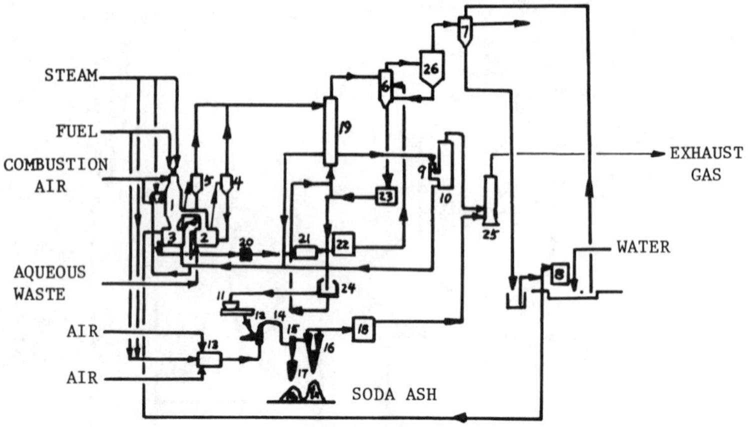

1 - burner-incinerator	10 - separator	18 - baghouse
2 - concentrator	11 - screw conveyor	19 - heat exchanger
3 - quench tank	12 - crusher	20 - tank
4 - mist eliminator	13 - air heater	21 - filter
5 - mist eliminator	14 - dryer	22 - tank
6 - flash drum	15 - primary cyclone	23 - tank
7 - condenser	16 - secondary cyclone	24 - centrifuge
8 - cooling tower	17 - rotary valve	25 - stack
9 - venturi scrubber		26 - mist eliminator

Figure 6-27. Sodium carbonate recovery system (reproduced from Reference 6-9, courtesy of Chemical Engineering Progress, NY).

Although organic compound emission from an incineration system usually is in an insignificant amount, there is public concern over certain organic compounds, such as 2,3,7,8-tetrachlorodibenzo-p-dioxin (2,3,7,8-TCDD), which is believed to be emitted from chemical waste incinerators. These compounds, in trace quantities, are believed to be extremely dangerous to human health. The formation of trace amounts of highly toxic organic compounds is not unique to incineration; other combustion sources, such as boilers, process furnaces, fireplaces, charcoal grills and diesel engines also contribute to the formation of these compounds. At the present time, only limited data are available to assess the generation of trace toxic compounds [13].

The primary end products of incineration are, in most cases, oxygen, nitrogen, carbon dioxide and water vapor. When wastes containing elements other than carbon, hydrogen and oxygen are incinerated, other combustion products are formed. For example:

- hydrogen fluoride from the incineration of organic fluorides,
- hydrogen chloride and small amounts of chlorine from the incineration of chlorinated hydrocarbons,
- hydrogen bromide and bromine from the incineration of brominated organics,
- iodine from the incineration of organic iodides
- sulfur oxides from the incineration of organic sulfur compounds,
- phosphorus pentoxide from the incineration of organic phosphorus compounds,
- nitrogen oxides from thermal fixation of nitrogen in the combustion air or from organic nitrogen compounds present in the waste, and
- particulates, including salts, metal oxides, etc.

The inorganic air pollutants can be classified into two groups: gaseous and particulate pollutants.

Gaseous Pollutant Removal Systems

There are three types of systems which are generally used to remove gaseous pollutants from incinerator flue gases: spray tower, packed bed tower and plate towers. All the systems are mass transfer devices for gas absorption.

Spray Tower

Spray towers are usually vertical chambers in which water is atomized by high pressure spray nozzles. The gas stream enters the bottom of the chamber and flows countercurrent to the liquid, although both concurrent and cross-current modes have been used. The gas may travel in a single path or may be directed by a series of baffles. The atomized liquid forms droplets, and mass transfer occurs at the droplet surface. The finer the droplets, the more gas absorption is enhanced. Impurities which are soluble in the scrubbing liquid can be removed by the gas absorption process.

Spray towers can be composite towers (as described in Chapter 5) if high-temperature flue gas is treated in the tower. They can also be made of low-temperature materials for low-temperature gases. The inlet gas temperature is determined by the maximal allowable temperature of the material of concentration.

Spray towers usually are used as cooling and quench towers only. Their absorption efficiency is usually lower than that of packed and plate towers.

Packed Bed Tower

Gaseous pollutants are removed in packed bed towers by a gas absorption process that depends on intimate gas/liquid contact. Packed towers are vessels filled with randomly oriented packing material such as saddles, rings and tellerettes® (a registered trademark of Ceilcote Company, Akron, OH). The scrubbing liquid is fed to the top of the vessel, with the gas flowing in either concurrent, countercurrent, or crossflow modes. As the liquid flows through the bed, it wets the packing material and thus provides interfacial surface area for mass transfer with the gas phase. A typical packed tower is illustrated in Figure 6-28.

Packed bed towers are a major air pollution control device for hazardous waste incinerators. The tower can be a composite tower (as described in Chapter 5) which can handle hot and corrosive incinerator flue gases. The packed bed tower also can be made of low temperature materials, such as fiberglass-reinforced plastics and thermal plastics. In this case, a quench system must be provided in front of the packed bed to ensure that the inlet gas temperature is below the maximal allowable limit of the tower materials.

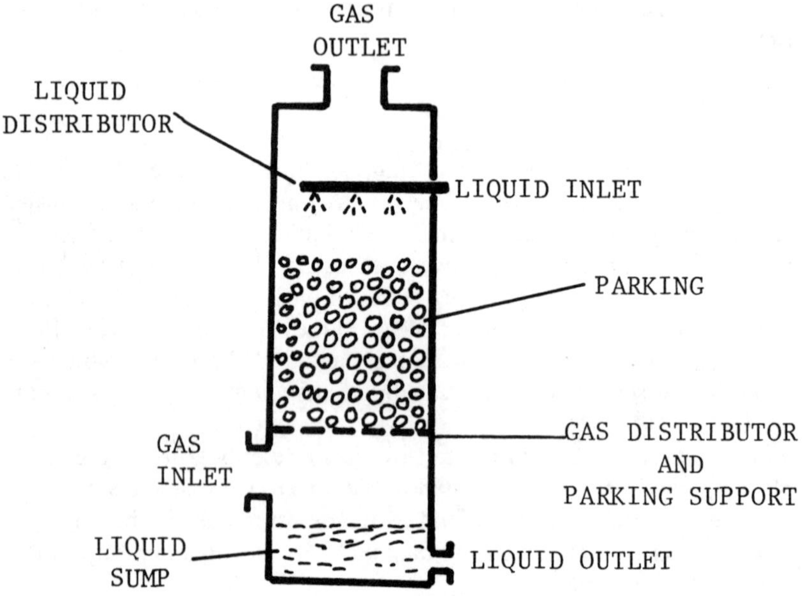

Figure 6-28. Schematics of packed bed scrubber.

In the absorption of gaseous contaminants, the rate of mass transfer is directly proportional to the concentration gradient driving force, and is restricted by both gas and liquid film resistance. The primary design variables for gas absorption are the depth of packing, minimal liquid rate and pressure drop across the bed.

1. *Packing depth.* The depth of packing required can be calculated by [14]

$$Z = N_{OG} \times H_{OG}$$

where Z = the packing depth
N_{OG} = the number of transfer units
H_{OG} = the height of a transfer unit.

The number of transfer units depends on the removal efficiency requirement. Under these circumstances, the number of transfer units can be calculated as

$$N_{OG} = \int_{y_1}^{y_2} \frac{dy}{y - y^*}$$

where y = the actual gas concentration of the contaminant,
y_2 = the concentration at the scrubber outlet,
y_1 = the concentration at the inlet, and
y^* = the gas concentration of the contaminant in equilibrium with the scrubbing liquid.

In industrial applications, the gaseous contaminant often is very soluble in the scrubbing liquid, as in the case of hydrogen chloride in water, or reacts very rapidly with the scrubbing liquid, as in the case of hydrogen chloride with caustic solution. For both of these cases, the equilibrium gas concentration is negligible and the number of transfer units can be calculated as:

$$N_{OG} = \ln\left(\frac{y_1}{y_2}\right)$$

where y_1 and y_2 are the inlet and outlet concentrations of the gaseous contaminant.

The height of a transfer unit is a characteristic of the particular system, and is influenced by the type and size of packing, gas and liquid flow rates, and gas and liquid physical and chemical properties. It is often taken as a constant over fixed ranges of operation and is given by the expression:

$$H_{OG} = \frac{G}{K_g a P}$$

where G = the total gas flow rate per unit cross-section of bed
K_g = the overall gas mass transfer coefficient
a = the interfacial surface area per unit volume of packing
P = the total pressure

Values of $K_g a$ for many of the more commonly used gas absorption processes have been published in the literature [15,16]. The height of transfer unit for Ceilcote 2-in. Tellerette® Type R packing is presented in Table 6-3. For a gas phase controlled absoprtion system, the height of the transfer unit can be estimated by gas diffusivity data:

$$\frac{H_{OG}}{H_{OGref}} = \frac{D}{D_{ref}}$$

where H_{OGref} = height of transfer unit of known gases
D_{ref} = diffusivity of known gases

The transfer unit concept can be used to calculate packing depth requirements if overall gas mass transfer coefficients are available. However, the mass transfer concept also can be used [17]. The height of a packed bed can be calculated, knowing the mass transfer coefficient $K_g a$ as

$$H = \frac{N}{K_g a A \Delta P_{ln}}$$

where N = moles of gas transferred
$K_g a$ = mass transfer coefficient
A = tower cross-sectional area

$$\Delta P_{ln} = \frac{P_1 - P_2}{\ln (P_1/P_2)}.$$

The mass transfer coefficient is a function of packing type, liquid flow rates and absorption system. $K_g a$ numbers for certain gases are shown in Table 6-4 [18]. $K_g a$ numbers for packings other than the 1½-in. Intalox saddle can be calculated as a ratio, based on the liquid rates. The $K_g a$ data for absorption of CO_2 with caustic soda are very complete for various packings, and thus are used as references.

Table 6-3. Height of Transfer Unit for Ceilcote 2 in. Tellerette® Type R Packing (Reproduced courtesy of Ceilcote Company, Akron, OH)

Gas	Scrubbing Medium	Height of Transfer Unit (gas) (ft)
SO_2	NaOH, Na_2CO_3	2.75
HCl	H_2O, NaOH	1.5
HF	H_2O, NaOH	1.2
Cl_2	NaOH	1.2
H_2S	NaOH	0.92

Table 6-4. Mass Transfer Coefficient of Typical Packings (6–18)[a]

Gas	Scrubber Liquid	K_ga (lb-moles/hr ft³ atm.)
O_2	H_2O/NaOH	25
HCl	H_2O	25
SO_2	H_2O/Na_2SO_3	7
SO_2	H_2O	0.317

[a] Packing Type: 1-½ in. Intalox saddle.
Liquid Rate: 5000 lb/hr/ft².

2. *Minimal liquid rates.* For each packing, there is a minimal liquid rate requirement. Below the minimal liquid rates, the packings cannot be wetted, and thus absorption efficiency will decrease. The minimal liquid rates are a function of packing type; e.g., the minimal liquid rates for saddles are between 1 to 2 gpm/ft², whereas those of Tellerettes are 5 to 6 gpm/ft² of tower cross-sectional area. An empirical method for estimating liquid rate is

$$L = 0.106a \text{ gpm/ft}^2$$

where a is the surface area of dry packing, ft²/ft³ packed area.

3. *Pressure drop across the packed bed.* Since the liquid rates are determined either by process requirement or by the packing minimal liquid rate requirement, the tower diameter becomes a function of the gas rate, using the pressure drop as the indicator. The pressure drop is an important design parameter. If the pressure drop is too high, the tower may flood and thus create high back pressure. However, if the pressure drop is too low, the gases may channel through the packing without

being scrubbed. Pressure drop must be high enough so that a reasonable tower turndown ratio (the maximum to minimum gas flow rates where efficiency is maintained) can be maintained. Pressure drops for the common commercial packings can be obtained from plots of pressure drop versus gas and liquid flow rates. These plots are available from packing manufacturers and should be used for more accurate estimating of pressure drop in the design evaluation process. The pressure drop also can be determined by the generalized pressure drop correlation:

$$\ln\frac{1}{\Delta P} = -11.76 - 2.695\ln X - 5.037\ln Y - 0.2549\ln X\ln Y$$
$$- 0.4586(\ln X)^2 - 0.7308(\ln Y)^2 - 0.0002628(\ln X\ln Y)^2$$
$$- 0.03471(\ln X)^3 - 0.0505(\ln Y)^3 + 0.0001543(\ln X\ln Y)^3$$

where ΔP = pressure drop, in. water column/ft packing

$$X = \frac{L}{G}\left(\frac{\rho_G}{\rho_L \rho_G}\right)^{0.5}$$

$$Y = \frac{G^2 F \mu_L{}^{0.1}}{\rho_G(\rho_L - \rho_G)}$$

L = liquid rate, lb/sec/ft^2
G = gas rate, lb/sec/ft^2
ρ_L = liquid density, lb/ft^3
ρ_G = gas density, lb/ft^3
F = packing factor
μ_L = viscosity of liquid, cP
g_c = 32.2.

Using the above correlation, the tower diameter can be determined, based on a preselected pressure drop. Normally, a packed tower should be designed to operate at the maximum economical pressure drop. Most scrubbing systems are set for maximum pressure drop at 60⅓ of flooding. The percent flooding of a packed tower can be determined by the following equations [19].

$$\log_{10}\phi = \left\{32.5496 - 4.1288\log_{10}\left[\frac{L^2 F \mu_L^{0.2}}{\rho_L^2}\right]\right\}^{0.5}$$

$$\%\text{ Flooding} = \left\{\frac{11.51}{D}\left(\frac{W}{\phi L}\right)^{0.5}\left(\frac{\rho_L}{\rho_G}\right)^{0.25}\right\}^2 \times 100$$

where D = the tower diameter
W = the gas rate in lb/hr.

Packing factor F, is a function of packing type. The packing factors for commonly used packings are listed in Table 6-5.

Plate Tower

Plate towers, like all wet scrubbers, remove gaseous contaminants in a gas absorption process that depends on intimate gas/liquid contact. The basic design of a plate scrubber is a vertical cylindrical column with a number of plates or trays inside [20]. Each plate has openings which can be in the form of perforations, slots or bubble caps. The scrubbing liquid is introduced at the top plate and flows across it, then down to the next plate (Figure 6-29).

A downcomer, located on alternate sides of each successive plate, permits the downward movement of the liquid. The scrubbing liquid exits along with the pollutants at the liquid outlet located at the tower bottom.

Incinerator gas enters the bottom of the tower and passes up through the plate openings, exiting at the top. The gas has enough velocity to prevent the liquid from flowing through the holes in the plates. Gas absorption is promoted by the breaking up of the gas phase into small bubbles which pass through the volume of liquid in each plate.

Plate towers may be divided into two classifications: the cross-flow plate and the counterflow plate (Figure 6-30). The cross-flow plates are used more because of their high scrubbing efficiency and greater operating range.

The diameter of a plate tower must be sufficiently large to handle the gas and liquid at velocities that will not cause flooding or excessive entrainment. The flooding velocity of a gas can be calculated as

$$V_f = C_p \left(\frac{\rho_L - \rho_G}{\rho_G} \right)^{0.5}$$

where ρ_L and ρ_G = densities of liquid and gases in lb/ft^3
V_f = the superficial gas velocity in ft/sec

In this case, the net cross-section area (total tower cross-section area minus the area taken up by downcomers) is used. The parameter C_f is a function of tray type.

Table 6-5. Packing Factors for Typical Packings (Wet and Dump Packed)[a] (Reproduced courtesy of Norton Company, Akron, OH)

		Nominal Packing Size (in.)										
Type of Packing	**Material**	¼	⅜	½	⅝	¾	1	1¼	1½	2	3	3½
Super Intalox	Ceramic	—	—	—	—	—	60	—	—	30	—	—
Intalox Saddles	Ceramic	725	330	200	—	145	98	—	52	40	22	—
Intalox Saddles	Plastic	—	—	—	—	—	33	—	—	21	16	—
Raschig Rings	Ceramic	1600[b,c]	1000[b,c]	580[d]	380[d]	255[d]	155[e]	125[b,f]	95[f]	65[g]	37[b,h]	—
Berl Saddles	Ceramic	900[b]	—	240[b]	—	170[i]	110[i]	—	65[i]	45[b]	—	—
Pall Rings	Plastic	—	—	—	97	—	52	—	40	25	—	16
Pall Rings	Metal	—	—	—	70	—	48	—	28	20	—	16
Raschig Rings, 1⁄32 in. Wall	Metal	700[b]	390[b]	300[b]	170	155	115[b]	—	—	—	—	—
Raschig Rings, 1⁄16 in. Wall	Metal	—	—	410	290	220	137	110[b]	83	57	32[b]	—

[a] $F \approx a/\in^3$ obtained in 16 and 30 in. i.d. tower.
[b] Extrapolated.
[c] 1⁄16 in. wall.
[d] 3⁄32 in. wall.
[e] ⅛ in. wall
[f] 3⁄16 in. wall.
[g] ¼ in. wall.
[h] ⅜ in. wall.
[i] Data by Leva.

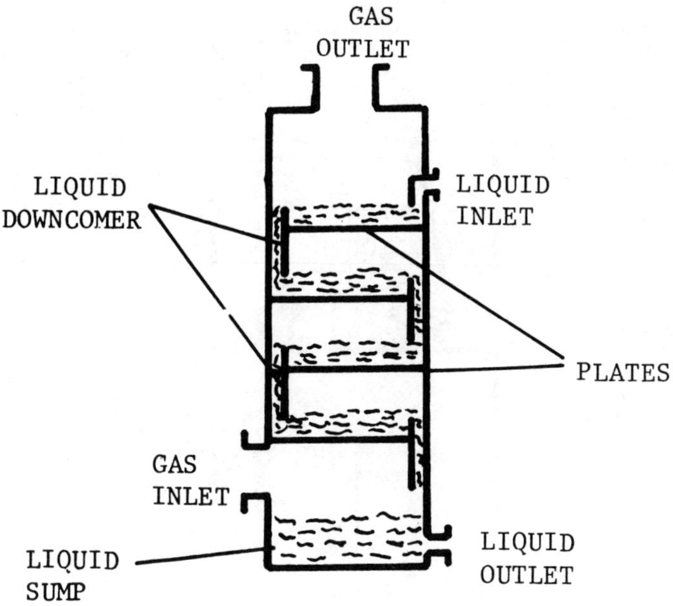

Figure 6-29. Schematics of plate scrubber.

For perforated trays

$$C_f = \left[a \log_{10} \frac{1}{(L/G)(\rho_G/\rho_L)^{0.5}} + b\right]\left[\frac{\sigma}{20}\right]^{0.2}\left[5\frac{A_h}{A_a} + 0.5\right]$$

where L/G = the liquid to gas ratio
σ = the surface tension
A_h = the hole area per tray
A_a = the active area of the tray

$$\left.\begin{aligned} a &= 0.062\,t + 0.0385 \\ b &= 0.0253\,t + 0.05 \end{aligned}\right\} \quad \text{for} \quad 0.1 < \frac{L}{G}\left(\frac{\rho_G}{\rho_L}\right)^{0.5} < 1$$

where t is the tray spacing in inches.

For bubble cap trays

$$C_f = \left[a \log_{10} \frac{L}{(L/G)(\rho_G/\rho_L)^{0.5}} + b\right]\left[\frac{\sigma}{20}\right]^{0.2}$$

where
$$\left.\begin{aligned} a &= 0.0041\,t + 0.0135 \\ b &= 0.0047\,t + 0.068 \end{aligned}\right\} \quad \text{for} \quad \frac{L}{G}\left(\frac{\rho_G}{\rho_L}\right)^{0.5} < 0.2$$

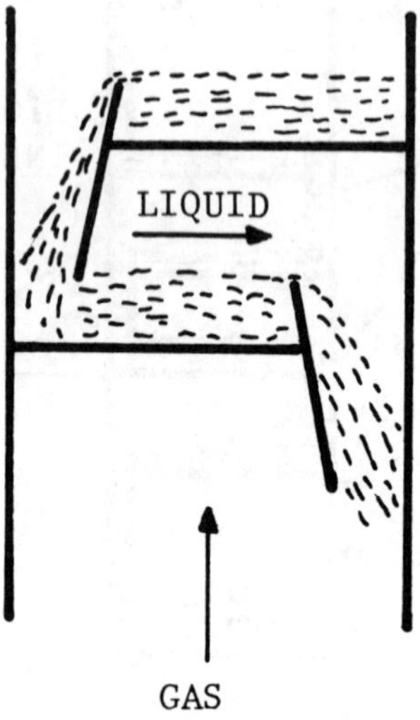

(a) CROSS FLOW TYPE

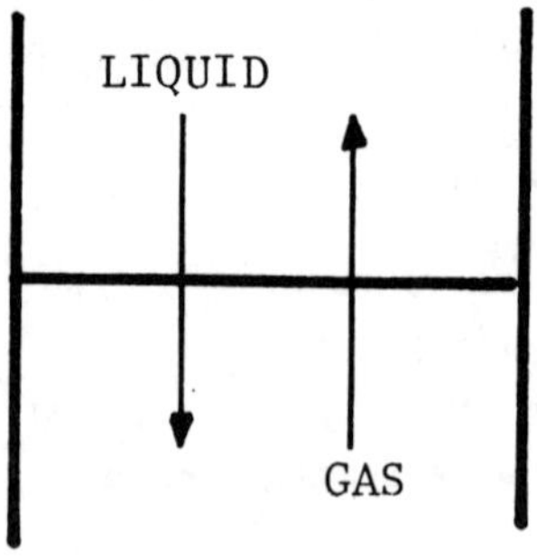

(b) COUNTER CURRENT FLOW TYPE

Figure 6-30. Plate types.

or
$$\left.\begin{array}{l} a = 0.0068\,t + 0.049 \\ b = 0.0028\,t + 0.044 \end{array}\right\} \text{for } 0.2 < \frac{L}{G}\left(\frac{\rho_G}{\rho_L}\right)^{0.5} < 1$$

The tower diameter is so chosen that the gas superficial velocity is lower than the flooding velocity.

The tray spacing is dependent on the tower diameter. A typical tray spacing requirement is illustrated in Table 6-6.

Table 6-6. Tray Spacing Requirement [14]

Tower Diameter (ft)	Tray Spacing (in.)
4	20
4–10	24
10–12	30
12–24	36

The pressure drop of a crossflow tray can be estimated as [14]

$$\Delta P = h_s + h_{ow} + 1/2\Delta H + h_D + h_r, \text{bubble cap tray}$$

$$\Delta P = h_w + h_{ow} + 1/2\Delta H + h_D + h_r, \text{sieve tray}$$

where h_s = height of liquid seal
h_{ow} = height of weir crest
ΔH = hydraulic gradient
h_D = height of liquid equivalent to pressure drop through gas dispersion
h_w = height of weir
h_r = residual pressure drop

as shown in Figure 6-31.

The range of operation of crossflow trays is

$$0.5 < V_{sup}\sqrt{\rho_G} < 2.5, \text{ sieve trays}$$

$$0.4 < V_{sup}\sqrt{\rho_G} < 2.3, \text{ bubble trays}$$

where V_{sup} is in ft/sec and ρ_G is in lb/ft^3.

Tray efficiency is the fractional capacity of an ideal tray which is attained by a real tray. The Murphree efficiency of a tray is defined as

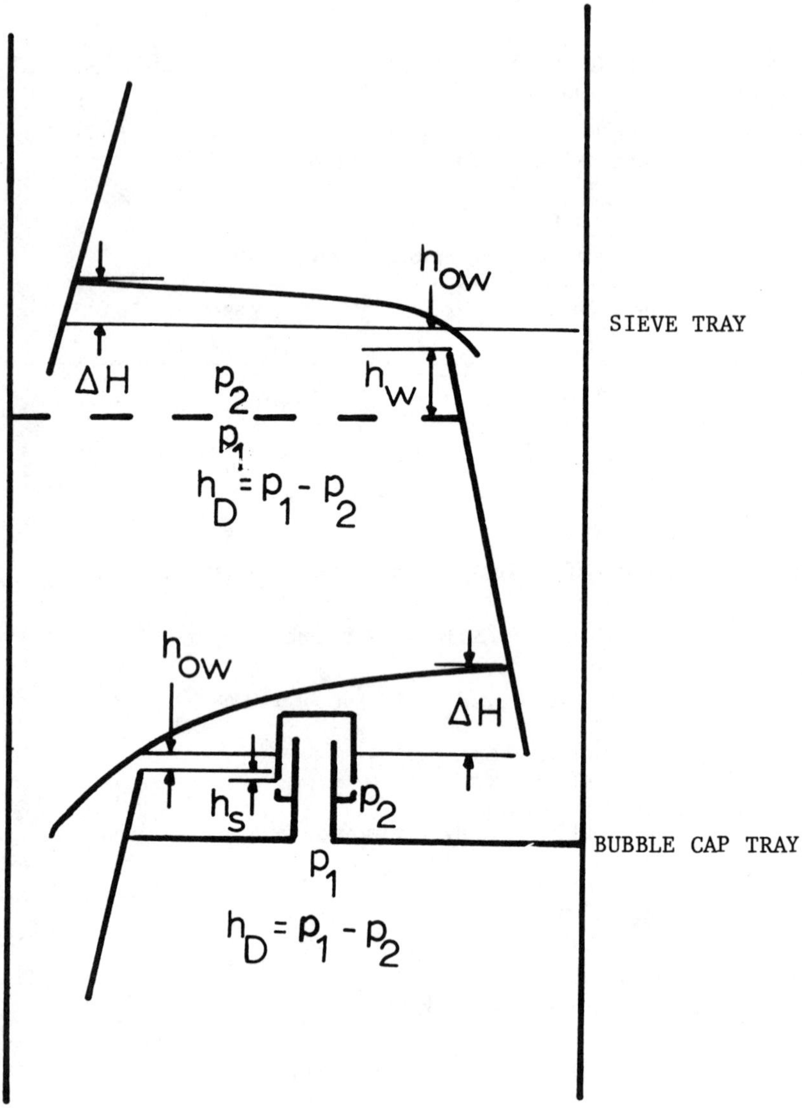

Figure 6-31. Parameters for pressure drop calculation across crossflow plate towers.

$$E_{MG} = \frac{Y_n - Y_{n+1}}{Y_n^* - Y_{n+1}}$$

where Y_n^* is the equilibrium value with leaving liquid of concentration x_n.

Neutralization Chemical Requirement

The stoichiometric caustic soda requirement for neutralization of acid gases is

Caustic Soda requirement (lb/lb waste) = 0.011 × Wt % Cl in waste + 0.0205 × wt % F in waste + 0.03775 × wt % P in waste + 0.0243 × wt % S in waste

Caustic Scrubbing of Chlorine

The chief problem associated with the caustic scrubber is corrosion. Usually, the use of caustic for removal of chlorine will give the following reaction:

$$2NaOH + Cl_2 \rightarrow NaCl + NaOCl + H_2O$$

It is the formation of hypochloride which causes the corrosion in plastic materials. The corrosion can be minimized by operating the tower at a low temperature, say 125°F, or, by using exotic materials, such as CPVC and Kynar®, as packing materials and high grade FRP or Kynar® lined steel as shell. If metallic materials are to be used, titanium is the best choice for either packed bed or tray towers.

Although caustic solution is used for illustration, the scrubbing liquid can be any alkaline solution, providing it will not generate a tower plugging problem.

Particulate Pollutant Removal Systems

The particulate pollutants in the incinerator flue gases can be removed by dry or wet systems. Many varieties of equipment are available for particulate removal [21]; however, only a few systems are used extensively in incineration application:

Dry Method: electrostatic precipitator
bag house filter

Wet Method: venturi scrubber
ionized wet scrubber
wet electrostatic precipitator

Electrostatic Precipitators (ESP)

Electrostatic precipitation is a process by which particles suspended in a gas are electrically charged and separated from the gas stream. In this process, negatively charged gas ions are formed between emitting and collecting electrodes by applying a sufficiently high voltage to the emitting electrodes to produce a corona discharge. Suspended particulate matter is charged as a result of bomardment by the gaseous ions, and it migrates toward the grounded collecting plates due to electrostatic forces. Particle charge is neutralized at the collecting electrode, where subsequent removal is effected by periodically rapping or rinsing. A majority of industrial ESPs used today are the single-stage, wire and plate type; charging and collection take place in the same section of the ESP. Two-stage ESPs, often called electrostatic filters, have separate sections for particle charging and collecting, and generally are not employed for controlling particulate emissions from combustion sources.

Electrostatic precipitators have been widely used in conjunction with utility boilers and municipal and industrial incinerators. ESPs have been employed by European facilities where hazardous wastes are incinerated, although the wastes generally do not contain highly chlorinated compounds. When halogenated wastes are incinerated, careful waste blending is employed to protect ESPs from corrosion, so that HCl concentrations do not exceed 1000 ppm, and usually average 300 ppm. Because dry ESPs are not capable of removing acid gases, facilities burning halogenated wastes must employ two-stage gas cleaning if ESPs are used for particulate emission control.

ESP components in direct contact with the process gas stream include the shell, electrodes, high voltage frames, rapper rods and gas distribution plates. On the basis of mild steel construction, such components constitute ~68% of the total precipitator weight and account for 45% of the total unit cost. Hence, applications requiring exposure to corrosive gas streams have substantial impact on ESP design and ultimate cost. Lead linings, used in acid mist ESPs, generally are not suitable for use in incinerator gas treatment due to their poor resistance to attack by gaseous halogens. Fiberglass reinforced plastic has been successfully utilized for inlet and outlet plenums as well as collecting electrodes; however the latter application requires provision of adequate conductivity to permit current flow to ground.

ESPs are carefully designed and constructed for maximum electrical safety; however, normal high voltage precautions must be observed. Design features such as interlocks between access doors and electrical elements should be incorporated. Also, access after deenergizing should be delayed to allow for static charge drainage.

Compared to wet scrubbers, pressure and temperature drops across ESPs are very small. The pressure drop across an ESP is typically <1.00 in. water column as compared with wet scrubbers which may operate with pressure drops up to 60.0 in. water column. Additionally, ESPs generally provide higher removal efficiencies for particles of <1 μ diam than do wet scrubbers. A standard gas temperature range is up to 700°F, and the voltage normally applied ranges from 30 to 75 kV.

The advantages of electrostatic precipitators are: dry dust collection, low pressure drop and operating cost and efficient removal of fine particles. Collection efficiency can be improved when the stream is treated (i.e., highly conducting dust treated with SO_2).

The disadvantages of ESP are: relatively high capital cost, sensitivity to changes in flow rate and particle resistivity affecting removal and economics.

Baghouse Filter

Baghouse filtration is one of the oldest methods of removing particulate matter from a gas stream. A baghouse filter consists of a permeable material through which a gas laden with particles is passed. The mechanisms of a baghouse filter for removing particles from a gas stream are:

1. sieving: filtration through the filter fibers,
2. interception: collision between the particles and the fibers of the filter media (>1 μ particles),
3. impingement: a sudden change in direction of the particle,
4. gravitational settling (5–10 μ particles),
5. electrostatic attraction: for the collection of small particles and
6. diffusion: for the collection of particles in the submicron range.

All baghouse filters operate in basically the same way: dirty gas is introduced to the unit where it is filtered by cloth tubes or bags. The filtering action usually removes $>99\%$ of the entrained particles. The bags must be cleaned of this collected material periodically. Methods and frequency of cleaning differs, depending on the type of baghouse filter.

Baghouse filters can be cleaned either intermittently or continuously. Intermittent baghouses cannot be cleaned while on-line, and thus are limited to low dust loadings or infrequent operation. They have the distinct advantage of being low priced. Continuous cleaning baghouses are more expensive but operate continuously and can handle high dust loadings.

Baghouse filters are characterized and identified according to the method used to remove collected material from the bags. Particle removal is accomplished in a variety of ways, including shaking the bags, reversing the direction of air flow through the bags, blowing a jet of air on the bags from a reciprocating manifold or rapidly expanding the bags by a pulse of compressed air [22].

The bags in shaker-type baghouse filters are supported by a structural framework (Figure 6-32). The framework is free to oscillate when driven by a small electric motor. Periodically, a damper isolates a compartment of the shaker baghouse filter so that no air flows. The bags in the compartment are then shaken for approximately one minute, during which time the collected dust cake is dislodged from the bags. The dust falls into the hopper for subsequent removal.

Reverse flow baghouse filters are equipped with an auxiliary fan that forces air through the bags in the direction opposite to filtration (Figure 6-33). This backwash action collapses the bag and fractures the dust cake. When the bag is reinflated by being brought back on-line, the fractured dust cake is dislodged into the hopper. If the unit operates under

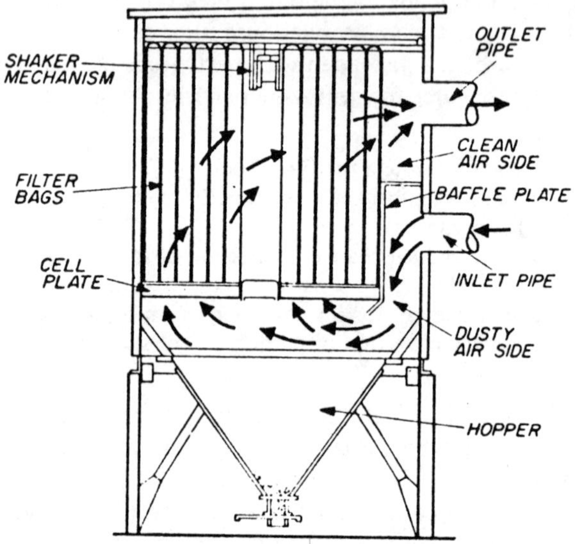

Figure 6-32. Shaker type baghouse filter (reproduced from Reference 22, courtesy of Pollution Engineering, Barrington, IL).

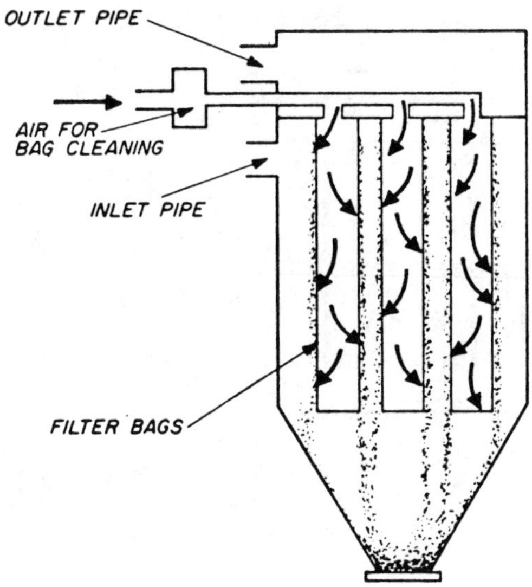

Figure 6-33. Reverse air flow baghouse filter (reproduced from Reference 22, courtesy of Pollution Engineering, Barrington, IL).

suction (the main fan is located on the "clean" side of the baghouse), reducing pressure in the baghouse may eliminate the need for an auxiliary fan.

Reverse jet baghouse filters (Figure 6-34) incorporate a jet case or manifold that surrounds each bag. The manifold travels the length of the bag in a constantly repeating cycle.

As it passes over the surface of the bags, a jet of high pressure air issues from orifices in the manifold and blows the dust cake off the bags.

Reverse pulse baghouse filters (Figure 6-35) utilize a short pulse of compressed air through a venturi, or diffuser, directed from the top to the bottom of the bag. This primary pulse of air aspirates secondary air as it passes through the venturi. The resulting air mass violently expands the bag and casts off the collected dust cake. A modification of this technique is the pressurized plenum type of cleaning. In this case, an isolated compartment above several rows of bags is supplied with pressurized air. The change in pressure differential across the bags when the damper is operated causes the bags to flex and cast off the dust cake.

Envelope type bags (Figure 6-36) capture the dust from the airstream outside the bag, which is prevented from collapsing by internal frames. This design offers the greatest surface area contact between cloth and air (made possible by close spacing of the envelopes). Occasionally, the dust

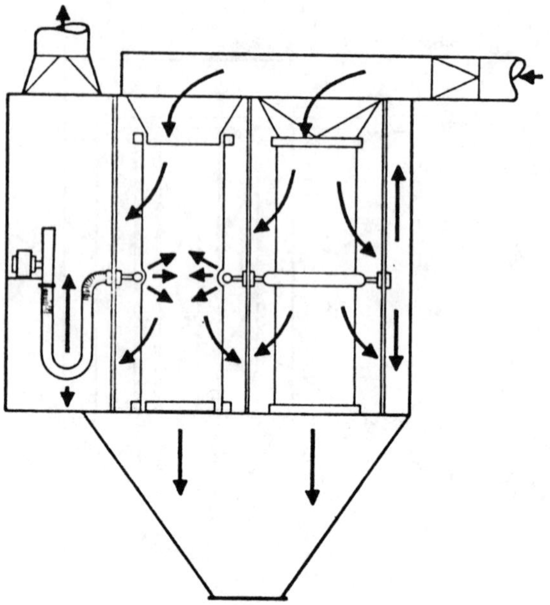

Figure 6-34. Reverse jet baghouse filter (reproduced from Reference 22, courtesy of Pollution Engineering, Barrington, IL).

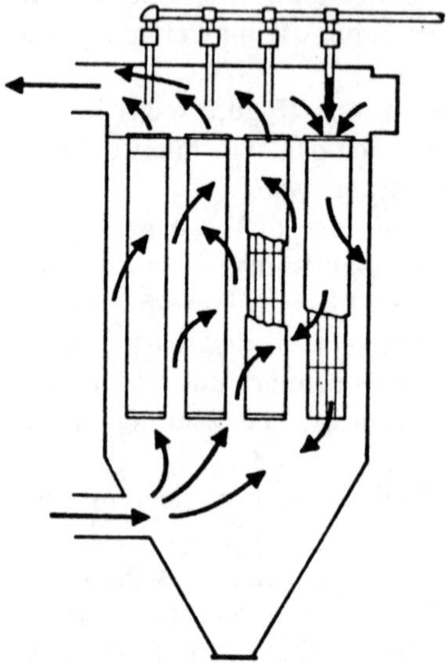

Figure 6-35. Reverse flow cleaning pulse jet baghouse filter (reproduced from Reference 22, courtesy of Pollution Engineering, Barrington, IL).

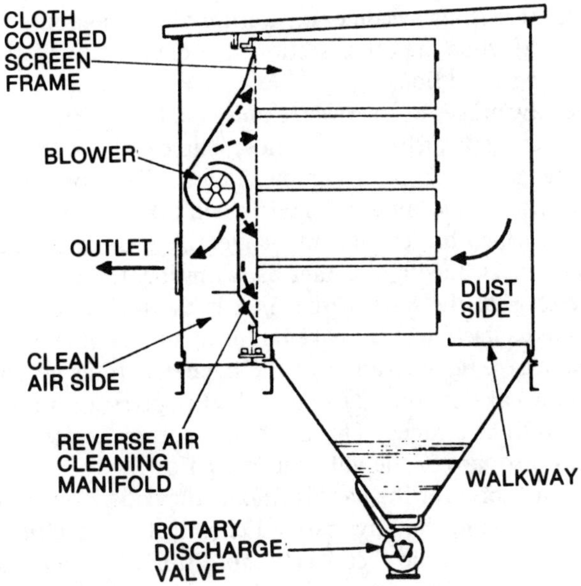

Figure 6-36. Envelope type baghouse filter (reproduced from Reference 22, courtesy of Pollution Engineering, Barrington, IL).

bridges or plugs the spacing between the envelopes, then it becomes necessary to remove every other bag. These units are most frequently used for low air flow applications.

The fundamental criterion used in applying any baghouse to any application is the air-to-cloth ratio (A/C), defined as the ratio of actual volumetric air flow rate to net cloth area.

$$A/C = \frac{Q}{A} = \frac{\text{Flow}}{\text{Area}} = \text{Velocity}$$

where A/C = air-to-cloth ratio, fpm
Q = volumetric air flow, acfm
A = net cloth area, sq ft.

A/C is the superficial face velocity of the air as it passes through the cloth. Shaker and reverse air baghouse filters normally operate at an air-to-cloth ratio of 1:1 to 3:1. Reverse pulse baghouse filters generally operate at an air-to-cloth ratio of from 3:1 to 6:1, although many are now operating in the range of 10:1 to 12:1. The lower ratio shaker and reverse air baghouses usually are equipped with extra compartments. In this arrangement, there is always an extra section of the baghouse to accommodate cleaning, while the other sections handle the full air flow under normal operating conditions.

One of the advantages of the reverse pulse baghouse filter is that it not only operates at high air-to-cloth ratios, but can be cleaned on-line, eliminating the need for extra compartments. Therefore, a baghouse filter with a pulse air-cleaning mechanism will take up considerably less space than one which has to be compartmentized for cleaning.

When a filter is cleaned and comes back on line, there is only a minimal pressure drop at the start of the filter cycle. (Filtration takes place through the media itself.) As the cake builds up on the filter and the pressure drop increases, the operation of the baghouse filter becomes more efficient. As the cake continues to build, higher pressures result and the baghouse needs to be cleaned. This cycle is important, since the pressure drop varies as a square of the volumetric air flow.

The choice of fabric for the bags is usually dependent on the temperature of the gas stream, the physical and chemical characteristics of the particles to be collected, the chemical composition of the gas carrier and the moisture content of the gas carrier. The rate at which a fabric media will deteriorate is generally related to the weight of the fabric in the filter and the composition of the gas stream.

Venturi Scrubber

Venturi scrubbers utilize the kinetic energy of a moving gas stream to atomize the scrubbing liquid into droplets. A venturi consists of four selections: a convergence section, a throat section, a divergence section and a mist separator (Figure 6-37). Liquid is injected into the high-velocity gas stream either at the inlet to the converging section or at the venturi throat. In the process, the liquid is atomized by the formation and subsequent shattering of attenuated, twisted filaments, and thin, cuplike films. These initial filaments and films have extremely large surface areas available for mass transfer.

Venturi scrubbers usually are designed for particulate collection, but they can be used for simultaneous gas absorption as well. However, the design of venturi scrubbers for removal of gaseous contaminants is dependent on the availability of applicable experimental data. There is no satisfactory generalized design correlation for this type of scrubber, especially when absorption with chemical reaction is involved. Reliable design must be based on full-scale data, or at least laboratory or pilot-scale data.

Correlations are available to design venturi scrubbers for particulate removal. The important design parameters are particulate loading and

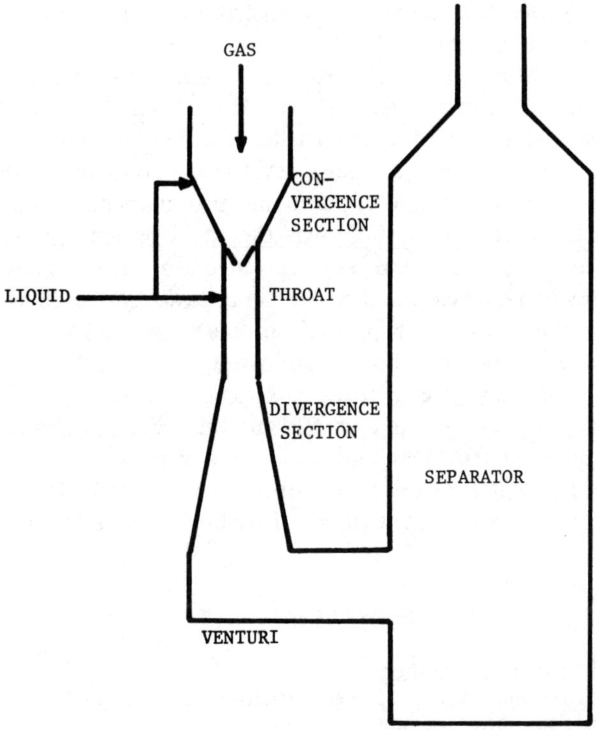

(a) FLAPPER TYPE VARIABLE THROAT VENTURI SCRUBBER

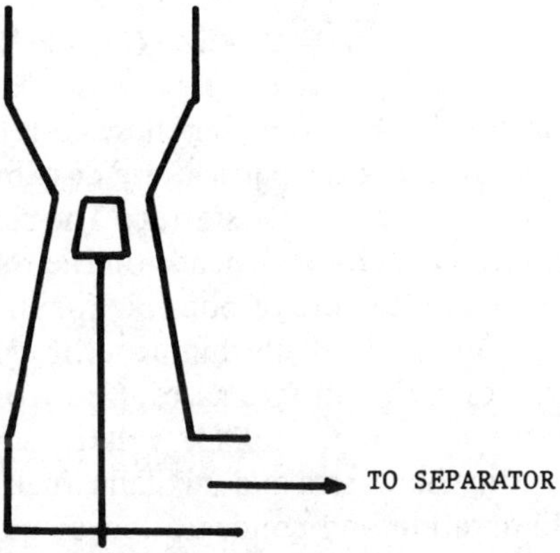

(b) INSERT TYPE VARIABLE THROAT VENTURI SCRUBBER

Figure 6-37. Schematics of venturi scrubber.

desired removal efficiency, particle size distribution, pressure drop, liquid-to-gas ratio and gas velocity.

1. *Particulate loading, size distribution, and removal efficiency.* If the particulate size distribution and desired removal efficiency are known, several correlations can be used to predict the required cut diameter for design purposes. Calvert et al. [23] have developed parametric plots of overall penetration versus the ratio of cut diameter to mass median diameter with geometric standard deviation as the third parameter. These plots can be used to determine the required cut diameter if the desired removal efficiency and particle size distribution are known. Cut diameter can then be related to pressure drop, liquid-to-gas ratio and gas velocity for design purposes, as described in the following subsection.

Hesketch [24] has also developed an empirical relationship between penetration of all particles $<5\ \mu$ in diameter and the pressure drop across venturis based on data from the collection of a variety of industrial dusts. Assuming that particles $>5\ \mu$ are collected with 100% efficiency, this relationship may be utilized with size distribution data to estimate overall penetration:

$$Pt = 0.065W\,(\Delta P)^{-1.43}$$

where
Pt = fractional penetration
W = the weight fraction of inlet particles of $\leq 5\ \mu$ diam
ΔP = pressure drop, in. water column.

The efficiency of a venturi is then determined as

$$E = \{1 - EXP(Pt)\} \times 100$$

The major drawback in applying these correlations to venturi scrubber design evaluation is that the particle size distribution rarely will be known until testing is performed after startup. The size distribution of particles emitted from an incinerator depends on the relative number of particles generated by several factors responsible for the formation of particulate emissions: (1) mechanical entrainment of combustible and noncombustible particles in the furnace gases, (2) pyrolysis of hydrocarbons and subsequent condensation, and (3) volatilization of metallic salts and oxides present in the wastes and auxiliary fuels. Further, particle growth due to agglomeration and condensation of moisture between the incinerator and the control device will affect the particle size distribution. It is not possible to predict particle size distribution resulting from waste incineration. While incineration of liquid wastes may result in mean particle diameters in the 0.5–3 μ range, mean particle diameters resulting from incineration of solid waste could range from 5 to 100 μ, depending on the size distribution of feed solids, their combustion characteristics and the incinerator design. If particle size distribution data are available, methods described in References 23 or 24 can be used to determine the required cut diameter.

2. *Pressure drop, liquid-to-gas ratio, and gas velocity.* As described above, particle cut diameter is a frequently used parameter for expressing and determining the particle collection performance of wet scrubbers. One reason is that plots of collection efficiency versus particle diameter tend to be rather steep in the region where inertial impaction is the predominant collection mechanism. Because the cut is fairly sharp for venturi scrubbers, a rough approximation of scrubber performance may be made by assuming that particles larger than the cut diameter are collected with 100% efficiency and those smaller will not be collected.

Pressure drop in venturi scrubbers is theoretically related to gas velocity and liquid-to-gas ratio, as shown in the following relation developed by Calvert [23]. This relationship assumes that all energy is used to accelerate the liquid droplets to the throat velocity of the gas.

$$\Delta P = 2.12 \times 10^{-5} (U_G)^2 L$$

where ΔP = pressure drop, in. water column
U_G = gas velocity, ft/sec
L = liquid-to-gas ratio, gal/1000 ft^3.

An alternative empirical approach by Hesketch [24] indicates that the pressure drop for venturis is proportional to $U_G{}^2$ and $L^{0.78}$, as well as to the gas density ρ_G (measured downstream from the venturi throat) and to $A^{0.133}$, where A is the cross-sectional area of the venturi throat:

$$\Delta P = \frac{(U_G)^2 \rho_G (A^{0.133}) (L)^{0.78}}{1270}$$

Pressure drop will be relatively insensitive to changes in A because of the small exponent, but density will be inversely proportional to the gas temperature. These relationships can be used as internal consistency checks for the proposed conditions of gas velocity, liquid-to-gas ratio and pressure drop.

Liquid-to-gas ratios for venturi scrubbers are usually in the range of 5–20 gal/1000 ft^3 of gas. At existing hazardous waste incineration facilities, liquid-to-gas ratios ranging from 7 to 45 gal/1000 ft^3 of gas have been reported. In many cases, a minimum ratio of 7.5 gal/1000 ft^3 is needed to ensure that adequate liquid is supplied to provide good gas sweeping. Typical venturi throat velocities for incineration applications are in the 300 to 400 ft/sec range.

The efficiency of a venturi can be improved by agglomeration of particles. One method is to saturate the incinerator flue gas with water and then condense the water vapor. The particles, in this case, will then serve as seeds for the condensation of the water droplets, and thus increase their size.

The divergence section is necessary for recovery of the pressure. A long and gradually expended section is preferred.

Ionizing Wet Scrubber

The ionizing wet scrubber [25] is a new development in fine particle removal technology. However, it has been gradually adapted by major commercial incineration facilities. A typical ionizing wet scrubber (IWS), as developed by Ceilcote Company, is illustrated in Figure 6-38. The IWS consists of a preconditioning tower, if required, a charge section and a crossflow packed bed scrubber.

The IWS utilizes high-voltage ionization to charge particulates in the gas stream before the particles enter a Tellerette® packed scrubber section where they are removed either by inertial impaction (Figure 6-39) or by attraction of the charged particles to a neutral surface. Particles $\geq 3\text{–}5\ \mu$ are collected through inertial impaction within the packing bed. As the smaller charged particles flow through the scrubber, they pass very close

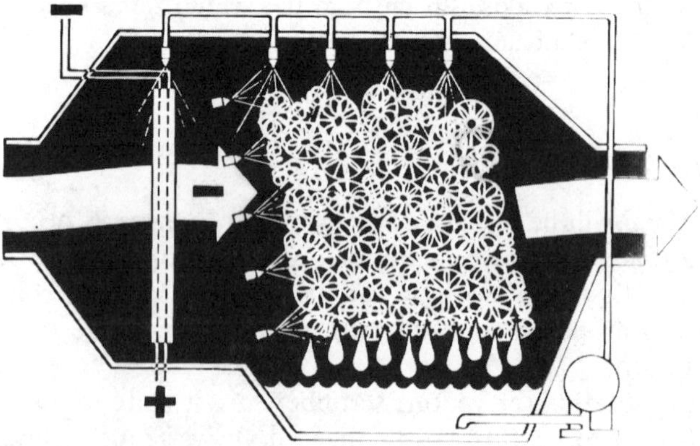

Figure 6-38. Schematics of Ceilcote ionized wet scrubber (reproduced courtesy of Ceilcote Company, Akron, OH).

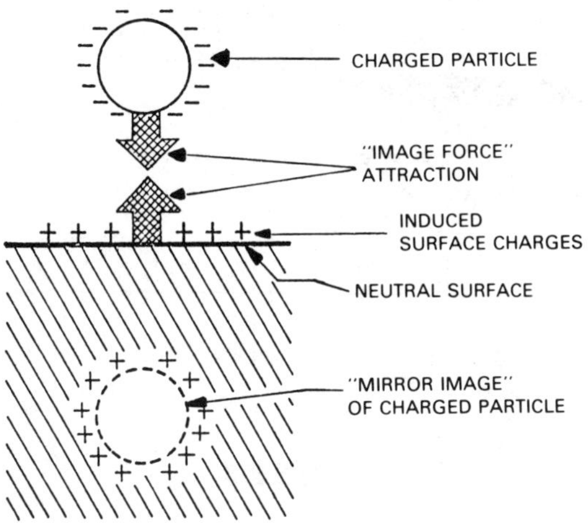

Figure 6-39. Image force attraction (reproduced courtesy of Ceilcote Company, Akron, OH).

to the surface of either a Tellerette® or a scrubbing liquid droplet. The particles become attracted to and attached to one of these surfaces by image force attraction. They are eventually washed out of the scrubber in the exit water. Gaseous pollutants are absorbed and reacted in the same scrubbing water.

IWS collection efficiency in the fine particle range decreases only slightly as the particles become smaller. The collection efficiency of a two-stage IWS is illustrated in Figure 6-40.

The IWS is a fractional collector. A single-stage IWS unit will remove a fairly constant percentage of incoming particles regardless of particle size distribution of the total loading. Where a higher collection efficiency is required than can be attained with a single-stage IWS, a two-stage IWS will receive a much smaller loading but will have similar particle size distribution to that which would have entered the single-stage IWS. Collection efficiency of the second-stage IWS will be approximately the same as the single-stage IWS despite the reduction in loading.

Shown in Figure 6-40 are typical collection efficiency curves for single and two-stage systems. Consider the application where a single-stage unit will remove 83% of the entering particulate. By adding a second-stage and obtaining a similar collection efficiency of 83%, an overall efficiency of 97% is achieved.

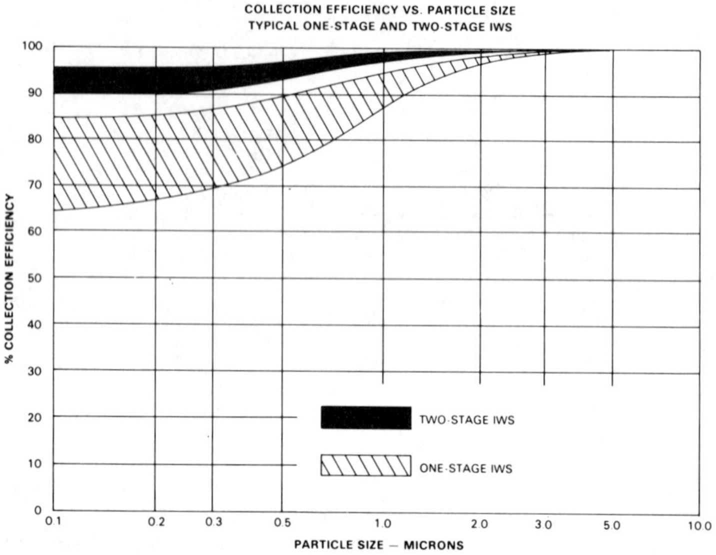

Figure 6-40. Collector efficiency of Ceilcote ionized wet scrubber (reproduced courtesy of Ceilcote Company, Akron, OH).

Wet Electrostatic Precipitator

The wet electrostatic precipitator (WEP) is a variation of the dry electrostatic precipitator design. The two major added features in a WEP system are: (1) a preconditioning step, where inlet sprays in the entry section are provided for cooling, gas absorption and removal of coarse particles, and (2) a wetted collection surface, where liquid is used to continuously flush away collected materials. Particle collection is achieved by the introduction of evenly distributed liquid droplets to the gas stream through sprays located above the electrostatic field sections, and migration of the charged particles and liquid droplets to the collection plates. The collected liquid droplets from a continuous downward-flowing film over the collection plates, and keep them clean by removing the collected particles.

The WEP overcomes some of the limitations of the dry electrostatic precipitator. Its operation is not influenced by the resistivity of the particles. Further, since the internal components are continuously being washed with liquid, buildup of tacky particles is controlled and there is some capacity for removal of gaseous pollutants. In general, applications of the WEP fall into two areas: removal of fine particles and removal of condensed organic fumes.

Data on capability of the WEP to remove acid gases are very limited. WEPs have been installed to control HF emissions from Soderberg aluminum reduction cells. With a liquid-to-gas ratio of 5 gal/1000 acf and a liquid pH between 8 and 9, fluoride removal efficiencies >98% have been measured. Outlet concentration of HF was found to be <1 ppm [26].

There are no WEP installations at hazardous waste incineration facilities. A potential application is to consider use of the WEP in conjunction with a low-pressure-drop venturi scrubber upstream, where a major portion of the gaseous contaminants and heavy particles will be removed. The WEP will then serve as a second-stage control device for removal of the submicron particles and remaining gaseous pollutants. Because of its limited application history, extensive pilot testing prior to design and installation may be necessary.

Nitrogen Oxides Removal

As described in Chapter 5, nitrogen oxides can be minimized by two-stage combustion. In this section, wet scrubbing nitrogen oxides (NO_x) are discussed.

The main problem in wet scrubbing of NO_x is getting nitrogen oxide (NO) into solution. Because of its inert nature and low solubility, getting an adequate rate of mass transfer is extremely difficult. Three approaches to improving mass transfer can be used [27].

1. Oxidize NO to NO_2 in the gas phase before scrubbing. Nitrogen dioxide is more reactive than nitrogen oxide.
2. Partially oxidize NO to NO_2 to give an equimolar mixture nitrogen oxide and nitrogen dioxide. This also is relatively easy to absorb because of nitrite formation.
3. Use a dissolved catalyst to promote adsorption of NO and conversion to nitrogen-sulfur compound.

The first two approaches are very expensive and impractical. The third approach is discussed here.

The catalyst normally used is ethylenediamine tetracetic acid (EDTA) plus ferrous ion and bisulfite. Although the chemistry is not entirely clear, it appears that the EDTA and iron form a complex with NO.

$$Fe^{++} - EDTA + NO \rightarrow Fe^{++} - EDTA - NO$$

and this reacts with bisulfite.

$$Fe^{++} - EDTA + NO + 3HSO_3^- \rightarrow Fe^{+++} - EDTA + NH(SO_3)_2^= + 1/2 S_2O_6^=$$

The $NH(SO_3)_2^=$ is an imido disulfonate and the $S_2O_6^=$, a dithionate. These are reacted in various ways to give end products such as ammonia, nitrogen, sulfite and gypsum.

Wet No_x scrubbing is not a widely used technology. Two-stage combustion is still the method for reduction of NO_x formation in incineration systems.

Controlling Steam Plume

The exhaust gases from scrubbers of an incineration system usually are saturated with water vapor. When mixed with cold air, the saturated gases cause condensation of water vapor; the condensed water vapor then forms a so-called steam plume. Usually, the size of the plume is determined by the temperature and degree of saturation of the exhaust gases. The steam plume generated thus is not harmful; however, it is usually a nuisance factor in industrial plant operation. The objection to a true steam plume is not its poisonous effect; it is a matter of appearance.

Formation of Steam Plume

To understand the plume formation mechanism, refer to the saturation curve illustrated in Figure 6-41. Any gases with water vapor concentration above the saturation line cause condensation. To study a system, an understanding of the mixing line is essential. The mixing line is defined as a straightline connection between the stack exhaust condition, as defined by temperature and water vapor partial pressure, and the ambient condition defined similarly. If the mixing line falls above the saturation line, condensation occurs. Given an ambient condition, there are four types of mixing lines, as presented in Figure 6-41. There is plume formation when Types 1 and 2 are applied. Type 3 is the critical line. Any mixing line above this line contains a fog-forming zone and any mixing line below this line is fog-free. It follows that the way to prevent plume formation is to move the stack exhaust condition to or below the critical line, so that the mixing line contains no fog formation zone. The mathematical expression for the critical line is

$$5038.13p_c/(T_c + 273)^2 = (p - p_a)/(T - T_a).$$

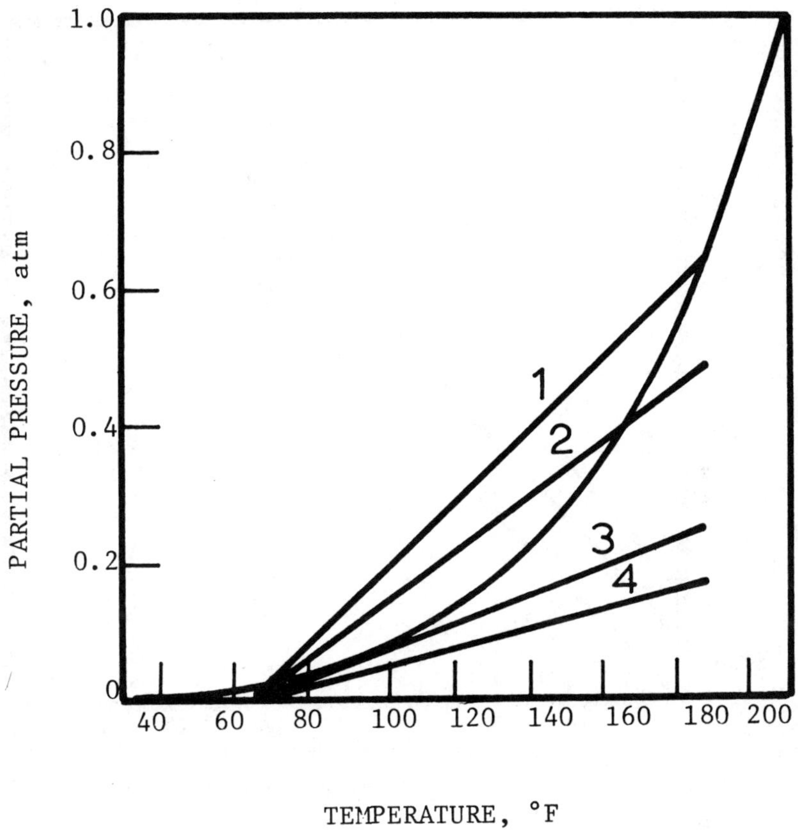

Figure 6-41. Saturation curve and mixing line of flue gases.

where p = partial pressure of water vapor, atm
T = temperature, °C
a = ambient condition
c = critical conditions.

The intersection of the saturation line and critical line is called the critical point. The curve in Figure 6-42 illustrates the critical temperature as a function of ambient temperature. The critical conditions are the solution of the critical line equation above, and the vapor pressure of water.

$$p = \exp[13.5091 - 5038.13/(T + 273)].$$

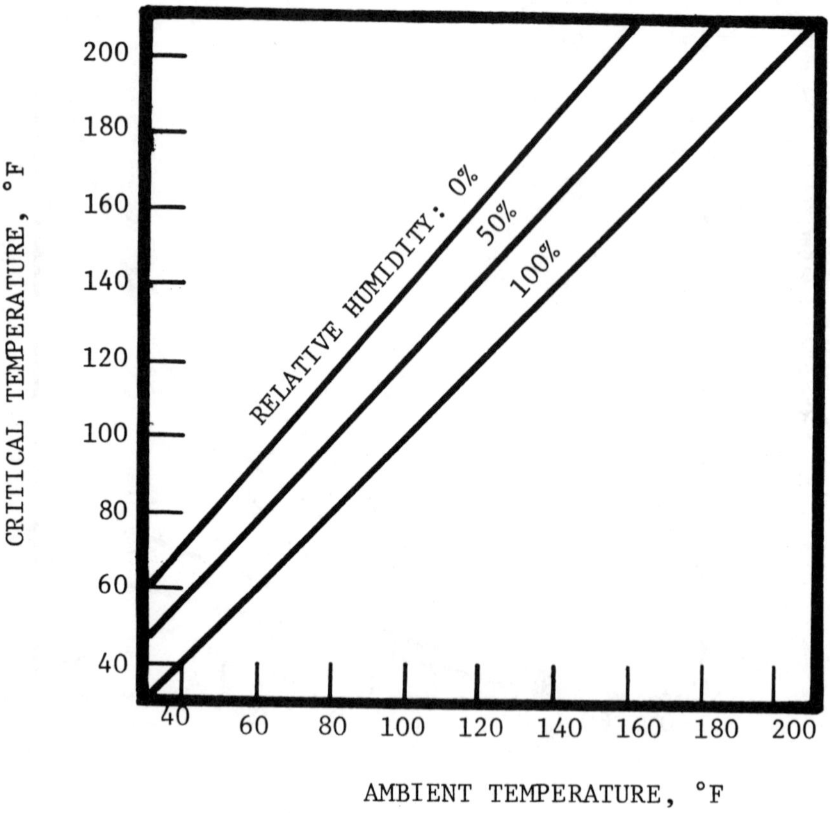

Figure 6-42. Critical temperature of flue gases.

Processes to Prevent Steam Plume

The options to move the stack exhaust conditions below the critical line are presented in Figure 6-43. Cooling is used in Option 1. The stack exhaust is cooled; thus water vapor is condensed, until the temperature reaches the critical temperature. In Option 2, heat is added to the stack flue gases. The temperature of the gases is heated over the critical line. Dilution is used in Option 3 to change the stack condition. Dilution usually causes some condensation and results in lower stack temperature.

The three options described above are the basic processes; a combination of them can be used to optimize operating and capital costs. The stack gases can be cooled and then heated so that the final stack condi-

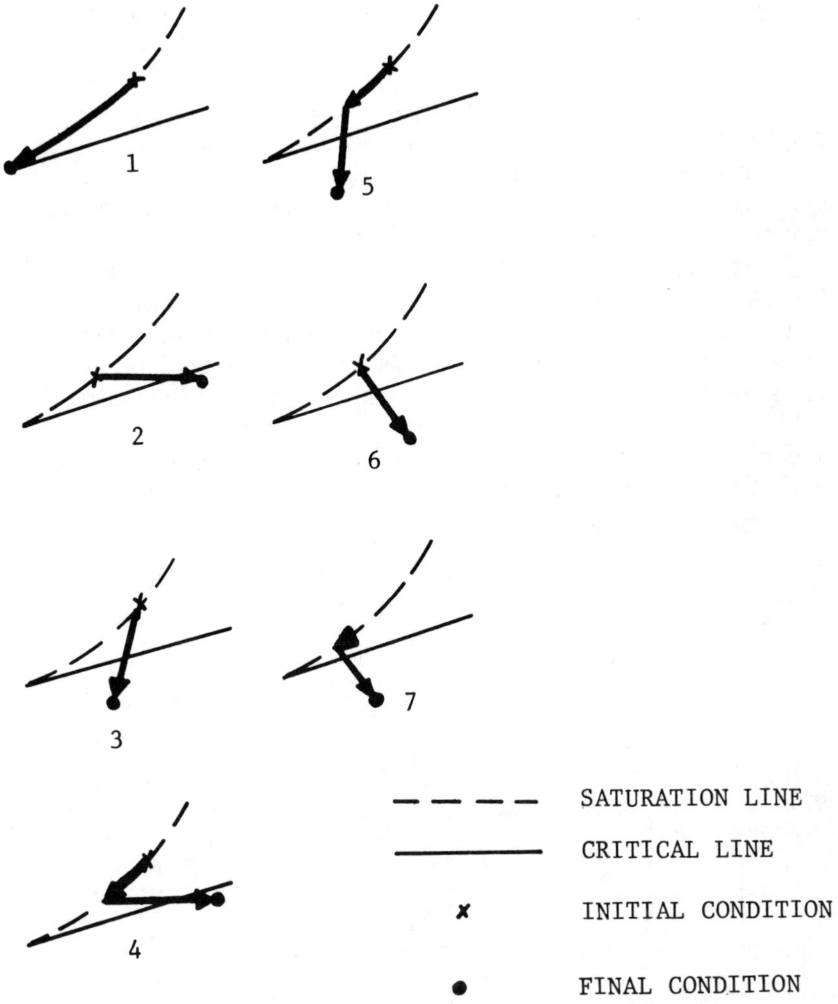

Figure 6-43. Steam plume control processes.

tion will be over the critical line; this is Option 4. Cooling and dilution are combined in Option 5. In Option 6, dilution of the stack flue gas with hot gases is applied. A combination of cooling, dilution and heating yields Option 7. Although seven options are available, the most widely used methods are based on Options 1, 2 and 7, discussed in detail in the following sections.

Cooling of Stack Gases. The practical cooling equipment can be a direct contact heat exchanger, such as packed towers and spray towers; or indirect heat exchangers, such as plate or shell and tube heat exchangers. The heat removal requirement is dependent on the temperature and degree of saturation of the stack gases.

Typical application of a direct contact cooler is illustrated in Figure 6-44. Although a countercurrent packed tower is shown in this application, it can be a cocurrent packed tower or other equipment such as a spray tower or tray towers. Water is usually used as the cooling medium. The advantage of using this type of system is the low equipment cost and, if water is readily available, low operating cost. Water quality is not an important factor if it does not generate its own stack emission problem. (For instance, it may become a problem if the cooling water contains

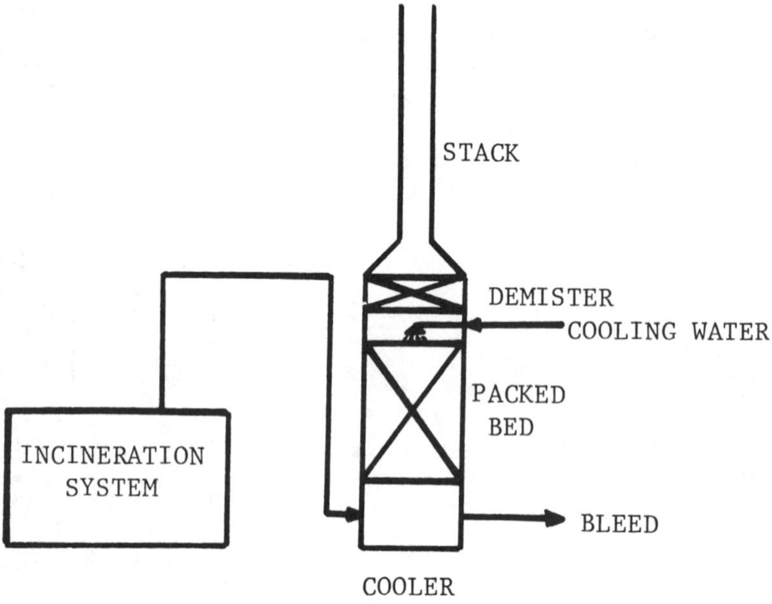

Figure 6-44. Direct contact cooling steam plume control processes.

organics.) Usually FRP or thermoplastics are suitable construction materials. The drawback in this method is the contamination of cooling water. Carbon dioxide, nitrogen oxides, sulfur oxides and other contaminants will blend into the water and lower the pH. However, when a large quantity of water is ued, this effect may not be apparent, especially when low grade water is used.

Figure 6-45 presents the application of an indirect heat exchanger to cool the stack gases. Both cooling air and cooling water can be used. The cooler is composed of condensation and gas to gas heat transfer sections. Usually, the indirect cooler requires a larger heat transfer surface and higher water consumption, compared to a direct contact cooler. The materials of construction are another critical area that may increase equipment cost appreciably.

Heating of Stack Gases. The stack gas temperature can be increased by either direct or indirect heating. In direct heating, fuel is supplied to burners, and the combustion gases are rapidly mixed with the stack gases. The burner can be fired into the stack (Figure 6-46) or into a separate combustion chamber, and the hot gases are then mixed with the stack gases. A simple material and energy balance can be used to determine the fuel requirement. Mixing is a critical design criterion in this

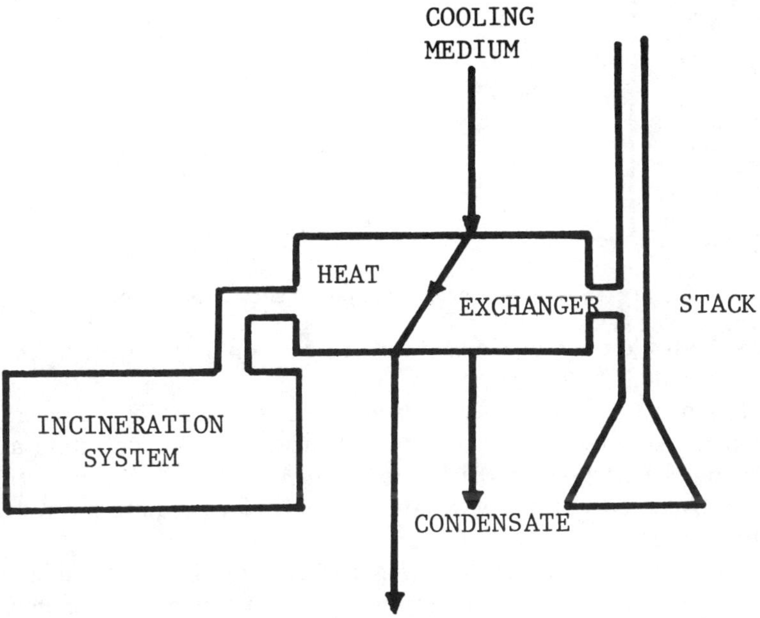

Figure 6-45. Indirect cooling steam plume control processes.

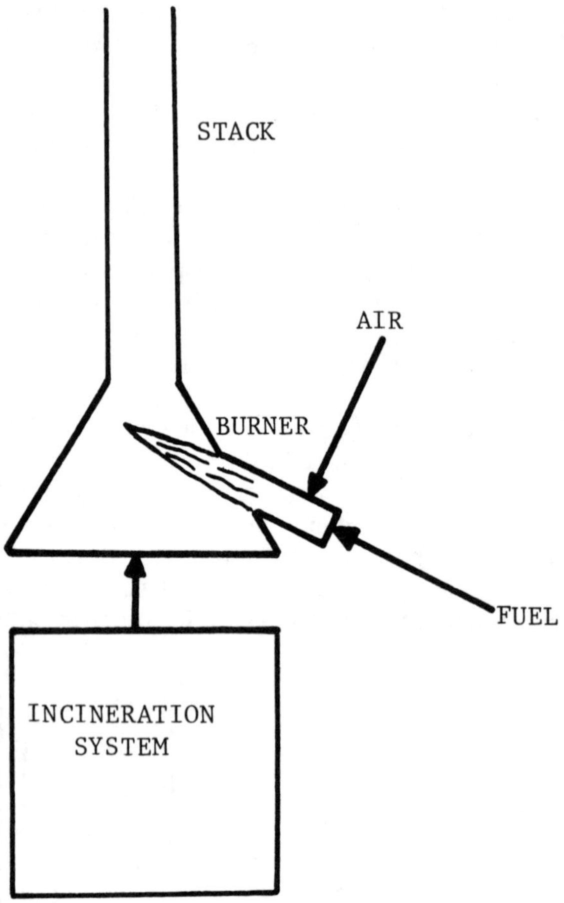

Figure 6-46. Direct heat steam plume control processes.

system. Also, the combustion system must include all the necessary shut-down functions to ensure safe operation.

The indirect heat exchanger can be installed in the stack or in a separate chamber. Any available fluid with a higher level of temperature and enthalpy can be used as the heating medium. Usually, steam gives a higher overall heat-transfer coefficient. Hot gases require more heat transfer surfaces.

Combination of Cooling, Heating and Dilution. If either heating or cooling alone is not an economical method to eliminate steam plume, a practical combination system (Figure 6-47) can be used. The stack gases are cooled and water vapor condensed in an indirect heat exchanger. The

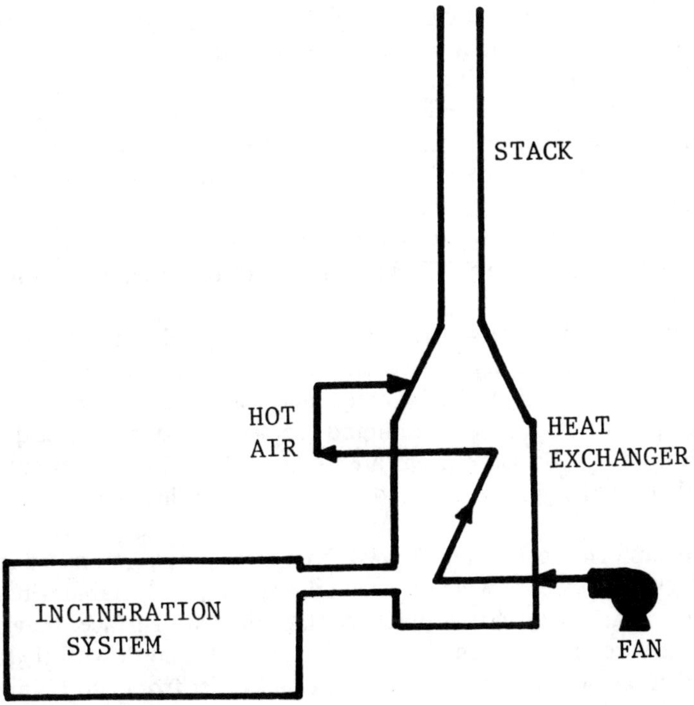

Figure 6-47. Combination steam plume control processes.

heat removed from the gases is used to increase the temperature of the dilution air. The hot dilution air is then mixed with the cooled stack gas. Proper design results in stack gas conditions below the critical line. This system can be either a forced draft system, as shown in Figure 6-47, or an induced draft system.

Mist Elimination

Mist eliminators are widely used to reduce emissions of liquid droplets from scrubbers. Mist eliminators are normally installed downstream from, or as an integral part of, the scrubbing system. In general, only one mist eliminator is needed. Where two or more scrubbers are used in series, intermediate mist elimination may be provided, but it is not considered necessary to prevent the release of liquid droplets to the environment.

The types of mist eliminators most commonly used in hazardous waste incineration facilities are cyclone collectors, simple inertial separators such as baffles, wire mesh mist eliminators and fiber bed mist eliminators. Cyclones are used for collecting very heavy liquid loadings of droplets $>10\ \mu$ such as those emitted from venturi scrubbers. The design of cyclone mist eliminators follows the principles of cyclone design for particles. For this type of mist eliminator, therefore, the collection efficiencies for liquid droplets and solid particles are about the same. Collection efficiencies of nearly 100% are possible for droplets in the 10–50 μ range, which is consistent with the liquid droplet sizes emitted from venturi scrubbers.

In the simple inertial separators, the primary collection mechanisms are inertial impaction and, to a lesser extent, interception. Devices such as louvers, zigzag baffles, tube banks and chevrons are simple inertial separators. The cut diameter for liquid droplet collection in these devices is typically 10 μ. Pressure drops are in the 0.02–0.12 in. water column, depending on the gas velocity and closeness in spacing of the collection surfaces.

Wire mesh eliminators are formed from meshes of wire knitted into a cylindrical open weave which is then crimped to give a stable wire configuration. As rising mist droplets contact the wire surface, they flow down the wire to a wire junction, coalesce, run off and flow freely to the bottom of the bed. The depth of the wire pad varies from 2 to 12 in. with 4–6 in. pods being most common. Pressure drops usually range from 0.02 to 4.0 in. water column, depending on the gas velocity, the wire density and the depth of the pad. In normal operation, the pressure drop is not likely to be more than 1 in. water column. The cut diameter for liquid droplet collection is a strong function of the gas velocity, and can range from 1 to 10 μ. Sizing of the wire mesh mist eliminator is based on the allowable gas velocity, calculated using the Souders-Brown equation:

$$U = k\sqrt{\frac{\rho_L - \rho_G}{\rho_G}}$$

where u = the gas velocity in ft/sec
ρ_L = the density of the scrubbing liquid
ρ_G = the gas density.

The value of K that is normally used is 0.35 for mesh density from 9 to 12 lb/ft^3. A value of 0.4 is normally used for the 5 lb/ft^3 high-capacity mesh styles and a K value of 0.3 is normally used for plastic mesh pads such as Teflon®* and polypropylene.

---

* Registered trademark of E. I. Du Pont de Nemours & Company, Wilmington, Delaware

The pressure drop across a wire mist eliminator is

$$\Delta P = \Delta P_D + \Delta P_T, \quad \text{in. of water}$$

where ΔP_D = pressure drop across a dry wire mesh pad

$$= fcla\rho_G \frac{v^2}{g_c E^2} \frac{27.7}{144}$$

ΔP_T = pressure drop due to liquid loading
fc = frictional factor
l = wire mesh thickness, ft
a = specific surface area, ft^2/ft^3
ρ_G = gas density, lb/ft^3
v = superficial gas velocity, ft/sec
g_c = 32.2
E = void fraction of wire mesh.

For collection of fine acid mists, fiber bed mist eliminators are most appropriate. In this type of device, large mist particles are collected on the fibers by inertial impaction and direct interception, whereas smaller particles are collected by Brownian diffusion. Since fiber bed mist eliminators are designed so that Brownian diffusion is the predominant mechanism for mist collection, extremely small particles, $<1\ \mu$, are recovered with high efficiency. Typical gas velocities through fiber bed mist eliminators range from 5 to 10.0 ft/sec, with corresponding pressure drops of 5–15 in. water column. Collection efficiencies are 100% for droplets $>3\ \mu$, and 90–99.5% for droplets $<3\ \mu$.

In wire mesh and fiber bed mist eliminators, plugging by solid deposition is a potential problem. This problem can be partially overcome by intermittent washing with sprays, by selection of a less densely packed design and by the use of sieve plate towers or cyclone separators upstream as an additional mist and particle collection device.

WATER POLLUTION CONTROL

When water scrubbers are used in an incineration system, proper treatment of the scrubber water is necessary to ensure environmentally safe discharge.

When acid water is discharged from the scrubber, a caustic solution or lime bed can be used to neutralize the acid. The neutralization can be accomplished either in the scrubber or off-site in a neutralization tank. Conventional neutralizing technology can be used.

Most of the time, the neutralized scrubber water can be discharged, if the suspended and dissolved solid content and chemical oxygen demand

(COD) meet effluent standards. Otherwise, the scrubber water must pass through a waste water treatment plant before final discharge or reuse.

For a well designed and operated incineration system, the organic compounds contribution of COD to the scrubber is insignificant. Most of the time, the scrubber water COD value is the result of inorganic compounds of the combustion products, such as sulfite solution and iron. Sometimes, on-site aeration systems can be used to reduce scrubber water COD content.

The quantity of scrubber water can be reduced by concentration within the scrubber system or by evaporation and concentration. Dry solid discharge is also possible; however, energy requirements usually make this approach uneconomical.

REFERENCES

1. Kiang, Y. "Waste Utilization Technology," (New York: Marcel Dekker, 1981).
2. Kiang, Y. "Energy Management for Low Btu Waste Incineration," American Institute of Chemical Engineers Symposium Series, Water 1978, 190(75):46 (1978).
3. Hung, W. "Results of a Fired Tube Test Boiler in Flue Gas with Hydrogen Chloride and Fly Ash," American Society of Mechanical Engineers WAM, Houston, TX, November 1975.
4. Fontana, B. J. *J. Am. Chem. Soc.,* 73:3348 (1951).
5. McCracken, C. Private communication (1981).
6. Fassler, K., et al. "Corrosion in Refuse Incineration Plants," Mitteilunger der V GB, 40 (2):126 (1968).
7. Nelson, W., and C. Cain. "Corrosion of Superheaters and Reheaters of Pulverized Coal-fired Boilers," Part 1, American Society of Mechanical Engineers Series A, 82:194 (1960).
8. Nelson, W., and C. Cain. "Corrosion of Superheaters and Reheaters of Pulverized Coal-Fired Series," Part 2, American Society of Mechanical Engineers Series A, 83:408 (1961).
9. Kiang, Y. "Liquid Waste Disposal System," *Chem. Eng. Prog.* 1:71 (1976).
10. Santoleri, J. J. "Chlorinated Hydrocarbon Waste Disposal and Recovery Systems," *Chem. Eng. Prog.* 69, 1:68 (1973).
11. Naidel, R. W. "Hydrogen Chloride Production by Combustion in Graphite Vessels," *Chem. Eng. Prog.* 62:53 (1976).
12. Zimmer, J. C., and R. Guxitella. "Incineration: Low Cost HCl Recovery," *Hydrocarb. Process.* (August 1976), p. 117.
13. Esposito, M.P., and D. R. Watkins. "Airborne Dioxins: The Problem in Review," paper presented at the 73rd Air Pollution Control Association Annual Meeting, Montreal, June 1980.
14. Perry, R. H. *Chemical Engineer's Handbook,* 5th ed. (New York, McGraw-Hill, 1973).

15. Sherwood, T. K., and R. L. Pigford. *Absorption and Extraction,* 2nd ed. (New York: McGraw-Hill, 1952).
16. Ekert, J. S., et al. "Absorption Process Utilizing Packed Towers," *Ind. Eng. Chem.* 52 (2):41 (1967).
17. Norton Company. "Design Information for Packed Towers," Bulletin DC-10R, Akron, OH (1971).
18. Eckert, J. S. "How Tower Packings Behave," *Chem. Eng.* (April 14, 1975), p. 70
19. Chen, N. S. "New Equation Gives Tower Diameter," *Chem. Eng.* (February 5, 1962), p. 109.
20. Treybal, R. E. *Mass Transfer Operations,* 3rd ed. (New York: McGraw-Hill, 1980).
21. "Engineering Handbook for Hazardous Waste Incineration," U.S. EPA, Cincinnati, 1980.
22. Cross, F. L. "Baghouse Filtration of Air Pollutants," *Poll. Eng.* 6(2):25 (1974).
23. Calvert, S., et al. "Wet Scrubber System Study, Vol. 1, Scrubber Handbook," U.S. EPA, EPA-R2-72-118a, Research Triangle Park, NC (1972).
24. Hesketch, H. E. "Fine Particle Collection Efficiency Related to Pressure Drop, Scrubbant and Particle Properties, and Control Mechanism," *J. APCA,* 24(10):939 (1974).
25. Ceilcote Company. "Ionized Wet Scrubber," Technical Bulletin 1255, Akron, OH (1973).
26. Rosealey, H. S., et al. "Past Combustion Methods for Control of NO_x Emissions," paper presented at the International Symposium on NO_x Reduction in Industrial Boilers, and Furnaces, Houston, TX, October 1979.

CHAPTER 7

MISCELLANEOUS AND DEVELOPING TECHNOLOGIES

Incineration technology is the most prevalent method currently used to thermally process hazardous waste. However, incineration is only one of many thermal processing technologies that can be used. This chapter discusses several less conventional methods, as well as some developing technologies that can be used as alternatives to incineration.

CATALYTIC INCINERATION

Catalytic incineration is an alternative process to thermal incineration of wastes, primarily applicable to gaseous wastes processing [1]. There are systems developed for the treatment of liquid chlorinated hydrocarbons [2]. Catalytic incineration always requires a lower oxidation temperature (600–1000°F) than thermal incineration (>1400°F). Catalysts are used to increase the oxidation rate. The catalytic reaction produces the same combustion products and liberates the same heat of combustion as thermal incineration.

The basic catalytic incineration system is illustrated in Figure 7-1. The system consists of a preheat/combustion/mixing chamber, a catalyst element, a hot gas chamber and a heat recovery unit. Various process schemes are illustrated in Figure 7-2.

The CATOXID system, developed by B. F. Goodrich Chemical Company, is illustrated in Figure 7-3. This system makes use of a fluidized bed for catalytic decomposition of liquid chlorinated hydrocarbon wastes.

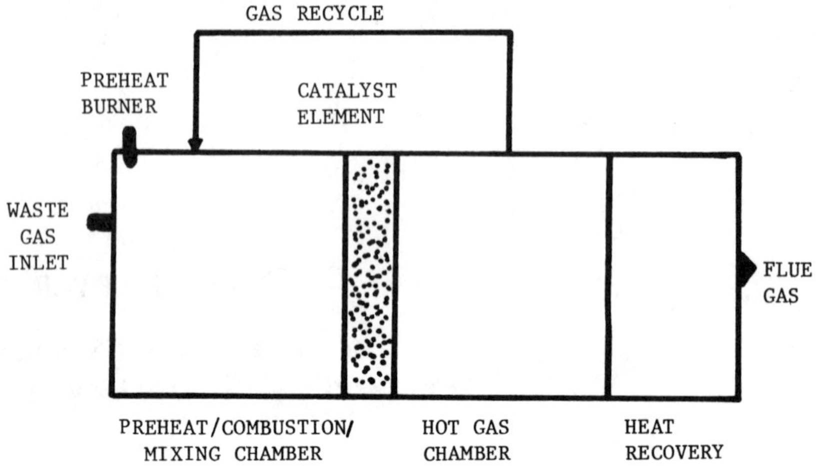

Figure 7-1. Basic catalytic incinerating process (reproduced from Reference 1, courtesy of Marcel Dekker, New York).

Process and Equipment Description

Characteristics of Catalysts

A catalyst bed is composed of three elements: the catalyst, the carriers and the promoters. The catalysts are metals or metal compounds. The oxidation performance of a catalytic incineration system depends heavily on the catalyst selected. Platinum is the primary choice for catalytic incineration applications. Other precious metals used are rhodium, palladium, iridium and gold, and sometimes precious metal alloys such as rhodium/platinum alloy, can be used. The precious metal catalysts usually consist of very small metal particles distributed uniformly on the surface of a support or carrier. The carriers are inert metal oxides of large surface area. Typical carrier materials are alumina, magnesia, asbestos, china clay, activated carbon, porcelain rods and metal wire or ribbon. Most catalytic incineration systems make use of monolithic supports, primarily ceramic honeycomb [3]. The activity of any one catalytic material may be increased by the addition of one or more components, known as promoters. For a particular catalyst used for a specific application, the reaction data are usually available through the manufacturer. Otherwise, pilot plant testing is required to obtain the necessary data.

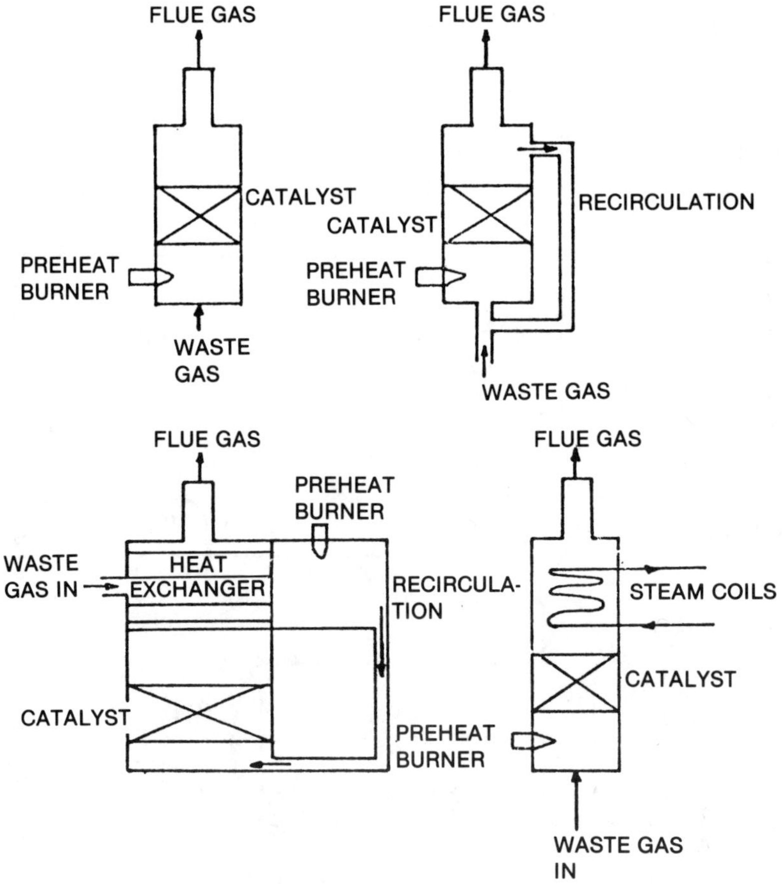

Figure 7-2. Schematics of several catalytic incineration processes (reproduced from Reference 1, courtesy of Marcel Dekker, New York).

Catalytic Reaction Mechanism

The gas phase catalytic reaction consists of the following steps:

- gas phase heat and mass transfer of reactants to the catalyst surface,
- diffusion of adsorbed reactants within the catalysts,
- chemical reaction between reactants,
- diffusion and desorption of reaction products, and
- gas phase heat and mass transfer of products leaving the catalyst surface.

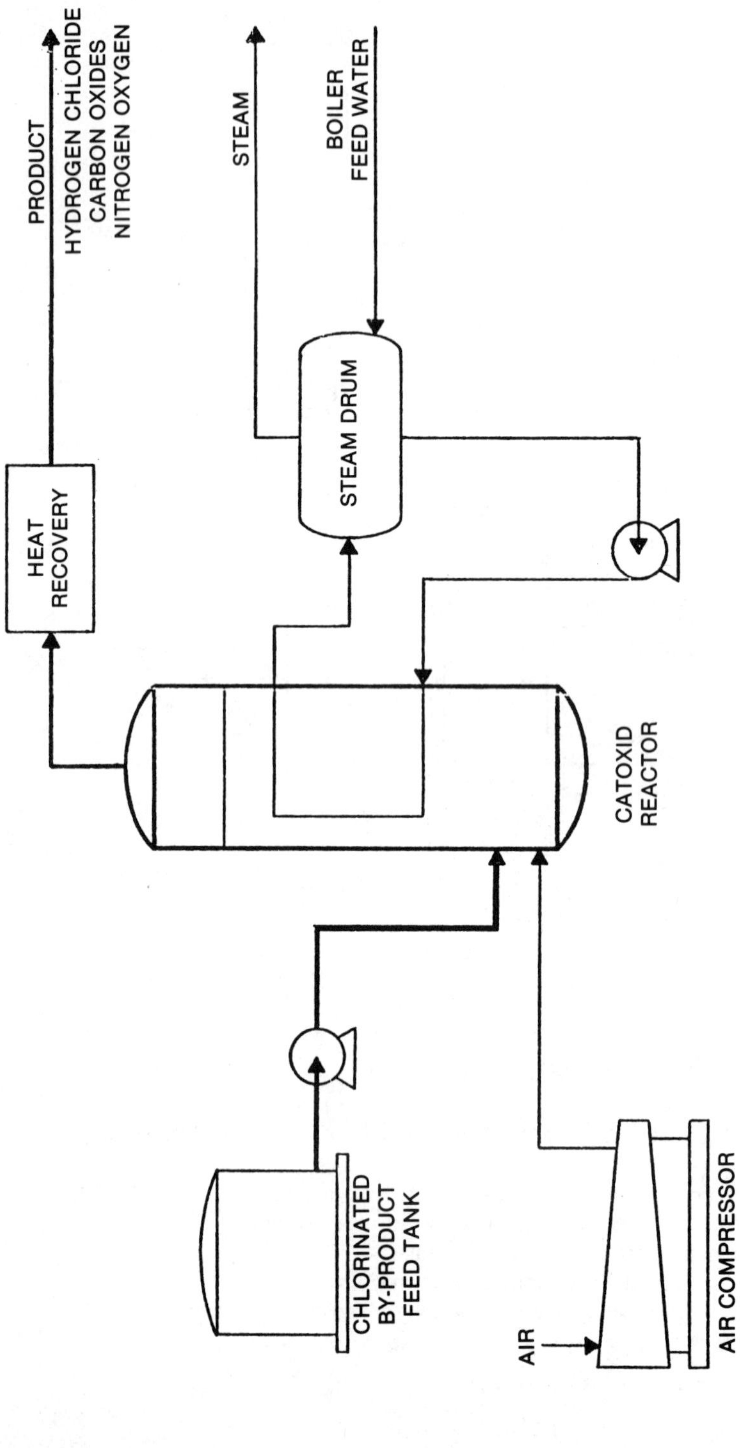

Figure 7-3. CATOXID process (reproduced courtesy of B. F. Goodrich Chemical Company, Cleveland, OH).

These are chemical and physical processes involved in the catalytic reaction, and the slowest of these controls the overall rate of reaction. In catalytic incineration application, heat transfer is important because catalytic incineration is an exothermic process. Since the incineration temperature must be kept constant, consideration must be given to heat transfer rates to and from the surface so that constant local surface temperature can be maintained.

Process Design

The performance of a catalytic incinerator depends not only on the catalysts used, but also on the geometric support of catalysts, incineration temperature, waste type and composition, and flow velocity.

The performance of a catalytic incinerator is dependent on the space velocity of the gas flow, the form of the catalyst element, the bed depth and the incineration temperature.

The space velocity is usually 10–20 ft/sec for a normal heat release system, and higher for high heat release systems. The form of the catalyst element is usually selected to give the optimal equipment design. The depth of the catalyst bed is dependent on the maximum allowable pressure drop, and the incineration temperature is usually fixed by the destruction efficiency requirement.

The gas passing to the catalytic reactor must be heated to the reaction initiation temperature by direct heat exchange. Where a substantial amount of heat is given out by the reactions which take place in the catalyst bed, the temperature of the gas leaving the reactor may be high enough for preheating the incoming gas to the reaction initiation temperature. If the heat given out by the catalytic reaction is insufficient, the incoming gas must be further heated after the heat exchanger by heating with an additional source of heat, such as a burner. Otherwise the reactor will cool down due to thermal losses, and the incoming gas will enter the reactor at a temperature below the reaction initiation temperature.

To maintain satisfactory temperatures of the reaction gas and catalyst in the reactor, temperature indicators must be used to indicate the temperature of the incoming gas immediately before the catalyst bed, of the reacted gas leaving the catalyst bed, and of the catalyst bed at one or more points.

In many cases, it is desirable to incorporate instruments for controlling one or more of these temperatures. For example, the temperature of the incoming gas immediately before the catalyst bed may be arranged to control an auxiliary gas burner so that, when the temperature falls below a set value, a burner is used to heat the incoming gas. Where a substantial temperature rise in the catalyst bed is caused by reaction with oxygen in the gas, the temperature at a point in the catalyst bed, or of the gas leaving the catalyst bed, can be used to maintain the desired oxygen content of the incoming gas.

The flow rate generally should not exceed the upper prescribed limit, and to ensure that, it is necessary to provide an indicating or recording flow meter.

Usually, before introduction of waste gases, the catalyst is activated by passing a treating gas (which may be different from the process gas) through the reactor at a required temperature until the catalyst becomes fully active.

Catalyst Deactivation

In practice, most catalysts deteriorate or gradually lose their activity over a period of operation. This reduction in catalytic performance is referred to as deactivation and depends on a number of factors.

Deactivation may be the result of overheating of the catalyst, resulting in change of the catalyst surface and rapid loss of activity. Deactivation also may be the result of normal thermal effects—such a recrystallization of the catalyst, the carrier or both—and is referred to as thermal aging or sintering. Thermal aging usually results in changing the catalyst surface area and in dispersion of the supported material, and it has an irreversible effect on catalyst activity. Prevention of thermal aging is usually achieved with over-design of the catalyst requirement, and the selection of right materials.

Deactivation also is the result of the combined effects of thermal condition and contamination; that is, the chemical reaction of a contaminant with the catalysts. This is called catalyst poisoning and its effect usually is irreversible. Lead, antimony, cadmium, zinc, phosphorous, arsenic and copper are usually considered to be poisonous to catalysts.

When the contaminants accumulate on the catalysts, their activity is decreased. This is defined as masking. Masking agents are high-molecular-weight organics, silica dusts, alumina dusts and those materials listed as catalyst poisons where thermal conditions are not favorable for chemical reaction. Masking can be prevented by properly designed filters in front of the catalyst bed.

Halogens, halogenated compounds, sulfur, sulfur compounds, nitrogen dioxide, and sodium salts usually are catalyst suppressants. Catalyst suppression is a temporary effect and is reversible.

Catalyst Regeneration

Catalysts can be regenerated to restore their activities. The fouling material on catalysts may be burned off by hot products of combustion of a fuel, or driven off by passing through a stream of superheated steam with or without the addition of air. Such treatment causes oxidation of the catalyst, and the catalyst may require activation by passing through a stream of hydrogen-containing gas with or without the addition of hydrogen sulfide [4].

Where fouling of the catalyst is known or likely to occur during operation, the following alternatives can be used:

1. *Using a single reactor:* New or regenerated catalyst can be periodically fed to the top of a catalyst bed and an equal quantity of fouled catalyst removed from the bottom of the bed while the reactor is in continuous operation.
2. *Using two reactors in series:* During normal operation, the gas flows through the reactors in series and the first reactor acts as a guard. Catalyst in the first reactor absorbs the fouling constituents in the gas. The first reactor can be periodically isolated from the gas stream, which then passes through only the second reactor for removal of the fouled catalyst.
3. *Using two or more reactors in parallel:* During normal operation, one or more reactors are in line with the gas stream. If more than one reactor is used, they are operated at different time intervals. One reactor is the standby reactor, and is isolated from the gas stream. When the catalyst in a reactor becomes fouled, this reactor is isolated from the gas stream and the standby reactor is connected to the gas stream. The fouled catalyst in the reactor which has been isolated may be regenerated in situ or may be withdrawn from the reactor and replaced by new or regenerated catalyst.

Applications

Catalytic incineration applications are primarily in the waste gas treatment. There are catalytic systems developed for chlorinated liquid waste treatment; however, this type of system has very limited applications. The fouling of catalyst is a major concern in the application of catalytic incineration and has to be studied before the selection of catalytic systems.

OXYGEN INCINERATION

Oxygen incineration is a recently developed alternative process for thermal incineration, using oxygen instead of air as oxidant. The oxygen incineration system relies on temperatures of 5000°F to dispose of hazardous wastes [5]. Since the mass flow is low, the unit is compact (about one-fourth the size of other incinerators).

This process is still in the development stage. Its advantages are: high temperatore, thus high efficiency at reduced residence time, and compact size. Its major drawbacks are the selection of high temperature materials for the furnace and the relatively higher cost of oxygen generation. High capital and operating costs may restrict the application of this technology.

PYROLYSIS

Pyrolysis is a starved air operation in that combustion is performed with air levels less than the stoichiometric requirement. The product gases from a pyrolysis furnace are combustible gases which can be used as fuel. A pyrolysis process may be exothermic or endothermic. For most materials, the process is endothermic at lower temperatures and exothermic at higher temperatures. The heating value of the product gases is the sum of the heating value of the original material and the net energy added during pyrolysis, for endothermic operations. For exothermic operations it is the difference of the heating value of the original material and the net energy used during pyrolysis.

Process and Equipment Description

Basic Chemistry

The chemical reaction in pyrolysis is very complicated. However, the goal of the pyrolysis process is to achieve the following reaction:

$$C_mH_n + \frac{m}{2} O_2 \rightarrow mCO + \frac{n}{2} H_2$$

Under certain conditions, free carbon may form through thermal cracking:

$$C_mH_n \rightarrow mC + \frac{n}{2} H_2$$

Other reactions which occur in pyrolysis processes are:

$$C_mH_n + (m + \frac{n}{4})O_2 \rightleftharpoons mCO_2 + \frac{n}{2}H_2O$$

$$C_mH_n + mCO_2 \rightleftharpoons 2mCO + \frac{n}{2}H_2$$

$$C_mH_n + \frac{n}{4}O_2 \rightarrow mC + \frac{n}{2}H_2$$

If a superheated steam is used in the process, the following chemical reaction may occur:

$$C_mH_n + mH_2O \rightleftharpoons mCO + (\frac{n}{2} + m)H_2$$

The objective of the pyrolysis process is to reduce free carbon formation. Free carbon can be reduced by the relatively slow secondary reactions.

$$C + CO_2 \rightleftharpoons 2CO$$

$$C + H_2O \rightleftharpoons CO + H_2$$

Pyrolysis Processes

There are two basic categories of pyrolysis processes: nonslagging and slagging. The nonslagging pyrolysis processes use conventional incinerators, operating under starved air conditions. The products from a pyrolysis furnace are product gases and chars. Chars can be mixed with the waste material and reintroduced into the furnace. Although there are nonslagging systems in pilot and commercial stages, the technology is not yet fully developed and further testing and development are required.

Slagging pyrolysis processes are characterized by very high operating temperatures (3000°F). Hot air (or oxygen) is passed into the base of the reactor (see Figure 7-4), where it reacts with a fraction of the waste. The supply of available oxygen is controlled to ensure that only limited combustion occurs, the hot gas products are drawn up through the descending waste, pyrolysing and—as the gas temperature falls—drying it. Product char formed then reacts with the limited oxygen supply producing temperatures high enough to slag the inorganics present. These are "tapped off", causing the waste to descend.

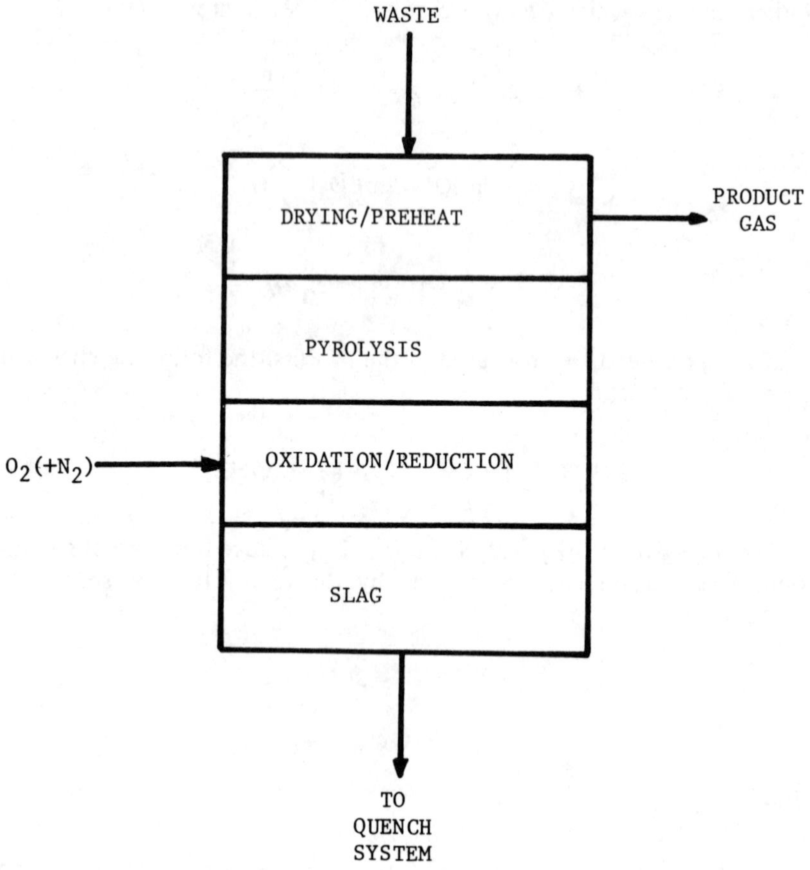

Figure 7-4. Slagging pyrolysis reactor.

Slagging pyrolysis systems achieve very high volume reduction of waste, 95–98%, as the void volume of the slag discharge is very low. They also offer high thermal efficiency. On the other hand, they involve high operating temperatures which can impose a higher level of maintenance in relation to molten slag reactivity versus refractory durability. Some other concerns such as gas channeling and ash fusion difficulties, etc. can only be resolved by full-scale operating experience.

Commercially, two processes are under development: Union Carbide's Purox System [6] and Carborundum's Torrax Process [7].

Applications

Pyrolysis is a viable alternative to conventional thermal incineration systems, offering these advantages:

- ability to burn the product gas in a combustion system separated from the waste, avoiding slagging problems and
- lower potential for air pollution.

However, the technology is still in the development stage. Large-scale operating experiences are required to establish the technical and financial feasibility of commercialization.

CALCINATION

Calcination is the conversion by thermal decomposition at elevated temperatures of aqueous liquids and sludges into solid materials, without any interaction with the gaseous phase (such as the air oxidation which occurs during incineration). For an aqueous solution, the first reaction that occurs is vaporization of the water, leaving a solid material that may be granular and free flowing or compacted. A similar process occurs in the initial treatment of a dewatered sludge. In many instances, it is possible to proceed further with the calcination to drive off volatile materials from the partially calcined solid, e.g., a salt, to form an oxide that is more stable or reusable.

Organic components can also be volatilized from metal organic materials, leaving the metal as a solid residue. The resulting solid may be in the form of a dry granular material that is readily handled, or on heating to a higher temperature the granules may be sintered into a solid mass. On still further heating, certain materials will melt or fuse into a glass-like material. Additives, such as silicates, borax or phosphates, can be used to decrease the leachability of certain components in the final solid or to assist in glass formation.

Sintering [8] can be defined as a limited form of calcination in which the physical structure, but not the chemical nature, of the solid is changed. For instance, dry powders may be heated to sinter them into a solid mass, usually with some reduction in volume. Additives such as silicates, which also sinter readily, can be added to improve this process.

Process and Equipment Description

Calcination can be a continuous process which generally operates at high temperature and atmospheric pressure. It can be applied to aqueous solutions, slurries, sludges and tars with the objective of producing a dry powder or solid material. It also can be used for solids and powders to produce a more acceptable form of waste, i.e., one which is less soluble and therefore does not represent a leachability problem after landfill. Calcination of mixed organic/inorganic wastes can be advantageous because combustion of the organic portion will provide some or all of the heat necessary to sustain the process.

The process results in a substantial volume reduction: ~90% in the case of liquids and 50–70% in the case of inorganic sludges. Only a minor reduction in volume occurs with the sintering of calcination of solids to drive off volatile components. In all cases, the solid material obtained after calcination generally is much more suitable for storage or landfill than the original uncalcined material. However, the calcine may still be toxic unless the toxic component was destroyed or was removed as a volatile material during the calcination. In the latter case, additional treatment would be required on the air or water effluents.

A major advantage of calcination is that several operations often can be carried out in a single step., i.e., concentration, destruction and detoxification. A potential disadvantage is the fuel requirement if the waste does not contain any combustible material. Calcination temperatures are generally in the 1600–2800°F range. The hot gas residence time at the 2800°F zone is 15–30 sec.

1. Open Hearth Calciner. The open hearth calciner in its simplest form is a tray that contains the material to be calcined. However, in this form, calcination is not very efficient because of the difficulty of exposing the material to the hot gases. Consequently, "rabble arms" are used, which rake through the material, constantly exposing fresh surfaces of the solid or sludge to the hot gases. Stationary hearths with rotating rabble arms and rotating hearths with stationary rabble arms are both used. A rotating hearth has the advantage that the solids are moved away from the feed area, thus preventing solid buildup at the feed point, and the stationary rabble arms generally can be simpler and of stronger design than the moving arms. Commercial equipment usually contains 3 to 12 multiple hearths stacked vertically. The feed is introduced at the top and is raked across each hearth by the rabble arms before falling to the next hearth to repeat the process. Several of the upper hearths are used for drying or preheating the material. The middle hearths are the

hottest and complete the calcination, and the lower hearths are used for cooling before discharge of the product.

2. Rotary Kiln Calciner. A rotary kiln (Figure 7-5) consists of a long metal tube lined with a refractory tube that can be up to 14 ft in diameter and 300–400 ft long in large industrial applications [9]. The tube is inclined toward the combustion source which is obtained by auxiliary fuel firing. It is supported at intervals along its length and continuously rotated by an external mechanism. Feed is introduced at the cool end of the calciner at the point where the gases and vapors are evolved. Because of the continuous rotation, a high degree of turbulence, agitation and surface-to-gas contact is achieved. Lengths of chain often are installed near the feed end of the kiln to increase surface agitation and improve heat transfer. With the inclination of the calciner, the partially calcined material travels slowly down the tube while being exposed to increasing temperature, and is finally discharged at the end nearest the heat source. Feed addition and product removal are continuous. Since the drive mechanism is outside the kiln, maintenance is low and there are no internal moving parts such as rabble arms, grates or plows.

3. Fluidized Bed Calciner. Fluidized bed calcination is a more modern process that is particularly advantageous for calcining liquids and slurries. The principle of fluidization is to pass gas through a bed of small particles at a sufficient rate to impart buoyancy to the particles. This causes the bed to expand until the buoyant force of the gas flow is balanced by the gravitational force exerted on the bed particles. The preheated fluidizing air is introduced through multiple orifices equally spaced in the air distributor plate at the bottom of the fluidized bed. Each orifice is surmounted by a cap which helps distribute the air more uniformly and minimizes backflow of solids when the flow of fluidizing air is stopped or reduced. Operation at a superficial fluidizing velocity between 1 and 2 ft/sec is generally satisfactory over beds with particle size range of 0.3 to 0.8 mm. Particle buildup occurs by deposition of already calcined materials on smaller particles, or if necessary, on inert materials which are introduced to form the fluidized bed. The material is exposed to several feet of hot bed with high turbulence and good air-to-gas contact, which provides rapid volatilization of liquids and complete calcination. Caking of the bed, particularly during start-up and shutdown periods, can be avoided by careful feed and temperature control. Residence time in the bed is usually 30–60 minutes and because the bed behaves like a fluid, temperatures are uniform throughout. Multicompartment fluid bed calciners often are used to conserve heat and provide heat exchange between incoming feed and exit gases.

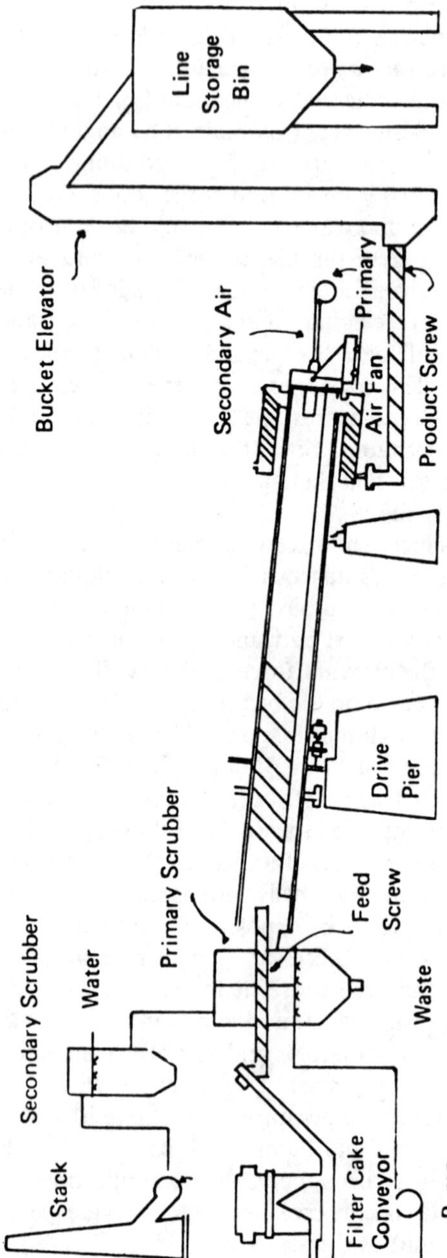

Figure 7-5. Rotary kiln calciner [9].

Applications

Calcination processes have been used in the recalcination of lime sludges from water treatment plants; coking of heavy residues and tars from petroleum refining operations; concentration and volume reduction of liquid radioactive wastes; and treatment of mixed refinery sludges containing hydrocarbons, phosphates and compounds of Ca, Mg, K, Na, S, Fe and Al.

Energy requirements generally are high, but depend on the water and organic content of the waste stream. Calcination of dry material requires about $1\text{–}3 \times 10^6$ Btu/ton of solid product; calcination of a sludge or slurry with 90% water requires about 20×10^6 Btu/ton of solid product. If the waste stream contains a combustible organic fraction, the energy requirements are reduced.

In general, calcination systems require fairly extensive air pollution control equipment including particulate-removal devices, wet scrubbers and possibly final gas adsorption systems.

Combustible hazardous waste also has been burned in commercial cement kilns as a fuel substitute. The burning conditions within the kilns are suitable, based on temperature and residence time, to destroy all combustible hazardous and toxic wastes. Wastes are introduced into the high-temperature burning zone of the kiln rather than into the tailend of the kiln where raw material is fed. Although burning conditions within the kiln are adequate to destroy hazardous toxic materials, the industry is concerned about quality control in the waste [10]. Of particular concern is the chloride content of the fuel which may lead to the condensation and freezing of chlorides in the cooler downstream portions of the kiln operation. At the present time, cement kiln operations limit the chloride content of the waste (up to 2% by weight). However, with more experimentation and the accumulation of knowledge, higher chloride feeds can be accommodated if burning conditions and/or certain designs are modified.

BOILERS

Coincineration of hazardous waste in power plant boilers is a viable method for hazardous waste disposal. There are different types of coal boilers, depending on the type of coal [11]; two types are shown in Figure 7-6. The excess air rate of anthracite coal boilers is 30–40% and that of bituminous coal boilers is 20–30%. The residence time inside the boiler is 3½–4½ sec for anthracite coal boilers and 2½–3½ sec for bituminous

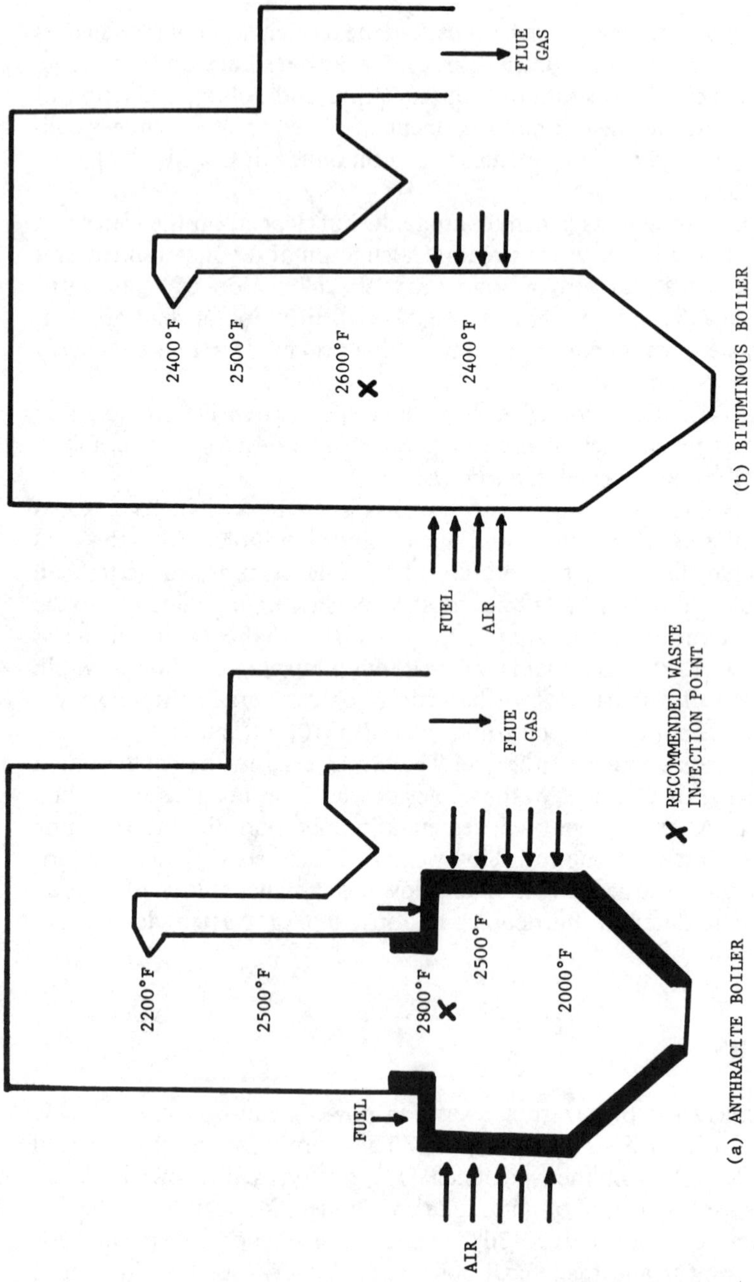

Figure 7-6. Coal boilers [11].

boilers. The temperature distribution of the furnace zone is illustrated in Figure 7-6. Present state-of-the-art of coincineration of hazardous wastes in coal-fired boilers is that the wastes will not exceed 15% total furnace heat duty and that the wastes are to be introduced into the high temperature zone of the furnace.

WET AIR OXIDATION

Wet air oxidation is the aqueous phase oxidation of dissolved or suspended organic substances at elevated temperatures and pressures. Water, which makes up the bulk of the aqueous phase, serves to catalyze the oxidation reactions so they proceed at relatively low temperatures (350–650°F), and at the same time it serves to moderate the oxidation rates removing excess heat by evaporation. Water also provides an excellent heat transfer medium which enables the wet air oxidation process to be thermally self-sustaining with relatively low organic feed concentrations.

The oxygen required by wet air oxidation reactions is provided by an oxygen-containing gas, usually air, bubbled through the liquid phase in a reactor used to contain the process. The process pressure is maintained at a level high enough to prevent excessive evaporation of the liquid phase, generally between 300 and 3000 psig.

Figure 7-7 shows a simplified flow scheme of a continuous wet air oxidation system [12]. A wastewater stream containing oxidizable contaminants is pumped to the system pressure by means of a positive displacement pump. The liquid passes through a heat exchanger where it is transferred against hot oxidized effluent. The temperature of the incoming feed is increased to a level necessary to support the oxidation reaction in the reactor vessel. The incoming liquid is mixed with air at the bottom of the reactor, and oxidation begins to take place. As oxidation progresses up through the reactor, the heat of combustion is liberated, increasing the temperature of the reaction mixture. The hot oxidized effluent, mainly steam, water, carbon dioxide and nitrogen, is cooled in the heat exchanger. The pressure is dropped through a specially designed automatic control valve. Next, liquid and noncondensables are disengaged in a separator drum and discharged separately.

Control of a wet air oxidation system is a relatively simple matter. The system is basically self-regulating in many respects; that is, oxidation takes place in a massive amount of water which serves as an effective heat sink and prevents the reaction from "running away". Should a surge or organic material enter the reactor, either the air would be depleted, or the heat liberated by the additional oxidation would be expended in forming more steam.

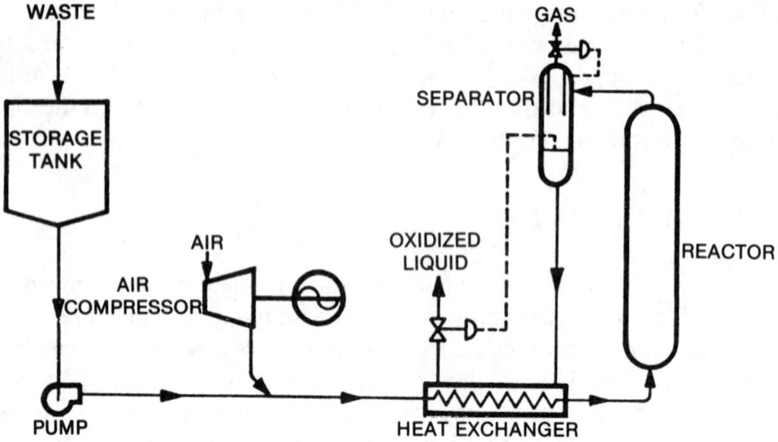

Figure 7-7. Wet air oxidation system ((reproduced from Reference 12, courtesy of Chemical Engineering Progress, NY).

A significant advantage of wet air oxidation is the minimal air pollution problems that it causes. Contaminants tend to stay in the aqueous phase. Such materials as sulfur compounds, chlorinated hydrocarbons or heavy metals end up in their highest oxidation state, i.e., sulfates, hydrochloric acid or a salt thereof.

Process and Equipment Description

The flow sheet shown in Figure 7-7 is the basic system, which can be varied almost infinitely. Figures 7-8 and 7-9 show variations for energy recovery. Figure 7-8 illustrates a cycle for generating saturated or slightly superheated steam at about 600 psig which may be combined with the cycle shown in Figure 7-9 for the production of electric power. The gas stream shown in Figure 7-8 may be passed through an expander coupled to the compressor. In this case, there would probably be only enough energy in the gas to recover a portion of the power required for compression.

Figure 7-10 shows a flow sheet for a high Btu waste stream, that is, one with an organic content $\gtrsim 10\%$. In this case, the heat liberated by the oxidation reaction might be sufficient to evaporate all the water. To avoid this, water condensed in the boiler is recirculated to the reactor.

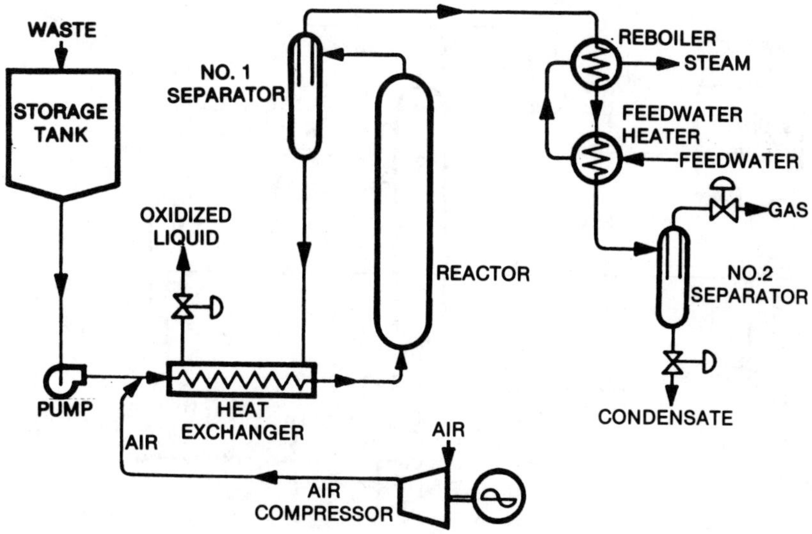

Figure 7-8. Wet air oxidation system for steam generation (reproduced from Reference 12, courtesy of Chemical Engineering Progress, NY).

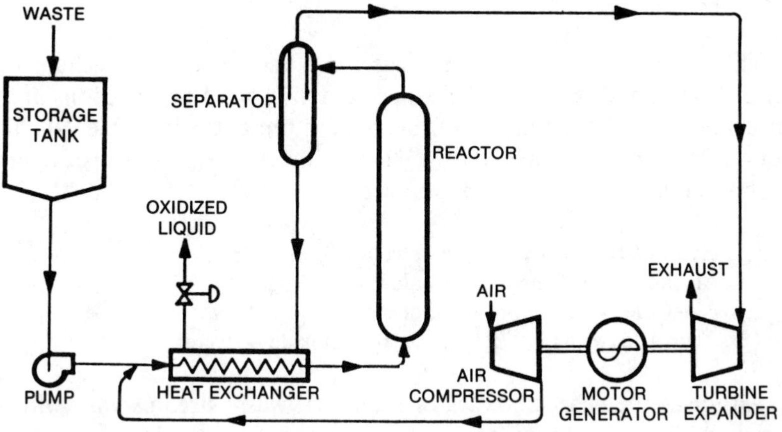

Figure 7-9. Wet air oxidation system for power generation (reproduced from Reference 12, courtesy of Chemical Engineering Progress, NY).

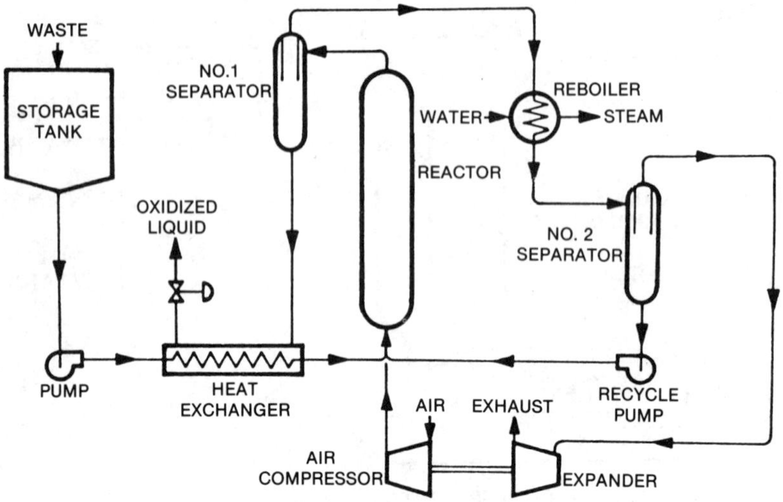

Figure 7-10. Wet air oxidation system for concentrated waste streams (reproduced from Reference 12, courtesy of Chemical Engineering Progress, NY).

Process Characteristics

The wet air oxidation process has three basic reaction mechanisms: hydrolysis, mass transfer and chemical kinetics. Brief explanations of the mechanisms and their major influences are presented in Table 7-1. The four basic steps [13] involved in eliminating the oxidation of a hydrocarbon pollutant by wet oxidation are:

Hydrocarbon + oxygen	→	alcohol
Alcohol + oxygen	→	aldehyde
Aldehyde + oxygen	→	acid
Acid + oxygen	→	carbon dioxide + water

Although the characteristics of industrial waste streams vary widely, nearly all have one thing in common: the organic materials break down into several intermediate compounds before complete oxidation occurs.

The process is efficient in total organic carbon (TOC) reduction for most compounds but not for acetates and benzoic acid. Evaluating waste streams for wet air oxidation treatment requires special effort to determine if difficult-to-reduce TOC intermediate compounds will be formed.

Table 7-1. Wet Air Oxidation Process Reaction Mechanisms[a]

Reaction Mechanism	Typical Effects	Strongest Influences
Hydrolysis	Dissolves solids Splits long-chain hydrocarbons	pH Temperature
Mass Transfer	Dissolves, abosrbs oxygen	Pressure Presence of liquid-gas interface
Chemical Kinetics	Oxidizes organic chemicals	Temperature Catalysts Oxygen activity

[a]Reproduced from Reference 13, courtesy of Plant Engineering, Barrington, IL.

Evaluating Process Applicability

A complete analysis of the specific waste stream is required to determine the suitability and probable performance of a wet-oxidation system. A representative waste sample is subjected to a series of autoclave tests, conducted at timed intervals at various pressures and temperatures. Chemical oxygen demand (COD) and TOC readings are recorded for each test. A series of graphs is then developed showing the correlation between time and the percentage of COD and TOC reductions. Typical oxidation rate data are illustrated in Table 7-2 and Figure 7-11.

Approximate installed cost of a full-size plant can be projected from the test data. If the preliminary data indicate that cost and peformance will be acceptable, a continuous pilot-plant test should be conducted. Corrosion tests should be run concurrently under actual operating conditions. Data from the pilot plant operation can be used to design the full-size plant.

Equipment Development

The type and construction of the individual equipment components depend to some extent on the nature and quantity of the waste to be processed. For sludges and abrasive slurries, a hydraulic exchange bag pump is employed. On cleaner materials, a piston or plunger type multiplex pump is used.

Heat exchangers are either double-pipe or shell-and-tube, depending on the fouling tendency of the waste. The heat exchanger system is the most expensive part of the wet air oxidation system.

Table 7-2. Destruction of Organics by Wet Air Oxidation[a]

Chemical	Temp. (°F)	Pressure (psig)	Contact Time (min)	TOC Reduction (%)
Aliphatics:				
Acetate	550	1500	30	24
Ethylene Gycol	550	1500	30	88
Formaldehyde	550	1500	30	97
Formate	550	1500	30	96
Fumeric Acid	550	1500	30	94
Glycolic Acid	500	1200	6	90
Aromatics				
Benzoic Acid	550	1500	30	17
O-Cresol	550	1500	30	84
Phenol	500	1200	6	90
P-Quinone	500	1200	6	89
Chlorinated Hydrocarbons:				
Carbon Tetrachloride	500	1500	30	99
DDT-25	550	1500	30	60
2, 4-Dichlorophenol	500	1200	6	81
O-Chlorophenol	500	1200	6	66
P-Chlorobenzoic Acid	550	1500	60	34
Pentachlorophenol	550	1500	30	94
Nitrogenous Organics:				
Aniline	550	1500	30	79
Cyanuric Acid	500	1200	30	49
Monoethanolamine	550	1500	30	88
P-Nitrobenzoic Acid	550	1500	60	65
Refractory:				
Diethylene Glycol	550	1500	30	66
t-Butyl Alcohol	550	1500	30	91
Chlorinated Organics	550	1500	30	78
Chlorinated Organics	550	1500	60	91
Chlorinated Organics	550	1500	30	93
Epoxy	550	1500	30	86
Epoxy	550	1500	30	94
Polyethylene	550	1500	30	67
Polyethylene	600	2000	30	74
Polyethylene	550	1500	30	81
Polyethylene	600	2000	30	90

[a]Reproduced courtesy of Astro Metallurgical Corporation, Wooster, OH.

Reactors are nonmechanically agitated vertical pressure vessels. Recent development work has illustrated the impracticality of using a single large reactor in wet air oxidation systems, because high operating pressures require thick-wall construction involving huge amounts of materials. Additionally, complex reactor interiors are necessary to ensure proper mass transfer and reaction kinetics. Multistage reactors are gradually replacing the single reactor concept in industrial applications. Reactors usually are connected in series with the number of units needed determined by the specific application. Each reactor is sized to minimize material and construction costs and optimize reaction kinetics and mass transfer.

Standard commercial compressors, pumps and motor controls can be used in wet air oxidation applications. Standard instrumentation also can be used. Smaller units employ reciprocating compressors; larger systems may have centrifugal or combined centrifugal/reciprocating booster air systems.

Selection of reactor material depends on the corrosiveness of the waste stream and the oxidation products.

Applications

Wet air oxidation can be used to oxidize any material, including inorganics with a COD value. Wet air oxidation also has been used in conjunction with biotreatment plant (Figure 7-12). In this type of system, only 50% oxidation is required. At this degree of oxidation, the solid residue is ~90% inert. The unoxidized organic matter is recycled to the inlet of the treatment plant. A feature of this system is the recycling of nutrients, which can reduce or eliminate the need to add nitrogen to the waste stream.

Wet air oxidation has been used to recover chromium in treatment of sludge from a glue manufacturer. A wet air oxidation system also has been used for recovery of reusable fillers from paper mill sludges (Figure 7-13). Cellulose fiber is oxidized or solubilized, and the remaining inert suspended solids can be reused in papermaking. Silver can be recovered from used photographic film by wet air oxidation. Wet air oxidation also can be used as a pulping process as illustrated in Figure 7-14. Wet air oxidation has been proposed for processing ores in the mining industry. If the ores were slurried and wet air oxidized, the sulfides in the ores would be converted to sulfates. The ore could then be processed in the usual way without obnoxious sulfur emissions.

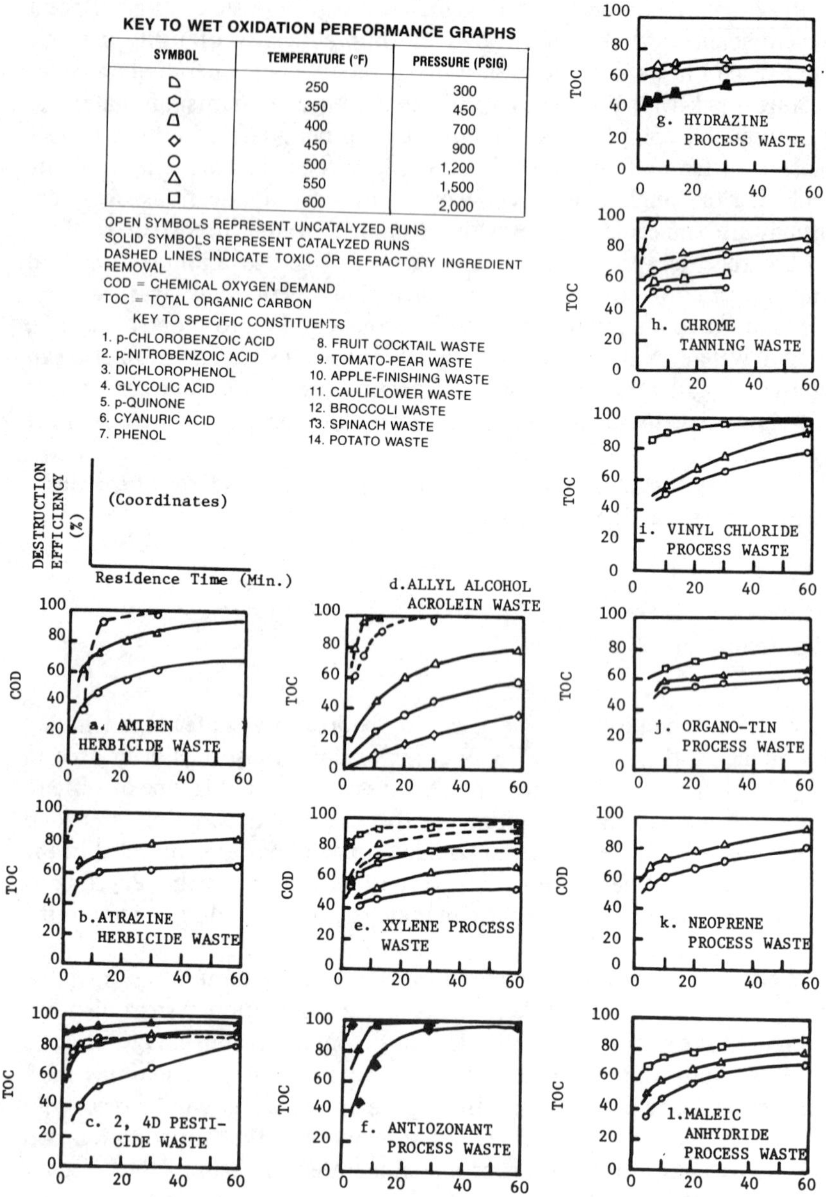

KEY TO WET OXIDATION PERFORMANCE GRAPHS

SYMBOL	TEMPERATURE (°F)	PRESSURE (PSIG)
◻	250	300
○	350	450
△	400	700
◇	450	900
○	500	1,200
△	550	1,500
☐	600	2,000

OPEN SYMBOLS REPRESENT UNCATALYZED RUNS
SOLID SYMBOLS REPRESENT CATALYZED RUNS
DASHED LINES INDICATE TOXIC OR REFRACTORY INGREDIENT REMOVAL
COD = CHEMICAL OXYGEN DEMAND
TOC = TOTAL ORGANIC CARBON

KEY TO SPECIFIC CONSTITUENTS
1. p-CHLOROBENZOIC ACID
2. p-NITROBENZOIC ACID
3. DICHLOROPHENOL
4. GLYCOLIC ACID
5. p-QUINONE
6. CYANURIC ACID
7. PHENOL
8. FRUIT COCKTAIL WASTE
9. TOMATO-PEAR WASTE
10. APPLE-FINISHING WASTE
11. CAULIFLOWER WASTE
12. BROCCOLI WASTE
13. SPINACH WASTE
14. POTATO WASTE

Figure 7-11. Wet air oxidation performance data (reproduced courtesy of Astro Metallurgical Corporation, Wooster, OH).

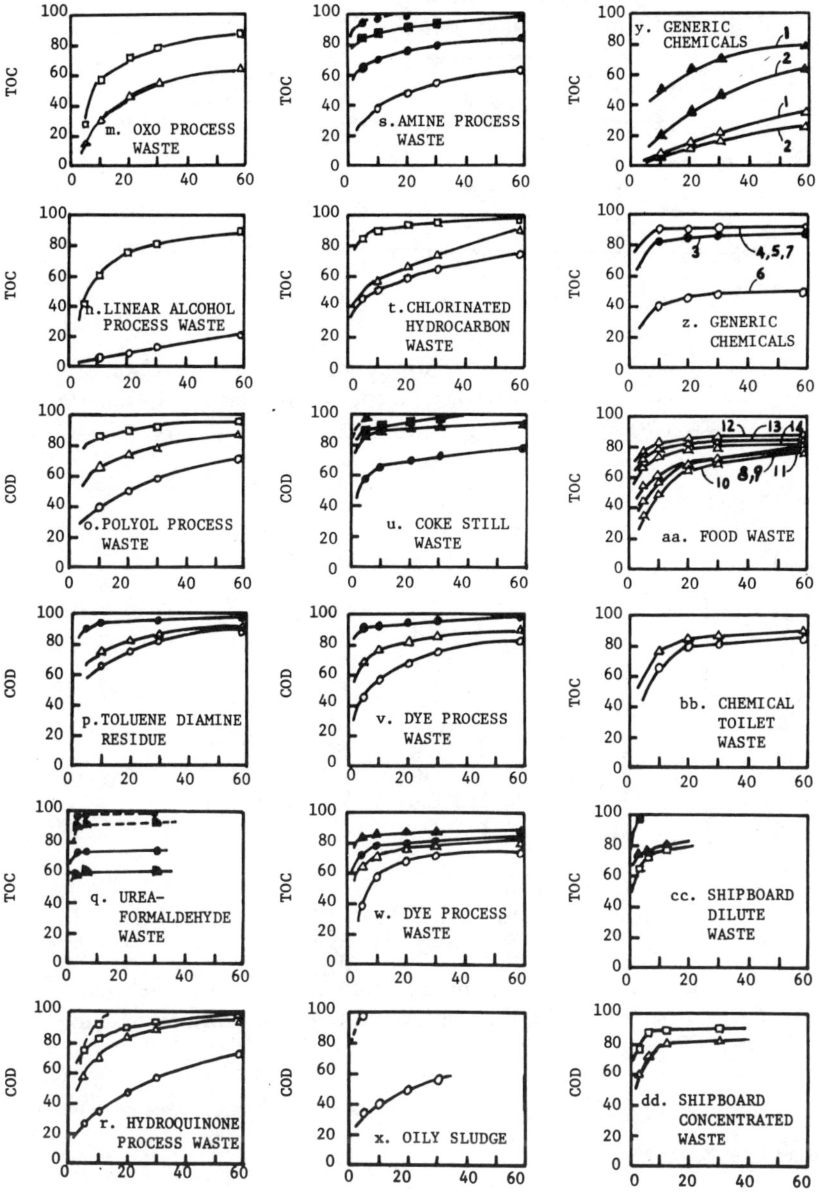
TOC
m. OXO PROCESS WASTE
TOC
s. AMINE PROCESS WASTE
TOC
y. GENERIC CHEMICALS
1
2
1
2
TOC
n. LINEAR ALCOHOL PROCESS WASTE
TOC
t. CHLORINATED HYDROCARBON WASTE
TOC
z. GENERIC CHEMICALS
3
4,5,7
6
COD
o. POLYOL PROCESS WASTE
COD
u. COKE STILL WASTE
TOC
aa. FOOD WASTE
12
13
14
10
8,9
11
COD
p. TOLUENE DIAMINE RESIDUE
COD
v. DYE PROCESS WASTE
TOC
bb. CHEMICAL TOILET WASTE
TOC
q. UREA-FORMALDEHYDE WASTE
TOC
w. DYE PROCESS WASTE
TOC
cc. SHIPBOARD DILUTE WASTE
COD
r. HYDROQUINONE PROCESS WASTE
COD
x. OILY SLUDGE
COD
dd. SHIPBOARD CONCENTRATED WASTE
0
20
40
60
80
100

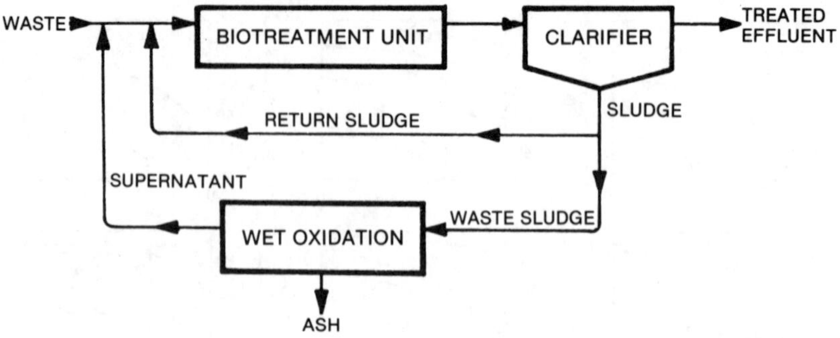

Figure 7-12. Biotreatment system incorporating wet air oxidation system (reproduced from Reference 12, courtesy of Chemical Engineering Progress, NY).

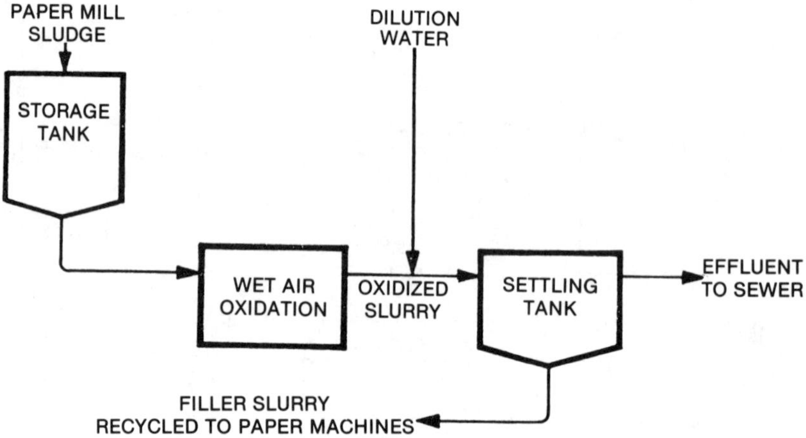

Figure 7-13. Filler recovery through wet air oxidation system (reproduced from Reference 12, courtesy of Chemical Engineering Progress, NY).

DISTILLATION

Distillation is a unit operational process often employed in industry to segregate, separate or purify liquid organic product streams, some of which contain aqueous fractions. Sometimes the operation is used to

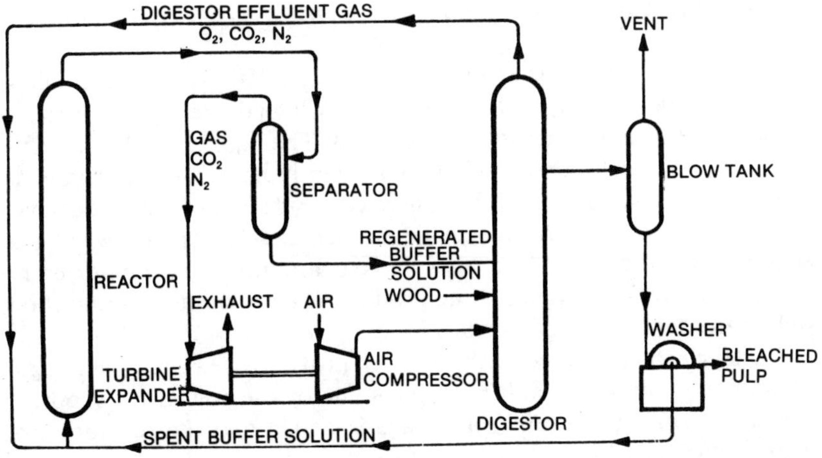

Figure 7-14. Wet air oxidation pulping system (reproduced from Reference 12, courtesy of Chemical Engineering Progress, NY).

recover one product; sometimes it is used to produce many desirable fractions from a process stream. Distillation usually is nondestructive and can produce products of any desired composition. Its practical limitations are primarily economic requirements, i.e., both operating and equipment costs.

Until now, organic solvent recovery has been justified only when economics warranted it. However, with the recent enforcement of stringent air pollution regulations, most organic solvents are prohibited from entering the atmosphere. This is being accomplished in a number of ways, such as direct condensation, demisting, absorption, etc. Often, regeneration of absorption media produces aqueous and/or organic streams. Distillation is often employed to recover the organics.

In the recovery of other waste solvents, such as painting or plating wastes or plastic coating wastes, distillation cannot directly compete with other recovery or disposal processes. However, this can be offset when favorable byproduct credits exist. With more and more stringent regulations on air pollution, liquid effluents and land site disposal, and with the rising cost of organic chemicals (i.e., increased byproduct credit) and the newer concept of waste management (resource recovery), distillation should become more competitive with other methods for liquid organic recovery or disposal.

Process and Equipment Description

1. Batch Distallation. The simplest form of distillation is a single equilibrium stage operation carried out in a still in which the reboiler equivalent consists of a steam jacket or a heating coil. The liquid is boiled and the vapor is driven off, condensed and collected in an accumulator (a condensed vapor collector) until the desired concentration of the product has been reached. As the remaining liquid becomes leaner in the volatile component and richer in the less volatile component, its volume diminishes. If the residual liquid is the product, then bottoms concentration will be the controlling parameter.

The batch still consists of a vessel which provides one equilibrium stage. By adding a condenser and recycling some of the condensed vapor, a second vapor/liquid equilibrium stage is added and the separation is improved (Figure 7-15).

2. Continuous Fractional Distillation (Figure 7-16). A steady stream feed enters the column. The column contains plates or packing (packing usually is used only in small-scale equipment) which provide additional vapor/liquid contact (equilibrium) stages. Overhead vapors and bottoms are continuously withdrawn. Vapor from the top plate is condensed and collected in a vessel known as an accumulator. Some of the liquid in the accumulator is continuously returned to the top plate of the column as

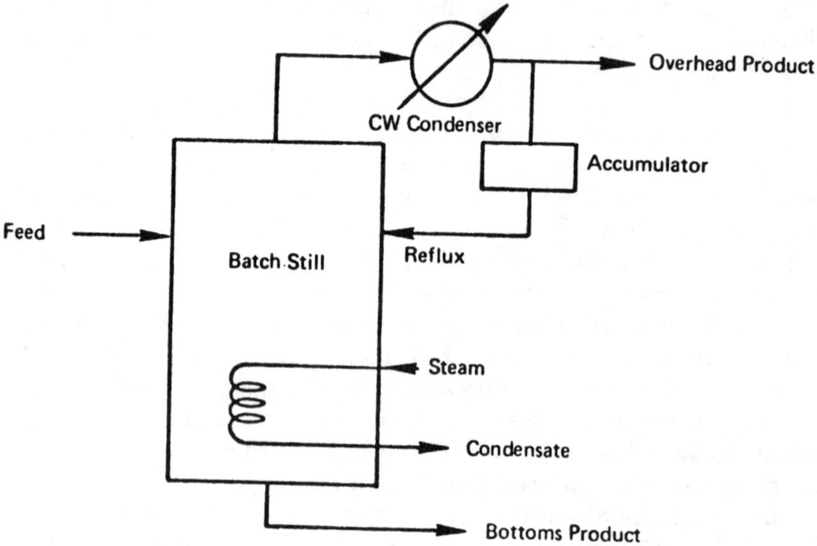

Figure 7-15. Batch distillation process [9]

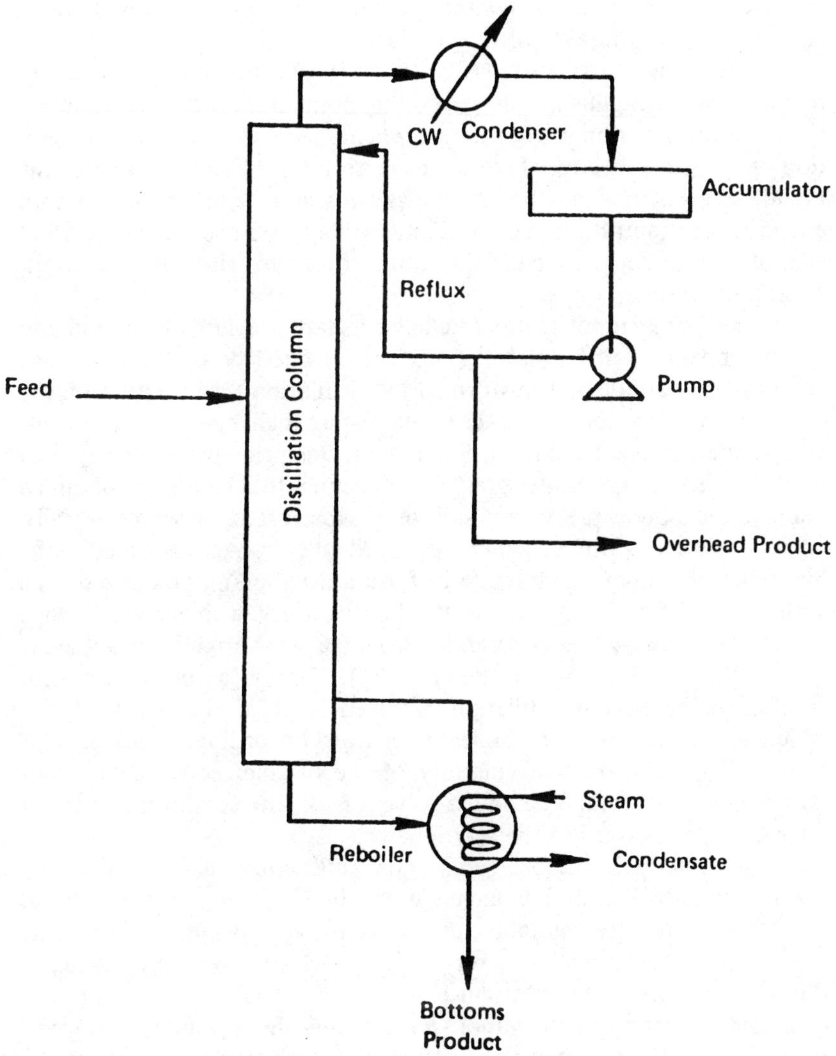

Figure 7-16. Continuous distillation process [9].

reflux, and the remainder is continuously withdrawn as the overhead product stream. At the bottom of the column, the liquid collects in the reboiler, where it is heated by steam coils or a steam jacket. The function of the reboiler is to receive the liquid overflow from the lowest plate and return a portion of this as a vapor stream; the remainder is withdrawn continuously as a liquid bottom product.

3. Azeotropic Distillation. (Figure 7-17). An azeotrope is a liquid mixture that maintains a constant boiling point and produces a vapor of the same composition as the mixture when boiled. Because the composition of the vapor produced from an azeotrope is the same as that of the liquid, an azeotrope may be boiled away at a constant pressure, without change in concentration in either liquid or vapor. Since the temperature cannot vary under these conditions, azeotropes are also called constant boiling mixtures.

An azeotrope cannot be separated by constant pressure distillation into its components. Furthermore, a mixture on one side of the azeotrope composition cannot be transformed by distillation to a mixture on the other side of the azeotrope. If the total pressure is changed, the azeotropic composition is usually shifted. Sometimes, this principle can be applied to obtain separations under pressure or vacuum that cannot be obtained under atmospheric pressure conditions. Most often, however, a third component—an additive, sometimes called an entrainer—is added to the binary (two-component) mixture to form a new boiling-point azeotrope with one of the original constituents. The volatility of the new azeotrope is such that it may be easily separated from the other original constituents.

4. Extractive Distillation (Figure 7-18). This is a multicomponent rectification method of distillation. A solvent is added to a binary mixture which is difficult or impossible to separate by ordinary means. This solvent alters the relative volatility of the original constituents, thus permitting separation. The added solvent is of low volatility and is not appreciably vaporized in the fractionator.

5. Molecular Distillation. Molecular distillation is a form of a very low-pressure distillation conducted at absolute pressures of the order of 0.003 mm of mercury suitable for heat-sensitive substances. Ordinarily the net rate of evaporation is very low, at a safe temperature, owing to the fact that evaporated molecules are reflected back to the liquid after collisions occurring in the vapor. By reducing the absolute pressure to values used in the molecular distillation, the mean free path of the molecules becomes very large (on the order of 0.4 in.). If the condensing surface is then placed at a distance not exceeding a few inches from the vaporizing liquid surface, very small molecules will return to the liquid, and the net rate of evaporation is substantially improved.

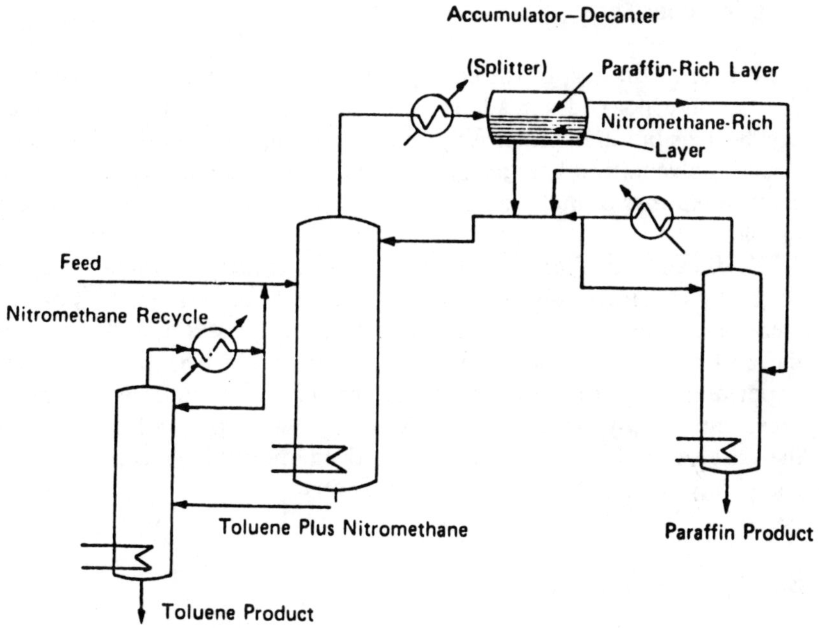

Figure 7-17. Azeotropic distillation process [9].

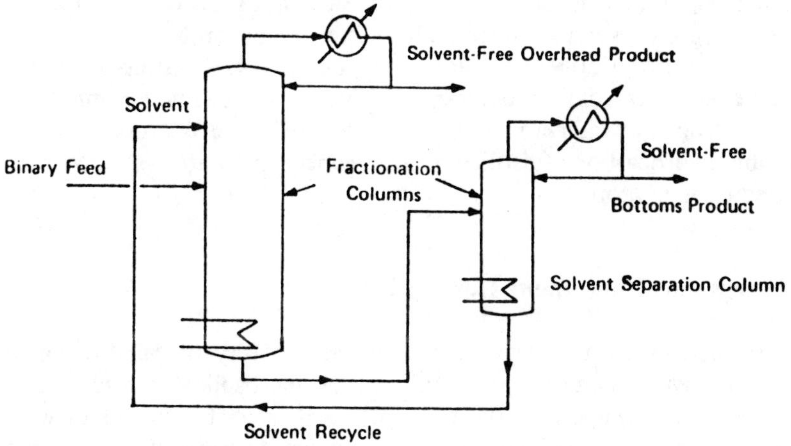

Figure 7-18. Extractive distillation process [9].

Applications

Because of the cost of the energy requirements, treatment of waste by distillation is not widespread. The only hazardous waste materials which can be feasibly and practicably treated are liquid organics, including organic solvents and halogenated organics, which do not contain appreciable quantities of materials that would cause operational or equipment problems.

Historically, distillable solvents have been recovered primarily as an economic consideration, but with imposition of more stringent government regulations for the disposal of hazardous wastes and increases in the cost of petrochemicals, byproduct credits will become even more important. Thus, the recovery of organic solvents should become more prevalent. If by-product credit offsets the higher cost of distillation vs the cost of other recovery methods, distillation will become a more competitive means of waste solvent recovery.

STEAM DISTILLATION

Steam distillation is a proven process for removing water-immiscible, volatile organic chemical compounds from waste streams. It is also used, in special cases, to recover heat-sensitive high-boiling-point water-soluble components from waste streams.

The process can be applied to any waste stream that can be adequately contacted with steam or water and that does not react or decompose in the presence of water or steam. The waste stream can be in the form of liquids, slurries, sludges or solids. The types of volatile components that can be removed from a process or waste stream include water-immiscible hydrocarbons, water-immiscible halogenated hydrocarbons, water-soluble hydrocarbons (distilled as azeotropes) and water-soluble hydrocarbons (nonazeotrope).

Process and Equipment Description

Steam distillation may be used for the recovery or purification of volatile organic material from liquid wastes, inert solids or in some cases slurries. The organic material to be removed from the process or waste stream must have a high enough vapor pressure to codistill with steam at a temperature low enough to prevent decomposition.

When steam distillation is used to reduce the concentration of a volatile component to very low levels, it is normally conducted as a batch or semibatch operation. In the case of a batch steam distillation, the still is filled with waste. The waste is heated to temperature and the distillation is conducted by bubbling steam through the liquid phase. In semibatch operation, the waste containing a high ratio of volatiles to nonvolatiles is fed to the still continuously for a given period of time while the volatile component is steam distilled from the mixture. After the last of the feed is introduced, the steam distillation is continued until the volatiles are reduced to the desired residual concentration.

Slurries, emulsions, sludges and bulk solids also may be treated by steam distillation to remove volatile organics. This unit operation may be conducted in the presence of heavy metals, provided there is no chemical reaction.

Reactivity of the process or waste stream with water or steam is a limitation of this process. It is not possible to recover some chlorinated hydrocarbons from organic waste streams, for example, since the water (or steam) removes the stabilizer normally used in the chlorinated hydrocarbon and peroxide formation and/or decomposition takes place. Nevertheless, some stabilizer systems are so designed that as the chlorinated solvent is steam distilled, the stabilizers are also steam distilled and are retained in the chlorinated solvent.

Steam distillation initially generates two output streams: the stripped waste (the bottom) and a vapor stream of volatile component and water vapor (the overhead product). The overhead product stream usually is condensed, and in the case of a water-immiscible organic, the immiscible liquids are separated to generate a second and third stream, a liquid stream of nearly pure volatile component and a waste water stream containing traces of the immiscible volatile component. In case of a water-soluble organic, the organic material may be recovered in a concentrated form by partially condensing the vapors, and then the pure product recovered by evaporation, distillation or other means.

The equipment used for steam distillation in waste treatment is usually a batch distillation system with provision for bubbling steam through the charge in the batch still. A typical arrangement for a steam distillation system is shown in Figure 7-19.

When sludges or liquids containing materials that may polymerize or precipitate out are treated by steam distillation, the batch still should be designed with removable tube heating bundles and adequate access to the still to facilitate removal of solid deposits.

Applications

Steam distillation is used in waste treatment to remove volatile organic material from liquids, solids, slurries or sludges. The volatile organic

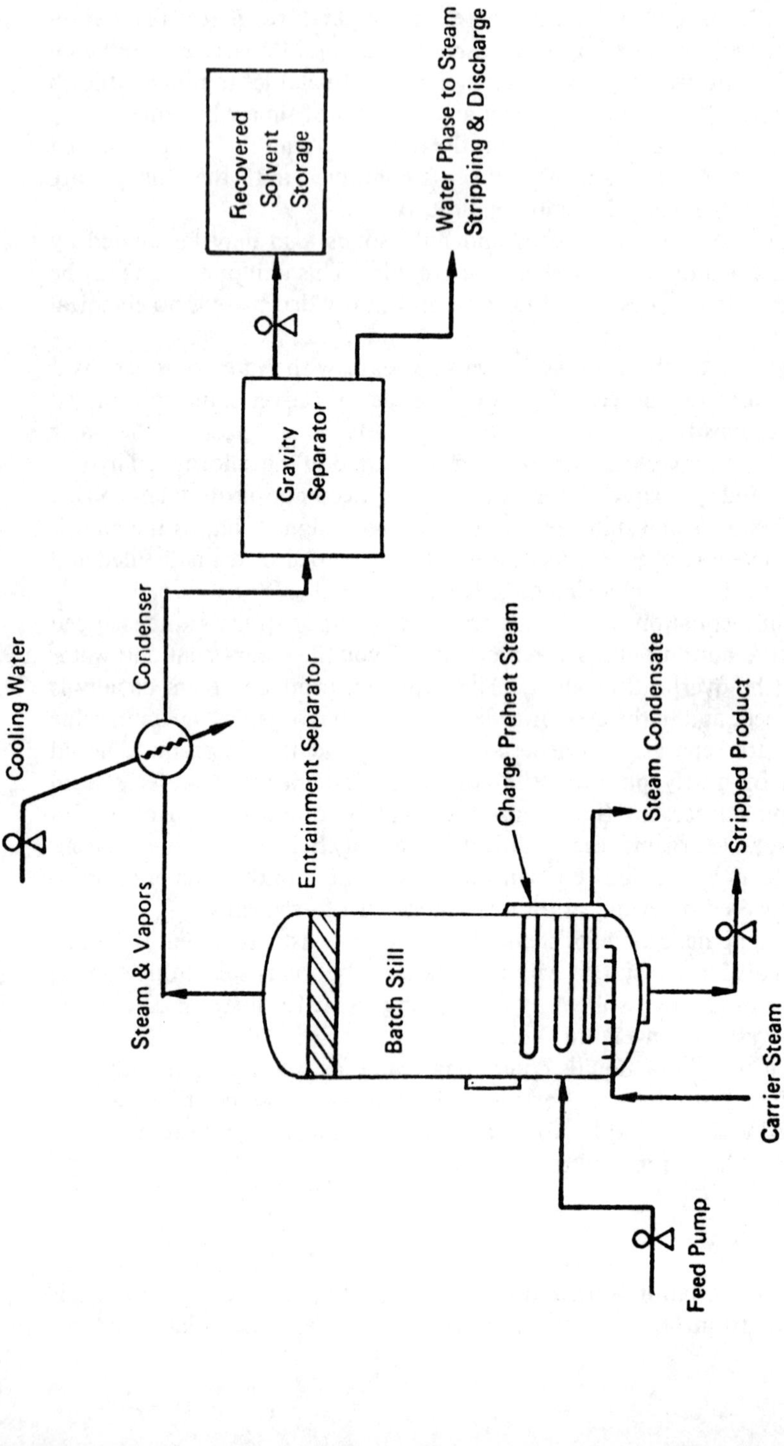

Figure 7-19. Flow diagram of a steam distillation system [9].

component is recovered for its value, and its residual concentration is reduced sufficiently to allow the resulting liquid, solid or sludge to be safely disposed of. Frequently, steam distillation is used for recovering a mixture of volatile hydrocarbons from a waste stream and the mixture of hydrocarbons then is further separated by conventional distillation.

EVAPORATION

Evaporation is a well defined, well established process, essentially omnipresent in industry. It is being used currently for the treatment of hazardous waste such as radioactive liquids and sludges and concentrating of plating and paint solvent waste, among many other applcations. It is capable of handling liquids, slurries and sometimes sludges, both organic and inorganic, containing suspended or dissolved solids or dissolved liquids, where one of the components is essentially nonvolatile. It can be used to reduce waste volume prior to landfill disposal or incineration.

Process and Equipment Description

Types of Evaporators

1. *Indirect evaporation* is a type of evaporation system where the heating medium is separated from the evaporating liquid by physical barriers. The heating medium may be confined by tubes, coils, jackets, flat plates, etc. By far the largest number of industrial evaporators employ tubular heating surfaces. Generally, in the tubular type the fluid to be evaporated is inside the tubes. Circulation of liquid past the heating surface may be induced by boiling or by mechanical means. In the latter case, boiling may or may not occur on the heating surface.
2. *Direct contact evaporation* is the type of system where the heating medium is in contact with the liquid to be vaporized. This type includes submerged combustion flue gas contact, immersed electrode evaporation and direct steam sparging.
3. *Natural evaporation* makes use of natural elements or phenomena to induced evaporation (e.g., solar energy or diffusion).

Evaporator Arrangements

Single-effect evaporators are used where the required capacity is small, steam is cheap, the vapors or liquids are so corrosive that very expensive materials of construction are required, or when the vapor is so contaminated that it cannot be reused. Single-effect evaporators may be operated in batch, semi-batch, continuous batch or continuous mode.

In *batch evaporators,* filling, evaporating and emptying are consecutive steps. This method of operation is rarely used, since it requires the evaporator body to be large enough to hold the entire feed charge and the heating element to be placed low enough so as not to be exposed when the liquid volume has been reduced during evaporation. The more usual method of operation in a single-effect evaporator is semibatch, wherein the feed is continually added to maintain a constant liquid level until the entire charge reaches the desired concentration.

Evaporators of *continuous batch* type usually have a continuous feed and, over at least part of the cycle, a continuous discharge. One method of operating in continuous batch mode is to circulate the charge from a storage tank to the evaporator and back until the liquid in the feed tank is at a predetermined concentration, and then to proceed to evaporate to the final product concentration by finishing in small batches.

The simplest, though not the least expensive, means of reducing the energy requirements of evaporation is to compress the vapor from a single-effect evaporator so that the vapor can be used as the heating medium in the same evaporator: the thermocompression evaporator (Figure 7-20). Compression may be accomplished by mechanical means or by a steam jet eductor. To keep the compressor cost and power requirements within reason, the evaporator must work within a fairly narrow temperature differential between the liquor and the compressed vapor, usually from 10 to 20°F. This means that a large evaporator heating surface area is required and, therefore, equipment cost is high.

The principal purpose for *multiple-effect evaporation* (Figure 7-21) is economizing on energy consumption. Most such evaporators operate on a continuous basis, although for a few difficult feeds a continuous-batch cycle may be employed. In a multiple-effect evaporator, steam from an outside source is condensed in the heating element of the first effect. If the feed to the first effect is at a temperature near the boiling point of the liquor in the first effect, one pound of steam will evaporate almost one pound of water. If the vapor produced in the first effect is the heating medium of the second effect which is operating at a lower pressure, another pound of water is evaporated which could go to a condenser if the evaporator is a double-effect. If the evaporation is a triple-effect, the vapor may be used as the heating medium of the third effect. This may be repeated for any number of effects. Each consecutive effect operates at a lower pressure than the preceding effect.

The feed to a multiple-effect evaporator is usually transferred from one

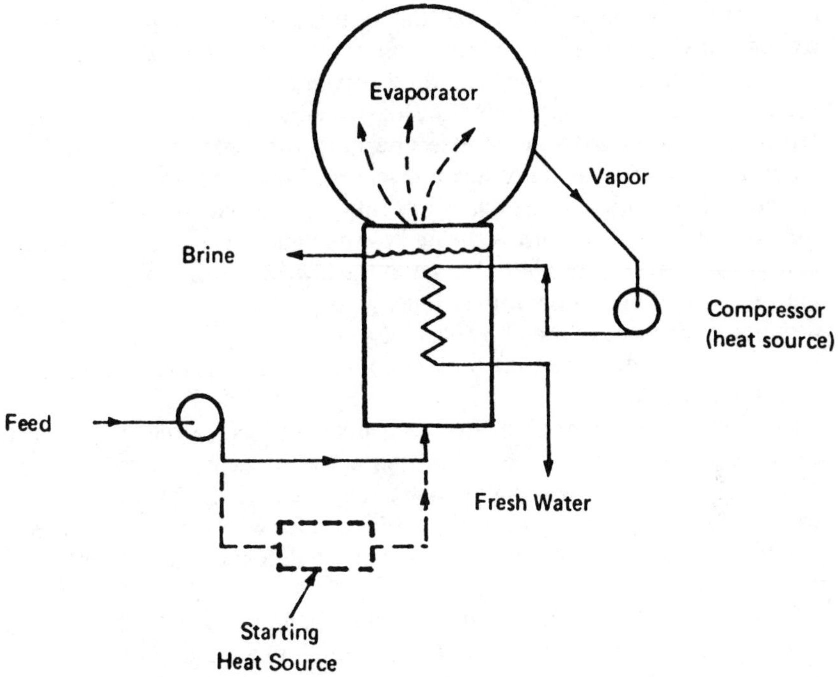

Figure 7-20. Thermo compression evaporator [9].

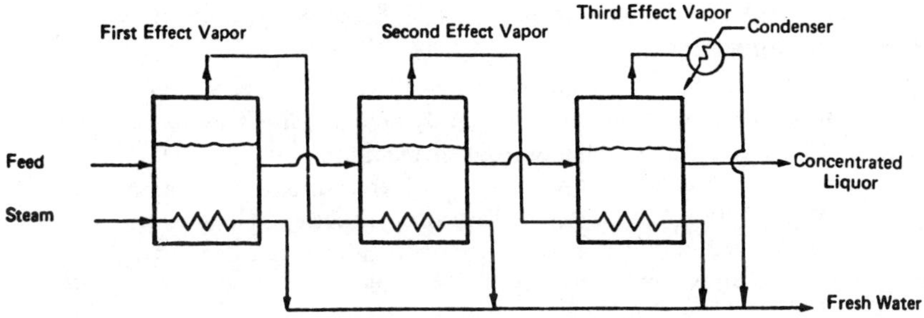

Figure 7-21. Multiple effect evaporator with forward feed [9].

effect to another in series, so that the ultimate product concentration is reached in only one effect of the evaporator. There are two modes of feeding the liquid: backward feed and forward feed.

In backward feed operation, the feed enters the last or the coldest effect. The discharge from this effect becomes the feed to the next and so on until the concentrated product is discharged from the first effect. This method of operation generally is advantageous when the feed is cold, since much less liquid must be heated to the higher temperature existing in the other effects. (The last effect is at the lowest pressure; therefore, at the lowest boiling temperature.) Backward feed also is used when the product is so viscous that high temperatures are required to keep the viscosity low enough to maintain reasonable heat transfer coefficients (i.e., high circulation rates).

In forward feed operation, raw feed is introduced in the first effect and passed from that effect to the next effect which is parallel to the flow of steam. Product is withdrawn from the last effect. This method of operation is advantageous when the feed is hot, or when the concentrated product would be temperature sensitive or would deposit scale at higher temperatures.

Forward feed simplifies operation because in most cases the liquor can be transferred by pressure difference alone, eliminating all intermediate liquor pumps. When the feed is cold, forward feed gives the lowest steam economy since the major portion of the heat content of the steam is required to heat the feed.

Applications

In the treatment of hazardous wastes, there are four basic potential uses for evaporation:

1. where no other treatment is currently practical, for example, concentration of TNT for simultaneous incineration;
2. where evaporation is preferable to other methods, for example, the concentration of radioactive wastes for disposal;
3. where evaporation is used as pretreatment, as an integral part of a process or as a polishing step, for example, spent molasses mash, dye stuff wastes and radioactive sludges and
4. for complete drying of wastewaters.

The application of evaporation to radioactive waste and to pulp and paper waste is illustrated in Figures 7-22 and 7-23.

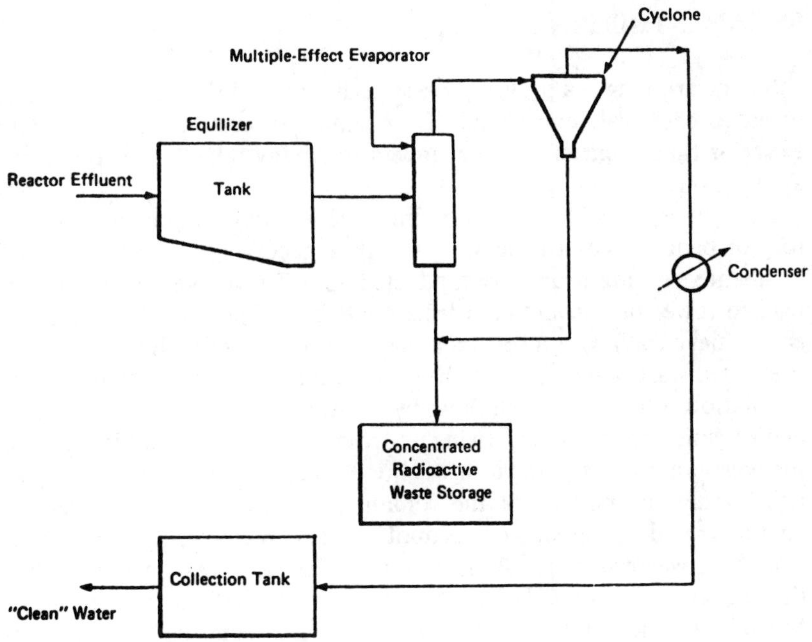

Figure 7-22. Concentration of radioactive wastes [9].

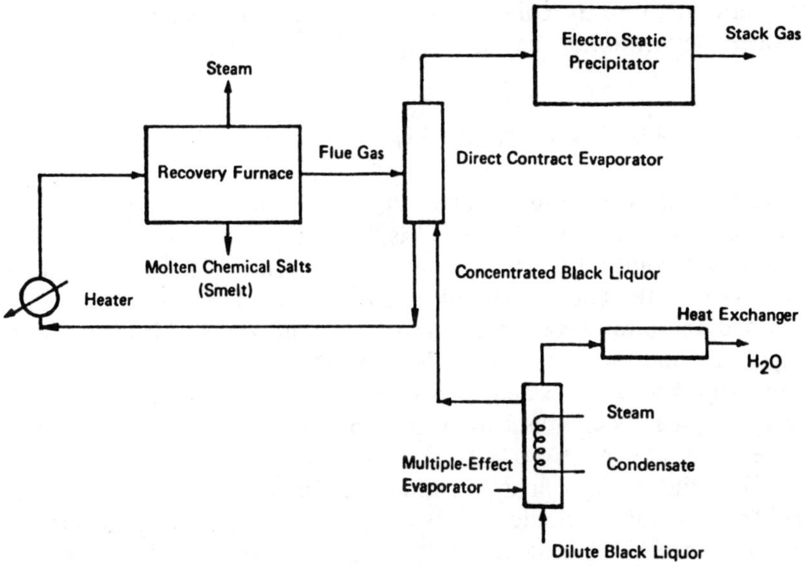

Figure 7-23. Waste liquor treatment and recovery for kraft pulp and paper process [9].

STEAM STRIPPING

Steam stripping is a proven process generally used for removing volatile (organic chemical) compounds from aqueous wastes. Sufficient data exist for the design of steam strippers for many waste water treatment applications.

For new applications involving multiple volatile components, laboratory or bench-scale investigation would be necessary.

Steam stripping usually is conducted as a continuous operation in a packed tower or conventional fractionating distillation column (bubble cap or sieve tray) with more than one stage of vapor/liquid contact. The preheated wastewater from the heat exchanger enters near the top of the distillation column and then flows by gravity countercurrent to the steam and organic vapors (or gas) rising up from the bottom of the column. As the wastewater passes down through the column, it contacts the vapors rising from the bottom of the column that contain progressively less volatile organic compound or gas until it reaches the bottom of the column where the wastewater finally is heated by the incoming steam to reduce the concentration of volatile components to their final concentration. Much of the heat in the wastewater discharged from the bottom of the column is recovered in preheating the feed to the column (Figure 7-24). Reflux (condensing a portion of the vapors from the top of the column and returning it to the column) may or may not be practiced depending on the composition of the vapor stream that is desired.

MOLTEN SALT INCINERATOR

Molten salt incineration is a recently developed technology for incineration of organic wastes. The system is illustrated in Figure 7-25. Organic wastes and combustion air are introduced beneath the surface of a molten salt bath. The molten salt bath is composed of 90% sodium and 10% sodium sulfates [14]. Hydrocarbons and air react inside the bed into carbon dioxide and water vapor. Hot gases rise through the molten salt bath, pass through a secondary reaction zone, and through the off-gas clean-up system before discharging into the atmosphere. The incineration temperature of a Na_2CO_3/NO_2SO_4 salt bath is in the range of 1500 to 1800°F. Other salts, such as potassium carbonate, allow for lower incineration temperature. Sodium carbonate is used to remove acidic gases, such as hydrogen chloride and sulfur dioxide. Sodium sulfate serves as the catalyst for the combustion of carbon. At normal incineration

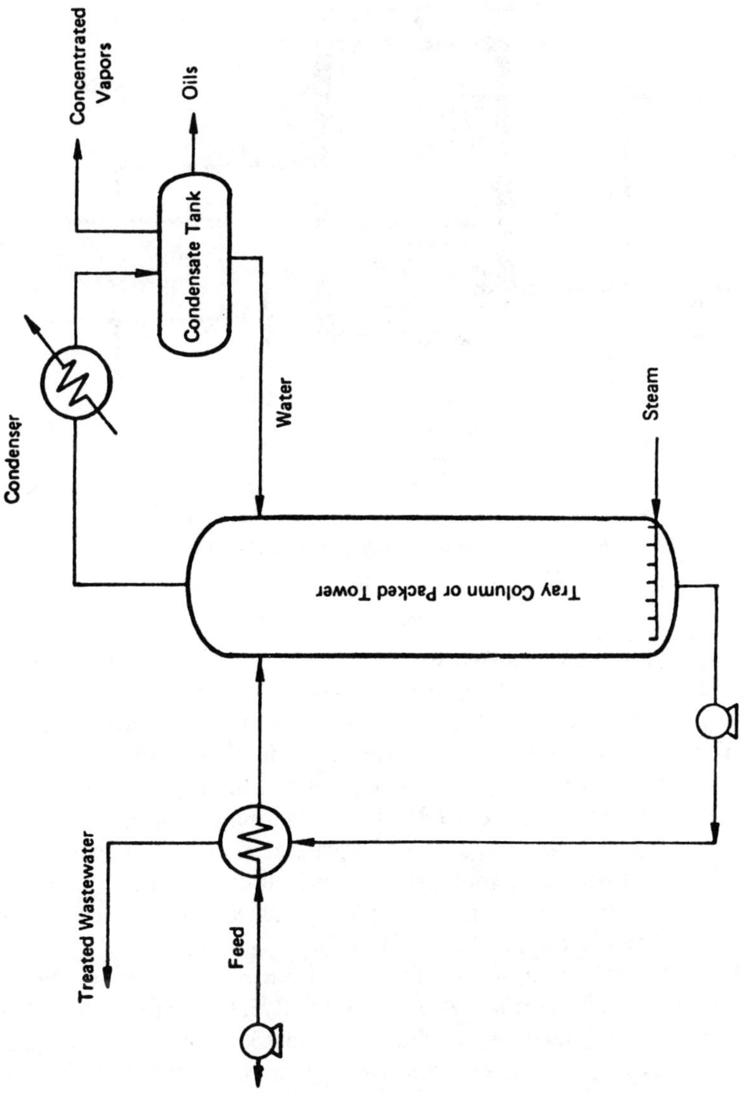

Figure 7-24. Typical steam stripping system [9].

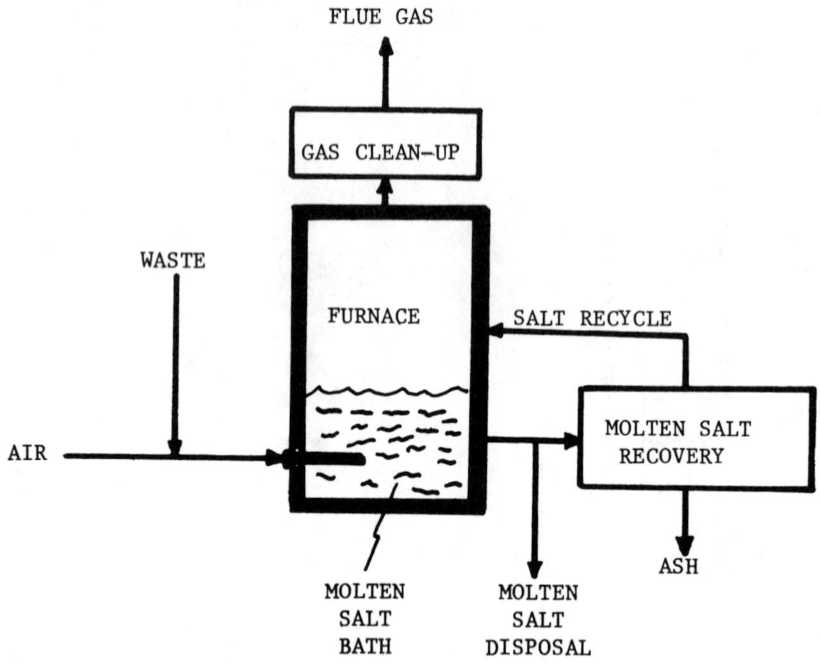

Figure 7-25. Molten salt incineration system.

temperatures, halogens react to form sodium halides. Phosphorus, sulfur, arsenic and silicon form their respective oxygenated sodium salts. Iron forms iron oxides. Because of the low temperature, nitrogen oxide formation is low. Other salt mixtures, such as sodium-hydroxide/potassium-hydroxide and sodium-carbonate/lithium-carbonate/potassium-carbonate, also can be used. The contaminated salt can be withdrawn batchwise or continuously and regenerated or land-disposed.

Liquid, free-flowing powders, sludges and shredded solid wastes can be fed directly into the incinerator. Typical destruction efficiency data of molten salt incinerator are illustrated in Table 7-3 [15].

A different configuration of a molten salt incinerator is illustrated in Figure 7-26 [16]. This configuration is essentially a box within a box. The inner box is a reaction chamber cooled and heated by floating on a bed of salt. The salts provide a fly-wheel effect in the incinerator. As heat is generated in the burning of wastes, it is absorbed by the salt. The heat stored in the molten salt is then used to combust the wastes.

Table 7-3. Typical Molten Salt Incinerator Data[a]

Chemical Wastes	Temperature (°F)	Destruction Efficiency (%)
PCB	1381–1650	99.994
Chloroform	1500	99.999
Trichloroethane	1540	99.999
Diphenylamine HCl	1690	99.999
Nitroethane	1640	99.993
Aqueous Slurry of Tributylphosphate	1720	99.99
Para-arsenilic acid	1695	99.999
DDT Powder	1650	99.998
Malathion	1650	99.9998
VX (Chemical Warfare Agent)	1705	99.99999
GB (Chemical Warfare Agent)	1695	99.999999
Mustard (Chemical Warfare Agent)	1700	99.99998

[a]Reproduced courtesy of Rockwell International, Canoga Park, CA.

PLASMA ARC PYROLYSIS

The plasma torch is a device that utilizes an electrical discharge to change minute quantities of almost any gas into the hottest sustainable flame known—up to 100,000°F.

Plasma arc pyrolysis is possible because the "plasma flame" can be generated in the total absence of oxygen. It is the oxygen (air) required to sustain safe combustion in conventional incinerator plants that makes pyrolysis in incinerators unattainable.

The plasma flame is generated by the following steps:

1. Gas (argon, helium, hydrogen, oxygen, etc.) is introduced in small quantity to create a swirling motion that keeps the plasma flame in the center of the torch, away from metal parts.
2. An electrical discharge is established (plasma arc flame) and maintained between the electrode inside the torch and any external electrical conductor.
3. The plasma flame then converts electrical energy into heat energy in an extremely efficient manner.

A typical plasma arc reactor is illustrated in Figure 7-27. In the plasma arc reactor, the ultrahigh arc temperature of 100,000°F is sustained to species. A plasma can be produced in several ways, the most common of

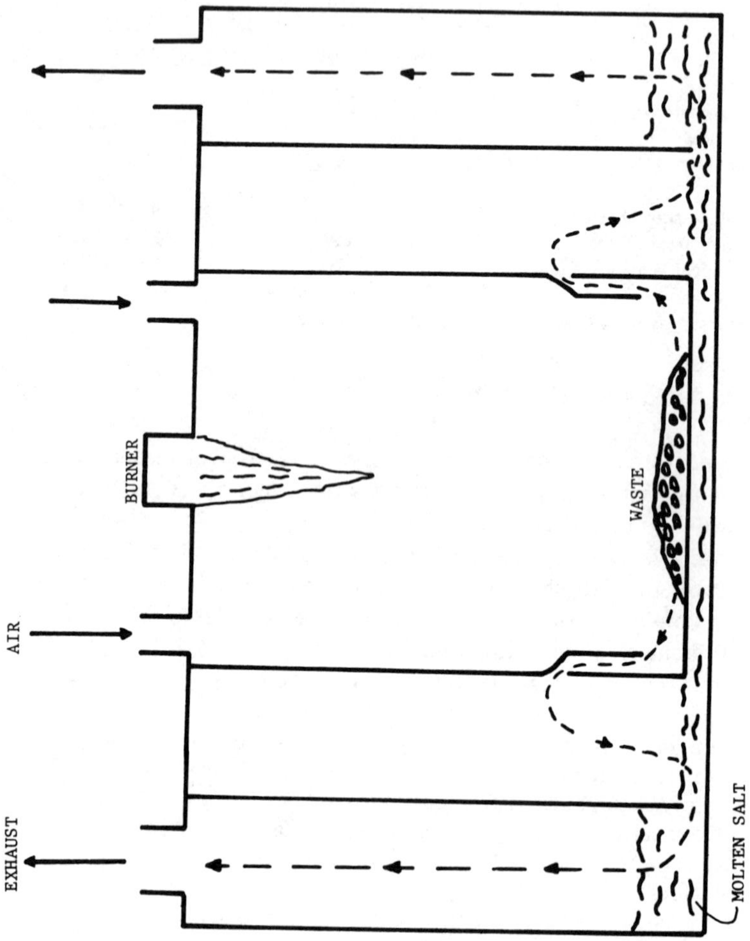

Figure 7-26. Molten salt incinerator (reproduced, courtesy of Anti-Pollution Systems, Inc., Pleasantville, NJ).

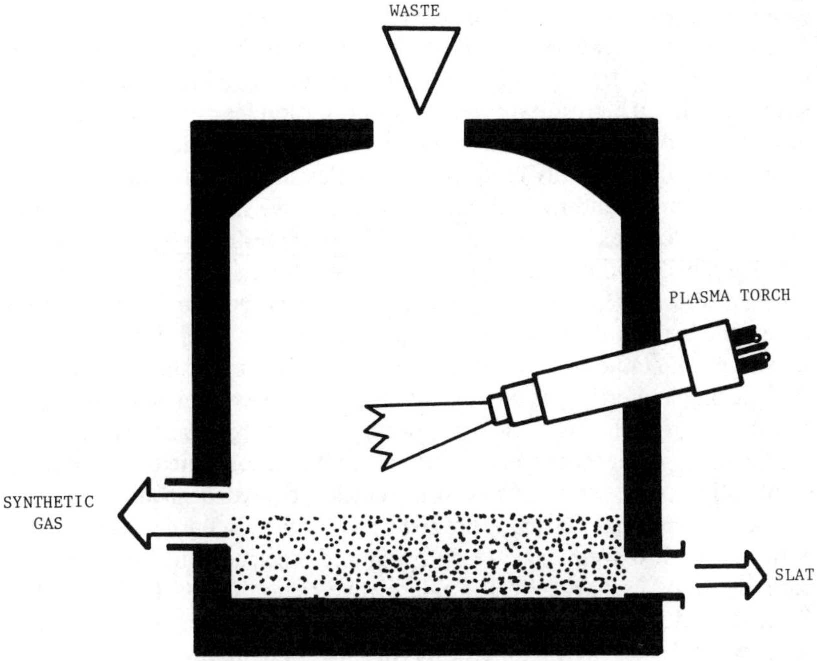

Figure 7-27. Plasma arc reactor.

provide the endothermic heat requirements of pyrolysis [17,18]. Intense ultraviolet radiation enhances volatilization and thermal cracking of organic matter.

In the pyrolytic zone, the high temperatures cause reduction of all species to atomic entities prior to recombination into low-molecular-weight gases. Plasma arc technology is applicable to most organic waste, in both solid and liquid form. Concurrently, the system could return energy up to five times the electrical energy input. Recovered energy will be in the form of sensible heat from the products and combustible by-products. The inorganic fraction of the wastes is recovered as slag.

MICROWAVE DISCHARGE SYSTEM

The use of a microwave discharge in the treatment of hazardous wastes [19] is a special application in the general field of plasma chemistry. A plasma is a partially ionized gas composed of ions, electrons and neutral which is a gaseous electric discharge. In a discharge, free electrons produced by a random or deliberate process pick up energy from an imposed electric field and transfer this energy, by collisons, to neutral gas molecules. The resultant molecular excitation leads to the formation of a variety of metastable, atomic, free radical and ionic species. These species are all chemically reactive, and under steady-state plasma conditions, generation and recombination of the active species proceed simultaneously. Plasmas produced by electric discharges have been used more for chemical synthesis of new stable compounds than for molecular decomposition. That is, the plasmas have been run under conditions where the excited decomposition products serve as intermediates in the formation of stable end-products, often of higher molecular weight than the starting material. In oxygen plasmas, however, particularly under conditions of high power density, decomposition products are typically oxidized to stable compounds similar to those obtained in complete combustion (e.g., water and CO_2 in the case of hydrocarbon feeds).

The conventional plasma is limited by available discharges, which were either dc or low-frequency ac and required electrodes in the discharge chamber and discharges in the microwave region (1000–10,000 MHz). Since the development of dc, low-frequency ac, or high-frequency microwave fields, high-temperature plasma is possible.

Plasmas can be initiated only in gases, but in gases of all kinds: inert gases (e.g., Ar, He), permanent gases (e.g., N_2, Cl_2, O_2, H_2, CO), inorganic vapors (e.g., H_2O, CO_2, $TiCl_4$, bCl_3, HCN, PF_3), organic vapors, and gaseous mixtures. Solids and liquids exposed to the reactive species in plasmas, particularly permanent gas plasmas, also have been shown to undergo chemical change.

The basic elements of a microwave discharge reactor are: (1) a microwave generator or source of power; (2) a wave guide which leads the microwave power from the generator to a resonant cavity, which surrounds the reactor; (3) a reaction chamber, which must be made of silica or quartz to minimize dielectric losses; (4) a system for generating or feeding vapors, or reactants or condensed phases into the reaction chamber; (5) a system for controlling pressure and flow; and (6) a system for collecting reaction products.

Specific reactor designs can vary considerably, depending on the application, and detailed equipment and apparatus descriptions are provided in the literature [20].

One of the major problems in the use of microwave plasmas for the treatment of hazardous wastes has been that the results are not predictable. The sometimes used term microwave plasma "decomposition" is misleading. As traditionally carried out, reactions in plasmas are as likely to lead to association products as to dissociation products, and the association products can be toxic. The problem recently has been overcome, however, through the use of intense oxygen plasmas that effectively bring about complete combustion of organics at low ambient temperatures. In other words, in an oxygen plasma at high power densities, rates of oxidation of dissociated species can be more rapid than rates of recombination.

Because hazardous wastes are unpredictable and inconsistent in composition, considerable research will be required to ensure the reliability of microwave discharge techniques for detoxification. In one of the first studies of the use of microwave to treat hazardous wastes, Lockheed used a 2450-MHz microwave power source delivering up to 2.5 kW to study the plasma decomposition of DIMP (diisopropyl methyl phosphonate) and DMMP (dimethyl methyl phosphonate), two compounds associated with nerve gas [21]. The DIMP and DMMP were introduced into the microwave discharge cavity in a helium or air carrier. Experimental conditions and results are summarized in Table 7-4. The percent conversion, which ranges from 62.4 to 99.5%, is based on residual DIMP or DMMP. The solid and liquid products even in the air plasma, however, still represent difficult disposal problems; they include phosphoric acid, methyl phosphonic acids, alcohols, plus unknown black liquids which may not be more suitable for landfill than the original agents.

Although condensed phase products of unknown composition formed from DIMP and DMMP in air plasma, the experiments on oxygen plasma ashing in analytical chemistry suggest that oxygen plasma reactions can be made to proceed essentially as low temperature combustion processes, with end products similar to those of incineration. More recent studies have demonstrated that this is in fact the case for a variety of organophosphorus and halogenated hydrocarbon compounds [22].

Oxygen plasma treatment of halogenated hydrocarbons can give rise to Cl_2O, $COCl_2$, HCl, Br_2, BrO_2 and Br_2O emissions. Nitrogen-containing organics are likely to give rise to nitrogen oxides. Metal fumes are likely to be less of a problem in oxygen microwave plasma systems than in high-temperature incinerators.

The outlook of this technique for hazardous waste treatment is encouraging, particularly for highly toxic materials that cannot be handled in any other way, or for recovery of high-value components.

Table 7-4. Microwave Discharge Reactor Data [22]

Toxic Agent	Carrier Gas	Power (watts)	Pressure (Torr)	Residence Time (sec)	Results
DMMP	He	50–200	3–55	1.5–2.4	Yellow solids and some black tarry deposit in the reaction tube; products collected in cold trap: trimethylphosphite; methanol; less than 0.5% DMMP.
DIMP	He	130–210	9–17	0.26–1.3	Predominant products were solids. Next in importance was a liquifiable gas, probably propylene. Liquid and solid residues had large amounts of H_3PO_4 and lesser amounts of methylphosphoric acid
DMMP	Air	140–510	29–62	0.12–0.15	Solids deposited in the reaction tube and probably contained methylphosphoric or phosphorous acids. A black viscous liquid deposited in the reaction chamber at high pressures, but no solids.
DIMP	Air	125–160	11–82	0.13–0.49	Products in discharge tube contained phosphoric and methylphosphoric acid. Liquid products had isopropanol and three unidentified gas chromatograph peaks.

REFERENCES

1. Cheremisinoff, P. N., and A. C. Moores. "Benzene, Basic and Hazardous Properties," (New York: Marcel Dekker, Inc., 1979).
2. Farbstein, S. B., and J. Elder. "Energy Conservation in the Chemical Industry through New Process Development—The B. F. Goodrich Catoxid Process," Federal Energy Administration Project Independence Hearing, San Francisco (October 1974).
3. *Kirk-Othmer Encyclopedia of Chemical Technology, Vol. 9, 3rd ed.* (New York: John Wiley & Sons, Inc., 1980).
4. Nonhekel, G. *Gas Purification Processes* (London: George Newnes Ltd., 1964).
5. J. B. Dicks and Associates. "Plasma Temperature Incineration of PCB's and other Hazardous Wastes," Information Circular 48, Tullahoma, TN, 1981).
6. Fisher, T. F., et al. "The PUROX System," Proceedings of the 1976 National Waste Processing Conference, Boston (1976), p. 125.
7. Page, F. J. "TORRAX—A System for Recovery of Energy from Solid Waste," Proceedings of the 1976 National Waste Processing Conference, Boston, (1976), p. 109.
8. *Kirk-Othmer Encyclopedia of Chemical Technology, Vol. 16, 2nd ed.* (New York: John Wiley & Sons, Inc., 1980).
9. Berkowitz, J. B., et al. "Physical, Chemical and Biological Treatment for Industrial Waste," Arthur D. Little for Hazardous Waste Management Branch, Office of Solid Waste, U.S. EPA (1977).
10. Mander, J. "Cement Kiln for Hazardous Waste Disposal," Seminar on Incineration of Hazardous Wastes, Harrisburg, PA (March 1981).
11. Watson, B. "Power Plant Boilers for Hazardous Waste Disposal," Seminar on Incineration of Hazardous Wastes, Harrisburg, PA (March 1981).
12. Pradt, L. A. "Developments in Wet Air Oxidation," *Chem. Eng. Prog.* 68(12):72 (1972).
13. Hulswitt, C. E. "Purifying Waste Water by Wet Oxidation," *Plant Eng.* (August 17, 1978).
14. "Molten Salt Decomposes Pesticide Wastes," *Chem. Eng. News,* (September 12, 1977), p. 44.
15. Rockwell International. "Molten Salt Destruction of Hazardous Wastes," Pub. No. 523-K-18-1, Rev. 4 (1980).
16. Greenberg, J. "Incineration of Wastes by Means of a Catalytic Salt Incineration," Private communication (1977).
17. Resource Recovery Corporation. "Plasma Refuse Converter," (1980).
18. Bartow, T. G., et al. "Destruction of Polychlorinated Biphenyls by Plasma Arc Pyrolysis," paper presented at the 2nd International Conference on Hazardous Waste Management, Denver, CO, October 1980.
19. Lockheed Palo Alto Research Laboratory, Contract with EPA-SHWRL, Cincinnati, OH.
20. "Chemical Reactions in Electrical Discharges," Advances in Chemistry Series 80 (Washington, DC: American Chemical Society, 1969).
21. Bailin, L. J., et al. *Environ. Sci. Technol.* 9:254 (1975).
22. Bailin, L. J. and B. J. Hertzler. "Development of Microwave Plasma Detoxification Process for Hazardous Wastes, Phase I," U.S. EPA Contract No. 68-03-2190, Final Report (October 1976).

PART 2

TREATMENT TECHNOLOGIES

CHAPTER 8

PROCESS AND SITE SELECTION REQUIREMENTS

CLASSIFICATION OF TREATMENT PROCESSES

In an Arthur D. Little study for the U.S. Environmental Proection Agency (EPA), 47 processes were investigated. Most were unit processes or operations, several of which would normally have to be linked in series to form a complete treatment system for a particular waste stream. Four of the processes—dialysis, electrophoresis, freeze drying and zone refining—were found to have little or no potential utility in a hazardous waste management system.

This left 43 potentially useful processes to be investigated. These processes fall naturally into four classes: (1) phase separation processes, potentially useful in volume reduction or resource recovery; (2) component separation processes, capable of physically segregating particular ionic or molecular species for multicomponent, single-phase waste streams; (3) chemical transformation processes, which promote chemical reactions to detoxify, recover or reduce the volume of specific components in waste streams; and (4) biological treatment methods, which involve chemical transformations brought about by the action of living organisms.

Phase Separation

Waste streams such as slurries, sludges and emulsions which are not single phase often require a phase-separation process (Table 8-1) before detoxification or recovery steps can be implemented. Frequently, phase separation permits a significant volume reduction, particularly if the hazardous component is present to a significant extent in only one of the

Table 8-1. Phase Separation Process[a]

Process Category[b]	Type of Waste to Which Process is Applicable: Settlable Slurries[c]	Colloidal Slurries[c]	Sludges[d]	Any Wastes With a Volatile Liquid Phase
V. Common in waste treatment	Sedimentation Filtration	Flocculation	Filtration	Solar evaporation
IV. Developed but not commonly used in waste treatment	Centrifugation			Distillation (with solvent recovery) Evaporation
III. Need further development for waste treatment	Flotation	Ultrafiltration	Freezing	
	High-gradient Magnetic separation			

[a]Source: NTIS-PB 275 054.
[b]Category descriptions:
I Process is not applicable in a useful way to waste of interest.
II Process might work in 5–10 years but needs research effort first.
III Process appears useful for hazardous waste but needs development work.
IV Process is developed but not commonly used for hazardous waste.
V Process will be common to most industrial waste processors.
[c]A slurry is defined as a pumpable solid-liquid mixture. It is settable if the phases separate on standing, and colloidal if they do not.
[d]A sludge is defined as a non pumpable solid-liquid mixture.

phases. When the hazardous portion of the stream is concentrated, subsequent processing steps are more easily accomplished. Phase-separation processes usually are mechanical, inexpensive and simple, and can be applied to a broad spectrum of wastes and waste components.

Emulsions generally are very difficult to separate. Heating, cooling, change of pH, salting out, centrifugation, API separators, etc., may all be tried, but there is no accurate way to predict what might work. Appropriate methods can only be developed empirically, specific to any given situation.

1. *Settlable Slurries.* Conceptually, the simplest separation process is sedimentation, or gravity settling. The output streams consist of a sludge and a decantable supernatant liquid. If the components of the sludge are at all soluble, the supernatant liquid generally is a solution. A closely related process—and the phase separation process in most common use—is filtration. Centrifugation is essentially a high gravity sedimentation process whereby centrifugal forces are used to increase the rate of particle settling. Flotation is used extensively in ore separation, and in fact has made it possible to recover value from lower and lower grades of metallic and nonmetallic ores. It has not been extensively studied for hazardous waste applications. High-gradient magnetic separation is a relatively new process that appears to have potential for separating magnetic and paramagnetic particles from slurries.

2. *Colloidal Slurries.* The basic concept in all the above processes for settlable slurries is to get the solid phases to drop out of the liquid phases, through the use of gravitational, centrifugal, magnetic or hydrostatic forces. Such forces generally do not act on colloidal suspended particles. The simplest and most commonly used colloidal separation process is flocculation. Ultrafiltration has many industrial applications, including waste treatment, and is expected to have many more within the next five years. Further development effort is required, however, to demonstrate its full potential.

3. *Sludges.* The major phase separation desired in the handling of sludges is dewatering. Vacuum filtration and press filtration are the processes in most common use. Some research has been done on simple freezing, but the process is not well developed and the work that has been done is not promising.

4. *Volatiles.* Sludges and slurries (colloidal or separable) in which the liquid phase is volatile may be treated by either evaporation or distillation. Solar evaporation is very commonly used. Engineered evaporation or distillation systems would normally be operated if recovery of the liquid is desired.

Component Separation

The many physical processes which act to segregate ionic or molecular species from multicomponent waste streams (Table 8-2) do not require chemical reactions to be effective. None are so commonly used as to be classified in Category V, but there has been a great deal of experience with most of them in the water treatment field. The majority of Category IV processes act only on aqueous solutions.

Chemical Transformation

The relatively few processes which involve chemical reactions (Table 8-3) are the only processes found potentially capable of detoxifying hazardous components in waste streams (in addition to recovering resources or reducing volume for land disposal). By far the two most common processes are neutralization and precipitation. Since there is usually a pH range where the solubility of heavy metal precipitates is at a minimum, neutralization (interpreted broadly as pH adjustment) and precipitation are in fact often used together.

Biological Treatment

Biological treatment methods (Table 8-4) are effective only in aqueous media, and are capable only of breaking down organic components. The four Category V processes are used essentially in polishing of soluble organics. The feed streams must be low in solids ($<1\%$), free of oil and grease, and nontoxic to the active microorganisms (e.g., heavy metal content <10 ppm). The processes yield a biomass sludge for disposal which contains heavy metals and refractory organics not decomposed by the biologically active species present.

The Category IV processes, anaerobic digestion and composting, are useful for more concentrated waste streams and will tolerate solid contents of 5–7% and 50%, respectively. Composting will decompose oils, greases and tars, yielding a concentrated metal sludge and a leachate containing partially decomposed organics.

SELECTION OF TREATMENT PROCESSES FOR GIVEN WASTE STREAMS

There are a variety of ways to approach the problem of selecting the appropriate process(es) for treatment of a particular waste stream. Indi-

Table 8-2. Component Separation Processes[a]

Process Category	Function of Process: Removal of Heavy Metal and Toxic Anions from Aqueous Solutions	Removal of Organics from Aqueous Solutions	Removal of Inorganics from Liquids, Slurries and Sludges	Solvent Recovery
IV. Developed, but not commonly used in waste treatment	Liquid ion exchange Electrodialysis Reverse osmosis Ion exchange	Ultrafiltration Solvent extraction Carbon adsorption Resin adsorption Steam stripping Air stripping		Distillation Steam Distillation
III. Needs further development for waste treatment			Freeze crystallization	
II. Needs further research	Ion flotation		Hi-gradient Magnetic separation	

[a]Source: NTIS-PB 275 054.

Table 8-3. Chemical Transformation Processes[a]

Process Category	Treatable Components and Waste Streams: Cyanides, Phenolics, Sulfides, Sulfites, and Organics in Aqueous Solution	Nitrates, Carbonates, Sulfates, Hydroxides, in Sludges, Tars, and Solids	Heavy Metals in Aqueous Solution	Organic Liquids, Sludges, Slurries Tars and Solids	Acids and Bases	Organic Liquids
V. Common in waste treatment			Precipitation		Neutralization	
IV. Developed but not commonly used in waste treatment	Oxidation Ozonation UV/ozonolysis UV/chlorination	Calcination	Reduction			
III. Requires further development for waste treatment			Electrolysis	Hydrolysis		Chlorinolysis
II. Needs further research	Photolysis Catalysis		Precipitate Flotation	Catalysis		Microwave

[a]Source: NTIS-PB 275 054.

Table 8-4. Biological Treatment Methods[a]

Process Category	Functions of Process: Decomposition of Soluble Organics in Dilute Aqueous Streams	Decomposition of Hydrocarbons (non-chlorinated)
V. Common in waste treatment	Activated sludge Aerated lagoon Trickling filter Waste stabilization pond	
IV. Developed but not commonly used in waste treatment		Composting Anaerobic digestion
II. Needs further research	Enzyme treatment	

[a]Source: NTS-PB 275 054.

vidual engineers, chemists, equipment manufacturers, salesmen, environmental managers, plant managers, regulatory authorities, etc., each have slightly different perspectives on the problem, different data needs, and different ways of manipulating the data to reach a final conclusion. No one approach is "right" for everyone.

We have formulated some questions to which various people might require answers before even beginning to match wastes with treatment processes. Next, we have provided a number of examples of possible steps in process selection for some typical wastes. The individual can decide what questions must be answered, and in what sequence, in order for him to develop a procedure for choosing the treatment processes applicable to particular waste streams. No matter how one approaches the problem of process selection, there are two seemingly conflicting criteria to keep in mind: to eliminate inappropriate processes from consideration at the earliest possible stage, but to maintain an open mind for consideration of advantageous processes as long as possible.

Background Questions for Treatment Process Selection

1. Nature of the Waste. Questions on the nature of the waste stream are asked for several reasons. One is to determine whether the waste stream characteristics match the feed stream requirements for various treatment processes. In a positive sense, this may be of interest to select

processes for further consideration; or in a negative sense, to rule out processes that are not and could not be made useful for the particular waste under any circumstances. Another is to determine whether the waste stream is compatible with typical treatment process equipment, materials of construction, pumps, throughput rates, temperature, size of pipes, etc. A third, reflected in the last question, is to determine whether air and water pollution controls, or the method of waste collection used, might in fact create a stream which is more difficult to treat than the waste originally generated in the manufacturing operation.

- What are the characteristics of the waste stream?
- Is it a liquid, an emulsion, a slurry, a sludge, a solid powder, or a bulk solid?
- What is its chemical composition?
- Which components are potentially hazardous for land disposal; or more generally, what is the problem?
- What are the physical properties of the waste stream—e.g., viscosity, melting point, boiling point, vapor pressure, Btu content, specific gravity, etc.?
- Is the waste stream corrosive?
- Over what range will the typical physical and chemical properties vary?
- What is the volume or mass of waste that will require treatment from a typical plant and/or region?
- Where does the waste stream originate and at what points could it be intercepted for treatment?

2. Objectives of Treatment—Desired Characteristics of the Output Stream. Questions on the desired characteristics of the output streams are asked to: (1) clarify the objectives of a treatment process; (2) explicitly learn what regulatory standards must be met; (3) help establish criteria for judging the usefulness of various treatment alternatives in meeting the objectives; and (4) establish a benchmark for improvement by identifying current practice.

- What is the present treatment/disposal method and why is this unacceptable?
- What are the objectives or goals of treatment, in order of priority, i.e., purification, resource recovery, detoxification, volume reduction, safe disposal to land, safe disposal to water, compliance with regulations?
- What are the air, water and other environmental quality regulations which must be complied with?
- What must be removed to make the waste stream amenable to disposal? What level of removal is necessary; i.e., what are the maximum allowable concentrations in the output stream(s)?

- What are the chemical and physical property requirements for recycle or reuse of the output streams?
- What are the physical and chemical property requirements for disposal to land or water?

3. Technical Adequacy of Treatment Alternatives. Questions about technical adequacy are asked to help distinguish processes that are technically feasible for use on the waste from those that are not.

- What processes, alone or in combination, are capable of meeting the treatment objectives?
- If a sequence of processes is needed, are the processes technically compatible?
- Can the key process selected for meeting the objectives handle the waste stream in its existing form? If not, can the waste stream be put into a form amenable to the process?
- What key processes are really attractive technically?
- Are there any components of the waste stream that would inhibit application of an otherwise technically attractive key process? Can these potentially inhibiting effects be minimized or eliminated?
- If no process, as presently conceived, can meet the objectives, can any process be modified to do the job?
- What function can each process perform, and how can the processes be grouped to achieve the objectives?
- Are there any processes that must be eliminated on technical grounds?

4. Economic Considerations. From the industry point of view, economic questions are paramount in selecting alternative treatment methods for in-plant use and in choosing a waste treatment contractor.

- What are the capital investment requirements for process implementation?
- What are the operating costs?
- Will credit for recovered material help offset operating costs? To what extent?
- How do projected costs for alternative treatments compare with current costs of disposal and with each other?
- Are the technically optimal operating parameters in the proper range for economical operation of apparently attractive processes?
- If process modifications are required, what will they cost?
- For technically and operationally acceptable processes with equal operating costs (including capital amortization), is there an economic reason to prefer the lowest capital cost alternative?
- What is the cost impact of any necessary environmental controls?

5. Environmental Considerations. Waste treatment processes, like any manufacturing process, almost always results in some residue for disposal. Environmental questions are directed towards tracing the fate of the hazardous components present in the waste feed stream to the point of ultimate disposal.

- Will air pollution control devices be required to clean up effluents?
- Will output streams require clean-up prior to discharge into water bodies?
- Will secured chemical landfill areas be necessary for solid residue(s) from process?

6. Energy Considerations. Questions of energy utilization are asked in order to ensure that treatment processes satisfy current national objectives of both environmental protection and energy conservation. Both the absolute quantity of energy required and the form of the energy required are important. Energy-intensive processes generally would be in disfavor, unless there were compensating benefits (e.g., materials recovery). Processes that use natural gas, which is in short supply, might be particularly unattractive. The economics of treatment processes for which energy costs represent a significant fraction of operating costs would, of course, be tied to the price of fuel, which has in the recent past been quite volatile.

- What are the energy requirements for process operation?
- What form(s) of energy will be used, i.e., electricity, natural gas, oil, coal, etc.?
- Are estimated energy costs more than 10% of operating costs?

7. Overall Evaluation. In final choice of a treatment system, the selection criteria will be weighted in each case according to specific circumstances and in accordance with the engineering judgment of the person making the decision.

- What factors are most important in selecting a treatment process?
- Are there any standard, state-of-the-art processes that can be used for baseline comparisons?
- Are costs "reasonable"?
- Does any process have clearly desirable (or undesirable) features that make it attractive (or unattractive) for treatment of a particular waste stream?

Examples of Process Selection Procedures

Selection Based on the Nature of the Hazardous Wastes

For the purposes of identifying possible treatment processes, and eliminating those not likely to prove useful, a given waste stream is conveniently characterized with respect to three broad dimensions:

1. Physical form: is the waste stream as generated a liquid emulsion, pumpable slurry (colloidal or noncolloidal), nonpumpable sludge, tar, bulk solid or powdered solid?
2. Hazardous components: Does the waste stream contain:
   - heavy "metal" cations (Sb, As, Cd, Cr, Hg, Pb, Zn, Ni, Cu, V, P, Be, Se, Mn, Ti, Sn, Ba, etc.)?
   - heavy metal anions (chromates, chromites, arsenates, arsenites, etc.)?
   - non-metallic toxic anions (cyanides, sulfites, thiocyanates, etc.)?
   - organics (hydrocarbons, organic acids, organic peroxides, esters, alcohols, aldehydes, phenols, chlorocarbons, amines, anilines, pyridines, organic sulfur compounds, organic phosphorus compounds, alkaloids, sterols, etc.)?
3. Other properties: For example,
   - Is the liquid phase primarily aqueous or nonaqueous?
   - What is the concentration of each of the hazardous components in each of the phases present?
   - What are the nonhazardous components in each phase?

For a given waste stream, characterized by physical form and hazardous components, the matrix presented in Table 8-5 may be used to select potentially applicable treatment processes. For example, liquid ion exchange (LIE) might be capable of removing heavy metals from solid powders. The matrix in Table 8-6 focuses on processes that are inapplicable for given waste streams. It provides some guidance for ruling out processes not likely to be technically feasible for certain types of waste streams.

Process Section Based on Desired Characteristics of the Output Streams

The output streams from any given treatment may or may not be suitable for reuse or amenable to disposal without further treatment. In evaluating and analyzing treatment processes that might be applicable to particular waste streams, it is usually necessary at some stage to define

Table 8-5. Treatment Processes for Hazardous Components in Waste Streams of Various Physical Forms[a,b]

Physical Form	Treatment Processes[c]: Heavy "Metal" Cations[c] and Metal Anions[d]	Nonmetal Anions[e]	Organics
Liquid	(IE), (FC), (UF), (ED), (RO), (Red), (LIE), (Ppt), (E1)	(CA), (LIE), (FC), (UF), (ED), (Oz), (RO), (Ox), (E1)	(CA), (RA), (Dis), (IE), (AS), (SS), (UF), (SE), (RO), (Ox), (Oz), (HY), (C1), (MW), (Pb), (UF)
Emulsion	(UF)		
Slurry	(FC), (UF), (Red), (HGMS)	(FC), (UF), (Ox)	(DIS), (AS), (SS), (UF) (Oz), (Hy)
Sludge	(LIE), (FC), (Red)	(FC), (Ox)	(Dis), (Cal), (Oz), (Hy), (Ox)
Tar	(Cal)	(Cal)	(Cal), (Hy)
Bulk Solid	(Cal)	(Cal)	(Cal)
Solid Powder	(LIE)	(Cal)	(Cal), (Hy)

[a]Source: NTIS-PB 275 054.

[b]Legend:

(AS) Air Stripping
(CA) Carbon Adsorption
(Cal) Calcination
(C1) Chlorinolysis
(Dis) Distillation
(HGMS) High-Gradient Magnetic Separation
(Hy) Hydrolysis
(IE) Ion Exchange
(LIE) Liquid Ion Exchange
(MW) Microwave Discharge
(Ppt) Precipitation
(RA) Resin Adsorption
(Red) Reduction
(RO) Reverse Osmosis
(SE) Solvent Extraction

(ED) Electrodialysis
(El) Electrolysis
(FC) Freeze Crystallization
(Ox) Oxidation
(Oz) Ozonation
(Ph) Photolysis
(SS) Steam Stripping
(UF) Ultrafiltration

[c]e.g., Sb, As, Cd, Cr, Hg, Pb, Zn, Ni, Co, V, P, Be, Se, Mn, Ti, Sn, Ba
[d]e.g., chromates, arsenates, arsenites, vanadates
[e]e.g., cyanides, sulfides, fluorides, hypochlorites, thiocyanates

Table 8-6. Applicability of Treatment Processes to Physical Form of Waste[a,b]

	Single Phase				Two Phase	
		Liquid				
	Solid	Inorganic	Organic	Mixed	Slurry[c]	Sludge
Phase Separation Processes						
Filtration	n	n	n	n	y	n
Sedimentation	n	n	n	n	y	n
Flocculation	n	n	n	n	n	n
Centrifugation	n	n	n	n	y	n
Distillation	n	n	n	n	y	y
Evaporation	n	n	n	n	y	y
Flotation	n	n	n	n	y	n
Ultrafiltration	n	n	n	n	n	n
HGMS	p	n	n	n	n	n
Precipitation	n	n	n	n	n	n
Component Separation Processes						
Ion Exchange	n	y	y	y	n	n
Liquid Ion Exchange	y	y	y	n	y	y
Freeze Crystallization	n	y	y	n	y	y
Reverse Osmosis	n	y	n	y	n	n
Carbon Adsorption	n	y	n	y	n	n
Resin Adsorption	n	y	n	y	n	n
Electrodialysis	n	y	n	y	n	n
Air Stripping	n	n	y	y	y	n
Steam Stripping	y	n	y	y	y	n
Ammonia Stripping	y	y	n	n	n	n
Ultrafiltration	n	y	y	y	n	n
Solvent Extraction	p	y	y	y	n	n
Reverse Osmosis	n	y	n	y	n	n
Distillation	n	n	y	y	y	y
Evaporation	n	y	y	y	y	y
Chemical Transformation Processes						
Neutralization	n	y	y	y	y	y
Precipitation	n	y	y	y	n	n
Hydrolysis	p	n	y	y	y	y
Oxidation	n	y	y	y	n	n
Reduction	n	y	y	y	n	n
Ozonolysis	n	y	y	y	n	n
Calcination	y	y	y	y	y	y
Chlorinolysis	n	n	y	y	n	n
Electrolysis	n	y	n	y	n	n
Microwave	n	n	y	y	n	n
Biological	n	n	y	y	y	y

Table 8-6, continued

	Single Phase				Two Phase	
		Liquid				
	Solid	Inorganic	Organic	Mixed	Slurry[c]	Sludge
Catalysis	n	y	y	y	n	n
Photolysis	n	n	y	y	n	n

[a]Source: NTIS-PB 275 054.
[b]y = yes, workable; n = no; p = possible.
[c]Slurry is defined here as a pumpable mxture of solids and liquids.

the objectives of treatment and the desired characteristics of the output streams.

For example, if the treatment objective is to convert the given waste stream to one or more streams that can be discharged legally to a water body, the federal and local water pollution control regulations will govern the characteristics of the output streams. If the treatment objective is recovery, those processes must be sought which either lead directly to a reusable resource or convert the waste to a form from which resources may be more easily recovered.

Table 8-7 provides some general characteristics of the output streams (end products) from various processes to aid in assessing their capability, alone or in combination, to meet defined objectives. Where processes are routinely or conveniently used in combination, follow-on steps are suggested, predicted on the assumption that the only hazardous components in the waste stream are those that the process listed can act on. If, for example, a waste stream containing both low-molecular-weight organic and heavy metal contaminants were treated by reverse osmosis (RO), only the heavy metals would be concentrated in one of the output streams (RO1), and the other output stream (RO2) would have to be treated further to remove or detoxify the organics.

Selection Based on Technical and Operational Adequacy of Treatment Alternative

Table 8-5 shows a number of treatment alternatives for various types of hazardous components in waste streams of different physical form.

Table 8-7. General Characteristics of the End-Products of Treatment Processes[a]

Treatment		Output Streams			
Type	Process	Code No.	Form	Characteristics	Possible Follow-On Steps
Phase Separation	Filtration	F 1	Sludge	15–20% solids	Landfill, calcination
		F 2	Liquid	500–5000 ppm total dissolved solids	Component separation
	Sedimentation, Centrifugation	S1	Sludge	2–15% solids	Decantation
		S2	Liquid	10–200 ppm suspended soids	
	Flotation	Fl 1	Stabilized	Particle-bearing froth	Skimming
		Fl 2	Liquid	Solution	Component separation
	HGMS	H 1	Slurry	Magnetic and paramagnetic particles	Recovery
		H2	Liquid	Solution	Component Separation
	Flocculation	Fc	Sludge or slurry	Flocculated particulates	Sedimentation, Filtration, centrifugation
	Distillation	Dis 1	Sludge	Still bottoms	Calcination
		Dis 2	Liquid	Pure solvent	Sale
	Evaporation	E 1	Solid	—	Resource recovery
			Liquid	Condensate	Recovery or disposal
Component Separation					
a. Inorganics	Ion Exchange	IE 1	Liquid	Concentrated solution of hazardous components	Precipitation, recycle, electrolysis
		IE 2	Liquid	Purified water with hazardous components at ppm levels	Discharge
	Liquid Ion Exchange	Similar to Ion Exchange			

	Carbon Adsorption	CA 1	Solid	Adsorbate on carbon	Chemical regeneration
		CA 2	Liquid	Purified water	Discharge
	Reverse Osmosis	RO 1	Liquid	Concentrated solution of hazardous components	Precipitation, electrolysis, recycle
		RO 2	Liquid	Purified solution, TDS > 5 ppm	To water treatment
	Electrodialysis	ED 1	Liquid	Concentrated stream, 100–500 ppm salts	Precipitation, metal recovery
		ED 2	Liquid	Dilute stream	To water treatment
	Freeze Crystallization	FC 1	Sludge	Concentrated brine	Recovery
		FC 2	Liquid	Purified stream, ~100 TDS	To water treatment
b. Organics	Carbon Adsorption	CA 1	Solid	Adsorbate on carbon	Thermal or chemical regeneration
		CA 2	Liquid	Purified water	Discharge
	Resin Adsorption	RA 1	Solid	Adsorbate on resin	Solvent regeneration
			Liquid	Purified water, < 10 ppm organics	To water treatment
	Steam Stripping	SS 1	Liquid	Aqueous steam concentrated in volatile organics	Recovery; incineration
			Liquid	Dilute aqueous stream with 50–100 ppm organics	To water treatment
	Solvent Extraction	SE 1	Liquid	Concentrated solution of hazardous components in extraction solvent	Recovery of extraction solvent
		SE 2	Liquid	Purified liquid; hazardous component concentrate < 10 ppm	Recycle or discharge
	Distillation	Dis 1	Sludge	Still bottoms	Incineration
		Dis 2	Liquid	Pure liquid	Sale

Table 8-7, continued

Treatment		Output Streams			
Type	Process	Code No.	Form	Characteristics	Possible Follow-On Steps
Chemical Transformation					
	Neutralization	N	Unchanged	Stream of altered pH	Component separation
	Precipitation	Ppt 1	Sludge	–	Landfill, calcination
		Ppt 2	Liquid	Supernatant with concentrations governed by solubility of precipitate	Depends on product stream Composition
	Oxidation Ozonation	O	Liquid	CO_2, H_2O and other oxidation products	Depends on product stream Composition
	Reduction	R	Slurry	Heavy metals and residual reducing agent	Filtration
	Calcination	Cal 1	Solid	Oxide and/or other residue	Landfill or recovery
		Cal 2	Gas	Volatiles (CO_2, NO_x, SO_x, hydrocarbons, fine particulates)	Wet scrubbing
	Hydrolysis	Hy	Liquid, slurry or sludge	Mixture of products that may or may not be toxic	Resource recovery
	Electrolysis	El 1	–	Cathode reaction products	Often a recovered metal
		El 2	–	Anode reaction products	Depends on nature of products
	Photolysis	P	Liquid	Solution of photodecomposition products	Depends on nature of products
	Microwave Discharge	M	Gas	Similar to incinerator emissions	Wet scrubbing
	Catalysis	Depends on Reaction Catalyzed			

Biological Treatment					
	Activated Sludge	AC 1	Liquid	Clean water	Discharge
		AC 2	Sludge	Heavy metals and refractory organics	Calcination
	Aerated Lagoon				
	Trickling Filter				
	Waste Stabilization Pond	W	Liquid	Clear water	Discharge
	Anaerobic Digestion	An 1	Sludge	–	Incineration
		An 2	Gas	CO_2, methane	Fuel recovery
	Composting	Com 1	Sludge	Concentrated in metals	Calcination or recovery
		Com 2	Liquid	Leachate solution of partially degraded organics	Component separation

[a]Source: NTIS-PB 275 054.

Tables 8-1 to 8-4 show that several of the alternatives function similarly, i.e., they remove or detoxify certain types of hazardous components. All processes which function similarly on similar types of waste streams are not necessarily technically equivalent, however. The allowable feed stream concentrations may differ. The treatment efficiencies and hence concentration of hazardous components in the output streams may differ. The degree of interference by other components in the waste stream may differ. Throughputs may differ; and the available experience with using the processes to treat hazardous wastes may also differ.

Table 8-8 compares treatment processes capable of separating heavy metals from liquid waste streams with respect to feed stream properties, output parameters and state of the art. Tables 8-9 to 8-11 provide similar comparisons for processes that separate organics from liquids and toxic anions from liquids. Table 8-12 compares procsses (other than phase separation processes) that can accept feed streams in the form of slurries or sludges. Table 8-13 compares processes that can accept feed streams in the form of tars, bulk solids or solid powders.

The vast majority of processes considered in this group operate mainly on liquids. Some can handle slurries and sludges, but in most cases, a liquid/solid separation would precede treatment and/or disposal. None of the processes can directly treat bulk solids contaminated by heavy metals, such as slag from the metallurgical industries (an enormously large waste stream in the aggregate). Few processes can work directly on tarry or even powered solid feeds. Unfortunately, water treatment sludges, still bottom tars, powdered particulate from air pollution control devices and oil-contaminated solids account for a larger fraction of the wastes destined for land disposal than do liquids.

Crushing, grinding and dissolution are therefore likely to play important roles in design of alternative hazardous waste treatment systems. Tars, which are often difficult to crush, grind or dissolve, might be reduced to smaller particle size by cryogenic cooling. The smaller particles thus formed should dissolve faster than the bulk tar removed from the reactor.

Selection on the Basis of Economic Considerations

Processes performing similar functions are compared with respect to capital and operating costs in Table 8-14. In deriving costs of alternative treatment systems (generally a sequence of processes) for any given waste stream, operating parameters specific to the particular situation should be taken into account; the costs in Table 8-14 only provide general guidelines.

SELECTION OF ENVIRONMENTALLY ADEQUATE DISPOSAL SITES

One of the most important and complex problems associated with the establishment of a hazardous waste disposal facility is selecting a suitable location. Typically, the overall selection process involves the following basic steps:

- developing site selection criteria,
- identifying candidate sites best meeting these criteria,
- initial review and evaluation of candidate sites,
- selection of sites for final evaluation,
- evaluation of regional awareness,
- final evaluation and ranking of sites,
- public involvement,
- site selection,
- public hearing and
- review.

The site-selection process is a complex system integrating public opinion and involvement and existing policy, while evaluating environmental, safety, economic and engineering feasibility. The relative importance of each of these factors is dependent on the basic selection of objectives; services to be provided by the facility; and pertinent local, state and federal regulations and policies.

The site selection process, therefore, requires:

- evaluating the selection objectives and constraints,
- evaluating regional and governmental awareness and
- establishing a site selection methodology in which criteria are determined and applied.

Objectives of the Selection Process

The basic objective of a hazardous waste disposal site selection process is to identify potential sites that are environmentally secure, economically and technically feasible to develop, and acceptable to regulatory agencies and the public. The site must ensure the present and future safety of the public and the protection of the environment.

Site selection criteria using environmental, socioeconomic and engineering factors have to be implemented in a manner responsive to exist-

Table 8-8. Comparison of Processes that Separate Heavy Metals from Liquid Waste Streams[a]

Process	State-of-the-Art	Required Feed Stream Properties	Characteristics of Output Stream(s)
Physical Removal			
Ion Exchange	Used but not common (Cat. IV)	Con. < 4000 ppm; aqueous solutions, low SS	One concentrated in heavy metals; one purified
Reverse Osmosis	Cat. IV	Con. > 400 ppm; aqueous solutions; controlled pH; low SS; no strong oxidants	One concentrated in heavy metals; one with heavy metal concentrations > 5 ppm
Electrodialysis	Cat. IV	Aqueous solutions; neutral or slightly acidic; Fe and Mn < 0.3 ppm; Cu < 400 ppm	One with 1000–5000 ppm heavy metals; one with 100–500 ppm heavy metals
Liquid Ion Exchange	Cat. IV	Aqueous solutions; no concentration limits; no surfactants; SS < 0.1%	Extraction solvent concentrated in heavy metals; purified water or slurry
Freeze Crystallization	Needs development (Cat. III)	Aqueous solutions; TDS < 10%	Concentrated brine or sludge; purified water, TDS ~100 ppm
Chemical Removal			
Precipitation	Common (Cat. V)	Aqueous or low viscosity nonaqueous solutions; no concentration limits	Precipitated heavy metal sulfides, hydroxides, oxides, etc.; solvent with TDS governed by solubility product of precipitates
Reduction	Cat. IV	Aqueous solutions; concentrations of heavy metals < 1%; controlled pH	Acidic solutions with reagent (oxidized $NaBH_4$ or Zn); metallic precipitates
Electrolysis	Cat. III	Aqueous solutions; heavy metal concentrations < 10%	Recovered metals; solution with 2–10 ppm heavy metals

[a]Source: NTIS-PB 275 054.

Table 8-9. Comparison of Treatment Processes that Separate Organics from Liquid Waste Streams[a]

Treatment Process	State-of-the-Art	Required Feed Stream Properties	Characteristics of Output Stream(s)
Carbon Adsorption	Used but not common (Cat. IV)	Aqueous solutions; concentrations <1%; SS<50 ppm	Adsorbate on carbon; usually regenerated thermally or chemically
Resin Adsorption	Cat. IV	Aqueous solutions; concentrations <8%; SS<50 ppm; no oxidants	Adsorbate on resin; always chemically regenerated
Ultrafiltration	Cat. IV	Solution or colloidal suspension of high molecular weight organics	One concentrated in high molecular weight organics; one containing dissolved ions
Air Stripping	Cat. IV	Solution continuing ammonia; high pH	Ammonia vapor in air
Steam Stripping	Cat. IV	Aqueous solutions of volatile organics	Concentrated aqueous streams with volatile organics and dilute stream with residuals
Solvent Extraction	Cat. IV	Aqueous or nonaqueous solutions; concentration<10%	Concentrated solution of organics in extraction solvent
Distillation	Cat. IV	Aqueous or nonaqueous solutions; high organic concentrations	Recovered solvent; still bottom liquids, sludges and tars
Steam Distillation	Cat. IV	Volatile organics, nonreactive with water or steam	Recovered volatiles plus condensed steam with traces of volatiles

[a]Source: NTIS-PB 275 054.

Table 8-10. Processees that Destroy Organics[a]

Process	State-of-the-Art	Required Feed Stream Properties	Characteristics of Output Stream(s)
Biodegradation	Cat. V	Dilute aqueous streams with soluble organics	Pure water
Oxidation	Cat. IV	Dilute aqueous solutions of phenols, organic sulfur compounds, chlorinated hydrocarbons, etc.	Oxidation products in aqueous solutions
Ozonation	Cat. IV	Aqueous solutions; concentrations $<1\%$	Oxidation products in aqueous solutions
Calcination	Cat. IV	Organics and inorganics that decompose thermally	Solid oxides; volatile emissions
Hydrolysis	Needs development (Cat. III)	Aqueous or non aqueous streams; no concentration limits	Hydrolysis products
Photolysis	Needs research (Cat. II)	Aqueous streams; transparent to light; components that absorb radiation	Photolysis products
Chlorinolysis	Cat. III	Chlorinated hydrocarbon waste streams; low sulfur; low oxygen; can contain benzene and other aromatics; no solids; no tars	Carbon tetrachloride; HCl and phosgene
Microwave Discharge	Cat. II	Organic liquids or vapors	Discharge products; not accurately predictable

[a]Source: NTIS-PB 275 054.

Table 8-11. Comparison of Processes that Separate Toxic Anions from Liquid Waste Streams[a]

Process	State-of-the-Art	Required Feed Stream Properties	Characteristics of Output Stream(s)
Physical Removal			
Ion Exchange	Cat. IV	Inorganic or organic anions in aqueous solution	Concentrated aqueous solutions
Liquid Ion Exchange	Cat. IV	Inorganic or organic anions in aqueous solution	Concentrated solutions in extraction solvent
Electrodialysis	Cat. IV	Aqueous stream with 1000–5000 ppm inorganic salts; and pH; Fe and Mn <0.3 ppm	Concentrated aqueous stream (10,000 ppm salts); dilute stream (100–500 ppm salts)
Reverse Osmosis	Cat. IV	Aqueous solutions with up to 34,000 ppm total dissolved solids	Dilute solution (~ 5 ppm TDS); concentrated solution of hazardous components
Freeze Crystallization	Needs development (Cat. III)	Aqueous salt solutions	Purified water; concentrated brine
Chemical Removal			
Oxidation	Cat. III-IV	Aqueous solutions of cyanides, sulfieds, sulfites etc; concentrations $<1\%$	Oxidation products
Ozonation	Cat. IV	Aqueous solutions of cyanides; concentrations $<1\%$	Cyanate solutions
Electrolysis	Cat. III	Alkaline aqueous solutions of cyanides or concentrated HCl solutions ($>20\%$)	Cyanides to ammonium and carbonate salt solutions; HCl to Cl_2 gas

[a]Source: NTIS-PB 275 054.

Table 8-12. Comparison of Processes that Can Accept Slurries or Sludges[a]

Process	State-of-the-Art	Required Feed Stream Properties	Characteristics of Output Stream(s)
Calcination	Used but not common (Cat. IV)	Waste stream with components that decompose by volatilization (hydroxides, carbonates, nitrates, sulfites, sulfates)	Solid greatly reduced in volume; volatiles
Freeze Crystallization	Needs development (Cat. III)	Low-viscosity aqueous slurry or sludge	Brine sludge; purified water
HGMS	Needs research (Cat. II)	Magnetic or paramagnetic particles in slurry	Particles adsorbed on magnetic filter
Liquid Ion Exchange	Cat. IV	Solvent extractable inorganic component	Solution in extraction solvent
Flotation	Cat. III	Flotable particles in slurry	Froth
Hydrolysis	Cat. II	Hydrolyzable component	Hydrolysis products
Anaerobic Digestion	Cat. IV	Aqueous slurry; <7% solids; no oil or greases; no aromatics or long chain hydrocarbons	Sludges; methane and CO_2
Composting	Cat. IV	Aqueous sludge; <50% solids	Sludge; leachate
Steam Distillation	Cat. IV	Sludge or slurry with volatile organics	Volatile, solid residue
Solvent Extraction	Cat. IV	Solvent extractable organic	Solution of extracted components; residual sludge

[a]Source: NTIS-PB 275 054.

Table 8-13. Comparison of Processes that Can Accept Tars or Solids[a]

Process	State-of-the-Art	Required Feed Stream Properties	Characteristics of Output Stream(s)
Calcination	Used but not common (Cat. IV)	Tars or solids that can be volatilized	Volatiles; char and/or metal oxides
Hydrolysis	Needs development (Cat. III)	Tars or solid powders	Hydrolysis products
Steam Distillation	Cat. IV	Solids contaminated with volatile organics	Purified solids; condensed organics
Dissolution	Cat. IV	Tars, solids, or solid powders that will dissolve in some reagent	Liquid solution for further treatment; solid residue
Crushing and Grinding	Cat. IV	Bulk solid	Powdered solid
Cryogenics	Needs research (Cat. II)	Tar, bulk solid	Reduced particle size

[a]Source: NTIS-PB 275 054.

Table 8-14. Approximate Treatment Costs[a]

Process	Annual Volume or Mass of Waste Stream Treated (typical) (gpd)	Capital Costs ($)	Operating Costs ($/1000 gal)	Fraction of Operation Costs Attributable to:			
				Labor	Energy	Materials	Other[b]
Phase Separation							
Sedimentation	5,000,000	—	$0.10-0.50	—	—	—	—
Vacuum Filtration	36,000	200,000	5-7	45	4	1	50
Centrifugation	36,000	140,000	5-7	35	5	17	43
Freeze Crystallization	50,000	280,000	6–12	52	16	—	32
Evaporation	20,000,000	1,300,000	1-2	3	92	—	5
Metal Removal From Liquids							
Precipitation	400,000	300,000	1-2	47	2	5	46
Electrodialysis	9,000	24,000	5-7	62	3	7	28
Ion Exchange	80,000	400,000	4–6	36	2	46	16
Liquid Ion Exchange	80,000	300,000	3–5	24	1	12	63
Reduction	2,000	230,000	150-200	32	21	15	32
Reverse Osmosis	3,000	12,000	9-11	29	6	—	65
Electrolysis	20,000	31,000	1-2	—	10-35	—	—
Organic Removal From Liquids							
Carbon Adsorption	100,000	1,200,000	5-20 (high figure with regeneration)	24	5-25 (high with thermal regeneration)	15	36-56
Resin Adsorption	67,000	720,000	11-13	11	40	Regenerating Solvent recovered	

Solvent Extraction	100,000	400,000	4-6				
Steam Stripping	720,000	500,000-850,000	~10	2	72	–	21
Steam Distillation	750	130,000	0.25-0.90	53	6	–	41
Distillation	1,000	230,000	264	14	12	–	74
Hydrolysis	30,000	320,000	20-30	57	17	–	26
Oxidation	1,000	100,000	229	44	4	15	37
Ozonation	800,000	330,000	0.40-1.00	26	20	–	54
Other							
Neutralization	1,000,000	1,050,000	2-3	15	1.5	59	24.5
Calcination	156,000	2,900,000	15-20	10	26	–	64
Chlorinolysis	20,000	5,500,000	3000	1	4	88	7

[a]Source: NTIS-PB 275 054 (1977).
[b]Capital amortization, water, maintenance, etc.

ing and new regulations, public opinion and concern, and the nature of current technology. Services to be provided and size of the facility are other factors affecting the overall objectives of the site selection process.

Specifically, the following must be considered:

- projected service area (e.g., local, regional, statewide, or multi-state);
- type of treatment, such as combustion, chemical stabilization, biological treatment, and land disposal;
- transportation access to the site;
- chemical and physical characteristics of the wastes accepted for disposal;
- planned life of the facility and
- long-range expansion or closure plans.

Regional and Governmental Awareness

Regional awareness for siting a hazardous waste disposal facility means presenting to the public and concerned government agencies a convincing statement of need along with a demonstration of ability to protect public safety and environmental quality. Due to the fact that initial public sentiment is generally against such a facility, regional awareness means involving representatives of the government and the people in the siting process. The opinions and issues of importance to local government can aid in developing an acceptable site selection methodology. Pressures to change the selection methodology may be experienced at the local level, with each locality suggesting another as a prime site area.

The federal Resource Conservation and Recovery Act (RCRA) provides for strong state and federal regulation of hazardous waste storage, treatment, recovery and disposal. Interfacing with state and federal regulatory agencies is, therefore, essential. In addition, RCRA provides the opportunity for public participation in the development, revision, implementation and enforcement of any regulation or program resulting from RCRA.

Methodology of Site Selection

The site selection of a hazardous waste disposal facility can be approached from two points of view. In either case it must be noted that final regulations have not yet been promulgated under RCRA and, therefore, complete regulations specifically related to hazardous waste disposal presently do not exist. Several states (such as California, Texas,

New Jersey, and Minnesota) have adopted comprehensive hazardous waste management programs; however, they may be subject to some modification as a result of RCRA.

The first approach requires that a series of site criteria must be established and evaluated with respect to their positive and negative effects; that is, the criteria must define what constitutes a good site and what does not. The major emphasis is on environmental adequacy and protection of public health. Basically, this first approach considers the technological and physical conditions of importance for public safety and protection of the environment. Particularly for states with little or no hazardous waste regulation, the results of such an approach most likely would not fit into the framework of the existing state regulations and policies specifically related to hazardous waste disposal. In this first case, the siting of a hazardous waste disposal facility is viewed as a specific problem requiring attention to specific details. The results of the siting study can be added to the existing governmental framework and can form the basis for changes to be made specifically for the establishment of chemical and hazardous waste policy.

The second approach to siting involves examination of existing governmental regulations and policies, even though they may not specifically pertain to hazardous wastes. The facility siting is guided by the limitations and interpretations of these policies which narrow the areas of site suitability. With the exception of those states having an existing comprehensive hazardous waste management program, a good site may be one that considers the existing political constraints first, and then evaluates the environmental adequacy and potential public health impact of the site. If the environmental and public health factors are not considered safe, then one or more of the policies must be changed.

This second approach may involve a site study conducted primarily within the political sphere, and considers the local and regional concerns of the various government entities. A site selected in this manner would be made to fit into the existing framework, allowing only case-by-case variances to be made within that framework. A determination must be made as to the nature of the existing state and local regulations and policies related to siting criteria for a hazardous waste management facility.

The first approach will be used to develop a site selection methodology because it is not constrained by the specifics of a particular state program. Priority objectives for site selection are stress, environmental adequacy and public health and safety.

Site selection criteria are necessary to provide a base from which any analysis can be completed. This allows a site or site area to be evaluated with respect to specific environmental concerns as well as many of the technological aspects of the proposed project. Social, economic and political constraints can also be added to the process by using the site selection criteria. Each set of criteria can then be evaluated to determine the positive and negative conditions with respect to siting a chemical waste facility. Essentially, an elimination process is developed by noting that certain factors are unfavorable for such a facility.

Initial analytical steps in the site selection process are to collect existing published data affecting the region proposed for the project, evaluate it and use it to limit the area of consideration. This represents an initial screening process to eliminate sites which exhibit unsuitable characteristics. Conversely, those sites with favorable siting conditions can be subjected to more detailed analysis which will lead to selection of the final site. Within this methodology, the selection process can begin by:

- identifying those factors pertinent to the siting of a chemical waste disposal facility,
- selecting the factors that would constitute a favorable site and
- identifying those factors that would constitute an unfavorable site.

The results of these considerations can be defined as the "site selection criteria." The physical, land-use and engineering conditions as they relate to land, water and air are included for consideration. Table 8-15 provides a summary of various factors that should be considered in the siting process and some of the favorable and unfavorable conditions associated with these factors.

Evaluation of Site Criteria

Applicable site characteristics as shown in Table 8-15 would be estimated from an accurate data source. Individual site criteria must be defined and processed in a form that can be related to other site criteria and data sources. The favorable or unfavorable factors must be derived from the physical area, first on a regional basis and then on a site-specific basis. The degree of precision of this calculation is strongly dependent on the type and quality of the data sources.

Table 8-16 reflects a typical matrix format that can be used to relate the relative suitability of several sites. In this example, five potential sites are evaluated on 15 site characteristics. A matrix format of this type offers flexibility so that weighting factors may be incorporated to promote certain site characteristics. The total sum of numeric values assigned to each characteristic for each site can be compared to determine relative suitability.

OPERATION OF HAZARDOUS WASTE FACILITIES

Once the facility is sited and constructed, proper operation is necessary to protect and prevent adverse impacts of the facility on the public health or to the environment.

Proper facility operation on a day-to-day basis includes proper handling of the waste; access to laboratory facilities for waste analysis, treatment and/or disposal; safety at the site; monitoring to ensure protection of the environment; operator training; and financial responsibility of the owner.

Waste Compatibility

Proper handling of the waste to include treatment and disposal is needed in order to prevent environmental damage. Without proper handling, there is a danger of fire, explosion and gas generation that can arise from the haphazard mixing of wastes which are not compatible. While empirical data exist concerning the consequences of reactions between pure substances under laboratory conditions, very little work has been done in the field of waste combination reactions. Very seldom are wastes pure substances. They are usually sludges, emulsions, suspensions or slurries containing many different components. In a landfill, these mixtures will not react in the same manner that the pure substances comprising them react in the laboratory. This is due to differences in concentration, rates of mixing, heat capacities of the surroundings, and the presence of other components in large or trace amounts which might accelerate or decelerate the reaction.

It is evident from existing data that the largest dangers inherent from incompatible reactions involve strong acids or bases. Large deviations of the pH of a waste from neutrality will interfere also with soil attenuation, and can solubilize and release heavy metals and other contaminants that might otherwise be bound. For these reasons, it is desirable that acids and bases be neutralized to within a pH range of 4.5 to 9 before being mixed with other wastes (possibly acidic and basic wastes could be mixed in a controlled manner to achieve pH neutrality). Even within this restricted pH range, acids should be segregated from acid-soluble sulfide and cyanide salts.

Wastes that are particularly toxic, including beryllium, asbestos and all pesticide wastes, should be segregated from highly flammable wastes, since fires provide a ready vector for these wastes to enter the immediate environment.

Table 8-15. Sample of Technical Site Selection Criteria

Category	Site Characteristic	Tolerance/Suitability for Chemical Waste Disposal: Favorable Conditions	Tolerance/Suitability for Chemical Waste Disposal: Limited or Unfavorable Conditions	Considerations
Land				
Soils and Topography	Topographic relief	Gently rolling terrain.	Hilly, or near steep slopes.	
	Soils: composition, engineering and site development	Suitable soils for dike construction, building construction, and linear development.	Poor foundation soils, unsuitable dike material; liner soils must be imported.	Limited conditions will likely add to facility development costs.
	Soils: slope, erodibility	Slopes (3-10%) to limit erosion potential.	Slopes $>10\%$ resulting in a high erosion potential	The exact slope limit needs to be defined on a site specific basis.
	Soils: texture	Clay to silt or loam (very fine to medium grain sizes.)	Fine sands to gravels (coarse grain sizes.)	
	Soils: agriculture uses	Soils with lesser agricultural value.	Prime agricultural land.	
	Subsoils: composition	Suitable soils for dikes, buildings and liner development.	Poor foundation conditions, unsuitable for dike materials; liner soils must be imported.	Cost is an important factor in this consideration.
	Subsoils: permeability	Silt soils with high clay content and with low permeabilities (≤ 10–7 cm/sec).	Clean sands and gravels, with permeabilities >10–5 cm/sec.	Here it is assumed that natural protection of low permeability deposits are more favorable than higher permeability deposits.

	Subsoils: thickness	Thick deposits of low permeable materials. Few or no sand and gravel lens. Uncompacted thickness no less than 4 feet.	Thin deposits of low permeable materials underlain by large thickness of sand and gravel.	Ideally, a site should be underlain by a good thickness of impermeable material. Underlying sands and gravels are less favorable.
Geology	Bedrock: depth	Bedrock covered by thick deposits of unconsolidated material.	Bedrock at or near surface.	
	Bedrock: subcropping formations	Shale or undisturbed very fine grained sedimentary formation.	Highly fractured limestone or dolomites; coarse grained, permeable sandstone.	The limitations introduced by this factor are dependent on the composition and thickness of the overlying unconsolidated material.
	Bedrock: structural conditions	No major structural variations within an area.	Areas of faulting, extreme fracturing or severe folding.	
Water	Ground Water: unconsolidated formations	No connection with surficial or buried drift aquifers. Low permeable materials to bedrock.	Underlain by surficial and buried drift aquifers of local and/or regional significance.	The limitations introduced by these factors are dependent on the composition and thickness of the unconsolidated material and are site specific.
	Ground Water: bedrock formations	Away from any recharge areas to major bedrock aquifers: no direct connection with a usable bedrock aquifer.	On a major bedrock aquifer recharge area; direct connection between a drift and usable bedrock aquifer.	Potential for polluting a usable aquifer is the primary concern here.
	Ground Water: flow direction	Local flow pattern.	Regional flow pattern.	

Table 8-15, continued

Category	Site Characteristic	Tolerance/Suitability for Chemical Waste Disposal: Favorable Conditions	Tolerance/Suitability for Chemical Waste Disposal: Limited or Unfavorable Conditions	Considerations
Man-Oriented	Land use: forested	Areas where existing forest may serve as a buffer.	Areas where significant amounts of existing forests may be removed are not as attractive.	Significant removal of forests is an additional cost factor.
	Land Use: cultivated land	Minor removal of land from current cultivation.	Areas where significant removal of prime agricultural land from cultivation is required.	Significant removal of prime agricultural land from cultivation can be a local socio-economic cost factor.
	Land Use: urban residential	Areas with little urban development.	Areas with high urban development.	Proximity to residences is considered less favorable.
	Land Use: extractive	Areas of no or low on-going activity.	Areas currently being mined or actively used.	Use of abandoned extractive areas is questionable and would require site specific investigation.
	Land Use: pasture	Areas that are currently prime pasture lands.	Significant pasturing activities.	Extent of pasturing determined by site specific investigation.
	Land Use: urban and nonresidential or mixed residential	Site specific.	Areas with minimal commerical, industrial or institutional development.	These factors can be considered exclusionary (schools, hospitals, airports).
	Land Use: parks, wildlife preserves, recreation areas	Very limited	Site location in any of these land types.	All federal, state, regional, county and local parks, preserves, historical areas, etc., are considered here. This factor is considered very limited area for a chemical waste disposal facility.

	Land use: transportation	Good conditioned roads (≥ 9 ton) in area, lower traffic volume; near railroad.	Roads in poor condition, high traffic volume, high hazard roads.	The absence of 9 ton roads is not exclusionary; however, upgrading of lesser roads may be a costly alternative.
	Land Use: historical, archeological	Dependent on site specific details.	Areas with confirmed historical or archeological significance.	This area will require some interpretation since areas of possible archeological significance have been designated. Services of a professional archeologist may be required.
	Socio-Economic Land Availability	Land available for purchase. Minimum amount of land owners involved.	Land unavailable or must be acquired through legal means, numerous land owners involved.	
	Location	Near the majority of the waste generators.	Away from waste generators.	Based on the waste generator/waste disposer relationship. This aspect can become matter of transportation economics.
Natural Conditions	Environmental: unique areas	Area of typical regional ecosystems.	Areas of unique ecological sensitivity, e.g., habitats of unique and/or endangered or threatened species.	This aspect is extremely site specific.
	Environmental: public health	Area where construction and operation will not adversely affect public health.	Areas where dust, noise, fire, explosion may create a public health and/or safety hazard.	Protection of the public is the primary consideration.
Non-development	Engineering Suitability: electric	Adequate electric power is relatively available in site area.		The economics of electrical transmission are a consideration.

Table 8-15, continued

Category	Site Characteristic	Tolerance/Suitability for Chemical Waste Disposal: Favorable Conditions	Tolerance/Suitability for Chemical Waste Disposal: Limited or Unfavorable Conditions	Considerations
	Engineering Suitability: sewer	Site near interceptor sewer or wastewater treatment plant.		Not required. . . but could be used to dispose of clarified effluent. This item becomes a matter of economics.
Water	Surface Water: water bodies and water courses	Limited	Placement of facility on or near.	
	Surface Water: flood plains, floodways	Limited	Placement of facility on or near.	
	Surface Water: wetlands	Limited	Placement of facility on or near wetlands.	
	Drainage: natural	Areas where surface drainage exists and can be controlled.	Areas of poor drainage or where ponding occurs; drainage areas requiring excessive engineered controls	Site drainage may be a major factor in preventing the unplanned spread of chemical wastes at the facility. Sites with suitable natural drainage conditions will be more favorable than those requiring large amounts of engineering and associated costs.
	Drainage: local watershed	Site location near a drainage divide where upstream surface area is small.	Site location where upstream surface area is great and engineering precautions to handle runoff become costly.	

Air	Ambient Air Quality	Good dispersive characteristics are important if the facility generates a discharge to the atmosphere.	Dispersion is not expected to be an important consideration for land disposal facilities.	
	Odor			These site characteristics are facility specific.
Climatology	Dust			Site and facility specific.

Table 8-16. Sample Site Selection Matrix for Hazardous Waste Disposal Facility

Potential Sites						
1	2	3	4	5	etc.	Site Characteristics
X	X			X		Compatibility with regulatory requirements
X	X	X				Thick deposits of low permeability soils
X	X	X		X		Permeability of soils and depth to ground water
X	X	X	X			Depth to bedrock: favorable
	X		X			Bedrock structural conditions: favorable
X	X	X	X	X		No adverse impact on usable aquifer
X	X		X			Low residential development in adjacent areas
X			X			Compatibility with present land use and zoning
	X	X		X		Compatibility with future local and regional plans
X		X		X		Desirable transportation access
X	X		X			Favorable air-dispersive characteristics
		X	X	X		Sewer available
	X	X	X			Water available
X	X	X	X	X		Electric available
X	X	X	X	X		No nearby historic, archaeological, or culturally significant areas

Also, wastes that react violently with water, or react with water to give off a noxious or toxic gas (wastes containing phosphorus trichloride, phosphorus pentachloride, thionylchloride, and elemental sodium, potassium or magnesium) must be encapsulated in a moisture-proof container before landfilling.

Facility operators should be aware of the problems that can arise from mixing incompatible wastes and should guard against such practices. If consistent mishandling occurs at a facility, the state can opt to revoke the operation permit.

The successful use of any compatibility system depends on the labeling of wastes to conform with the generic names used in the system. These matrices will be modified and updated as further information concerning waste compatibility becomes available.

Monitoring

In order to protect against pollution of surface and groundwater, the site should have monitoring equipment. Samples should be taken of the surface water and ground water to determine if the facility is polluting the water. In the event pollution is detected, corrective steps can be taken. Also, monitoring of the air quality and noise levels at the site should be undertaken.

Personnel

Training of waste management facility personnel in safety, first aid and facility operation is an important aspect of overall facility management. All site personnel should undergo training either in a classroom environment or on the job site. The type and degree of the training will vary with the responsibilities of the site personnel.

A hazardous waste facility should have a manager, a supervisor and a technical advisor (although one person may be able to perform more than one of these functions). The manager is responsible for the overall management of the hazardous waste facility, is knowledgeable about site operations and equipment design, and is able to give specific waste handling instructions and safety precautions to the supervisor and equipment operators on a continuing basis in consultation with the technical advisor.

The supervisor directs the everyday waste treatment/disposal activities and ensures that proper waste handling procedures are followed and safety regulations are enforced. Other site personnel—heavy equipment operators and laborers—are under his direct supervision.

The technical advisor should be available to answer questions relating to waste compatibility and the hazards of chemical toxicity, flammability, reactivity, etc.

Many in the hazardous waste management-service industry believe that the most important safety precaution is the proper characterization and identification of hazardous waste. Therefore, the facility supervisor must be able to recognize the hazards associated with each of the chemical wastes managed at the site. Training of management personnel should focus on operational procedures of the facility, special handling procedures for the hazardous waste, occupational safety, first aid and industrial wastes.

Employee safety is an important aspect of proper facility operations. OSHA standards for safety in the workplace should be enforced, and any violations recorded in the event of permit review. State environmental officials may need to highlight for state or federal occupational health agencies the unique problems involved at waste management facilities.

The supervisory/management personnel should have either a degree in chemistry or chemical engineering or have a strong background in the subject matter. All site employees should be given training on facility operations by the plant management. In addition, site employees should be required to attend a safety course that includes instruction in accident prevention, occupational safety, first aid and hazardous waste handling procedures. A basic safety course, "Safety in Chemical Operations," currently is offered by the National Safety Council. Because each facility may have unique operations and handling requirements, it will be necessary for management personnel to provide additional training unique to the site involved.

Fiscal Responsibility of Owners—Insurance

The owners and operators of any waste management facility have a responsibility to the public to operate in a manner that will not adversely affect the environment or the public health. Within the broad realm of this responsibility is the financial protection against liability. The amount of financial protection required by the waste management facility should be the amount of liability insurance available from private sources. It is assumed that the private insurance industry will be able to provide adequate liability coverage. A hazardous waste management facility ideally should be required to obtain coverage over all aspects of operating a hazardous waste facility including transportation, contamination incidents and other risk activities associated with long-term consequences, even after closure of a facility and/or a change in ownership. The protection should extend to any persons who may be legally liable for a hazardous waste incident.

The policy should cover liability for bodily injury and property damage, and should contain a single aggregate limit of liability for all losses and loss expenses for bodily injury and property damage arising during the policy period.

The service firm, as a condition for seeking insurance, would be required to meet all state and EPA standards associated with the operation of a hazardous waste facility. By the same token, a permit application must contain the names and addresses of the applicant's current or proposed insurance carriers, including copies of insurance policies in effect.

CLOSURE OF FACILITIES

Landfills for hazardous waste disposal ultimately reach capacity and must be closed, but the potential for harmful occurrences remains.

Because hazardous waste constituents may enter the environment after the day-to-day maintenance of the facility has ceased, the owners of the facility must plan for site closure and long-term surveillance, and the state must consider future uses of the land. The funding requirements of the plan must be estimated, and a means derived to acquire the necessary funds.

Long-term Liability

Regardless of the kind of firm originally or currently owning such a facility (whether public or private), liability for damages is an important fact or burden that someone will have to bear. The possibility certainly exists that the owner and operator of a closed hazardous waste facility still under his ownership could be held liable for long-term damages. The problem is more complex when ownership has changed. In order to provide protection in the event of future occurrences after closures, the liability insurance requirement might include coverage for long-term damage regardless of whether ownership is retained or not.

The advantages of this system are as follows:

- it is easy to implement and involves minimal cost to the government;
- the private sector (insurance carriers) operates the liability insurance mechanism;
- it is self-enforcing; that is, if a company cannot afford the insurance, it does not qualify for a permit; and
- it provides current and future liability protection against hazardous waste occurrences.

The disadvantages of this system are as follows:

- the insurance cost may be very expensive, and lead to an uneven cost burden within the private sector;
- the cost may force firms out of business;
- firms may be unwilling to buy insurance after they close or sell a facility;
- the insurance coverage from the private sector may not be adequate to protect the public health and the environment; and
- adequate amounts of insurance per facility and per incident are unknown.

Planning Long-term Care

The owners of a hazardous waste management facility need to plan for long-term care which should address: decontamination of equipment and structures prior to sale; removal and disposal of remaining hazardous materials; modification to disposal areas to render the site secure; and expected resource commitments or requirements. In addition, a long-term care plan (for disposal area only) should be developed and implemented after closure of the site. It should include monitoring, sampling, analysis of ground water and surface waters in the vicinity of the site, maintenance of the site (cap maintenance or replacement), containing operations to prevent leachate from reaching the ground water and surface waters, and identification of officials response for implementation of the plan.

Sufficient funding to implement this plan generally can be secured via a posted bond, a perpetual care fee, or a combination of both mechanisms. A mutual trust fund also may be used.

Future Land Use of Closed Facilities

The state should require that the use of a site for a hazardous waste management facility be recorded on the deed to the property. This information is necessary to prevent future improper uses of the land. After use as a land disposal facility, the site should not be an area zoned for commercial or residential construction. Construction of any structure on the site should be limited to only those areas where waste was not disposed of. The use of the site for a recreational area or park may be the best use for the land. However, the location of the facility in a highly industrial area may limit the appeal of such a recreational facility. In the planning stages of the hazardous waste management facility, state decision makers should decide if future land use restrictions will be necessary in the context of what uses of the land can serve.

ACKNOWLEDGMENT

The material in this chapter is derived in part from information in a study by Joan B. Berkowitz, et al. of Arthur D. Little, Inc., prepared for the Hazardous Waste Management Division, Office of Solid Waste, U.S. Environmental Protection Agency, NTIS Publication PB275054 (1977); and from "State Decision Makers Guide for Hazardous Waste Management," U.S. Environmental Protection Agency, SW-612 (1977).

CHAPTER 9

PHYSICAL TREATMENT

Physical treatment processes discussed in this chapter are primarily phase separation unit operations. Seventeen processes are discussed in alphabetical order in the following sections: adsorption (activated carbon and resin), centrifugation, dialysis, electrodialysis, electrolysis, electrophoresis, filtration, flocculation (precipitation and sedimentation), flotation, freeze crystallization, freeze drying, freezing (suspension), high gradient magnetic separation, reverse osmosis, stripping (air), ultrafiltration, and zone refining.

ADSORPTION

Activated Carbon Adsorption

The term "activated carbon" applies to any amorphous form of carbon that has been treated to produce high adsorption capacities. Typical raw materials include coal, wood, coconut shells, pulp mill residues, petroleum base residues and char from sewage sludge pyrolysis. A carefully controlled process of dehydration, carbonization and oxidation yields the product called activated carbon, though it is not pure carbon. This material has a high capacity for adsorption, due primarily to the large surface area (500–1500 m^2/g), resulting from a large number of internal pores. Pore sizes generally range from 10 to 100 Å in radius. Most of the available surface area is nonpolar, but the interaction with oxygen (in production) does produce specific active sites which give the surface a slightly polar nature.

Adsorption on activated carbon occurs when a molecule is brought up to its surface and held there by physical and/or chemical forces. This process is reversible, thus allowing activated carbon to be regenerated and reused by proper application of heat and steam, or solvent [1,2].

After initial contact between activated carbon and a solution, an equilibrium will eventually be reached where the rates of solute adsorption and desorption are equal. The amount of solute adsorbed per unit weight of carbon increases as the concentration of the solute is increased. In general, adsorption equilibria are governed by two types of interactions: solute-adsorbent and solute-solvent. Thus, the forces favoring dissolution and the forces favoring adsorption are in competition; any change in a system which tends to decrease the dissolution forces or increase the adsorption forces will shift the equilibrium toward higher adsorption per unit weight of carbon.

Some important, but general, rules result from considerations relating to the above factors:

- Greater surface area produces greater adsorption capacity.
- Larger pore sizes produce a greater adsorption capacity for large molecules.
- Adsorptivity increases as the solubility of the solute (in the solvent) decreases. Thus, for hydrocarbons, adsorption increases with molecular weight.
- For solutes with ionizable groups, maximum adsorption will be achieved at a pH corresponding to the minimum ionization.
- Adsorption capacity decreases with increasing temperature (since adsorption is an exothermic process). In practice, this effect generally is small.

The above factors all relate to adsorption capacity; the rate of adsorption is also an important consideration. For example, while capacity is increased with the adsorption of higher molecular weight hydrocarbons, the rate of adsorption is decreased. Similarly, while an increase in temperature decreases capacity, it may—depending on the rate-limiting step in the overall process—increase the rate of removal of solute from solution.

One additional point to remember is that biological activity usually takes place in a carbon bed. If the concentration of adsorbed species is high enough and the material is biodegradable and nontoxic to the bacteria, then biological degradation may significantly increase the effective removal capacity.

Operating Characteristics

In general, carbon adsorption is applicable only to single-phase fluid waste streams, e.g., liquid solutions or gas mixtures. In actual applications, both aqueous and nonaqueous liquids are treated with carbon. The nonaqueous streams include petroleum fractions, syrups, animal and vegetable oils, and pharmaceutical preparations; color removal is the most common objective in such cases. Current waste treatment applications are limited to aqueous solutions.

Suspended solids in the influent (which lead to premature pressure drops in a carbon bed) should generally be <50 ppm to minimize backwash requirements; a downflow carbon bed can handle much higher levels (up to 2000 ppm), but frequent backwashings would be required. Backwashing more than two or three times a day is not desirable; at 50 ppm suspended solids, one backwash per day often will suffice. In any upflow packed bed excessive suspended solids can lead to clogging. Oil and grease should be less than ~10 ppm.

Technically, there are no limits on the concentration of the solute(s) in the feed stream, but in practice the highest concentration influent that has been treated on a continuous basis contained ~10,000 ppm total organic carbon (TOC).

A wide variety of organic and inorganic solutes may be efficiently adsorbed on activated carbon. Applications involving organic solutes are more prevalent, and are more attractive when the solutes have a high molecular weight, low water solubility, low polarity and low degree of ionization. Highly water-soluble organics, which often contain two or more hydrophilic groups, are difficult to remove. For example, the adsorption of glycols from an industrial waste stream was found to be unfeasible in one recent study due to the low capacity of the carbon for the glycols [3]. In another case, the treatment of wastewater from a polyvinyl chloride production plant was found to be impractical; poor adsorption characteristics were attributed to the presence of long-chain organic soaps in the wastes [4]. Figure 9-1 is a schematic showing the adsorption process for phenol and acetic acid.

Carbon adsorption of inorganic compounds, e.g., the removal of cyanide [5] and chromium [6] from electroplating wastes, has been found to be practical. Other sources [1,7–9] indicate that a wide variety of other inorganics will adsorb on activated carbon. However, adsorption may be quite variable from chemical to chemical; it is likely to be highly pH-dependent, and thermal or chemical regeneration may not be feasible. In general, strong electrolytes will not be adsorbed on carbon.

Energy, Environment and Economics

Energy requirements include electricity for pumps and fuel for the regeneration furnace. Energy costs may be 25% (or more) of the total operating cost where concentrated waste streams are being treated and

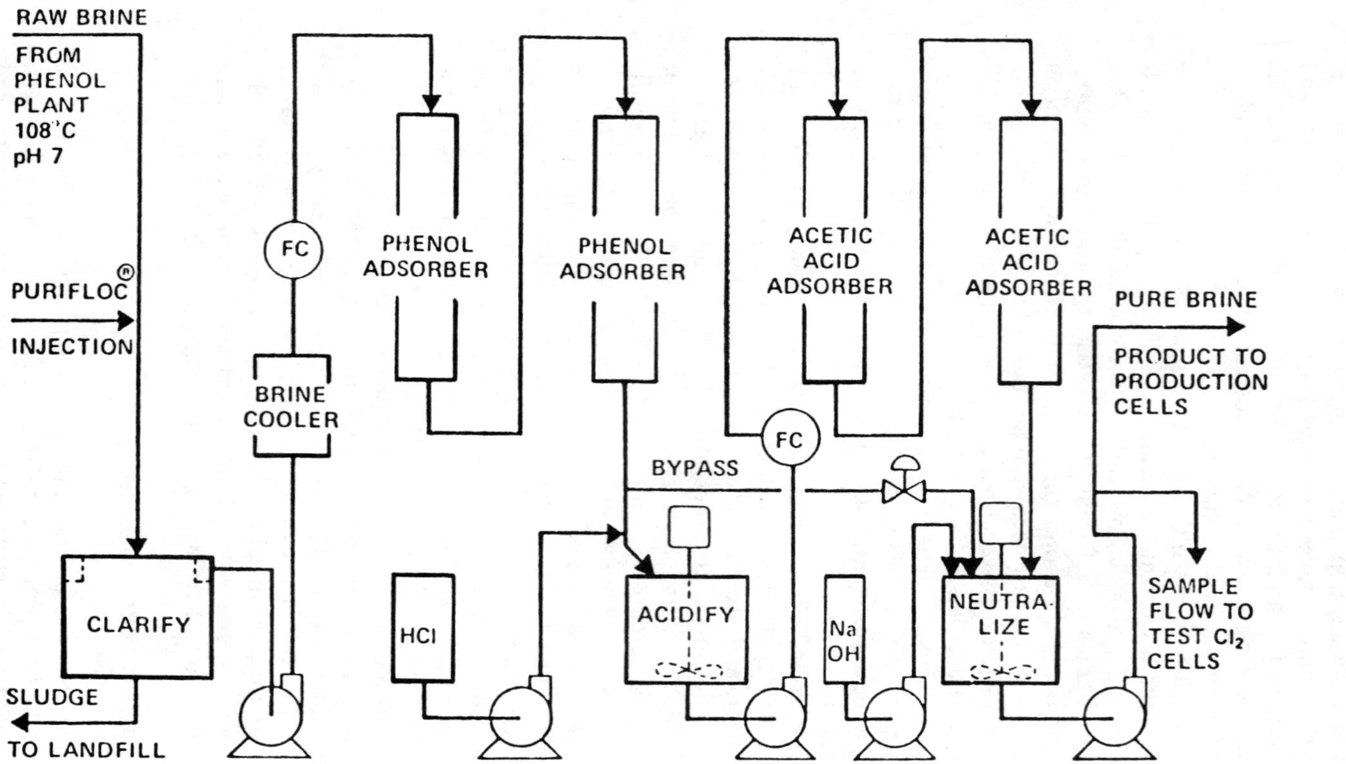

Figure 9-1. Schematic flowsheet of adsorption process for phenol and acetic acid to be followed by chemical regeneration and solute recovery (Source: NTIS-PB 275 054).

the carbon is thermally regenerated. Energy may constitute no more than 5% of total operating costs if regeneration is nonthermal.

Capital costs for a 100,000 gpd facility would be ~$1,000,000. Total operating costs would be in the range of $5–20/1000 gal.

If spent carbon is not regenerated, it presents a problem for disposal. If it is thermally regenerated, the regeneration furnace usually will require an afterburner and a scrubber, and sometimes a dust filter.

Resin Adsorption

In many respects, adsorption on resins is similar to adsorption on carbon; thus, researchers are investigating both types of adsorbents for treatability studies on industrial waste streams. A combination of both carbon and resin adsorption has been proposed as being particularly attractive in some situations; this alternative should be kept in mind.

Waste treatment by resin adsorption involves two basic steps: (1) contacting the liquid waste stream with the resins and allowing the resins to adsorb the solutes from the solution; and (2) subsequently regenerating the resins by removing the adsorbed chemicals, often by simply washing with the proper solvent.

The chemical natures of the commercially available resins can be quite different; perhaps the most important variable in this respect is the degree of their hydrophilicity. The adsorption of a nonpolar molecule onto a hydrophobic resin (e.g., a styrene-divinyl-benzene-based resin) results primarily from the effect of Van der Waal's forces. In other cases, other types of interactions such as dipole-dipole interaction and hydrogen bonding are important. In a few cases, an ion-exchange mechanism may be involved; this is thought to be true, for example, in the adsorption of alkylbenzene sulfonates from aqueous solution onto weakly basic resins; e.g., a phenol-formaldehyde-amine based resin.

Equipment and Materials

Equipment requirements for resin adsorption systems are relatively simple. The adsorption system generally consists of two or more steel tanks (stainless steel or rubber-lined) with associated piping, pumps and (perhaps) influent hold-up tank. Regeneration takes place in the same tanks, and thus the only extra equipment needed for regeneration would be solvent storage tanks, associated piping and pumps, and solvent (and perhaps solute) recovery equipment, e.g., a still. Up to three stills may be required in some systems, such as the one shown in Figure 9-2.

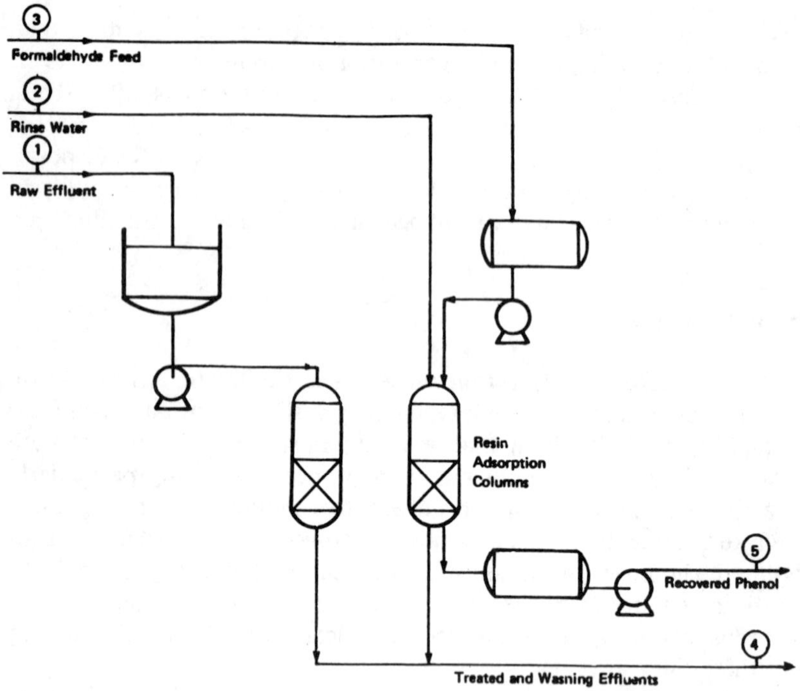

Figure 9-2. Phenol recovery process—formaldehyde regeneration system (Source NTIS-PB 275 054).

Materials needed include a regenerant solution (e.g., aqueous caustic solution or organic solvent) and resin. In one full-scale installation for the removal of organic dye wastes from water [10–13], two different resins are employed. In this case, the waste stream is first contacted with a normal polymeric adsorbent and then with an anion exchange resin.

Energy, Environment and Economics

Energy requirements are small when the regenerant is not recycled. When both solvent and solute are recovered, the steam requirements for distillation (up to three stills required) are significant. If the regenerant is not recycled, it must be disposed of. If the regenerant is recycled (e.g., by distillation), the still bottoms remain to be disposed of.

Capital costs are moderately large; although no furnace is needed for regeneration (an expensive item with carbon systems), resin costs are high. Operating cost may be <$1/1000 gal in some applications, but may reach $5–20/100 gal when concentrated waste streams are treated and the solute recovered. Credit for recovered solute can allow a system to operate at a profit in favorable cases.

CENTRIFUGATION

Process Description

Centrifugation is a physical process in which the components of a fluid mixture are separated mechanically by rapidly rotating the mass of fluid within a rigid vessel. Centrifugal forces acting on the revolving mass of fluid radiate outward from the center of rotation and would pull the mass of fluid apart if it were not contained within the vessel.

As noted in the sections on precipitation, flocculation and sedimentation, there are many forces acting on particles suspended within a fluid. These include gravity, inertia and electrostatic and interionic forces. If the forces acting on a particle in a fluid are in equilibrium, the particle will remain suspended. If an external force is applied to the particle, the particle will tend to migrate in the direction of that force (provided, of course, that there is a relative difference in density between the particle and the fluid). In the case of centrifugation, if a particle is more dense than the fluid, it will migrate in the direction of the centrifugal force, i.e., toward the periphery of the rotating vessel. If the particle is less dense than the fluid, there will be a tendency for the particle to remain near the center of rotation and for the fluid to migrate toward the periphery of the vessel. Either way, particles that were uniformly dispersed throughout the fluid before centifugation would then be concentrated in a specific place in the centrifuge where they can be removed as a more concentrated mixture. The centrifugal force is analogous to gravitational force in the sedimentation process. In centrifugation, however, forces equal to several thousand times the force of gravity are often generated.

Centrifuges are in widespread use throughout industry for a variety of process and waste treatment applications. The many different applications have resulted in a large number of equipment configurations. Fundamentally, centrifuges fall into two categories: sedimentation centrifuges and filtering centrifuges. In the sedimentation centrifuge the solids accumulate in a layer or "cake" on the inner wall of the rotating vessel. In the filtering centrifuge a cake of granular solids is deposited on a filter medium held in a rotating basket. Some representative types of centrifuges are described below [14] and shown in Figure 9-3.

1. *Tubular Centrifuge.* In the tubular centrifuge, a sedimentation type centrifuge, the fluid enters the bottom through a stationary nozzle. The

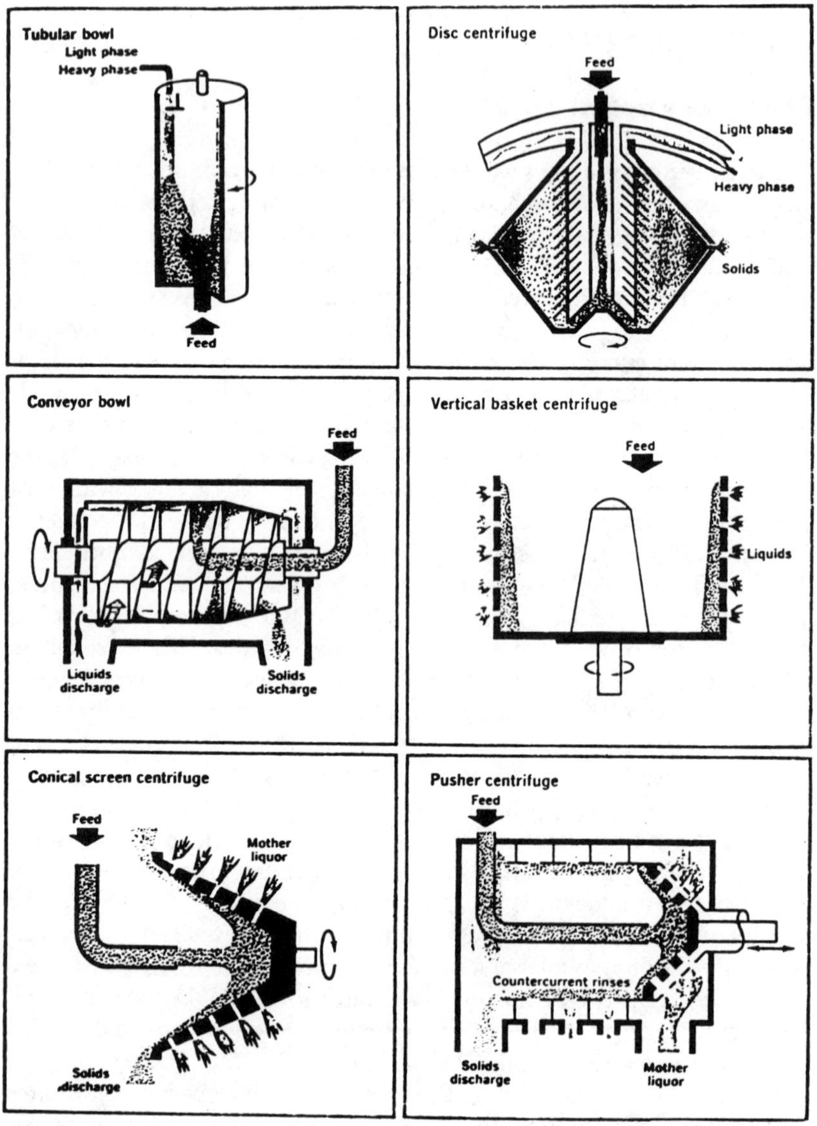

Figure 9-3. Representative types of centrifuges (Source: NTIS-PB 275 054).

fluid accelerates to the speed of the revolving tubular bowl. Solids contained within the fluid migrate to the periphery of the bowl and form a layer on the inner wall of the bowl. The separated fluids usually are continuously displaced by the incoming feed.

2. *Disc Centrifuge.* The disc centrifuge, a sedimentation type centrifuge, consists of a revolving bowl which contains a series of conical discs that divide the feed into layers, usually not more than 0.05 in. thick. This "thin strata distribution" increases the rate of solids separation. There are several variations of this type of centrifuge. In the "nozzle bowl" type, solids are continuously discharged through nozzles built into the bowl wall. In the "self cleaning" type, the bowl's bottom section slides downward for a fraction of a second to discharge the solids.

3. *Conveyor Bowl Centrifuge.* Also a sedimentation type centrifuge, the conveyor bowl centrifuge employs a rotating screw within the rotating centrifuge bowl. The screw rotates in the same direction as the bowl in which it is contained, but at a slightly lower speed. Solid particles accumulated on the inner wall of the bowl are directed by the rotating screw to the discharge point. The liquid is discharged from the other end of the centrifuge through adjustable ports. Conveyor bowl centrifuges are available in a number of configurations. The axis of rotation can be either horizontal or vertical, and the bowl may be either cylindrical or conical. The bowl configuration affects the clarity of the outlet liquid and the dryness of the cake.

4. *Batch Centrifuge.* The batch centrifuge is the simplest type of filtering centrifuge. It generally consists of a perforated metal basket that rotates about a vertical axis. Liquid flung against the inner wall of the basket is forced through the perforations by the centrifugal force, while the solids are retained, and accumulate in a layer on the inner wall. After a sufficiently thick layer has accumulated, the machine is stopped, the solids removed, and the basket washed and spun dry. Although a batch machine, it is often automated so that little labor is required for its operation.

5. *Conical Basket Centrifuge.* In this variation of the filtering centrifuge, a conical screen is rotated about a horizontal axis. As in the batch centrifuge, solids are retained on the rotating screen while the liquid passes through. Due to its geometry, the conical basket centrifuge is a continuous machine. The force of the incoming feed, along with the force vector along the direction of the cone, causes the accumulated solids to be pushed out the wide end of the cone.

6. *Pusher Centrifuge.* The pusher centrifuge is a filtering basket centrifuge, as described above, which employs an oscillating piston that travels the length of the bowl and displaces solids from the basket. It operates in

a continuous mode as in the case of the conical basket type, but also has the capability of washing the cake in a "continuous" mode.

While there are many more variations, under a large number of trade names, the general types of centrifuges described above embody the basic elements of most centrifugation equipment. As mentioned, the centrifuge configuration greatly determines the type of fluid and particles that can be successfully separated. To provide perspective on the types of particles that can be separated by centrifugation and the nature of the resulting cake, a summary of general applicability, available equipment capacity, etc. [15], is given in Table 9-1.

Applications to Date

Probably the main application for centrifuges at present is the dewatering of waste sludges. Some other common applications of centrifugation are in separating oil and water mixtures; clarification of viscous gums and resins; classification and removal of oversize particles and unground pigment from lacquers, enamel and dye paste; clarification of essential oils, extracts, and food products such as homogenized milk and fruit juices; separation of microorganisms from fermentation broths, recovery of finely divided metal such as silver from film scrap and platinum from spent catalyst; separation of acid sludges from the acid treatment of petroleum; recovery of crystalline solids from brine; dewatering of fibrous solids such as paper pulp and chemical fibers; dewatering and removal of starch from potato fibers, etc. Figure 9-4 presents a flow diagram of a centrifugation process.

Energy, Environment and Economics

Power requirements for centrifugation are typically 0.3–1.2 hp/gal/min of inlet waste feed. Power consumption is equal to or slightly greater than for other sludge dewatering processes.

For most sludge dewatering purposes, centrifugation is generally cost-competitive with other dewatering processes such as vacuum filtration or press filtration.

A conveyor bowl centrifugation system capable of dewatering 6 ton/day of sludge (dry basis) would have an installed capital cost of ~$140,000 and a total operating cost (including amortization) of $34.50/ton of solids dewatered. In most applications, costs range from $20–$45/ton.

Table 9-1. Application Range of Centrifuges[a]

Characteristic	Tubular	Disc (Nozzle Type)	Conveyor Bowl
A. Sedimentation Type Centrifuges			
Minimum Particle Size (μ)	0.1	0.25	2
Maximum Particle Size (μ)	200	50	5,000
Allowable Concentration of Feed Solids (%)	0.1	2–20	2–60
Condition of Cake	Pasty, firm	Fluid	Firm, pasty
Typical Solids Handling Rate (lb/hr)	0.1–5	10–30,000	100–100,000
Typical Liquid Rate (gpm)	0.25–20	1–800	1–500
Characteristic	**Batch Vertical**	**Conical Basket**	**Pusher**
B. Filtering Type Centrifuges			
Minimum Particle Size (μ)	10	250	40
Maximum Particle Size (μ)	1000	10,000	5000
Allowable Concentration of Feed Solids (%)	2–10	40–80	15–75
Condition of Cake	Pasty	Relatively dry	Relatively dry
Typical Solids Handling Rate (lb/hr)	0.1–1.0	5–40	0.5–5.0

[a]Source: NTIS-PB 275 054.

DIALYSIS

Process Description

Dialysis is one of several membrane separation procedures which consist, in essence, of (1) a barrier which preferentially passes certain components of a fluid mixture or solution, and (2) a driving force to cause such transfer to take place. Table 9-2 lists the processes and the function of the membrane and type of driving force in each. Dialysis uses a semipermeable membrane capable of passing small solute molecules (such as salts and small organic species) while retaining colloids and solutes of higher molecular weight. The driving force for this transfer is the concentration gradient—the difference in chemical activity of the constituents on either side of the membrane. The transfer through the membrane is by diffusion, that is, the process of individual molecules, rather than by the hydrodynamic flow that would occur through a porous medium.

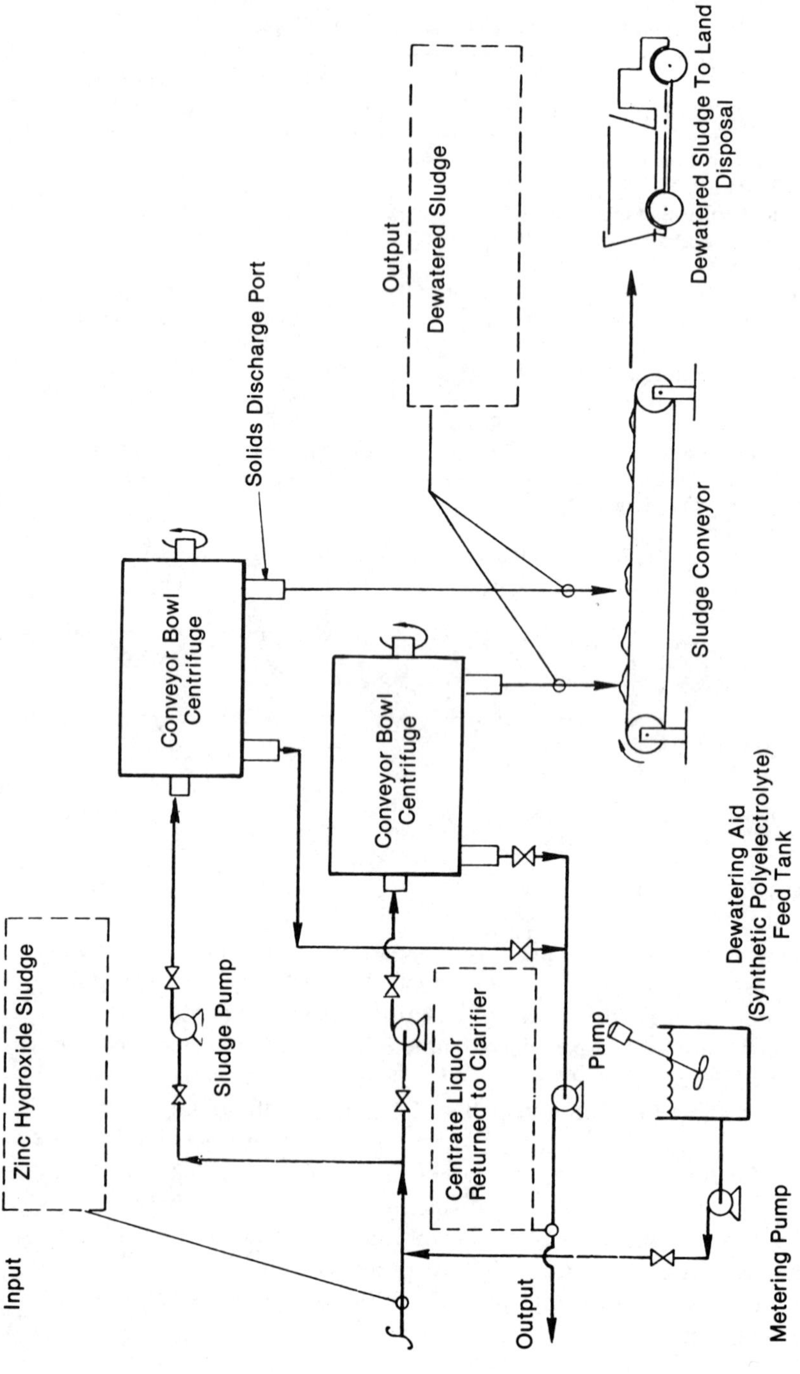

Figure 9-4. Centrifugation of waste sludge: an illustrative flow diagram of zinc hydroxide sludge (Source: NTIS-PB 275 054).

Table 9-2. Membrane Separation Process and Principal Driving Forces[a]

Process	Function of Membrane	Principal Driving Force
Reverse Osmosis	Selective transport of water	Pressure
Ultrafiltration	Discriminates on the basis of molecular size, shape and flexibility	Pressure
Electrodialysis	Selective ion transport	Electrical potential gradient
Dialysis	Selective solute transport	Concentration
Gel Permeation Chromatography	Retard high molecular weight solute penetration	Concentration
Liquid Permeation	Selective transport of liquids	Concentration

[a]Source: NTIS-PB 275 287.

Dialysis was first investigated over one hundred years ago as a means of separating colloidal materials from species in true solution. For many years, membranes of animal gut were employed, replaced eventually by parchment paper, then rubber nitro-cellulose. Today, membranes are of regenerated cellulose (cellophane) and synthetic resin such as polyvinyl chloride. These new materials improve transfer rates and also permit the use of dialysis in more concentrated acid or base media. It has been discovered that interaction of the solvent with the membrane to cause swelling will greatly increase the mobility of solute molecules within the membrane, and thus improve transfer rates. This characteristic is particularly exploited in the use of cellulosic membranes in dialysis of caustic solutions, which cause a high degree of membrane swelling.

Requirements for a membrane are good transfer rates, suitable mechanical strength and durability, resistance to chemical degradation, and low cost. Thermal stability also may be desirable, since transport rates for solutes follow the general formula $W = Ae^{-E^*/RT}$ for temperature dependence of diffusion processes. Thus there are advantages to carrying out dialysis at somewhat elevated temperatures, is based on cellulosic or vinyl materials in either tubular, flat sheet or, recently, hollow fiber form.

Although dialysis occurs under "static" conditions, concentration gradients develop on either side of the membrane, and this retards the transfer. To prevent this, it is common practice to provide stirring or high flow rates at the membrane surfaces, which minimizes stagnant film thickness. Commercial dialysis usually involves the flow of the solute-containing stream across one face of the membrane and the flow of the second, higher-volume wash stream on the other side (see Figure 9-5).

Because concentration gradient is the sole driving force, dialysis is generally suited only to concentrated streams (5–20%) in which large concentration gradients may be achieved. Also, the concentration of solute at the feed stream outlet (known as the dialysate) is greater than that of the exiting wash stream (known as the diffusate), except under exceptional circumstances.

Applications to Date

The best known current application of dialysis is hemodialysis, which removes salts, urea and other wastes from the blood of people suffering from chronic kidney failure. Since the 1920s, dialysis has been used in the rayon industry to separate caustic soda from hemicellulose wastes. There are also other, smaller-scale applications in pharmaceutical and biochemical laboratories for special production and purification. Dialysis equipment is available commercially.

Energy Environment and Economics

Energy requirements of dialysis are low, being limited to the pumping of feed and wash streams.

The two diluted product streams could present difficult disposal problems if not reusable.

Capital costs depend more on the amount of material to be separated than on the waste stream throughput. A commercial dialyzer separating 1000 lb/day of solute would cost about $3000.

ELECTRODIALYSIS

Process Description

The general function of electrodialysis (ED) is the separation of an aqueous stream (more concentrated in electrolyte than the original), and a depleted stream. Success of the process depends on special synthetic membranes, usually based on ion exchange resins, which are permeable only to a single type of ion. Cation exchange membranes permit passage

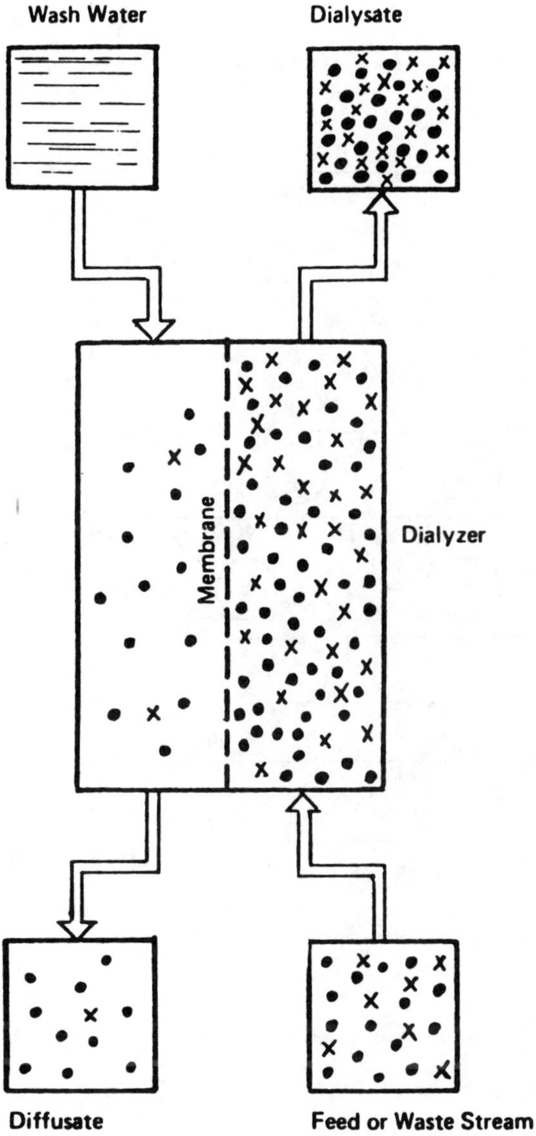

Figure 9-5. Schematic diagram of dialysis (Source: NTIS-PB 275 054).

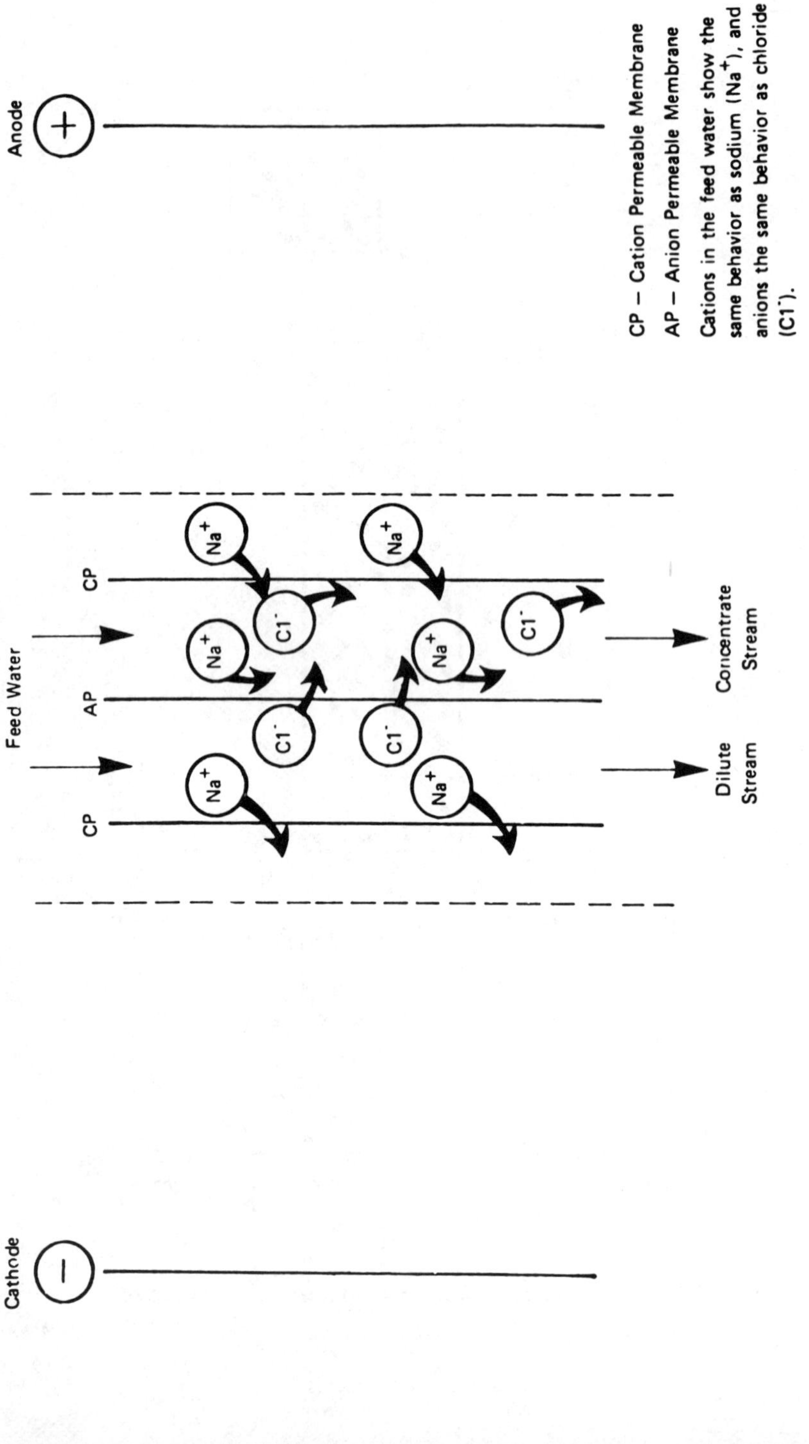

Figure 9-6. Diagrammatic representation of electrodialysis (Source: NTIS-PB 275 054).

only of positive ions under the influence of the electric field, while anion exchange membranes permit passage only of negatively charged ions.

The feed water passes through compartments formed by the spaces between alternating cation-permeable and anion-permeable membranes held in a stack. At each end of the stack is an electrode having the same area as the membranes. A dc potential applied across the stack causes the positive and negative ions to migrate in opposite directions. An operating plant usually contains many recirculation, feedback and control loops and pumps to optimize the concentration and pH at different points for most efficient operation. Feed material is first filtered to remove suspended particles that could clog the system.

Applications to Date

Electrodialysis has been used for desalination since the 1950s. Most installations produce potable water from brackish well water or river water. Hundreds of such units, some with a capacity exceeding 10^6 gpd, are in use throughout the world.

In the food industry, electrodialysis is used for desalting whey and deashing sugar. The chemical industry uses the technique for enriching or depleting solutions, and for removing mineral constituents from product streams.

Energy, Environment and Economics

Electrical requirements vary, but conventional ED systems take about 5 kWh of energy for each 1000-ppm reduction of salt in each 1000 gal purified product water and up to 3 kWh to pump each 1000 gal products.

The capital costs for electrodialysis are modest, ~20–25% of the total cost in the case of water treatment. Both capital and direct operating costs are dependent on the volume of water treated and on the salts removed. Total water production costs of $<\$.50/10^3$ gal are reported for salt reduction from 2000 ppm to 500 ppm in plants treating $\geq 10^6$ gpd. Other plants may have higher costs or may receive significant credits for reclaimed material.

A typical electrodialysis system to treat rinse tanks from an acid nickel plating line might cost $\sim\$6.000/10^3$ gal.

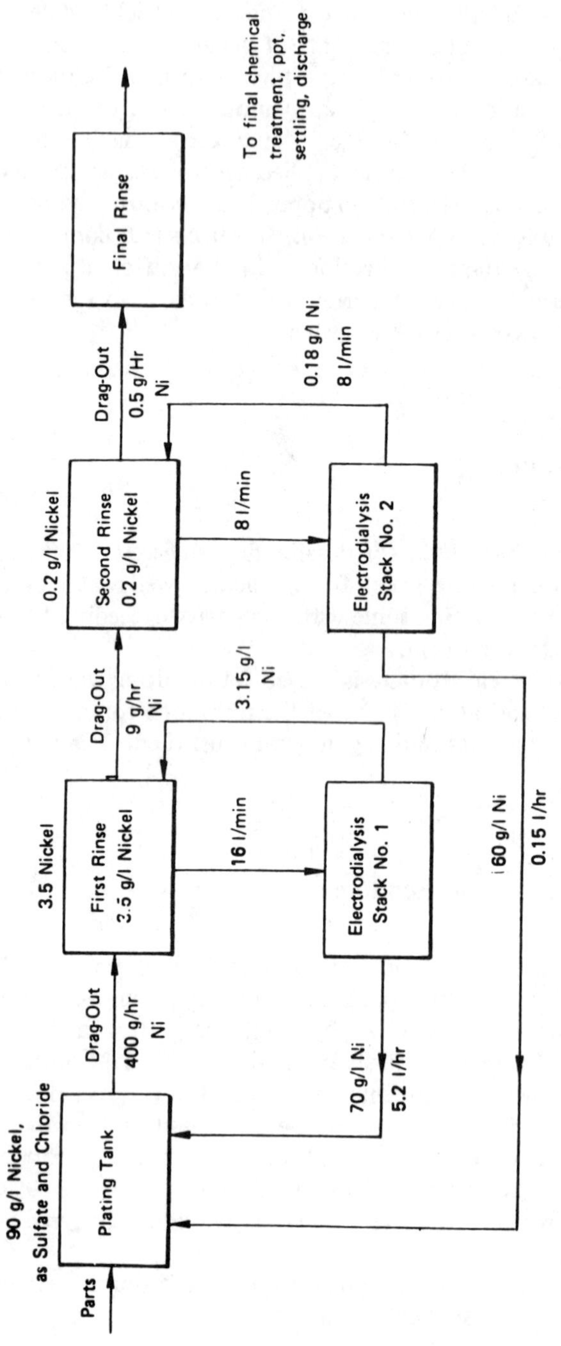

Figure 9-7. Electrodialysis reclamation of $NiSO_4$ from noncascaded rinses of nickel plating line (Source: NTIS-PB 275 054).

ELECTROLYSIS

Process Description

The terms electrolysis and electrolyte reaction are applied to those reactions of oxidation or reduction which take place at the surface of conductive electrodes immersed in a chemical medium, under the influence of an applied potential. At the negative electrode, or cathode, the reactions may include the reduction of a metal ion to the metal itself, M^+ $M^+ e^- \rightarrow M$, or, in aqueous media, the reduction of the hydrogen ion or water to hydrogen gas

$$2H+ +2e^- \longrightarrow H_2\uparrow$$

or

$$2H_2O + 2e^- \longrightarrow H_2\uparrow + 2OH^-$$

The potential at which each such reaction takes place at 25°C with all reactants and products at unit activity is termed E° for that reaction (E° measured versus the normal hydrogen electrode as a reference point). For conditions in which all reactants and products are not at unit activity, the required potential is given by the Nernst equation.

$$E = E° - \frac{0.0592}{n} \log Q$$

where n = the number of electrons required in the reduction (or oxidation) step and Q = the product of activities of product materials divided by the activities of the reactants.

Oxidation reactions, including

$$2Cl^- \longrightarrow Cl_2\uparrow + 2e^-$$

or

$$2H_2O \longrightarrow O_2\uparrow + 4H^+ + 4e^-$$

or

$$4OH \longrightarrow 2H_2O + 4e^- + O_2\uparrow$$

may be described likewise.

Values of E° for most oxidation and reduction reactions in aqueous solution range from about +3 to −2 volts, but many cannot be utilized due to the low potential, 1.23 V, at which water electrolyzes into hydrogen and oxygen.

From the Nernst equation, it is apparent that for an aqueous solution containing several species at various concentrations, the potentials of the various possible electrode reactions may be sufficiently close in value that several reactions could take place at a single electrode. As a result, in practical situations it is common to speak of the efficiency of an electrode reaction, i.e. that percentage of the current that results in the desired reaction rather than in other possible side reactions. Obviously, for maximum economy high current efficiency is desirable; values from 10% to virtually 100% may be found in the electroplating industry.

The applied voltage necessary to promote a desired electrode reaction is not only dependent on the theoretical cell voltages (and overvoltages) mentioned above, but also contains corrections for concentration changes in the neighborhood of the electrodes and simple infrared (IR) losses due to the electrolytic resistance of the solution itself. For this reason, commercial electrochemical cells generally contain some form of stirring to reduce concentration effects, and narrow electrode spacing to minimize resistance.

The table below shows the calculated values of the maximum diffusion-limited current for copper deposition at various levels of copper concentration. At current densities approaching this maximum, the current efficiency falls off significantly.

Cu^{++} Concentration (moles/1 ppm(as Cu))		Maximum Current Density (A/cm_2)	Maximum Copper Deposition ($g/cm_2/hr$)
10^{-1}	6300.00	1.4×10^{-2}	17.00 mg
10^{-3}	63.00	1.4×10^{-4}	.17 mg
10^{-5}	0.63	1.4×10^{-6}	.0017 mg

Although dimensional changes in the cathode due to metal deposition are more predictable, other more subtle changes may take place. For example, a cathode substrate chosen to have a high overvoltage for hydrogen evaluation in order to permit operation at higher voltages and thus higher currents will, upon being plated with metal "M", begin to exhibit the characteristics of an "M" electrode. Cathode efficiency may thus fall.

The most common, least predictable, and most difficult to control form of electrode deterioration is that generally referred to as fouling. By this is meant the accumulation at the electrode surface of a coating of insoluble salts, oxides, organic materials and biological films which interpose a high resistance barrier to the desired electrolytic barrier. For example, an inefficient cathode evolving hydrogen according to the equation

$$2H_2O + 2e^- \longrightarrow H_2\uparrow + 2OH^-$$

is also developing a region of high pH which may cause precipitation of species which are in solution at the pH of the feed. Likewise, organic film or slime may deposit. These may be slowly accumulated and may be present in the feed only in minute quantities. Also, variations in feed may be enough to push the chemistry at an electrode surface from a nominally nonfouling condition to a fouling one.

Applications to Date

Electrolysis, including electroplating and anodizing, has been an important process of industrial chemistry for many years. Chlorine production, for example, depends on electrolysis, and many commercial metals are refined by electrolytic processes. Metals may be obtained from primary ores, and magnesium and aluminum are processed by electrolysis in molten salt baths. Electrolysis for waste treatment has been employed to a limited extent, depending largely on costs. The most frequent application is the partial removal of concentrated metals such as copper from waste streams for recycle or reuse. Other applications which have been successfully pilot-tested include oxidation of cyanide wastes and separation of oil-water mixtures. An example of the electrolysis process is shown in Figure 9-8.

Energy, Environment and Economics

Electrical energy costs range from 10 to 35% of total operating costs, with treatment of concentrated metals at the low end, and dilute streams or cyanide treatment at the high end.

Gaseous emissions may exist; some may be vented to the atmosphere, others may have to be scrubbed or otherwise treated. The process wastewater may be reusable or disposable, or may have to undergo further processing.

Costs are highly dependent on the concentration and nature of the undesirable material. Electrolysis may offer significant trade-offs between capital and operating costs, depending on chemical and economic variables.

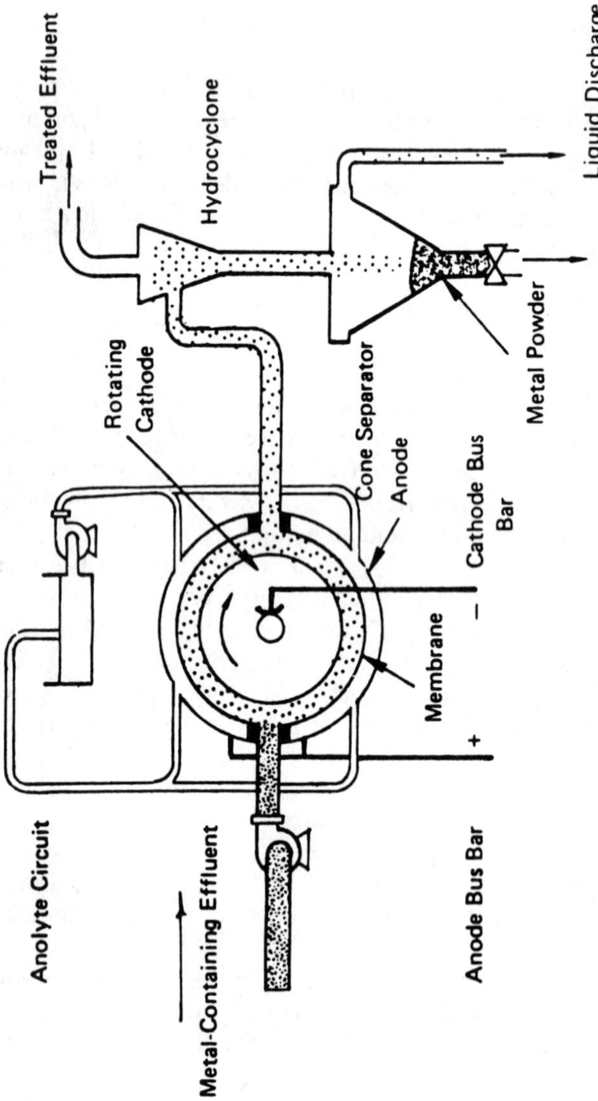

Figure 9-8. Electrolysis system (Source: NTIS-PB 275 054).

ELECTROPHORESIS

Process Description

Electrophoresis is the deposit of electrically charged particles under the influence of a dc electrical field. The particles may be complex macromolecules and colloids or particulate matter, either living cells (such as bacteria or erythrocytes) or inert material (such as oil emulsion droplets or clay), indeed almost any particulate. This section considers electrophoresis for removing electrically charged particles from liquids.

The general principle is based on the migration of charged particles, as a result of the applied dc electrical field, to a collecting plate for subsequent removal (see Figure 9-9). Because the charged particles are not allowed to reach the electrode, reactions at the electrode do not take place. Particles without charge—isoelectric particles—are not collected. The net result of electrophoretic deposit is thus a reduction of the volume of liquid in which a hazardous material is contained. The membranes which stop the migration of particles are essentially dialyzing membranes (e.g., cellulose) which allow only water and small ions to pass through.

For migration to occur, suspended material must carry an electrical charge, and the liquid phase must carry an opposite charge to preserve electrical neutrality. The source of this apparent charge on the suspended matter is not always evident; it may arise from a partial ionization of one substituent group on a molecule or it may be due to the sorption of ions or ionizable substances onto the suspended material.

Electrodecantation (electrogravitation) is based on the difference in density created by transport depletion of any impurity and the difference in resistivity caused by the transport depletion of ionic species. The first effect causes a film of less dense liquid to rise along the membrane surface on the depleted side and a film of more dense material to fall on the concentrated side. This density difference is amplified by heating effects associated with differences in conductivity of the two films. (The less dense film has a lower conductivity and thus increases in temperature, which further decreases its density.) Thus filtration, which is essentially continuous, is effected by collecting the less dense (purified) liquid at the top of the membranes and the more dense (concentrated) liquid at the bottom of the membranes. (Electrodecantation is sometimes classified as a variation of conventional electrodialysis, rather than a form of electrophoresis.) Electrodecantation was used commercially for a time by Dunlop Rubber Company for creaming of rubber latex and DuPont has used the process for the concentration of Teflon®* latex.

---

*Registered trademark of E. I. duPont de Nemours & Company, Inc., Wilmington, Delaware.

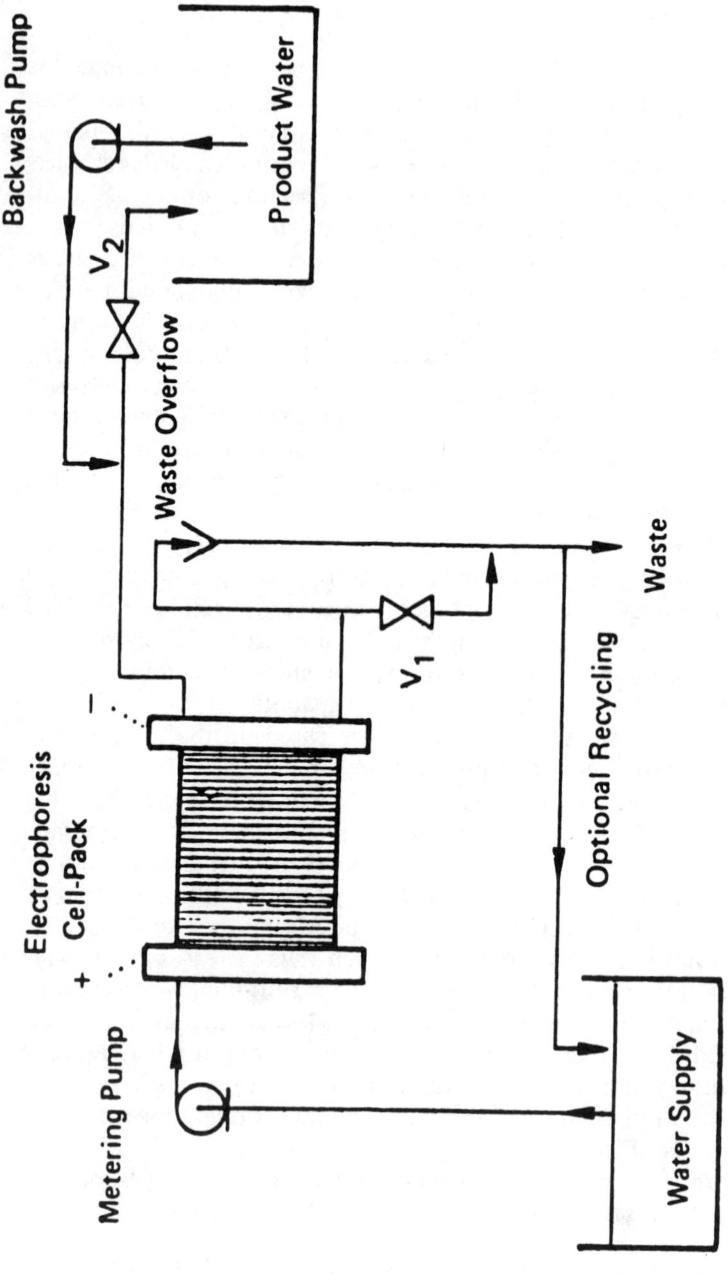

Figure 9-9. Schematic presentation of a proposed pilot plant for water purification (Source: NTIS-PB 275 054).

Applications to Date

Electrophoresis is used extensively as a laboratory tool in the analysis and separation of proteins, polysaccharides, and nucleic acids. It has also been used commercially for creaming of rubber latex, and for fractionation of animal sera for veterinary vaccines. Numerous proposed applications have been researched and shown to be technically feasible. These include deposition of paints, polymers, ceramics and metals. The process has also been considered for water purification (e.g., for separation of emulsions, and for color, virus and algae removal).

Energy, Environment and Economics

In aqueous systems, the electrical energy requirements are on the order of 7 kWh/1000 gal.

The process may evolve gases from electrode reactions. Both the concentrated sludge and the "treated" liquid may require subsequent disposal.

Capital costs would be lower than the costs for electrodialysis. Operating costs might be in the range of $0.50–2.00/1000 gal, depending on the application.

FILTRATION

Process Description

Filtration is a well-developed liquid/solid separation process currently applied to the full-scale treatment of many industrial wastewaters and waste sludges. For the treatment of hazardous wastes, filtration can be used to perform two distinctly different functions:

1. removal of suspended solids from a liquid (usually aqueous) waste stream with the objective of producing a purified liquid and
2. increasing the solids concentration, and thereby reducing the volume, of a high concentration liquid/solid mixture (sludge) by removing liquid from the mixture (sludge dewatering).

As a wastewater treatment process, filtration usually follows some form of flocculation and/or sedimentation. Filtration is usually technically and economically competitive with other dewatering processes for sludge.

Filtration is a physical process whereby particles suspended in a fluid are separated by forcing the fluid through a porous medium. As the fluid passes through the medium, the suspended particles are trapped on the surface and/or within the body of the medium. A filter medium can be a thick barrier of a granular material, such as sand, coke, coal or porous ceramic; a thin barrier, such as a filter cloth or screen; or a thick barrier composed of a disposable material such as powdered diatomaceous earth or waste ash. The pressure differential to move the fluid through the medium can be induced by gravity, positive pressure or vacuum. The intended application has great relevance to both the type of filter and its physical features.

1. *Granular Media Filters.* Granular media filtration, one of the oldest and most widely applied types of filtration for the removal of suspended solids from aqueous liquid streams, utilizes a bed of granular particles (typically sand or sand with coal) as the filter medium. The bed is contained within a basin or tank and supported by an underdrain system which allows the filtered liquid to be drawn off while retaining the filter medium in place. The underdrain system usually consists of metal or plastic strainers located at intervals on the bottom of the filter. As suspended-particle-laden water passes through the bed of the filter medium, particles are trapped on top of and within the bed, thus reducing its porous nature and reducing the filtration rate at constant pressure, requiring increased pressure to force the water through the filter. The filter material must then be backwashed to restore the effectiveness of the filter. The suspended solids concentration of the backwash water is far greater than that of the liquid filtered. Granular filtration essentially removes suspended solids from one liquid stream and concentrates them into another, but much smaller, liquid stream. Depending on the specific process configuration, backwash water itself can be treated to remove suspended solids by flocculation and/or sedimentation or by returning it to the portion of the process from whence the liquid stream subjected to filtration originated, e.g., a settling pond.

2. *Fixed Media, Continuously Renewed Surface Filtration.* A very large number of filtration devices can be categorized under this term, including rotary drum vacuum filters, microstrainers and disk filters. Probably the most common and most representative type of filter within this general group is the rotary vacuum filter.

In the rotary vacuum filter (Figure 9-10), the filter medium consists of a continuous belt of fabric or wire mesh. The belt is stretched over a steel cage-like drum which rotates around a central trunnion. Part of the belt sometimes revolves around a small roller. The best-covered drum is partially submerged in a trough containing the liquid to be filtered. The

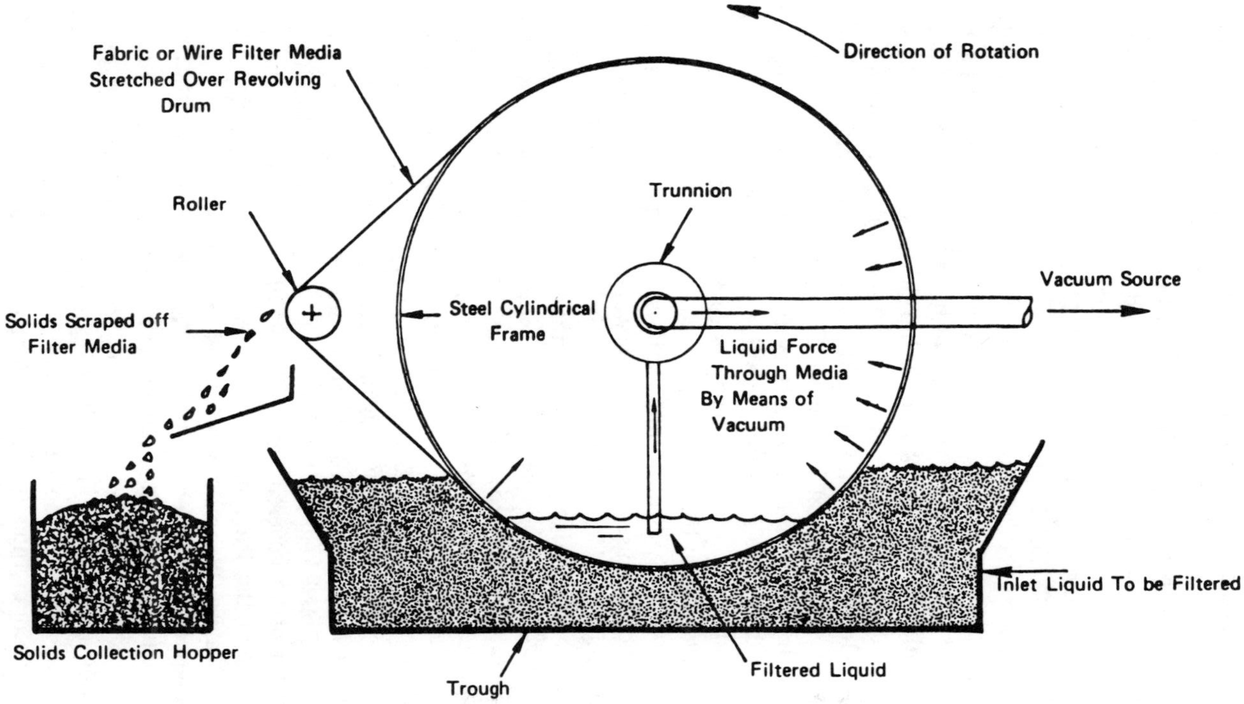

Figure 9-10. Rotary drum vacuum filter (Cross-sectional side view) (Source: NTIS-PB 275 287).

drum, driven by an electric motor, slowly rotates within the trough of liquid. A vacuum is applied to the inside of the drum by means of a connection within the central trunnion. The vacuum causes the liquid in the trough (and the liquid adhering to the media as it rotates out of the trough) to be forced through the filter medium, leaving wet solids adhering to the outer surface. The filtered liquid, or filtrate, is collected from the inner bottom portion of the drum through a vacuum connection. As the belt passes over the smaller roller, a blade scrapes off the adhering solids into a collection hopper.

A variation of this application is the precoated vacuum filter. Typically a layer of powdered material, such as diatomaceous earth, is deposited on the surface of the previously described vacuum filter as a slurry. Solids are then trapped on the surface of this layer as it rotates, dipping in and out of the trough. To prevent clogging, a thin layer of the precoat material (along with the entrapped solids) is continuously cut away by a slowly advancing blade. When the entire layer has been removed, the filter is taken out of service, given a fresh precoat, and is then ready to resume filtration. The fine pore structure of the precoat material enables much smaller particles to be removed, as compared to an uncoated vacuum filter.

In many vacuum filtration applications, filter aids such as lime and ferric chloride are used to improve dewaterability of certain sludges. Their use improves filterability by precipitating a coating (ferric hydroxide) onto the fine sludge particles, making them larger so that they have less tendency to clog the filter media. The use of lime and ferric chloride also reduces the suspended solids concentration of the filtrate.

3. *Chamber Pressure Filters.* The filter press is the most common and representative of this group. The filter press consists of a series of plates and frames, alternately arranged in a stack and "pressed" together by a large screw jack or hydraulic cylinder, hence the term "filter press". Referring to Figure 9-12, the liquid to be filtered enters the cavity formed by frame B. Pressed against this hollow frame are plates A and B, perforated metal plates covered with a fabric filter medium. As the liquid flows through the filter medium, solids are entrapped and build up within the cavity. When the solids build up to a certain level, the plates and frames are separated, the solids scraped away into a receiving hopper, the media washed, and then the whole assembly returned to service by pressing the plates together and resuming the flow of liquid.

In certain applications, the medium is precoated with a powdered filter aid such as diatomaceous earth. As in the case of the previously described vacuum filter, the precoat material enables the removal of smaller particles. Lime and ferric chloride filter aids are also frequently

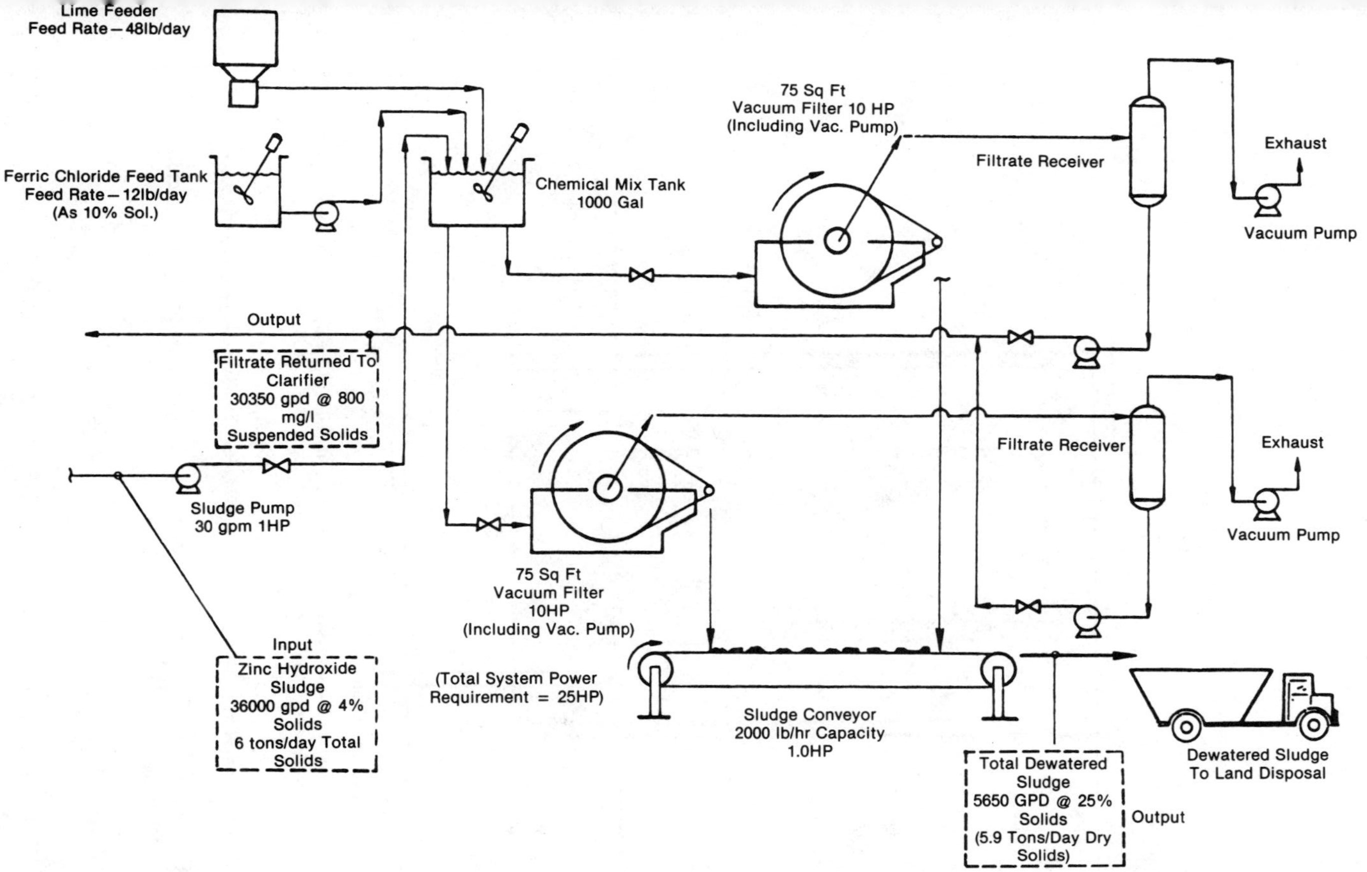

Figure 9-11. Vacuum filtration of waste sludge. Illustrative flow diagram of waste stream with zinc hydroxide sludge (Source: NTIS-PB 275 287).

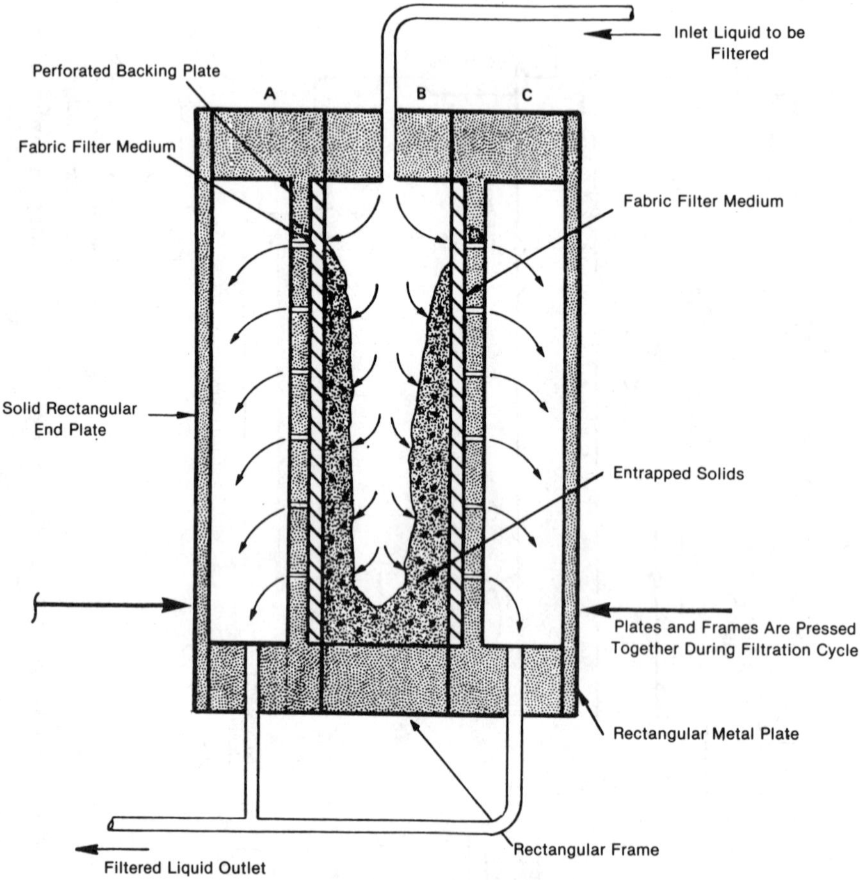

Figure 9-12. Filter press (cross-sectional view of one rectangular chamber) (Source: NTIS-PB 275 287).

used in filter press applications to effect more complete removal of solids.

Applications to Date

The inorganic chemical industry employs various forms of filtration to separate precipitated products from waste material. They are commonly used in the manufacture of titanium dioxide, sodium dichromate, aluminum sulfate and magnesium. The organic chemical industry also employs filter techniques, e.g., removal of acetylene carbon particles from aqueous quench streams, and removal of dye particles from the reaction bath. Rotary vacuum filters are used to remove impurities in the processing of sugar. Vacuum filtration often is used to remove impurities from lubrication oils. Boiler feed water and many types of industrial process water have stringent specifications on suspended solids. Filtration often is used in conjunction with precipitation, flocculation, and sedimentation to remove these solids. Filtration also is used as the final step in many industrial wastewater treatment plants.

Energy, Environment and Economics

Energy requirements for filtration are relatively low. A vacuum filtration system capable of dewatering 36,000 gpd of sludge containing 6 tons of solids will have a power requirement of only 25 hp.

The cost of treatment for both vacuum filtration and press filtration is usually in the range of $20–45/ton of solids treated (dry basis). For liquid purification the cost of filtration by granular media filters usually varies from $0.10–0.50/1000 gal of wastewater treated.

FLOCCULATION, PRECIPITATION AND SEDIMENTATION

Process Description

Precipitation, flocculation and sedimentation are discussed in a single section because in waste treatment they are most commonly used together, as consecutive treatments to the same stream (see Figure 9-13). Precipitation transforms a substance in solution into the form of solid particles that may be small or even colloidal. Flocculation transforms

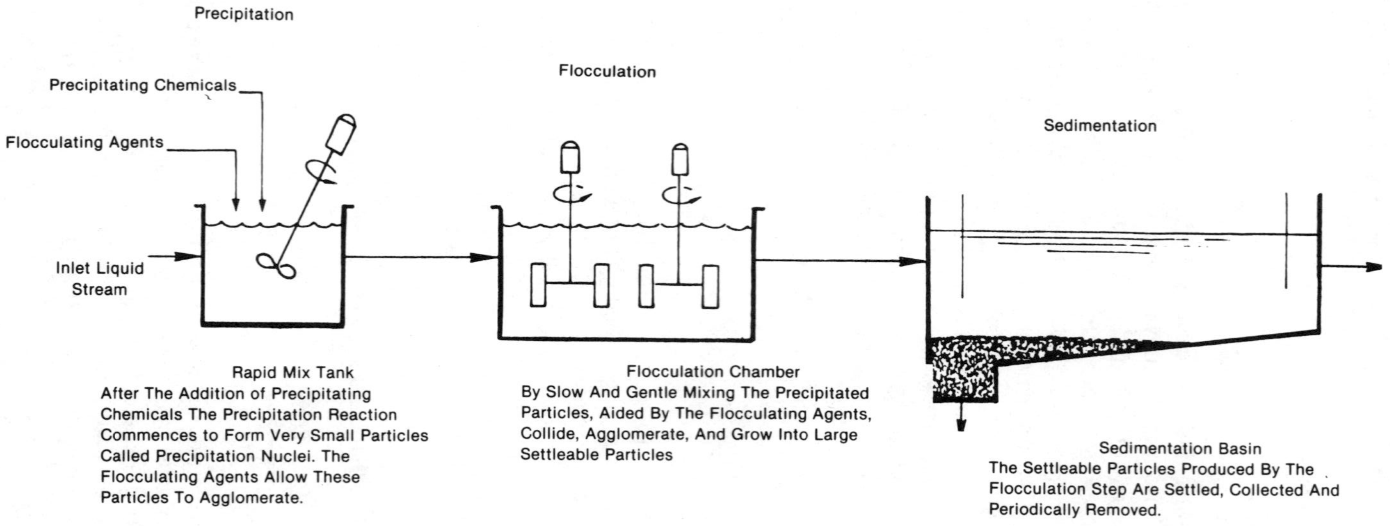

Figure 9-13. Representative configuration employing precipitation flocculation and sedimentation (Source: NTIS-PB 275 287).

small suspended particles into larger suspended particles so that they can be more easily removed. Sedimentation removes the suspended particles from the liquid.

Precipitation

Precipitation, in the context of this analysis, is a physicochemical process whereby some or all of a substance in solution is transformed into a solid phase, and thereby removed from solution. Precipitation involves an alteration of the chemical equilibrium affecting the solubility of the component(s), achieved by a variety of means. Most precipitation reactions for industrial or waste treatment purposes are induced by one or a combination of the following steps:

- adding a substance that will react directly with the substance in solution to form a sparingly soluble compound.
- adding a substance that will cause a shift in the solubility equilibrium to a point which no longer favors the continued solubility of the substance in solution.
- changing the temperature of a saturated or nearly saturated solution in the direction of decreased solubility; since solubility is a function of temperature, this change can cause ionic species to come out of solution and form a solid phase.

The most common precipitation reactions involve the removal of inorganic ionic species from various aqueous media. For instance, zinc chloride is highly soluble in water, as is sodium sulfide. Zinc sulfide, however, has an extremely low solubility in water. Thus, if an aqueous solution of zinc chloride is mixed with an aqueous solution of sodium sulfide, zinc ions and sulfide ions will rapidly combine to form solid zinc sulfide particles,

$$Zn^{2+} + 2CL^{-} + 2Na^{+} + S^{2-} \longrightarrow \underset{\substack{\downarrow \\ \text{(solid)}}}{ZnS} + 2Na^{+} + 2Cl^{-}$$

The mixing of the two solutions creates an unstable, highly supersaturated solution of zinc sulfide, which rapidly readjusts itself toward equilibrium by the creation of a solid zinc sulfide phase. The resultant liquid/solid mixture is essentially a suspension of solid ZnS in a saturated but necessarily very dilute solution of zinc sulfide. In this reaction, as in most precipitation reactions, the governing equilibrium relationship is the solubility product (K_{sp}) of the substance that eventually forms the solid phase. The solubility product is basically an expression of the maximum concentration of ionic species that will be in equilibrium with the respective solid phase. For this example, the solubility equilibrium expression would be

$$[Zn^{2+}][S^{2-}] = k_{sp}$$

If solid zinc sulfide is contacted with water, dissolution will occur, putting zinc and sulfide ions into solution until the product of the ionic zinc concentration and the ionic sulfide concentration is equal to the solubility product. Both precipitation and dissolution involve an approach toward the solubility equilibrium or "saturation point". In dissolution, equilibrium is approached from a state below the saturation point; in precipitation, equilibrium is approached from a state above the saturation point. The equilibrium point itself can be a function of a number of variables (e.g., temperature and ionic strength), and often is influenced by the presence of other dissolved species, which can enter into additional completion and/or solubility relationships.

In many precipitation and dissolution reactions, pH is a master variable affecting the equilibrium concentration of ionic species. This is particularly true where the respective solid phase is a hydroxide or carbonate compound. Since the hydroxide concentration of a solution is pH-dependent (by definition), many precipitation reactions can be induced by varying the pH of the original solution. For example, if solid ferrous hydroxide is contacted with water, the following dissolution reaction will occur (but only slightly),

$$Fe(OH)_{2(s)} = Fe^{2+} + 2OH^-$$

and the equilibrium expression can be written as,

$$[Fe^{2+}][OH^-]^2 = k_{sp}$$

Thus, solid ferrous hydroxide will continue to dissolve until the product of the ferrous ion concentration and the square of the hydroxide ion concentration equals the respective solubility product. If a strong acid is added to the equilibrated solution (thus lowering pH), the hydroxide ions will be neutralized and the solution will no longer be in equilibrium with the solid phase. Instead, it will now be below the saturation point. Equilibrium is again attained as more ferrous ions go into solution. Thus, as the pH is lowered, more and more ferrous ions will go into solution.

Approaching equilibrium from the reverse direction, if a strong caustic such as sodium hydroxide is added to an aqueous (and necessarily slightly acidic) solution of ferrous ions, the solubility product of $Fe(OH)_2$ will be exceeded, thus causing the creation of a solid ferrous hydroxide phase as the solution returns to equilibrium.

In certain industrial applications, precipitation of a desired product material is induced by chilling a saturated solution. Since most salts are less soluble at lower temperatures (calcium carbonate and calcium sulfate being two notable exceptions), chilling a saturated solution of such salts causes the equilibrium to be disturbed. The equilibrium is readjusted by the removal of ions from solution and the creation of a solid phase. This technique has very limited applications for waste treatment purposes, mainly due to the fact that solubility of most slightly soluble compounds used in precipitation schemes is a weak function of temperature, and therefore, very large differences in concentration usually cannot be achieved.

Physically, most precipitation reactions are carried out by adding the appropriate chemicals to the solution and mixing thoroughly. Although most precipitation reactions take place extremely rapidly, a moderate amount of time is usually required to allow the chemicals to be dispersed throughout the solution. Characteristically, the solid particles, when first formed, are very small. Depending on the nature of the chemical system involved and the types of further treatment applied, the solid particles can remain as submicroscopic precipitation nuclei or very small colloidal particles, or they can grow into larger particles. The particles may be either crystalline or amorphous.

Flocculation

The terms "flocculation" and "coagulation" have been used indiscriminately and interchangeably to describe the process by which small, unsettleable particles suspended in a liquid medium are made to agglomerate into larger, more settleable particles. Distinctions between the two terms frequently appear in the water- and waste-treatment literature; however, the definitions used are often conflicting [16,17] and the result is that there are no precise and universally accepted technical definitions of these terms. For the purpose of this study, the term "flocculation" shall encompass all of the mechanisms by which the above-mentioned suspended particles agglomerate into larger particles. As a general term used in this study, no distinction will be made between coagulation and flocculation.

Many liquid-solid separation processes, such as sedimentation, are based on the use of gravity and/or inertia to remove solid particles from a liquid. It is generally true that the larger the particle size, the easier will be the removal of the particle from the liquid.

In flocculation, as defined, there are a variety of mechanisms whereby small particles are made to form larger particles. Most of these mechanisms involve surface chemistry and particle charge phenomena. In simple terms, these various phenomena can be grouped into two sequential mechanisms.

- chemically induced destabilization of the repulsive surface-related forces, thus allowing particles to stick together when they touch and
- chemical bridging and physical enmeshment between the now nonrepelling particles, allowing for the formation of large particles.

Typically, chemicals used to cause flocculation include alum, lime and various iron salts (ferric chloride, ferrous sulfate). Relatively recently, organic flocculating agents, often referred to as "polyelectrolytes" have come into widespread use. These materials generally consist of long-chain, water-soluble polymers such as polyacrylamides. They are used either in conjunction with the inorganic flocculants, such as alum, or as the primary flocculating agent.

The inorganic flocculants, such as alum, lime or iron salts, make use of precipitation reactions. Alum (hydrated aluminum sulfate) is typically added to aqueous waste streams as a solution. Upon mixing, the slightly higher pH of the water causes the alum to hydrolize and form fluffy, gelatinous precipitates of aluminum hydroxide. These precipitates, partially due to their large surface area, enmesh small particles and thereby create larger particles. Lime and iron salts, as well as alum, are used as flocculants primarily because of this tendency to form large fluffy precipitates or "floc" particles. Many precipitation reactions, such as the precipitation of metals from solution by the addition of sulfide ions, do not readily form floc particles, but rather precipitate as very fine and relatively stable colloidal particles. In such cases, flocculating agents such as alum and/or polyelectrolytes must be added to cause flocculation of the metal sulfide precipitates.

Once suspended particles have been flocculated into larger particles, they usually can be removed from the liquid by sedimentation, provided that a sufficient density difference exists between the suspended matter and the liquid. An illustrative flocculation process is shown and described in Figure 9-14.

Sedimentation

Sedimentation is a purely physical process whereby particles suspended in a liquid settle by means of gravity and inertia acting on both

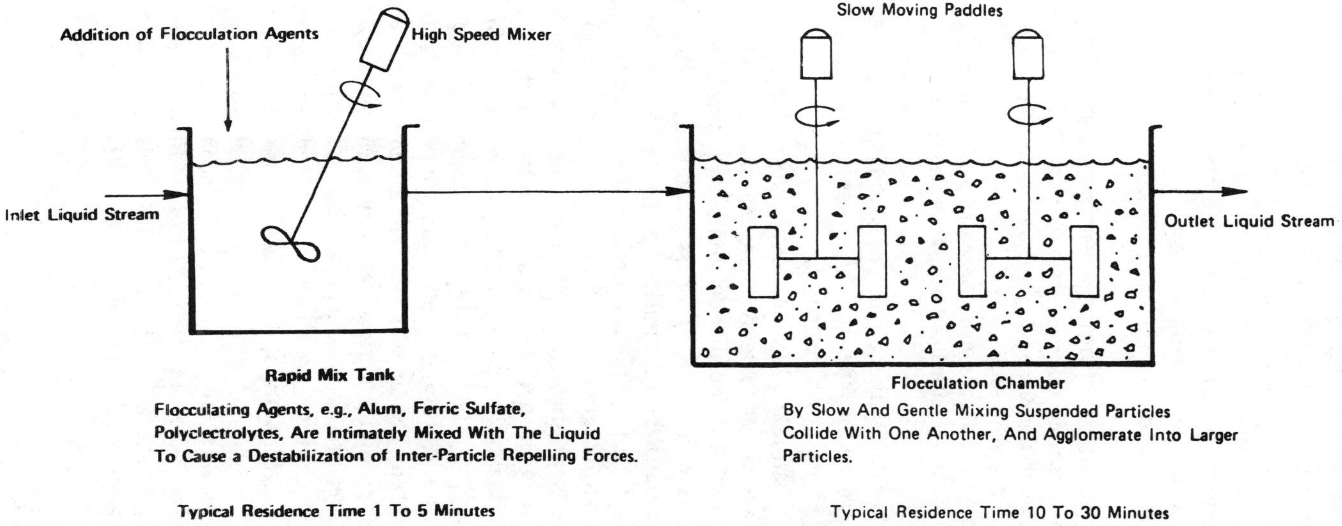

Figure 9-14. Flocculation process (Source: NTIS-PB 275 287).

the particles suspended in the liquid and on the liquid itself. Basically, particles are made to settle out of a liquid by creating conditions in which the forces acting on the particle in the desired direction of settling are greater in magnitude than the various forces (drag forces, inertial forces) acting in the opposite direction. This force differential causes the particles to travel in the desired direction.

The fundamental elements of most sedimentation processes are:

- a basin or container of sufficient size to maintain the liquid to be treated in a relatively quiescent state for a specified period of time.
- a means of directing the liquid to be treated into the above basin in a manner conducive to settling.
- a means of physically removing the settled particles from the liquid (or the liquid from the settled particles, as the case may be).

Sedimentation can be either a batch or a continuous process. Continuous processes are by far the most common, particularly when large volumes of liquid are to be treated.

Sedimentation can take place in rudimentary settling ponds, conventional settling basins, or in more advanced clarifiers which often are equipped with built-in flocculation zones and tube-like devices that enhance settling (see Figure 9-15). In settling ponds, the liquid is merely decanted as the particles accumulate on the bottom of the pond and eventually fill it. Often the pond is periodically emptied of particles by mechanical shovels, draglines or siphons. Sedimentation basins and clarifiers are more sophisticated and usually employ a built-in solids collection and removal device such as a sludge scraper and draw-off mechanism. Sedimentation basins tend to be rectangular in configuration, usually employ a belt-like collection mechanism, and tend to be used mostly for the removal of truly settleable particles from a liquid.

Clarifiers generally are circular, and are usually used in applications that involve precipitation and flocculation, in addition to sedimentation. Very often all three processes take place within the same piece of equipment, since many clarifiers are equipped with separate zones for chemical mixing and precipitation, flocculation and, of course, settling. Certain clarifiers are equipped with low lift turbines which mix a portion of the previously settled precipitates with the incoming feed, as this practice has been shown to enhance certain precipitation reactions and promote favorable particle growth. (This type of clarifier often is used in water softening applications involving the precipitation of calcium as calcium carbonate).

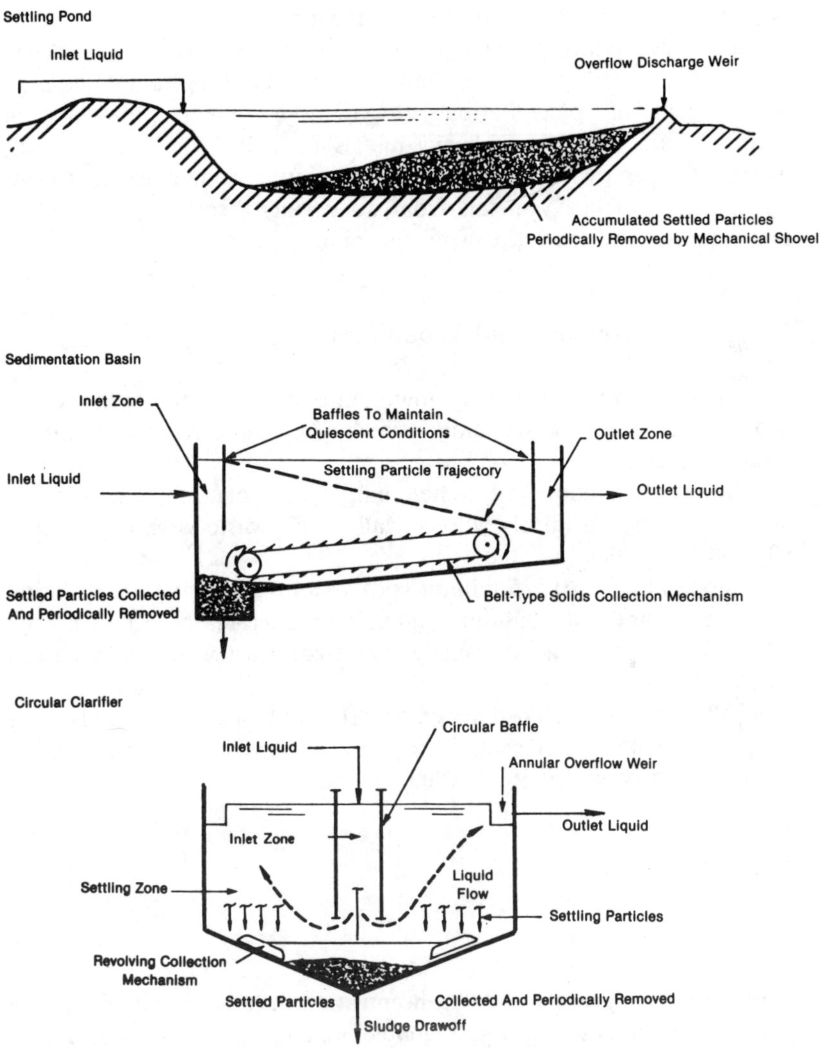

Figure 9-15. Representative types of sedimentation (Source: NTIS-PB 275 287).

Applications to Date

These processes have long been widely used in a variety of industrial applications, such as the manufacture of many organic chemicals, the preparation of metal ores and sugar refining.

Almost every industry that discharges a process wastewater stream contaminated with suspended and/or precipitable pollutants employs some form of precipitation, flocculation and/or sedimentation. Examples are: removal of heavy metals from iron and steel industry wastewater; removal of fluoride from aluminum production wastewater; and removal of heavy metals from wastewaters from copper smelting and refining, and from the metal finishing industry.

Energy, Environment and Economics

Energy consumption is very low compared to other processes. The processes produce a waste sludge, which often can present a serious disposal problem.

A large (>5 million gpd) system employing only sedimentation with no flocculating chemicals will typically treat wastewater at a cost of $0.10–0.50/1000 gal treated.

A moderate size (0.5–5 million gpd) system employing precipitation, flocculation and sedimentation and using moderate dosages of precipitating/flocculating agents usually will treat wastewater at a cost of $0.50–3.00/1000 gal.

Small, specially designed systems (<0.5 million gpd) using high dosages of precipitating/flocculating agents can have costs that are higher, but these rarely exceed $6.00/1000 gal.

FLOTATION

Process Description

Flotation is a process of ore concentration developed and used principally by the mineral industry. Valuable ore constituents are separated as a "concentrate" from the waste products, called "tailings".

The process is a physicochemical method (carried out in a wet environment) for concentrating finely ground ores. A necessary and important step in preparing the ore for flotation is crushing and grinding, designed for each particular application to separate the individual mineral particles that make up the ore by reducing them to their natural grain size. Also, in some cases, removal of "slime" is necessary before flotation.

The flotation process itself involves chemical treatment of an ore pulp or slurry to create conditions favorable for the attachment of selected mineral particles to air bubbles formed therein. The air bubbles carry the selected minerals to the surface of the pulp and form a stabilized froth which is skimmed off while the other waste minerals remain in the pulp.

The process of contacting the ground ore pulp with reagents is called "conditioning" and is usually done with reagents being added in an agitator for mixing with the pulp just before flotation. However, at times, benefits are obtained by adding reagents in the grinding stage.

Variations of the Process and Adaptations

Although the flotation process has been applied principally to mineral processing, there have been a number of applications in related areas. Some of these are briefly described below.

1. *Flotation of Microorganisms.* Research has shown that bacteria can be floated and concentrated from the aqueous phase [18]. For the organisms used in this study, sodium chloride acted as a collector and the organisms could be floated.

2. *Flotation of Waste Paper.* Flotation is used to treat paper pulp mixtures of magazines, newspapers and other paper rejects to remove ink, pigments and coatings. The clean cellulose fiber can then be reused to make specialty grade papers.

3. *Precipitate Flotation.* It is possible to float precipitates that have been made in a solution and recover them as a froth concentrate. In this application the metal to be removed from solution is precipitated before the addition of a collector.

One example of this in the mineral processing industry is the leach-precipitation-flotation process (LPF) which is used on mixed oxide-sulfide copper ores. In the LPF process, the ore is treated with sulfuric acid which dissolves the oxide copper minerals. Powdered iron is then added to the slurry, and the copper precipitates as metallic copper particles. The whole mixture is then floated and the precipitated copper, as well as the unaffected sulfide copper particles, is collected as a froth concentrate.

Another possible application of precipitate flotation is the flotation of complexed cyanide as a means of removing cyanide from solutions or mixed suspensions. If ferrous iron is added to a cyanide-containing solution, a ferro-cyanide precipitate can be formed which can then be floated from the solution. Test results in one case [19] indicated that ~95% of the complexed cyanide could be removed under the proper conditions.

4. *Agglomerate Flotation (Emulsion Flotation).* The typical flotation process takes place on ground ores where the top particle size is ~40 mesh (~400 microns). It is difficult for an air bubble to pick up a particle much bigger than that. However, coarser particles up to about 10 mesh in size (2000 microns) can be floated after conditioning by carrying out the separation on a vibrating table or similar device. This is called agglomerate or table flotation, and is practiced in the phosphate industry where coarse apatite particles are separated from quartz grains using a fatty-acid/fuel-oil emulsion as a collector.

5. *Ion Exchange Flotation.* Ion-exchange resins can be contacted with solutions to pick up or exchange particular ions in the solution. The resin particles can then be removed by flotation. There is no application of this process as far as we know. Resin particles can usually be more simply removed by screening.

6. *Ion Flotation.* In ion flotation a surfactant ion of opposite charge to the inorganic ion to be removed from solution is added in stoichiometric amounts. The surfactant "collector" must be added in such a way that it exists in solution as simple ions. The collector reacts with the inorganic ion to form an insoluble "soap" which can be levitated to the surface with a gentle bubbling action to form a foam or scum, then removed.

Energy, Environment and Economics

The typical conventional flotation plant is a relatively large consumer of energy, averaging ~15 kWh/ton milled. Only ~15% of the total is consumed in the flotation step, with most of the energy used for crushing and grinding.

Air emissions are not significant, since flotation is a wet process. Dust emissions occur at the ore crusher and at conveyor transfer points but are controlled with collecting hoods and water sprays. The waste effluent goes to a tailings dam from which water may be recycled, especially in arid areas.

Costs depend on the size and nature of the process. Operating costs for sulfide ore flotations vary from $4/ton of ore processed for a 500 ton/day plant to $1.50/ton for a 10,000 ton/day plant.

FREEZE-CRYSTALLIZATION

Process Description

Freeze-crystallization has been successfully tested for desalination of brackish waters in pilot plants. It has been demonstrated in the laboratory for hazardous waste treatment, and is expected to find commercial applications in the near future.

Freeze-crystallization involves formation of "pure" ice crystals from a solution, and concentration of dissolved solutes in a residual brine. The ice crystals may be separated mechanically from the brine, then washed and melted to yield fresh water (or solvent).

When an aqueous solution containing dissolved salts is frozen, "fresh" water ice crystals form and the salts are concentrated in the remaining brine solution. The ice crystals can be separated from the brine by mechanical means, and washed and melted to yield fresh water [20,21]. The remaining brine may contain potentially hazardous substances which can be treated further or disposed of. The freezing process resembles the distillation process in that heat transfer is a very important element of the process, and a change of phase is involved.

With a suitable means of separating the ice crystals from the mother liquor, freezing can yield a concentrated waste product stream and high-quality water (99+% pure). Since most of the developments in freeze crystallization have been based on aqueous streams, or descriptions refer mostly to ice. Theoretically, at least, these processes can be applied to nonaqueous streams as well.

Although the process generally is considered to be a demineralization technique, it is capable also of removing organic materials from water.

Freeze crystallization (see Figure 9-16) involves the following steps:

- heat exchange
- freezing
- washing
- melting and
- refrigerant or energy recovery.

There are basically two forms of the freezing process:

1. vacuum-flash/vapor-compression (VFVC) in which water itself is the refrigerant; and

2. secondary refrigerant freezing (SRF) in which butane or a halogenated hydrocarbon such as Freon®* is the refrigerant.

Barduhn [22] and others [20,21] have reviewed these processes. Several variations have been proposed and demonstrated. Most closely associated with the VFVC has been Colt Industries; most closely associated with the SRF system have been AVCO Systems and University Engineers, Inc.

Applications to Date

A number of freeze-crystallization processes have been developed for desalination, but none have become commercial. Waste treatment applications tested in the laboratory include: sulfite liquors; plating liquors; paper mill bleach solutions; arsenal redwater; solutions containing acetic acid, methanol and aromatic acids; ammonium nitrate wastes; and cooling tower blowdown.

Energy, Environment and Economics

Electrical energy requirements are in the range of ~60–75 kWh/1000 gal of product water.

The major environmental problem is associated with further treatment, or disposal, of the brine. Some emissions of refrigerant (e.g., butane or Freon) are possible.

Capital costs are estimated to be in the range of $600,000–800,000. Operating costs might be in the range of $6–12/1000 gal of product water.

FREEZE-DRYING

Freeze-drying is a process for subliming frozen water from a material under high vacuum. Basic equipment consists of a vacuum chamber, a vacuum source and appropriate refrigeration and heating equipment. Suitable feeds include wet solids, sludges and slurries.

The largest current use of this process is in the preparation of freeze-dried coffee, which commands a premium price in the marketplace. It is

---

*Registered trademark of E. I. du Pont de Nemours & Company, Inc., Wilmington, Delaware.

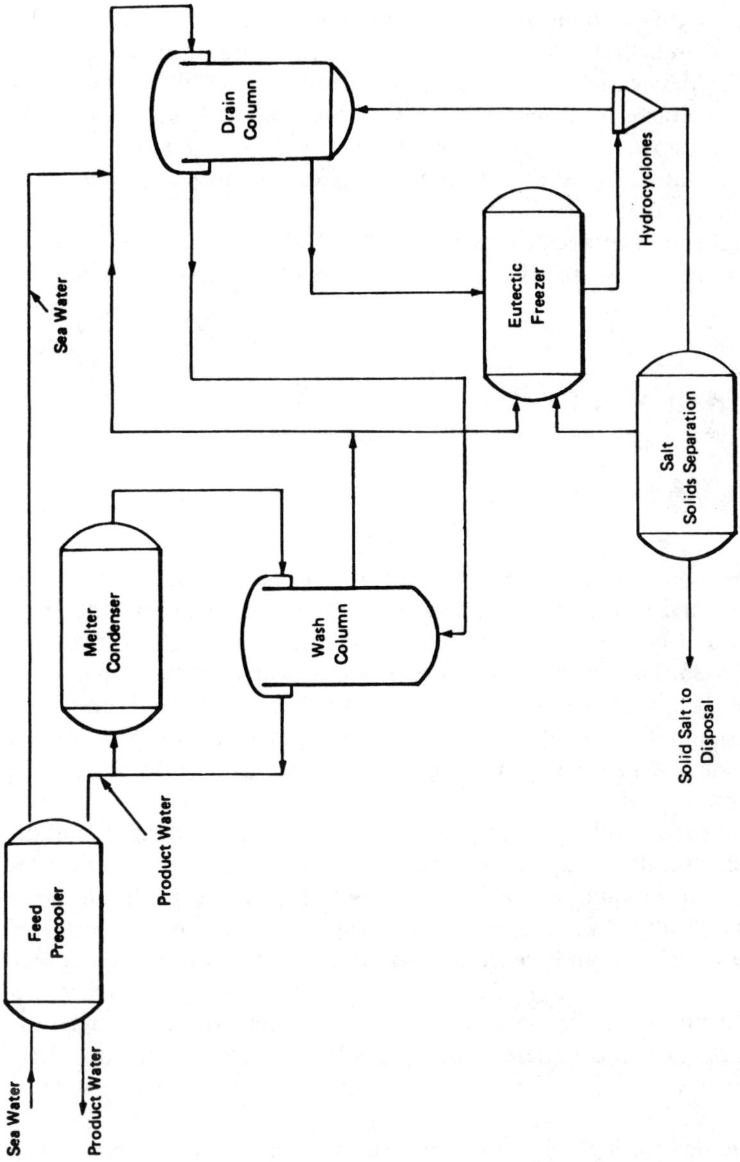

Figure 9-16. Conceptual design for a single-stage eutectic-freezing plot plan (Source: NTIS-PB 275 287).

also used in the manufacture of pharmaceutical and biological preparations.

Freeze-drying (lyophilization) has no apparent potential for treating hazardous industrial wastes. Although freeze-drying is used commercially for desiccating biological and sensitive materials, it does not appear adaptable to economical waste processing on a large scale. The process is slow, costly and energy-intensive, with limited use for removing water. There are no known applications to waste treatment, and none are under development.

Capital equipment costs range from $300,000 to 500,000. Its pollution potential is low, except for secondary effects of energy generation.

SUSPENSION FREEZING

Process Description

Suspension freezing, either by natural freezing or refrigeration, was proposed and investigated for treating sludges and gelatinous materials as early as 1940–1950 [23]. Both these early and more recent investigations [24–30] have been aimed primarily at dewatering municipal water treatment plant sludges which are difficult to process. In order to permit handling and disposal of water treatment sludges, which can vary from 1 to 5% solids depending upon their source, concentration by dewatering is necessary.

Regulations preclude directly returning potentially hazardous sludges and waste solids to surface waters. Current practice is first to dewater sludge by techniques which include gravity thickening in drying beds, vacuum filtration, filter pressing and centrifugation. The concentrated solids are collected and placed in a landfill. Water is processed and then returned to surface waters essentially free of organic and inorganic materials. Chemical pretreatment and filter aids may be used to hasten separation of solids. These treatments all suffer from inherent operational limitations, so that an efficient treatment and disposal system is still needed.

Freeze dewatering has been proposed as a method which might even eliminate the need for chemical preconditioning treatment with alum, lime and polymer, and might make separation of solids and water more economical.

Underlying Principles

The freezing point is the temperature at which a liquid becomes a solid. Suspension freezing may provide a freeze separation process in two ways:

1. *Crystallization.* As a liquid mixture freezes, the solid that forms first usually has a different composition from the liquid, and formation of the solid changes the composition of the remaining liquid, usually in a way that steadily lowers the freezing point. This principle is used in purifying mixtures, successive melting and freezing gradually separating the components. This method is discussed elsewhere.
2. *Freeze-Conditioning.* Freezing of a sludge is directed toward accomplishing physical and mechanical changes in the suspended solids or gel particles, rather than crystallization of dissolved salts. Although crystallization of some soluble material may occur in the sludge, crystallization of water to ice is the mechanism utilized, since sludge already contains solid particles of material. There are several ways freezing alters solid particles; the processes are complex and vary with the nature of the sludge and manner of freezing. It has been shown that freezing a sludge causes the suspended solids to agglomerate and form relatively large floc particles [25]. Upon thawing, these floc particles settle and occupy significantly less volume than before freezing, leaving a clear supernatant. Filterability is increased. The conditioning effect can be explained as the result of dehydration and pressure exerted on the sludge particles by the ice structure, causing agglomeration and densification [31]. This treatment was found to be effective on all types of sludges: primary, secondary, activated and digested.

In spite of the recurrent interest in freeze dewatering, the literature is rather limited. Work and literature concerned with soil freezing and frost damage prevention are allied to sludge dewatering problems, and have contributed to sludge dewatering concepts [32].

Applications to Date

No commercial suspension freezing or freeze dewatering applications exist. Freezing alum sludges typical of wastewater treatment plants has been the center of interest in the laboratory. Development of freezing for other materials has not been advanced.

Energy, Environment and Economics

Energy requirements for natural freezing outdoors are small; mechanical refrigeration requires large energy expenditures. Suspension freezing is essentially a phase separation process, and both the separated solids and the supernatant liquid generally would require further treatment before disposal.

Reliable cost data are not available, but can be expected to be relatively high.

HIGH-GRADIENT MAGNETIC SEPARATION

Process Description

High-gradient magnetic separation (HGMS) is a new technique for separating weakly paramagnetic materials* and nonmagnetic suspended solids (down to colloidal particle size) from gas or liquid streams, on a large scale, at flow rates over one hundred times faster than the flow rates possible in ordinary filtration, and at lower cost and energy requirements. Magnetic separators capable of removing highly magnetic (i.e., ferromagnetic) particulates have existed for some time; HGMS extends the capabilities of magnetic separation to include particles that are only weakly magnetic.

HGMS uses fine ferromagnetic filament material containing 95% void space (felted or woven steel fabric, compressed steel wool, expanded metal, etc.), and magnets capable of generating high-intensity fields, up to 20,000 gauss (G), in large spaces. The impurities are collected in the filter by magnetic attraction as the feed stream passes through the unit. When the magnet is turned off, the filter matrix may be washed clean. A continuous process is shown in Figure 9-17.

The magnetic field intensities used in conventional HGMS are in the range from 1 to 20 kG; superconducting machines could be built to operate in the range from 20 to 100 kG. The magnetic field gradients in conventional HGMS machines are on the order of 1 kG/μm. In comparison, conventional magnetic separators have field of $\sim$1 kG and field gradients of $\sim$0.1 kG/cm.

---

* Paramagnetic materials are those in which an applied magnetic field is slightly increased by the alignment of electron orbits. Thus, the magnetic field induced in paramagnetic materials will increase monotonically as the applied magnetic field increases.

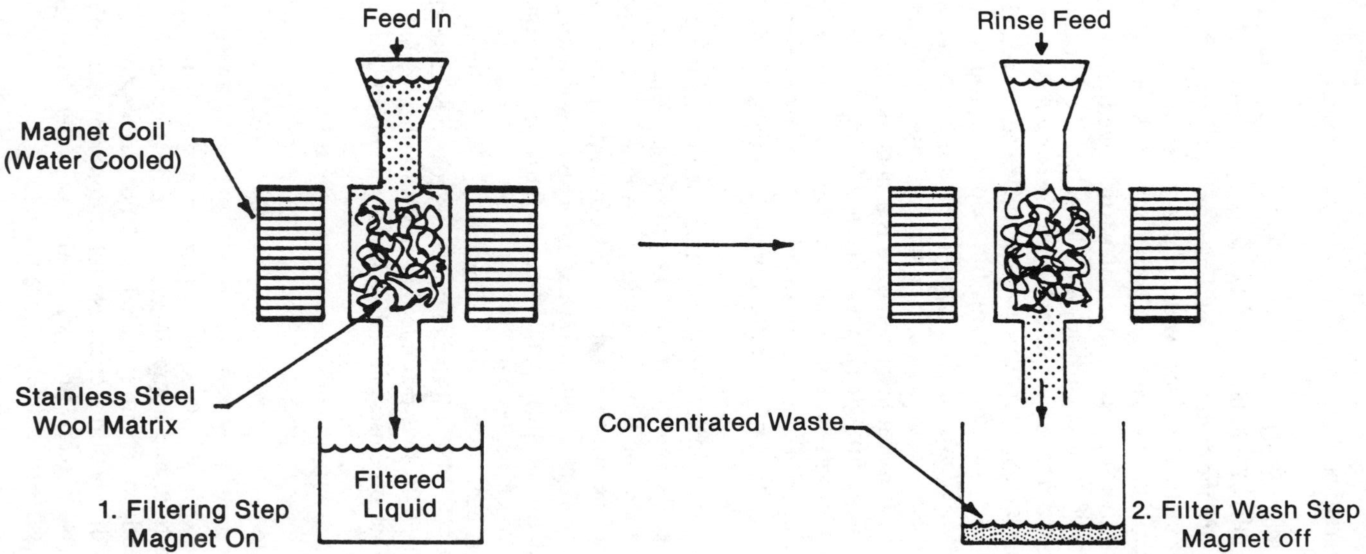

Figure 9-17. Schematic representation of high-gradient magnetic separation (Source: NTIS-PB 275 287).

Operating Characteristics

1. *Feed Streams.* HGMS is effective in removing waste stream particles with diameters as small as 1 μ (0.001 mm). In comparison, conventional magnetic separators are ineffective for particles much below 100 μ in diameter. When filter matrices of steel wool are used (as is common), the wool may typically be 100 μ in diameter. Tests have indicated that this matrix is mostly effective for the removal of particles with diameters about 30 μ and that it will remove particles with diameters as small as 1 μ. At a packing density of a few percent, the average interstrand distance is on the order of 500 μ, which limits the treatable particle size to about 100 μ or less. Larger particles will cause serious filter clogging problems.

2. *Process Operation.* HGMS may be operated as either a cyclic or a continuous operation; both methods are in commercial use. Cyclic units are preferable when the material being removed is a small percentage of the total volume passing through the system and/or high operating pressures are needed. Conversely, continuous operation may be preferable when high operating pressure is not needed and the material being removed is a large percentage of the total volume passing through the system.

3. *Output Streams.* The principal emission from the process is a concentrated waste stream. Particulates removed from air can be easily collected in a compact state for reuse, recycle or disposal. If matter is removed from liquid, the waste stream is a slurry with high solids content; in recent tests with steel mill effluents, the aqueous waste stream contained 30% solids (by weight). After vacuum filtration, the solids may be reused, recycled or disposed of.

A minor emission is heat, usually in the form of hot water from the magnet cooling coils. HGMS units in current use generally raise the water temperature 20–30°F. It is possible that this waste heat could be recycled for use in other processes, including heating and cooling.

Applications to Date

Current applications include clay whitening (removal of a small, colored, magnetic fraction) and upgrading of low-grade iron ore.

Applications currently being investigated, but not yet commercial, include: beneficiation of other ores, coal desulfurization, removal of flue dust in air streams from blast furnaces, and wastewater treatment (including municipal wastes and steel mill wastewaters).

Energy, Environment and Economics

Energy requirements may be relatively large, especially if high magnetic fields are required. Electromagnets, used to generate fields of up to 20 kWe, have power ratings of ~400 kW for the larger machines. Disposal of the filter wash solution, if the material is not recovered, and additional treatment of the treated stream may also be required.

Capital costs may be as high as $800,000 if high magnetic fields are required; they may be as low as $5,000 if the material being removed is ferromagnetic. Operating costs for high-volume applications are expected to be ~$10–50/1000 gal for removal of ferromagnetic materials, and of the order of $1–5/1000 gal for removal of weakly paramagnetic materials.

REVERSE OSMOSIS

Process Description

Reverse osmosis (RO) employs a semipermeable barrier which will pass only certain components of a solution and a driving force to separate these components at a useful rate. The membrane is permeable to the solvent but impermeable to most dissolved species, both organic and inorganic. The driving force for its separation is an applied pressure gradient (see Figure 9-18).

Conventional "forward" osmosis transfers solvent through a semipermeable separator from more dilute to more concentrated solution, driven by the difference in solvent vapor pressure on either side of the separator. The osmotic pressure π, or magnitude of this driving force, is given by the equation:

$$\pi = \frac{RT}{v} ln \frac{P_1}{P_2}$$

where
- R = the gas constant
- T = the absolute temperature
- v = the molar volume of the solvent
- P_1, P_2 = the solvent vapor pressure in the solutions on either side of the membrane.

(Note that π is independent of the specific membrane material.)

If a pressure equal to π is applied across the membrane counter to normal solvent flow, no transfer will take place. If a pressure greater than π

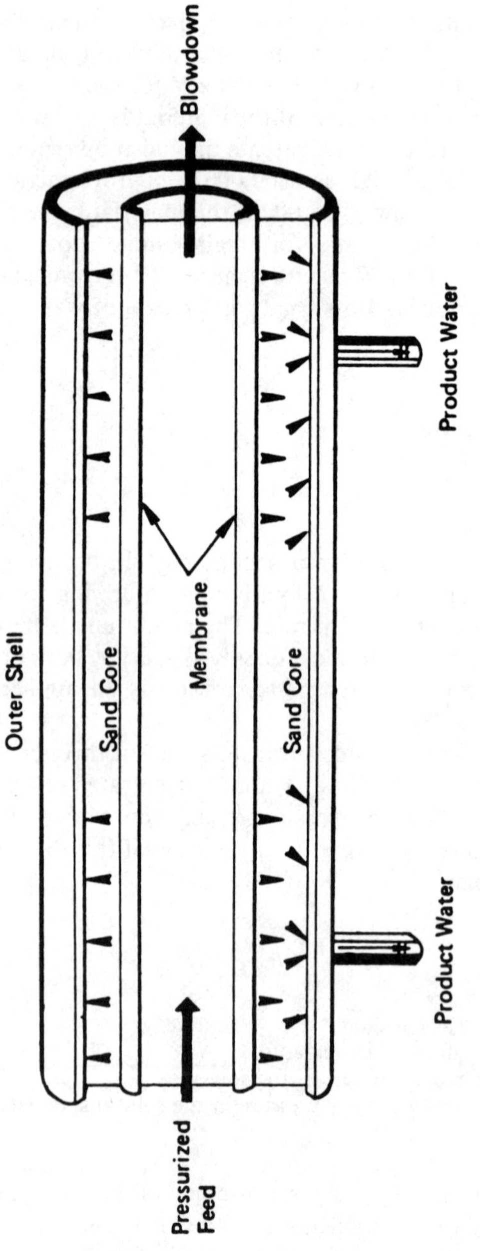

Figure 9-18. Sand-core type of reverse osmosis module (Source: NTIS-PB 275 287).

is applied, solvent will be transferred from the more concentrated to more dilute solution, resulting in both a concentration of solute and purification of solvent. This is reverse osmosis.

The dilute solvent flux, J (frequently expressed in gallons/ft²/day) is given by:

$$J = K(\Delta P - \pi)$$

where ΔP = the applied pressure
K = a constant for the membrane-solvent system.

As can be seen from this equation, the product-water flux rate decreases with increasing salinity (increasing osmotic pressure) of the feed solution. Thus, the difficulties (and cost) of recovering clean water also increase with increasing salinity of the feed stream.

The design of the modules containing the RO membranes is crucial to the efficient operation of the process. As solute is rejected by the membranes, it concentrates at the membrane surface and results in a situation known as "concentration polarization," where the concentration at the membrane surface is many times higher than in the bulk feed solution. Since the driving force for water transport $(\Delta P - \pi)$ decreases with increasing concentration, polarization can have a very deleterious effect on water flux.

Concentration polarization can be minimized by high fluid shear at the membrane surface to aid the back-transport of polarized solute into the bulk of the process stream. This is accomplished by flowing the feed stream at high velocities in thin channels to promote laminar shear, or in wide channels to produce turbulence.

The chemical nature of the membrane material is important, because it affects the transport of solvent and rejection of solute. There have been two major hypotheses regarding the functioning of an RO membrane: the pore theory and the diffusion theory. The pore theory suggests that the membrane surface contains pores only a few angstrom units in diameter, and molecules are selected for passage on the basis of size. In addition, according to the pore theory, a layer of pure water is formed at the membrane surface by the repulsion of ionic species from the surface by their "reflected charge," and this layer of pure water is drawn off through the pores.

The diffusion theory proposes that the surface of the membrane is in fact a thin homogeneous film and that membrane specificity or rejection is the result of widely diffusing permeation rates of solvent and solutes across this layer. The weight of the support has swung to the side of the diffusion theory, on the basis of its ability to predict correctly the effect of changes in pressure and concentration or rejection rates.

Reverse osmosis also differs from "conventional" filtrations in that the flow of the feed is not normal to the membrane surface but tangential to it in an effort to keep it clean of debris and to reduce surface concentration effects. Reverse osmosis membranes do not become "plugged" but may become fouled by film-forming organics or by insoluble salts and scaling. Much of the prefiltering of the feed water is, in fact, aimed at preventing the narrow flow channels of the assembled device from becoming plugged.

Cellulose acetate membranes remain the most popular. Ion exchange membranes produce specific selectivity but are rarely used; polyamide materials, nylons and polyarylsulfones have recently appeared [33]. Because of the need for maintaining high solvent flux rates while withstanding high pressure differentials, most membranes in use today are of the "skinned" type in which membrane casting technique is controlled to produce a very thin homogeneous film or skin upon the more open porous substrate of the same material.

Operating Characteristics

Total dissolved solids (TDS) in the feedwater may be as high as that of sea water (34,000 ppm) and product water TDS as low as 5 ppm.

Cellulose acetate membranes have been the most frequently used in the past, but polysulfones and polyamides (nylon) are increasingly popular for use at high pH values. The hollow fiber type of module has gained rapid acceptance and in terms of total operating units may be the most prevalent.

Because of the susceptibility of the membranes to chemical attack and fouling, and the susceptibility of the flow system to plugging and erosion, it is common to preprocess feed water as necessary to remove oxidizing materials (see Figure 9-19). These include iron and manganese salts to filter out particulates and to remove oils, greases, and other films. If there is likelihood of fouling by living organisms, chlorination or UV treatment may be employed as well, to ensure that maximum flux rates may be obtained.

Applications to Date

There are about 300 full-scale plants worldwide using RO for desalination of sea or brackish water. It also has been used very successfully in

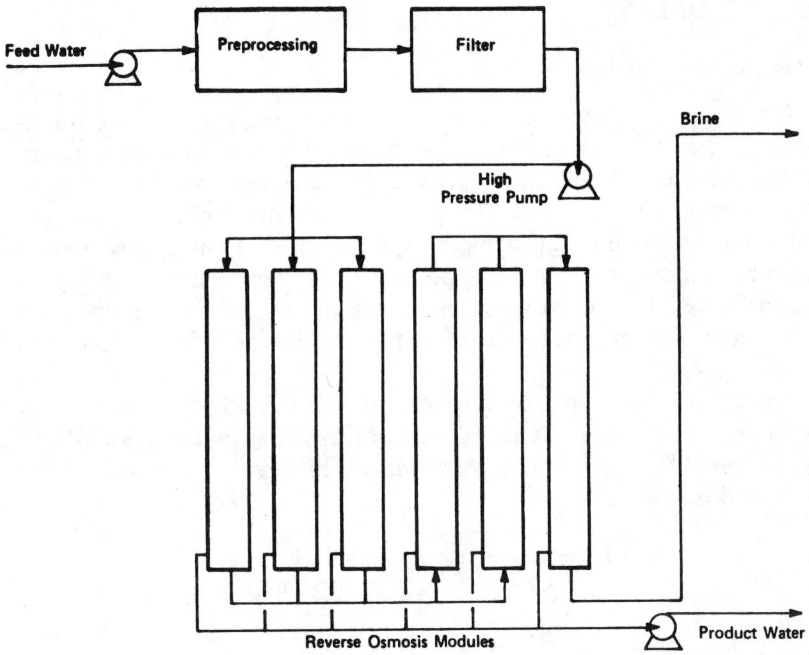

Figure 9-19. Reverse osmosis plant flowsheet (Source: NTIS-PB 275 287).

the treatment of electroplating rinse waters, not only to meet effluent discharge standards, but also to recover concentrated metal solutions for reuse. A limited number of other full-scale uses can be found in the treatment of sulfite streams from the paper industry and in food processing.

Energy, Environment and Economics

Energy requirements are of the order of 10 kWh/1000 gal of product water.

The concentrated brine or solute solution presents a disposal problem if not recoverable.

Capital costs range from ~$0.50 to 4/gpd of purified water output, depending on the volume of waste to be treated. Total operating costs are in the range of $1–5/1000 gal.

AIR STRIPPING

Process Description

Air stripping of ammonia from biologically treated domestic wastewater is being developed as a means of reducing nitrogen content. Ammonia removal efficiencies of over 90Δ have been obtained in pilot-scale tests using packed towers and a wastewater containing 60 ppm (ammonia) nitrogen. Air stripping systems other than packed towers (such as holding ponds, holding ponds with surface agitation and spray ponds) have been investigated as means of stripping ammonia from wastewater, but the packed tower appears to be the most compact and efficient [34].

Ammonia is quite soluble in water, but this solubility is temperature-dependent. Data from the *Handbook of Chemistry and Physics* [35] on the solubility of ammonia in water at different temperatures are presented below:

Temperature (°C)	gNH_3/g water (at 1000mm Hg)
0	1.094
20	0.629
40	0.386

The relationship between temperature and the solubility of ammonia for dilute ammonia solutions is expressed by Henry's Law:

$$y = Mx$$

where y = mole fraction NH_3 in the vaopr
x = mole fraction NH_3 in the liquid
M = Henry's constant.

Henry's constant (M) is a function of temperature. Raising the temperature of the wastewater increases the vapor pressure of the ammonia removal efficiency.

Another factor in ammonia removal efficiency is the pH of the wastewater. A portion of the ammonia dissolved in the water reacts with the water to give the following equilibrium:

$$NH_3 + H_2O \rightleftharpoons HN^+{}_4 + OH^-$$

By increasing the pH (concentration of OH^-) the equilibrium is shifted to the left, reducing the concentration of NH_4^+ and increasing the concentration of free dissolved ammonia.

To obtain reasonable ammonia removal efficiencies (or rates) by air stripping, either the temperature or the pH of the wastewater must be increased. In steam stripping ammonia from "sour water" the temperature of the wastewater is increased from ~38°C to ~110°C. The pH of the "sour water" ranges from 8 to 9 (unless it is not acidified to aid release of the H_2S).

In air stripping of ammonia from dilute wastewater, the air temperature limits the effectiveness of heating the wastewater. Ammonia removal efficiency is enhanced instead by increasing the pH.

Figure 9.20 is the flow diagram for the air/ammonia stripping system as applied to the treatment of domestic wastewater at the Orange County, California Water District. This same system could be used for treating other wastes containing aqueous ammonia or volatile organics, but would be subject to air emission regulations and the fact that the ammonia or organic in the dilute air stream leaving the towers could not be economically incinerated or recovered.

Applications to Date

Full-scale packed towers have been used at two locations in California for treating domestic wastewater.

Energy, Environment and Economics

Electric power requirements for treating 15 million gpd are in the range of 1600 to 1800 kWh/hr. The recalciner requires about 8 million Btu (8000 ft^3) natural gas/ton of feed, or 192 million Btu/day.

When the ammonia concentration is about 23 ppm and the air-to-water ratio is 500 ft^3/gal, the concentrated ammonia in the saturated air leaving the tower is about 6 mg/m^3, well below the odor threshold. Disposal of about 25 ton/day of sludge requires a significant amount of land, but does not pose an environmental hazard.

The capital investment would be about $7.8 million; fixed costs would be $1,420,000, and variable operating costs would be $940,000/year.

ULTRAFILTRATION

Process Description

The basic operating principle of ultrafiltration is illustrated in Figure 9-21. Flowing by a porous membrane is a solution containing two

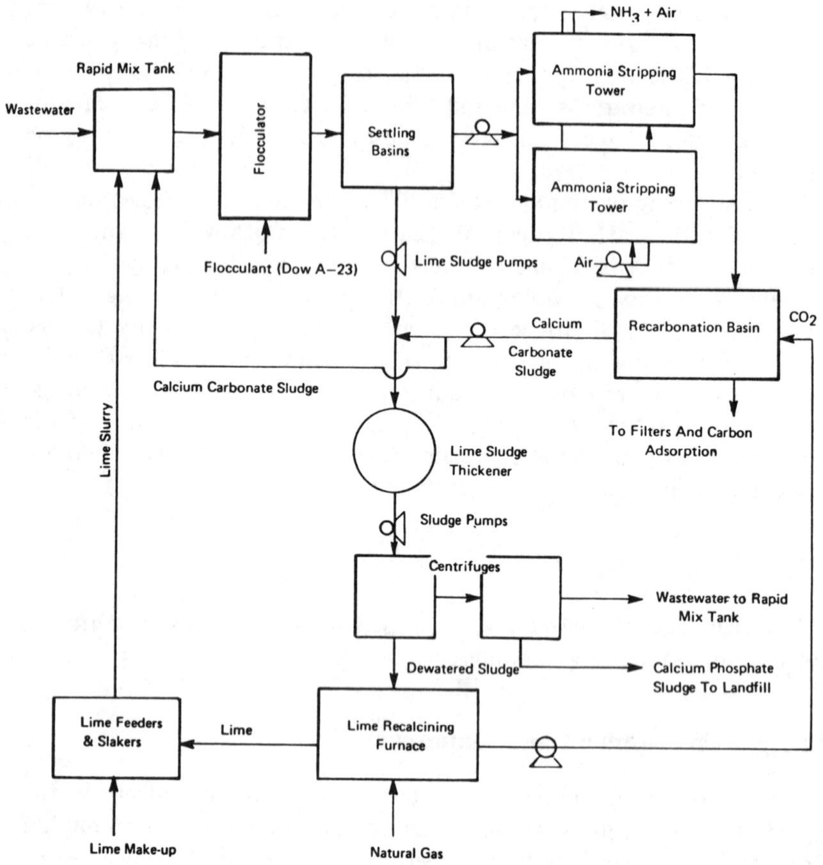

Figure 9-20. Air stripping of ammonia from biologically treated domestic wastewater (Source: NTIS-PB 275 287).

solutes: one of a molecular size too small to be retained by the membrane, and the other of a larger size allowing 100% retention. A hydrostatic pressure, typically between 10 and 100 psig, is applied to the upstream side of the supported membrane, and the large-molecule solute or colloid is retained (rejected) by the membrane. A fluid concentrated in the retained solute is collected as a product from the upstream side, and a solution of small-molecule solute and solvent is collected from the downstream side of the membrane. Of course, where only a single solute is present and is rejected by the membrane, the liquid collected downstream is (ideally) pure solvent.

Retained solute (or particle) size is one characteristic distinguishing

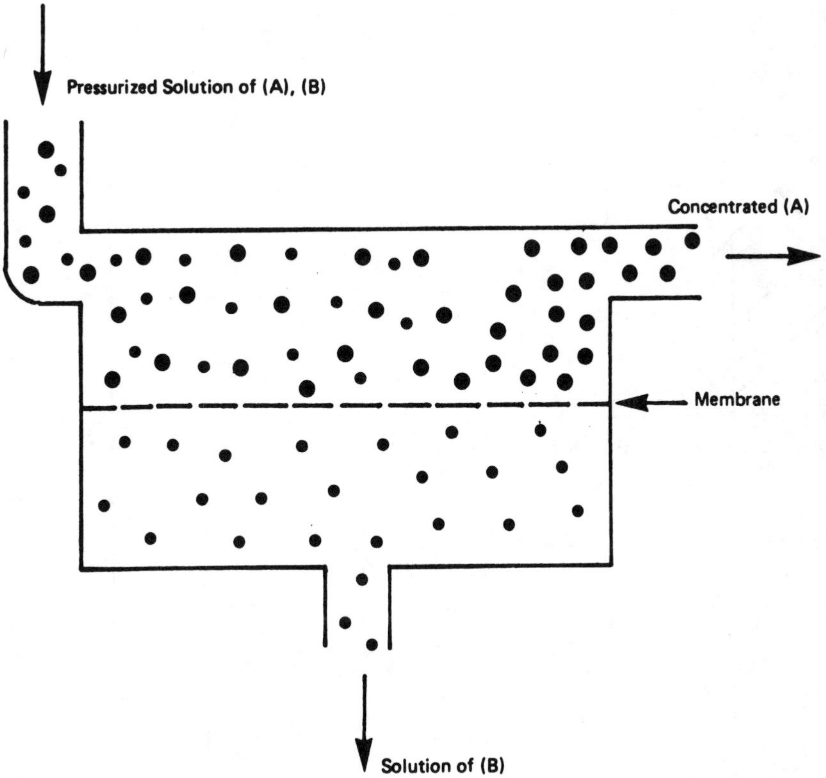

Figure 9-21. Schematic diagram of membrane ultrafiltration process (Source: NTIS-PB 275 287).

ultrafiltration from other filtration processes. Viewed on a spectrum of membrane separation processes, ultrafiltration is only one of a series of membrane methods which can be used. For example, reverse osmosis, a membrane process capable of separating dissolved ionic species from water, falls farther down the same scale of separated particle size. In Figure 9-22, that size spectrum is shown as a function of filtration flux. At the small-molecule/low-flux end of the spectrum lies the commercial cellulose acetate RO membrane, with the capability of retaining hydrated sodium and chloride ions. Next come ultrafiltration membranes with pores that cover a size range of $\sim 10^{-3}$ to 10^{-2} microns (10–100 Å) with filtration fluxes of $\sim$0.5–10 gal/ft^2/day/psi of pressure driving force. Microporous filters capable of virus and bacteria retention cover the pore size range of $\sim$0.01–1.0 μ, with fluxes of 10–1000 gal/ft^2/day/psiΔp.

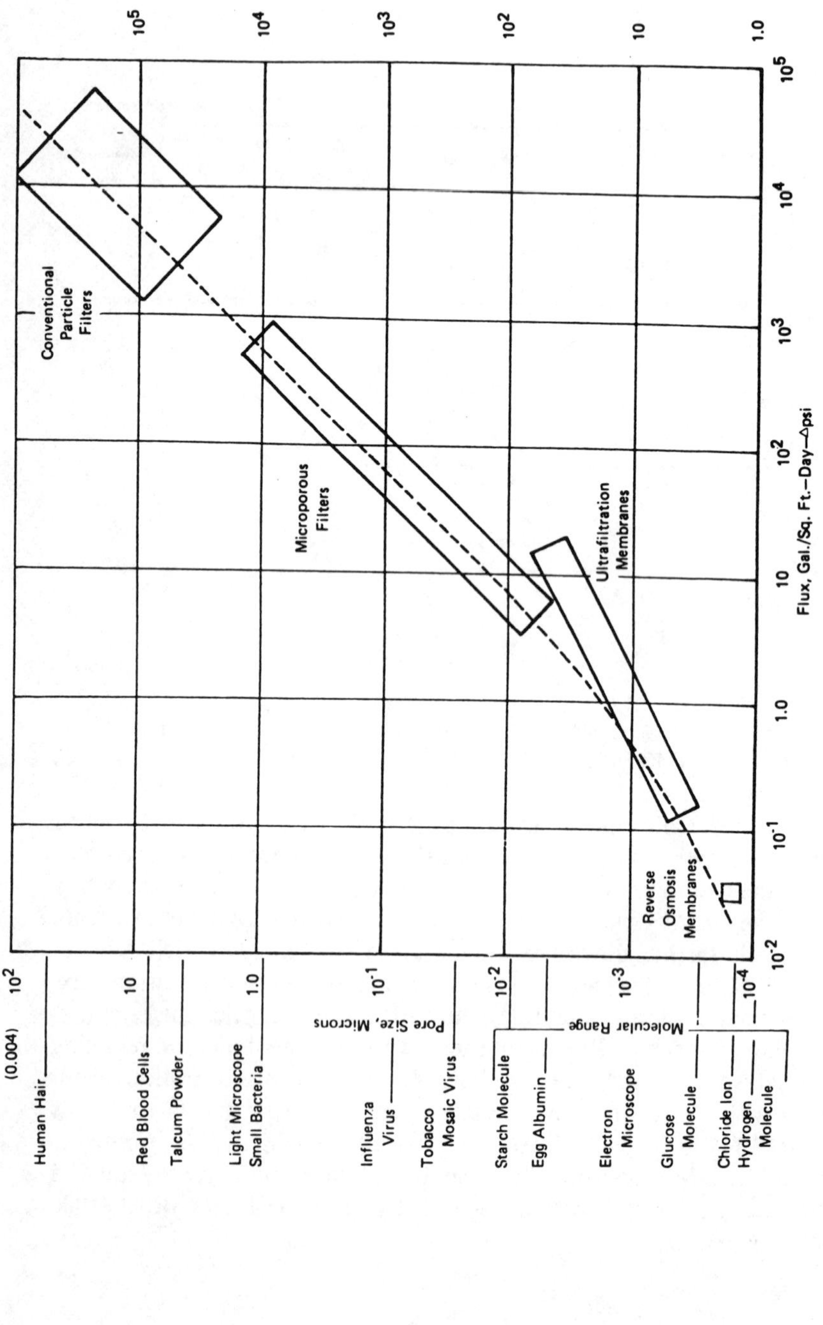

Figure 9-22. Pore size vs flow rate for separation media (Source: NTIS-PB 275 287).

In a sense, any RO membrane also ultrafilters, although perhaps at very low flux states. In turn, some ultrafiltration membranes may exhibit a slight degree of retention of ionic species.

Ultrafiltration membranes are asymmetric structures, possessing an extremely thin selective layer (0.1–1.0 μ thick) supported on a thicker spongy substructure. Controlled variation of fabrication methods can produce membranes with desirable retentive characteristics for a number of separation applications. Indeed, it has become possible to tailor membranes with a wide range of selective properties. For example, tight membranes can retain organic solutes of 500–1000 mol wt, while allowing passage of most inorganic salts. Conversely, loose membranes can discriminate between solutes of 1,000,000 vs 250,000 mol wt.

Ultrafiltration membranes are different from so-called "solution-diffusion" membranes, which have been the subject of study for a wide variety of gas- and liquid-phase separations. The latter group possesses a permselective structure which is nonporous, and separation is effected on the basis of differences in solubility and molecular diffusivity within the actual polymer matrix. Reverse osmosis membranes generally fall into this category.

Membranes can be made from various synthetic or natural polymeric materials. These range from hydrophilic polymers, such as cellulose, to very hydrophobic materials such as fluorinated polymers. Polyarylsulfones and inorganic materials have been introduced to withstand high temperatures and pH values. Membranes of this type are similar to RO membranes, except for the openness of their pores. Other forms and materials are available as well, including porous zirconia, deposited on a porous carbon substrate and on a porous ceramic tube, which is also useful at very high pH values and temperatures.

Applications to Date

As shown in Tables 9-3 and 9-4, ultrafiltration is used for electrocoat paint rejuvenation, rinse-water recovery, protein recovery from cheese whey, and metal machining oil emulsion treatment, with capacity to handle $\sim 100 \times 10^6$ gal/yr for each application. There are also smaller (on the order of 10×10^6 gal/yr) plants for treatment of textile sizing waste and wash water from electronic component manufacturing, and for production of sterile water for pharmaceutical manufacturing.

Table 9-3. Commerical Applications of Ultrafiltrations[a]

Application	Function
Electrocoat Paint rejuvenation and rinse water recovery	Fractionation
Protein recovery from cheese whey	Concentration and fractionation
Metal machining, rolling and drawing—oil emulsion treatment	Purification
Textile sizing (PVA) waste treatment	Fractionation
Electronics component Manufacturing wash water treatment	Purification
Pharmaceuticals manufacturing sterile water production	Purification

[a]Source: NTIS-PB 275 287.

Table 9-4. Developmental Applications of Ultrafiltration[a]

Application	Function
1. Dye waste treatment	Concentration and purification
2. Pulp-mill waste treatment	Concentration and purification
3. Industrial laundry waste treatment	Purification and fractionation
4. Protein recovery from soy whey	Concentration
5. Hot alkaline cleaner treatment	Fractionation and purification
6. Power-plant boiler feedwater treatment	Purification
7. Sugar recovery from orange-juice pulp	Fractionation
8. Product recovery in pharmaceutical and fermentation industries	Concentration
9. Colloid-free water pollution for beverages	Purification

[a]Source: NTIS-PB 275 287.

Energy, Environment and Economics

Electrical energy for pumping to maintain flow at operating pressures may be as much as 30% of total direct operating costs.

Ultrafiltration residues are typically a concentrate of the undesirable or hazardous components and usually require further processing. However, sometimes valuable by-products can be recovered.

Capital and operating costs are dependent on the specific application and the capacity of the system. For large plants, capital costs may be

$1–4/gpd; operating costs may be $5–10/1000 gal. Coupled with the economics of reuse of salvaged materials, these costs often are acceptable.

ZONE REFINING

Process Description

Zone refining is a fractional crystallization technique in which a rod of impure material is purified by heating so as to cause a molten zone to pass along its length. Basic equipment consists of a material support or ingot holder to contain the sample, a feed or travel mechanism, and a source of heat. The process may include a cooling step. It can be used on solids, liquids and mixtures such as slurries. High-viscosity and reactive materials are not suitable.

Details of the principles of zone refining and the zone refining operation and problems are reported in the literature [20,36–40]. Gouw and Jentoft have compared the efficiencies of normal freezing, column crystallization and zone melting [41].

When a liquid mixture is cooled, the solid that crystallizes out usually has a composition different from that of the liquid. The purification of substances by zone refining depends on this difference. Two simple types of solid-liquid equilibrium reveal some of the conditions that arise during zone refining. In a system the cooling of liquid of composition J will cause crystallization of pure component A when the temperature corresponding to point L is reached. On the other hand, if the original composition corresponds instead to point J_1, the first solid to separate will be pure component B.

Zone refining, at present, is only useful for processing small quantities (up to 10 kg) of relatively pure material. Processing rates are < 10 cm/hr. The process is not practical for the complex mixtures that characterize most waste streams. Even for specialized applications, the process is only operationally feasible if the distribution coefficients permit segregation of impurities.

Energy, Environment and Economics

Zone refining is an energy-intensive process and therefore expensive to operate.

Its pollution potential is low. Equipment costs are not presently available, as most equipment is being engineered on a custom basis.

REFERENCES

1. Hasler, J. W. *Purification with Activated Carbon* (Bronx, NY: Chemical Publishing Company, Inc., 1974).
2. Weber, W. J., Jr. "Sorption from Solution by Porous Carbon," in *Principles and Applications of Water Chemistry,* S. D. Faust and J. V. Hunter, Eds. (New York: John Wiley & Sons, Inc., 1967).
3. Zeitoun, M. A. and W. F. McIlhenny. "Treatment of Wastewater from the Production of Polyhydric Organics," U.S. EPA Project No. 12020-EEQ.
4. "Wastewater Treatment Facilities for a Polyvinyl Chloride Production Plant," U.S. EPA Project No. 12020 DJI.
5. "An Investigation of Techniques for Removing Cyanide from Electroplating Wastes," U.S. EPA Water Pollution Control Research Series No. 12010EIE 11/71.
6. Smithson, G. R., Jr. "An Investigation of Techniques for the Removal of Chromium from Electroplating Wastes," U.S. EPA Water Pollution Control Research Series No. 12010 EIE 03/71 (1971).
7. Nelson, F., H. O. Phillips and K. A. Kraus. "Adsorption of Inorganic Materials on Activated Carbon," in Proceedings of 29th Industrial Waste Conference, Purdue University, Lafayette, IN (1974), pp. 1076–1090.
8. Cheremisinoff, P. N. and A. C. Moressi. "Carbon Adsorption," *Poll. Eng.* 6(8):66–68 (1974).
9. Lin, Y. H. and J. R. Lawson. "Treatment of Oily and Metal-Containing Wastewater," *Poll. Eng.* 5(11):45–48 (1973).
10. Kennedy, D. C., V. Stevens and J. W. Kerner. "Decolorizing Dye Wastes," *Am. Dyestuff Reporter* (August 1974).
11. Montanaro, R. A. and A. H. Nobel. "Removal of Color and Heavy Metals from a Dyestuff Waste Stream by Adsorption," paper presented at the American Association of Textile Chemists and Colorists Symposium, Washington, DC, May 22–24, 1973.
12. "Color, Heavy Metals Removed by Adsorption," *Chem. Process.* (September 1972).
13. Harrington, C. H. "Historic Dye Plant in Major Changes," *Providence Sunday Journal* (July 9, 1972).
14. Brooks, K. "Centrifuges," *Chem. Week* (September 16, 1970), pp. 33–48.
15. Day, R. W. "Techniques for Selecting Centrifuges," *Chem. Eng.* (May 13, 1974), pp. 98–100.
16. *Water Quality and Treatment,* 3rd ed. Prepared by the American Water Works Association (New York: McGraw-Hill Book Company, 1971), pp. 72–73.
17. Weber, W. J., Jr. *Physicochemical Processes for Water Quality Control* (New York: Wiley-Interscience, 1972), p. 63.
18. "Froth Flotation," *50th Anniversary Volume AIME* (1962).
19. Grieves, R. B. and D. Bhattachoryya. "Precipitate Flotation of Complexed Cyanide," Proceedings of the 24th Industrial Waste Conference (1969).
20. *Encyclopedia of Chemical Technology,* 2nd ed. (Kirk-Othmer, 1974), p. 22.

21. *Desalting Handbook for Planners* (Bureau of Reclamation and Office of Saline Water, U.S. Department of the Interior, May 1972).
22. Barduhn, A. J. "The Status of Freeze Desalination," *Chem. Eng. Prog.* 71(11):80–87 (November 1975).
23. Clements, G. S., R. J. Stephenson and C. J. Regan. "Dewatering by Freezing with Added Chemicals," *J. Inst. Sew. Pur.* 4:318 (1950).
24. Logsdon, G. S. and E. Edgerly, Jr. "Sludge Dewatering by Freezing," *J. Am. Water Works Assoc.* 63(11):734–740 (1971).
25. Katz, W. J. and D. G. Mason. "Freezing Methods Used to Condition Activated Sludge," *Water Sew. Works* 117(4):110–114 (1970).
26. Farrell, J. B., J. E. Smith, Jr., R. B. Dean, E. Grossman, III, and O. C. Grant. "Natural Freezing for Dewatering of Aluminum Hydroxide Sludge," *J. Am. Water Works Assoc.* 62(12):1145–1147 (1970).
27. Cheng, C., D. M. Updegruff and L. W. Ross. "Sludge Dewatering by High-Rate Freezing at Small Temperature Differences," *Environ. Sci. Technol.* 4(12):1145–1147 (1970).
28. Randall, C. W., M. Z. Alikhan and N. T. Stephens. "Waste Activated Sludge Conditioning by Direct Slurry Freezing," *Water Research,* Vol. 9 (Elmsford, NY: Pergamon Press, Inc., 1975), pp. 917–925.
29. Osterkamp, T. E. "Waste Water Sludge Ice," *J. Glaciol.* 13(67):155–156 (1974).
30. Garinger, L. E. "Freeze-Thaw Conditioning of Biotreatment Plant Sludge," M.S. Thesis, University of Alaska, Fairbanks, AK (1973).
31. Dorsey, ed. *Properties of Ordinary Water Substance* (Reinhold Publishing Co., 1940).
32. Chamberlain, E. J. *Freeze-Thaw Consolidation of Fine-Grained Materials* (Hanover, NH: U.S. Army Cold Regions Research and Engineering Lab, 1974).
33. Kesting, R. E. *Synthetic Polymeric Membranes* (New York: McGraw-Hill Book Company, 1971).
34. Gonzales, J. G. and R. L. Culp. "New Developments in Ammonia Stripping," *Public Works* (May 1973), pp. 78–84; (June 1973), pp. 82–85.
35. Hodgman, C. D., R. C. Weast and C. W. Wallace. *Handbook of Chemistry and Physics,* 35th ed. (Cleveland, OH: Chemical Rubber Publishing Co., 1953), p. 1610.
36. Pfann, W. G. *Zone Melting,* 2nd ed. (New York: John Wiley & Sons, Inc., 1966).
37. Herington, E. F. G. "Zone Refining," *Endeavour* (October 1960), pp. 191–196.
38. Wang, E. Y., "Analysis of Zone Melting Processes," *J. Electrochem. Soc.: Solid-State Science and Technology* 121(12):1671–1672 (1974).
39. Nicolau, I. F. "Purification Process by Solution Zone Passages: Part I, Process Theory," *J. Materials Sci.* 5:623–639 (1970).
40. Fischer, D. "Diffusion and the Influence of Separating the Impure End," *J. Applied Physics* 44(5):1972–1982 (May 1973).
41. Gouw, T. H. and R. E. Jentoft. "Evaluation of Efficiencies of Normal Freezing, Column Crystallization and Zone Melting," *Anal. Chim. Acta* 39:383–391 (1967).

CHAPTER 10

CHEMICAL TREATMENT

As discussed in Chapter 8, selection of treatment processes for given waste streams depends on the nature of the waste, desired characteristics of the output stream, technical adequacy of the treatment, and economic, environmental and energy considerations.

This chapter discusses major chemical treatment processes applicable to hazardous waste: these include (1) chemical oxidation, (2) chemical reduction, (3) hydrolysis, (4) liquid-liquid solvent extraction, (5) neutralization, (6) ozonation and (7) photolysis.

CHEMICAL OXIDATION

The processes discussed here are based on chemical oxidation as differentiated from thermal, electrolytic and biological oxidation. Although oxidation using air or oxygen in solution can be used for waste treatment on sulfites, sulfides and ferrous iron, these oxidations typically are catalyzed with small amounts of materials such as cobalt to increase the reaction rate. Also, the oxidation reactions discussed here should be distinguished from the higher temperature, and typically pressurized wet oxidation processes, which are not included in this study.

Reduction-oxidation ("redox") reactions are those in which the oxidation state of at least one reactant is raised while that of another is lowered. In reaction (1) in alkaline solution:

$$(1) \qquad 2MnO_4^- + CN^- + 2OH^- \rightleftarrows 2MnO_4^{2-} + CNO^- + H_2O$$

the oxidation state of the cyanide ion is raised from -1 to $+1$ (the cyanide is oxidized as it combines with an atom of oxygen to form cyanate); the oxidation state of the permanganate decreases from −1 to −2 (permanganate is reduced to manganate). This change in oxidation state implies that an electron was transferred from the cyanide ion to the permanganate. The increase in the positive valence (or decrease in the negative valence) with oxidation takes place simultaneously with reduction in chemically equivalent ratios. Figure 10-1 illustrates the oxidation process.

Fluorine is a powerful oxidizing agent. The other halogens, including chlorine, are also good oxidizing agents. The positive ions of noble metals are good oxidizing agents. Many of the oxygenated ions, such as BrO_3^- and NO_3^- are strong oxidizing agents in acid solution. There are, then, many oxidizing agents; however, only a few are convenient to use. The ones more commonly used in waste treatment are listed in Table 10-1.

Oxidizing agents vary in strength as illustrated by the following half-reactions arranged in order of decreasing oxidation potentials (i.e., tendency to pick up electrons):

Half-Reaction	Oxidation Potential (E_0) (volts)
$F_2 + 2H^+ + 2e^- \rightarrow 2HF$ (aq.)	3.06
$H_2O_2 + 2H^+ + 2e^- \rightarrow 2H_2O$	1.77
$MnO_4^- + 4H^+ + 3e^- \rightarrow MnO_2 + 2H_2O$	1.695
$Cl_2 + 2e^- \rightarrow 2Cl^-$	1.359
$Cr_2O_7^{2-} + 14H^+ + 6e^- \rightarrow 2Cr^{3+} + 7H_2O$	1.33
$2H^+ + 2e^- \rightarrow H_2$	0

Some oxidations proceed readily to CO_2; in other cases the oxidation is not carried as far, perhaps because of the dosage of the oxidant, the pH of the reaction medium, the oxidation potential of the oxidant, or the formation of stable intermediates. The primary function performed by oxidation in the treatment of hazardous wastes is essentially detoxification. For example, oxidants are used to convert cyanide to the less toxic cyanate or completely to carbon dioxide and nitrogen. The oxidant itself is reduced. For example, in the potassium permanganate treatment of phenolics, the permanganate is reduced to manganese dioxide. A secondary function is to ensure complete precipitation, as in the oxidation of Fe^{++} to Fe^{+++} and similar reactions.

Table 10-2 lists the more common oxidation reactions for cyanide treatment and their reaction products. Oxidation reactions for other wastes appear throughout the text.

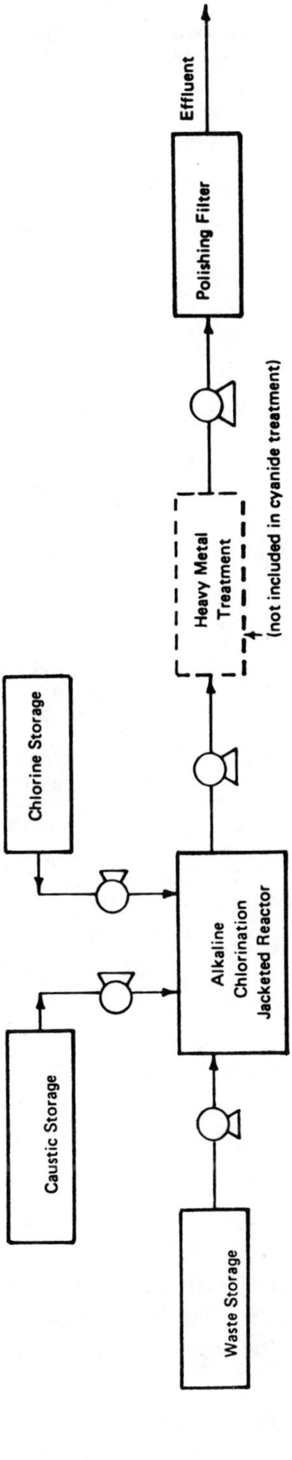

Figure 10-1. Example process flowsheet—oxidation (Source: NTIS-PB 275 287).

Table 10-1. Waste Treatment Applications of Oxidation Identified[a]

Oxidant	Waste
Ozone	—
Air (atmospheric oxygen)	Sulfites ($SO_3^{=}$) Sulfides ($S^{=}$) Ferrous iron (Fe^{++})—very slow
Chlorine gas	Sulfide Mercaptans
Chlorine gas and caustic[b]	Cyanide (CN^{-})
Chlorine dioxide	Cyanide Diquat } pesticides Paraquat } pesticides
Sodium hypochlorite	Cyanide Lead
Calcium hypochlorite	Cyanide
Potassium permanganate	Cyanide—organic odors Lead
Trace quantities only	Phenol Diquat } pesticides Paraquat } pesticides Organic sulfur compounds Rotenone Formaldehyde
Permanganate	Manganese
Hydrogen peroxide	Phenol Cyanide Sulfur compounds Lead
Nitrous acid	Benzidene

[a]Source: NTIS-PB 275 287.
[b]Alkaline chlorination.

Operating Characteristics

Stream Characteristics

Liquids are the primary waste form treatable by chemical oxidation. The most powerful oxidants are relatively nonselective; therefore, any easily oxidizable material in the waste stream will be treated. If, for

Table 10-2. Conventional Waste Treatment Oxidation Reactions[a]

Cyanide destruction using chlorine gas:

$$\underset{\text{sodium cyanide}}{2NaCN} + \underset{\text{chlorine}}{5Cl_2} + \underset{\text{sodium hydroxide}}{12NaOH} \rightarrow \underset{\text{Nitrogen}}{N_2} + \underset{\text{sodium carbonate}}{2Na_2CO_3} + \underset{\text{sodium chloride}}{10NaCl} + \underset{\text{water}}{6H_2O}$$

Cyanide destruction using hypochlorites:

$$2\,NaCN + \underset{\text{sodium hypochlorite}}{5NaOCl} + H_2O \rightarrow N_2 + \underset{\text{sodium bicarbonate}}{2NaHCO_3} + 5NaCl$$

$$4NaCN + \underset{\text{calcium hypochlorite}}{5Ca(OCl)_2} + 2H_2O \rightarrow 2N_2 + \underset{\text{calcium bicarbonate}}{2Ca(HCO_3)_2} + 3CaCl_2 + 4NaCl$$

Conversion of cyanide to cyanate using permanganate:

$$2NaCN + \underset{\text{potassium permanganate}}{2KMnO_4} + KOH \rightarrow 2K_2MnO_4 + NaCNO + H_2O$$

Conversion of cyanide to cyanate using chlorine gas:

$$NaCN + Cl_2 + 2NaOH \rightarrow \underset{\text{sodium cyanate}}{NaCNO} + 2NaCl + H_2O$$

Conversion of cyanide to cyanate using hypochlorites:

$$NaCN + \underset{\text{sodium hypochlorite}}{NaOCl} \rightarrow \underset{\text{sodium cyanate}}{NaCNO} + NaCl$$

Conversion of cyanide to cyanate using hydrogen peroxide:

$$NaCN + \underset{\text{hydrogen peroxide}}{H_2O_2} \rightarrow \underset{\text{sodium cyanate}}{NaCNO} + H_2O$$

[a] Source: NTIS-PB 275 287.

instance, an easily oxidizable organic solvent were used, little of the chemical effect of the oxidizing agent would be spared for the hazardous constituent. This essentially limits the most commonly used oxidants to treatment of aqueous wastes.

Gases have been treated by scrubbing with oxidizing solutions for the destruction of odorous substances, such as certain amines and sulfur compounds. Potassium permanganate, for instance, has been used in certain chemical processes, in the manufacture of kraft paper and in the rendering of fats. Oxidizing solutions also are used for small-scale disposal of certain reactive gases in laboratories [1].

Oxidation has limited application to slurries, tars and sludges. Because other components of the sludge, as well as the material to be oxidized, may be attacked indiscriminately by oxidizing agents, careful control of the treatment by multistaging the reaction, careful control of pH, etc., is required.

The chlor-alkali industry is reported to use chemical oxidative techniques to remove mercury from ores as well as from the cell wastes. Mercury removal rates of >99% are claimed for concentrated ore, and residual mercury levels of <0.1 ppm for chlor-alkali sludge.

However, the Pacific Northwest Environmental Research Laboratory, Corvallis, Oregon, has reported that it could not duplicate these results on a laboratory scale, perhaps simply because of the variability of the sludges. In a study which recommended the use of sulfide precipitation to remove the mercury [2], the use of sodium hypochlorite and chlorine as accessory reagents was tested. The intent was to oxidatively convert the elemental mercury and insoluble mercurous compounds in the brine sludge to a stable, soluble mercuric complex as follows:

$$Hg + ClO^- + 3Cl^- + H_2O \rightleftharpoons HgCl_4^= + 2OH^-$$

Other reactions include:

$$2Hg^+ + ClO^- + 7Cl^- + H_2O \rightleftharpoons 2HgCl_4^= + 2OH^-$$

$$Hg^{++} + 4Cl^- \rightleftharpoons HgCl_4^=$$

The results indicated that the hypochlorite dissolved nearly as much of the sludge solids as the mercury. Other kinds of treatment would be required to remove the remaining mercury from the residue.

Work has been done using sodium hypochlorite for leaching mercury from low grade ores. Residual mercury was present, which suggests that the reaction may be incomplete. The extent to which this technique could be extended to the treatment of industrial wastes may be limited because of the inefficiency of the oxidant and the incompleteness of the removal of mercury from sludge solids.

Powders and other solids usually would be put into solution prior to the use of chemical oxidation. However, as with many chemical reactions such as neutralization of acids with limestone, reactions may be possible that depend on a reaction between a liquid and solid phase.

Chemical oxidation can be used to treat both organic and inorganic waste components. Since some oxidizing agents may react violently in the presence of significant quantities of readily oxidizable organic material, either the organic matter or the oxidizing agent should be added in small quantities, so that large momentary excesses are avoided. Widely varying concentrations of nonoxidizable ions of heavy metals are well tolerated. In fact, the primary use of chemical oxidation for waste treatment is in the conversion and destruction of cyanides from plating operations where metals such as zinc, copper and chromium are present.

Operation

The first step in treating a solution by the chemical oxidation process is the adjustment of the pH. In the use of chlorine gas to treat cyanides, for instance, this adjustment is required because acid pH has the effect of producing hydrogen cyanide and/or cyanogen chloride, both of which are poisonous gases. The pH adjustment is done with an appropriate alkali sodium hydroxide, for example. This is followed by the addition of the oxidizing agent and mixing with the waste. Because some heat often is liberated, concentrated solutions require cooling. The agent can be in the form of a gas (chlorine gas) or a solution (hydrogen peroxide), or perhaps a solid if there is adequate mixing. Reaction times vary but are on the order of seconds and minutes for most of the commercial-scale installations. Additional time is allowed to ensure complete mixing and oxidation. At this point, additional oxidation may be desired and, as with cyanide destruction, this often requires readjustment of the pH followed by the addition of more oxidant. Once reacted, this final oxidized solution generally is subjected to some form of treatment to settle or precipitate any insoluble oxidized material, metals and other residues. A treatment for the removal of what remains of the oxidizing agent (both reacted and unreacted) may be required. A product of potassium permanganate oxidation is manganese dioxide (MnO_2) which is insoluble and can be settled or filtered for removal.

While some stream components may be added or removed, the output stream from chemical oxidation is very similar to the input stream. Oxidizing agents such as potassium permanganate and potassium dichromate introduce to the reaction mixture ions that are not easily separable from the product streams. Oxidizing agents such as oxygen and hydrogen peroxide have the advantage that they introduce no such foreign ions to the reaction mixture. Oxidizing agents often have a reaction product, such as MnO_2, that is insoluble and can be removed by filtration.

Equipment and Materials

Only very simple equipment is required for chemical oxidation. This includes storage vessels for the oxidizing agents and perhaps for the wastes, metering equipment for both streams, and contact vessels with agitators to provide suitable contact of oxidant and waste. Some instrumentation is required to determine the concentration and pH of the water and the degree of completion of the oxidation reaction. The oxidation process may be monitored by an oxidation-reduction potential (ORP) electrode. This electrode is generally a piece of noble metal (often platinum) which is exposed to the reaction medium, and produces an electromagnetic field (EMF) output that is empirically related to the reaction condition by revealing the ratio of the oxidized to the reduced constituents.

Calgon, DuPont, and Oxymetal Industries are among numerous companies that have commercial units for the removal of cyanides from industrial effluents. Calgon uses cupric ions to catalyze cyanide oxidation. DuPont uses Rastone (41% H_2O_2 and formaldehyde) to convert cyanide to cyanate. Oxymetal Industries has a package unit which oxidizes 5 lb sodium cyanate/hr [3]. All of these units offer the user a preengineered system for a specific waste or range of wastes.

The common, commercially available oxidants that we have identified are: potassium permanganate, chlorine gas, calcium hypochlorite, sodium hypochlorite, hydrogen peroxide (35% solution), chromic acid (CrO_3). Since varying amounts of these chemicals are required for treatment of specific wastes, the oxidizing agent that is least expensive on a weight basis would not necessarily be the least expensive overall treatment system. The characteristics of a number of common oxidizing agents are described in the following paragraphs.

1. *Potassium Permanganate* ($KMnO_4$). Potassium permanganate has been used for destruction of organic residues in wastewater and in potable water. Its usual reduced form, manganese dioxide (MnO_2), can be removed by filtration. Potassium permanganate reacts with aldehydes, mercaptans, phenols and unsaturated acids. It is considered a relatively powerful oxidizing agent.

2. *Hydrogen Peroxide* (H_2O_2). Hydrogen peroxide has been used for the separation of metal ions by selective oxidation. In this way it helps remove iron from combined streams by oxidizing the ferrous ion to ferric, which is then precipitated by the addition of the appropriate base. In dilute solution ($<30\%$) the decomposition of H_2O_2 is accelerated by the presence of metal ion contaminants. At higher concentrations of hydrogen peroxide, these contaminants can catalyze its violent decomposition. Hydrogen peroxides should be added slowly to the solution and mixed well. This caution also relates to other oxidants. If the follow-on treatment involves distillation or crystallization, the absence of all unspent peroxides must be confirmed, since these techniques tend to concentrate the unused reagent. Hydrogen peroxide has also been used as an

"anti-chlor" to remove residual chlorine following chlorination treatment.

3. *Chromic Acid* (CrO_3). Chromium trioxide, CrO_3, is commercially called chromic acid. It is used as an oxidizing agent in the preparation of organic compounds. It is often regenerated afterward by electrolytic oxidation. In the oxidation of organic compounds, CrO_3 in a solution of sulfuric acid is reduced and forms chromium sulfate [$Cr_2(SO_4)_3$].

Applications to Date

Oxidation reactions are among the most common of chemical reactions. The experience with these reactions for waste treatment is primarily related to removal of trace contaminants in water effluents and for cyanide treatment from operations such as plating and metal finishing. The former are of interest only as they identify potential oxidants and types of materials that can be oxidized. The latter, although often relating to dilute cyanide rinse wastes, can be extended to be more concentrated solutions. Some selected examples of the application of chemical oxidation to hazardous waste management problems are described here.

Oxidation of Cyanide Effluents

Numerous plating and metal finishing plants use chemical oxidation methods to treat their cyanide wastes. Cyanides and heavy metals often are present together in plating industry wastes. Their concentration and their value influence the selection of the treatment process. If the cyanide and heavy metal are not commercially recoverable by a method such as ion exchange, the cyanide radical is converted either to the less toxic cyanate or to CO_2 and N_2 by oxidation, and most heavy metals are precipitated and removed as a sludge.

Chemical oxidation is applicable to both concentrated and dilute waste streams, but the processes are more numerous for the concentrated streams. These methods include thermal and catalytic decomposition of the cyanide, and decomposition using acidification.

In treating cyanide waste by oxidation, hypochlorite or caustic plus chlorine (alkaline chlorination) may be used to oxidize the cyanide to cyanate or to oxidize it completely to nitrogen and carbon dioxide. It is a fast reaction which is adaptable to either batch or continuous operation. Smaller volumes would be treated as a batch for simplicity and safety. Figure 10-2 describes a batch process to destroy cyanide.

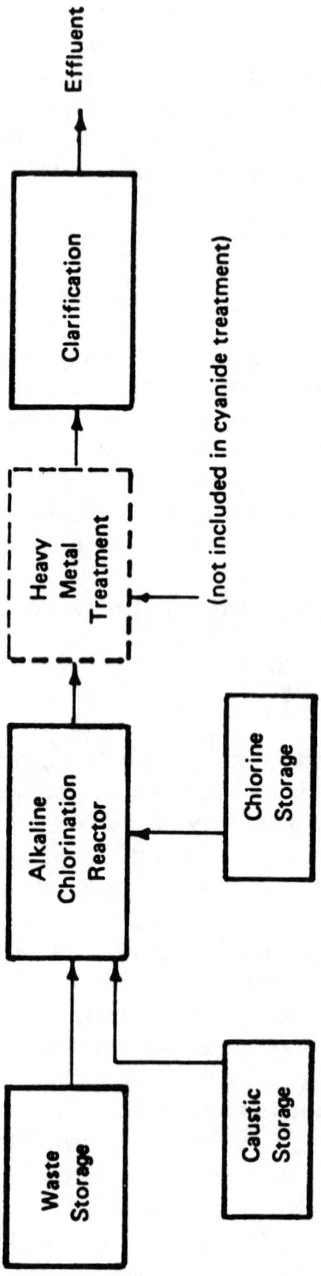

Figure 10-2. Cyanide waste treatment using alkaline chlorination (Source: NTIS-PB 275 287).

The destruction is believed to proceed according to the following equations:

(1) $$NaCN + Cl_2 \rightarrow CNCl + NaCl$$

(2) $$CNCl + 2NaOH \rightarrow NaCNO + NaCl + H_2O$$

(3) $$2NaCNO + 4NaOH + 3Cl_2 \rightarrow 6NaCl + 2CO_2 + N_2 + 2H_2O$$

The rate of the second reaction is dependent on pH and proceeds rapidly at a pH of 11 or higher. About 8 parts chlorine and 7.3 parts sodium hydroxide are required per part of cyanide. Neutralization is required after treatment because the waste generally is alkaline.

Calcium, magnesium and sodium hydrochlorite are frequently used in place of gaseous chlorine even though the chlorine causes a more rapid reaction and costs about half as much as the hypochlorites. This is because they are easier and safer to use and do not require the addition of supplementary alkali. Calcium hypochlorite will give more sludge than sodium hypochlorite if certain anions such as sulfate are present.

There are problems associated with alkaline chlorination of cyanide if soluble iron or certain other transition metal ions are present. The iron forms very stable ferrocyanide complexes which prevent the cyanide from being oxidized.

Potassium permanganate and hydrogen peroxide also are used to oxidize cyanide wastes. Potassium permanganate ($KMnO_4$) is not used widely for the destruction of cyanide. However, oxidation by permanganate is a method of cyanide removal which has been reduced to commercial practice. One advantage of the use of permanganate is that there is no need to monitor pH. Once the pH adjustment has been made there is continuous formation of the hydroxide ion:

$$2KMnO_4 + 3CN^- + H_2O \rightarrow 3CNO^- + 2MnO_2 + 2OH^- + 2K^+$$

to constantly keep the reaction medium on the alkaline side. This is fortunate because otherwise there is the danger that if the pH drops to between 6 and 9, hydrogen cyanide and/or cyanogen, both poisonous gases, may be formed. With other oxidative methods the addition of alkali is used to maintain an alkaline reaction medium. The use of permanganate oxidizes the waste cyanide only to the cyanate. Simple acid hydrolysis can be used to further treat the cyanate, converting it to CO_2 and N_2.

Potassium permanganate is a powerful oxidizing agent. Since it is relatively expensive, it has not been widely used because there are other less expensive oxidants available. A small plater could find application for this material, however, because there is little need for instrumentation or testing to monitor the reaction and there is no large capital investment.

Lawes and Mathre [4] describe a process which uses a combination of H_2O_2 and formaldehyde with the addition of a magnesium salt, for the detoxification of cyanide wastes. The temperature and pH are important variables in this reaction. The preferred reaction temperature is 10–82°C and the pH of the waste should be in the range of 9 to 12.5. The waste treatment was designed specifically for treatment of wastewaters from zinc plating operations. When the rinse waters are treated, the settled or filtered basic zinc salts can be recycled to the zinc electroplating step. Previously, peroxygen compounds could not be used effectively and economically for cyanide destruction without the use of a catalyst. A catalyst that is often used is a metal ion such as Cu^{++}. Indeed, Cu^{++} is often found in plating solutions; however, it is a pollutant which must eventually be removed. Also, because of the decomposition of the H_2O_2 that occurs in dilute aqueous solutions (<30%), which is accelerated by the presence of metal ion contaminants, addition of a metal ion to catalyze the reaction may make the reaction less efficient. It should be noted that although metal ions cause decomposition in dilute solutions, they actually may catalyze violent decomposition in higher concentration solutions of H_2O_2 (70–90%) even though present in only trace amounts. This type of reaction of powerful oxidants is not uncommon. Therefore these properties of oxidants should be considered when thinking of treating concentrated wastes such as those normally incinerated or disposed of on land.

Oxidation of Phenol

Oxidation reactions involving phenol are often complex, since the reaction products depend upon the substituents. The reactions are believed to involve as a first step the removal of the hydroxyl hydrogen to yield a phenoxy radical:

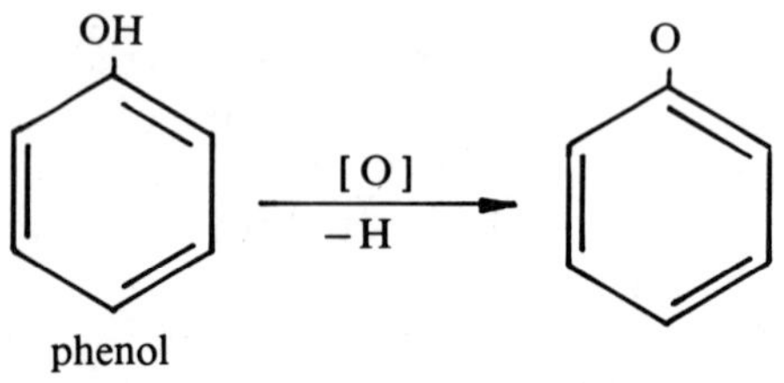

The eventual reaction products can include quinone which is considered more toxic than phenol. The one commercial reaction, for instance, the oxidation of phenol with chromic acid is designed to yield quinone:

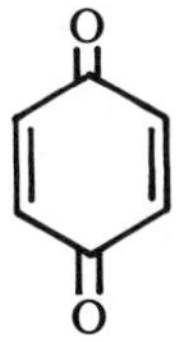

Spicher and Skrinde [5] propose that the reaction mechanism involves first the production of the quinone and then the rupture of the ring followed by the oxidation of the ring fragments if sufficient oxidant is present. The reaction does not usually go quite as far as Spicher and Skrinde suggest in their proposed reaction using potassium permanganate:

$$3C_6H_5(OH) + 28KMnO_4 + 5H_2O \rightarrow 18CO_2 + 28KOH + 28MnO_2$$

although the reaction usually does go to the stage of opening the ring.

Chemical oxidation of phenols has found application to date only on dilute waste streams. Potassium permanganate is one of the oxidants that is used. After it is added, some further time is allowed for the phenol to be oxidized to carbon dioxide and water [6]. The $KMnO_4$ is reduced to manganese dioxide (MnO_2) which is a filterable solid. In one application the product MnO_2 has been found to act also as a coagulant aid to settle other material from the waste stream. Because of the high potential for formation of chlorophenols, chlorine gas is not frequently used.

When phenol is present only in trace quantities, the economics appear favorable for chemical oxidation. It has been used in the treatment of potable water. Removal of 1 ppm phenol in this application can be accomplished by the addition of 6–7 ppm potassium permanganate [7].

Oxidation of Other Organics

Chemical oxidizing agents have been used for the control of organic residues in treatment of wastewaters and potable water. Among the organics for which oxidative treatment has been reported are: aldehydes, mercaptans, phenols, benzidine and unsaturated acids. For these applications sodium hypochlorite, calcium hypochlorite, potassium permanganate and hydrogen peroxide have been reported as oxidants. In one application nitrous acid was used.

Benzidine, an organic used in the manufacture of dyes, is considered a carcinogen, and its concentration is generally reduced to parts per billion in wastewaters prior to discharge for this reason. Nitrous acid oxidation is used to achieve this effluent quality. While biodegradation, carbon adsorption, radiation, oxidation by ozone and oxidation by other chemicals such as H_2O_2 have been suggested, only the oxidation (commonly called diazotization) using nitrous acid has been used on a full-scale basis [8]. The reaction of benzidine with an excess amount of nitrous acid in a strong acid reaction medium yields the quinone form, 4,4′-dihydroxybiphenyl and/or similar products. The reaction products cannot revert back to benzidine. The quinone product is toxic also, but considered less so than benzidine. Since the effluent stream is very dilute, no secondary treatment is required.

The reaction of formaldehyde with potassium permanganate in neutral or mildly alkaline solutions is as follows:

$$3HCHO + 4KMnO_4 \rightarrow H_2O + 3CO_2 + 4KOH + 4MnO_2$$

The reaction is the basis for a simple gas washing apparatus in the processing of permanent-press fabrics.

Because a strong oxidant (such as potassium permanganate) may be decomposed by alcohols and some other organic solvents, as well as acting as oxidants for them, it is believed that their use on concentrated organic wastes would not be cost-effective. This does not rule out the possibility that some types of organic waste might be converted on a commercial scale to usable products via oxidation reactions similar to those used in the organic chemicals industry. However, it does not appear that wastes in general are susceptible to this form of treatment.

Oxidation of Sulfur Compounds

Much of the oxidative treatment of sulfur compounds focuses on odor removal. Scrubbers using oxidizing solutions of potassium permanganate, for example, remove organic sulfur compounds from air. Thiophene is one of these compounds, in which the molecule is unsaturated and susceptible to complete degradation.

$$2KMnO_4 + 3C_4H_4S + 4H_2O \rightarrow 2KMnO_2 + 12CO_2 + 3SO_4^{=} + 2O\ OH^-$$

Chlorine and calcium hypochlorite have been used to prevent accumulation of soluble sulfides in sewer lines [9]. If an excess of chlorine is added to a wastewater containing sulfide, the sulfide will be oxidized to sulfate.

$$HS^- + 4Cl_2 + 4H_2O \rightarrow SO_4^{=} + 9H^+ + 8Cl^-$$

For a waste stream containing only small concentrations of sulfide and no other substances susceptible to oxidation, the chlorine requirement would be nearly 9 parts (by weight) for each part of sulfide. In streams where there are other oxidizable constituents, this requirement may rise to 15–20 parts.

Hydrogen peroxide also has been used for this application of sulfide oxidation. In a wastewater which contained about 6 mg/l total sulfide, the addition of 30 mg/l hydrogen peroxide (H_2O_2) reduced the concentration of sulfide to <1 mg/l. The average retention time was about 2 hr [9].

Oxidation of Pesticides

Because of the resistance of pesticides to biodegradation, chemical oxidative methods have been investigated to remove pesticide residues from water. Gomaa and Faust [10] experimented with potassium permanganate, chlorine, and chlorine dioxide to remove residual Diquat® and Paraquat® from water.

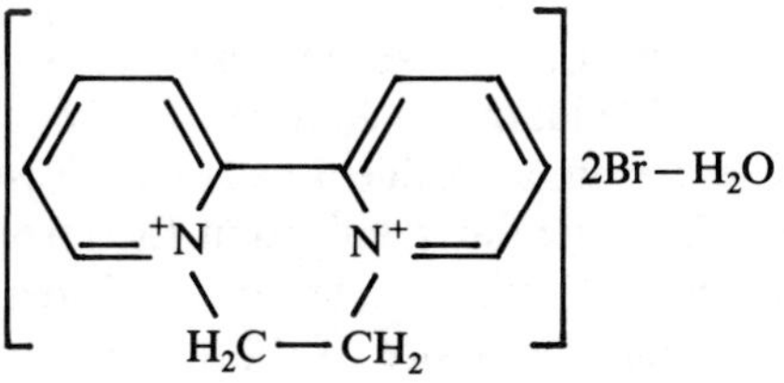

Diquat

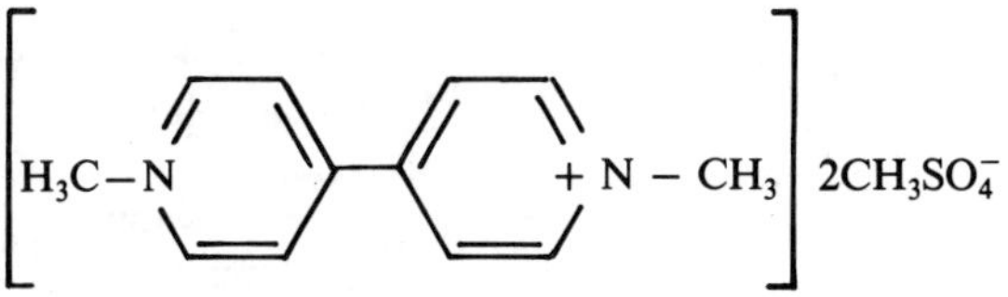

Paraquat

With potassium permanganate oxidation, manganese dioxide was precipitated as expected. The application of $KMnO_4$ at a molar concentration 25 times that of the two pesticides causes fairly complete oxidation to oxalate, ammonia and water. The reaction is said to go through several intermediate stages, and the reaction rates are pH dependent—being faster above pH 8. In an alkaline medium

$$3(C_{12}H_{12}N_2)^{2+} + 40MnO_4^- + 2OH^- \rightleftharpoons$$
$$40MnO_2 + 18C_2O_4^= + 6NH_3 + 10H_2O$$

Diquat

$$(C_{12}H_{14}N_2)^{2+} + 14MnO_4^- \rightleftharpoons 14MnO_2 + 6C_2O_4^= + 2NH_3 + 4H_2O$$

Paraquat

When chlorine dioxide was used as the oxidizing agent on these substances in concentrations of 15 and 30 mg/l, the reactions were complete in less than one minute. These rates were observed at pH values above 8.

Oxidation of Lead

Although other methods have so far been considered more practicable, the use of chemical oxidative techniques for the removal of trace quantities of soluble lead from an effluent has been investigated on a laboratory scale [11]. In this particular application the insoluble lead was already removable by other techniques to acceptable levels. However, in order to meet effluent regulations, more of the soluble lead had to be removed. Potassium permanganate, hydrogen peroxide and sodium hypochlorite were tested and found to convert portions of the soluble lead as described below:

	Initial Soluble Lead Concentration (ppm)	Final Soluble Lead Concentration (ppm)
Potassium permanganate	14	4–7
Hydrogen peroxide	14	9
Sodium hypochlorite	14	9–10

The chemical oxidation processes did not appear economically practical for the application in question; reagent costs alone would have exceeded $1 million/yr.

CHEMICAL REDUCTION

Chemical reduction is of interest because metals often can be reduced to their elemental form for potential recycling or converted to less toxic oxidation states. One such metal is chromium, which, when present as chromium (VI), is a very toxic material. In the reduced state, chromium (III), the hazards are lessened and the chromium can be precipitated for removal. At the present time, chemical reduction is applied primarily to the control of hexavalent chromium in the plating and tanning industries and to the removal of mercury from caustic/chlorine electrolysis cell effluents.

Reduction-oxidation, or "redox" reactions, as described in the previous section, are those in which the oxidation state of at least one reactant is raised while that of another is lowered. In reaction (1)

$$2H_2CrO_4 + 3SO_2 + 3H_2O \rightarrow Cr_2(SO_4)_3 + 5H_2O$$

the oxidation state of Cr changes from 6^+ to 3^+ (Cr is reduced); the oxidation state of S increases from 2^+ to 3^+ (S is oxidized). This change of oxidation state implies that an electron was transferred from S to Cr(VI). The decrease in the positive valence (or increase in the negative valence) with reduction takes place simultaneously with oxidation in chemically equivalent ratios. Reduction is used to treat wastes in such a way that the reducing agent lowers the oxidation state of a substance in order to reduce its toxicity, reduce its solubility or transform it into a form that can be more easily handled.

The base metals are good reducing agents. This is evidenced by the use of iron, aluminum, zinc and sodium compounds for the reduction treatments identified in this chapter. Sulfur compounds also appear among the more common reducing agents. They are listed in Table 10-3 along with identified applications.

Table 10-4 lists the common reduction reactions for chromium (VI) treatment and their reaction products. Reduction reactions for other wastes appear throughout the text.

Operating Characteristics

Liquids are the primary waste form treatable by chemical reduction. The most powerful reductants are relatively nonselective; therefore, any easily reducible material in the waste stream will be treated. For example, in reducing heavy metals to remove them from waste oil, quantities of

Table 10-3. Waste Treatment Applications of Reduction Identified[a]

Waste	Reductant
Chromium (VI)	Sulfur dioxide (often flue gas)
	Sulfite salts sodium bisulfite sodium metabisulfite sodium hydrosulfite
	Ferrous sulfate
	Waste pickle liquor
	Powdered waste iron Powdered waste aluminum Powdered metallic zinc
Mercury-containing	Sodium borohydride ($NaBH_4$)
Tetra-alkyl-lead	Sodium borohydride
Silver	Sodium borohydride

[a]Source: NTIS-PB 275 287.

Table 10-4. Conventional Waste Treatment Reduction Reactions[a]

Cr^{+6} to Cr^{+3}—using sulfur dioxide:

$4SO_2$	$+ 4H_2O \rightarrow$	H_2SO_3	$+ 2CrO_3$	$+ 3H_2SO_3 \rightarrow$	$Cr_2(SO_4)_3$	$+ 3H_2O$
sulfur dioxide	water	sulfurous acid	chromic acid		chromic sulfate	

Cr^{+6} to Cr^{+3}—using bisulfites:

$4CrO_3$	$+ 6NaHSO_3$	$+ 3H_2SO_4 \rightarrow$	$2Cr_2(SO_4)_3$	$+ 3Na_2SO_4$	$+ 6H_2O$
chromic acid	sodium bisulfite	sulfuric acid	chromic sulfate	sodium sulfate	

Cr^{+6} to Cr^{+3}—using ferrous sulfate:

$2CrO_3$	$+ 6FeSO_4$	$+ 6H_2SO_4 \rightarrow$	$3Fe_2(SO_4)_3$	$+ Cr_2(SO_4)_3$	$+ 6H_2O$
chromic acid	ferrous sulfate	sulfuric acid	ferric sulfate	chromic sulfate	

[a]Source: NTIS-PB 275 287.

esters large enough to cause odor problems may be formed by the reduction.

Gases such as chlorine dioxide and chlorine have been treated by reducing solutions for small-scale disposal in laboratories. For reduction of fluorine, instead of a solution, a scrubber filled with solid bicarbonate, soda lime or granulated carbon is recommended. Reduction has limited application to slurries, tars and sludges. Because of the difficulties of achieving intimate contact between the reducing agent and the hazardous constituent, the reduction process would be very inefficient.

In general, hazardous material occurring as powders or other solids would have to be dissolved before chemical reduction.

The first step of the chemical reduction process is usually adjustment of the pH of the solution to be treated. With sulfur dioxide treatment of chromium (VI), for instance, the reaction requires a pH in the range of 2 to 3. The pH adjustment is done with the appropriate acid, sulfuric, for example. This is followed by the addition of the reducing agent. Mixing is provided to improve contact between the reducing agent and the waste. The agent can be in the form of a gas (sulfur dioxide), a solution (sodium borohydride) or perhaps a finely divided powder if there is adequate mixing. Reaction times vary for different wastes, reducing agents, temperatures, pH and concentrations. For commercial-scale operations for treating chromium wastes, reaction times are on the order of minutes. Additional time usually is allowed to ensure complete mixing and reduction. Once reacted, the reduced solution generally is subjected to some form of treatment to settle or precipitate the reduced material. A treatment for the removal of what remains of the reducing agent may be included. This can be unused reducing agent or the reducing agent in its oxidized state. Unused alkali metal hydrides are decomposed by the addition of a small quantity of acid. The pH of the reaction medium is typically increased so that the reduced material will precipitate out of solution. Filters or clarifiers are often used to improve separation.

While some stream components may be added or removed, the output stream from a chemical reduction treatment is not very different from the input stream. Reducing agents such as sodium borohydride and zinc introduce to the reaction mixture ions that are not easily separable from the product streams. The effluent solution is typically acidic and must be neutralized prior to discharge with materials such as hydrated lime, caustic soda or soda ash.

Equipment and Materials

Very simple equipment is required for chemical reduction, identical to that described in the previous section on oxidation. This includes storage vessels for the reducing agents and perhaps for the wastes, metering equipment for both streams, and contact vessels with agitators to provide suitable contact of reducing agent and waste. Some instrumentation is required to determine the concentration and pH of the waste and the degree of completion of the reduction reaction. The reduction process may be monitored by an oxidation-reduction potential (ORP) electrode. This electrode usually is a piece of noble metal (often platinum) which is exposed to the reaction medium and which produces an EMF output that is empirically relatable to the reaction condition by revealing the ratio of the oxidized and reduced constituents. Figure 10-3 shows a process flow diagram for a typical chemical system.

There are numerous commercial units on the market for the treatment of chromium (VI) in industrial effluents. All of these units offer the user a preengineered system for a specific waste or range of waste streams.

The chemical reducing agents commonly used, and commercially available are: sulfur dioxide, sodium bisulfite, ferrous sulfate and sodium borohydride.

Since varying amounts of these are required for treatment of a specific waste (because of reducing potential or other characteristics of the chemical), it is not necessarily true that the least expensive on a weight basis is the least expensive to treat a specific waste. Additional information is required. The following table illustrates how chemical requirements vary for a specific chromium-containing waste [12]:

Chemical	Amount Required of Component (lb)
Sulfur dioxide	1.9
Sodium bisulfite	3.0
Sodium metabisulfite	2.8
Ferrous sulfate	8.8

In addition to the reducing agent, approximately 1.1 lb of hydrated lime is required to neutralize 1 lb of reduced chromic acid.

Applications to Date

Some selected examples of the application of chemical reduction to hazardous waste management problems are described here.

Reduction of Chromium (VI) to Chromium (III) in Effluents

Numerous plating and metal finishing plants treat their chromium (VI) waste using chemical reduction methods. Cyanides and chromium are often present together in plating industry wastes [12]. The concentrations of these substances and their potential recovery value influence the selec-

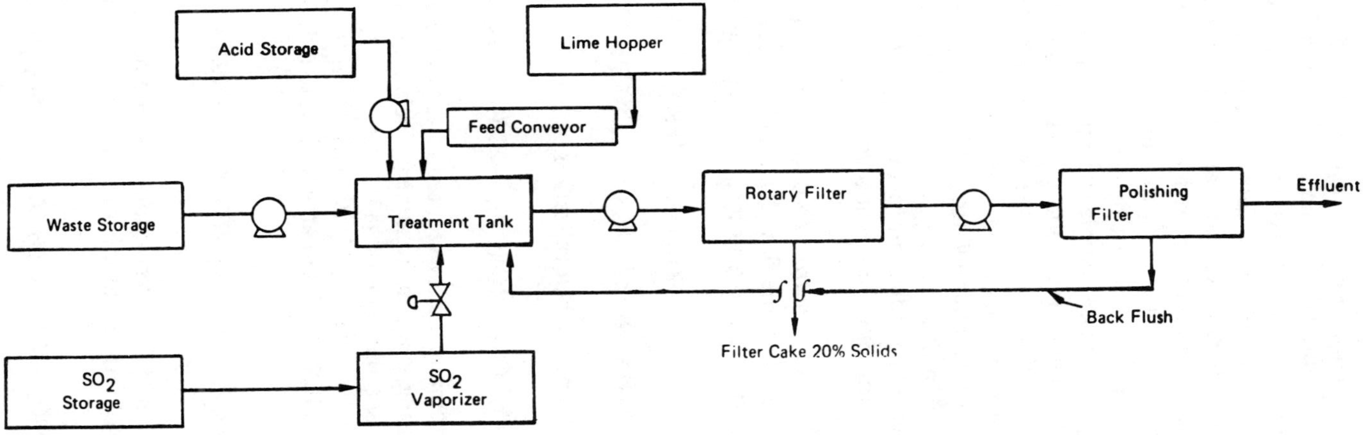

Figure 10-3. Typical process flowsheet for chemical reduction (Source: NTIS-PB 275 287).

tion of the treatment process. If the cyanide and chromium are not economically recoverable by a method such as ion exchange, the cyanide radical is first destroyed or converted to the less toxic cyanate by oxidation and the chromium (VI) is converted, by subsequent reduction, to chromium (III), which precipitates and is removed as a sludge.

Hexavalent chromium can be reduced to chromium (III) by a variety of reducing agents including sulfur dioxide, sulfite salts and ferrous sulfate. In industry the most widely used reducing agent for this purpose is sulfur dioxide. Because soluble chromium (III) compounds are themselves toxic, chromium reduction processes usually are followed by a precipitation operation in which the chromium (III) is precipitated as Cr $(OH)_3$ with either lime or sodium carbonate. In the tanning and plating industries, sludges containing from 10 to 80% solids obtained from prior concentration of chromates are often redissolved by acidification and then subjected to reduction followed by precipitation to obtain the chromium in an insoluble, concentrated form.

1. *Reduction Using Sulfur Dioxide.* Figure 10.3 in the preceding section presents a schematic flow diagram for chromium waste treatment using sulfur dioxide. The reaction equations are as follows:

$$SO_2 + H_2 \rightarrow H_2SO_3$$

$$2H_2CrO_4 + 3H_2SO_3 \rightarrow Cr_2(SO_4)_3 + 5H_2O$$

Using hydrated lime the neutralization is:

$$Cr_2(SO_4)_3 + 3Ca(OH)_2 \rightarrow 2Cr(OH)_3 + 3CaSO_4$$

Hexavalent chromium can be reduced to the range of 0.7–1 mg/l in the effluent by using such a treatment including reduction, chemical precipitation and sedimentation [13].

2. *Reduction with Sodium Metabisulfite (and Bisulfite):* About 3 lb of sodium metabisulfite ($Na_2S_2O_2$) are required to reduce 1 lb of hexavalent chromium.

$$4H_2CrO_4 + 3Na_2S_2O_5 + 3H_2O + 6H_2SO_4 \rightarrow 2Cr_2(SO_4)_3 + 6NaHSO_4 + 10H_2O$$

3. *Reduction with Ferrous Sulfate.* Because of the sludge volume produced, this use of ferrous sulfate is rare in large-scale treatment facilities.

$$2H_2CrO_4 + 6FeSO_4 + 7H_2O + 6H_2SO_4 \rightarrow Cr_2(SO_4)_3 + 3Fe_2(SO_4)_3 + 50\ H_2O$$

Removal of Mercury from Effluents

Reduction/precipitation processes are being used increasingly to treat wastewater containing mercury when the flow rate is relatively small and intermittent. Because of its value, and because it is not amenable to disposal, the elemental mercury produced by reduction processes is usually recovered and recycled. Depending on the process, a cyclone, filter or perhaps a furnace and mercury condenser may be used.

In a reduction/precipitation process which has been commercialized, a caustic solution of sodium borohydride ($NaBH_4$) is mixed with mercury-containing wastewater. The ionic mercury is reduced to metallic mercury which precipitates out of solution. The following reaction occurs:

$$4Hg^{2+} + BH_4^- + 8OH^- \rightarrow 4Hg + B(OH)_4^- + 4H_2O$$

In theory, 1 lb of sodium borohydride can reduce 21 lb of mercury. In actual operation this is closer to 10 lb of mercury. If the mercury solution is in the form of an organic complex, the driving force of the reduction reaction may not be sufficient to break the complex. In that case, the wastewater must be chlorinated prior to the reduction step in order to break down the metal-organic bond. This reduction process compares favorably with the sulfide precipitation treatment for mercury removal. It does not produce a large volume of waste residue. The efficiency is slightly lower in lab scale tests, however, and the $NaBH_4$ is more costly [14]. Ventron Corporation holds patents for the use of sodium borohydride for heavy metal removal [8,9,15,16]. Commercial-scale facilities are listed in the references.

Using other metals to reduce mercury ions merely trades one problem for another. Zinc reduction of mercury, for instance, is accompanied by the presence of zinc ions in the effluent stream; however, the zinc compounds are usually found to be less toxic than mercury compounds.

Figure 10-4 describes the process steps required for mercury removal.

Removal of Lead

1. *From Effluents.* Removal of dissolved lead compounds, including organo-lead salts, in wastewater from the manufacture of tetra-alkyl-lead compounds is now being done on a commercial scale. The reduction process, using an alkali metal hydride as reductant, lowers the lead content in the waste stream by altering the chemical form of the lead so that it can be precipitated. The reaction is believed to go partially to elemental lead and partially to an alkyl-lead compound that is not stable over long

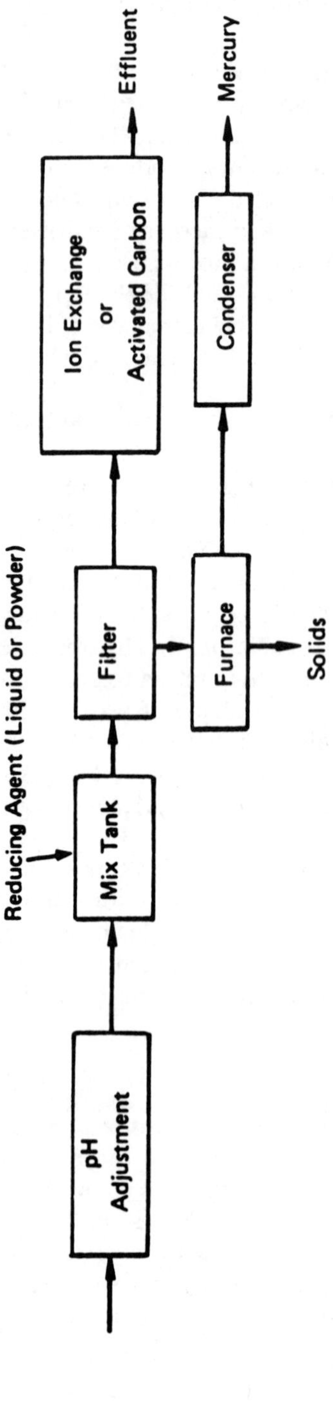

Figure 10-4. Mercury removal using chemical reduction (Source: NTIS-PB 275 287).

periods of time [15] and some of which is eventually converted spontaneously to elemental lead. As the element, the lead precipitates and can be removed by settling or filtration.

The concentration range in the effluents to be treated by the reduction process are 2–300 ppm. The lead is mostly in the form of soluble organo-lead compounds which will not precipitate with pH adjustment alone, with some other lead in the form of soluble inorganic lead compounds.

After treatment with an alkali metal hydride (sodium borohydride is preferred in this reaction [15]) insoluble lead products are formed. They include hexa-alkyl-di-lead compounds (which may with time decompose to elemental lead), which are formed from the soluble alkyl-lead compounds, and elemental lead from the soluble inorganic lead components.

Low concentrations of borohydride are preferred because one of the characteristics of the material is that it hydrolyzes with evolution of hydrogen, and with an accompanying loss in its reductive properties. This is partially true at higher temperatures, pH below 8 or 9, and in the presence of certain catalysts. For this reaction, a pH of 8 to 11 is preferred.

The following table gives information developed in laboratory experiments [15].

Reaction Time (hr)	Lead Concentration (ppm)	
	Sample A	Sample B
0	8.2	8.2
1	5.8	5.2
2	5.1	4.6
4	3.2	2.6
16	2.4	0.45

(Note: Sample A contained 1.0 ppm of sodium borohydride ($NaBH_4$) as the reducing agent. Sample B contained 2.5 ppm $NaBH_4$.)

2. *From Waste Oil.* An oil recovery firm has tested the use of a metal hydride for the removal of heavy metals, including lead from waste oil, by reduction. The product had an odor, probably caused by the production of esters. This was part of a study for the EPA (Contract No. 68–01–0177).

Removal of Silver from Effluents

Alkali metal hydride ($NaBH_4$) is being used to recover silver from photographic waste effluents.

Removal of Other Metals

Applications are being investigated for the use of sodium borohydride for the removal of trace quantities of other metals from waste streams as either the reduced ion or the element.

Treatment of Inorganic Anions

While not used for waste treatment, the use of $NaBH_4$ for reduction of chlorates (OCl^-) and iodates (IO_3^-) has been studied for analytical purposes.

HYDROLYSIS

Hydrolysis as a chemical process has been used since the earliest days of soapmaking. The addition of alkali to hydrolyze heated fats in the production of soap is still practiced today. Processes involving hydrolysis are common in industry, although frequently they are called by different names (for example, the hydrolysis of fats mentioned above is termed saponification). Hydrolytic processes have commercial manufacturing applications in such diverse industries as food, paper and petrochemicals.

Inorganic hydrolytic reactions in which a salt reacts with water to form acid and base are usually the reverse of neutralization. The trivalent metal salts of aluminum and iron undergo a different mechanism of hydrolysis; during a series of reactions with water, various multivalent hydrous oxides are formed [17]. These charged species are important in floc formation and in the treatment, by coagulation, of turbid waters.

Although water by itself can bring about hydrolysis, most commercial processes employ elevated temperatures and pressures to promote reaction. Acids, alkalies and enzymes are commonly used as catalysts, although an alkali also can participate frequently as a stoichiometric reactant. Hydrolytic reactions may be broken down into five classes, [17] (see Figure 10-5):

1. pure hydrolysis with water alone;
2. hydrolysis with aqueous acid, dilute or concentrated;
3. hydrolysis with aqueous alkali, dilute or concentrated;
4. alkali fusion, with little or no free water, but at high temperatures—the reaction is the same as class 3, with a decreased ratio; and
5. hydrolysis with enzymes as catalysts. For example, in the biological degradation of carbohydrates, fats and proteins, hydrolysis by

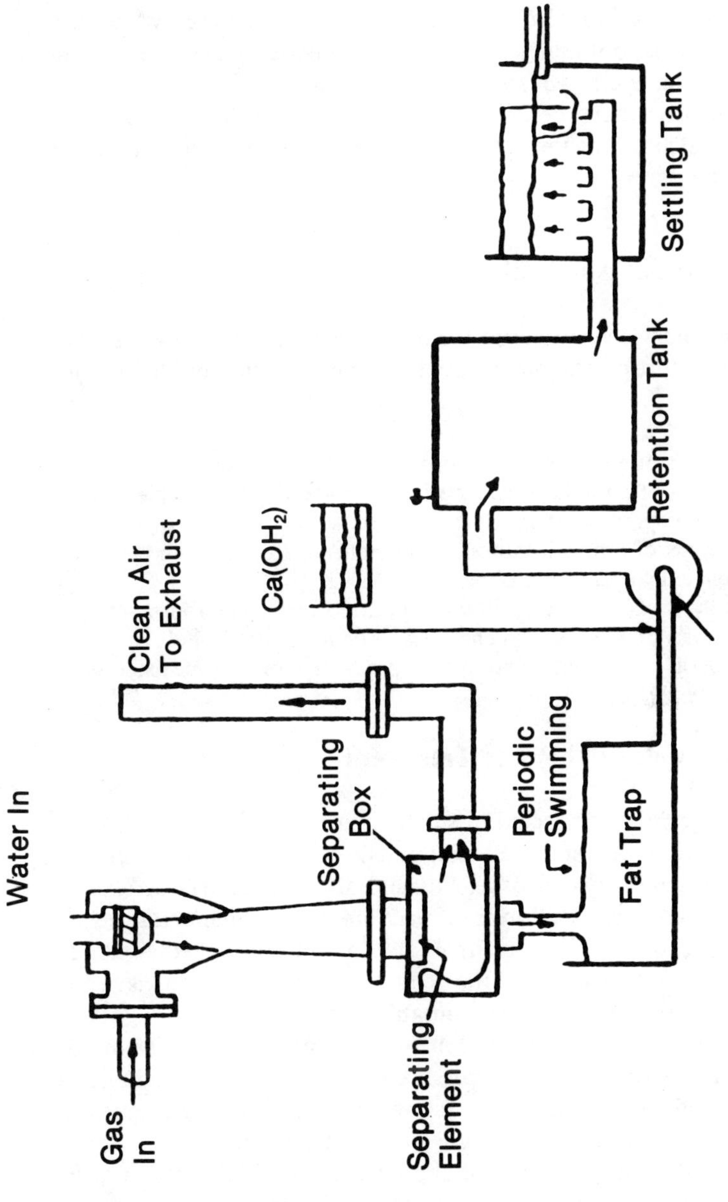

Figure 10-5. Hydrolysis of fats (Source: NTIS-PB 275 287).

enzymes is often the first step to degrade these compounds to a size which can pass the cell membrane of bacteria [18].

The agents for acid hydrolysis most commonly used are hydrochloric and sulfuric acids, but many others are of potential use (formic, oxalic, benzenesulfonic, etc.). Alkaline hydrolysis utilizes sodium hydroxide most frequently, but the alkali carbonates as well as appropriate potassium, calcium, magnesium and ammonium compounds could find applications.

Principal Current Applications

Hydrolysis has been employed for many years, and finds extensive use in the manufacture of organic materials. Some general examples of applications are:

1. hydrolysis of ethers: ethylene oxide from ethylene glycol,
2. hydrolysis of carbonates: conversion of wood cellulose to edible sugars and decomposition of starch to dextrose,
3. hydrolysis of aromatic sulfonic acids: phenol from sodium benzene sulfonate by alkali fusion,
4. hydrolysis of aliphatic halides: amyl alcohols from chloropentanes,
5. hydrolysis of amyl or allyl chlorides: production of alcohols and
6. hydrolysis of ethylene chlorohydrin: production of ethylene oxide and ethylene glycol.

Outlook for Industrial Waste Treatment

Hydrolysis can be conducted in simple equipment (in batches in open tanks) or in more complicated equipment (continuous flow in large towers). The handling of strong acids and alkalies requires care, but is not of undue concern. Performing reactions at high temperatures and pressures necessitates close control and monitoring of the process. However, the equipment and knowledge for such operations is readily available and presents no insurmountable difficulty.

As treatment process for hazardous wastes, hydrolysis can be applied to a wide variety of physical forms. It can be adapted to handle liquid, gaseous or solid materials. With few exceptions, hydrolysis does not appear to be promising for disposal of inorganic materials. Its importance is in handling a wide range of aliphatic and aromatic organics, such as esters, ethers, carbohydrates, sulfonic acids, halogen compounds, phosphates and nitriles.

The capital costs vary considerably, depending on the equipment. Operating costs also vary as a result of the required severity of operating conditions. Higher temperatures/pressures lead to increased energy costs for heat by electricity and/or steam. Raw material costs usually are small.

A potential disadvantage of hydrolysis is the possibility of undesirable reaction products. Each case must be examined in detail as to economics and acceptability of the products which result. It frequently will be necessary to conduct a preliminary laboratory-scale investigation of the reaction, to determine the appropriate temperature, pressure, reaction time, hydrolyzing agent and concentration. The possibility of side reactions and the toxicity of any suspect products also should be studied.

LIQUID-LIQUID SOLVENT EXTRACTION

Liquid-liquid solvent extraction, hereinafter referred to simply as solvent extraction, is the separation of the constituents of a liquid solution by contact with another immiscible liquid. If the substances comprising the original solution distribute themselves differently between the two liquid phases, a certain degree of separation will result and this may be enhanced by use of multiple contacts.

This process description deals only with the extraction of relatively unionized species where the primary forces of attraction between the solute and the solvent are not ionic.

Solvent extraction generally is applicable to the removal of certain organic chemicals, primarily from water or, much less commonly, from other solvents (see Figure 10-6).

Principal Current Applications

Solvent extraction is in limited use both in commercial processing and in waste treatment applications.

Commercial Process Applications [6,18]

Commercial process applications of solvent extraction include:

1. manufacture of lubricating oil from crude oil; saturated paraffins are extracted in a dewaxing operation with such solvents as phenol, furfural, propane, nitrobenzene, benzene and cresylic acids;

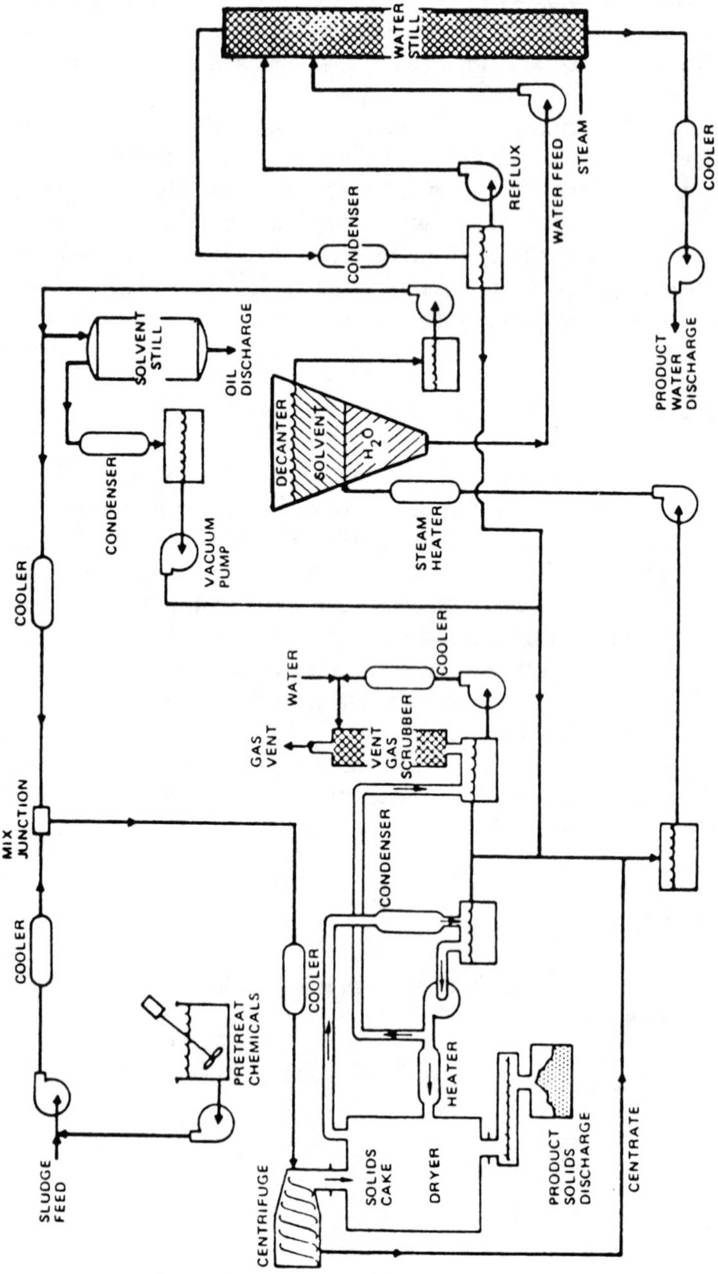

Figure 10-6. B.E.S.T. process for solvent extracting water and oil from sludges (Source: NTIS-PB 275 287).

2. upgrading of gasoline, which involves the separation of aromatics from low-octane paraffins; diethylene glycol may be used as the solvent;
3. extraction of sulfur compounds from gasoline; the solvent can be an aqueous sodium hydroxide solution, a methanol-water mixture, or others;
4. recovery of valuable products (from waste streams) and purification of recycle solvents in the plastics industry;
5. refining vegetable oils and fats;
6. manufacture of fine chemicals and pharmaceuticals;
7. dehydration of acetic acid; and
8. acetic acid recovery by neutral sulfite semichemical pulping plants and cellulose acetate plants; ketones, ethers and esters have been used as the extracting solvents.

Waste Treatment Applications

Solvent extraction should be regarded as a process for treating concentrated, selected and segregated waste streams primarily where material recovery is possible to offset process costs. Solvent extraction on concentrated waste streams seldom produces a treated effluent (raffinate) that can be directly discharged to surface waters; some form of final polishing usually is needed. Solvent extraction cannot compare economically with biological oxidation or adsorption in the treatment of large quantities of very dilute wastes, and it would have trouble competing with stream stripping for the recovery of volatile solutes present in moderate to low concentrations.

Nevertheless, solvent extraction is a proven method for the recovery of organics from liquid solutions and the process of choice in some cases. Table 10-5 summarizes areas of actual and potential applicability (see Figure 10.7).

Outlook for Industrial Waste Treatment

There are relatively few insurmountable technical problems with solvent extraction. The most difficult problem is finding a solvent that best meets a long list of desired qualities including low cost, high extraction efficiency, low solubility in the raffinate, easy separation from the solute and adequate density difference with raffinate that has no tendency for emulsion formation, and that is nonreactive and nonhazardous. No one solvent will meet all the desired criteria, and compromise is necessary. A wide range of extraction equipment is available today, and space requirements are not a problem.

Table 10-5. Areas of Actual and Potential Applicability of Solvent Extraction for Organics Removal and Recovery[a]

Physical Form	Solute Recovered
Wastes that have been treated	
Aqueous Solution[b]	Phenol Acetic acid Salicylic and other hydroxy aromatic acids Petroleum oils
Organic Solution[b]	Methylene chloride from isopropyl alcohol Freon from oil and alcohol (or acetone) Mixed chlorinated hydrocarbons from alcohol or acetone
Wastes that might be treated	
Aqueous Solutions[b] (containing one or just a few solutes)	Any valuable organic solute present in moderate to high concentration. Candidates might include phenols, acids, alcohols, amines, glycols, tetrahydrofuran, dimethyl-formamide and others.
Organic Solutions[b] (containing a mixture of water soluble and non-water-soluble components)	Will often be able to recover both water-soluble and non-water-soluble components. Water-soluble components include low molecular weight alcohols, ketones, amines, ethers, phenols, etc. Non-water-soluble components include simple hydrocarbons, halogenated hydrocarbons, oils, and other *high* molecular weight organics which may contain a hydrophylic functional group.

[a]Source: NTIS-PB 275 287.
[b]Some degree of emulsification and suspended solids may be tolerated.

Process costs are always a determining factor with solvent extraction, and they have thus far limited actual applications to situations where a valuable product is removed in sufficient quantity to offset extraction costs. These costs are relatively small when a single-stage extraction unit can be used (e.g., a simple mixer-settler) and where solvent and solute recovery can be carried out efficiently. In certain cases, the process may yield a profit when credit for recovered material is taken. Any extraction requiring more than the equivalent of about ten theoretical stages may require custom-designed equipment and thus will be quite expensive.

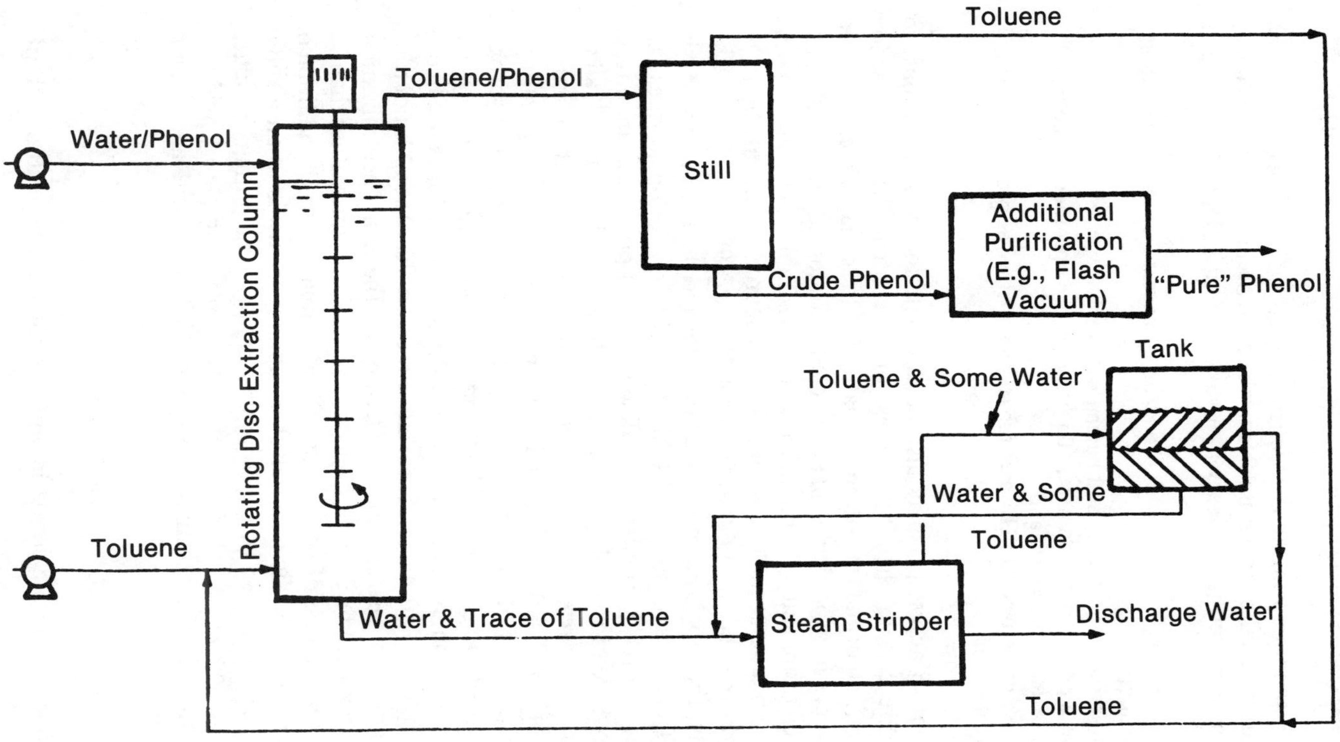

Figure 10-7. Example of liquid–liquid solvent extraction of organics: removal of phenol from water with toluene (Source: NTIS-PB 275 287).

NEUTRALIZATION

Many manufacturing and processing operations produce effluents that are acidic or alkaline in nature. Neutralization of an excessively acidic or basic waste stream is necessary in a variety of situations, for example:

1. to prevent metal corrosion and/or damage to other construction materials;
2. to protect aquatic life and human welfare;
3. as a preliminary treatment, allowing effective operation of biological treatment processes; and
4. to provide neutral pH water for recycling either as process water or boiler feed.

Treatment to adjust pH may also be desirable to break emulsions, to insolubilize certain chemical species, or to control chemical reaction rates, e.g., chlorination. Although natural waters may differ widely in pH, changes in a particular pH level could produce detrimental effects on the environment. To minimize any undesirable consequences, the effluent limitations guidelines for industrial sources set the pH limits for most industries between 6.0 and 9.0 for 1977 to 1983.

Simply, the process of neutralization is the interaction of an acid with a base. The typical properties exhibited by acids in solution are due to the hydrogen ion $[H^+]$. Similarly, alkaline (or basic) properties are a result of the hydroxyl ion $[OH^-]$. In aqueous solutions, acidity and alkalinity are defined with respect to pH, where $pH = -\log [H^+]$ and, at ambient temperature, $pH = 14 + \log [OH^-]$. In the strict sense, neutralization is the adjustment of pH to 7, at which level the concentrations of hydrogen and hydroxyl ions are equal. Solutions with excess hydroxyl ion concentration (ph $>$ 7) are said to be basic; solutions with excess hydrogen ions (ph $<$ 7) are acidic. Since adjustment of the pH to 7 is not often practical or even desirable in waste treatment, the term "neutralization" is sometimes used to describe adjustment of pH to values other than 7.

The actual process of neutralization is accomplished by the addition of an alkaline to an acidic material or by adding an acidic to an alkaline material, as determined by the required final pH. The primary products of the reaction are a salt and water. A simple example of acid-base neutralization is the reaction between hydrochloric acid and sodium hydroxide:

$$HCl + NaOH \rightarrow H_2O + NaCl$$

The product, sodium chloride in aqueous solution, is neutral with pH =7.0.

Operating Characteristics

Neutralization finds its widest application in the treatment of aqueous wastes containing strong acids such as sulfuric and hydrochloric, or bases such as caustic soda and ammonium hydroxide. However, the process can be used with nonaqueous materials (for example, acidic phenols, which are insoluble in water). Although neutralization is a liquid-phase phenomenon, it also can treat both gaseous and solid waste streams. Gases can be handled by absorption in a suitable liquid phase, as in the case of alkali scrubbing of acid vapors. Slurries can be neutralized, with due consideration for the nature of the suspended solid and its dissolution properties. Sludges are also amenable to pH adjustment, but the viscosity of the material complicates the process of physical mixing and contact between acid and alkali which is essential to the treatment. In principle, even tars can be neutralized, although the problems of reagent mixing and contact are usually severe, making the process impractical in most instances. Solids and powders that are acidic or basic salts also could be neutralized if dissolved.

Neutralization can be used to treat both inorganic and organic waste streams that are either excessively acidic or alkaline. A neutralization process often used to precipitate heavy metal ions, e.g., Zn^{++}, Pb^{++}, Hg^{++} or Cu^{++}, involves addition of an alkali (usually lime) to a waste stream. Organic compounds which can be treated include carboxylic acids, sulfonic acids, phenols and many other materials.

The basic principle behind neutralization is simple—the mixing of an acid with an alkali. Neutralization may be carried out in tanks, ponds, absorber columns or in a variety of other types of reaction equipment either in batch or continuous-flow operations, depending in part on the volume and rate of flow. Although many different chemicals can be neutralized, certain principles are common to most systems.

The addition of the neutralizing agent is monitored and adjusted by pH measurement and control. In batch treatment an operator can take samples, measure the pH, and add the required dose of acid or alkali. In a continuous flow system, automatic pH monitors check the acidity or alkalinity and control the feeding of neutralizing agent. The number of neutralization units and the location of pH sensors are determined by the stability of the waste stream pH. Where pH levels vary widely, several reaction units plus additional monitoring equipment may be required. A stream with large fluctuations in pH might also be preceded by an equalization basin which would yield a more homogeneous effluent with a narrower pH range for treatment.

The selection of a neutralizing agent is dictated by a number of factors such as economics, availability and process compatibility. Commonly, the choice of an acid for neutralizing alkaline wastes is between sulfuric and hydrochloric acids [17]. Because of its lower cost, sulfuric acid is usually preferred, but it does entail the possiblity of forming relatively insoluble salts (e.g., calcium sulfate) with the attendant problems of scaling and solids handling. The products of neutralization with hydrochloric acid are usually soluble (as are the salts of nitric acid). However, there are legal discharge limits on soluble species which may be added by neutralization.

The choice of alkali for neutralization of an acid is generally between reagents containing sodium, calcium or magnesium. In the selection of an alkali, an important element is the "basicity factor" which is the number of grams of calcium oxide equivalent in neutralization capacity of a particular alkali [17]. Solid sodium hydroxide (76% Na_2O) has a basicity factor of 0.687; thus, it is somewhat less effective (on a weight basis) than calcium oxide with respect to neutralization. However, caustic soda has the advantage of being very soluble, thus allowing the use of concentrated solutions. In addition, the product salts of neutralization are also highly soluble, precluding any solids problems.

The disadvantage of caustic soda is the relatively high raw material cost. The lime/limestone reagents, such as high-calcium hydrate, $Ca(OH)_2$, high-calcium quicklime, CaO, and high-calcium limestone, $CaCO_3$, have basicity factors of 0.710, 0.941 and 0.489, respectively; they are less expensive than sodium hydroxide but because of their low solubility often require increased capital investment. These solids are usually fed as slurries on the order of 15% solids. In the presence of sulfuric acid, insoluble calcium sulfate is formed, and the accompanying problems of sludge and scale occur. It should be noted that limestone is the least effective neutralizing agent (on a weight basis) described thus far. Sodium carbonate (soda ash) also has only a moderate basicity factor of 0.507, but it is much more soluble—as are the products.

The use of magnesium in the oxide or carbonate form as a reagent can be beneficial in many instances. In particular, the neutralization of sulfuric acid by a magnesium-based alkali produces a soluble magnesium sulfate (as opposed to the insoluble calcium salt). Magnesium oxide is more effective as a neutralizing agent than calcium oxide (on a weight basis), as is dolomitic quicklime, $CaO \cdot MgO$ (basicity factor of 1.110). Also, dolomitic limestone, $CaCO_3 \cdot MgCO_3$, is an improvement (basicity factor of 0.564) over calcium limestone.

In some cases, it may be feasible to use a plant's acid or alkaline waste stream as a neutralizing agent for other effluents. Economically, such reuse of waste materials as acid or alkali reagents is usually superior to other alternatives. In industries producing both acid and basic wastes, as in plating installations, pH is adjusted by proper mixing of streams. Carbon dioxide from flue gas is also used in pH treatment simply by bubbling the gas through an alkaline waste stream. Acetylene sludge (an impure lime formed in the manufacture of acetylene) is used as an inexpensive alkali to treat acid wastes, e.g., pickle liquor from a steel mill [19].

The neutralization process is subject to the influence of temperature and the resulting heat effects common to most chemical reactions. Generally, in water-based reactions, increasing the temperature of the reactants increases the rate of reaction. In neutralization, the interaction of acid and alkali is frequently exothermic (evolves heat), with an accompanying rise in temperature. An average value for the heat released during the neutralization of dilute solutions of strong acids and bases is 13,360 cal/g mole of water formed. Controlling the rate of addition of the neutralizing reagent may dissipate the heat produced and minimize the temperature increase. For each reaction, the final temperature depends on: the initial reactant temperatures, the chemical species participating in the reaction (and their heats of solution and reaction), the concentrations of the reactants and the relative quantities of the reactants. In general, concentrated solutions can produce large temperature increases as the relative quantities of the reactants approach stoichiometric proportions. This can result in boiling and splashing of the solution and accelerated chemical attack on materials. In most cases, proper planning of the neutralization scheme with respect to concentration of neutralizing agent, rate of addition, reaction time and equipment design can alleviate the heating problem.

The products of neutralization can be liquid, solid, gaseous or a combination. A product's physical form is not related to the form of the reactants, but to its own chemical composition and that of its environment. The chemical species present in the neutralized stream may include the original components of the waste stream, in addition to material from the neutralizing agent. The concentrations of the individual species depend on the solubility of the products formed during reaction. For example, neutralizing hydrochloric acid with lime yields dissolved calcium chloride as a product remaining in the stream; however, neutralizing sulfuric acid with lime produces solid calcium sulfate as a slurry or sludge, which removes most of the calcium and sulfate from solution. In the case where a solid product is present, further treatment to separate the material is necessary. Gaseous products can be toxic, as in the case of hydrogen sulfide gas formed during the acid neutralization of a basic stream containing sulfide salts. Provision must be made for the containment and disposal of hazardous vapors if their formation cannot be avoided.

Equipment and Materials

The equipment required may be as varied as the reactions that can be classified as neutralizations. A few examples will indicate the range of possibilites: absorption towers to neutralize acid flue gas with aqueous alkali (venturi scrubbers), filter beds of limestone granules [18] to neutralize certain acidic liquid wastes, and aeration systems to introduce carbon dioxide into alkaline streams. But the most commonly occurring scheme for neutralization is the addition of a chemical, in either liquid or solid form, directly into the wastewater stream. The required equipment for this form of treatment is simple, i.e., storage and reaction tanks with accessory agitators, and delivery systems. The tanks may be of any shape but must be properly baffled to allow adequate mixing and prevent "short-circuiting". Frequently the neutralization is carried out in a series of reactors to provide better control of the final pH. Such a system with three units is shown in Figure 10-8 [20]. There are two addition points for neutralizing agent, controlled by pH monitors. Most of the neutralization occurs in the first reactor with adjustment to the final desired pH taking place just before discharge. In large-scale operations the tanks are often built below ground level, of lined concrete.

Appropriate instrumentation must be provided and include pH measurement (and possibly recording) devices with appropriate sample pumps. The feed of neutralizing agent may be regulated automatically by the pH monitoring unit, depending on the requirements of the individual system. There are two common modes of control: feedback and the more sophisticated feedforward [20]. The feedback mode allows a measurable error before instituting control. When the error is detected, it alters its output until the measured pH and the set point value agree. This can result in undesirable oscillations in the pH of the neutralized mixture. By monitoring the influent stream (by pH measurement or titration), a feedforward controller can take action before deviations in the effluent pH occur, thus preventing excessive fluctuations.

The design of storage facilities depends on the chemical reagents employed in the treatment process [17]. Caustic solutions and acids may be stored in the open, but quicklime should be kept in waterproof silos, hoppers or even bags. Delivery systems depend on the physical form of the reagents. Liquids may be transferred with pumps, and slurries can be moved through gravity piping, pumps or open flumes. Ancillary equipment might include installations such as equalization basins, clarifiers or vapor removal systems, depending on the specific neutralization scheme.

In dealing with acids and alkalies, corrosion-resistant construction materials are required to provide reasonable service-life for equipment.

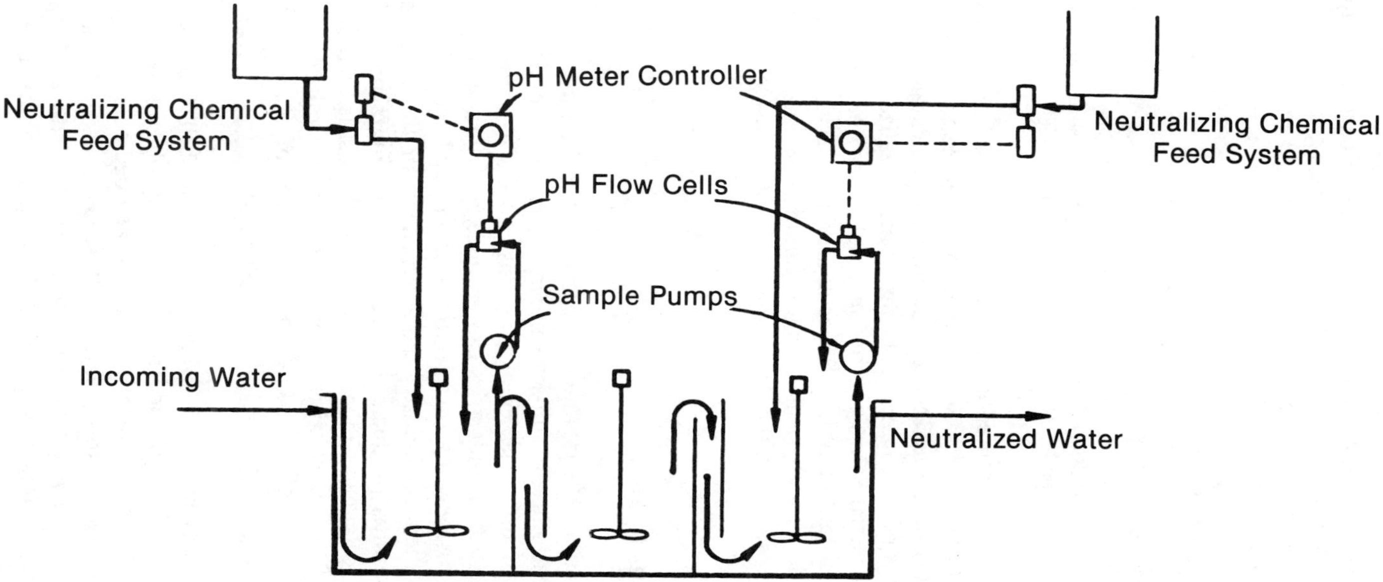

Figure 10-8. Continuous flow neutralization (Source: NTIS-PB 275 287).

In many cases, the specific concentration of a reagent is important in selecting the correct material used in pumps, pipes, tanks, etc. Examples of materials recommended for handling different acids and alkalies at ambient temperature are [20]:

- Sulfuric acid (75–95%): lead
  (<10%): lead or rubber
- Hydrochloric acid (concentrated or dilute): rubber
- Sodium hydroxide (concentrated): 316 SS or rubber
  (dilute): 316 SS, rubber, carbon steel or cast iron
- Calcium hydroxide: 316 SS, rubber, or carbon steel.

Other less commonly used materials include: glass, metal alloys such as monel, plastics (e.g., PVC) and even wood. The expense of such materials frequently precludes their use except on a small scale or in situations where there is no alternative. It is important to realize that a vessel need not be constructed entirely of one material; it may be merely lined with corrosion-resistant materials. Expected length of service, temperature of operation, desired physical strength, liquid flow rate and mechanical abrasion are some of the other factors to be considered in material selection.

Applications to Date

Neutralization is a treatment process of demonstrated technical and economic feasibility, in full-scale use in a wide spectrum of industries. A sample list of industries employing this process is presented in Table 10-6. As illustrated, industries can produce a wide range of pH in their wastewaters, depending on specific products and manufacturing processes. The chemical industry alone accounts for the creation of such diverse wastewater products as those from the manufacture of TNT (pH = 2.6) and reclaimed rubber (pH = 11.5). The list is therefore only an indication of the many existing applications of neutralization.

Examples of applications for pH treatment of acidic and alkaline wastes are described in the following paragraphs.

Acid Exhausts [20]. Industrial processes that utilize acids, e.g., sulfuric, nitric, or hydrochloric, frequently have problems with acid mist in the exhaust. Scrubbing with water on packed bed columns produces an acid-free gas, but the spent water must be neutralized. Alkali is usually added automatically to produce a water stream with a pH of 6.5–7.5 which can be discharged or recycled. In similar systems, flue gas desul-

Table 10-6. Industries Using Neutralization[a]

Industry	Wastewater pH Range
Pulp and Paper	Acidic and Basic
Dairy Products	Acidic and Basic
Textiles	Basic
Pharmaceuticals	Acidic and Basic
Leather Tanning and Finishing	Acidic and Basic
Petroleum Refining	Acidic and Basic
Grain Milling	Acidic and Basic
Fruits and Vegetables	Acidic and Basic
Beverages	Acidic and Basic
Plastic and Synthetic Materials	Acidic and Basic
Steel Pickling	Acidic
By-product Coke	Basic
Metal Finishing	Acidic
Organic Chemicals	Acidic and Basic
Inorganic Chemicals	Acidic and Basic
Fertilizer	Acidic and Basic
Industrial Gas Products	Acidic and Basic
Cement, Lime and Concrete Products	Basic
Electric and Steam Generation	Acidic and Basic
Nonferrous Metals—Aluminum	Acidic

[a]Source: NTIS-PB 275 287.

furization units absorb and neutralize sulfur oxides with alkalies such as lime, limestone, dolomite or caustic soda.

Petrochemical Waste Streams [21]. Neutralization is applied to: (1) washwaters, acid or alkaline, (2) spent caustics, (3) acid sludges from alkylation, sulfonation, sulfation and acid treatments and (4) spent acid catalysts. Sulfuric acid and carbon dioxide from flue gases are both used to treat spent caustic wastes. Pits filled with lime, limestone and even oyster shells (a source of calcium carbonate) are utilized to neutralize spent acid sludges.

Sulfuric Acid Pickle Liquor [6]. In small-scale operations (< 5000 gpd) neutralization of pickle liquor from steel cleaning operations can be performed in a batch, usually with quicklime. Typically, pickle liquor contains on the order of 70 g iron and 170 g sulfate/l liter (~5% sulfuric acid by weight). Large waste streams can be handled in continuous flow systems (as shown in Figure 10-9), and other suitable alkaline agents may be employed. If calcium-based materials are utilized in the neutralization, calcium sulfate will form a sludge, which is usually dewatered by vacuum filtration or placed in a lagoon. The formation of a flocculated ferrous hydroxide precipitate (at neutral pH) can produce a

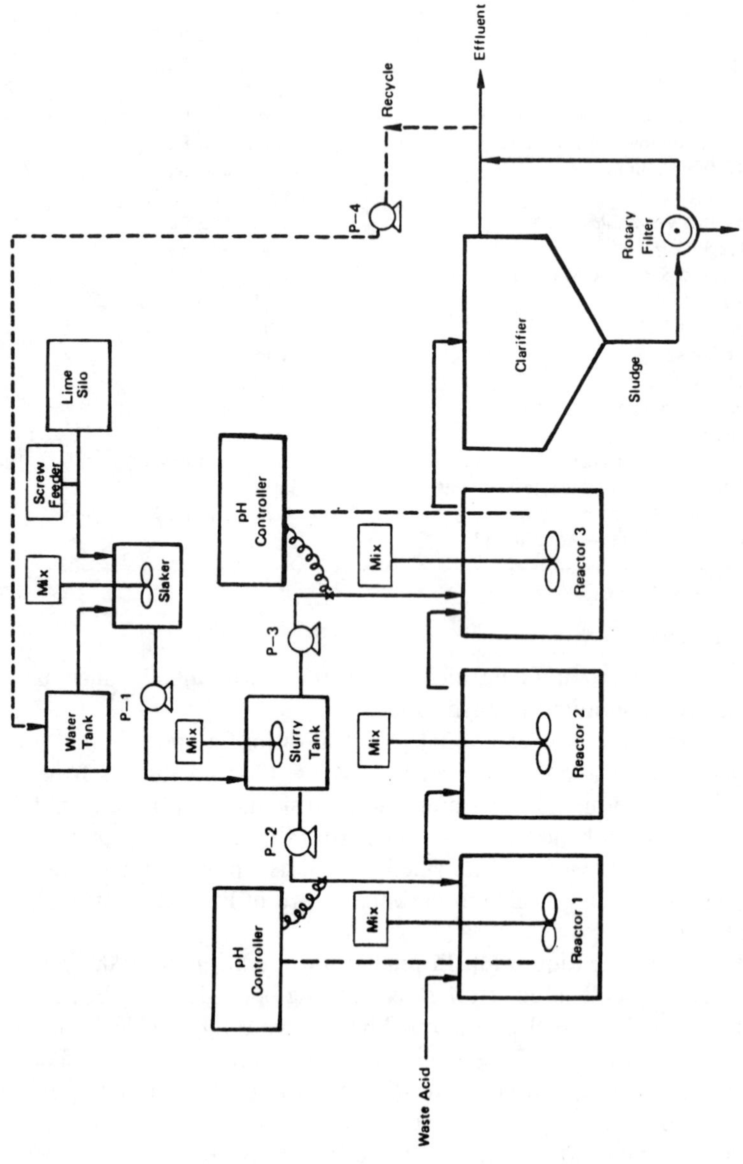

Figure 10-9. Lime neutralization of sulfuric acid waste (Source: NTIS-PB 275 287).

solid with poor settling and filtering properties. Thus an oxidation step is often employed since ferric hydroxide is very insoluble, and there is an optimum ratio of ferric to ferrous ions at which the sludge can be handled most readily.

Hydrochloric Acid Pickle Liquor [15]. Although in the past hydrochloric acid was not as widely used as sulfuric acid in steel pickling operations, today there is a trend toward conversion to HCl. Up to 1500 gpm of acid rinse waters, containing up to 0.5 g/l free hydrochloric acid and up to 0.87 g/l ferrous chloride, are treated. An aeration step is included in the process to oxidize the iron which then precipitates as ferric hydroxide. This precipitate and unreacted limestone are the only solids to be handled since the major product, calcium chloride, is quite soluble. Temperatures $>49°C$ and a 25% excess of limestone are employed to increase the system's efficiency.

Limestone Beds [6]. Upflow limestone neutralization beds are used at a resin manufacturing plant in New York to treat wastewater containing hydrochloric acid and some sulfuric acid. The unit is capable of operating at flows of up to 13.6 gpm/ft^2 with 1% hydrochloric acid. The limestone beds are 3 ft deep with a cross-sectional area of 113 ft^2. Present design would call for substantially deeper beds.

Metal Finishing Operations [6]. A plant manufacturing automobile bumpers in Ohio produces wastewater containing sulfuric, phosphoric, hydrochloric and chromic acids, as well as metal ions. Combined with alkaline wastes, the final waste stream pH is between 1.5 and 3.0 with a flow rate of about 1000 gpm. Neutralization is carried out in a series of three lead-lined reactors, each of almost 7500 gal capacity. A slurry of dolomitic lime is added to the first and third reactors, to produce an effluent with a pH of 8.0–8.5.

Plating Wastes. A large plating shop in Massachusetts presents a good example of small-scale neutralizations, both batch and continuous flow. As part of an electrolytic treatment scheme for cyanide rinse waters (about 20,000 gpd) a final pH adjustment is necessary before discharge. This neutralization occurs in a gravity sump equipped with a mixer and pH controller. Either dilute sulfuric acid or dilute caustic soda is added as required to produce a final pH of 6.5–8.5. Also, a batch neutalization is practiced on acid and spent chromate dips, and on spent alkalis and floor spills. There is no automatic pH control; the appropriate level is reached by sampling and subsequent addition of the required quantity of acid or alkali.

Acid Mine Drainage [22,23]. In many underground mines (particularly coal mines) iron pyrite (FeS_2), is oxidized in the presence of air and water to sulfuric acid and ferric sulfate. Treatment of such an acidic stream usually entails various combinations of neutralization, aeration, settling and sludge disposal. Due to the large quantities of wastewater to be treated, selection of a neutralizing reagent is of prime importance if the process is to be economically feasible. Also, one must consider the handling of large quantities of sludge which can be produced during neutralization. Different limes and limestones have been used, with varying amounts of success.

As stated earlier, many neutralizations follow the same theme, addition of a neutralizing reagent to an acidic or basic waste stream. The previous examples have described the types of materials treated and diverse schemes for carrying out the treatment. The list is not meant to be all-inclusive, but to convey the basic similarity of the methods commonly employed.

OZONATION

Ozonation consists of treatment with ozone (O_3), an extremely reactive gas. Ozone cannot be shipped or stored, and must be generated on site immediately prior to its application.

Ozone is a very powerful oxidizing agent. Organic chemists have long made use of the ability of ozone to cleave carbon-carbon bonds in synthetic and structure-determination procedures. There are abundant literature references to the mechanisms and products of ozonation of a variety of organic compounds. References to reactions of inorganic chemicals with ozone are fewer, but not scarce. These literature data can be used to make preliminary choices of industrial waste streams suitable for ozonation (see Figure 10.10).

In addition to high chemical reactivity, ozone has powerful antibacterial and antiviral properties. The disinfecting and oxidizing powers of ozone have been responsible for virtually all of the large-scale applications of ozone to date. Ozone is widely used in Europe for application, at doses of a few ppm, to millions of gallons per day of aqueous streams. This technology is therefore highly developed and can be readily adapted to treatment of selected industrial waste streams.

Ozone is a powerful oxidizing agent, as illustrated by the following redox potentials:

$$O_3 + 2H^- + 2e^- \rightarrow O_2 + H_2O \quad E_0 = 2.07\nu$$

$$MnO_4^- + 4H^+ + 3e^- \rightarrow MnO_2 + 2H_2O \quad E_0 = 1.70\nu$$

$$\tfrac{1}{2}Cl_2 + e^- \rightarrow Cl^- \quad E_0 = 1.36\nu$$

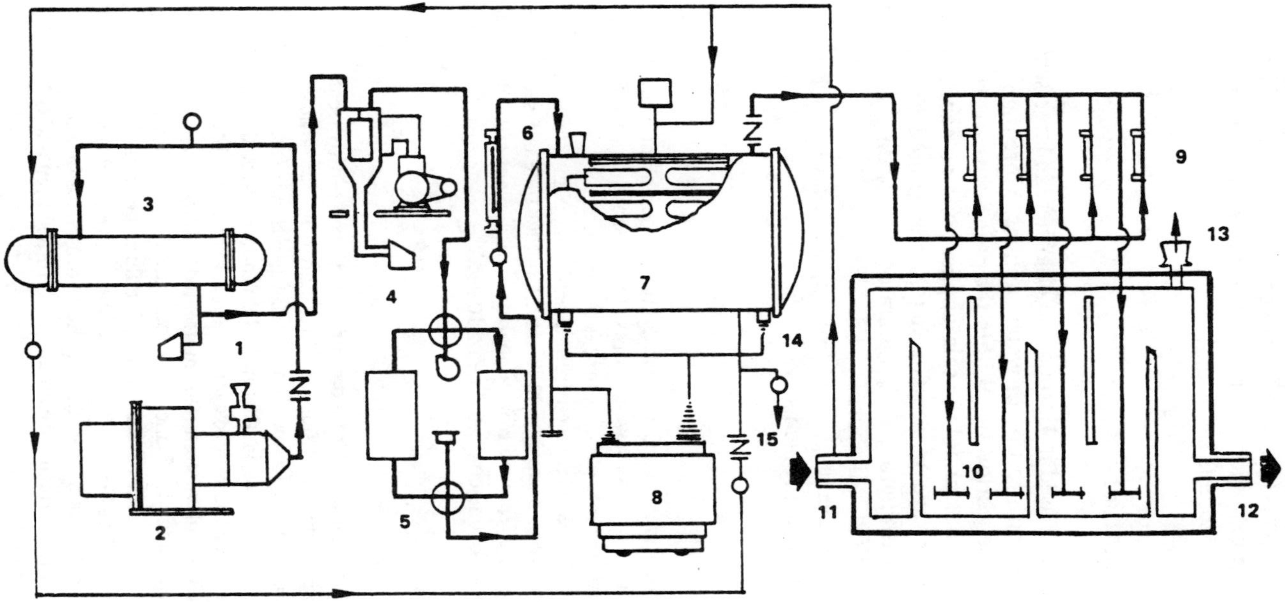

1	Air Inlet	7	Ozoniser	12	Outlet Ozonised-Air-Water Emulsification
2	Rotary Air Compressor	8	H.T. Transformer	13	Air Return to Atmosphere
3	Air Cooler	9	Ozonised-Air Measurement	14	Cooling Water Supply
4	Refrigerator	10	Porous Diffusers	15	Cooling Water Discharge
5	Air Drier	11	Inlet Ozonised-Air-Water Emulsification Tank		
6	Air Flow Measurement				

Figure 10-10. Ozonation plant schematic arrangement (Source: NTIS-PB 275 287).

It is sufficiently strong to break many carbon-carbon bonds and even to cleave aromatic ring systems (e.g. conversion of phenol to 3 molecules of oxalic acid). Complete oxidation of an organic species to CO_2, H_2O, etc., is not improbable if ozone is sufficiently high.

Principal Current Applications

Ozone treatment has been used in Europe and elsewhere in large-scale installations for years, for disinfection of water supplies. More than 500 such installations are in use worldwide. Within the past few years, there have been a number of pilot and full-scale applications of ozone to treatment of municipal sewage plant effluents in the United States, including Blue Plains, Washington, DC; Indiantown, Florida; Woodlands, Texas; and Springfield, Missouri.

The following are some selected samples of application of ozone to hazardous waste management problems.

Gaseous Effluents

1. Wet oxidation ozonation is used to treat 50,000 m^3/hr of odorous gaseous effluent from a Swiss sewage works. Ozone dosage is 10–40 mg ozone/m^3 of treated air. Contact time is 5 sec.
2. Sulfide and other odors are removed from a rendering plant effluent (25,000 cfm) at an ozone dosage of 42 lb/day. Contact time is 5 sec.
3. Fermentation odors are removed from a pharmaceutical plant effluent (80,000 cfm) with an ozone contact time of 10 sec.

Liquid Effluents: Cyanide

1. At an installation in Kansas, 350 lb/day of ozone are used to treat effluent containing cyanides, sulfides, sulfites and other hazardous components. This ozonation follows biological waste treatment.
2. At the Michelin tire factories in Clermont-Ferrand, France, 3.5 lb ozone/lb cyanide are used to reduce cyanide levels in effluent from 25 mg/l to 0 mg/l. A flow of 90 gpm is being treated.
3. At a large chemical plant in France, UV/ozonation (Houston Research) is being used to treat several hundred gallons per minute of waste containing 6 mg/l of $Fe(CN)_6^{-3}$. The effluent stream meets the standard of <0.1 mg/l total cyanide. In the process, oxidation of organics also occurs; the influent stream has TOC of 800 ppm and the effluent has a BOD of 30 ppm.
4. In the northeastern United States a small ($<10,000$ gpd) electroplating

facility uses ozonation as the primary treatment process in reducing CN-levels (60 ppm) in plating wastes to below detectable levels.

Liquid Effluents: Dyestuffs

In Japan, a combination of ozonation and activated carbon adsorption has been used to remove color, BOD and COD from 3300 m^3/day of waste dyeing water.

Liquid Effluents: Phenols

1. An ozonation process for oxidation of phenols in code oven wastes was developed for Allen Wood Steel in Conshohocken, Pennsylvania. An ozone dosage of 10 ppm reduces phenol from 10 ppb to <0.5 ppb.
2. An ozonation process for oxidation of phenols in wood products waste at Blandon F.P., Grand Rapids, Michigan. An ozone dosage of 10 ppm reduces phenol from 300 ppb to <10 ppb.
3. At the Cities Service Refinery in Bronte, Ontario, Canada, ozonation is used for final removal of phenols from biologically treated effluents. The ozone is applied to 20–40 ppm and reduces phenol from 380 to 12 ppb.

Benefits and Limitations of the Process

1. Ozonation is suitable for streams with a low concentration of oxidizable material. Such dilute streams are most difficult to treat by bulk removal processes such as solvent extraction or precipitation.
2. Technology for large-scale generation and application of ozone to aqueous and gaseous streams is well developed.
3. Ozone has been demonstrated as effective in a number of hazardous waste applications.
4. Ozonation systems are relatively capital-intensive. Operating costs are not especially high and consist of the cost of power for ozone generation.
5. Ozone treatment is likely to be cost-effective when compared to other advanced treatment processes, such as activated carbon adsorption, which are viable alternatives for similar wastes.
6. Energy requirements for ozone generation are substantial, but may be no more than those for competitive processes.
7. The pollution potential of the process will vary with the particular application, but is not excessively high.
8. Provided that excess ozone itself is not allowed to escape, ozonation produces no emissions in either the gaseous or the liquid effluent streams.

PHOTOLYSIS

Photolysis is a process in which chemical bonds are broken under the influence of light. In the primary photochemical process, the target species is converted to an electronically excited state, usually a diradical, which is sufficiently energetic to undergo chemical reaction. The fate of the excited molecule, and therefore the effectiveness of a photolysis treatment process, depends on its chemical structure and on the medium in which the reaction is carried out.

In order that a proposed photolysis process be effective in treatment of an industrial waste stream, the following criteria must be met:

1. The radiation source must be sufficiently energetic to produce electronic transitions.
2. The radiation must be absorbed by the target species.
3. The ultimate photochemical products must be less toxic than the original stream component.

Principal Current Applications

1. *Dow Chemical Company: UV-Chlorination.* Dow Chemical, with joint funding from the EPA, has developed a UV-chlorination process to remove acetic acid from 200 gpm of a brine stream. The brine is recycled to Dow's chlor-alkali process. The acetic acid is oxidized to CO_2 and CH_3Cl by a combination of Cl_2 and irradiation. High-pressure mercury arcs are immersed in quartz wells in the 12,000 gal tank, maintained at above ambient temperature. Residence time in the reactor is ~1 hr. This facility consistently achieves better than 90% acetic acid removal. Cost data show that the process is at least competitive with carbon absorption for acetic acid removal.

2. *Houston Research, Inc.: UV-Ozonolysis.* Houston Research, Inc. has developed UV-Ozonolysis treatment units for oxidation of refractory materials such as complexed cyanides, organic nitrogen compounds and acetic acid. It is claimed that the addition of UV radiation to the process enhances the reaction with ozone 10^2- to 10^4-fold. A variety of UV sources are used depending on application. Facilities capable of treating 100 gpm have been installed, with removal efficiencies of >90%. Residence times are 0.5–1 hour. Not only the particular hazardous component(s), but the total organic carbon is reduced in concentration; through control of ozone and UV levels, complete conversion to CO_2, H_2O, etc., is claimed.

ACKNOWLEDGMENT

The technical discussions in this chapter are adapted in part from a two-volume report prepared by Arthur D. Little, Inc., for the U.S. Environmental Protection Agency (PB-275 287, 1977) in which 47 unit engineering processes were evaluated for applicability to the task of treating hazardous industrial wastes.

REFERENCES

1. *Laboratory Waste Disposal Manual* (Washington DC: Manufacturing Chemists Association, 1974), p. 140.
2. Perry, R. "Mercury Recovery from Contaminated Waste Water and Sludges," U.S. EPA Report 660/2-74-086 (1974).
3. Cheremisinoff, P. N., and Y. H. Habio. "Cyanide—An Assessment of Alternatives for Water Pollution Control," *W & SW* R-95 to R-197 (1973).
4. U.S. Patent 3,617,582.
5. Spicher, R. G., and R. T. Skrinde. *J. Am. Water Works Assoc.* 57(4):472–484 (1965).
6. "Cleaner Waste," *Indian Chem. Eng.* 15(4):21 (1974).
7. Anderson, C. E. "Potassium Permanganate Control of Certain Organic Residues in Air and Wastewater," 1972 Symposium: Progress in Hazardous Chemicals Handling and Disposal, Institute of Advanced Sanitation Research International.
8. Keinath, T. M. Unpublished draft: Benzidine: Wastewater Treatment Technology, 1975.
9. "Process Design Manual for Sulfide Control in Sanitary Systems," U.S. EPA Technology Transfer (October 1974).
10. Gomaa, M. H., and S. D. Faust, "Kinetics of Chemical Oxidation of Dipyridylium Quaternary Salts," *Agric. Food Chem.* 19(2):302 (1971).
11. Ethyl Corporation. Report to Texas Water Quality Board, Houston, TX (January 1972).
12. Battelle Memorial Institute "A State-of-the-Art Review of Metal Finishing Waste Treatment" (1968).
13. *Poll. Eng.* 5(11):45–48 (1973).
14. O'Neill, F. "Facing Up to Pollution," *Plating* 57:1211–13 (1970).
15. Battelle Memorial Institute. "An Investigation of Techniques for Removal of Cyanide from Electro-Plating Wastes," (1971).
16. Diggens, A. "Instrumentation and Automatic Control of Cyanide Waste Treatment," *Poll. Eng.* (March 1976).
17. "Promising Technologies for Treatment of Hazardous Waste," U.S. EPA Report 670/2-74-088 (November 1974).
18. Arthur D. Little Inc.
19. Cali, G. V. and B. J. Galetti. "A Practical Approach to Plating Waste Control Instrumentation," *Poll. Eng.* (March 1976).
20. *Laboratory Waste Disposal Manual* (Washington, DC: Manufacturing Chemists Association, 1974), p. 143.

21. Farb, D. and S. D. Ward. "An Inventory of Hazardous Waste Management Facilities," HWMD, OSWMP, U.S. EPA (1975).
22. Druschel, E. F., J. F. Zeivers and W. Zaben. "Continuous and Batch Treatment of Industrial Wastes from the Manufacture of Electric Typewriters at IBM, Lexington, Kentucky," *Eng. Bull. Purdue Univ.* 44 (5) (September 1960).
23. Barnes, G. E. "Disposal and Recovery of Electroplating Wastes," *J. Water Poll. Control Fed.* 40(8) (August 1968).

CHAPTER 11

BIOLOGICAL TREATMENT

GENERAL CONSIDERATIONS

Basic Principles

Biological treatment processes involve placing a waste stream in contact with a mixture of microorganisms, so that the organic compounds in the waste stream are decomposed. Typically, the microorganisms used in the process are present in the influent waste stream. The process optimizes the microbial environment, so that natural degradation is enhanced. Methods for optimizing biological degradation include controlling the dissolved oxygen level, adding nutrients, increasing the concentration of microorganisms, and slowly increasing influent waste concentrations so that an acclimated microbial population develops within the process.

Biological treatment is applicable to aqueous waste streams with organic contaminants. The organics may be either solvent or solid in the influent waste stream to be amenable to biodegradation. Water is essential in the waste stream. The microorganisms rely on enzymes to catalyze organic decomposition reactions, and the enzymes require water to remain active. In aerobic biological treatment processes, both simple and complex organics can eventually be decomposed to carbon dioxide and water. Oxygen is essential to the decomposition of long-chain and aromatic hydrocarbons. In anaerobic biological treatment processes, only simple organics such as carbohydrates, proteins, alcohols and acids can be decomposed.

Biological treatment processes usually do not alter or detroy inorganics. In fact, concentrations of soluble inorganics should be kept low so that enzymatic activity is not inhibited. Trace concentrations of inorganics may be partially removed from the liquid waste stream during the biological treatment, because of adsorption onto the microbial cell coating. Typically, microorganisms have a net negative charge and therefore are able to perform cation exchange with metal ions in solution. Anionic species, such as chlorides and sulfates, are not affected by biological treatment.

Microorganisms are known for two biochemical processes involving energy transfer, and together they describe metabolism: assimilation (anabolism) and dissimilation (catabolism). In assimilation, organisms synthesize organic compounds from CO_2, water and other components. The process is endothermic, and primarily involves reduction. Dissimilation, on the other hand, is exothermic and primarily involves oxidation and hydrolysis. During dissimilation, organisms decompose organic compounds to CO_2 and water, or partially decompose organics to lower molecular weight organics, i.e., alcohols to aldehydes or acids.

The organisms which perform assimilation are autotrophic, while those which perform dissimilation are heterotrophic. Autotrophic organisms may assimilate photosynthetically using sunlight for their energy source, or chemosynthetically using the energy from chemical reactions wherein inorganic elements are oxidized. Heterotrophic organisms obtain their energy from the decomposition of organics.

For the most part, the biological systems prevalent in waste treatment are heterotrophic. They may coexist with other types of organisms and partially depend upon them. In the instance of waste stabilization ponds, the heterotrophic organisms obtain some of their oxygen from algae as the algae photosynthesizes organics and releases oxygen. Nitrifying bacteria, which are present in activated sludge systems, are autotrophic and able to chemosynthesize nitrate from ammonia.

Heterotrophic organisms may be either aerobes, obligate anaerobes or facultative anaerobes. Aerobes require molecular oxygen for their respiration and synthesis; obligate anaerobes require the complete absence of oxygen, while facultative anaerobes obtain their energy for growth either in the presence or absence of oxygen. Aerobic synthesis proceeds faster than anaerobic synthesis and has a higher growth yield of cells resulting in more biomass sludge residual.

All of the biological systems require carbon as a food source. Some organisms are able to utilize a wide range of organic substances as their primary food source, while others are more specific. All microorganisms require certain ratios of nutrients. The essential macronutrients are nitrogen, phosphorus, sulfur, potassium, calcium and magnesium. These are so-called macroelements because of the quantity in which they are required. Micronutrients are just as essential as the macronutrients, but they are needed only in trace amounts. Micronutrients essential for growth include, for example, iron, boron, copper, manganese, zinc, chromium and cobalt.

Water is the medium of life for microorganisms. The organisms synthesize water-soluble organics. Water is also an indispensable factor of plant life in temperature control, as nutrient solvent and in maintenance of correct pH values, control of osmotic pressure, hydrolysis reaction, oxidation reactions and transport of ions and compounds.

Energy Requirements

Energy demands for biological treatment vary by process. In waste stabilization ponds, energy requirements are for pumping of influent and effluent waste streams to and from the process. Energy requirements for trickling filters are for pumping, dosing and wastewater recirculation. For the activated sludge treatment and aerated lagoon treatment processes, energy demands are from pumping, mixing and aeration of the waste stream/microorganism mixed liquor. Anaerobic digestion requires energy to pump, mix, heat and recirculate the waste stream. Composting energy requirements are for pumping, dosing and heavy equipment (dozer/shovel earth moving machine).

Chemical requirements for biological processes are limited. Chemicals may be needed for pH adjustment, metals precipitation and/or nutrient additions. In systems operating on a uniform waste stream with sufficient biodegradable organic substrate and neutral pH, need for chemical additives such as nitrogen and phosphorus varies according to the waste origin.

Economic Analysis

Costs of biological treatment vary for the type and scale of process and the influent-effluent organic concentrations used as a design basis. Total costs vary from 5¢ to more than $15/1000 gal influent waste. Generally, costs increase as the influent organic concentrations increase and longer retention times are required. Waste stabilization ponds, for example, handle the most dilute waste streams of the biological processes considered. Total waste stabilization pond treatment costs range from ~5¢/1000 gal for a very dilute waste stream of <50 ppm biochemical oxygen demand (BOD) handled in earth-constructed ponds, to nearly $1.50/1000 gal for a waste stream of ~300 ppm BOD handled in ponds with plastic lining. Activated sludge treatment can accept waste streams of higher organic loading utilizing lower retention times because there is designed control of the level of dissolved oxygen and the concentration of microorganisms in the system. Total costs for activated sludge treatment range from ~20¢/1000 gal for a waste stream of ~300 ppm BOD, to nearly $2/1000 gal for a waste stream of ~4000 ppm BOD. Anaerobic digestion handles more concentrated waste streams than the above processes; total cost for digesting an organic waste of ~5% solids content is ~$11/1000 gal of influent. Composting handles the most concentrated waste streams (up to 50% solids content) and requires the longest retention periods. The total cost for composting a waste stream of ~5% solids content is ~$30/1000 gal. Since this report is concerned with industrial processing waste, often a highly variable composition, the above costs include equalization and neutralization prior to biological treatment.

Outlook for Industrial Waste Treatment

In general, biological treatment processes are probably the most cost-effective techniques for treating aqueous waste streams containing organic contaminants. In order to be useful in industrial waste treatment, fairly uniform influents to the biological processes must be maintained. Therefore, biological processes generally should be preceded by neutralization and equalization facilities. Since soluble inorganics are inhibitory to microbial activity, preliminary treatment should be employed to lower the levels of these toxicants to threshold concentrations tolerated by acclimated microorganisms present in various processes.

Of the four biological wastewater treatment processes (activated sludge, aerated lagoon, trickling filter and waste stabilization pond), the activated sludge treatment system is best suited for handling industrial wastes with organic constituents. The system is the most compact of the four, and the continuous circulation of biomass (activated sludge) allows development of an acclimated microbial population. The activated sludge system, especially pure oxygen process modifications, allows the greatest control of dissolved oxygen levels so that variable organic loadings can be accommodated without the system becoming oxygen-deficient.

The anaerobic digestion process is not well suited for industrial waste treatment of varying influent compositions. The process is not able to treat complex hydrocarbons, including long chain and aromatic compounds. Also, the microbial population contains highly sensitive methane bacteria, which cannot tolerate fluctuations in influent organic levels.

The composting treatment process employs long retention periods to decompose very high organic loadings. It is the optimum biological process for treatment of semisolid industrial wastes of variable composition and concentration. Nearly all types of organic compounds are eventually biodegradable, although halogenated aromatic hydrocarbons may inhibit the microbial population.

Enzyme treatment has no potential for the variable industrial waste streams being considered here. The technique has potential only if there are significant quantities of one organic substrate such that resource recovery can be employed, e.g., municipal trash has sufficient cellulose to realize recovery of glucose through enzyme treatment.

An overview of biological treatment processes is presented in Table 11-1. More detailed discussion of each process follows in this chapter: activated sludge, aerated lagoons, anaerobic digestion, composting, enzyme treatment, trickling filters and stabilization ponds.

ACTIVATED SLUDGE

Process Description

The activated sludge process treats aqueous organic waste streams having $<1\%$ suspended solids content. In general the process is unsuited for slurries, solids, tars or viscous waste streams. The process is described as having flocculated, biological growths which are continuously circulated and contacted with organic wastewater in the presence of oxygen. (Figure 11-1). The process was patented in England about the turn of this century, and has steadily undergone modification and development. Much of the process modification has involved improved methods of maintaining aerobic conditions under varying organic loadings.

The process relies on continuous recycling of living microorganisms (biomass) acclimated to the wastewater environment. The recycled biomass is a mixed culture of aerobic heterotrophic bacteria which decompose organic matter. The presence of fungi is not significant to the process. Protozoa and rotifers reside within activated sludge systems by feeding on the bacteria. Since the protozoa and rotifers are strict aerobes and sensitive to toxicants, operation monitoring of activated sludge systems includes routine microscopic observations of the mixed liquor for their presence as a sign of healthy activated sludge activity.

Bacteria in activated sludge systems can be thought of as "bags of

Table 11-1. Overview of

Biological Process	Principal Microbial Population	Optimum Temperature	Range (in pH)	% Solids in Waste Stream	Average Retention Time
Enzyme Treatment	None	Mesophilic	1.5–9.5 varies per enzyme	<50	Nil
Activated Sludge Treatment	Aerobic heterotrophic baceria	Mesophilic	6–8	<1	<1 Day
Trickling Filter	Aerobic heterorophic bacteria	Mesophilic	6–8	<1	<1 Day
Aerated Lagoon	Aerobic heterotrophic bacteria and facultative anaerobic heterotrophic bacteria	Mesophilic	6–8	<1	2–7 days
Waste Stabilization Pond	Aerobic heterotrophic bacteria and autotrophic algae	Mesophilic	6–8	<0.1	3–6 Months
Anaerobic Digestion	Obligate anaerobic heterotrophic bacteria	Thermophilic	6.4–7.5	<10	2 Weeks
Composting	Aerobic heterotrophic bacteria and facultative anaerobic heterotrophic bacteria and fungi	Mesophilic and Thermophilic	5–8.5	<50	3–6 Months

[a] Source: NTIS-PB 275 054.

Biological Treatment Processes[a]

Organic Decomposed	Estimated BOD Upper Limits Effectively Handled (mg/l)	Effluent	Residue	Energy Demand (% of total cost)	Chemical Demand (% of total cost)	Total Cost ($/1000 gal)
All can be decomposed by a series of enzymes	No limit	CO_2 and water if complete treatment, otherwise intermediate decomposition products	None	<10	<10	Prohibitive production and immobilization cost
All but oil, grease and halogenated aromatics, nitrogen compound	<10,000	CO_2 and water, 5–15% influent BOD remains	Biomass sludge	>10	>10	<5
All but oil, grease and halogenated aromatics, nitrogen compound	<5,000	CO_2 and water, 10–20% influent BOD remains	Biomass sludge	<5	>10	<3
All but oil, grease and halogenated aromatics, nitrogen compound	<5,000	CO_2 and water, 10–30% influent BOD remains	Biomass sludge	>10	>10	<3
Mostly carbohydrates proteins, organic acids and alcohols	<100	CO_2 and water, 1010% influent BOD remains	None	<5	<5	<2
Mostly carbohydrates proteins, organic acids and alcohols	Not applicable	Mixed liquor of biomass and interstitial water; 40–50% influent volatile sludge solids remain	"Stabilized" sludge	<5	<5	<15
All organics, phosphorus compounds and nitrogen compounds	No limit	Leachate with soluble organics	None	<5	>10	<30

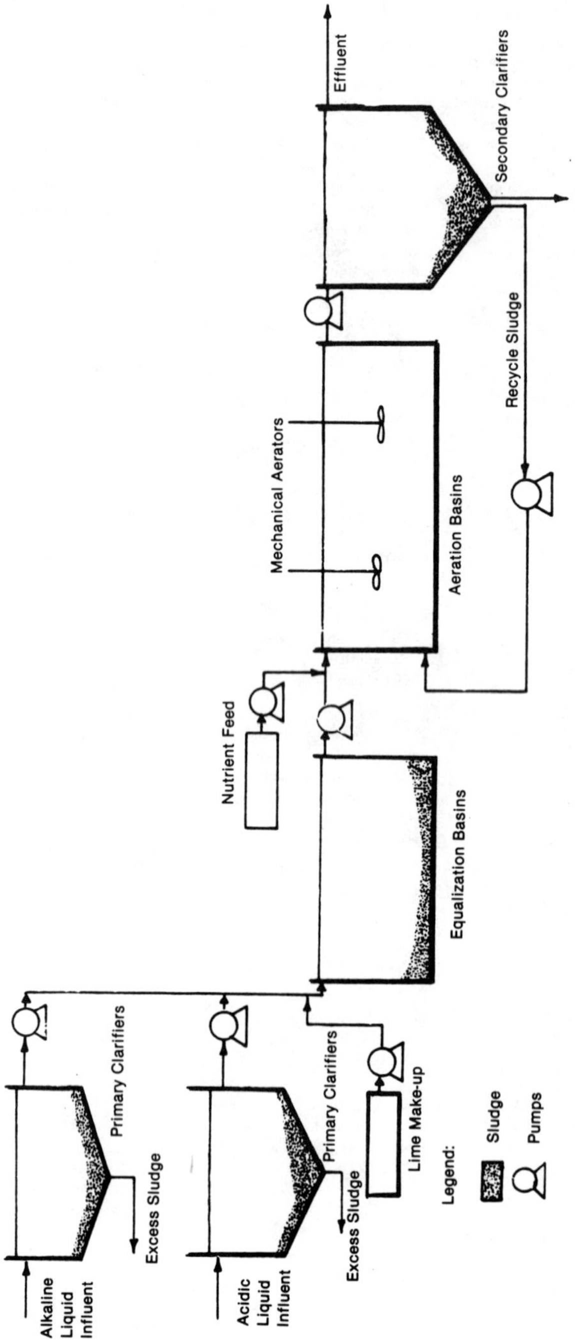

Figure 11-1. Activated sludge treatment flow diagram (Source: NTIS-PB 275 054).

enzymes" capable of performing hydrolysis and oxidation reactions. Complex hydrocarbons are oxidized to lower molecular weights by oxygenase enzymes which incorporate oxygen directly into the long chain or cyclic hydrocarbon molecule. Polysaccharides, fats and proteins are degraded from their polymeric state to monomeric units via hydrolysis. Both the oxidation of complex hydrocarbons and hydrolysis of polysaccharides, etc., occur outside the cell, and are catalyzed by exoenzymes secreted from the cell wall into the surrounding aqueous environment. Oxidation is conducted by aerobic organisms which use dissolved oxygen present in the biological system. Hydrolytic reactions are caused by aerobic organisms using water present in the biological system.

Organics which can be decomposed by aerobic microorganisms include: polysaccharides, proteins, fats, alcohols, aldehydes, fatty acids, alkanes, alkenes, cycloalkanes and aromatics [1]. Isoalkanes, halogenated hydrocarbons and lignin are more resistant to microbial decomposition; however, decomposition does occur at a slower rate under appropriate conditions and with the right microbial population [2]. Aqueous feed streams with low (<1% solids having organic contaminants are applicable.

Not all of the organics removed from the wastewater influent are decomposed. For example, polychlorinated biphenyl (PCB) is known for its chemical stability and low biodegradability. Microorganisms do not naturally possess the enzymes necessary to decompose these synthetic organic compounds. PCB has been studied for its effects on the activated sludge treatment process [3]. Concentrations of PCB up to 10 μg/l were added to acclimated and unacclimated activated sludge microbial systems. Oxygen uptake activity of sludge acclimated to PCB tended to be higher than the unacclimated sludge. The PCB was removed from the wastewater by concentration in the sludge biomass; however, no biodegradation of PCB was observed.

Metals present in concentrations nontoxic to bacteria in activated sludge systems are concentrated and separated by the treatment process. Most insoluble metals, i.e., metal oxides and hydroxides, are removed by sedimentation before activated sludge treatment (Table 11-2). Dissolved metals and fine metal particulates are concentrated in the biomass, primarily through adsorption onto the activated sludge surface [4,5]. It is suggested that the biomass surface is coated with a polysaccharide slime, consisting of polymers of glucuronic acid and neutral sugars [6]. Metal ions form salts with the carboxyl groups present in the slime coating and are electrostatically attached to the hydroxyl groups [6].

In a study by the Washington State University, researchers found that arsenic is bioconcentrated through assimilation and adsorption [7]. They

Table 11-2. Average Values of Total Heavy Metal Concentration and Removal Efficiency by Activated Sludge Treatment at the Dallas Demonstration Plant (4-Month Average)[a]

	Activated Sludge Influent (mg/l)	Activated Sludge Effluent (mg/l)	Activated Sludge % Removal of Influent
As	0.016	0.012	23
Ba	0.156	0.083	47
Cd	0.013	0.008	39
Cr	0.215	0.093	57
Cu	0.092	0.062	23
Fe	1.047	0.299	72
Hg	0.00051	0.00016	69
Mn	0.067	0.050	25
Ni	0.073	0.058	21
Pb	0.095	0.042	56
Se	0.0141	0.0028	79
Zn	0.320	0.112	65

[a]Source: NTIS-PB 275 054.

found a linear correlation existing between the concentration of arsenic in the influent and the concentration of arsenic in the biomass. For the amounts of arsenic studied, ranging from 0 to 156 μg/l, biota could concentrate arsenic in proportion to the amount available (see Table 11-3).

Metals can have an adverse effect on microbial metabolism because they inhibit enzyme catalysis. The metals affect enzymes by binding at the enzyme-active site or causing conformational changes in the enzyme [8]. Normally, microorganisms can tolerate only a few milligrams per liter of heavy metals [1]. Numerous studies have been made on the inhibitory effect of metals on various microorganisms, but results are difficult to compare, as some researchers looked at metal inhibition on unacclimated cultures while others viewed acclimated cultures. In addition, studies on pure cultures do not readily relate to the mixed population of microorganisms present in activated sludge systems. For example, *Nitrosomonas* bacteria in a pure culture were reported inhibited by copper concentrations of <1 mg/l, while *Nitrosomonas* in mixed activated sludge required 4 mg/l of copper to produce the same level of inhibition [9].

The activated sludge process involves an aeration step followed by a sludge-liquid separation step, with recycling of a portion of the sludge. The basic system has an open tank for the mixture of the active biomass with influent wastewater and air, followed by a clarifier. A portion of the

Table 11-3. Arsenic Removal by Biomass—Washington State University Laboratory Study[a]

Sample No.	Concentration (μg As/1) Influent	Effulent	Reduction of Arsenic in Activated Sludge Treatment (%)	Arsenic in Biomass (μg As/g biomass)
1	2.99	0.80	73	3.08
2	3.10	1.70	45	5.18
3	2.99	0.50	83	7.23
4	2.10	1.00	52	4.87
5	2.75	1.00	64	4.30
6	30.00	18.50	38	23.40
7	33.00	18.50	44	35.00
8	40.00	29.00	28	27.90
9	53.00	22.00	59	23.60
10	42.00	26.00	38	28.30
11	128.00	70.00	46	31.50
12	156.00	61.00	61	83.50
13	144.00	63.00	56	96.50
14	112.00	36.00	68	126.90
15	124.00	53.00	57	129.00

[a]Source: NTIS-PB 275 054.

biomass, called activated sludge, is recycled to the open tank to maintain the food-to-mass (F:M) ratio (organic substrate to microorganism ratio). The conventional plug-flow system mixes wastewater and return sludge at the head of the aeration tank; the so-called mixed liquor flows through the tank in a plug-flow fashion with some longitudinal mixing.

Process Modifications

Process modifications of conventional activated sludge include the following:

- contact stabilization: used where BOD is rapidly removed from the aeration step by biosorption, and involves aerating the activated sludge on its return trip to the aeration tank so that sorbed inorganics are decomposed.
- step aeration: used to equalize influent organic loading along the course of flow of the mixed liquor, and involves admitting influent wastewater at multiple points along the aeration tank.

- completely mixed: used to equalize load variations and improve distribution of dissolved oxygen, and involves operating mechanical aerators in the aeration tank to achieve almost instantaneous distribution of untreated wastes throughout the tank.
- extended aeration: used where there are low organic loadings and it is desirable to minimize sludge residue, and involves longer aeration retention periods so that endogenous respiration of the biomass is achieved.
- pure oxygen: used where there are high organic and trace metal concentrations to maintain a high dissolved oxygen level and a high biomass concentration, and involves a closed staged aeration tank with mechanical mixers receiving concurrent flow of wastewater and oxygen gas.

Various researchers have reported threshold concentrations of metals for mixed activated sludge cultures [10]. The threshold concentrations are limits of metals above which there is significant decrease in treatment efficiency. Treatment efficiency is measured by the chemical oxygen demand (COD) of the effluent, enzymatic activity or the respiratory rate of the culture. In Table 11–4, Srinath [9] presents a list of critical threshold metal concentrations based on review of available literature.

A summary of activated sludge plants treating petrochemical and organic waste in Table 11–5 indicates the representative type of mixed waste that could be treated by activated sludge, and the effluent quality obtained by such process.

AERATED LAGOONS

The technique of aerated lagoons developed from adding artificial aeration to existing waste stabilization ponds. The aerated lagoon process (Figure 11–2) employs mechanical or diffused aeration equipment similar to that found in the activated sludge treatment process. In fact, the process has been called a "dilute activated sludge" treatment process. The major difference with aerated lagoon treatment is that microorganisms are not continuously circulated from final clarifiers back to the head of the process.

Because aerated lagoons usually are not as well mixed as activated sludge processes, a low level of suspended solids is maintained in the process mixed liquor. Mixed liquor volatile suspended solids (MLVSS) of aerated lagoons generally range from 50 to 150 mg/l [11]. However, lower levels of mixing and aerating can be increased to levels comparable to activated sludge treatment so that higher MLVSS loadings can be supported.

Table 11-4. Threshold Concentration for Various Metals in the Air Activated Sludge Process[a]

Metal Ion	Concentration (mg/l)	Type of Activated Sludge
Silver	<0.03	Carbonaceous
Vanadium	10.0	Carbonaceous
Zinc	2.0	Carbonaceous
	5–10	Carbonaceous
	1.0	Nitrification
Nickel	1.0–2.5	Carbonaceous
	1.0	Nitrification
	2.0	Nitrification
Chromium, $^{+6}$	10.0	Carbonaceous
	1.0	Nitrification
	10.0	Nitrification
	1.0	Nitrification
Chromium, $^{+3}$	10.0	Carbonaceous
Lead	10	Carbonaceous
Iron (Ferric)	15	Carbonaceous
Copper	1.0–10.0	Carbonaceous
	1.0	Nitrification
	2.0	Nitrification
Cadmium	1.0	Carbonaceous
	5.0	Nitrification

[a]Source: NTIS-PB 275 054.

The most important modification of the aerated lagoon process occurs when aeration is not sufficient to maintain aerobic conditions throughout the lagoon. A portion of the suspended solids, including biomass, is allowed to settle to the bottom of the basin and undergo anaerobic microbial decomposition. Lagoons having this characteristic are called aerobic-anaerobic or facultative lagoons. At the settled-sludge/wastewater interface, facultative anaerobic bacteria decompose simple organics such as carbohydrates and proteins to volatile organic acids. These, in turn, are decomposed by obligate anaerobic bacteria which release methane as a product of anaerobic metabolism. (The section on anaerobic digestion presents a more complete description of anaerobic microbial metabolic reactions.)

The aerated lagoon system requires retention times that are slightly longer than those for activated sludge treatment. Retention times decrease as aeration facilities are improved to maintain dissolved oxygen levels comparable to activated sludge treatment. For facultative anaerobic lagoons, longer retention periods are necessary to support the

Table 11-5. Activated Sludge Treatment of Industrial Organic Wastes[a]

Product and/or Process	Flow (mgd)	BOD In (mg/l)	BOD Out (mg/l)	BOD Rem (%)	COD In (mg/l)	COD Out (mg/l)	COD Rem (%)	Organic Loading lb BOD5/day / lb MLSS	Nutrients Required	Remarks
Refinery, Natural Gas Liquids, Chemical Specialties, Sanitary Sewage	4.87	90	20	78	200	90	55	0.1	None	Effluent phenol 0.05 Effluent oil 0.5 mg/l
Phthalic Anhydride, Pehnol, Salicylic Acid, Rubber Chem., Aspirin, Phenacetin	2.54	45.7	6.1	86.7				0.031	None	Brush aeration, treats trickling filter effluent, 55% sludge return
Refinery, Detergent Alkylate	2.45	345	50–100	71 - 85.5	855	105–200	7.6.-82.5	0.08	PO_4	Phenols in = 160 mg/l Sulfide in = 150 mg/l Lab scale
Butadiene Maleic Acid	2.0	2000	25	98.8	2990	480	84	0.24	NH_3	
Butadiene Alkylate	1.5	1960	24	98.8	2980	477	98.3			
Butadiene, Maleic Anhydride Fumaric Acid, Tetrahydrophthalic, Anhydride, Butylene Isomers, Alkylate	1.5	1960	24	98.8	2980	51	84	0.24 (MLVSS)	NH_3	Surface aerators, wastes contain: alcohols, maleic acid, fumaric acid, acetic acid, C_1–C_4 aldehydes, furfural, water soluble addition products

Ethylene Propylene, Benzene	1.44	600	90	85	700	105	85		None	Oily waters: C_4–C_{10} oils, 90% phenol removal
Naphthalene, Butadiene, Phenol, Acrylonitrile, Soft Detergent Bases, Resins, Other Aromatics	0.43	500	60	85–90	600	90	80–85	1.5	NH_3 PO_4	Sour waters: oil in = 500 mg/l; phenol in = 65 mg/l pH adjustment, preceded by trickling filter; phenol removal = 99.9%
Phenol, 2, 4-D Aniline, Nitro-benzene, Rubber Chem., Polyester Resins, Misc. Chem.	0.97	370	76	76.2				0.4	NH_3 PO_4	Accelator pilot plant sewage added in ratio 1:600 once/wk
Ethylene, Propylene, Butadiene, Benzene, Polyethylene, Fuel Oils	0.63	85	10	99	200	75	62.5			Quench waters, polyethylene and benzene wastes: preceded by trickiing filter, effluent phenol = 0.01 ppm
Refining Processes	0.51–0.63	125	15–25	80 – 88			65 – 80	0.28–0.4	PO_4	Phenol removal = 85–94%; oil removal = 75–85%; effl. phenol 0.5 mg/l; effl. oil 1–2 mg/l; temp. = 30°C
Nylon	0.4	1540	250	83.8						
Petroleum Products	0.27	440	5	98.8	500	60	88			Phenol in = 25 ppm Phenol out = 1 ppm

Table 11-5, continued

Product and/or Process	Flow (mgd)	BOD In (mg/l)	BOD Out (mg/l)	BOD Rem (%)	COD In (mg/l)	COD Out (mg/l)	COD Rem (%)	Organic Loading lb BOD5/day / lb MLSS	Nutrients Required	Remarks
Acrylic Fibers	0.252	2260	118–226	90–95				0.4		Wastes contain acrylonitrile, dimethylamine, dimethylformamide, formic acid; temp. 35–37°C; return sludge 10–50%, mechanical aeration
Acetone, Phenol p-Cresol, Ditert.-Butyl-p-Cresol, Dicumyl Peroxide	0.216	3560–4400	1030–750	71–83				0.89–1.1		Waste phenol, 600 ppm; waste BOD 7500–8000; waste diluted with effluent or water; pilot plant
Resins-Formalin, Aminoplasts, Phenol-Formald., Epoxy Resins, Textile Aux.	0.2	890	444–266		50–70			0.8–1.2		Diffused-air; domestic waste added; trickling filter follows 100% recycle sludge
Ethylene and Propylene Oxides, Glycols, Morpholines, Ethylene-Diamines, Ethers, Piperazine	0.15	1950	20	99	7970–8540	5120–5950	25–40	0.51	None	Lab scale; extended aeration; high nonbiodegradable fraction followed by stabilization ponds

2, 4-D 2, 4, 5-T (Acid Wash Wastes)	0.1	1670	125	92.5	2500	500	80	0.78 (MLVSS)	NH_3 PO_4	1:1 mixture of acid; wash streams diluted 9:1 prior to treatment to reduce chlorides toxicity, lab scale

[a]Source: U.S. EPA Report-670/2-73-053-I, (August 1973).

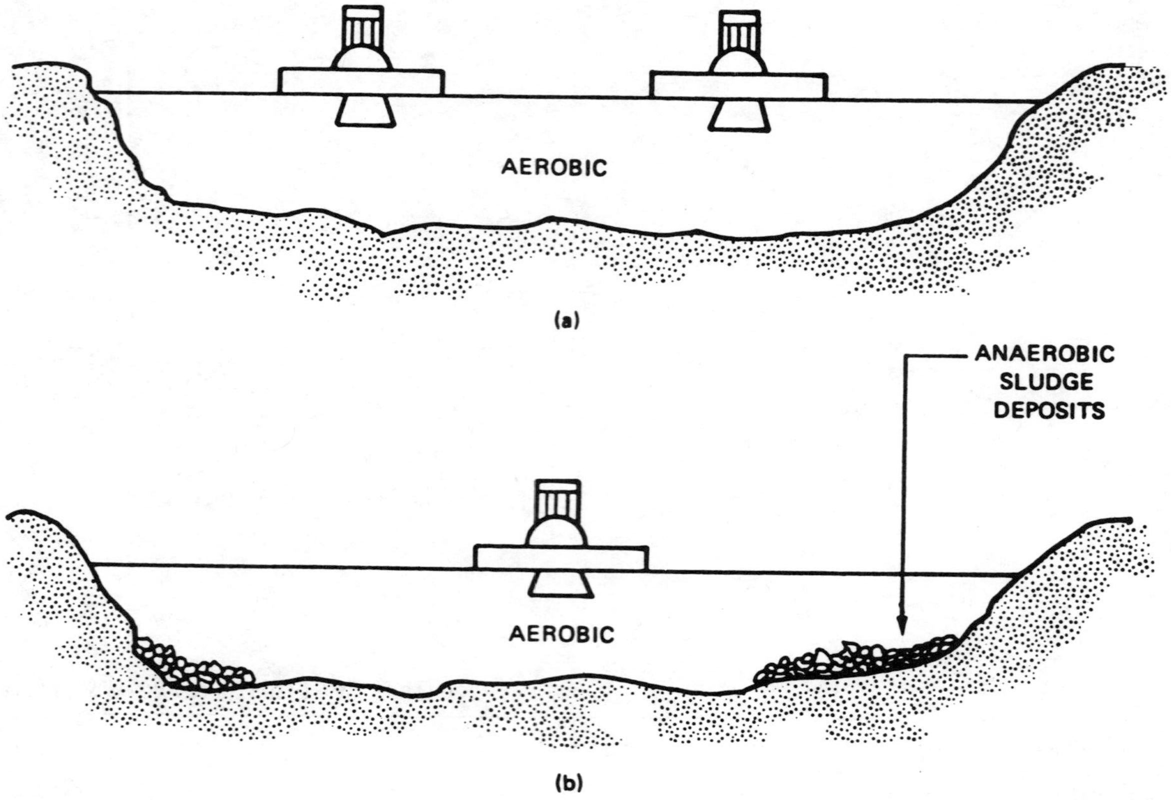

Figure 11-2. Schematic of (a) an aerobic lagoon and (b) an aerobic-anaerobic lagoon (Source: NTIS-PB 275 054).

slower metabolic rate of anaerobic microorganisms. Aerobic lagoons may require up to two days retention, while facultative anaerobic lagoons may need more than four days of retention time.

The typical aerated lagoon is a relatively deep (6–17 ft) earthen basin with mechanical aeration. The side walls of the basin are diked at a 3:1 slope. Clarification of the suspended solids in lagoon effluent is considered part of the total process.

For the treatment of industrial wastes, it may be necessary to line the basin. Recent linings for waste lagoons consist of pigment-filled polyethylene or polypropylene. Hypalon®* is excellent except for some solvents, ketones and chlorinated solvents. The necessity for lining depends on the composition of the influent waste and the in situ soil permeability.

ANAEROBIC DIGESTION

Anaerobic digestion traditionally has been a supporting process in the field of biological treatment, in which the organic solids and biomass sludges from primary clarification and biological wastewater treatment are processed to reduce their volume and improve stability. The process allows hydrolysis and fermentation to occur under anaerobic conditions, resulting in production of methane gas and reduction of the substrate carbon. The process depends on the symbiotic relation of two classes of microorganisms: acid-forming bacteria and methane-forming bacteria.

Acid-forming bacteria hydrolyze polysaccharides to monosaccharides and oxidize these to organic acids and alcohols, carbon dioxide and hydrogen [2]. The acid-forming bacteria are primarily obligate anaerobes, although some facultative anaerobes may be present in the mixed microbial population [12]. They perform oxidation by utilizing nitrites, nitrates, sulfates and organics as oxygen sources [1]. Therefore, the oxygenase enzyme catalysts in the microbes are accompanied by reductase coenzymes.

Methane-forming bacteria utilize end products of the acid-forming bacteria's degradation of organics. All of the methane-forming bacteria are obligate anaerobes, capable of reducing acids and carbon dioxide to methane [12]. The methane-forming bacteria rely on the acid-formers for their substrate. It appears that they also rely on the acid-formers for their nutrients. For example, ammonia is produced from organic nitrogen compounds through the activity of acid-forming bacteria, and methane

*Registered trademark of E. I. duPont de Nemours & Company, Inc., Wilmington, Delaware.

bacteria studied thus far require it as their main nitrogen source [13]. They appear unable to utilize the original nitrogen compounds, such as amino acids, for a nitrogen source.

The anaerobic digestion process results in low production of waste sludge. The volume of the influent sludge is substantially reduced, because organics are finally converted to gaseous end products of methane and carbon dioxide. Part of the microbial population incompletely hydrolyzes the substrate to alcohols and acids, resulting in little conversion of carbon to new cell growth. Another part of the microbial population converts the alcohols and acids to methane, which is rapidly discharged from the system because of its extremely low solubility in water. The continued removal of carbon from the system results in anaerobic cultures utilizing 10–20% of the substrate carbon for cells. For comparison, an aerobic microbial population may use as much as 50% of the carbon substrate for conversion to cell mass [12].

The conventional anaerobic digester (Figure 11-3) is a closed tank having no agitation mechanisms. Sludge is received in the middle zone of the tank where it is actively digested by the microbes. Methane and carbon dioxide are released from the microbial metabolic activity; these gases rise to the surface of the supernatant, lifting some sludge particles and some undigested greases, oils and fatty acids. As a result, a scum layer forms above the supernatant. The digested sludge is removed from the middle zone by gravity settling. Due to stratification in the digester, digested sludge can be removed through the base of the tank and gas from the roof of the tank. Conventional digesters require a retention time of 30–60 days. The conventional process accepts up to 0.1 lb volatile solids/ft^3 of digestion capacity/day. The influent sludge is reduced in volume by 40–60%.

High-rate anaerobic digesters are closed tanks with provisions for mixing. Mixing may be accomplished by mechanical agitators, gas circulation or pumping. There is no stratification of digested sludge, supernatant and scum as there is in conventional digestion. Frequently the high-rate digester may appear in series with an unmixed digester, so that settling of digested sludge and clarification of supernatant may occur. The high-rate anaerobic digester requires a minimum retention period of 3 days, and averages 14–16 days. The process may accept up to 0.5 lb volatile solids/ft^3 of digestion capacity/day.

Temperatures in the digester are typically maintained at 31–35°C for conventional anaerobic digestion, and at ~37°C for high-rate anaerobic digestion. Significant increases in gas production and volatile solids destruction accompany increases in temperatures, provided sufficient time is allowed for microbial population to maintain the balance of acid-

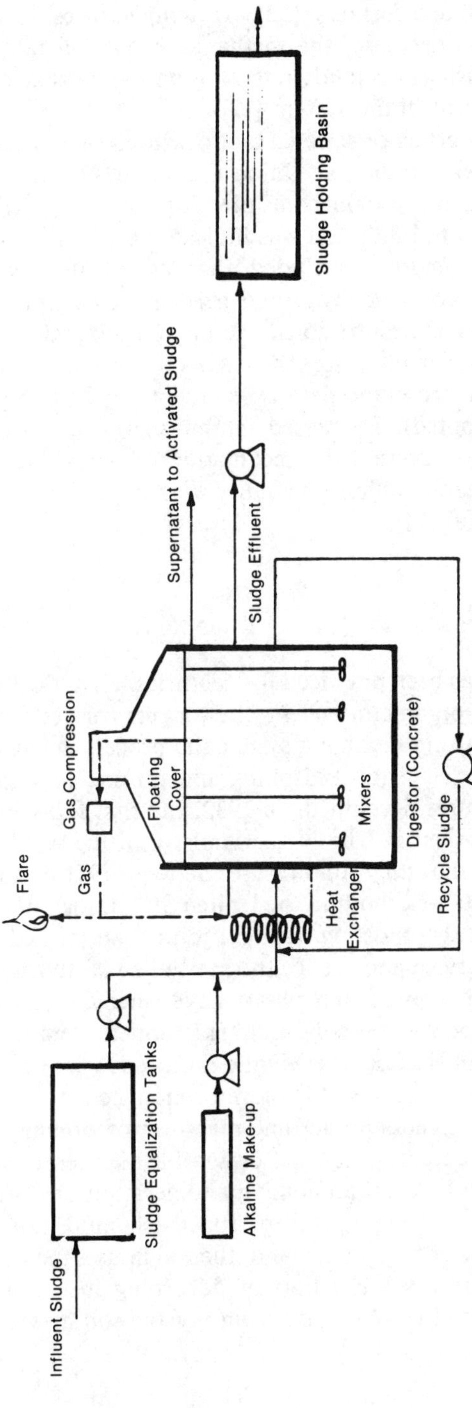

Figure 11-3. High-rate anaerobic digestion flow diagram (Source: NTIS-PB 275 054).

formers to methane-formers [12]. If temperatures in the anaerobic digestion process decrease, the methane production rate can be maintained by increasing the solids retention period so that more methane-formers are present in the system [12].

The inhibitory effect of selected hydrocarbons on unacclimated anaerobic digestion was studied at Union Carbide [14]. Since the methane-forming bacteria are recognized as the most sensitive microorganisms in anaerobic digestion, inhibition was indicated by the rate of methane gas production. The study concluded that all of the aldehydes tested (formaldehyde, crotonaldehyde and acrolein) created inhibitory problems at 50 mg/l concentrations. Acrolein exhibited the most severe effects. Table 11-6 summarizes the results of the study. In general, inhibition was most pronounced in systems having high organic loadings (nonsubstrate limited). Decreased inhibition was evidenced as volatile acid concentration decreased. Acclimation of anaerobic digestion processes to the organic inhibitors studied was shown to be slow and relatively unsuccessful [14].

COMPOSTING

Composting has been practiced for centuries. Historically, composting involved leaving organic matter in piles or pits for decomposition prior to reuse. Composting became a systematic process in India and Italy in the 1920s, when the sequential piling and turning of vegetative matter and animal manures developed. In 1932, the first full-scale composting plant was established in The Netherlands, utilizing windrow piling for the decomposition of unground refuse. Between 1951 and 1969, eighteen composting plants were built in the United States, including the Johnson City, Tennessee, composting facility jointly sponsored by the U.S. Public Health Service and the Tennessee Valley Authority in 1966 [15]. Most of the U.S. composting plants have since closed due to lack of viable markets for the soil-conditioning product. Composting has been more successful in Europe, the Middle East and Asia, where the need to add organic matter to the soil is more pronounced.

Composting is essentially aerobic digestion of organics. It may take place within a structure, i.e., a silo or aerobic digester, or it may be conducted on the land. Adequate mixing and aeration of waste is provided so that aerobic microorganisms perform decomposition of organics. When composting occurs on the land, the soil houses the microorganisms and performs an added function of adsorbing metals and refractory organics. Sequential mixing and turning of the soil mass maintains aer-

Table 11-6. **Identified Problem Concentrations of Tested Materials**[a,b]

Chemical	Problem Concentration: Substrate Limiting (mg/l)	Problem Concentration: Non substrate Limiting (mg/l)
n-Butanol	–	>1000
sec-Butanol	–	>1000
t-Butanol	>1000	>1000
Allyl alcohol	–	>1000
2-Ethyl-l-hexanol	500–1000	–
Formaldehyde	–	50–100
Crotonaldehyde	~200	50–100
Acrolein	–	20–50
Acetone	–	>1000
Methyl isobutyl ketone	>1000	100–300
Isophorone	>1000	–
Diethylamine	–	300–1000
Ethylene diamine	–	100–300
Acrylonitrile	150–500	100
2-Methyl-5-ethylpyridine	>1000	100
N,N-dimethylaniline	>1000	–
Phenol	>1000	300–1000 (~400)
Ethyl benzene	>1000	–
Sodium benzoate	–	>300
Ethylene dichloride	150–500	–
Ethyl acrylate	600–1000	300–600
Sodium acrylate	–	>500
Dodecane	>1000	–
Dextrose	>1000	>1000
Ethyl acetate	>1000	–
Ethylene glycol	>1000	>900
Diethylene glycol	–	>1000
Tetralin	>1000	–
Kerosene	–	>500
Cobalt chloride	–	>1000

[a]Source: NTIS-PB 275 054.
[b]Compound was arbitrarily classified as a problem when the activity ratio was <0.5. The 0.5 level was considered to be a decrease of >50% of the total gas production.

obic conditions. Because of the adsorption advantages of composting on land, most of this discussion focuses on that process modification.

The composting system (Figure 11–4) relies primarily on long retention periods and acclimated aerobic microorganisms which perform hydroly-

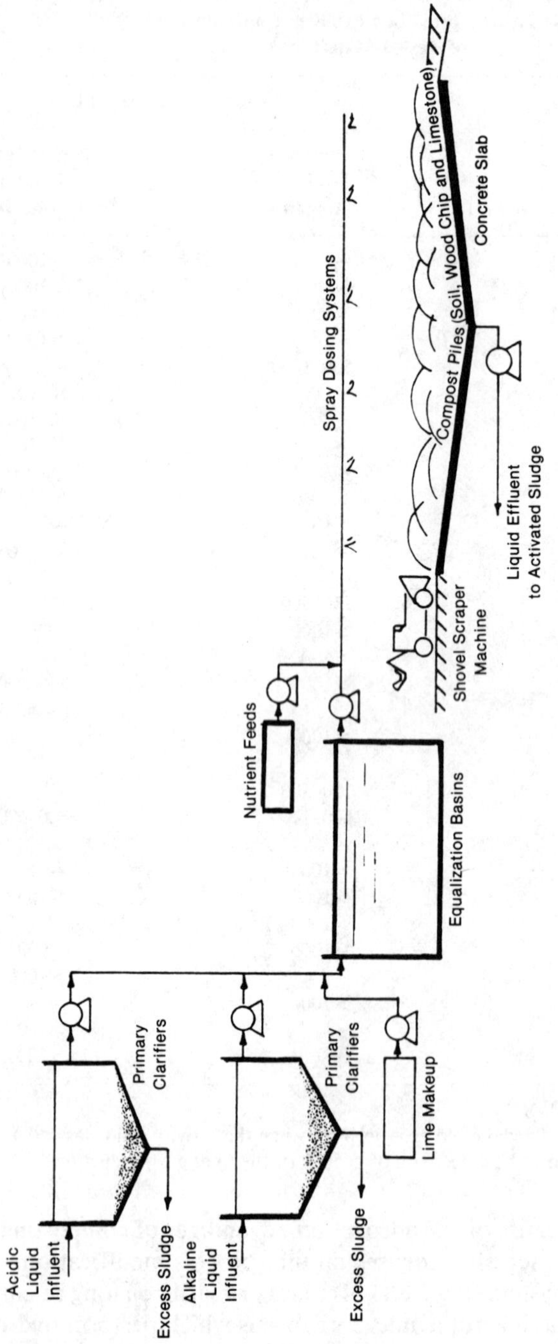

Figure 11-4. Biochemical bed-compost system flow diagram (Source: NTIS-PB 275 054).

sis and oxidation reactions to decompose organics. If the composting takes place in a soil media, fungi and facultative anaerobic microorganisms also may be present. When the waste and soil piles are not turned adequately to maintain aerobic conditions, some anaerobic hydrolysis and oxidation of carbohydrates and proteins occurs. Microorganisms necessary for composting activity are present in the original substrate. In windrow piling, they are present in the soil as well as the organic substrate. Addition of microorganisms from foreign sources has proved to be of little value [15].

When composting begins, the microorganisms are predominantly mesophilic. As temperatures increase to >40°C, thermophilic microbial species predominate.

In systems employing soil media for composting, metal inhibition of microorganisms has not been apparent. At the Hyon Waste Management Services, Inc., facility which employs composting of hazardous wastes, metals have not inhibited microbial activity. The pH levels are kept neutral to alkaline, and the compost beds are sequentially spread and piled to maximize aerobic conditions. As a result, metals are present as oxide, hydroxide and carbonate precipitates, if they are not adsorbed or exchanged onto the soil or organic media [16]. In land farming of oils, lead concentrations between 7000 and 15,000 ppm were shown to have no effect on the soil's microbial flora [17]. Similar studies on vanadium concentrations in oils showed no effect on microbial flora [16].

The mixed microbial system is able to destroy nearly all types of organic compounds. Oils are commonly applied to the soil in land farming of petroleum refinery wastes, and are susceptible to being oxidized by soil microorganisms within several years [18]. The primary mechanism for microbial decomposition is enzyme catalysis of oxidation, with exoenzyme oxygenases secreted from the cells. Within one year, oil concentrations in soils were proved reduced by 50–90% of their original levels [19]. Raymond, et al. demonstrated the oxidation of paraffinic cycloparaffinic and aromatic hydrocarbons by soil microorganisms, as long as more simple organics were present as substrate for cell growth [20]. Intermediate byproducts of the microbial oxidation included organic acids, alcohols, aldehydes and ketones. Some of the aromatics may polymerize to form resins which then take longer to biodegrade.

To date, halogenated aromatic hydrocarbons have been found the most resistant organics to significant degradation by typical microbial populations [21]. At the Hyon facility, only the halogenated hydrocarbons (i.e., polychlorinated biphenyl) are not applied to the compost beds and are, instead, incinerated [21]. On the other hand, a microbial population may be developed and acclimated to handle even these most refractory organics. Although pentachlorophenol is cited as one of the most refractory organic compounds, an aerobic bacterium has been shown to metabolize pentachlorophenol as a sole source of organic carbon and energy [22,23].

Operating Characteristics

Applied loading rates for composting are not readily established. Acceptable loading depends on the biodegradability of the organic constituents, the microbial acclimatization to the influent waste, substrate, nutrient availability and climate.

In land farming of refinery activated sludge, Exxon applies 70 tons of dewatered (~15% solids) sludge per acre per month and believes 100 tons monthly will be assimilated by the land [21]. The applied loading was equivalent to about 0.4 gal/ft^2/month dosing rate with 15% solids.

Land farming of oily sludges, containing 33% oil, in an EPA demonstration project involved applying 70 barrels/acre/month [24]. This was equivalent to ~0.07 gal/ft^2/month. Land farming of oils added in a single application for investigative purposes [19] by Sun Oil involved a loading of 11.9 m^3/4 $\times$ 10^3 m^2. This was equivalent to ~0.07 gal/ft^2.

At Hyon, loadings of 10 gal/ft^2/month of aqueous waste streams averaging 3–5% solids are applied to the compost beds [21].

Moisture content is an important criterion for compost optimization. Excess moisture restricts aeration, while limited moisture deactivates microbial enzymes. Studies on municipal refuse have established moisture contents between 63–79% as optimum. Higher moisture contents are permissible for porous mixtures of straw and manure [25]. Addition of pulverized limestone further increases acceptable moisture levels [21].

Temperature is the fundamental parameter for measuring composting activity. At the beginning of composting, temperature in the waste is the same as ambient air temperature. As the organisms dissimilate organics and synthesize new cells, heat is released and temperatures in the compost pile rise. At ~40°C, mesophilic microorganisms die off, to be replaced by thermophilic microorganisms. As temperatures increase to as high as 70°C, microbial activity accomplishes rapid decomposition of organics. Once the waste substrate is fully decomposed, temperatures in the pile return to ambient levels [26]. The sequence of spreading-dosing the compost bed, then farming the windrow piles should be scheduled to optimize thermophilic microbial activity.

Alkaline aerobic conditions are maintained in composting so that metals are not soluble, and therefore potentially toxic to microorganisms. Nutrients are added, as needed, to supplement the carbon-nitrogen-phosphorus ratio of incoming wastes. Wood chips, manure, etc., are provided to maintain a simple organic substrate for cell growth.

The windrow pile composting process operates continuously year-round. Total retention times necessary for organic wastes to be degraded average three to four months. Within one year, even refractory organics should be oxidized. An optimum composting procedure, as established at Hyon, would follow the following steps:

1. 3–4 weeks: Spread the media and organisms into flat beds ~2-in. thick. Dose with waste, lace with nutrients (nitrate) and alkalines (lime and calcium carbonate).
2. 7–10 days: Pile media, organism and waste mass into compost windrow forms ~4 in. high.
3. Repeat flattening of beds for aeration.
4. Repeat waste dosing, nutrient addition and pH adjustment.
5. Repeat windrow piling.

Location of windrow piles is alternated so that the biochemical bed bottoms do not get mucky and impervious. An aerated pervious bed bottom allows continuous leachate drainage.

ENZYME TREATMENT

Enzyme treatment of industrial processing wastes is totally impractical. Enzymes catalyze specific reactions and cannot adapt well to the varying composition of typical waste streams. Furthermore, enzyme production is very expensive.

Enzymes are highly selective chemical catalysts which act on specific molecules. The urease enzyme, for example, breaks down urea into carbon dioxide and ammonia. A hydrolase enzyme derived from yeast has been shown to oxidize phenol to carbon dioxide and water. The cellulose enzyme, produced by a stream of fungus, Trichoderma viridi, catalyzes the hydrolysis of cellulose to glucose.

There are no known full-scale applications of enzyme treatment processes in hazardous waste management. There are commercial applications in meat tenderizing, dehairing of hides prior to tanning, cheese-making, pharmaceutical manufacture and detergent production.

The U.S. Army Natick Research and Development Command is operating a 1000 lb/month pilot plant to convert waste paper into glucose. A number of government, university and industrial laboratories are investigating the use of lactose for recovery of monosaccharides from cheese whey. Groups at Oak Ridge National Laboratories and the University of Pennsylvania have studied the enzyme decomposition of phenol.

Enzyme treatment may be useful for specialized industrial applications, particularly in cases where salable reaction products result. Enzymes, however, have little or no potential in general waste treatment.

TRICKLING FILTERS

In the trickling filter process (Figure 11-5), wastes are sprayed through the air to absorb oxygen and are allowed to trickle through a bed of rock or synthetic media coated with a slime of microbial growth. The microbial slime is able to decompose organic matter in the waste stream. Process modifications employ various media and depths of media to retain the microorganisms under varying hydraulic conditions.

The trickling filter process relies on media support of immobile microorganisms which receive their organic substrate as waste is trickled over their cell surface. The primarily metabolic processes are aerobic, and the trickling filter system utilizes the same types of aerobic heterotrophic bacteria as the activated sludge system. In fact, in the petroleum industry, trickling filters precede the activated sludge unit and produce a continuous population of microorganisms for activated sludge treatment [1]. The aerobic microorganisms produce enzymes which perform oxidation and hydrolysis catalysis for the decomposition of simple and complex organics. Intermediate decomposition by-products, namely organic alcohols and acids, are utilized by the bacterial cells for both metabolic energy and substrate for cell synthesis.

The microbial slime which coats the trickling filter media remains aerobic primarily at its surface where air and water interface with the cells. The underlying portion, adjacent to the media, may become anaerobic. Some anaerobic decomposition results, as simple organics are hydrolyzed to organic acids, and in turn are oxidized to methane and carbon dioxide.

Periodically, the microbial slime coating sloughs off the trickling filter media. This sloughing off may occur for several reasons. As the microorganisms grow and reproduce, the slime coating may become too heavy to remain adhered to the media. Also, as the substrate becomes limited to the underlying microorganisms, endogenous respiration becomes prevalent. Under endogenous respiration, the microorganisms become more dense and their adhesive polysaccharide cell coating diminishes.

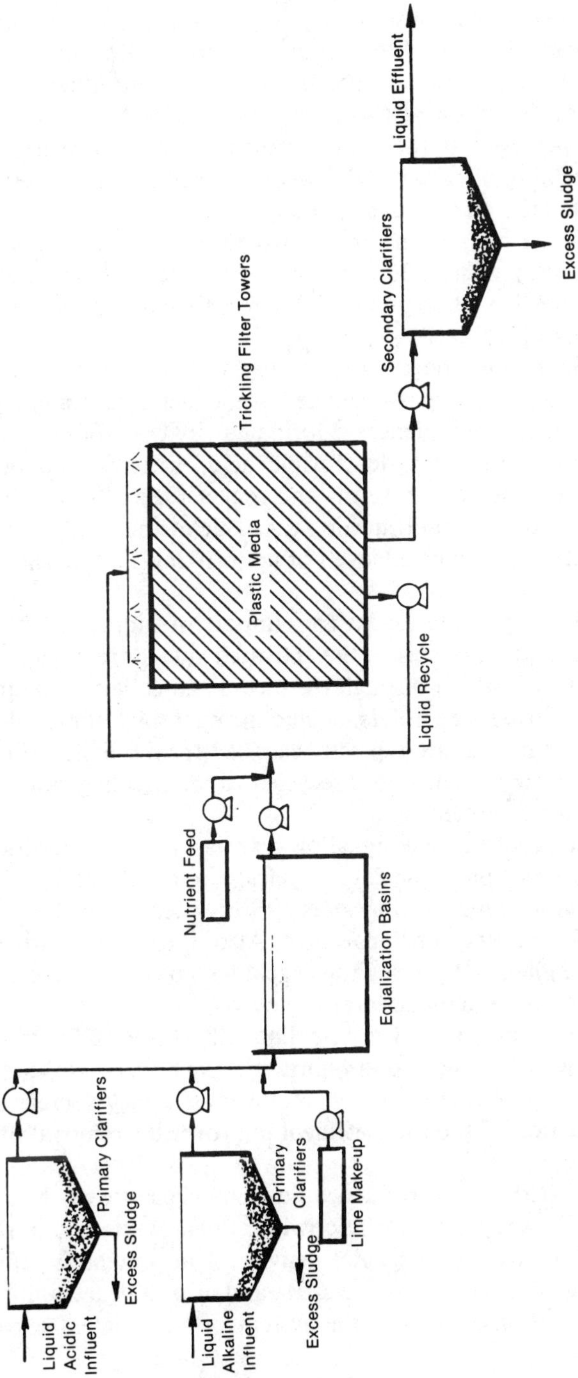

Figure 11-5. Super rate trickling filters flow diagram (Source: NTIS-PB 275 054).

Trickling filters decompose all types of organics, as does activated sludge treatment. Because of the relatively short residence time of wastewater contact with microorganisms, however, the percentage removal of organics is not as complete as in activated sludge treatment. Greater removals are achieved as the depth of media and the recycle ratio are increased. Trickling filters with 30-ft depth of media and recycle ratios of 3:1 are not uncommon in industry today [27].

Trickling filters have been used satisfactorily to decompose oil and phenol. In refinery wastes, 30 mg/l of oil have been effectively decomposed [28]. Trickling filter pilots of 3:1 recycle have decomposed ppm phenol to 0 ppm [27].

Trickling filters are reported to have handled successfully the following waste constituents: acetaldehyde, acetic acid, acetone, acrolein, alcohols, benzene, butadiene, chlorinated hydrocarbons, cyanides, epichlorohydrin, formaldehyde, formic acid, ketones, monoethanolamine, propylene dichloride, resins and rocket fuels [29]. Study on the trickling filtration of nitrilotriacetic acid, which is normally used in the building of detergents, showed levels of up to 16 mg/l not harmful to the process [30].

Trickling filters provide media for support of biomass, rather than having suspended biomass as in the activated sludge treatment process. The wastewater is trickled through the media and collected in an underground drain. Suspended solids, including microbial slime which has sloughed off the media, are typically clarified from the underflow. The clarified underflow may be either recycled to the trickling filter head or sent to following treatment units.

Media used in filter packing allow various process modifications. Rock media used to pack the filters typically allowed depths of 3–8 ft. The use of synthetic media allows deep filters because of their lessened tendency to clog and become anaerobic. Also, their comparatively light weight allows higher packings. Filter packings up to 40-ft deep are reasonable where synthetic media are employed.

Hydraulic loading rates for trickling filters generally are <0.5 gpm/ft^2; however, loadings up to 4 gpm/ft^2 have been employed [11]. As the hydraulic loading rate increases, removal efficiency decreases. Generally, recirculation of the filter effluent improves the removal of biodegradable organics.

It appears that the short residence time characteristic of the trickling filter process allows greater variations in influent waste composition to occur without inhibiting microbial activity. The process is reputed to handle shock loadings of organic wastes, and also to be less inhibited by metals concentrations. In fact, the system often is called a roughing filter, used to level loads and reduce biodegradable organics concentrations prior to other biological treatment processes.

STABILIZATION PONDS

Waste stabilization ponds (Figure 11-6) are large, shallow basins which provide aerobic and facultative anaerobic decomposition of organics. The ponds rely on long retention periods and natural aeration for the aerobic microorganisms to decompose organics to carbon dioxide and water. Natural aeration is encouraged by wind action and algal photosynthesis. The facultative anaerobic decomposition which sometimes occurs in the ponds takes place at the benthic sediment-water interface.

Waste stabilization ponds support aerobic and facultative anaerobic microorganisms, as well as algae. There is a symbiotic relationship between the aerobic microorganisms and the algae. Algae synthesize new cells by using the sun as an energy source and carbon dioxide and amine as a food source. The algae provide dissolved oxygen for aerobic bacteria respiration. Aerobic bcteria hydrolyze and oxidize organics to carbon dioxide and intermediate amine by-products.

Waste stabilization pond activity varies with changes in temperature. During warm seasons, the symbiotic relationship between the aerobic bacteria and algae is most efficient. As temperatures fall, the algae produce less oxygen. If the temperature declines sufficiently for ice to form on the pond, both surface wind aeration and algal access to sun energy is limited. During cold seasons, facultative bacteria may shift to the anaerobic mode of metabolic activity, obtaining oxygen from selected inorganic and organic compounds. Nitrites, nitrates and sulfates are the three principal sources of inorganic oxygen [1]. Only simple organics, such as carbohydrates and proteins, are decomposed by anaerobic microbial activity and the rate of decomposition is less than under aerobic conditions.

Anaerobic activity increases with pond depth [31,32]. With pond depths of 8–12 ft, anaerobic biodegradation of simple organics occurs at the benthic sediment/water interface. Although methane gas is produced by methane-forming bacteria (see the discussion of anaerobic digestion biological treatment for further description of microbial reactions which occur anaerobically), no odor is evident provided the aqueous medium above contains a dense algal population [31]. Both the interface of the benthic sediment, which comprises settled organic matter, and the top 4 in. of the sediment are actively involved in anaerobic activity, witnessed by the formation of volatile acids [31]. Increased anaerobic activity is

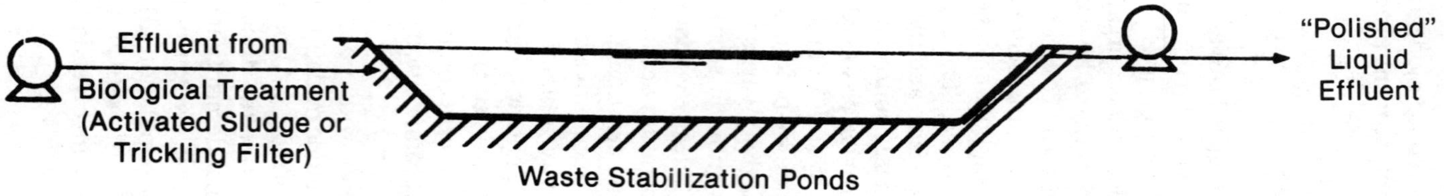

Figure 11-6. Waste stabilization pond flow diagram (Source: NTIS-PB 275 054).

evident in the early summer, as microorganisms digest the winter's accumulation of settled dead zoo- and phyto-plankton and bacterial cells [31].

Since methane production is an important means of ultimate removal of carbon from a waste stream, deep ponds which promote anaerobic digestion of settled sludge may offer some advantages. Carbon dioxide, which is anaerobically and aerobically produced, is utilized by the algae and therefore does not represent ultimate removal of carbon from the system.

Waste stabilization ponds are capable of decomposing all types of simple and complex organics. Significant decomposition of phenols in steel industry waste waters has been proven [33], although the influent concentrations demonstrated are low, <1 ppm phenol. Photosynthetic algae are able to oxidize anaerobically produced sulfides and utilize the volatile acids which were anaerobically produced and not converted to methane [33]. Chlorophenols and chlorphenoxy acids have been decomposed by waste stabilization ponds; influent levels of 12 mg/l and 50 mg/l, respectively, were treated [34].

Operating Characteristics

Waste stabilization ponds provide quiescent retention of dilute wastewater streams so that dispersed microorganisms decompose organics through their metabolic processes. No aeration or mxing is mechanically provided. Wind activity and seasonal temperature induce stratification, and turning provides aeration and mixing. As a result, the waste stabilization pond process is very sensitive to temperature and wind velocity for removal efficiencies.

Retention times for waste stabilization range from days to months. The pond depths are generally shallow so that aerobic conditions are maintained. Sunlight is essential to the algal production of oxygen, and optimum pond depths for sunlight penetration would be 6–18 in. [11]. Wind aeration coupled with algal aeration might lead to optimum pond depths of ~ 4 ft for fully aerobic conditions to be ensured. At depths >5 ft, waste stabilization of settled sludge occurs anaerobically.

The long retention periods and shallow depths lead to large land requirements for the process. Waste stabilization is limited to rural areas having extensive acreage. Maximum organic loadings of 100–300 lb of BOD_u/acre/day are recommended by Eckenfelder [11].

Metals concentrations appear to be more significant in waste stabilization ponds than in any of the other biological treatment processes discussed in this chapter. Metals inhibition is evidenced by decreased respiration of the mixed microbial population, and results in lower BOD removal efficiencies. Copper was shown to seriously affect pond performance at concentrations ≥ 0.25 mg/l. Sensitivity to chromium was less, and chromium concentrations >50 mg/l were shown to appreciably affect pond performance [35]. The investigations of copper and chromium indicated that sludge doses of these metals reacted with the natural buffering system, causing a pH depression and a significant carbon dioxide gas evolution [35]. These factors upset the delicate symbiotic relations of the mixed microbial population and seriously hampered removal efficiencies.

ACKNOWLEDGMENT

The material in this chapter is derived in part from information in a study by Joan B. Berkowitz, et al. of Arthur D. Little, Inc., for the Hazardous Waste Management Division, Office of Solid Waste, U.S. Environmental Protection Agency, NTIS PB 275054 (1977).

REFERENCES

1. *Biological Treatment of Petroleum Refinery Wastes* (New York: American Petroleum Institute, Division of Refining, 1963).
2. Dugan, P. R. *Biochemical Ecology of Water Pollution* (New York: Plenum Press, 1972).
3. Kaneko, M., K. Morimoto and S. Nambu. "The Response of Activated Sludge to a Polychlorinated Biphenyl (KC-500)," *Water Research,* Vol. 10 (Elmsford, NY: Pergamon Press, Inc., 1976), pp. 157–163.
4. Oliver, B. G. and E. G. Cosgrove. "The Efficiency of Heavy Metal Removal by a Conventional Activated Sludge Treatment Plant," *Water Research,* Vol. 8 (Elmsford, NY: Pergamon Press, Inc., 1974), pp. 869–874.
5. Esmond, S. E. and A. C. Petrasek, Jr. "Trace Metal Removal," *Ind. Water Eng.* (May/June 1974), pp. 14–17.
6. Steiner, A. E., D. A. McLaren and C. F. Forster. "The Nature of Activated Sludge Flocs," *Water Research,* Vol. 10 (Elmsford, NY: Pergamon Press, Inc., 1976), pp. 25–30.
7. Johnson, W. F. and E. Hindin. "Bioconcentration of Arsenic by Activated Sludge Biomass," *Water Sew. Works* (October 1972), pp. 95–97.
8. "Optimizing a Petrochemical Waste Bio-Oxidation System Through Automation," U.S. EPA (June 1975).
9. Srinath, E. G. Personal communication and site visit, Union Carbide Corporation, Tonawanda, NY.

10. Barth, E. F., M. B. Ettinger, B. V. Salotto and G. N. McDermott. "Summary Report on the Effects of Heavy Metals on the Biological Treatment Processes," *J. Water Pol. Control Fed.* 37 (January 1965).
11. Eckenfelder, W. W., Jr. *Water Quality Engineering for Practicing Engineers* (New York: Barnes & Noble, Inc., 1970).
12. Hockenhull, D. J. D. *Progress in Industrial Microbiology, Vol. 9* (Cleveland, OH: CRC Press, Inc., 1971).
13. Pohland, F. G. *Anaerobic Biological Treatment Processes* Advances in Chemistry Series 105 (Washington, DC: American Chemical Society, 1973).
14. "Identification and Control of Petrochemical Pollutants Inhibitory to Anaerobic Processes," U.S. EPA (1973).
15. Breidenbach, A. W. "Composting of Municipal Solid Wastes in the United States," U.S. EPA (1971).
16. Bruns, R. G. and J. A. Meindl. Personal communication and site visit, Hyon Waste Management Services, Inc., Chicago, IL.
17. Raymond, R. L. Personal communication, Sun Oil, Marcus Hook, PA.
18. Harstine, J. and E. Evans. Personal communication and site visit, Skelly Oil Refinery, El Dorado, KS.
19. Raymond, R. L., J. O. Hudson and V. W. Jamison. "Oil Degradation in Soil."
20. Raymond, R. L., V. W. Jamison and J. O. Hudson. "Hydrocarbon Cooxidation in Microbial Systems," *Lipids* 6(7): 453–457 (1971).
21. Bruns, R. B. International Hydronics Corporation, Princeton, NJ.
22. Chu, J. P. and E. J. Kirsch. "Metabolism of Pentachlorophenol by an Axenic Bacterial Culture," *Appl. Microbiol.* (May 1972), pp. 1033–1035.
23. Kirsch, E. J. and J. E. Etzel. "Microbial Decomposition of Pentachlorophenol," *J. Water Poll. Control Fed.* 42(2) (1973).
24. Kincannon, C. B. "Oily Waste Disposal by Soil Cultivation Process," U.S. EPA Office of Research and Monitoring, Project 12050 EZG.
25. Jeris, J. S. and R. W. Regan. "Controlling Environmental Parameters for Optimum Composting," *Compost Sci.* (March/April 1973).
26. Poincelot, R. P. "A Scientific Examination of the Principles and Practice of Composting," *Compost Sci.* (Summer 1974).
27. Selm, R., J. Butler, J. Ascher and R. Riordan. Personal communication and site visits, Lockheed, Marietta, GA: Boeing, Wichita, KS; Skelly Oil Refinery, El Dorado, KS.
28. Davis, J. B. *Petroleum Microbiology* (New York: Elsevier Publishing Company, 1967), pp. 375–392.
29. TRW report.
30. Cleasby, J. L., et al. "Trickling Filtration of a Waste Containing NTA," *J. Water Poll. Fed.* 46(8):1873–1887 (1974).
31. Brockett, O. D. "Microbial Reactions in Facultative Oxidation Ponds—I. The Anaerobic Nature of Oxidation Pond Sediments," *Water Res.,* Vol. 10 (Elmsford, NY: Pergamon Press, Inc., 1976), pp. 45–49.
32. Brockett, O. D. and T. A. Orchard. "Microbial Reactions in Facultative Oxidation Ponds—II. Biochemical Activity of Facultative Oxidation Pond Sediments," *Water Research* Vol. 10 (Elmsford, NY: Pergamon Press, Inc., 1976), pp. 315–321.

33. "Anaerobic Treatment of Synthetic Organic Wastes," U.S. EPA (January 1972).
34. "Biological Treatment of Chlorophenolic Wastes," U.S. EPA (June 1971).
35. Azad, H. S. and D. L. King. "Evaluating the Effect of Industrial Wastes on Lagoon Biota," 20th Industrial Waste Conference, Purdue University, Lafayette, IN (1965), pp. 410–422.

INDEX